Eloquence in Trouble

Volumes Published

Eloquence in Trouble

The Poetics and Politics of
Complaint in Rural Bangladesh

JAMES M. WILCE

New York   Oxford

Oxford University Press

1998

Oxford University Press

Oxford   New York
Athens   Auckland   Bangkok   Bogotá   Buenos Aires   Calcutta
Cape Town   Chennai   Dar es Salaam   Delhi   Florence   Hong Kong   Istanbul
Karachi   Kuala Lumpur   Madrid   Melbourne   Mexico City   Mumbai
Nairobi   Paris   São Paulo   Singapore   Taipei   Tokyo   Toronto   Warsaw

and associated companies in
Berlin   Ibadan

Published by Oxford University Press, Inc.
198 Madison Avenue, New York, New York 10016

Oxford is a registered trademark of Oxford University Press

Library of Congress Cataloging-in-Publication Data
Wilce, James, MacLynn, 1953– .
Eloquence in trouble: the poetics and politics of complaint in rural Bangladesh
/ James M. Wilce.
p.   cm. — (Oxford studies in anthropological linguistics ; 21)
Includes bibliographical references and index.
ISBN 0-19-510687-3
1. Sociolinguistics—Bangladesh.   I. Title.   II. Series.
P40.45.B3W55   1998
306.44'0954'92—dc21   98-18338

1 3 5 7 9 8 6 4 2

Printed in the United States of America
on acid-free paper

PREFACE

This book is my attempt to come to grips with the eloquence of Bangladeshis even in times of trouble, and with the trouble besetting Bangladeshi genres of "troubles talk." Though "medical" does not adequately describe all of the contexts for troubles talk (talking about one's troubles, Jefferson 1980)—in fact, troublesome conflicts and questions should not be medicalized—it is one of them. The story of my interest in medical discourse in Bangladesh begins with my interest in medicine. Sitting at age five in the lap of my grandfather, a cardiologist and a football coach at Ohio State University, I wanted more than anything to become a doctor. Just after high school that plan fell by the wayside as I imagined other ways of being with troubles, with suffering. I have been unable to completely disengage myself from medicine, however, even when my experiences of physicians and other healers have been, at times, traumatic. That is not an idiosyncratic experience, even in Bangladesh.

Religious Confessions

My first days in Bangladesh were spent as a missionary. I am one of those who once thought that studying anthropology would make him a better missionary, only to find anthropology displacing my old worldview. In 1979, before being appointed a missionary, I had a two-week introduction to Bangladesh. It came after teaching English for six months in Pakistan, and after I had finished seminary studies in theology, Hebrew, Greek, and mission history. I was convinced that Christians could do much better than they had in relation to the Muslim world—better "represent Christ" and more successfully foster mutual understanding. In our two weeks in Bangladesh, my wife and I saw the material conditions of life in Bangladesh as a challenge, but also sensed that people were always ready for religious discussion. We sought to be appointed to Bangladesh by the relatively ecumenical American Baptist Churches and its partner churches in Bangladesh. In June 1981 our first daughter was born and we were formally appointed to Bangladesh, to strengthen churches and to share our faith. Finally, in June 1983, we arrived in Dhaka. Determined to identify from the onset with Bengalis rather than with expatriates, we completely avoided the latter for our first ten days. Ramadan is the month in which Muslims fast during daylight hours; our first three days fell in the middle of that month. They were spent with a well-to-do Muslim family whose son Karim (a pseudonym) I had met while I was studying in California between 1981 and 1983. His family's fluency in English and their plush air-conditioned home cushioned the shock of our arrival. Karim and his sister gave us a few powerfully generative Bangla phrases that would help us toward deeper social and linguistic involvement. After four days, the family dropped us off at a bus station, whence we boarded a bus for Jaydebpur, about an hour from Dhaka. In Jaydebpur we found the farm of a Bengali Baptist farmer/pastor, where our two-year-old daughter Rebekah was introduced to the hard nose of a cow. The pastor's teenage son taught me some questions useful for generating verbs in context.

Thus it was that after seven days we were on our way to using the little Bangla we had learned, and to escaping the expatriate ghettos that dot Bangladesh. For the next six months, I continued to learn Bangla in the streets and in shops along Green Road in Dhaka. Our four years (1983–1987) with the mission saw me doing various tasks, but always eating, speaking, and worshiping regularly with Bengalis. I was there to share my faith, as I said; I fulfilled that sense of call by sitting in small towns at tables laden with tracts and receiving the many curious visitors and the few who came to seriously engage in dialogue. Though I told myself at the time that it was possible for some to reorient their spiritual lives without disrupting their traditions and social allegiances, I no longer see the two as separable and feel more comfortable listening to spiritual journeys than sharing my own utterly confused journey. Commonly, I found myself on the receiving end of Muslim attempts to convert me. During such religious dialogues I learned a great deal about Islam, and particularly Bengali Sufism.

Although much of my work was fulfilling and I had some rewarding relationships with Bengalis and with expatriates, there were ample sources of stress. Bangladesh did not find in me an answer to its problems, and I felt a sense of guilt and pervasive disquiet throughout those years. Those who asked me for help challenged the limits of my charity. But one stressful experience in particular probably influenced the selection of my research topic years later. My wife and I had a nightmarish encounter with a Brahmin doctor during a medical emergency that took us from our mission "post" to Calcutta. My wife was told by two expatriate doctors in Bangladesh that her fetus had died, but was not spontaneously miscarrying, and that her life would be at risk unless she received prostaglandins to abort the dead fetus she was carrying. Prostaglandins could not be administered to Gretchen at that time in Bangladesh. So we traveled to the Calcutta hospital we had already contacted, which assigned her a doctor; we presented to him the findings of our doctors in Bangladesh. When we left Calcutta, after my wife had spent four days under his "care," we were both in tears. He reluctantly performed the delivery, asking me to leave in the middle. When he emerged, he "showed" me what he thought would convince me that the fetus had probably not been dead, and that our rushing him was the cause of a sin (murder), and of my wife's pain. Like a fanatic somehow representing the worst nightmares of both sides of the U.S. abortion debate, he thrust something bloody at me and I wandered off in a kind of dissociated state. Like those who occupy later pages, we had to deal with loss; unlike them, we were not privy to a tradition of poetic public weeping. This book probably displays some envy of the tradition it describes (though I have been exploring hybrid genres—poetic-expressive-musical—bringing their influence home for myself). My wife was in pain from the procedure, and felt that the doctor had gone out of his way to hurt her. Colleagues who comforted us over the next days speculated that we must have offended him and provoked his rough treatment by telling *him* the problem and the procedure we had been sent to receive. We did not meet his expectation that patients be passively dependent on his diagnosis and recommendations. Patients and clients, including myself, who encounter Bengali doctors with this attitude either conform or have conflictual experiences like mine. When I had recovered from shock, I was angry. Yet, because it was balanced by my inbred respect for physicians such as my own grandfather, this experience attuned me to signs that Bengali patients were dissatisfied with their relationships to practitioners, without rendering my view of practitioners completely jaundiced.

We left what we had originally thought would be our first four-year term of service in Bangladesh in mid-1987. We were to return in a year, but it became a year of re-evaluation. Feeling uncomfortable with the tasks—such as the Bengali translation of texts written in other countries—that the mission was asking me to return to do, and seeing increasing opposition to the mission from the government of Bangladesh, I resigned from the mission in 1988 and entered graduate anthropology training. At this remove, the religious motivation to my brief missionary career seems hard even for me to understand. Yet for a time, I silently "lamented"—a theme of this book—the loss of my center, my certitude, my community. As James Peacock reports having said to religious people asking him about his faith on two different fields, "anthropology is our religion" (President's comments, Society for Cultural Anthropology meetings, 1990). From 1991 on, when Bangladeshis asked what my *dharma* (religion) was, I replied *mānab dharma* (a term for humanism associated with Bengali Bauls [Capwell 1986]). The more I said it, the better it seemed to fit me. Yet it is clearly not the same. Choosing (along with other anthropologists) to "love the question and live into the answer" (in the words of the poet Rilke) is a very different love than loving the Answer. At the same time, I still often sense (along with Bangladeshis) a spirit that questions us and our questions; the "sensorium" of my spirit struggles with my mindset. I have new laments, new celebrations, and a new reference group; "loving the question" makes as much sense as anything these days.

During graduate school, as I anticipated returning in a new capacity to Bangladesh, I gradually forgot how stressful my years there had been. In 1991 and again in 1996—in the days leading up to my first and second periods of fieldwork, respectively—the amnesia began to wear off. Still, I assured myself that I would not arouse less anxiety and fewer expectations in my new role! I could go about my work, I hoped, without people resenting the religious influence I brought or looking to me for what a missionary might provide. For the most part, my experience with anthropological fieldwork allows me to cope better with conditions in Bangladesh, to develop sympathetic engagements and even friendships, and to love questions.

Are there continuities? I would not have revealed this past, somewhat disconnected with academic anthropology, were there no point and no continuities. One of those is my longstanding appreciation for biblical Psalms of lament, and for those dimensions of religion that facilitate working through grief and working toward deeper "connection." When Bangladeshi Muslims have dared to reveal to me their deepest spiritual feelings, perhaps my religious background has prepared me better than some to appreciate them. This is a book about the social roots of discourses such as off-the-cuff complaint and lament; about social identities formed and revealed in such discourse; and about personal and even national historic shifts that are sometimes wrenching, that may motivate laments, but that also may in some degree be managed or processed in such discourse and interaction. But, indirectly, it is about my transformation and also a means by which I make sense of the personal history into which I have given you a window. And my own disturbing experiences as I grew apart from my religion, my religious career, and eventually my wife—a three-fold alienation well underway during my missionary years—shape the way I hear and feel-with Bangladeshi troubles tellers. Elinor Ochs says the vast majority of oral narratives around the world is probably about something troubling and that narrative serves a function not unlike that of prayer (discussant comments, American Association for Applied Linguistics 1998). Complaint narratives are also theodicies—theological "why?" discourses aimed at explaining how bad or at least mysterious the world is—and are thus central to culture (Good 1994). My experience of losing old certainties drew me to the particular religious-theodical-moral aesthetic entailed in lament.

Lament says "I don't understand"; that was a theme of the laments of Latifa represented in this book. It asks "Why?" Perhaps I returned to Bangladesh as an anthropologist because I had begun to find the questions (expressed in lament songs I had stumbled upon as a missionary) and the richness of pursuing the questions more satisfying than being "the answer man" as a missionary. Once more, as at age 18, I was seeking a new way of being with troubles.

In April 1991, as I awaited word on funding and was required to affiliate my research with an institution in Bangladesh, two Bangladeshi demographers in Los Angeles—Omar Rahman and Mizanur Rahman "Mizan" (the two are unrelated)—led me to write the International Centre for Diarrheal Disease Research, Bangladesh (ICDDR,B). [1] Through Sushila Zeitlyn at ICDDR,B and H. K. Arefeen at Dhaka University I found my field assistant, Gazi Nazrul Islam Faisal, who has become a true friend. I spent time with Faisal and Arefeen when I did more fieldwork in 1996. Omar, Mizan, Faisal, Arefeen, Karim, and I still correspond. The choices an anthropologist makes early in his career shape his relationships for years to come; the choices I have described were fortunate ones.

On Representing Bangla Conversation

After settling in to fieldwork in 1991, I began taping conversations and transcribing them in hopes of bringing Bangladeshi voices to bear in presentations such as this one. My Bangla transliteration system is adapted from Bagchi (1996), but my transcription system (see page xiii) derives from conversation analysis. For a detailed explanation of my approach to transcribing Matlab speech, see the appendix.

For some readers, beauty lies in consistency of form. For me and for Ochs (1979), transcripts must rather vary their form according to what needs to be highlighted. Thus, for example, some of my transcripts represent monologic speech; in those cases, I put speaker's text in one column and glosses in another. But, where I draw attention to one "protagonist," and treat her interlocutors as a contrast unit, I juxtapose their lines—together with glosses—with the protagonist's. My use of italics varies depending on whether or not English glosses are in the same column as Bangla text.

The list of key characters presented on page xv and table 1-1 in chapter 1 provide a reference point for the many Bangladeshi persons and places invoked in this book.

J. M. W.

Flagstaff, Arizona
June, 1998

Rice and potatoes are Matlab's staple crops.

ACKNOWLEDGMENTS

The list of those who have contributed to my efforts, without whose help I could not have completed this book, is a long one. I thank the Department of Anthropology at UCLA for funding my pilot study of Bengali household interaction in Los Angeles in 1989–1990. My fieldwork in Bangladesh in 1991–1992 was supported very generously by the Institute of International Education (a Fulbright grant) and the American Institute of Bangladesh Studies (AIBS). Analysis of the data was supported by the National Science Foundation's Dissertation Improvement Grant DBS-9919127; Paul Chapin of the NSF has consistently encouraged me since completion of my dissertation. The Fulbright grant carried me to the field and sustained me, and the generous support of AIBS (administered in-country by the Centre for Development Research, Bangladesh [CDR,B) enabled me to purchase a laptop and video camera and to pay field assistants. In addition, both of those organizations came with kind personal assistance attached, in the form of U.S. Embassy personnel in the case of Fulbright and CDR,B staff in the case of the AIBS grant. The CDR,B staff in Dhaka were always very encouraging to me and eager to hear of my progress.

Further logistical and moral support in the form of helpful consultation during the period of fieldwork was provided by the International Centre for Diarrheal Disease Research, Bangladesh (ICDDR,B). Many thanks to friends currently or formerly affiliated with ICDDR,B, especially Mike Strong, Sushila Zeitlyn, and Jerune VanGinneken—three of the fine social scientists in that stronghold of biomedicine. M. Sarder, G. Chakraborty, and K. M. A. Aziz provided me with much needed field supervision, personal sponsorship, and advice. I also thank Bangladeshi friends and former neighbors in Los Angeles—particularly Farooq Ameen, Omar Rahman, and Mizanur Rahman—for steering me toward Matlab and toward their kind and hospitable relatives in Bangladesh.

Beyond my colleagues in ICDDR,B and CDR,B, I received enormous help from Rezwana Quaderi of the Institute for Post-Graduate Medical Research and from Rajib Humayun, Anis Ahmed, Syed Hashemi, Hidayetul Islam, and especially Helaluddin Khan Arefeen, who sent along Gazi Md. Nazrul Islam (Faisal).

I am grateful to the people of Bangladesh—particularly to the people of Matlab—for putting up with endless questions and the intrusions of microphone and lens. Among those, I owe a special debt of gratitude to the families with whom I lived and ate rice—the extended family of Habibur Rahman of Baghmar village (pseudonyms) who graciously housed and fed not only me but also my field assistant(s) at various times, and to Mr. and Mrs. Rejak Khan (pseudonym), who generously cared for me during my days in Dhaka.

To field assistants Faisal, Lopa, and Rani, a separate thanks for sweating and empathizing, for sharing life in the field and all that that entailed. Gazi Md. Nazrul Islam (Faisal) lived and worked with me in the Rahman settlement and its surrounding villages from January through June of 1992. He transcribed tapes with me until his ears ached. I have continued to refine the transcription of my recordings, and in that work in the United States, Kazi Asadul Mamun, Faisal Rahman, and Imtiaz Hossain have been of immense help.

The members of my doctoral committee—Nancy Levine, John Kennedy, Keith Kernan, and Stanley Wolpert—gave generously of their ears and eyes as I shared drafts of the dissertation from which this book emerged. Paul Kroskrity, chair of the committee, did yeoman's service to clarify my thinking, improve my writing, and steer the process, giving me countless hours of advice along the way, not limited to the dissertation. I thank Katherine Ewing for her careful reading of the whole manuscript at an earlier stage, and for her suggestions. Alex Bolyanatz Bob Desjarlais, Elizabeth Keating (who coined the term, "dis-cursive *parda*"), Leila Monaghan, and Jill Dubisch have also given generously of their friendship, encouragement, and editorial advice on one or more chapters. Graduate assistants Neill Hadder, Gretchen Ndousse-Fedder, and Aigli Pittaka gave valuable suggestions on all or part of the manuscript, as did reviewers of chapters previously published—Ken George, Susan Wadley, and Joe Boles. I gratefully acknowledge the editorial assistance of Louella Holter at Northern Arizona University on the whole manuscript, and the assistance provided by editors of the journals in which some of this material has appeared—Don Brenneis and Michael Herzfeld (*American Ethnologist*), Gay Becker (*Medial Anthropology Quarterly*), and Byron Good and Mary Jo Delvecchio Good (*Culture, Medicine, and Psychiatry*).

Finally, I cannot begin to express my thanks to my daughters Rebekah and Charissa and my ex-wife Gretchen for their support and encouragement through the difficult separation entailed by fieldwork and the mental separation entailed in writing such a book. My parents, Phyllis and Jim, also did much to make this possible. The book is dedicated to Taqbir, who died of stomach cancer at the age of four in 1993, and to Latifa, whose poetic and musical work has shaped much of my thinking and feeling about lament.

CONTENTS

TRANSCRIPTION CONVENTIONS

The form of the second-person pronoun (or verb marking that agrees with it) varies in Bangla, something like *vous* and *tu* in French, with an additional third level. In the translations in this book, I have indicated these levels of respect-marking as follows:

V   Bangla *āpni* = respect-distance, like French *vous*

T   Bangla *tumi* = equality-solidarity, like French *tu*

sT   Bangla *tui* = extreme affection/intimacy or condescension/power asymmetry

/xxx/   Overlapping speech segments are shown between slashes on both of the lines that overlap.

(???)   Inaudible words. The number of x's or ?'s approximates the number of inaudible words.

( )   Words within parentheses are alternative or problematic/uncertain hearings of the taped words.

[ ]   Sound segments within brackets are not realized in the pronunciation on tape but are included for ease of recognition by Bangla speakers and Indologists. Gestures and other actions relevant to the ongoing speech interaction are also noted within brackets, as are words that are necessary for the gloss but lacking in the Bangla original. Brackets also contain words needed in the gloss but lacking in the Bangla.

(1.5)   Length of pauses is shown in seconds and tenths of seconds.

(())   Double parentheses surround notes on the prosodic features of utterances.

=   Latching of utterances—the near overlap of two utterances by the same or different speakers.

:   Colon indicates lengthening of the preceding sound segment; in the Matlab dialect of Bangla this is stylistic, not phonemic.

ital   Represents code mixing— typically an English word in Bangla discourse. When an English word is uttered in Bangla discourse, and the gloss line is italicized, the code-mixed word is in roman to show the contrast. Italics can also mark change of speaker in the transcript of a multiparty interaction, or set off gloss from text where the two occupy the same column.

CAST OF

KEY CHARACTERS PRESENTED

Pseudonym	Description/Relation to Others
Aesha Begum	Wife of Durim, mother of eight; sister-in-law of Habibur Rahman
Ahmed Dada	Habibur Rahman's father's brother; chronic parasitic infection causes great pain periodically
Ali	Ayurvedic-herbalist-*kabirāj* in a village of Matlab 3 hours from Sonargaon; sees Yasmin as his patient
Amina	Daughter of Habibur Rahman and Rani; mother of Rajib
Bokul	Habibur Rahman's father's brother's son
Bonhi	Los Angeles–based Calcutta woman who said, "My whole body hurts"
Bozlu "Pagla" ("Ecstatic")	Spiritual preceptor, fakir; can teach disciples never to lose consciousness
Buji ("Granny")	Bokul's father's wife (stepmother); had growths on front of both hips; hospitalized for surgery
Bun	Sister/grandmother or great-aunt to Latifa; Ahmed Dada's wife
Delwar Kari	Diviner in a village of Matlab 2 hours from Sonargaon
Durim ("Distant")	Habibur Rahman's youngest brother; Aesha's often distant husband
Faisal	My long-term field assistant and roommate; M.A., Dhaka University
Farhad	Heykal called him "brainless"; diarrhea patient
Fatima	Sometimes mute, almost exorcised; live near ICDDR,B's clinic in Sonargaon
Habibur Rahman	My host and "father," husband of Rani; father of Tuslim and Amina
Hawladar	Astrologer, palmist, gem specialist; is called "Professor"

xvii

Heykal	Respected "doctor" in Sonargaon bazaar; affine of Habibur Rahman
Izzat ("Honor")	Second most educated person in the compound; college student in 1991
Jahangir	Cigarette vendor and part-time exorcist; was called to exorcise Fatima
Jalu	Neighbor and affine of Habibur Rahman; employee of the man who arranged for me to stay with Habibur Rahman
Karim	Son of wealthy businessman; his father calls himself the "friend" (not disciple) of Baba, a Pir; met author while studying in California
Karim Baksh	Father who criticizes his feverish son for "miaowing" for his mother; character from Isahaque 1955
Khaleja	Rani and Habibur Rahman's daughter Samia's daughter, living with them
Krishna Daktar	Practices allopathic medicine in Sonargaon bazaar
Latifa	Father's brother's son's daughter's daughter of Habibur Rahman; sings laments
Loqman	10-year-old boy who died of bloody dysentery
Meherban ("Kind")	Youngest of the brothers Rahman; called attention to irritations of joint-extended family life; criticized folklore; *Imām* of Baghmar mosque
Petuli	Samia's infant daughter
Rajib	7-year-old son of Amina and Musadeq; cousin of Tuslim
Rani	My field "mother"; wife of Habibur Rahman; mother of Tuslim, Amina, etc.
Rejak Khan	My Dhaka host; his children are all in the United States
Said	Habibur Rahman's elder brother, the eldest of the four
Samabedanā ("Sympathy")	Sensitive to Latifa's suffering; 14-year-old granddaughter (SD) of Ahmed
Samia	Eldest daughter of Rani and Habibur Rahman; mother of Petuli
Shefali	Possession-medium and "patient" of female Islamic spirit (*pari*); neighbor of ICDDR,B community health worker
Sufia	Heykal's patient who miscarried; lump remains in her abdomen; sent back by husband to live with parents
Suleyman	Calls himself "Mad Emperor"; Durim's affine
Suraya	Nurse, runs a women's clinic in Sonargaon; Taqbir's mother

Taqbir   Son of Suraya; played outside his mother's clinic; shook
                    head "no" when asked if his body felt okay

Tuslim   Son of Habibur Rahman and Rani; my 20-year-old periodic
                    housemate in Baghmar

Yasmin   Ali's patient who died (of cancer?); told Ali, "I haven't told
                    half of it."

Taqbir: 1989–1992.

Eloquence in Trouble

1

TROUBLING OURSELVES WITH BANGLA TROUBLES TALK

"Man invented language to satisfy his deep need to *complain*," or so says comedienne Lily Tomlin (quoted in Pinker 1994: 32; emphasis added). An effective study of troubles telling is one contribution that linguistic anthropology should make toward theorizing medicine and the social organization of power, emotion, and troubles-management strategies, which include "medicine," broadly construed. How are the realities and ideologies of power and of person-hood constructed when Bangladeshi people tell troubles?

This book seeks to answer that question and, in doing so, uniquely yokes linguistic and medical anthropology in the service of ethnography. It is a book about small linguistic acts of resistance in Bangladesh. It deals with the telling of troubles, with local perceptions of the troubles-in-the-telling process (communi-cative competence), and with my perception that many speech genres—which not only carry personal signs of grief, but also potentially serve as hidden transcripts of social protest—are themselves in trouble, or at least make trouble for the teller. Much of the troubles talk reflected herein represents resistance to the forces that structure the lives of the women and men who are speaking. Acts of resistance are often political, but some of the actors described here are better described as resisting illness, trouble, and death. As Byron Good reminds us, there is another sense of resistance in illness narratives and other forms of troubles talk: They tell of ways in which *reality resists us* as we experience and confront illness, disease, and injustice as "brute facts" in the world (1994: 177). It is true in Bangladesh and elsewhere that families, communities, and larger social units constrain and sometimes forcibly repress troubles talk, but life also resists resolution (Kleinman 1992). Thus these strips of talk and all their polysemy and multivocality resist attempts by myself or anyone else to represent them as romanticized hidden transcripts of political resistance. They clearly speak of existential suffering that cannot and ought not to be squeezed into a purely (micro)political frame, even if all of life is political in some sense.

I include many examples of lament in this book about troubles talk, and lament prototypically thematizes separation or death. The various senses in which I speak of troubles talk as resistant are well captured in the words of

Seremetakis regarding women's laments on the Greek island of Mani. Rather than following the social anthropological tradition of "reading" death rituals and laments to catch social organization in the act of "dominating death," she sees "the defamiliarization of social order through the optic offered by death" (1991: 15).[1] Caraveli (1986) and Holst-Warhaft (1992) imply that women's communication with the dead—for that is what lament often seems to be—inverts social convention. Not only does such communication step outside of the everyday, but what women sing in laments often constitutes a challenge to the powers that control women's lives, sexuality, and economic security. To a greater or lesser extent, troubles talk has a similar prismatic potential to re-present (and perhaps challenge) prevailing visions of life in Bangladesh.

There are multiple anthropological arguments for devoting increased attention to complaints. First, the complaint theme is heard in popular culture. Complaining and the suppression of complaining have been increasingly salient in the late twentieth century in the United States. Means have perhaps always existed for making pejorative references to complaints—bellyaching, whining, and bitching (this latter indexes the link between characterizations of complaints and of gender)—and new forms are arising in pop culture. One sees buttons iconically prohibiting whining:

QUIT IT!

More important, exploring the form, function, and ideologizing power of complaints can help create a new linguistic-medical anthropology, responding to calls from Kleinman, Das, and Lock (1996) and Rhodes (1990: 172) to "shift our perception of boundaries" and focus on suffering rather than illness.

Life in Matlab

In 1991–1992 and for a month in 1996, I did fieldwork in the Chandpur district, which is a 4-hour ferry trip from the capital city of Dhaka (see table 1-1) in the *upajilā* (subdistrict) of Matlab (Fauveau 1994; Habte 1990). The staff of the International Centre for Diarrheal Disease Research, Bangladesh (ICDDR,B) helped me make initial contacts with medical practitioners in Matlab. The Matlab subdistrict of Chandpur is approximately 50 kilometers southeast of Dhaka and is reachable by river. It is home to at least 300,000 persons and is the site of field projects in demography, epidemiology, and basic science that have led to hundreds of publications (Habte 1990).[2] As far as I know, no studies of the Matlab Bangla dialect have been published (but see Wilce 1995). Because I wanted to understand the idioms and experiences of Matlab troubles tellers,

Table 1-1. Bangladeshi place names cited (real and fictitious).

Place	Description/Relation	Further Notes
Baghmar (pseudonym)	"Tiger killed [here]"; village of my residence with Habibur Rahman	One of several villages in North Sonargaon union
Chandpur (actual name)	"Moon Town"; the district of which Matlab is a part	City threatened by erosion from river
Dhaka (actual name)	The capital of Bangladesh	Home of Rejak Khan
Dukkhapur (pseudonym)	"Sad village"	Home of Latifa
Matlab (actual name)	Literally, "attitude, opinion"; an upazilā or subdistrict of Chandpur	Town location of major ICDDR,B diarrhea hospital
Sonargaon (pseudonym)	"Golden village"; name of market area at the heart of the union on the Dhonagoda River	Location of most of the practitioners I interviewed

especially of those whose troubles could count as medical, I settled in an area—the Sonargaon Union[3] of Matlab, centered in the bazaar (market) of Sonargaon—with a great variety of practitioners. After settling in, I was able to meet patients of those practitioners and develop my own contacts with the sick and the healthy during their everyday-life activities. These contacts arose as I participated in the life of one extended family, including their troubles talk (a term I have borrowed from Jefferson, e.g., 1981), and became a neighbor of their neighbors. When people heard of my interest in illness, possession, and ethnomedical practice, they sometimes led me to incapacitated relatives or neighbors. My involvement with some of them became long term.

Bangladesh—once East Bengal, then East Pakistan, and then a secular republic after achieving independence from Pakistan—embraced Islam as the religion of the state in the late 1970s. Sunni Islam dominates all but a few small areas of the country, although some Shi'a-derived observances are evident, such as Ashura, the commemoration of the death of Hasan and Husein. The mosque, located within a few yards of my extended family's compound, is presided over by my adopted uncle, and Islamic idioms figure largely in local politics (Wilce 1997).

One hears many borrowed Perso-Arabic words in the Bangla speech of Muslims. These include one word for lamentation, *jāri* (Dunham 1997),[4] which in Bangladesh denotes a genre of call-and-response songs that my consultants in Matlab say are rousing and enjoyable, despite being performed during Ashura. From *jāri* is derived another Bangla word, *āhājāri*, which denotes the violent mourning (falling down, beating oneself) seen at times of loss among Muslims in Bangladesh but also among Punjabi Hindus (Das 1996).[5] Men, the rightful inhabitants of public spaces and public speaking roles in Bangladesh, can be heard reciting poetry and singing on occasion.

Matlab in many ways reflects its region, northern South Asia. My adoptive field family of prosperous peasants grows rice, potatoes, and jute, which are the dominant crops in Matlab and in most of Bangladesh. Village exogamy, virilocal residence, and patrilineal kinship reckoning help create a form of gender hierarchy—sexual segregation and exclusion of women from public domains—which is justified locally in terms of Islam but contrasts strongly with South Indian patterns. The situation for women in Matlab is indeed difficult. The Population Crisis Committee (1988) once ranked the status of women in Bangladesh as the lowest in the world. Female literacy then was 24 percent. One in five girls died before her fifth birthday, one woman in six did not survive her childbearing years, and female life expectancy was 49 years. Papanek (1990) aphoristically described their status: "To each less than she needs, from each more than she can do." Within residential compounds, each nuclear family lives and cooks in a separate dwelling, but they share a common courtyard. Marriages are arranged, and the older Islamic norm of bride-price governing marital negotiations in Bangladesh before 1940 has given way to a dowry, and in fact to demands for ever-larger dowries (Rozario 1992). A prenuptial agreement (*kābin*) specifying the sum of money that the groom will owe to the bride's family if he divorces her is another part of these complex negotiations. For men to divorce women is not uncommon in rural Bangladesh—men often divorce their wives if the couple fails to have children, or sons in particular. Divorce in Matlab, like most other forms of conflict, is managed by informal open-air gatherings of concerned parties, with local power brokers attending as mediators. The position of women is related to their speech roles. One reader of this manuscript considers its depiction of "discursive *pardā*" (her term) one of the book's key contributions.

Matlab is intersected by the Dhonagoda, a branch of the river Meghna. Annual flooding has ceased on the western side since the construction of an embankment.[6] Baghmar, where I lived and worked, lies on the east side, where seasonal flooding still governs agricultural cycles. Extended virilocal families living in *bāṛis* (compounds) cultivate rice, wheat, and lentils, along with harvesting fruit from their shade trees and collecting greens to add to their curries. Some families in the villages that I frequented own a surplus of land with fish ponds, grow cash crops such as potatoes and jute, and have at least one educated household member who provides an income to the family through salaried employment. But landlessness is now growing in Bangladesh so that almost half of the people subsist by selling their labor in others' fields.[7]

Problems of Ethnographic Representation

A word about the problematics of a white Western male representing the words of Muslim women in Bangladesh is appropriate. Rather than representing these women as "voiceless and oppressed"—a rhetorical strategy used by the British to justify colonial intervention (Raheja and Gold 1994: 4) and more recently by the West to portray Islamic societies as backward—or even claiming to "give voice" to certain women or men in Bangladesh, I simply want to present dialogues in which I was but one participant. As Mannheim and Tedlock (1995) have argued, if "the critique of representations" either results in a new excuse to ignore native words or obscures the fact that discourses and even objectifying discourses predate the arrival of the ethnographer, it will have done anthropology no service. We must not let elaborate academic discourses characterizing bondage lull us into thinking that academics are the only "authors" of incisive commentary on and rejection of injustice.[8] Among the more significant problems with concluding that "the subaltern cannot speak" (Spivak 1994) is that this conclusion obviates listening. In keeping with the agenda of the important subaltern studies movement, but differing in method—relying on ethnographic recordings of complex contemporary discourse more than on historical archives—I want to join Raheja and Gold in countering "assumptions about the passivity of Indian women" (1994: 17). The fact that the Bangladeshi Muslim women I quote herein are subject to veiling, gender segregation, and violent silencing is quite relevant to my account, but it is not unique to Islam, although the ideological justification for some of this can appeal to a particular form of Islamic thought. Nor is Bangladeshi Islam unique among religious traditions in both motivating resistance and simultaneously becoming the target of resistant discourse. Religion is always available as a resource for heteroglossic conflict.[9] But hegemony does not eliminate resistance—it spawns it.

The voices of women and certain men in Bangladesh are often actively hushed. It would be highly misleading to call Bangladeshi women silent, but powerful actors do silence women who get out of hand, if they can. As I have mentioned, I had limited and sometimes obviously filtered access to any Bangladeshi voices. I feel that I owe it to those who were at times forcibly silenced, however, to continue my dialogue with them herein; as great as the moral risk might be in my claim to represent their resistant words, I have no choice but to continue the dialogue in book form. When I revisited some of these people in 1996, I received explicit instructions from as many as possible as to how, and how much, I should represent them. For some these instructions were to include photographs and tell their stories boldly. Others, particularly practitioners who evidently felt that my Western identity represented a scientific-cosmopolitan cultural threat to their particular practice of troubles-solving, asked me to depersonalize my account of their words and activities.

Bangla Speech

Bangla is a member of the Magadhan or eastern branch of the Indo-Aryan language family.[10] It is thus very closely related to Assamese and Oriya, and less closely to Hindi. As an Indo-European language it is distantly related to the Greek, Latin, Romance, and Germanic languages, including English. Because of centuries of contact between Dravidian and Indo-Aryan speech communities, some diffusion of features has occurred. Bangla phonology thus bears evidence of Dravidian influence (Chatterji 1934). Despite the great typological gap between the Indo-Aryan languages and Arabic, Indo-Aryan borrowing of Arabic words has a long history. Typically, words of Arabic origin have passed into Indic languages via Persian.[11] Bangla syntax does not seem to have been influenced by the syntax of Arabic or Persian, but rather reflects Indo-Aryan patterns. For instance, in Bangla, subjects are normally the first noun phrases of sentences, followed by direct objects, if any, with the verb usually last (subject-object-verb word order). Bangla, as a "pro-drop" language, allows subjectless sentences. Subjects, particularly pronominal subjects, can be unrealized (unexpressed) without serious consequence; ambiguities are blocked, to some extent, by the "rich system of verb-agreement" typical of such languages (Crystal 1991: 279).

The form of the second-person pronoun (or verb marking that agrees with it) varies in Bangla; the significance of such phenomena has long been a favorite topic of sociolinguistic investigation (Brown and Gilman 1960). Bangla has a respect form and a form expressing solidarity—something like *vous* (*āpni*, a V-form) and *tu* in French (*tumi*, the T-form)—but also a third level beyond the T-form, *tui*, which entails extreme affection/intimacy or condescension/power asymmetry and is commonly used in addressing one's children, domestic workers, or other social subordinates; *tui* may also be exchanged between lovers.

The inflected passives of Old Bangla have disappeared in modern language. But passivization of sentences is still possible, and seems to be a strategy for maintaining distance or keeping agents unmentioned, often with politeness as a motivating factor for the indirection.[12] The common question people asked me as I passed through their rice fields— "Where are you going?"—is phatic rather than intrusive, whatever form it takes.[13] Avoiding even the appearance of being intrusive is likely to explain why some farmers passivized that question, asking me the Bangla equivalent of "where will [the traveling] be gone today?" (*āj kothā-e jāwā habe?*).[14]

Klaiman (1981) has written about the semantics of agency and volitionality in Bangla. She describes the "dative subject" construction that is often used to express troubles.[15] Along with passives and certain participles, dative subject constructions either bar the realization of agents or express a state involving no action or agent per se. Indo-Aryan linguists refer to "dative" subjects, because in most Indo-Aryan examples of this construction (for example, utterances corresponding to the English statement, "I don't feel good") the subject receives dative case marking (Masica 1991: 346). In the Bangla language, however, such subjects take genitive, or possessive, case marking. In semantic terms, dative subjects are experiencers, not agents, and I will refer to them as "experiencer subjects."[16] Klaiman (1981: 84) argues that Bangla participial constructions, passives, and experiencer subjects form a trio indicating a sense of nonvolitionality. All three constructions indicate weakened or nonexistent "volitionality" in the "subject" noun phrase, if any subject is realized. "Volitionality has become a grammatically significant semantic parameter of the Bangla language in relatively recent times." Klaiman argues that this semantic parameter constrains discourse-grammatical processes. Bangla speakers, for example, cannot use an experiencer-subject construction to portray assertive agents at work. Bangla grammar—or, to use Whorf's felicitous term "fashions of speaking" (1956: 158) that transcend grammar as commonly conceived—constrains the projection of subjecthood and agency.

Indeed, it is not grammar alone or grammar per se that is always the most significant factor in an inquiry into the relation of habitual thought and behavior to language (Whorf 1956). Three aspects of Bangla speech-in-use are particularly relevant to the linguacultural construction of actors and action: the greeting ritual, the expression of acknowledgment or gratitude, and cursing. The words used in greetings vary according to the religious-communal affiliation of the speaker and the addressee. I want to call attention to greetings as acts of deference. As Fuller (1992) notes in his study of the Hindu *namaṣkāra* (greeting) ritual in India, the ritual action reproduces the hierarchy that is characteristic of Hindu society—the inferior always greets the superior with words and at least a symbolic dusting of the feet. In contemporary greeting patterns we see that pre-Islamic (Hindu) hierarchical structure has outlasted pre-Islamic ideologies among Bangladesh's Muslims. In fact, a perceived superior creates a problem for his subordinate by greeting him first; it sets off an attempt not only to give the return greeting but also to issue a new greeting as if the subordinate had initiated the ritual.

"Thank you" and even its Bangla gloss, *dhanyabād*, is a recent innovation or a marker of Westernization in the rare Bangla speech in which it occurs. The traditional means of acknowledging another's kindness is to say, *[āpnāke] kaṣto dilām* (I've given you trouble). The response, "No—I've given *you* trouble"—is both semantically and syntactically more reciprocal or parallel to the first member of the adjacency pair[17] than is the English response, "you're welcome." Hence the analysis by Duranti and Ochs (1986) of a Samoan sociolinguistic parallel applies to the Bangla situation. In traditional speech settings, Samoans contextualize actions as shared or mutual achievements by a reciprocated acknowledgment. Any change toward an unreciprocated recognition of achievement makes possible a more autonomous or individualistic construction of personhood suited to competitive social situations imported along with other aspects of Western culture. Bangla mutual acknowledgments similarly highlight the relationship between the speakers rather than the autonomous goodwill of one actor.

Curses also differ from English patterns. The common American curse, "fuck you," certainly has Bangla counterparts that are often heard among males—for example, *śālā*, literally "wife's brother" but connoting "he whose sister I am sleeping with," or "the inferior exchange partner who gives [me] his sister in marriage." Other street language includes more explicit, though empty, threats to rape the other's mother or sister. The difference between Bangla and American cursing is that the implicit sexual-aggressive threat is aimed not directly at the addressee or his sexuality but at his womenfolk. As in the case with greetings, there are areal-typological parallels extending into Pakistan. The significance is clear to the student of gender and symbolic capital. In an economy that measures a family's status by the degree of control its men exercise over its women and their reproduction, the gravest threat one can make to a man is through his sister's sexuality. Thus, even in the tension exemplified by cursing during heated interactions, language use wraps Bangla speakers tightly in relational bonds.

A commonality among experiencer-subject constructions such as troubles talk, greeting, thanking, and cursing, as Bangla fashions of speaking, is their tendency to foreground relationality and background personal autonomy. Bangla patterns of cursing and thanking remind us not to assume that even Bangla complaints assert that autonomy unproblematically.

A Complex Historical Moment in Bangladesh

Bangladeshi society is currently passing through a phase of history whose complexity defies easy reading. The mass media—including cable television from the West and India, and Hindi videos now shown on some rural river ferries—have increased penetration of even such places as Matlab. Economic forces, I suspect, have conspired to make family planning appear rational to more and more women and men. Girls as well as boys are staying in school longer than ever, and rates of literacy and overall participation in school are rising. As LeVine and his colleagues (1993) have argued, the schooling of South Asian girls often alters their expectations for the future, weakening their loyalty to older ideals of domesticity. At the same time, legal protections for women's rights have yet to be enforced, so that women seem to suffer from violence more and more, partly due to modernity's impact on the dowry system. Dowry claims pressed by grooms' families in South Asia sometimes include requests for gifts such as payment of all expenses for sending the groom's brother overseas for sweatshop employment (repatriated wages account for an ever-increasing share of Bangladesh's economy), a motorcycle, or a television (Rozario 1992). Broken dowry promises can put brides at risk of death or disfiguration. New stresses can result in shifting manifestations of *pāgalāmi* (madness)—one young Baghmar man's manic symptoms included imitations of oriental martial arts stars he had seen in movies. Yet traditional avenues of resistance—including expressive genres and perhaps forms of madness as well (depending on the eye of the beholder)—are under threat. In 1996 Bangladeshis told me of things that once were but are no more (perishing within the memory of today's older generation)—a class of women who were once paid to lament at funerals (Devi 1994), storytellers who once sang ballads, and so on. Such expressive genres are challenged, increasingly, by urbanization (which cuts people off from the contexts in which, say, tuneful, texted weeping once seemed natural) and the influence of Middle Eastern versions of Islam. Thus this historical moment that undercuts tradition seems also to cut into spaces traditionally reserved for cultural improvisation (Sawyer 1996), areas of culture previously shielded from at least some forms of surveillance.

My 1996 fieldwork also confirmed the impression, gained in 1992, that a wide range of expressive genres—from possession-mediumship and women's noncommercial healing practices to *bilāp* (tuneful, texted weeping)[18]—is "becoming extinct" (*bilupto haiye jācche*). A vital tradition of tuneful narrative (the singing of tales or ballads for which some use the label *sāhir*) is dead, for all practical purposes. What Matlab men call *sāhir* (songs associated with boatmen and laborers that were often bawdy) are now heavily critiqued and rarely performed. Women's *thāṭṭā-tāmāśā* (teasing) songs, once commonly performed in cities and villages all over the Bengal region during prenuptial *gāye-halud* ceremonies ("painting the body with turmeric"; cf. Raheja and Gold 1994), have almost vanished from elite weddings in Dhaka and are less common even in villages (Professor H. K. Arefeen, personal communication 1996). Most of the genres mentioned were, like *bilāp*, tuneful; many were the domain of women. These gendered "genre wars" remind us that in contemporary rural Bangladesh, women's health complaints are often ignored, cut off, or construed as malinger-ing (Hashemi and Schuler 1992; Wilce 1995), and the legal testimony of two women is needed to counterbalance that of one man, in a rape case, for instance.

Modernist/Islamic reformism began to influence the Bengal region pro-foundly in the nineteenth century, condemning as local impurities such practices as the "riotous reading of *marsiyā* poems on the death of the martyrs" on the day of Ashura (Mannan 1966: 171), as well as a Muslim cult of *Manasā* and *Śitalā* (the Hindu snake and smallpox goddesses), "to whom they pray for relief from disease or other misfortune and for the fulfillment of their desires" (168). If this cult of emotion (riotousness) and of goddesses among Muslims represented a substrate of resistance to Islam insofar as it was once perceived as a religion foreign to Bengal and its values, its elimination was and is understandably a high priority for Middle East–inspired Islamists. Women's status in general is im-pacted by histories of ideological struggle beginning in the nineteenth century and lasting into the present.

My Entry into This History—My Research

I set out in 1991 to listen to troubles talk for what it could teach me of the meaning of persons and relationships in Bangladesh. I took audio and video recording equipment, although I would often hear troubles talk so fleeting that recording it mechanically was out of the question. But I did record those words in my fieldnotes, and I was able to mechanically record about 50 other troubles-telling encounters. With help from my field assistant Faisal and others, I tran-scribed about 20 of them in whole or in part. These recordings were made in a variety of circumstances. I sought out medical encounters in obvious places, such as the shops of pharmacists or biomedical practitioners (called *ḍāktārs*) and sites where traditional healers see patients. On some occasions field assistants helped me conduct interviews, and we transcribed the tapes together. As to how representative the transcripts are, my involvement with some persons was long enough to judge transcribed excerpts of their interaction as typical. In the cases of patients whom I did not encounter more than once, I derive contextualizing evidence from hints in the encounters themselves, and from other ethnographic knowledge, including long-term relationships with practitioners. With regard to the "illness careers" (Goffman 1961) and social relationships represented, I make no strong claims about how the transcribed encounters affected illness careers, but wherever possible I will describe the outcome of each case as I heard it narrated and saw it lived out.

It is odd to be a foreigner fairly fluent in Bangla. Foreigners' status is liminal even in a place like Matlab, which has been fairly overrun by researchers associated with ICDDR,B for about 25 years. The Bengal region bore the brunt of British colonialism, and its effects are enduring. Being a white-skinned, English-speaking foreigner cannot help but link one with this history of domina-tion and repression. Identified in this way, I heard in the Bangla talk all around me elements of what Scott (1990) calls the "public transcripts" and "hidden transcripts" of the dominated. I often heard two types of discourse that frankly trouble me, two ways of speaking—public enough for me to hear them but pulsing with subterranean tensions. The first is praise of foreigners, which is disturbing because it is part of an invidious comparison wherein some Bangla-deshis disparage their countrymen (see Maloney 1988). The second more openly challenges the power of persons like myself. I call it "hangtang foreigner talk." It is hidden only in that crowds and distances preserve the anonymity of those who "throw" such sounds at the quickly passing foreigner. "Hangtang" is my typification of the nasalized, nonlinguistic sounds that students in Matlab College (grades 11–12) and younger boys make, evidently as a bitingly playful representation of the sounds they perceive as produced by non-Bangla speakers. Although the effect seems to me more like Chinese than English, it is evidently understood to be English in some sense. Hidden within crowds, boys thrust these words at rich foreigners, challenging the status often ascribed to them and resisting their hegemonic role in foreign-aid-dependent Bangladesh. I raise this issue both to situate myself in this postcolonial fieldwork situation and to introduce the theme of resistance as a functional substrate in Matlab's culture of communication. Hangtang made me as uncomfortable as the idea of being laughable made George Orwell in Burma (Scott 1990: 10).

The Sound and Significance of Bangladeshi Troubles Talk

Given the long tradition in anthropology of grounding one's analysis within locally named realities, I must admit that "complaint" does not pass that test, at least not at the level of single-word (lexicalized) category terms. Complaining is for Bangladeshis a "hypocognized" activity (Levy 1973), a last resort for the vulnerable. Women *in extremis* do tell troubles, but to do so is to take risks. Self-assertion of this sort is a necessary evil, "evil" not in itself but due to the risks it poses. For Muslim men, complaining is a less risky option, surrounded by few if any sanctions. Imagine a taxonomic hierarchy with inclusiveness at the top and specificity at the bottom (Hanks 1990: 151). Admittedly, there is no inclusive Bangla term for the complaints category, nor, at the bottom of the hierarchy, are there terms for some of the most specific varieties that can be recorded. But for that matter, the English term "complaint" is too broad for my purposes; English forces me to resort to phrases such as "troubles talk" or "state-of-being com- plaint" to exclude accusations from the broad sense of complaints. Yet it is sig- nificant that people commonly use several midlevel terms to identify some types of complaint.[19] Bangla speakers use labels for criticism/accusation (*nāliś, abhijhog*), crying (*kānnākāṭi*), lamentation (*bilāp*), and chanting or calling "God, God" (*Āllāh Āllāh karā*).[20]

Named practices such as *Āllāh Āllāh karā* and *bilāp* exert some gravitational pull on unnamed practices,[21] or at least on the ways people refer to practices. That is, even when there is no clear agreement (on the scene or in consultants' post hoc reflections) that someone is "doing x" (a named speech act), named acts or genres influence both actor-speaker and interpreter-hearer. Thus when an old man's singsong speech breaks through to a fully melodic text—of a secular nature—one sees the influence of *Āllāh Āllāh karā* and *bilāp* on the chanting. This performance in some ways defies categorization, using as it does linguis- ticomusical forms with religious connotations in an evidently secular way. Hence post hoc consultants, after hearing the tape, and naturally (given the nature of cultural models of cognition) finding their minds filled with recognized categories rather than category-blurring performances, apply known labels that match best, if only approximately (Briggs and Bauman 1992).

Although the category closest to "complaints" is expressed in Bangla by phrases like *asubidhār kathā balā* (speaking words of trouble) rather than one lexeme, there are certain structural characteristics of complaints noticeable to the analyst (not necessarily to actors in the thick of it). Elements contributing to an integrated set of practices—complaints—are found at several levels. Complaint clauses are typically constructed with stative verbs taking experiencer subjects. The near-obligatory "grammar of complaint"—the omnipresence of experiencer- subject construction in framing illness narratives and much of troubles talk— does not determine the experience of troubles but does stand in dialectical relationship with it. Notably, the experiencer-subject construction—contrasting with the transitive English grammar of "I caught a cold"—does not prevent Bangladeshis in actual discourse from holding someone responsible for becom- ing ill. In one utterance, one can narrate the act that rendered the sick person vulnerable—traveling at night, sitting on the windy top deck of a launch, moving too close to a tree, or violating some other taboo. In the next utterance, such a speaker logically concludes, "And thus so-and-so was struck by illness," though the latter will be phrased literally, "And thus, to him, illness struck." While the grammatical preference reflected in this "striking" Bangla inference does not preclude the first "blaming" utterance, Bangla fashions of speaking do seem to sustain perceptual habits that decouple discrete agency from the experience of illness, if not from suffering in general.[22]

Besides the clause-level grammatical preference for the experiencer-subject construction, lexical and phonological elements also contribute to the integrity of the nonlexicalized inclusive-level category. There is a paradigm class of interjections, including *hāy* (typically doubled, *hāy hāy* [woe, woe!]), *māgo* (oh, mother!), and *iś* (ouch!)—which speakers use to complain (express distress) or to commiserate.

Bangladeshi troubles talk is emotion talk, reflecting not only on problematic external realities but also on inner states (Ochs and Schieffelin 1989). At least potentially, a complaint causes its audience to know or empathically experience something to which it might otherwise have no access. Complaints thus move inner states from subjective experience into social space, turning private concerns into interpersonal concerns. So complaints often heard in Bangla discourse—*bhālo lāge nā* ("good feel not") is typical of them—deserve analytic attention as unique bridges between subjectivity and intersubjectivity. The words *bhālo lāge nā* may precede an exposition of a variety of troubles, somatic, psychic, or social (see table 1-2). Also, a variety of complements may precede the verb *lāge* (feel; literally "strike"). Table 1-2 thus lists common symptoms that may "strike" Bangla speakers. These complaints never cease to be social signs; the responses they evoke, including criticism, are also central to my analysis.

What do complaints about inner states mean? Or, better, what is it that persons *do* when they complain about body or soul, about their state of being? I went into the field looking for evidence that Bangladeshis make explicit or implicit links between somatic symptoms and psychosocial distress. Suffering and accounts of it are topics worthy of anthropological attention whether or not sufferers make such links. But if—through local accounts or some defensible interpretation of behavior—we find links with social relations, complaints take on all the more importance for our field. Phenomenological anthropology argues that persons experience their bodies not in a presocial but in a social form of consciousness (Csordas 1990). Moreover, the bodily experience becomes even more clearly social as it is topicalized in social interaction (Wilce 1997).

Table 1-2. Pre-complements of *lāge*: "Striking" Bangla complaints.

Bangla	Gloss
man(e) khārāp	emotionally down
bhay	fear
asthir	unsettled, upset
asahya	intolerable
byathā	pain
durbal	weak
jvar	inner heat (feverish)
māthā bhāri	heavy-headed
kāś	cough
thāndā sardi	cold/runny nose
mājhe jvālā jantranā	abdominal pain/discomfort
peṭ [p]hāpā [p]hāpā	bloating of stomach
peṭe dheyu/dheku	burps

Complaints As Interactively Constructed,
Personally Historicized

This book is not about complaints as symptoms, as reified signs of disease. Rather, I disclose here the social and discursive dynamics of complain*ing*, or troubles telling. I explore the degree to which troubles bear the stamp of social interaction—that is, the extent to which they receive their meaning and even their form in the process of conversational interaction. If the very grammar of sentences composing a narrative may owe as much to the eye gaze and attentive-ness/inattention of interlocutors as to any prior design the speaker might have conceived (Goodwin 1979), troubles talk must also reflect the emergent qualities of interaction, those qualities that make face-to-face interaction, like a partially improvised dance or jam session, impossible to script completely.

At the same time, the semiotic processes through which we convince our-selves that we are stable as selves across time and context (Ewing 1990) include participation in repetitive speech. One woman presented here performed *bilāp* (lament), repeating a theme with variations over the course of a week. Her audience clearly had a role in shaping each performance, sometimes even the content of a particular poetic line of the lament text; still, this woman Latifa (and her audience) frequently stepped out of the performative-emergent moments to frame her weeping in terms of the history of her life. That is, troubles tellers like Latifa do not lack a sense of self, continuity of self, or personal-experiential-narrative history simply because their troubles are necessarily coconstructed in emergent talk. Put differently, discursive strands of individuation and of relationality are woven together in this South Asian setting (oversimplified renderings of Asian "selfless personhood" in the anthropological literature not-withstanding) and in Western settings as well (Battaglia 1995b). Thus I attempt here to faithfully represent discourse in its Bangladeshi context while daring to take narrative representations of (seemingly centered, personal) identity seri-ously as they claim a listenership.

Troubles Telling in the Literature

In his essay "The Sick Who Do Not Speak," Basil Sansom has provided nega-tive ethnographic evidence confirming the indexical connection of troubles talk or illness narration to self and society: "Amongst Aborigines of Darwin fringe camps ... each episode of serious illness leaves behind its signs," key among which is the transfer of the right to tell its story to the one who is chiefly respon-sible for playing the hero's role in nursing a critically ill person back to health ("You can['t] tell about that time you bin sick"; 1982: 184). That transfer of rights is the counterpart of the judgment that, during the illness event, the sick "do not speak"; whatever utterances are heard from their mouths represent the illness itself speaking through them. Their words are thus "discreditable" (Goff-man 1963; see example 25). Such a view of the transferability of speaking rights reflects the egalitarian arrangement of aboriginal social life. The taboo on telling one's own tale of serious illness reflects a concept of "ownership" very different from that in (post) industrial societies, a view suited to a mobile egalitarian band. As Sansom puts it, "such signs [of sicknesses past] are essential to the creation and perpetuation of relationships of long-term indebtedness amongst a community of people who have no property but rely instead on verbal warranties (called 'the word') to carry indebtedness over from the past into the present and so to transform local fields or networks of social relationships by locating obligations of enduring indebtedness within them" (1982: 183–184).

Sansom's account buttresses my argument that troubles talk and evaluations of it are governed by cultural concepts of selfhood, and thus relativizes a Western sense of personal rights to illness narratives. The sense of ownership of one's own story is not universal, and ought not be projected onto Bangladeshi troubles tellers. Still, we must see Sansom's case in a comparative ethnological framework. His aboriginal consultants were reflecting a way of life in which words seem to represent the most valuable commodities in a particular economy of symbolic and material goods. Theirs is a mode of production and sociality in which forms of wealth must be transportable (keeping them to a minimum) and status distinctions minimized. The symbolic-material economy and concomitant flexibility of social order sharply distinguishes Australian Aboriginal society from Bangladeshi society. The question of talking rights in Bangladesh should be approached empirically. When I argue that Bangladeshis do value the opportunity to tell their own stories and do resent interruptions, I appeal to evidence internal to the transcribed interactions themselves.

Rather than simply expecting that some societies—like Sansom's Aboriginals—see talk as a burden and others see it as a privilege, it is likely that talk is cast as privilege or burden by particular parties for strategic purposes. Thus, Bangladeshis could cast presenting a complaint as a burden in order to support the practice of indirection, while at other times those who tend to be "spoken for" resist others' attempts to speak for them as if speaking were more a privilege than a burden (cf. Irvine 1989). The tendency for men to speak for women in medical settings is part of a system that redundantly deprives women of the right to speak. Admittedly, neither overlapping speech nor even speaking for another in Bangladesh is always "aggressive." I did not feel violated by my field mother Rani telling my troubles, putting words in my mouth, when I was too sick with a cold to feel very talkative. But the more hidden, internal, or subjective the symptoms, the greater the danger of others misrepresenting a patient's experience.

Those who have paid serious attention to troubles telling (Jefferson 1980, 1981, 1984a, 1984b) fall into two camps—those who investigate marked genres such as laments, and those who interpret the telling of troubles in everyday talk. The latter follow Radcliffe-Brown (1964) in dichotomizing unmarked "natural" crying and "ritual" weeping, which is often texted and constitutes an extreme end of the troubles telling continuum I describe here. Recent work on laments uncovers their poetry, structure, and power (in both aesthetic and political senses); thus laments must be taken as a key site for the construction of aesthetics, personhood, emotion, and gender politics (Briggs 1992a, 1992b, 1993; Das 1990, 1996; Feld 1990; Feld and Fox 1994; Grima 1991, 1992; Herzfeld 1993; Kaeppler 1993; Seremetakis 1990, 1991; Urban 1996). Jefferson (1980) and others who explore everyday interaction in which troubles-talk emerges also find such encounters to be structured. If everyday troubles talk is interactively and aesthetically structured (Good 1994), the converse is also true: ritual weeping makes no sense to participants in the absence of semiotic linkages between marked and unmarked crying (as Urban 1988 argues with regard to Bororo-Amazonian weeping).

I find it problematic to label even the laments represented here—or, in fact, those represented in the literature—as "ritualized," without raising important caveats. For analytic purposes, it is useful to locate "ritual" and "improvisation" as two poles of a continuum, following Sawyer (1996) who traces the system-atically contrastive tendencies of performances that actors locate at the ritual versus improvisational poles. Ritual and improvisation are characterized con-trastively by ossification versus revivalism, low creative involvement versus high, indexical reflexivity versus indexical entailment, narrow versus broad genre definition, large versus small "ready-mades,"[23] low versus high audience involvement, resistance versus receptivity to novelty, changes that are long lasting versus short lived, and high versus low cultural valuation. The utility of this model, however, rests in its ability to explicate the gray areas between the poles even as it acknowledges the polarity of the ideal types. Seremetakis (1991), analyzing Greek antiphonal funerary laments by women, labels them ritualized even while acknowledging their improvisational ethic, but never directly addresses the paradox. In contrast, my analysis of the resistant quality of laments—and certainly less marked forms of troubles talk as well—is enhanced by Sawyer's model. While we must keep in mind the improvisational quality of much if not all ritual (Duranti, personal communication, 1992), the polarity seems to inform actors, shaping folk criticism as well as performances.

Troubles Talk As Social Trouble and Resistance

The telling of troubles disturbs listeners. In a series of experiments, health psy-chologist Pennebaker has discovered that Americans who write about or narrate past trauma can experience health benefits reflecting enhanced immunocompe-tence (Berry and Pennebaker 1993; Pennebaker, Kiecolt-Glaser, and Glaser 1988; Pennebaker 1990). Troubles recipients (Jefferson 1984a), by contrast, ex-perience anxiety while hearing relatives and friends express ongoing trauma or grief after such events as losing a loved one or going through an earthquake. In the San Francisco Bay area after the Loma Prieta earthquake, T-shirts appeared saying, "Please refrain from telling me your earthquake story" (Pennebaker 1993: 211). Pennebaker acknowledges that this psychological defensiveness is a social construct, but we must go beyond that to analyze the relationship between psychological and sociocultural defenses. There is an analogous pattern—"moti-vation to disclose" and "avoidance by the listener"—in Bangladesh.

One of the things this book does is to ask why potential audiences increasingly criticize a variety of traditional ways of speaking in Bangla (and they have since the nineteenth century; Banerjee 1989). To reduce all explanations of attacks on particular performances, genres, or performers to purely personal motives would be a mistake. However, it would be equally wrong to limit our explanations to a structural-functionalist analysis, for instance, of the modernist-Islamist critique of Bangladeshi folklore as if broad social patterns were not reflected at the personal level. My discomfort in hearing hangtang hurled at me like a weapon must be similar to the experiences of those relatively powerful Bangladeshis whom I saw silencing others' laments, complaints, and unorthodox prayer songs. Not only were these social actors moved to stop traditional lament performances in particular situations, but they also felt deeply that their actions were necessary or right—they were personally motivated by locally and socially constituted values. Although the laments ranged over many themes, some who silenced them sensed that the laments were directly or indirectly critiquing or lampooning them. [24]

The experience of defensive anxiety—and here I am indebted to Eagleton's perspective on the "affective dimensions of ideology" (1991: 221)—can be a personal reflex of socially positioned ideological defensiveness. To hear blasphemy or politically subversive words, for instance, arouses anxiety—particularly in circumstances where blasphemy or subversion is coercively suppressed and even physical proximity to those who utter it is therefore dangerous. It is no surprise that laments may, at least in the Punjab and in Bangladesh, be construed as acts of resistance when they sometimes contain challenges to religious worldviews (Das 1996: 80). Even to complain in less marked speech is to present a public challenge, something that the politically weak often avoid via "hidden transcripts" of resistance (Scott 1990: 154). If the performance of troubles talk or even marked genres like lament were perfectly predictable, these forms might arouse less anxiety. It is the nature of improvisation, however, that its outcome is emergent and unpredictable. Opportunities for subversion—or perceptions of the riskiness of speech acts—thrive on that kind of indeterminacy.

Troubles talk itself—"complaining," if we can use the term without its typically pejorative connotations—is resistant in several senses. Even the most somatic or psychological of complaints tends to be either metatheological—comments on dominant worldviews, but comments that share with those worldviews a common theological idiom—or political. And, "the religious convictions of the 'disprivileged' reflected an implicit protest against their worldly fate" (Scott 1990: 157). It is not difficult at all to perceive the resistant subtext in, say, an African-American spiritual song, in which religious conviction takes on a decidedly this-worldly tone. Even within an extended family in Bangladesh, a disgruntled member's complaint can take on metatheological overtones, as though the trouble itself is a way of distinguishing the teller from recipients of the troubles talk. The troubles teller seems to be asking, "If your theology is valid, why am I experiencing this?"

De Certeau (1984) has described everyday life in terms of "resistance."

Troubles talk, illness narratives, and complaints are tactical in de Certeau's sense without being conscious (socially explicit); they are self-assertive without necessarily being linked with the centered, bounded self projected in certain Western discourses. Complaints are worth studying because they resist, and resistance is ontologically necessary in the interface of self and society, not so much because resistance is functional in a bio-individualistic sense but because it is the naturally elicited mirror image of culture/organization/sociality/hege-mony. That is, complaints index resistance to enculturation, particularly the enculturation of suffering. At the same time, they can scarcely avoid reflecting and reproducing those processes of enculturation. Scott writes that

> We are all familiar with grumbling as a form of veiled complaint. Usually the intention behind the grumbling is to communicate a general sense of dissatis-faction without taking responsibility for an open, specific complaint. It may be clear enough to the listener from the context exactly what the complaint is, but, via the grumble, the complainer has avoided an incident and can, if pressed, disavow any intention to complain. (1990: 154)

Grumbling is indeed safer than shouting. And complaining about illness symptoms is safer than attacking structures that either produce those symptoms, as in the unequal social and ethnic distribution of disease brought about through environmental policy (Feierman 1985), or provoke embodied signs of protest (Lewis 1975). Still, if we follow Scott's (1990) metaphor of the "hidden tran-script," we do find the protest, hidden but nonetheless transcribed within com-plaints.

Nichter (1981) has described a range of symptom narrations (or mere men-tions) as idioms of distress. We should not take this phrase to mean that a range of idioms neutrally expresses some formless content of distress any more than we should interpret Scott's comments on the strategic choice of forms of protest as an affirmation that the protest is without any particular content or aim, or that the form protest takes has no bearing on the outcome. With these caveats in mind, I frame my theory of troubles talk in terms of such choices of idioms, narrative frameworks, or semiotic modalities. Although troubles talk is much more than veiled protest, this resistant dimension of complaints is neglected in discussions of illness and disease in Bangladesh and therefore has received particular emphasis in this book.

Agency, Repression, and the Practice of Troubles Telling

Troubles tellers often occupy relatively weak roles, although they may gain some benefits along the way, particularly in the work-disability system of any society (the system, however informal, that grants relief from responsibility to those recognized as sick; Kleinman 1986). Yet even apparent passivity may be a resource exercised by Bangladeshi persons as moral agents—particularly trou-bles tellers. This book explores the subjecthood and agency of Bangladeshi troubles tellers and *rogī*—that is, those who have a *rog* (illness), patients or sufferers. As persons, they are not simply acted upon by illness, practitioners of healing, or significant others. They act. Semanticists call direct objects "patients" or "experiencers" of a verb's action, and the semantic subject of a transitive verb its "agent." But the patients in my field experience were themselves agents.[25] To cast them as agents does not make them liars, malingerers, or even unilateral manipulators, but rather persons engaged in conflict and negotiation to maintain well being.

Sufferers and medical patients, as linguistic subjects, exercise some degree of agency by telling their troubles, but never in a vacuum. Troubles recipients respond in various ways. Critical listeners—particularly those whose responses uphold such aspects of social structure as gender hierarchy—share in reproducing old hierarchies. Though it shares some of the qualities of literary or art criticism—critics of troubles tellers may cite violations of the aesthetics of everyday management of the body-mind (Wikan 1990; Desjarlais 1992)—criticism of complainers is political nonetheless. It plays a role in managing power relations at the micro level. The political significance of criticizing troubles tellers is seen also in the way that such criticism reinforces a gendered distribution of emotions and emotionality, and in the discourses that link violations of "heart management" (*man śakto karāno*, making the heartmind hard;[26] cf. Wikan 1990 and Desjarlais 1992) to the aesthetic realm as well as the health of persons and polities.

This is to say that troubles tellers can be complaining subjects/agents but can also become objects of others' (meta) complaints. Two strategic means by which troubles talk is discouraged are proscription of complaints as inauspicious acts of ingratitude toward the divine and of self-assertion as egotism, and honoring suffering in silence or wordless sighs when the sufferer is a woman.

The suppression of complaints used as requests for expensive treatment is explained locally in terms of resource constraints. But this is only one locally salient motivation for silencing troubles talk. Casual listeners in the streets of a bazaar may criticize those who say, off the cuff, *bhālo lāge nā* ([I] don't feel good). Certainly family members criticize even an elder when his expression of trouble becomes desperate enough to violate the accepted norms of theology or polite speech.

How Medicine (De)Values Sufferers' Words and Delegitimizes Complaints

Although doctors still depend on patients to give some account of their troubles, biomedicine has increasingly attended to visible signs produced by instruments, resulting in a long-term trend to relegate patients' narratives to a lower order of certainty (Reiser 1978). The strongly technological orientation of biomedicine reflects and sustains the dominant ideology of Western societies (Mishler 1984) and typically neglects the meanings of illness in patients' lives (Waitzkin 1991). Bangladeshi practitioners—even nonbiomedical ones—follow this trend. If biomedicine is at best ambivalent toward patients' speech, it is not surprising that doctors interrupt their patients. In the political economy of speech[27] in doctor-patient relations, metacommunicative privileges, including the right to assign labels or evaluate processes, are typically held by the doctor. Conversation analysis holds talk to be governed by turn-taking rules; attuned to the actions of copresent others, conversationalists cooperatively produce order and meaning. Interruptions stand out as potential examples of conversational noncooperation; but interruption must be distinguished from benign overlap. Both would seem to be violations of unspoken turn-taking rules. Upon closer examination, we note that some overlapping speech entails a harmonious coproduction of structure. In some speech communities listeners may contribute to the overall effectiveness of communication through a cooperative "conversational duet"; partners may encourage each other with overlapping speech (Falk 1979; Tannen 1979: 100). By contrast, interruptions represent a breakdown of communicative cooperation; an interrupter indeed cuts off the previous speaker, dismisses the old topic, and imposes a new one.

Edelsky's (1981) research on conversational interaction in institutional settings helps unpack the concept of "floor." While the unequal distribution of speaking rights is clearly an issue deserving investigation, there is not just one kind of floor in any given setting or any culture, let alone around the world. In academic committee meetings, Edelsky found that women participated most intensely when the floor shifted to sequences of short turns in which more than one speaker contributed to building a thread of talk. Men dominated a kind of floor characterized by longer turns. Gal (1989) calls for attention to the issue of how differently empowered persons manage to shift floor types. In Bangladeshi medical complaints, practitioners and the guardians accompanying women who visit medical settings sometimes shift not only topic (interrupting women) but also floor types (making it less likely that women's speech is heard).

In relationships such as that of patients to doctors, asymmetrical control of topic (one conversational partner doing all the interrupting) reflects an asymmetry of power. Powerlessness means loss of control. The interruptions relevant to the cases explored in this book are the "sudden and unilateral topic changes" that male physicians often make, particularly with female patients (Ainsworth-Vaughn 1992; Fisher and Groce 1990).[28] Often, the effect is to limit patient responses to the minimum, even the monosyllabic—yes or no. It is patients who attempt to add detail to their minimal responses—or pursue psychosocial themes beyond the limited opportunity typically given to describe their problems (the "exposition exchange")—whom American doctors are most likely to cut off. Many such patients are less likely to appear for follow-up appointments, comply with instructions, or experience positive overall outcomes (Putnam and Stiles 1993).

Biomedical encounters are not homogeneous. The quality of the practitioner-patient relationship or the extent of domination varies with sex of the practitioner (Ainsworth-Vaughn 1992). Often, but not always, stereotypic gender relations can predict power moves in conversation,[29] and gender inequality exacerbates doctor-patient asymmetry when a female patient consults a male doctor. Medical relationships also vary across institutional sites, such as private allopathic pharmacies versus Ayurvedic shops or even possession-mediums' homes in Bangladesh, and private clinics versus public hospitals in the United States (Lazarus 1988).

Human distress is not experienced by disembodied minds, soulless bodies, or unsocialized creatures, but rather by fully embodied, socially engaged persons. Csordas (1990) has offered "embodiment" as a new paradigm for anthropology, whereas Kleinman (1992) and Good (1994) have argued that we must do more to link embodied suffering with social context. Anthropologists have also called attention to the risk of the reductionist delegitimation of suffering entailed in much biomedical practice (Ware 1992). Medicalization of realities traditionally considered part of the normal range of variation in human life is partly to blame for the widespread use of labels such as "alexithymia" (no words for feelings) or "somatization" (the physical-symptomatic expression of non-specific distress) for patterns of behavior (manifesting distress through non-verbal means) that are better described in interactive terms (Kirmayer 1984). Dramatic, embodied "acting out" of distress, or even simply verbally dramatic animation of the sick role, can be vulnerable to medicalizing redefinition: "Such drama indicates that the problem is in their head."

On the other hand, those in pain can find that dramatizing their troubles is quite necessary. It was in Los Angeles during my doctoral coursework that I found troubles telling as a topic of study. I had made a videotape in a Bangla-speaking home—the sort of dinner table conversation video so often used by conversation analysts. During repeated viewing of the videotape, my attention was drawn to the way the woman of the house, Bonhi, suddenly introduced a note of trouble. She not only said "my whole body hurts," but the vowels in the sentence creaked like painful joints, and she used her body effectively to point out and enact the pain. I was to spend many hours viewing the tape and discussing what I was transcribing with Bonhi herself. Neither she nor the Bangla-speaking friends to whom she introduced me could come up with metalanguage for the vocal quality she used, which phoneticians call "whispery creak." What Bonhi did do for me was to describe its function; she said it was part of a sort of *nāṭak* (drama), a process of dramatization. Whence comes this dramatization, and her choice to refer to it as such? As with somatization, we should recognize dramatization as both an on-the-ground idiom or strategy available to troubles tellers and a typification (Schutz 1970) of that strategy, and typification can distort as well as represent practice.

Bangladeshi troubles talk, particularly genres like lament, may be in trouble on the ground, but in academic and medical discourses in the West and in Bangladesh, patients' complaints are vulnerable to officially empowered typifications—they may be delegitimated. Both immediate/folk and medical/academic metadiscourses delegitimize the original. Still, despite the risk entailed in calling any complaints "somatization," there are reasons to use the concept.

Anthropologists like Comaroff (1985) regard somatization as symbolic. Following Victor Turner (1964), Comaroff, Kleinman, and others advocate a view of much suffering as sociosomatic—"somatized signs of a wider social malaise" (Comaroff 1985: 182). Still, Fabrega (1990) views the psychiatric definition of somatization as a problematic, culture-bound notion. Those social psychiatrists who use the notion of somatization have tended to associate it with non-Western peoples and with economically marginal populations in the West. A diagnostic category once common in the West, neurasthenia, is regarded by contemporary psychiatrists as one label for the somatization of distress. Kleinman (1986:152) argues that neurasthenia in China continues to be a relevant "cultural idiom of distress and an interpersonal coping process" because it is simply less problematic politically and socially to express distress in a somatic idiom than in some more direct idiom. His more general point is that "learned daily life pattern[s] of communicating distress and seeking help" are culturally variable, and that these patterns include relative preferences for psychological, somatic, or sociopolitical idioms of distress.

An ideology of language (or, more broadly, of semiosis) that ranks referential linguistic expression of emotion above its performance (Urban 1996: 175) requires that the comparison of various idioms of distress be invidious. It need not be so. We ought not ignore the semiotic diversity of cultures of emotion, subjectivity, distress, or dis-ease. Cultural scripts can rather explicitly devalorize discursive expressions of discontent, encouraging subtler forms of acting out distress, perhaps even prodding actors to choose between that sort of dramatization and somatizing. When Bangladeshi children wail or adults perform *bilāp* they are following social norms of self-dramatization that contrast starkly with those of the Eskimos described by Briggs (1970). For Bangladeshis, the option of verbalizing distress in emotion-jargon is no more salient than it was in pre-Freudian Vienna; psychologizing idioms have only recently penetrated the speech of the urban well-to-do. Hence, multinational drug companies have launched advertising campaigns to spread messages like *bhiṣannatā ekṭā rog* (depression is an illness).

What I am pointing to are the ways in which Bangladeshi bodies are "good to think" social thoughts with (Scheper-Hughes and Lock 1987), but I am also denying that this somatization is a strategy to which they are limited by illiteracy. In fact, Bangladeshis inherit nondualistic body-mind theories of medicine in the Ayurvedic textual underpinnings of contemporary thought and practice surrounding health and healing. The idiom of Ayurvedic medicine is predominantly somatic, although the very cosmos itself is linked to the soma therein.

Still, though I deconstruct a psychiatric discourse built on an invidious comparison of somatization with psychologization, I also point to local discourses that delegitimize complaints. Kirmayer (1984) and Fabrega (1990) have problematized somatization as a psychiatric category, particularly as applied to non-Western societies. When Fabrega claims, however, that South Asian discourses on emotion or illness lack "an epistemology much less a technology that serves to validate illness independent of its report" (664), he does a double injustice to the region. He underestimates both the sophistication of its epistemological and metalinguistic resources in general and the specific extent to which patriarchy licenses powerful males to question the significance of complaints authored by females (to cite but one example of a class of persons whose expressions of dis-tress may be doubted). The epistemological and practical rejection of women's complaints in Bangladesh has been documented by Hashemi and Schuler (1992).

During a visit to Dhaka in 1992 I brought up the subject of *bilāp* with my hosts, Mr. and Mrs. Rejak Khan. Mr. Khan pointed out that there once was a class of women, *rudālī*, who were paid to lament at funerals (cf. Devi 1994).[30] Mr. Khan said that the purpose of hiring such people was to enable even those who might not be distraught over the death at hand to do the proper thing. Mrs. Khan was scandalized by what her husband was saying. She argued that people would certainly realize why some people would hire another party to grieve for their departed loved one instead of doing their own grieving.

Mr. Khan then asked rhetorically, "You don't really believe *bilāp* is ever sincere do you? It's just the same ritual emotion, the same putting on a good show, as you've seen when so-and-so reads the Qur'an and weeps ritual tears."

Mrs. Khan still would not agree. To her, recitation of the Qur'an and funeral wailing are two very different speech acts (the former more adequately charac-terized as "ritual," I gather). She accepted the possibility that a proper display of religious sentiment might need to be intentionally managed; but to her, one either truly grieves for a loved one or one does not—no one would believe in the sincerity of someone who hired a wailer.

If Fabrega's (1990) critique of the concept of somatization risks glossing over empirical evidence from Bangladesh, so does a global assertion that edu-cated elites tend to psychologize, intellectualize, or verbalize, whereas working-class persons tend to somatize. A psychiatrist friend allowed me to be present during her clinical interview with Nellie, a brilliant but troubled student from Dhaka University. Nellie complained that her hands trembled uncontrollably, particularly when she faced a group or had to give a talk. Her description was devoid of emotion terms; it was confined to a description of a physical symptom. The psychiatrist's feedback, however, included such remarks as *āpnār bhay lāge* (You feel afraid/nervous/anxious). Nellie left the room when her psychiatrist told her the interview was over. My psychiatrist friend and I began to discuss what had happened in terms of its broader significance. I asked her what signs in a patient's speech and so forth she considered evidence that the physical symp-toms being described pointed beyond themselves to an emotional problem. I had phrased the question with her own previously expressed psychiatric theory in mind, but I intentionally avoided reinserting the term "somatization" into our discussion. But the doctor reintroduced it herself and volunteered the opinion that somatization is common among the illiterate and in the Third World in general.

How well does Nellie, a graduate student at the best university in Bangla-desh, represent the Third World? While her idiom might conceivably be used to buttress the generalization that, regardless of social class, people of the Third World are less likely to use psychological idioms than are their postindustrial world counterparts, there is another issue here. My psychiatrist colleague was unaware of the role of her own translation of physical symptom descriptors into emotion language (*bhay*, fear) and of the contrast between this generalization and the case of the person who had just left. The young woman was highly educated, yet spoke in a somatic idiom, describing physical symptoms. If the doctor herself was psychologizing, she was unaware of it. If anything, Nellie demonstrated that somatization is not the exclusive domain of the uneducated. Yet her discourse also demonstrated the absence of psychological idioms in everyday usage (the more so in rural Bangla),[31] constraining the use of somatic, social, or religious idioms of distress.

The Semiotic Perspective Taken in This Book

Throughout this book, I turn to the semiotics of Charles Sanders Peirce (1839–1914) to help me grasp the verbal and nonverbal modes of Bangladeshi inter-action around times and themes of distress. In particular, I rely on some of his taxonomies of signs and sign relations. Thus, I argue in later chapters that pronouns are only one choice among several indexical options whereby troubles tellers can delimit reference—indexical signs (in this case words) being those whose ability to represent relies less on an arbitrary denotative sense than on a particular relationship to context.

I will not review Peircean semiotics here or even its utility for linguistic anthropology. That has been effectively done by others (Daniel 1984; Hanks 1996; Mertz and Parmentier 1985, 1994). Peirce's "semiotic" offers heuristic devices for the interpretation of communicative behavior in any mode, in any society. Its dynamism enables it to resist the reductionism to which Saussurean semiotics falls prey along with most other paradigms. However, my eclectic brand of semiotics is indebted to phenomenology, ethnomethodology, and translinguistics (Bakhtin 1981), as well as to Peirce. It is axiomatic to me that experience is "semiotically mediated" (Mertz and Parmentier 1985)—shaped, though not determined, by pervasive semiotic habits.

2

LISTENING IN MATLAB: WHERE TROUBLES TALK LED ME

Fashions of speaking and thresholds of tolerance change with social conditions. For example, Fatima and Yasmin, whose *diffuse* (less assertive, less confrontational) somatic complaints and their indexicality are explored in chapter 4, are past childbearing, members of a generation in which schooling was unavailable to rural women. By contrast, Latifa's relatively assertive protest against her brothers' behavior, embedded in a 1992 lament, is that of an educated young woman (chapter 4). And Rehana, who attained an M.A. from Dhaka University in 1991, is one of two Bengali persons who ever complained to me spontaneously of depression; this psychological idiom reflects her engagement with modernity.

Idioms and social space change in tandem. For many rural women the space in which they live is confined to their husband's compound and that of their father, which they may periodically visit (though in the past 10 years, even rural Bangladeshi spaces have become ever more closely linked with modernizing urban centers). Any communication of discontent that takes place in those spaces—the natural home to such intimate stories of trouble, spaces of resistance that are "won and defended in the teeth of power" (Scott 1990: 119)—is less likely to be quashed or co-opted than is public expression of resistance. On the public-hidden continuum the louder the speech or song, the more likely it is to be defined in Bangladesh as public communication, even in domestic space. Loud discourse in which one is defined as performing alone—despite the real extent of the audience's role in coconstruction—is particularly vulnerable. Performances by raconteurs and lamenters that Bangladeshis define as loud and tuneful are in danger.

This book is indeed concerned with endangered genres of tragic eloquence and with literally unsung eloquence occasioned by everyday troubles, speech shielded from publicity. An interview far too multiparty to label "private," yet which took place inside closed doors away from the adult men of the residential compound, is a good example of unmarked troubles talk. I turn now to an account of that interview with Aesha.

Encounters with Aesha in the *Bāṛi* Courtyard

In the dry months of fall 1991 when I began my fieldwork, hard-packed dirt courtyards would send up dust to filter the sunlight coming through the fruit trees that provide shade in at least the better-off *bāṛi* (compounds). While walking each day through my adoptive home, I would often see Aesha, my "aunt" (my host's sister-in-law), passing through the courtyard (see figure 2-1) into her cooking hut, or standing in it to bathe one of her eight children or prune her fruit trees. At times she would approach and even speak with me where the courtyard blended into the packed earth foundation of my house, standing outside the room in which I had my writing table. Not having known whether it would be possible for women or even men to open up to me, a foreign man, I was glad that Aesha was breaking the ice, although I was also uncomfortable with the role of patron that she seemed to cast me in. This is illustrated by a conversation we had about three weeks after I had moved into her village. That day I made an entry in my fieldnotes, describing what she said to me as she stood outside my open "office" in the presence of several of her adult nieces:

Figure 2-1. The *bāṛi* courtyard: Social space and space for crops.

Aesha has warmed up to me. Today she asked me for a Taka 650 loan ($15, perhaps what her son sent each month) if neither her husband nor her police-man son send money. Aesha said, "I'm the poorest of all in the *bāṛi*, so you don't know me as well."

Jiban is her eldest son. She admitted him to the 11th and 12th grade diploma program at Daudkandi College but says she is not able to give him money for books to study further, so he got a job with the police force requiring only a high school diploma.

She was having a loud argument earlier in the morning with an adult male nephew about fish she wasn't receiving from the family ponds, though she was owed a share of the catch. She complained to me that she wasn't able to feed her eight children properly, that they were sick, etc. And "the others" (her husband's three brothers) are each focused on their own families (Bengali *saṅsār*, Sanskrit *saṃsāra*) and thus "don't do anything for" her.[1]

Aesha said, "What should I feed them (my children)? What medicine can I give them? For two or three days, this one (pointing to a child in her arms) has had a fever that won't go away." Her brother died recently. Her mother is also dead, and her father "shakes." Her husband has little income and is going blind from fine-tailoring work, and they have been forced to sell parcels of his land to eat. There is also some kind of problem with a cow.

She said, "No one watches out for me. I have no one left."

Aesha's Status in the Compound

From small talk in my adopted *bāṛi*, I gained the impression that Aesha, the wife of the youngest of Habibur Rahman's brothers, Durim, was a prototypical occupant of the most tenuous adult role in a rural Bangladeshi *bāṛi*, the weakest adult in the extended family from a structural viewpoint. Despite folklore that makes young brides symbols of propitious fertility in raising family and crops, the recent impact of intensive family planning campaigns—added to the structural realities making Aesha a weak member of the family—resulted in Aesha's stigmatization. Old and young residents alike spoke aloud of her excessive number of children, shouting at the children or at Aesha when they were too boisterous. Her husband Durim—participating in the modern cash economy, and one of an increasing number of men dislocated by it—worked far away in Chittagong and visited only once during my seven months at the *bāṛi*. Never did I hear the family make Durim the target of the criticism; it was the woman Aesha whom they criticized for having had so many children. As if she had somehow conceived the children alone, she alone was held responsible.

Six weeks after the "office" courtyard conversation, I decided to tape an open-ended life history interview with Aesha. The informal conversation described in my fieldnote was typical of many that happened so quickly and spontaneously, that interrupting the talk to dig out my tape recorder would have been disruptive. Still, if in those circumstances there were advantages in simply listening without recording, relying on my own memory has its disadvantages. By contrast, mechanical recording facilitates transcription, such as the transcript (see example 1) representing a segment of the life history interview with Aesha.

(For a complete explanation of transcription conventions, see the appendix.) Aesha evidently conceives of this as a formal narrative, opening it as she does by invoking the name of God in the Arabic words with which Muslims begin important tasks (see line 25). The narrative turns on the theme of grief and hardship. How would she characterize what she was doing in this interview? What might she call the sort of speech she engaged in? What native category underlies my focus on complaints? Piecing a phrase together from her own words, we can call this speech genre *dukkho-kaṣṭer kathā* (grief-and-hardship words). Complaints in ethnomedical–therapeutic–problem-solving contexts are called *asubidhār kathā* (problem words).[2]

Example 1. Life history interview with Aesha.

A = Aesha; J = the author/ethnographer

21 A—Uncle,[3] what should I tell? Tell about our home [natal family]?[4]
22 Khaleja (Aesha's niece)—What happened in your life, tell that.
23 A—The whole time, what's happened in my life? That?
24 J—Yes.
25 A—*Bismillāh errahmān errahim e āssālāmu ālāykum, ei* (In the name of Allah, the Merciful, the Compassionate, Peace be with you. There!)
26 J—Not right up close ... [referring to the mike] a little further will do ... It will be
27 better if you keep the mike a little further—Yes.
28 A—What happened in my *sanisāra* [family of procreation], [shall I tell] that now?
29 J—Yes, tell of your life from any, from any direction.
30 A—In my life, in my childhood my mother died, then my father remarried.
31 Then when I was still little he gave me away in marriage. So then I was
32 married. From then on [my life has carried on] in grief and hardship (*dukkho*
33 *kaṣṭe).* [My life] has passed in much hardship. Then my son Jiban was
34 born. Then they all [gesturing to children present] were born. After that I
35 passed my days in grief and hardship; that was when there was grief and hardship.
36 J—For instance?
37 A—From then on, [I] have been in grief and hardship. After that—[I] used to
38 have a brother, Salam—he, too, died. Now my father is still alive but very
39 old, my mother is gone and so is my brother. There is no one.

Rural Bangladeshis are not very familiar with the interview as a speech event, and throughout my fieldwork I was aware that relying on this speech event as my primary learning tool might lead to odd results at best (Briggs 1986). So I tried to record the sorts of speech events that have roots in the soil of Bangladesh, or—if I did need to learn by asking questions—to do so in a way that conformed to local models of talk and learning. At times these efforts left a door open for participants other than the person from whom I wanted to hear directly. Such a participant's question is seen in the transcript of the interview with Aesha, continued in example 2. It touches a painful memory from Aesha's past. All of the local participants (other than outsiders Rehana and myself) were children or unmarried youths, and it was one of these who asked Aesha about her past struggle with *pāgalāmi*, a Bangla category we may gloss as madness.

Example 2. Life history interview with Aesha, second excerpt.

? = Unidentified participant (one of the dozen or so children or adolescents present)

55   J—No, won't you say more?
56   ?—Speak!
57   A—What more do I say?
58   ?—The story of [when you were afflicted with] madness [i.e., tell about when you
59   were mad].
60   A—Bah! What are you [sT][5] saying, you ... mixed up words ...
61   They say I am, or I went, mad. Whatever happened—what tomfoolish words.
62   ?—No, no—it went bad, your body got sick.
63   A—Yes.
64   J—No, you can speak about whatever ...
65   A—This is what people will say—lots of different things[6] ... thoughts, feelings—
66   how many different kinds of heartmindish (*mānasik*) things happen. No, if your
67   body gets weak ... how much can happen! How many things people say!—People
68   say "mad," that's what they say ... I don't [??] with anyone, that is, I don't get upset. If the person[7]
69   is good [mentally healthy?] nothing comes of it, whoever says they're mad. Don't
70   they say "mad, mad"? But they might not be aware that maybe God is watching
71   [them saying that?].
71   Whoever says whatever, let them say it. Right, Uncle? If someone gets ill, what a
72   lot of ... Folks look down on (*hiṅsā kare*) others.
73   You [T][8] said I have too many little kids, these eight you see. And my husband
74   has taken a second wife. My patriline has no prestige; my husband's line has no
75   glory. Local folks
75   speak condescendingly (*hiṅsār kathā*). All these different words! Let them speak. I
76   don't fight
76   with people. Whatever God does with me, I will float above the water[9] like that.
77   Though people say one thing ... whatever—what pain is in people's heartminds!
78   Why do people look down on others? Let them! I won't be like that.
79   Let their mouths say whatever they will today—today they'll say good things,
80   tomorrow they'll lie. They'll slander you. When they're not in your presence ...
81   Why should they get any reward [from God?]? God made all people one sort [that
82   is, equal], whatever people may say.

The younger people of the *bāṛi* had told me that Aesha had been *pāgal*, and I *did* want to hear about it. I wanted to hear Aesha's own perspective on the events. I had hoped she would spontaneously raise the issue, but the children decided to help me by bringing it up themselves. Responding to their blunt questions (lines 58–61), Aesha framed her experience as a bout with serious illness (lines 62 and 72). This might entail a *denial* that she was mad, or mad at least for any reasons

more profound or "endogenous" (Bhattacharyya 1986) than for example a passing fever.

There is a reflective and evaluative tone in this second excerpt that is absent
in the first; here moral evaluation replaces the cataloguing of sorrows evident in
the first. I include both excerpts to draw attention to several dimensions of troubles talk. First, these two narratives are linked by Aesha's mention of hardship,
which clearly takes on an emotional, existential sense in the second segment—
"what pain (*kaṣto*) is in people's heartminds (*mane*)!" Although it is by no
means mentioned in every example I recorded, the word *kaṣto* captures the local
integrity of the events I call troubles tellings or complaints.

Second, Aesha's narrative makes clear the impossibility of making sharp
distinctions between various sorts of troubles—troubles of the body, the *man*
(heartmind), the family, or its economy. Troubles telling interactions like this
one provide privileged access to locally relevant models of the body-mind and
the social body. Aesha eagerly agreed with whoever suggested that her episode
of *pāgalāmi* had resulted from bodily weakness. The implicit model of troubles
expressed here is somatopsychic rather than psychosomatic; that is, the body is
portrayed as the source of her *mānasik* (heartmindish, roughly parallel to our
"mental") trouble. Despite its appeal to a bodily origin, the model of distress that
Aesha and her interlocutor jointly construct is far from being biologically reductionist. Aesha's illness narrative holistically incorporates social and religious
dimensions of physical and mental distress.

The two points I've made here ought to be viewed together. We should
notice the inclusion of a discourse of values in Bangladeshi troubles talk. When
we look at the problem of how talk achieves meaning, we must transcend the
insights of linguistics regarding the systematicity of language per se as well as
those of hermeneutic social science, which tend to read talk merely for the way
it reflects social context, ignoring language form. For this thesis (language as sui
generis) and its antithesis (the "relationality" of language to its context emphasized in the social sciences), Hanks recommends the synthesis of practice as the
nexus of "the law of system, the quick of activity, and the reflective gaze of
value" (1996: 11). To look at troubles talk as practice, as this book does, is to
hold these three elements together in our analysis. Aesha's talk is shot through
with value and ideology as well as with the systematicity of the grammar typifying Bangla complaints and relational links to her shared history with those
who are either present or discursively invoked.

A third important aspect of Aesha's complaint is the way it illustrates multiple functions of language, and of this sort of language in particular. Obviously,
complaints presented at a pharmacy or the home of an herbalist might include a
description of symptoms, or more neutrally, problems to be treated. Troubles
talk at home—for example Aesha's listing of her hardships in example 1—is
similar to a patient's description of symptoms in that it refers beyond itself to
situations rather than reflexively to language itself. We take this referential
function of language so much for granted that we must make a special effort to
realize the many other things language does. In the spontaneous complaints that

Aesha voiced in the later months of my stay, she also mentioned foot pain and difficulty breathing. There her intent certainly included referring to physical problems that might respond to treatment, but her descriptions of symptoms sometimes led to requests for medicine, if I should have any. In contrast with that extralinguistic referential focus on things beyond talk itself, much of Aesha's talk in example 2 is a complaint about others' talk. Complaints can include not only symptom narratives or stories of loss and trouble, but also responses to the way others have spoken of one's problem. Aesha spoke much about how others characterized her troubles as *pāgalāmi*.

The "madness" label deserves our attention. Bangladeshi *pāgalāmi*, which would be labeled mental illness in the West, is not described in publications other than Bangladeshi psychiatric journals. No psychiatric morbidity studies of Bangladesh are known to me, nor are there any other ethnographic studies of madness there (but see Bhattacharrya 1986 on West Bengal). The phenomenon of *pāgalāmi* is not precisely glossed in terms of mental illness, since at least some of my 1996 interviewees deny that it is an illness. The period in Aesha's life in which she became mad, according to others, was the time her husband took a second wife. Was even her madness a form of resistance?

As an anthropologist concerned with language, I find that the words of people like Aesha have a powerful appeal. The troubles talk in example 2 exemplifies the reflexive dimension of language—its ability to refer to itself (for instance, quoting others' labels or insults)—which makes it such a powerful mode of symbolization. Linguistically, troubles talk has pragmatic dimensions as well as referential meaning; that is, it aims to do something in the world like making a request or an accusation, rather than simply referring to something in the world. Complaints indicate some conflicts and create others. Further, Bangladeshi troubles talk offers us privileged access to local models of the self—heartmind, body-mind, feelings-thoughts—and significant relationships.

Yet it was also for personal reasons that speech events like the one tran-scribed above appealed to me more than requests for medicine by Aesha or others. I hesitated to dispense medicine even in response to common complaints, such as cold symptoms or foot pain. I'm sure such encounters left both troubles teller and troubles receiver dissatisfied; I know I was uncomfortable when I received requests. In contrast, the very act of listening to those whose pain was not so easily treatable seemed a service I could perform. I imagined a solidarity between us, a communion of emotional pain—the pain of being away from loved ones, the pain and loneliness of being seen as different, the pain of feeling like a disappointment to others. I disappointed others' expectations by not giving money or medicine; some of those I listened to disappointed their families by becoming so ill as to be unable to fulfill standard productive and reproductive roles. In particular, the poignancy of the complaints of those labeled *pāgal* (mad, insane) drew me to return to them again and again.

If troubles telling interactively helps to heal a person in distress—or, in other cases, creates distress in listeners (Pennebaker 1993)—it also exemplifies discourse as a social phenomenon. Whatever self is formed in a complaint

interaction is indeed allowed or disallowed to form—it is legitimated or sanctioned. Rules of group identity, of belonging and exclusion, thus silently or
explicitly inform complaint interactions. To be "a person" in the sense of a
recognized social agent is a gift of the group (Harris 1989); all the more does
healthy personal existence depend on group life and norms. And, this being so,
troubles talk always takes place within the larger field of ongoing negotiations of
legitimation and power.

In the remainder of this book I describe the "problem words" spoken mostly
by kin and neighbors of Habibur Rahman. I jotted down some complaints as
soon as possible after hearing them, trying to memorize the linguistic form of the
brief, spontaneous examples I heard or overheard. Most of those presented herein were mechanically recorded, some by video camcorder. Some of the recorded
events took place in the *bāṛi*, many in medical settings in the nearby *bāzār*
(market) in the town I call Sonargaon, some 20 kilometers away in the town of
Matlab, a few in Dhaka, and one event in a Bangla-speaking household in Los
Angeles.

In most of this troubles talk we hear the voice of a person at least potentially
in conflict, a self (a center of experience, Harris 1989) in distress, the multiple
voices (self-projections) that a single speaker can animate, and talk whose meaning emerges in interaction, with reference to the strategies of individual participants, but transcending them (Battaglia 1995a; Hanks 1996: 12; Mannheim and
Tedlock 1995). Indologists have made claims regarding the selflessness of South
Asian persons that lend themselves to misunderstanding and that call for ethnographic contextualization. Here I provide a context in which to hear the voices of
selves that, though clearly embedded in relationships without which the voices
would be lost and meaningless, are projected nonetheless as *byakti* (individuals)
with their own varied, if not unique, biographies and agendas. They indeed have
their own stories that, though they share common themes, are in some ways
unique. In telling her troubles, each person I describe negotiates the form of her
ongoing self-in-relation. As one dances with her interlocutors and as the two
shift their stances, moving between dependency and assertiveness—as one
complains—she is simultaneously creating a presentational self and declaring
that self to be linked with the interlocutor. It is urgent that anthropology transcend sterile dichotomies—autonomy versus embeddedness, egocentricity
versus sociocentricity, the West versus the Rest—through recognizing empirical
complexities that defy simple categorization.

In devoting analytic attention to the "I" or self of troubles tellers and to their
speech *as discourse*, I hope *not* to distance the reader or myself from their
human suffering. There is a link between the inability to complain openly—or
say "I"—and the very social matrix that gives rise to at least some of the complaints. Whatever else they might accomplish, for some people complaints are
the only sort of resistance or protest available. My exploration of troubles talk
aims to amplify the existential and political protests of persons who have varying degrees of authorization to speak, and does so by offering ways both to
understand and to feel with the troubles tellers.

3

SIGNS AND SELFHOOD ·

The South Asia reflected in the anthropological literature until recently was trapped at either of two extremes between which this book steers. I avoid the homogenizing tendency of Indological literature on selfhood that eschews variation at the individual level, [1] but I also eschew the tendency on the part of psychoanalytic ethnographers of India to reduce emergent social interaction to individual psychology. Focusing on transcribed interaction discourages psycho-logical reductionism, while also calling more attention to interpersonal varia-bility than is possible within structuralist and ethnosociological accounts of India. The linguistic constitution of both intersubjectivity and individually variable participant strategies becomes visible to us through careful analysis of the transcripts. As we familiarize ourselves with those transcripts we thus discover what I call the dialogical self.

Language offers a privileged window on the self and society. Peirce wrote that "my language is the sum total of myself" (quoted by Singer 1994: 3814). Peircean semiotics offers a dynamic model of signs in social use—just what is needed for looking at such things as troubles talk. What we call "the self" is, in a Peircean frame, the sign relation present when we have a feeling-thought with meaning (Hoopes 1991: 8). That the self is an inference arising in communica-tion with others is well illustrated in the following example: Peirce argues that children come to the inference that they have a self through others' testimonies about the world. Someone tells them that the stove is hot. Not content to hear that, the child touches it. Through defiant experimentation, the child realizes past ignorance and posits a self that was indeed ignorant. "It is necessary to suppose a *self* in which this ignorance can inhere. So testimony [language socialization, one could say] gives the first dawning of self-consciousness" (Peirce 1991: 44).

Peirce wrote that "the self sign is, among other things, a material quality or organic bodily state interpreted as constituting one's self" (54). In one of his better-known essays, "Man's Glassy Essence," Peirce argues against behavioral determinism even while affirming materiality of the mind. He concludes not only that persons are general ideas but also that those general ideas "have per-sonality even when they pertain to organizations and institutions" (Hoopes 1991: 229). Peirce writes that "all that is necessary, upon this theory, to the existence of a person is that the feelings out of which he is constructed should be in close enough connection to influence one another" (1991: 229). What is this "person"? It is clearly *not* reductively psychological, individualistically cognitive. Peirce's semiotic model of the person as idea is a radically social one; he writes that "*esprit de corps*, national sentiment, [and] sym-pathy, are no mere metaphors" (230).

How do the problematics of self-construction in Bangla become evident to the careful listener? Where did structuralist approaches to South Asia fall short, and just how does a semiotic or interactionist perspective contribute to addressing the problems of earlier approaches?

Bangla Self-Construction: Revisiting a Problem in South Asian Studies

A series of conversational vignettes will help to convey some dimensions of everyday self-construction in Bangladesh, particularly the key role played by nonpresent "figures" animated (Goffman 1974: 518–529) in such narratives.[2] In these vignettes, Bangla speakers "triangulate" their identity and value to me through the lens of third parties who love them.[3]

Soon after I moved to a Matlab village, a wealthy rural businessman assured me that everyone in the area *tāke ādar kare* (showed him affection). On a visit to Dhaka, my Bangladeshi hostess there wanted to be sure I noticed that her mother-in-law had given her some of her tea—evidence of how much her in-laws loved her. When the paternal grandmother of a well-trained rural nurse died, the nurse told me a story of how this woman, who had practically raised her, had once put off her own lunch until her granddaughter had come home from nursing school—at 4:00 PM. My field assistant Faisal on one occasion elicited a reaffirmation from workers at the clinic where we had once had an office that they still cared about us even after we had rented another office a kilometer away from them. On another occasion, Faisal seemed too exuberant in telling someone (who, as Faisal complained privately, damaged our work seriously) how much that man's fellowship (*āntarikatā*), cooperation (*sahajagitā*), and care had meant to us. On yet another day, that object of Faisal's mixed feelings told me an illness story. He stressed the importance of being with those who love you; particularly when gravely ill, men long for their mothers (or at least he had). Then there were the two men in their seventies, weeping in my presence. The first wept over his sinful life, but assured those sitting with him in the clothing shop that his offspring loved him. The other old man cried out with abdominal pain on the great festival of Eid ul-Uzha, complaining that his family was neglecting him, celebrating without him.

In all of these incidents from my field notes, people assigned great weight to others' feelings toward them. Rarely did I hear Bangladeshis abstractly reflect on their feelings toward others, whereas they often reflected on others' feelings. Although the reality is that many, if not all, Americans base their self-image on others' evaluations of them—is it really possible to do otherwise?—they are told by various authorities to affirm *themselves*. At least in some contexts, some

Americans claim not to care about how society views them. In further contrast
with Bangladeshis, one commonly hears Americans flaunting their feelings for
others, evidently affirming their own value—for example, as parents—by loudly
proclaiming their love for their children.[4]

How the Problem Has Been Addressed Previously

In the context of South Asian ethnography, dependency and autonomy are
significant themes that surround the expression of selfhood and of troubles. The
suppression of complaints and particularly of self-assertion is not unique to
Bangladesh, but a comparative perspective on it is useful. American selfhood, as
public discourse, projects and presumes personal autonomy. Hindu personhood
publicly presents a socially embedded or sociocentric face. In Pakistan, a
dominant public ideology demands homage to hierarchy, but private family
interactions accommodate individual needs; indeed, those that do not accommodate persons produce pathology, according to Ewing (1991: 145).

   Both personal ambitions—albeit only partially acknowledged—and hierarchy pervade social relationships (Dumont 1970; Fuller 1992; Kurtz 1992;
Roland 1988). The form of psychological autonomy manifested at least by
Pakistanis seems better described as intrapsychic than interpersonal (Ewing
1991). That is, in an environment in which interpersonal autonomy is explicitly
devalued, particularly for women, women do nonetheless harbor an "intrapsychic autonomy." Ewing argues that they carry with them images of affirmation that enable them to endure stress and maintain the sort of intrapsychic
strength necessary in the sometimes tense relationships in their in-laws' homes.
Conflict is associated with hierarchy. Kakar (1978) and Roland (1988) have
argued that the dependency of boys on their mothers for nurture, and of mothers
on sons for future support, creates conflict in families and in the experience of
individual members. In fact, psychoanalytically oriented anthropologists have
offered this sort of conflict (which often has sexual dimensions) as one explanation for gender hierarchy: sons, fearing excessive closeness to their mothers,
take on a habitually aggressive stance, distancing themselves from women
(Herdt 1987).

Dumont and His Influence on More Recent Studies

How well equipped are older renderings of South Asia by social scientists to
explain the relative tendency of Bangladeshis to triangulate the self, to project a
selfward gaze *from a constructed other*? Among the older theories, I particularly
raise the question vis-à-vis the structuralist approach to the South Asian person
that derives from Dumont. Still older theoretical treatments of the self that
would have given those studies a better grounding, particularly the works of
Peirce and of George Herbert Mead,[5] were neglected by the Dumont generation's studies of the self in South Asia:

To say that the world of caste is a world of relations is to say that the particular caste and the particular man have no substance: they exist empirically, but they have no reality in thought, no Being ... at the risk of being crude ... on the level of life in the world the individual *is* not." (Dumont 1970: 272; emphasis in original)

Despite Dumont's stature and contributions to the field, the empirical foundations of his portrait are uncertain. How true to life on the ground—to the lives of all sorts of people in and out of the caste system—is it? And, if indeed South Asians—Hindus, Muslims, and others—see social wholes where others see individual parts or actors, how does that come about?

Since the publication of Dumont's *Homo hierarchicus,* several studies have addressed those issues. Shweder and Bourne, agreeing with Dumont that Hindus at least *conceive* of persons as embedded in social wholes, nevertheless find it important to ask how they come to do so.

How do people live by their world views? It is instructive to reflect, for example, on the socialization of autonomy in the West. We find it tempting to argue that Western individualism has its origins in the institution of privacy... Socialization is terroristic. The young are subject to all sorts of invasions ... It is sobering to acknowledge that our sense of personal inviolatability is a violatable social gift, the product of what *others* are willing to respect and protect us from ... the product of rights and privileges we are granted by others in numerous 'territories of the self' [for example, adults in the West] knocking on the door before entering the child's personal space, his private bedroom, another replica of the assertion. (1984: 194)

Implicitly, Shweder and Bourne argue that such fundamental experiences as those of "territories of the self" (not necessarily defined in individual terms but perhaps in neutral terms),[6] or habitual uses of the body in social space, go a long way toward imparting concepts of the self. My fieldwork leads me to believe that practices involving sharing of spaces and possessions have the inverse effect. Such sharing of spaces and things—beds, for example—helps in "weakening interpersonal barriers" in Bangladesh, as in Japan (Caudill and Plath 1974: 147). The treatment of domestic space does not seem greatly different among Bangladeshi Hindus and Muslims.

Recently, Kurtz (1992) has combined Dumont's structuralism with a revisionist psychoanalytic approach to the self in Hindu families. Kurtz traces the means by which Hindu children are led to the profound group identification that could be called an immersion of self in the group. In his fruitful revisiting of older ethnographies of Hindu households, Kurtz argues that common patterns of weaning and of passing babies from the mother to other caregivers also teach children, from an early age, the larger lesson of weaning themselves from selfish attachment to their biological or nursing mothers. Hindu children, he argues, learn to identify profoundly with the larger group of women (and men?) to whom they are passed both literally and symbolically. Still, Kurtz's study is not a new contribution to the ethnography of the interactions in which social selves are constituted.

Although Dumont (1970) argued that Muslims in South Asia must be seen as only peripherally influenced in behavior by Hindu hierarchy as an ideology, others find more profound similarities. Dumont argued that the ascetic renouncer within Hinduism was the rare individual in Indian society. Werbner argues that the figure of the Sufi Muslim saint is like the Hindu renouncer in that he represents the achievement of a unique individuality. Whereas in the West this individuality is absolutized as a desideratum for everyone in the society, "autonomous religious individuality-cum-knowledge—the direct personal access to God valorized by the Protestant Puritan sects—is regarded as a rare achievement by Sufi disciples" (Werbner 1996: 105). Whereas the moral individual is the goal defended by the institutions of Western society, the role of the moral individual (moral because persuaded or coerced) in Islamic society is to uphold the Islamic state; there, the family, not the individual, is foundational:

> What vision of personhood and society is entailed in this Islamic approach, and what impact does it have on social practice? Clearly, the movement shares a great deal with Calvinism: the emphasis laid on worldly asceticism, antihedo-nistic lifestyles, moral and sexual puritanism, the role of the elect, a rational, total life project, direct individual worship of God, individual responsibility, and a 'disenchantment of the world'—a rejection of elaborate ritualistic prac-tices or priestly intercession as a means of salvation. Absent, however is the final compromise with capitalism. (Werbner 1996: 108)

As useful as such a structuralist analysis may be at some level, it does not match all the forms of discourse one hears in the give-and-take of everyday South Asian Muslim social life. A contrasting stream in the discourse of self-construction in South Asia asserts independence. At times this seems confined to fantasies, though these may be actively cultivated (Derné 1995). According to Mines (1988), Indian men increasingly act out fantasies of autonomy as they move into later stages of adult maturity. South Asian Muslims, more than Hindus, embrace personal autonomy and financial independence as ideals (see, for example, Prindle 1988). Many Muslims are likely to display an aversion to the notions of social stratification and hierarchical dependence, apart, perhaps, from an affirmation of the rule of elder males over their patrilineal homesteads.

Dependency relationships in India also foster expectations of patron empathy and client indirection. Ethnographers and psychotherapists who have worked in India note that subordinates have strong expectations that their superiors will not only offer support in return for loyal obedience, but will even intuit their needs (Roland 1988). Family elders are expected to know junior members' needs through refined powers of empathy (which must entail careful attention to subtle hints and verbal indirection). Ethnographic accounts of these expectations resonate with my observations of troubles talk, though one finds cases in which subordinates' troubles explode into direct confrontations with their superordinates.

Beyond Dumont: Models from Recent Ethnographic
Writing on South and Southeast Asia

There has been a shift in the focus of theoretical treatments of South Asia—from structure to process and from harmony to conflict—reflecting broader trends in social theory (Bourdieu 1977b; Giddens 1979). Wikan (1990) challenges us to rethink portraits of social behavior that fail to incorporate personal agency. What is at stake for Balinese persons in trouble, she argues, goes beyond their need to maintain an appearance in order to uphold a cultural ideal or carry out a culturally composed dramatic script of some sort ("the show must go on," as Geertz [1984] implies); in fact, deferring to authority and hiding negative feelings may help the actor avoid death by sorcery (Wikan 1990). Behavior that might be interpreted by Geertz or Dumont as the performance of a script requiring sociocentricity might, if we ask the person involved, mask (or help cope with) fear for his or her very life.

Similarly, Hindu society, long essentialized as the home of persons fixed in stable groups, has recently been reexplored as the site of conflict and everyday resistance (Haynes and Prakash 1991). Prior to the shift toward conflict approaches, the holism of Dumont's theory—its vision of all things Hindu, including secular power, being encompassed by the principle of hierarchy—had enchanted two previous generations of scholars including, to some extent, Shweder and Kurtz. The empirical question, however, remains: What evidence have we that everyday experience or common voices echo the song of holism, or that everyday experience is truly captured by this concept? Since the 1980s, a number of ethnographies have attuned us to a different sort of music, much more polyphonous and complex. Whereas South Asians' voices were absent from Dumont's published accounts, they receive print space and scholarly attention in more recent work.

Post-Freudian ethnographers of South Asia have questioned accounts, such as those of Dumont, that project an unproblematic acceptance of the ideology of hierarchy and the authority of both caste and male heads of families. Finding, as I do, evidence of tensions within close families in South Asia, Ewing (1991), Roland (1988), and Derné (1995) use post-Freudian theory to describe the ontogeny of sociocentric selves but also to demonstrate other dimensions of self in the South Asians they know. Chodorow (1974) argued that women often find separation-individuation either less necessary or more difficult than men do, given the unbroken intimacy girls enjoy with their mothers at least until they leave home. Applying a similar model to South Asia, Roland and Ewing describe the results of certain individuals' failure to develop a mature intrapsychic autonomy (Ewing 1991: 132). Crucially, rather than using the individuation model to critique South Asian hierarchies or sociocentric self-structure, Ewing distinguishes this intrapsychic autonomy—a universal need—from the individualistic *external* autonomy to which few Pakistani women aspire. Intrapsychic autonomy, defined by Ewing as "the ability to maintain enduring mental representations of sources of self-esteem" (for example, images of parental care), is a tentative psychological universal. Failure to achieve it—which is as exceptional in Pakistan as in the West, Ewing implies—results in psycho-pathology.

Still, selfhood is a gendered discourse. Ewing describes the depression that haunts a few Pakistani women whose intrapsychic autonomy she regards as pathologically underdeveloped. This, it seems to me, is an apt metaphor for Fatima (see example 9 in chapter 4), an unschooled, timid, overburdened woman who is afflicted with a spirit of mutism, and whose abortive exorcism left her nonspecific complaints untreated. Women in Bengal, according to a male Hindu informant, are expected to be selfless in their suffering and labor, to suppress complaints. If Bengali women fulfilled that ideal, we should nonetheless have to ask why. Complaining itself—or prolonged weeping—is sometimes punished. A married woman may publicize or veil her troubles;[7] regardless, any perceived signs of disability or infertility could lead her husband to divorce her (an example of this is Sufia's case cited in chapter 10). Feldman argues that women are motivated to "hide whatever health difficulties they do have" lest they be seen to have lost their potential to contribute to production and reproduction in their husbands' families. For poor women, to be divorced often means to become homeless (1983: 1891).

Thus, the sociocultural ethos renders Bengali women in general vulnerable, though this vulnerability varies with life experience, as Ewing argues. Many rural women I know (and elderly men like Suleyman, see example 10) find themselves constrained by their vulnerability even if they should desire to assert their needs. Junior members of households throughout South Asia believe that their elders should intuit what they need; this ideal construes assertiveness as not only unnecessary but also insulting. Yet, when elders betray that trust, the contract implicit in family hierarchy suffers; their frustrated dependents struggle to turn up the volume of their complaints while staying within the acceptable range of communicative options (hinting and beyond; see Roland 1988: 122, 220–229). Selfhood, here the strong self-indexing entailed in troubles telling, can be conceived of as an unequally distributed privilege rather than as a biological given.[8]

Because hierarchy pervades Muslim Bangladeshi households—but not their intergroup relations as in Hindu India—we find some degree of Muslim ideological preference for entrepreneurship over employment (viewed as service to another) but none for individuals forming autonomous households. Particularly among Muslim farming families in Bangladeshi villages, autonomy is not the goal of an ideal developmental trajectory. Instead, hierarchical complementarity (sons offering respect, fathers bestowing blessings) is viewed as the abiding framework of father-son relationships, although sons owe fathers economic support in their old age. Revealingly, the most prevalent positive uses of the Bangla glosses for the English terms "independence" and "self-reliance" arise out of the newspeak introduced by foreign aid organizations. *Svanirbhar* and other such terms of self-reliance have a decidedly neologistic and foreign ring to them; such foreignness contributed to the 1993 Islamist backlash against non-governmental developmental organizations. Still, even in development discourse, self-reliance is projected only as a goal for social groups—particularly village self-help cooperatives and Bangladesh as a nation.

What can troubles talk—indexing experiences at the outer edges of normalcy—tell us about the ebb and flow of Bengali life, the private and public lives of Bengali souls? My experience in Bangladesh validates the claims of other anthropologists regarding cross-cultural variation in concepts of the person, in the forms of self-presentation, and perhaps even in the self itself as a center of subjective experience. The extent of variability, however, has been exaggerated and its nature sometimes distorted. The methodological and theoretical problems plaguing the literature—the Orientalist tendency to simplify variability in the self by dichotomizing "the West and others" and to conflate behavior or self-presentation with psychic structure, experience or self-representation—are serious ones (Spiro 1993). Thus I balance or constrain a particularistic social-constructionist perspective with cross-cultural evidence and a discourse-centered approach. Do naturally occurring social interactions support the clinically based report that South Asians depend so heavily on hierarchical superiors to intuit their needs that they do not complain or explicitly state needs (Roland 1988)? Not quite.

Complaining is a self-assertive act, and self-assertion is recognized in greater or lesser degrees in most societies as a survival need—once it stops crying, a hungry baby is doomed. Hence the Bangladeshi saying:

Example 3. A proverbial understanding of the importance of crying.

Bāccā nā kãdle dudh pāy nā.
If a baby does not cry, it gets no milk.

Revealingly, it was during a dispute involving adults, who were vigorously arguing for their entitlement to a welfarelike benefit, that I first heard the proverb used. On the surface the very currency of such a proverb—particularly if it is typically used to warrant self-assertion—seems to fly in the face of other anthropological representations of South Asian sociocentric persons. Specifically, it contrasts with Roland's report that elders' intuition is perceived to obviate crying or the verbalization of distress. Admittedly, the on-the-ground social reality is that babies and adults who cry too much are lightning rods for criticism—despite the proverb. The many babies of Durim and Aesha in Habibur Rahman's compound attracted almost constant criticism for their crying, though the prime target of the criticism was Aesha, the victim blamed for overproducing and undermanaging. Local perceptions of the anthropologist and his interests can yield insights of their own. My fictive brother Tuslim characterized the sort of speech I was recording as nothing but *kæ kæ*, summing up all the instances of natural conversation and complaints as mere noise and irritating whinings. As an icon or onomatopoeia the phrase is untranslatable, but the low front vowel sound

/æ/—particularly when nasalized—is, for Bengali speakers, a sound symbol of
"things that irritate" (Dimock 1989). Repetitive or excessive speech of any
kind—particularly nagging and whining—are iconically referred to as *pyānpyān*
(phonetically, *pæ̃npæ̃n*) *karā*. So, despite the proverbial acknowledgment that
crying gets you somewhere, that complaining potentially works as a pragmatic
strategy, the Bangla language also encodes conventionalized pejorative means of
referring to complaining.

How are we to understand these two conventionally encoded language
ideologies,[9] the one affirming the need to gripe, the other stressing how alienat-
ing it is? What do these two attitudes reveal about local models of person and
social group? Before I untangle the knots and lay out my lines of understanding,
I need to show that individual strands of socioemotional expression do not point
unambiguously in the direction we might assume them to. What is needed is an
effort to problematize some of our own folk models and explore more complex
analytic models.

I have grown up associating anger with aggressive self-assertion. Anger
may strike the distant observer as being out of place in troubles talk as opposed
to accusations. Yet troubles talk often follows and points to frustrating disrup-
tions in the self. Rural South Asian societies have in the past provided ritualized
channels for venting frustration and anger—lamentation, for one. But Bengali
persons grieving a loss other than death—for example, an unhappy divorce, or a
mental or physical disability—may conventionally find that their laments meet
with less sympathy. Such "eccentric" laments are repressed, adding to the
sufferer's frustration. Anger is palpable in the laments represented in this book,
not to speak of the aggressive actions taken by one old man who sang laments
(see example 10).

For Bangladeshis and for Americans, anger originates in a self that is pain-
fully aware of its boundaries and of threats (see example 12). But for Americans
it originates in egalitarian ideals and less-than-egalitarian practices, whereas for
South Asians it originates in the disappointed expectations of superordinates'
beneficence. Anger that persists, goes underground, and resurfaces—as symptoms, backbiting, or sorcery fears—is a normal frustration response for bounded
selves, selves encountering obstacles. I speak here of Bengali anger (and Indian
anger, Roland 1988) but evoke its kinship to what I know in America. Still,
while angry action is in some sense another name for self-assertion in both
societies, it may also serve as a defense against the psychic disorganization
entailed in a loss such as the death of a significant other. And loss is a problem
only to the extent that lives are entangled with each other, is it not?

To feel loss, in contrast with anger, is to testify to a bond. Loss indirectly
indexes connectedness, communion, sociality. Complaints bespeak loss—for
Latifa the loss is her love; for Suleyman, a son; for Fatima, a secret visitor (see
example 9); for Yasmin (see example 13) her hope for life itself. Loss is salient
in Bangla troubles talk, indicating the relational quality of Bengali selves. It is
especially salient in those examples of the traditional genres of lamentation—
bilāp and *bāramāsyo*—that thematize *viraho* (separation, longing). As Sufi

Muslim poets showed in their own versions of the *viraho bāramāsyo*, even the absence of the beloved can be resung in an Islamic idiom. Still, most complaints, while they do involve social relationships and a longing for support, focus unromantically on immediacies—the loss of health or, in the case of meta-complaints, the loss of voice and communion through interruptions and other glitches. Loss is indeed an index of connectedness. But, as is most obvious when it is blamed on injustice, a sense of loss becomes tied up with anger. And thus to associate anger directly or exclusively with a relational self (even to construe relational selfhood as an essence radically distinct from another essence, ego-centric selfhood) is problematic.

Dependency behavior also projects a troubles teller's relational self-stance. Some complaints of dependents function as indirect requests, or lead to direct requests. Children, younger siblings, and most women lack control over finan-cial resources. They relate to elders as clients do to patrons. Clients, fictive kin, and blood kin occasionally ask their patrons to buy them old familiar medicines or—when no one seems sure of a diagnosis—to take them to practitioners. Dependency, after all, is naturalized and idealized in the Hindu caste ideology that shaped traditional Bengali thought, and intergenerational dependency is still idealized by all but the most cosmopolitan or impoverished Bangladeshi Muslims. Any affirmation of dependency occasioned by illness could be framed as an example of the hierarchical embeddedness of caste persons described by Dumont (1970). Dependency leaves patrons in a powerful position, which some abuse. But men and other powerful persons are not villains in medical inter-actions; they do expend energy and cash in trips to pharmacies to present such complaints and bring back medications for their children and their women. Bangladeshis in dependent positions use client status only as an expedient; the dominant ideology notwithstanding, their ambition is to attain the kind of autonomy enjoyed by their patrons. Thus, poor rural women who gain any sort of financial autonomy—through the ever-increasing network of cottage indus-tries supported by development organizations—are quick to seek their own medical care, bypassing their husbands and other male patrons (Hashemi and Schuler 1992).

For Bangladeshis, talk reveals conflict between assertion and dependency, both of which find some ideological affirmation. The next chapter explores what troubles talk tells us about personhood and the dialectic of autonomy and dependency.

4

PERSONHOOD: THE "I" IN THE COMPLAINT

How do narratized experiences of being a person vary cross-culturally, and what relation do those experiences have to cultural models of the self (Hollan 1992; Spiro 1993)? Comparing the way that various Bangla speakers deploy literal tokens of "I" in discourse points us to the referents of "I" projected and constituted by language.

In the last 60 years, hundreds of essays and dozens of books concerned with the self or person have been written by social scientists and philosophers (reviewed recently by Ochs and Capps 1996). Linguistic and cultural anthropologists have revealed significant cross-cultural variation in concepts of the self and in the linguistic forms in which those concepts take shape. An even thornier problem than that of idealized cultural conceptions of the self is that of the self as a phenomenological locus of experience, as reflexive awareness or consciousness. Hollan distinguishes between "simplified and idealized cultural conceptions of the self [and] descriptive accounts of subjective experience" (1992: 283). This difference is only one among many, including that between discourse and experience; accounts of subjective experience are still rhetorical constructions. Battaglia (1995a) quite rightly denies that rhetoric reveals essential, pre-existing objects or selves. Nor do narrative self-acts pertain only to the narrator; rhetoric, instead, has profound capacities to create what Ricouer calls "social entanglement" (Battaglia 1995a: 11). Thus we ask a narrower question than, "What form does the self take cross-culturally?"

Talk of pain or other such inner states is a complex social action in that it makes subjectivity public and indexes the bounds and experiences of the psychobiological organism (Spiro 1993), presumably not accessible to interlocutors, while simultaneously challenging or remaking boundaries by attempting to create intersubjectivity. In fact, even the subjective partakes of the intersubjective and is publicly constituted. Both subjectivity and intersubjectivity (mutual attunement) are shaped or achieved through language deployed in interaction. [1] Even when actors agree to refer to a trouble as belonging to a particular person among them, some of what Bangladeshis label *byārām* (phonetically, *berām*) or *rog* (illness) becomes an illness *because it is labeled as such*. To some extent, Bangladeshi persons also become their illness label (Zola 1992). The one labeled might or might not agree that he or she is sick. Some actors, particularly some of the women I recorded in the patient role, point indirectly to the role that others play in shaping their troubles talk, and their (meta)complaints—here, complaints about their troubles not being listened to—shift attention (temporarily and partially) to the behavior of their guardians and practitioners (Wilce 1995).

What sort of evidence should be taken as relevant to the question of the form of the self as it varies within and between societies? What forms of selfhood are rhetorically projected in cultural discourses (Battaglia 1995b)? Our approach to self-acts in Bangladeshi encounters should start with questions raised in and by Bangla discourse, local questions touching on selfhood. Troubles-telling encounters invite analysis as rhetorical self-acts. As discussed by philosophers (Cavell 1987), linguists (Benveniste 1971), and social scientists (Mead 1934; Urban 1989), the use of pronouns is central to the linguistic con-struction of self. Thus, close attention to complaints—which might be expected to make considerable use of pronominal indexes but in fact, as is crucial to my analysis, need not do so in Bangla—helps us approach Bangladeshi answers to those questions with greater sophistication and experience-nearness than has been seen in previous anthropological writings on South Asian personhood.

The previously cited Bangla proverb, "If a baby does not cry, it won't get any milk," recognizes the occasional need for self-assertion by complaining, although on the other hand superfluous complaining is criticized as *alakṣmi* (*Olok: ʰi*) (inauspicious). Bangla has no single word for complaints about states such as illness or sadness. Everyday complaints about such states are referred to by the phrase *asubidhār kathā balā* (speaking about inconveniences). Marked or extreme forms of complaining, such as ritualized texted weeping (*bilāp*), are salient enough to enter the lexicon on their own. Some styles of complaining make listeners uncomfortable, particularly those shading into nagging and begging. *Pyānpyān* designates such repetitive whining. In his article on Bangla sound symbolism, Dimock (1989) notes that many iconic descriptors for unpleasantness contain the vowel /æ/ and that its grating effect is heightened by nasalization. Though it is only those marked forms that are lexicalized (have their own words), everyday complaints are still recognizable. In addition to sharing semantic themes, everyday complaints are typically realized through experiencer-subject constructions.

The Complaining Self in Social Context

During my time in Bangladesh, I got to know a few dozen people well enough that I could narrate major parts of their life stories or characterize them across the events in which I have known them. My life's course has blended with theirs, and there is between us a strong recognition of shared humanity. Still, at times misunderstanding, hurt feelings, and profound commitments to divergent values nurtured over centuries of cultural history highlight the gap between our experiences of life. Troubles telling can bridge that gap. A person who can laugh, but also complain, about a headache or pervasive discouragement, appears enough like myself to invite further interaction. The troubles telling

events I transcribe help establish that sense of commonality, but they also stretch
the Western reader's understanding or empathic ability, particularly to the extent
that unexamined and ideologically grounded notions of ourselves limit empathy.
Such troubles telling, however, is only one speech genre. Moreover, we should
see it against the background of other ways that Bangla speakers project self and
other and build relationships.

Troubles talk differs from the triangulated self-constructions narrated
earlier. Rather than constructing self-worth, troubles talk starts from some challenge to the self. For instance, one brilliant Bangladeshi son of a privileged
family, telling me of a past that still surrounds him, relates how he has been
dogged by a sense of incompetence. These words are reassuring if mystifying to
hear, as I and others are in awe of his abilities. Another, much older man, with
few years of schooling but decades of farming experience, tells me that his
"heart" keeps him awake until he feels he will be driven to suicide (as were his
father and *his* father before him) if sleep eludes him even one more night.
Although his reference to this sleep disturbance with suicidal thoughts as a *hrid
rog* (or disease of the heart) is at first difficult to understand, since I was waiting
to hear a reference instead to anxiety, I can soon enough translate his idiom of
distress (Good 1977). When others speak of pains, shortness of breath, a lingering cough, or a cold—or when they complain that people do not treat them
right—I understand. More challenging to empathy or *Verstehen* is the troubles
narrative I heard from several persons in rural Bangladesh—that a spirit choked
or at least stifled them.[2] Still, even if we have had no similar experiences, we can
listen to their attempts to explain the phenomenon. We also tend to interpret it in
terms familiar to us.

For the most part, then, troubles telling reassures me of a potential for intersubjectivity and intercultural understanding. I tend to assume that complaints
index "a self like mine." That assumption is tested here by exploring whether, or
how, such a self might be both revealed and constituted in complaint interactions. It is revealed and constituted in that every interaction re-creates socially
structured action out of the very elements that are thought by actors to presuppose basic social realities (Giddens 1984; Silverstein 1976). Such an analysis
requires that we consider not only the content but also the form of complaints
and their interactive contexts. While the anecdotes reported above show something of the diverse contents of complaints, some easy and some difficult for
Western readers to identify with, troubles telling *forms* also need probing. One
reason is that form cannot be separated from content in any neat and clean way.
Linguistic and interactive forms claim our attention because they reveal dimensions of troubles tellers' social lives that no content analysis could uncover.

Men's Relational Selfhood in Matlab

A useful relationship to examine in South Asia, for a view of negotiations between needs for self-assertion or agency and relatedness or communion, is that

between fathers and sons. Three complaints I heard indicate the parameters of such negotiations.

The first case involved Grandfather Ahmed—my host Habib's father's brother—who was doubled up with abdominal pain on the high feast day, Bakr Id ("goat Id," Arabic *'id ul azha*). In between groans we heard him utter three "response cries" (Goffman 1981), two of which could be considered, even in their very form, as calls for the presence of an Other. His *hāy hāy* (woe, woe) was mingled with cries of *Āllāh* (God!) and *māgo* (oh mother!). It is the expectation of every old person that he or she will live and eat with supportive children and grandchildren until death. The celebration of Eid—going on without him—made Ahmed's physical suffering more painful. Ahmed's perception of his son's failure to give him adequate attention completed his misery.

In the second case, two griefs fueled the "heatiness" or *pāgalāmi* (madness) of Suleyman, a more distant relative of Habib, in 1992. The first was the disappearance of his son in Pakistan some years before. His family could not explain the sudden cessation of letters from the young man, who had been sent to Pakistan to work and to repatriate his wages for the support of his family. There seemed to be evidence that he was still alive and well in Pakistan; yet, mysteriously estranged from his family, he was still causing great pain in 1996. Suleyman's second source of grief in 1992 was the complicity of another son in binding him with chains during his manic periods. Bereft in these ways of the respectful love of his sons, he cried out, "*God* is not with me."

In the third case of filial stress, the suffering of a son was central. During a violent village conflict, Jalu Miah was threatened with a loaded pistol *in the presence of his son*; as a result, the boy had to be treated for *dar* (fear), which takes on a life of its own,[3] conceptualized as an evil force threatening the victim's vitality. Jalu's neighbor, an old woman with knowledge of herbs and incantations, treated the boy for several weeks. At stake was the boy's relational self—entwined, as it is, with his father's life.

Broader Patterns of Behavior and Ideology in Bangladesh

The surface reality in rural compounds is one of conformist homogeneity. At least in Bangladesh in the 1970s, personal preferences of couples were less significant than the will of the head of the *bāṛi* when it came to deciding whether or not to use family planning (Rahman 1986). The fabric of those residential compounds was tight. But sometimes fabrics unravel, leaving family members more autonomous than they would be in a prototypical extended family. For example, one of Habibur Rahman's cousins supports a reputedly immoral local politician, the nemesis of the losing Islamist candidate who is supported by most of the men in the compound.

Another conflict in that compound over issues of autonomy and control is better known to me. It involves Habib's own brother Meherban, whose frustration with the task of farming itself is inextricably linked with his expressed frustration with his brothers' behavior toward him. Meherban is the second youngest of the four Rahman brothers. His older brother sold Meherban's seed potatoes to get some quick cash, but the seller informed only Habib (the eldest), not Meherban. Habib, instead of informing Meherban of this when Meherban expressed misgivings about going ahead with the coming season of planting, withheld the information. Only after Meherban had committed his resources to planting did Habib tell him the bad news. Meherban's frustration results from his sense that his personal rights, property, and ambition are clashing with his brothers' "behavioral ideology" (Vološinov 1973) reflecting a corporate sense of ownership (see example 40). Of course the ultimate in family fission, frequently seen in the landless classes, occurs when siblings decide to split up and subsist on their own means rather than struggling along jointly.

At an ideological level, persons (and sometimes groups, factions, or political parties—all glosses for the Bangla word *dal*) are believed to act in many cases out of *svārtho* or self-interest. Teastall conversations and political discourses bemoan this trend, seen in the corruption (*durnīti*) and divisive partisan factionalism perceived to pervade economic and political life. Such an ideology underlies the political graffiti I saw on a wall in Dhaka:

> Bektir-ceye dal baṛo, daler-ceye deś baṛo.
> Group above person, country above group.

Such ideological statements work upstream against the political economy in which contracts and other manifestations of capitalism separate individuals from groups. At the same time, they evoke corporate identities that are at once old and new as they combine traditional senses of solidarity with an identification with party and nation-state.

A Translinguistic-Semiotic Approach to South Asian Personhood

In the previous chapter's survey of South Asian ethnography, I intentionally omitted discussion of recent works that I find most congenial, which I will now briefly summarize to frame this chapter's translinguistic approach to the narrative self in troubles talk. In the 1980s and 1990s, several ethnographers of India have sought more explicitly to undermine monistic and monolithic accounts of South Asian culture and Hindu forms of selfhood. Those to whom I will now turn have described selfhood in terms of conflicts generated by the encounter with colonialism (Nandy 1983), tensions inherent in Tamil social structure and cultural forms (Trawick 1990a), or the dialectic of signs (Daniel 1984).

As Appadurai (1986) points out in his review of works by Daniel (1984), Khare (1984), and Nandy (1983), the South Asian self that they thematize is not so neatly embedded, nor does it transcend conflict and complexity to abide in a nonempirical world of holism. Rather, the three explore complex histories and forms of common discourse in which concepts of the self emerge and live. Khare's (1984) ethnography of untouchable Chamars in Lucknow shows how they construct for themselves a positive self-concept that constitutes a challenge to the notion of hierarchy. Nandy's (1983) stress on the colonial experience historicizes the loss of self in India; turning away from putative religious roots of selflessness, Nandy situates Indian senses of self in the eddies of history and particularly its violent encounter with colonialism. Daniel's (1984) and Trawick's (1988, 1990a, 1990b) studies in Tamil Nadu offer an even better model for asking questions about self and other and the often fluid boundary between them. Their works showcase intracultural variation, replacing the vision of holism with one of multivocality. Their semiotic and, in Trawick's case (1988), translinguistic approach to discourse results in ethnographic representation of the many voices that are heard even in a single Tamil speaker's utterance. By "explor[ing] the consciousness of everyday Indians" (Appadurai 1986: 749)— indeed, a multivocal consciousness—these contributors to South Asian ethnography rediscover the individual, not, perhaps, as conceived in the West, but no longer submerged in the whole. Here, "at least one kind of 'part,' the South Asian person, may provide the logical and semiotic foundation of the 'whole,' the caste system, rather than vice versa" (758). By their "tilt toward the pragmatic rather than the lexical dimensions of language," these newer studies reorient us to societies as organizations of diversity (755, 759; Wallace 1961).

Trawick has pioneered the translinguistic analysis of South Asian speech and song. Translinguistics denotes the discourse theory of Bakhtin (1981) and Vološinov (1973). Bakhtinian translinguistics explores transpersonal ownership of utterances, transpersonal histories and shared meanings, and transpositions of discourse from the mouth of one speaker to that of another in reported speech. Far from being limited to the obvious turn-taking pattern of conversation or any other mundane sense in which discourse is interactive, Bakhtinian analysis uncovers the "inner dialogism" of every individual utterance, the way each word is replete with echoes of other utterings. It is a misinterpretation of Bakhtin to claim that in stressing speakers' interorientation to each other, he does away with the concept of the speaker or speaker's intention altogether. What he does, however, is to rescue the notion of the speaker from a lonely vision of the person as radically autonomous in the formation of utterances. Thus translinguistics opens a means of uncovering the social, yet personal, voices audible in any given complaint.

In her particularly fruitful application of translinguistics, Trawick probes the way that untouchable Paraiyar women not only merge the voices of the characters they animate in song but also merge those voices with their own. She links this with the Tamil sense of the rich possibilities of fusion of spirits. Her analysis is exemplary in anchoring interpretation to linguistic form. Trawick argues persuasively that it is the singer's use of grammatical case (1988) and careful placement of pronouns and persons' names within poetic lines (1990b) that conjures up the sense of multivocality and the vision of spirits fusing. It is noteworthy (and reminiscent of Bangla troubles talk) that one singer, in a paradigmatic lament, referred to herself in the dative case while crying out to others in the vocative case.

What I am calling a translinguistic-semiotic anthropology of personhood in Bangladesh is one that takes the self as a linguistic-interactive sign linked complexly to materiality, and that prefers (a) as its source of evidence, the speech of common people in everyday settings; (b) as its interpretive strategy, a tacking back and forth between what can be construed as speaker's intentions and the multivocality or inner dialogism of utterances; and (c) as its standard, attention to both the data of linguistic and interactive form and the larger questions that theory poses.

Forms and Functions of Complaints

Since troubles talk is a form of social semiosis, it would be naive to understand complaints as the autonomous productions of individuals, though the tendency to do so is common in biomedicine and in Western ideologies of language. We see those ideologies in the practice of reading complaints as if they reflected, more or less accurately, something that is internal to the speaker. True, there is a strongly egocentric dimension to the act of complaining. It is *my* body, *my* heart, *my* sorrow to which my complaint draws attention—unless the complaint is an accusation.[4] When someone says, "It hurts *here*," that act of deictic reference indexes a spatial field of which the speaker is the center. My choice of English examples is intentional; my argument here does not apply to Bangla discourse alone. In troubles talk, we do see linguistic, specifically deictic, egocentrcity—in pronouns, demonstratives, and nonverbal indexical acts like pointing to where it hurts. Still, there is some theoretical significance to particular South Asian patterns of linguistic egocentricity, given the exoticizing depictions of selfless persons extant in the ethnographic literature on Asia, particularly on Hindu and Buddhist communities.

Nevertheless, to speak of linguistic egocentricity is shorthand for a phenomenon that is fundamentally social. Complaints are linguistic forms of social engagement. While this is obviously true of accusation-complaints, it is no less true of state-of-being complaints. Even such complaints find expression within social relationships, typically long-term relationships. Troubles talk, like all talk, is designed for particular recipients, so that the utterance is best seen as interactively emergent.[5] Recipients can and do shape complaints by their ongoing engagement in conversation with the troubles teller. Thus the egocentrism is embedded in interactive engagement. Also, the repertoire of linguistic forms used in complaints is conventionalized, a set of public symbols; and these conventions are socialized in myriad ways.

Boas (1911) found much significance in the fact that every human language makes possible the act of referring to speaker and listener, self and interlocutor, along with third parties; that is the functional significance of the universality of first-person, second-person, and third-person pronouns.[6] Pronouns, including the Bangla pronoun *āmi* and the English I, are useful tools in constructing characters that may be quite imaginary or projected. Recognizing this does not detract from the significance of pronoun use, but adds to it. To say "we" is to project a group identity; invoking an inclusive we is a crucial tool in the politics of identity. What Silverstein calls "the trope of 'we'ness" helps create—for instance, in the context of a conflict-resolution meeting[7]—the frame of being gathered together for a unified purpose, acting together as a cohesive group. Likewise, to say I is to project an individual but engaged, relationally located self, or rather one of many sorts of discursive selves (for example, principal, animator, figure; Goffman 1974, 1981) arising within a particular strip of interaction.

The referents of first-person and second-person pronouns are always grounded in and relative to shifting contexts of interaction. Thus I may seem always to refer to the speaker, but note that the referent changes as different participants speak (Silverstein 1976); moreover, by saying "I," a speaker can animate any number of other characters (Goffman 1974; Urban 1989). This is true of reported speech, especially in direct discourse. It is natural for us to think of deixis—the use of I or you, of here or there—as though all such references were fixed, but, at the same time, subjective and egocentric. Yet, such indexes are social symbols and make sense only within an interactive process that creates intersubjective realities. Every utterance of I contains the implicit message, "You are listening to me, and know it is this speaker who is thus referring to himself." In fact, deictic usage, including utterances of I, is fundamentally relational, intersubjective, sociocentric, and dialogical.[8]

How does all this illumine Indological discussions of the self? To say that selves are created—or, more accurately, creatively projected—in Bangla (or Mayan, or English) interactions offers a new perspective on ethnosociology (Marriott 1976). The interactionist approach avoids the two extremes of either denying the existence of individuated selves in South Asia or claiming that the self is an invariable universal entity grounded in the biological individuality of each human being regardless of culture. It also shifts the grounds of discussion from the unusual—religious texts and rites of passage—to everyday discourse. Regarding exchanges, it shifts attention from the abstracted structure of nonverbal acts involved in prestations and economic encounters to verbal interaction. By focusing on Bangla verbal interactions we open ourselves to hearing ways in which participants in exchanges interpret those very exchanges.

Achieving understanding is an interactive task. Delimiting reference is a key task of linguistic communication, and one that is thoroughly context-sensitive. What information do one's interlocutors have available to them when one tries to refer to some ache or pain? Complaints must be recipient-designed if they are to succeed at referential specificity. In example 4, Habibur Rahman's daughter Amina complains about her leg: She raises the topic without much prior context for her complaint; the only contextualization she offers is the first phrase of line 72A, *rojā thāikkā* (keeping the fast). Perhaps due to the relative lack of contextualization, the topic noun-phrase of line 72A does indeed begin with the first-person pronoun *āmār* (my). But a style of reference equally common in my corpus appears in line 74A. There, "leg" is no longer delimited by a pronoun, but only by the postposed definite article /-ṭi/.

Example 4. Amina's leg complaint, with and without a pronoun.

72A	rojā thāikkā āmār pāwṭi āijjā	[From] keeping the fast, my leg today
73A	eman bhār [h]ai(ye) ch e	got so heavy as I sat for a long time.
	bai[s]yā thāikkā. (.8)	
74A	pāwṭi ekkebāre e ram[9]	The leg got completely like this.

Though Amina does not always use a possessive pronoun to index her ownership of her leg, we have no question about whose leg is being discussed— context makes it clear. By contrast, the speaker in example 5 illustrates the way that even such words as I and my may not be the inalienable possessions of speakers—but, rather, may bear such strong echoes of others' speech as to create a complex dialogical self. In other words, Shefali's speech, in which she identi- fies herself as a patient under treatment, calls for a translinguistic-semiotic analysis. That analysis indicates that the I of troubles talk is but an egocentric special case of the rule—sociocentric discourse—and that the social underpin- nings of these I's are evident in Shefali's culturally patterned resort to a quotative-performative I-of-possession.

Shefali

Shefali came to my attention when her neighbor—a community health worker and fellow affiliate of ICDDR,B—mentioned her as a *kabirāj* (traditional healer; in Matlab, one who practices any of several sorts of medicine from herbalism to exorcism). Shefali has a reputation specifically as a possession-medium.[10] My colleague said that she *jinn cālāy*, she "drives" or controls a jinn or Islamic spirit. Her possession episodes recur every Thursday night and always begin with Shefali's practice of a loud form of *dhikr* (repeating the name of Allah(u) with every breath; literally, "remembrance"),[11] a Sufi Muslim breathing tech- nique, inhaling "Alla" and exhaling "HU!" After some 15 minutes of this ritual hyperventilation (Lex 1979), she enters a trance (see figures 4-1 and 4-2) and is possessed by a spirit. Technically, it is not a jinn that possesses her, since jinns are male, and the possibility that a male spirit would be intimate with Shefali would be scandalous. It is a *parī*, or female Islamic spirit.[12]

Whether or not Shefali actually practices healing became a matter of much discussion with Shefali herself when, on several occasions, my field assistants and I met her. At two of those meetings with Shefali, she was not there—that is, after an exhausting *dhikr* session, she fell into the trance state that enables her to act as a possession-medium and at times provide or pronounce cures for others. Is she, then, a practitioner? It is not that simple. Shefali proudly declares herself the patient of her *parī*, as she explains below. It is in that sense that she joins the ranks of troubles tellers. However, it is not simply Shefali's self-designation as "patient/sick one"—*rogī* (left unglossed throughout the transcript)—which makes her discourse so instructive. Rather, it is the remarkable grammar of this self-description, involving a radical de-centering of reference—reference to herself in the voice of her guardian *parī*.

Figure 4-1. Shefali in a trance; her gestures accompany glossolalia.

Figure 4-2. Shefali lies down in her trance state.

More than any of the others, this transcript deals explicitly with the meaning of being a *rogī*, and of being a self-in-relationship. In the interview my field assistants tried to integrate the strands of what Shefali herself said with the impressions conveyed to us by her neighbor, Apa, who was also present during the interview. In this and other interviews, Shefali creates for us a picture of her life since the onset of her possession, or visitation, by a *parī*. She achieves this narrative self-construction, however, partly through contrasting herself with various other *rogīs*. By the end of her narrative, we see how she stands out against the run-of-the-mill passive sort of *rogīs* who beg her for help (lines 10S–15S).

Example 5. Interview with Shefali.

S = Shefali; F = Faisal, senior field assistant, male.

Note: Faisal's words are italicized to set them apart from Shefali's.

9F	*rogī māne rogī to āpni: nā /x/.*	Rogī *means—* rogī *is you, right?*
10S	āmi *rogī* to er maddhye to ābār anno tafāt āche to	I am a *rogī* but within that category there are of course differences.
11S	xx ay onārā āi[ye]che nā ane. herā o je rogī nā.	They did not come [into my state]. They are not that *rogī* [like me].
12S	to er maddhye ā i[s]ye jadi kae	Even so, if they come and say,
13S	to (xxxx) dey (de[k]hen) nā	"Hey, won't you look,"
14S	(māne to āre de[k]hen),	that is, "Hey there, look—
15	e āmār ki rogḍā, ektu cān.	I have this illness, please take a look."
16S	ektu kākati minati kare kailei (.)	If they beg and talk like that,
17S	(beyāg eḍā) kaiyā diyā jāy gā ār ki (.)	[the spirit] tells all of them [what's wrong] before [third person] leaves.
18F	*o.*	*Oh.*
19S	diyā to ei rog. āmi kichu pārtām nā.	[The spirit] gives [the knowledge that it is] this illness. I cannot do that [in and of myself].

After 36 lines (not shown here), Shefali begins speaking again—as in lines 13–15—in another's voice.

55S	((louder)) "āmār rogīr janno [h]ay[e]che dharā jāy ni tor	"They have come for my 'patient'; no touching!
56S	tor ghare āi[s]yā bisrāitāche-re	They come looking in your [sT] house."
57F	*ā rogī māne āpni.*	*Oh,* rogī *means you?*
58S	hyā. "āmār rogīr janno ā i[ye]che,	Yes. "They have come for my 'patient'.
59S	dharā jāy nā to āmār rogīr dāre	No touching [or coming] close to my *rogī.*
60S	mānse tāre mando kawto	If people spoke badly of you,
61S	(māde) bandte pārti nā	You could not tie patients up in the courtyard [a common treatment for epilepsy].
62S	tui jadi mānus	If you
63S	māre anos	bring [a lot of people] in[to your house],
64S	māinse tore mando kaybo.	people will speak ill of you.

65S	jei śunto je owṣadh dey,	Whoever heard that I gave out medicine [through you],
66S	āmār rogīrā more khārāp kaibe,	those people would speak ill of my *rogī*,
67S	mānuṣ ā[s]wā jāwi karle beśi.	[that is,] if people were coming in and out [of my secluded female space of honor] too much."

In line 66 Shefali breaks frame and resorts to an unmarked form of self-reference ("of me"). When my excerpt resumes after 19 deleted lines, Shefali is answering Faisal's question (line 87), but in a way that is grammatically odd (*).

86F	*hedāre jigāi[ye]che cācā-e*	*Didn't Uncle*[13] *question it [the spirit]?*
87S	*nā jān.* jiṅāile āmrā kailām,	I don't know. Whether or not someone asked the spirit something, we said ...
88S	āmi to kaite[p]āri nā e janno /(nā likh[e]chi)/	I can't say; that's why /(I wrote it??)/
89F	*o ta[k]han āpni kichu kaite [p]ārten nā.*	*Oh, then you can't say anything.*
90S	āmār jñāna pāy nā to.	I'm not conscious.
91S	je āmnār jadi āmār jadi (byārām-ḍā) uḍḍi (1)	If (my illness) rises
92S	āmnārā jadi gharo āi[s]yen (1) ābār āmā-e huś nā haite	and you come to the house and before my consciousness
93S	nā haite	returns [<1]
94S	jadi āmnārā jān gā (1), āmi kait[e p]ārtām nā, jāi	you leave, I wouldn't be able to say.
95F	*ācchā ta[k]han ayje māne rogīrā (jhārā gocchā) dey tey,*	*Uh, then you mean you give a (magical sweeping treatment) to* rogī.
96F	*e (xx) karen to āpni: ei sab/guli/.*	*You do /all that/.*
97S	/hā/.	/Yes/.
98F	*āpnār hāt diye /x/*	*By your hand /[the spirit acts]/.*
99S	/āmār/ hāt diyā āmār mukh diyei (.) kare.	/By my/ hand, by my mouth [it] acts.

Shefali's statement in lines 91S–94S, like Fatima's in 21 (example 9), is deceptively transparent; at first glance it appears to confine the complaint to a sort of dissociation or post-trance amnesia. A more complete treatment of this event, however, would problematize this seemingly transparent statement. Isn't she saying more? And, in fact, isn't the speaking subject problematized in lines 9–11? On the one hand, Shefali does call her trances a *byārām*, a disabling illness. Still, the disability is transient, manageable, and in many ways advantageous. In the trance state, she says, she cannot be subject to normal expectations. She is not present as an acting subject. During one of Shefali's trance-possession events, my associate Faisal called her by her name. The spirit, speaking "by my [Shefali's] mouth" (line 99S), chided him with a reminder that Shefali was not there. So when Shefali was later asked to describe specific aspects of an event at which she was not consciously present (namely, those altered states), she pleaded ignorance. For example, she *can't say* whether or not my assistants and I were even present in her home as her guests during the trance-possession.

What, then, makes Shefali the *rogī* (patient)? It is her relationship to the familiar spirit, reaffirmed each Thursday night for the public through her mediumship. Shefali explicitly constructs herself as *rogī*, and describes her weekly trances as *byārāmḍā uḍḍe* (standard Bangla, *byārāmṭā oṭhe* ([times when her] illness rises). But is it Shefali's self that is under construction, or her relationship with the *parī*? Where do we draw the line between Shefali's self and her *parī*? Shefali gives us to understand that the *parī* has made her what she is, a *rogī*. Thus, in lines 58, 59, and 66, the voice behind the referring act (*āmār rogī*) is not the speaker's (Shefali's). Instead, what we hear is the reported speech of Shefali's *parī*. And in this context, like that of Puerto Rican Spiritist healers, the *rogī* identity is a badge worn proudly, part of a "[valued] rhetoric of complaint" (Gaines and Farmer 1986: 305; Koss-Chioino 1992: 79).[14] Her helpless succumbing to the *parī*'s weekly influence constitutes her as patient; but the usage here is an index of the identity Shefali acquired in the "initiation illness" marking the onset of her periodic possession by the *parī*.

How do we compare this illness, which is homologous with shamanic initiation illnesses,[15] with the complaints of the others presented herein? Admittedly, we must treat Shefali's complaint in itself as a mark of her new and valued identity. Her speech to us is like a testimony of a convert to a spirit cult like the *zār* in East Africa (Kennedy 1967). For her, weakness and confusion lie in the past, and are associated with the initiation illness. Shefali's patienthood now consists of the altered state she enters in which she finds her status enhanced. I am convinced that, had we met Shefali immediately before and again during the onset of her possession "illness" (*rog/byārām*), we would have discovered more similarities with the other cases. At other points in interviews with Shefali, she describes the early days of her possession, the confusion it brought, and the tense negotiations between the *parī* and her husband that followed. The outcome of the negotiations was a compromise: Her trances would be limited to a weekly occurrence—rather than daily, as the *parī* had desired (for maximum intimacy with her *rogī*), or monthly, as her husband had proposed. From what she told us and from my anecdotal evidence of women's status in Matlab, we can justly assume that Shefali had previously experienced severe restrictions on her right to narrate and, particularly, to tell troubles. In that light we can see that Shefali's illness opened up new communicative possibilities for her.[16] Thus, what we hear from her today is a thoroughly transformed complaint, a pseudocomplaint reflecting her satisfaction with things as they stand as much as it indirectly reflects a gendered order of communication that she is managing rather effectively. The illness now embraced becomes a kind of health.

In sum, the *parī*'s presence has evidently improved Shefali's status in relation to her husband and neighbors—kin and nonkin. Shefali's possession is not pathological; if it can be seen as a dissociation, it is dissociation in the service of the relational self. On the other hand, insofar as it has not radically altered her psychosocial situation, it may also be seen as an example of the sort of indeterminate, contingent, and incremental healing described by Csordas (1988). Ironically, Shefali's *parī*, while in some ways empowering Shefali to speak more assertively, also reinforces Islamic discourse. In lines 58–67, even the *parī* seems not to speak for itself but to reflect the voice of the generalized social other, who will speak ill of Shefali if she violates social norms. Both voices—that of the *parī* and that of Shefali—are co-opted. In the end, their resistance itself is taken into, and becomes a part of, the discourse of gender segregation and hierarchy. Shifting from Bakhtin (1981)—whose focus is on multiple voices within even a single utterance—to Foucault (1985), we see that both "voices" are parts of a single order of discourse.

Shefali's narrative, while containing references to herself as a sick person, is unusual in many ways. In relation to my corpus of complaints, it is neither spon-taneous nor directed primarily at a local audience. It is offered to neither practi-tioner nor kin. Despite her reference to herself as a *rogī*, Shefali takes no action to change that status by getting better. She does not speak of any need for a cure. What her narrative does for my overall account, however, is to neatly illustrate the complexity, constructedness, and sociocentricity of I's and other pronouns in patients' discourse, particularly the multivocality in Shefali's utterance, "my patient." This pronoun that Urban (1989) calls de-quotative reflects the projec-tive I of Shefali's trance-possession.

Urban describes a range of I's. First, there are the unreflecting everyday tokens of I for which traditional semiotic analysis is unproblematic. These are indexical-referential; that is, their referent shifts as speakers take turns becoming I. On the other hand, when one quotes another speaker and represents his or her I in a direct quotation, the quoted I is *not* indexical. Shefali uses decentered quoted I's; she does not help her listeners, however, by framing the quote! Had she introduced her decentered I (or my) with the matrix clause, "The *parī*, referring to me, said, ...," few interpretive problems would have arisen. When she did not thus frame her quotation of the spirit, we took her my as directly indexical of herself, as a possessive derivative of a centered I. But the fact is that when Shefali spoke the word "my," the possessing I was decentered from the speaker—it was the *parī's* perspective, the spirit's I, that controlled the refer-ence. Pronouns like that my are more anaphoric than indexical—they are coreferential with a third person designated in a matrix clause (never spoken by Shefali) rather than pointing indexically to an I who is speaking in the here and now. If Shefali had spoken the frame ("The spirit said ..."), this I would have been anaphoric. But, in Urban's (1989: 36) taxonomy of I's, this one is de-quotative because it lacks a matrix clause. The de-quotative I occurs in utter-ances in which the quotative frame is effaced in progressively more extreme forms of heteroglossia or decentering, as in theatrical performance and spirit possession.

Urban argues that it is through quoting and imitating the speech of others—through anaphoric first-person pronouns that refer to other I's—that the I be-comes a truly cultural self (cf. Mead 1995a: 90). It is through such uses that "the anaphoric self that is a substitute for a discourse character allows an individual to fit into a culture-specific text" (Urban 1989: 49). The texts to which he refers can be compared with cultural schemas (Holland and Quinn 1987); trance-possession is such a schema, widely available to rural Bangladeshis. That is, when Matlab residents hear that someone "drives a jinn," they can imagine a series of scenarios, a set of events conjured up in the form of a stereotyped frame for action. There are many links between trance-possession and theater and myth performances. In the drama of possession and myth enactment, actors animate powerful roles. Shefali's projective I parallels the I of myths recorded by Urban, who says that "the projective 'I' of origin myth telling is an 'I' that aligns speaker/narrators with past 'I's" (Urban 1989: 45). The I of Shefali's female guardian spirit is one that aligns her with the pre-Aryan peoples of India, whose deities were female (Blanchet 1984).

The taming or socialization of the I, however, is limited. Urban rightly points out that when individuals grasp the tension between the everyday referential-indexical I and anaphoric, de-quotative, or projective I's, possibilities for manipulation open up. These possibilities mean that "the individual is not entirely subject to the reign of culture through received texts" (1989: 49). Urban draws an analogy between the insights at which psychoanalysts and semioticians respectively aim. The play of various I's, whether it is achieved through under-going personal analysis or through "the semiotic capacity to grasp the two 'I's, also opens a dialogue within the individual over everyday 'I' and the 'I' of discourse" (50).[17] The impact of other selves on one's own linguistic self-formation comes through ways of imitating others' speech while maintaining consciousness that it still somehow belongs to the other; it is, in fact, in such interaction that selves emerge (Mead 1934). In these forms of discourse and pronoun usage, there is some "control that the imitated other exercises over the speaker ... This metaphorical 'I' can become a kind of 'ideal' of the self" (Urban 1989: 36). Thus it is not so surprising that in the very act of saying "I," Shefali tends to speak for her community's Islamic conscience and to subject herself to it. The *parī*'s I and its speech is not the product of Shefali's private imagination but in some ways distills "spirit discourse" that Shefali heard on others' lips even before her spirit visitations began. If the *parī*'s I closely resembles the idealized identity of the local Muslim community, Shefali's participation in discourse explains it.

The question of Shefali's significance, particularly the representativeness of her case, arises immediately. In Urban's terms, her narrative's use of I is toward the extreme end of a continuum. It is, however, a continuum and in some ways even a circle. Here I refer to the fact, pointed out by Urban (1989), that the projective I—unless clearly marked as the I of a possessing spirit, etc. (and Shefali's was *not* marked as such in any grammatical or lexical way)—is extremely hard to distinguish from the "ordinary indexical referential 'I'" (42). On the other hand, we ought not take the everyday end of the continuum of I's of discourse as qualitatively different, or radically egocentric in comparison with the boundary-blurring sociocentric I of anaphoric (clearly quotative) and de-quotative (minus the matrix "She said" clause) I's including the theatrical I and the projective I of spirit-possession. Hanks (1990) has demonstrated the interactive grounding of all indexical references, including reference to ego's body or other aspects of the self or I.

What we have arrived at, then, is a recognition that the I of troubles talk and *rogī*-talk (a) is a special, egocentric, form of sociocentric discourse;[18] (b) may reflect others' I's through quotation and the influence of the imitated I on the discourse in which it becomes embedded; (c) is therefore a cultural phenomenon, which does not preclude the possibility that (d) it may also entail complex manipulative forms of play between given cultural forms and situationally specific goals of the person.

Latifa: A Self Magnified in the Light of Fire

One has only to think of the role of reported speech in Latifa's troubling performance to see that Shefali's speech is not unique. Latifa and others strengthen their authority by borrowing others' words. Not even Latifa's frequent first-person pronouns are all tokens of the everyday indexical-referential I. In fact, some echo the stories *that others tell about her.* Yet in her speech we also meet the limits of the inner dialogism of the I and of interpretations of Bakhtin that deny the role of authorial intentionality of which he wrote. Granted that every utterance, including the word "I," contains echoes of others' usage such that no word belongs to one speaker alone. Yet Latifa's various I's, collecting other voices together with her own as they do, are strategic marshalings undergirded with determined intentionality. She marshaled those voices to persuade her family to undo her divorce, since, as she told me in 1992, she regretted having complained (albeit mildly) about mistreatment during the first months of her marriage in 1990. A significant factor in that mistreatment was the $1500 in dowry money that Latifa's brothers had promised but failed to give to her husband's family.[19] At any rate, that mistreatment had largely ceased by the time her brothers intervened to force a divorce and claim for themselves the cash settlement.

One of the most profoundly disturbing experiences of my fieldwork occurred in late March, 1992. But before describing that experience, and examining Latifa's complaint transcript, it is important to tell something of her story. I had lived in the *bāṛi* of Habibur Rahman's clan in the village of Baghmar since November 1991. Three of Habib's cousins (his father's brothers' sons [FBSs]) and three brothers shared the Rahman lineage compound with him, and the older sons of his FBSs were my fictive brothers and real companions. Habib's father's brother's daughter lived with her husband, her sons (her husband is deceased), and their formerly married daughter Latifa, 10 miles from Baghmar in the village of Dukkhapur.

I had visited Dukkhapur in December 1991, meeting only Latifa's brothers. Because *parda* (gender segregation) is the norm in rural Bangladesh, and particularly so in Muslim villages, it would have surprised me at that time if the women of that unfamiliar household had sat down, along with the men, to chat with me. After my first visit, there seemed to be little correspondence between the two distant households. Then in March, when I returned to Matlab from a weekend in Dhaka, the Rahman family told me that they had a guest who was *pāgal* (mad, insane). My field assistant Faisal introduced her to me as Latifa, a woman of the household we had visited in Dukkhapur, about 20 years old, now visiting her mother's brothers' compound. Faisal had spent some hours listening to the story she had to tell, and over the next two weeks I also heard it from her and others. Within the relative freedom of my own adopted compound, the norms of cross-sex modesty were relaxed sufficiently to allow us the opportunity to speak with her.

Latifa came to our *bāṛi* after experiencing what Finkler (1991) calls one of "life's lesions," events in the lifeworld that frequently form the context of health complaints. Some two years before the visit to Baghmar, she had been married to an *imām* (Islamic cleric; a Qur'anically trained teacher and prayer leader) and had gone to live with him. Before marrying, in her high school career, she had won a reputation as a fine student. She resisted the marriage proposal. In fact, her brothers forced the marriage upon her, although most Bangladeshis would say that Islam forbids such coercion. A sum of 50,000 Taka ($1200) was set as the figure she would receive as a *kābin* (settlement) in case of a divorce.

Not surprisingly, Latifa had difficulty adjusting to life in her husband's natal home. During the months she resided there, Latifa sent word to her brothers that she was being mistreated by her in-laws. Yet somehow, she began to get used to the situation and even to feel a strong romantic attraction toward her husband. Her brothers, however, taking her former reports seriously—and (according to Latifa, her mother, and nonkin informants) desiring to receive the *kābin* promised in case of divorce—took it upon themselves to arrange a divorce as they had arranged the marriage.

Their arrangement was imposed on the bride and groom with violence. Latifa's brothers beat the *imām* and worked, through village councils, to receive the *kābin*. They brought Latifa back to their home. In this, as in her marriage, she was unwilling: She protested and wept loudly but was ignored. Her brothers' attempts to receive the cash settlement resulted in suffering for all but the mediators; the *imām* paid up, the mediators pocketed the money, and Latifa's family was left with only bitterness. When I met her two years later, Latifa was still grieving. Some of those in her extended family construed her weeping as a sign of love madness caused by charms purportedly planted around her father's house by her ex-husband.

Bangladeshi friends tell me that, Islamic strictures notwithstanding, such events are not unusual. It *is* rather unusual, however, for such a woman to be found lamenting her former husband years later. Latifa and her brothers have been in constant conflict since they carried her back home. They claim that her passion for the *imām* indicates the continued effects of the powerful love charms that he must have used to win her. This, they say, explains both her change of heart in the last weeks of her marriage and her enduring feelings for him. Because they see in her the effects of an unwelcome force, they pay for her to

receive treatment by a *kāri*, an expert in Islamic texts who can use that knowledge for healing.[20] She, on the other hand, asks us, "Am I sick, that I should
receive such treatment?" And her brothers—evidently impatient with the
progress of her therapy and losing face with every word of protest and lamentation that Latifa utters—respond with more violence, binding her with chains and
beating her.[21]

This brings me back to her visit to our compound in March 1992. At that
time, Latifa walked the 10 miles from her brothers' home in Dukkhapur to visit
her mother's brothers' compound in Baghmar village—my field home—for two
weeks. She came to her mother's kin to seek their support in her efforts to over-
ride her brothers and be reconciled and reunited with her beloved. For this she
would need her uncles' moral and financial help; they would need to apologize
to the *imām* for the beating he had suffered and also to repay the *kābin*. More
urgently, she needed help in resisting their efforts to marry her to yet another
man against her wishes.[22] Latifa's appeal to her mother's brothers should be
seen against the background of the warmth and hopes attached to that kin category in Bengali culture, encoded in this proverb:

> Nāi māmār ceye kānā māmā bhālo.
> Better a blind mother's brother than no mother's brother at all.[23]

Latifa's other relationships, especially with her brothers, were both close
and problematic. Her brothers had arranged her marriage, and they had ended it.
She also has a younger sister who is married and lives in Dhaka; having seen
them talk intimately and urgently about Latifa's troubles, my sense is that Latifa
would derive emotional support from the sister if she lived nearer. Yet, when
Latifa asked her sister to visit her ex-husband, the sister passed this request to
my field assistant and me. He said that taking Latifa back was inappropriate for
an *imām*. He also expressed doubts about her mental or spiritual health, though
something about him made Faisal wonder about his own normalcy. At any rate,
Latifa's sister's transfer of that responsibility to Faisal colors my perception of
the relationship between the sisters, and contributes a note of ambiguity to my
role as well. Bengali tradition depicts ego's mother's brothers as ego's support-
ers. Thus, that Latifa sought their support was not remarkable, but what about
the timing of her visit during my residence? This timing raises the question of
how Latifa perceived me, beyond calling me "brother," as did her maternal
cousins. Even before March, she had learned of my presence there, since I had
visited her brothers' home in January. Finally, their father was alive in 1992, but
not visibly involved in these matters. His absence from Latifa's discourse will
remain a mystery; he died in 1994.

It probably became apparent to Latifa, early in the two-week visit to her
uncles' compound, that hers was a desperate struggle, doomed to failure unless
she resorted to extreme measures. When I arrived on the scene, she was spend-
ing most daylight hours away from the compound, claiming that her uncles
would otherwise beat her and force *kabirāji* (herbal, Ayurvedic, or other traditional) medicine upon her.[24] Faisal and I recorded three separate occasions on

which Latifa added words and a melody to her weeping. At the end of the second week of her stay with us, late in what had been a peaceful evening, Latifa's
sobs and screams had a more urgent occasion, although even then the elements
of rhythm, melody, and rhetorical formulaicity were not missing. The men of the
Rahman compound were threatening her openly. Their tolerance exhausted, her
mother's brothers were now about to forcibly remove her. Whatever formulaic
lament she now uttered was, in her male cousins' words, *sei purān kāndāi* (that
[same] old crying).

At 10:00 P.M., two men about 30 years old—Latifa's distant cousin and a
next-door neighbor of the Rahmans—seized her arms and legs and carried her
out of the compound as she screamed, her clothes, hair, and persona in disarray.
Most of her male cousins (my "brothers") followed their fathers in whipping up
their angry resolve to remove her. Habib's own brother and that brother's
daughter objected meekly, but the crowd of some 30 people gave at least passive
assent to the shouting men. Finally, they carried Latifa out of our compound and
forbade Faisal and me to accompany them. The next day, my fictive brothers
told me that after Latifa had been carried a few hundred yards, she walked the
rest of the 10 miles home with the men and she was thus delivered there that
night.

Faisal and I visited her a month later. Her mother and sister reported that
she was "crying less now." We asked Latifa. "Yes," she said; "I don't cry—I
don't want to be beaten anymore!"

People I spoke with were universally pessimistic about Latifa's chances for
redress. Sympathetic voices spoke in a whisper on the night she was forcibly
removed to her natal home. When one female cousin said to another that the
male neighbor carrying Latifa by her legs "is not of good character," the second
woman shushed her. The day after Latifa's abduction, I reported the event to
some health workers who had some acquaintance with Latifa and her village,
hoping to inspire someone to intervene. Some men immediately said it was
divine justice; she had been unhappy with the marriage in the first place, so in
the end she got what she had wanted—a divorce. One woman spoke of Latifa's
fine reputation as a high school student; she also said Latifa was a "good girl."
Males in the room seized on the theme of girls' schooling to point out how
common it is for educated women to be assertive, thereby threatening rural
norms. These educated women are seen as a sort of nouveau riches group in a
nation where female literacy is 24 percent and where fewer than 10 percent of
girls ever finished high school in the 1980s. A male medical practitioner at the
ICDDR,B's Sonargaon clinic said that educated girls in Bangladesh often
haven't "digested" their education, and that they cause problems. Well before
Faisal visited the ex-husband, the people I spoke with predicted that he would
never take Latifa back; he had lost face as well as money. This group and others
laughed at my suggestion that the courts or village councils would help her, and
all politely agreed that the women of the area needed to unite to help each other.
Regarding Latifa herself, they predicted that she would eventually be forced to
commit suicide; that, they say, is what her brothers want, since Latifa has

become a burden to them.[25] Hearing me tell this story, some in Matlab said that her brothers could not be human—*orā mānuṣ nā* (they are inhuman).

Midway through Latifa's visit in March of 1992, I recorded her performing a lament that complained of bitter pain and condemned her brothers for destroy-ing her life. She wept for her lost husband. Her weeping had formulaic elements about it; it canalized her experience (Obeyesekere 1975) of loss, grief, and be-trayal. (Emotions can be a threat to social orders, and the canalizing—"leading in a desirable direction" [Compact Oxford English Dictionary 1991]—of emo-tion is a good thing from a social-functionalist perspective.) The setting (see figure 4-3) was the house of her mother's aunt—the eldest woman in the Rahman compound. Gathered about Latifa on the "sitting bed" were some 10 women and children. Outside were another 10 men and women. One of the young men remarked aloud that it was shameful for Latifa to carry on about a lost affine and to defame her own brothers. He openly discussed with his mother and sisters the question of her sanity. For days she had been loosely referred to as *pāgal*. But when she stopped weeping and argued her case with some rhetori-cal force the young man said, "She is not mad after all." Still, the sincerity of the weeping was not taken for granted by those standing outside.

Self and Fire in Latifa's Texted Weeping

Latifa's linguistic self-indexin contrasts starkly with that of Fatima (see example 9). Whereas Fatima succeeded at specifying references to her own body and symptoms largely without the help of first-person pronouns, Latifa's lament is filled with them. The lament is not much longer and has just a few more possible instances of first-person indexicals than the recorded speech of Fatima—37 as compared with Fatima's 21. Yet, while Fatima used 2 first-person indexicals, Latifa used 33! That count does not include Latifa's decentered references to self, those in which she reports the speech of others about herself—and thus the

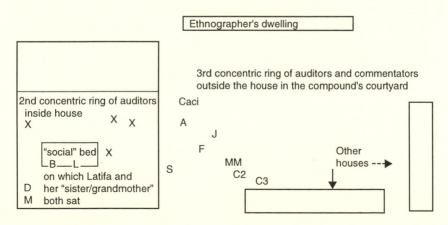

Figure 4-3. Latifa and her audience(s): performance setting, the night of March 26, 1992.

reference to self is transposed from first to second person, or to a nonindexical form like *mānuṣ* (translated as "one" in line 3). Latifa's varied forms of self-reference are underlined in the following example; •hh represents a sobbing inbreath marking the end of one of Latifa's poetic lines; and, contrary to my usual practice (because example 6 is sung), question marks indicate grammar and not intonation.

Example 6. Latifa begins to lament.

2   āmāre ni deśe deśe [p]hirāigo bun •hh   They took me from land to land,
    bun go o o bun •hh   sister, O sister.

3   āmi ni "kāro bārit jāwnā mānus" •hh   [They said] I was, "A person who
    āchilām bun •hh   goes to others' homes," sister,
    bun go o o bun •hh   sister, O, O sister.

4   kono mān[u]ṣe tay āmāre kono din   Yet no person ever saw me,
    de[k]he nāi •hh   sister, O, O sister.
    bun go o o bun •hh

5   man[u]ṣe dekhle nā i āmāre •hh   If people [do] see me [now],
    kay "āpner ki o go [h]ai [ye]che" •hh   they ask "What on earth happened
                                                    to you?"
    bun go o o bun.   sister, O, O sister.

6   āmār śaril dekhle man[u]ṣe   If they see my body,
    [ś]hirbā diyā •hh   people shiver,
    uḍe •hh bun o o o go •hh   sister, O sister.

Latifa's performance is referred to locally as a tuneful type of weeping. There are named lament genres with long written histories that have been de-scribed in the scholarly literature. I make no claim here that Latifa's spontaneous performance bears all the marks of poetry in classical *bilāp* (laments). In Mukun-daram's (1589) *Phullera's 12-Monthly Sorrows*, for instance, we find rhyme, a creative lexical variety representing the literate end of the diglossic spectrum (Ferguson 1959), and an absence of self-indexing in first-person pronouns. Latifa's performance lacks rhyme, exploits a limited lexical range all drawn from everyday usage, and foregrounds the self as victim, through its frequent first-person indexicals. Still, there are powerful elements of verbal artistry in her performance and even possible evocations of genres of old—including ancient written forms of lament—and of newer genres such as Hindi film songs.

In line 13 Latifa introduces an idiom that is powerful for her audience be-cause of its echoes of medieval Indo-Islamic piety (echoes that become louder in lines 42–43):

Example 7. The fire theme in Latifa's lament.

13   āmi e āgun kemte sahyo   How can I this fire
     go karbo •hh   bear?
     bun go a: a: ((crying voice)) bun. •hh   sister, O sister?

14   dhum rānāy āmāre   Tell me—will the smoke
     bujhāibā •hh   (not sear) me,
     bun go o o bun. •hh   sister, O sister?

Lines 13–14 introduce the image of fire to evoke the destruction, pain, and anger that Latifa experiences. Later (in line 42), Latifa returns to the theme of fire and more openly exploits the theological and mystical histories of the figure's use. In all her mentions of fire as an image for pain, Latifa evokes the theme of the particular fiery pain associated with separation from the object of love in Muslim *bāramāsyo* (calendrical laments; Vaudeville 1986: 38).[26]

Bāramāsyo is a recognized genre of oral and written literature in most of the Indo-Aryan languages (Vaudeville 1986; cf. Wadley 1983), a genre with several centuries of written history. A *bāramāsyo* is a calendrical lament for the absent beloved, prototypically a husband. In classical examples,[27] the image of rain linked with reunion was appropriate not only because seasonal rain brings relief (from spring heat), but also because rain served as a metaphor for sexual fluids (which serve, themselves, as a cultural metonym for both love and vitality). In its origins in oral performance, therefore, *bāramāsyo* might have provided women an avenue for the assertive expression of their longings.[28] After the classical period of *bāramāsyo* composition, some were also penned by Sufi Muslim men. Squeamish about both the affirmation of sex and the assertiveness of the woman's voice in conventional *bāramāsyo*, they substituted the imagery of fire for that of rain. Fire represented the pain of separation. The figurative richness of that usage derives from Sufi Muslim literature, in which it points to the mystic's desire for union with God through ascetic practices and Qur'anic recitation. Vaudeville describes the Sufi poets' tendency to transform the Hindu notion of *viraho* (separation-longing) into Arabic *'ishq* (love). Because such love was typically not fulfilled, pain was an apt metonym for it—and fire for the pain of love—"an inextinguishable fire, a mortal torment consuming those whom it possesses, bearing them inexorably towards death" (1986: 38).

What this history provides is a warrant for interpreting the fire image in conjunction with the theme of Latifa's song—grief over her ex-husband. The Hindu and Muslim variants of the genre also testify to the conflict that the language of lament can represent and engender. Latifa's self-assertion might be indexed through her frequent first-person pronouns, but it doesn't end there. The polysemy of fire leverages for Latifa the authority of Islam—its regional poetic traditions as well as its scriptural traditions—in her confrontation with her brothers. Later in her texted weeping, she sang these lines:

41	āmāre nā kiyā karlo •hh	What they have done to me,
	bun o go •hh	sister, O sister!
42	hāśarero māḍer matan kairā go •hh	The fire of judgment day
	ānlo go bun •hh	They've brought down, sister—
	bun go bun •hh	sister, O sister.
43	hāśarero māḍer matan kairā go	It's like the day of judgment,
	bun o go •hh	sister, oh!

Is this fire again the fire of her inward pain, the fire searing her soul? Fire here evokes not only pain but also rage. These lines cannot only refer to her subjectivity. The frightening eschatological vision of *Hāśarer maṭh*[29]—the field on

Eloquence in Trouble

which God's judgment will burn hotter than a sun, descending onto the very heads of those gathered—is a reminder. It reminds all those who hear it that human actions, including her brothers', will be judged in this fiery scene. Latifa's verbal skills certainly include the ability to draw on various voices to support her cause, the ability to manipulate key symbols.

Hence we have the possibility that Latifa's self was magnified by fire, cast up, so to speak, on a wall like a tremendous, shifting shadow of a person standing in front of a bonfire. The fire of pain helped drive her song with its constant references to how "they have killed *me*." In a second sense, Latifa's is not just a lonely, unsupported voice, but one magnified through its subtle participation or identification with the fire of God. While never leaving the plane of relationships, the self of this complainer takes on a form that is bigger than life in the very process of performing her complaint. It is quite likely that Latifa's magnified projections of self helped bring down her family's wrath—the beatings, but particularly the labeling as *pāgal*—for to magnify self is deviant.

Counting Grammatically Superfluous Pronouns

Let us assume here that persistent patterns of self-referencing by means of first-person singular pronouns constitute a privileged site for the linguistic construction of personhood both as concept and as experience, and that the frequency of first-person indexicals in a text or a corpus sheds some light on the sense of self. Such an approach would be simplistic unless we put that frequency in the context of expected or possible instantiation of first-person pronouns. What sorts of functions are performed by those indexicals that do occur? Given the number of possible tokens of a first-person indexical, how many actual tokens of those indexicals are found in transcripts of various types of speech? Such frequencies are not necessarily simple reflexes of egocentricity as a stable personality variable.

Starting a complaint with a sentence-initial first-person singular possessive pronoun (*āmār*) is usually superfluous, but it characterizes the elaborated code of standard spoken Bangla, reflecting written usage.[30] The following is an example of the experiencer-subject construction from Klaiman (1980: 276); the elicited example refers to the same body part as the one in Amina's spontaneous complaint, the leg, with a phonological shift in the standardizing direction— Amina's nonstandard *pāw* becomes *pā*.[31]

> Example 8. Standard complaint grammar with a pronoun.
>
> | āmār pā-e | culko-cch-e |
> |---|---|
> | my leg-ERG[32] | itch-ing-is |
> | "My leg itches." | |

In English complaints, verbs would agree with subjects of sentences, including pronouns—for example, "I feel sick/he feels sick." In pro-drop languages such as Bangla, subjects need not be overtly expressed since they are reflected in verb endings marking agreement with the (optionally expressed) subject. Thus the pronoun in complaints like those in the above examples is optional, and absent more than it is present in Bangla as it is commonly spoken in Bangladesh. But there is variation; the pronoun may appear. In a corpus of 101 complaints recorded not mechanically but from memory, verbatim, within minutes of my hearing them (see chapter 8), only about a dozen complaints—none of those I recorded *myself* uttering, in order to record others' responses—included the optional pronoun. Its presence indexes the status and perhaps the worldview associated with standard Bangla of Calcutta and Dhaka. Allegiance to those urban centers of capitalist penetration correlates with a Western style of self-hood, perhaps egocentricity.

Further analysis of Bangla verb agreement will illuminate my discussion. Not only is the pronoun optional, but also in the experiencer-subject construction typifying Bangla troubles talk, the verb is impersonal; that is, it only occurs in the third person and is thus never marked for subject agreement. The uninflected verb *lāge* (seem; strike) is very common in this construction (cf. Masica 1991: 346–358). Thus, even if a pronoun does occur in Bangla troubles talk, it usually occurs neither in the unmarked nominative case as the sentence's semantic agent, nor as the sentential subject that would control verb agreement (Li 1976; Comrie 1981).

In the large corpus of complaints discussed in Chapter 8, there is a positive correlation between the status of the audience and pronoun use. Complaints made to a higher-status audience were more likely to contain first-person pronouns. Perhaps superfluous pronoun use is a form of standardization, like increased r-pronunciation among "hypercorrecting" New York English speakers (Labov 1972); a higher-status audience seems to elicit more pronouns. If so, Bangla pronoun use betrays sensitivity to social context of usage rather than an autonomous egocentricity.

Troubles-talk utterances I heard in the bazaar as opposed to the *bāṛi* (residential compound) tended to use *āmār* (my). Remember that almost no women are seen in rural marketplaces. Also, noise and the lack of a conversational context prevent the listener from presupposing that any malady the speaker might express is his own. In fact, it is typical for acquaintances passing each other on the street to inquire about a whole list of each other's kin; that custom would make no sense during a social visit in one's home. Those who meet on the streets must take special measures to nail down referential specificity and avoid the ambiguity potentiated by dropping pronouns.

Fatima's troubles talk is remarkable, however, for its lack of pronouns.

Fatima: A Self Compromised by "Something Loose"

Fatima is a woman with grown children, living—as do most women in Matlab—with her husband's family in their compound. That compound includes four households. Fatima's daughters live with their husbands, too, when they are lucky enough to be fed by them. Her 25-year-old son, on whom she would otherwise depend for her economic security, is retarded (*sidhā*). Although she is only about 40, the intense physical and emotional stress of her life in poverty shows on her thin, anxious face. During the interviews I conducted at Fatima's home, sisters-in-law usually spoke for her. On occasion—for instance, during my 1996 visit—Fatima herself would deny having the sorts of problems for which an exorcist's services might be needed. Fatima's motivation for denial became clearer with the revelation that her sisters-in-law called her problem a *māthār byārām* (disabling illness of the head). They indicated that her symptoms have a long history. Fatima had a frightened look about her as she shrank before her more forceful affines.

There seems to be a mismatch between Fatima's focus on physical discomfort in her abdomen and head—in 1996 she reported a *cākā* (lump), or tumor, in her abdomen, though an MRI exam in the city revealed nothing—and the others' stories of speechless spells in which she gets a terrified look on her face and bites her tongue (seizures?). Perhaps this can be explained by recourse to Fatima's "loss of consciousness" during such episodes (although epilepsy seemed to be ruled out by an EEG, done along with the MRI) or as an example of necessarily positioned, and thus differing, rhetorical strategies in the conarration of illness. The first explanation privileges the sisters-in-laws' knowledge; the second highlights the conflicting interests of various parties in the narrative representation of illness (Good 1994). In any case, among the stakes to which these narrative tensions point is a public appraisal of Fatima's personal competence—that is, her ability to fulfill the responsibilities accompanying her roles as wife (though her husband died in 1995), mother, mother-in-law of some very demanding sons-in-law, and now head of the household. My sense is that for some time Fatima's sisters-in-law have sought to establish their representation of Fatima as incompetent, though I fail to see what they might gain by doing so.

As of 1996, Fatima was not quite getting by economically. When I asked about her *abasthā* (situation, position, standing), she began to weep, saying "I don't even have anything you can call an *abasthā*." I gave Fatima small gifts in 1992 and 1996. Since her husband's death, she has been forced to accept the charity of neighbors and sometimes to labor for them in return for some rice.

It was shortly after I had moved to Matlab in November 1991 that I first met Fatima. News of my interest in spirit illness and exorcism had spread quickly; specifically, it reached Jahangir, whom Fatima's family had called to perform an exorcism. At roughly 30, Jahangir is exceptionally young among local exorcists. The other exorcists I met in Matlab are at least 50; all three are men. Jahangir makes his living selling cigarettes and betel leaves in the Sonargaon bazaar and told me that he performs exorcisms at no charge, in accord with a vow to his guru.[33] Fatima and her kin confirmed that they paid Jahangir nothing, perhaps because the exorcism was aborted. Before that day I had met neither exorcist nor "patient," but, having heard of my interest, Jahangir and a friend came to meet me and they invited me to come with them to Fatima's compound. When we arrived there I received permission to record the whole consultation with Fatima. After the initial awkwardness during the setting up of the microphones, the consultation moved smoothly. When Jahangir concluded that Fatima's condition was not caused by a spirit, the consultation came to an end and we left. I re-visited Fatima's compound twice in 1992 to gain a better understanding of the encounter and what had led to it. In preparation for those interviews, my male and female field assistants decided how we could best ask the women there about Jahangir's style, his questions, and his conclusions. On no occasion did anyone interview Fatima *alone*; the idea of a private consultation between a local woman and any party that includes unrelated men is almost unthinkable in Matlab.

Jahangir was quite sure of his conclusion that Fatima was not possessed or troubled by a spirit. Walking along the homeward path, he listed some of the deviant behavior patterns that he expected in cases of possession but had not seen that day. It was only when I visited without Jahangir that Fatima and her sisters-in-law described her symptoms over the last several years, which had prompted them to seek treatment for a spirit illness, particularly her bouts of speech loss that they blamed on a *bobā* spirit (fainting [Good 1994: 148 and 149] and also interacting with personages invisible to others). On those later occasions I found the women relatively free from work; both of our interviews lasted an hour. Jahangir had left after 15 minutes, perhaps because he relies on income from his shop and no one was minding it for him that day. Perhaps, in his inex-perience, he was unaware of the varieties of *spirit illness* as distinct from posses-sion. Given the likelihood that Fatima's family would have felt obliged to offer Jahangir *something* for an exorcism, I credit Jahangir's integrity for declaring that his services were not needed. Some of the women in Fatima's compound had enough experience to know that expatriates (like me) might give gifts and require none in return. More than any fault of Jahangir's, these factors probably explain why the women gave me information they had not given him.

Rain forced us indoors for my ethnographic interviews, but during the consultation with Jahangir all participants had sat in the pleasant November sun in the courtyard shared by the four thatch dwellings of the compound (see figure 4-4). The women provided three chairs for us while they themselves sat on the ground. I listened while Jahangir tried to gain all the information he needed from Fatima herself. Fatima's sisters-in-law repeatedly "helped" or mediated in the interview. Jahangir resisted this characteristic of Bangladeshi folk-medical interviews, perhaps because he could read the discomfort on my face each time the sisters-in-law would interrupt or berate Fatima. Or he might have considered a recorded event too formal for interruptions.

The transcript excerpt (see example 9) shows the question-and-answer exchange typifying ethnomedical encounters in Bangladesh. I have underlined two points in the exchange at which Fatima might have been expected to use a first-person pronoun but did not (these are symbolized by ∅), and one point at which she seems to have used at least an idiosyncratic form of such a pronoun. (For a discussion of the relationship between my transliteration, standard Bangla pronunciation, and the nonstandard Matlab phonology characterizing speech represented in example 9, see the appendix.)

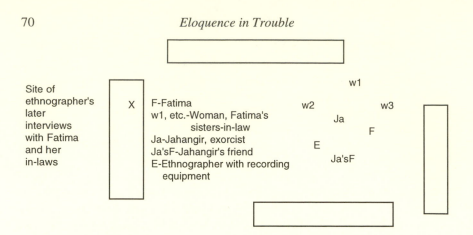

Figure 4-4. Fatima's compound: setting for an exorcist's consultation.

Example 9. Fatima's encounter with Jahangir, an exorcist.[34]

F = Fatima; J = Jahangir; w = one of several women present (Fatima's sisters-in-law)

20J	āpnār ki abasthā lāglo.
	How did your situation begin?
21F	[ø] ki rakam lāge.
	What [it] felt like ...
22F	[ø] sārinṭā śarīr kāippā jeman āẏ śarīr
	ekkebāre ki ra[ka]m je lāge,
	The whole body [was] trembling like—
	my body completely—it felt like ...

Shortly after this exchange, Jahangir forced to the surface the issue that, he believed, had brought him there to perform an exorcism—the issue of *ālgār kichu* (something loose):

49J	ācchā tā haile ki ālgār kichu āsari
	mane karen āpnārā nā ki.
	Hmm, so then do you all think that
	something "loose" is possessing [her]?
50w	āche.
	There is.

Families do not call in a healer, let alone an exorcist, if they interpret the behavior of the person in question, or the events befalling the family overall, as normal and untroublesome. What was troubling these people finds expression in the term *ālgār kichu* (something loose). Whatever is loose is not bound, at least not to what it should be; it is free from its moorings and thus free in a troubling sense, free to transgress boundaries by wandering where it shouldn't. People who explained the metaphor to me mentioned cows getting loose, wandering from their rightful place into a field that could be damaged—the more problem-atic if the field does not belong to the cow's owner. *Ālgā* can also mean extra, or extraneous. A nurse at an ICDDR,B clinic told this to a woman patient:

Your blood pressure is a little high. Stop eating *ālgā* salt. Don't take [any extra pinch of] salt with your rice. Just [eat] whatever [salt] you put in the curry, got it?

Like loose animals and excessive salt, those influenced or possessed by something loose transgress behavioral limits and pose a threat—typically, to the social order. Paradoxically, transgressive selves of this sort are to some degree forgiven because they have been compromised by the presence of something loose. Looseness here is thus linked with permeability. What is loose can slip into the cracks of the self.

Fatima's frightened look and spent strength had analogues in her speech. Of the 31 potential occurrences of first-person pronouns in her speech—moments in her speech when they would have been appropriate and might have been used by others—Fatima used only two. One of these is somewhat idiosyncratic, though her *āy* might have been intended as *ay* (that) rather than as the pronoun "my" (*āmi*, see example 9). While I do not claim that her speech therefore fails to refer clearly to her self or to particular possessions, alienable or inalienable—her house that shakes during her episodes, or her head that buzzes—the absence of explicit self-indexing is still significant.

It was Fatima to whom I alluded at the beginning of this chapter in my reference to complaints that challenge our understanding; it was she who was periodically choked or robbed of the ability to speak by a *bobā* spirit. Fatima's sisters-in-law, who had let the *bobā* go unmentioned during the exorcism consultation, discussed it with me in my later interviews. At least a year before Jahangir's visit, an *ālim* (male Muslim cleric) appeared privately to Fatima and only to her, forbidding any revelation of his presence. Fatima and her sisters-in-law attribute her transient mutism to her violation of this injunction. Her unfaithfulness, it would seem, transformed the *ālim* spirit into a *bobā* spirit.

In unmarked usage *bobā* refers to a person whose hearing and speech impairment has natural causes. The marked usage describes a speech-blocking spirit that typically visits at night; this sort of *bobā* presses on the victim's chest, literally choking off speech but sparing the hearing. Thus, Fatima's experience of being mysteriously silenced is not isolated.[35] She was one of the three persons who described for me their experiences with *bobā* spirits. All three took spiritual measures aimed at delivering themselves from the unwanted visitations, but— for Fatima, who had lost speech for a number of days at a time, and for the other person, who had almost nightly episodes—the *bobā* problem proved refractory.[36]

How do Latifa's case and Shefali's case compare with Fatima's? Both Fatima and Latifa are under pressure. Yet Latifa's angry assertion of self is as different from Fatima's bouts with silence as Latifa's outstanding high school performance is from Fatima's illiteracy. Two different selves were shaped in two contrasting careers, and continue to be constituted in their ongoing interactions with others. The families offer unflattering labels for both women, but the labels are also contrastive. Whereas Fatima's history of visions, mutism, and dizziness has led to her being labeled the victim of a *māthār byārām* (disabling illness of the head), Latifa's more assertive complaints have gained her a reputation as *pāgal* (mad, insane). Latifa's label is more pejorative in its moral connotations, whereas those are absent from *māthār byārām,* which conveys hopelessness.[37]

Notice the contrast in the role of supernatural visitors in the life stories of Shefali and Fatima. The *ālim* visitor in Fatima's story is paradigmatically male—an *ālim* is a male religious leader with special Qur'anic training. The spirit who visits Shefali is a *parī,* a female Islamic spirit.[38] Shefali tells us (and everyone) about the spirit without anxiety; she is *not* sworn to secrecy. If anything, her *parī* makes her unusually assertive. In Fatima's case, the male *bobā* spirit effectively silences her. A *parī,* by contrast, enables Shefali to utter what she normally could not say. Leaving the question of agency suspended, Shefali's mouth is not held to normal standards of respect (for her husband) or politeness (toward her neighbors) during trance-possession. The correlation between the spirits' respective genders and their actions is clear: The male spirit shuts up one woman while the female spirit loosens the tongue of the other.[39] Fatima's situation and her condition did not improve between 1991 and 1996; her speech does little more than confirm her weak position in her social world. Shefali's case appears to be an inversion of Fatima's in that they both experienced altered states, after which they were "unable to say" what had happened. Yet, the whole tone of Shefali's narration of this recurring event is proud, whereas Fatima's is distressed.[40] From what Shefali herself says about the early days of her relationship with her *parī,* the contrast with Fatima might not always have been so strong. The contrast strikes us nonetheless, and it can be explained, partly, with reference to the respective positions of the two women. While neither has a powerful son to look after her, Fatima is the youngest wife in her husband's joint family and the mother of a retarded son. This double vulnerability in Fatima's position in her household is mirrored in her vulnerability vis-à-vis the *bobā* spirit.

Suleyman

It is not only women like Fatima and Latifa who suffer or complain. In Latifa's former in-laws' village lives Suleyman, a well-educated, 65-year-old Muslim man, whose "head trouble" led to his being shackled. My encounter with him followed a networking process like that through which the exorcist Jahangir took me along on his house call to see Fatima. Throughout my stay with the Rahmans in Baghmar, residents and neighbors asked about my research. It was no small challenge for me to describe in Bangla an ethnomethodological approach to troubles talk! Often, I would mention those who visit the *kabirāj* for *mānasik asubidhā* (mental problems), as a focus of my interest. My self-presentational strategy reflected not only my interest in psychotherapy but also my sense that those whose troubles had obvious psychosocial or even micropolitical elements would be more likely to present them to "folk psychiatrists" than to local representatives of biomedicine. Thus it was that the young men of Baghmar knew early on of my interest in *pāgalāmi*; hence, they told me of Suleyman, their elder affine[41] (see figure 4-5).

Figure 4-5. A man of Suleyman's generation prays expressively.

Naturally, I listened with interest to their story of how Suleyman, while visiting a mosque very near my adopted home, had violently usurped the role of the *muezzin* (one who gives the call to prayer). As the hapless man who was the regular *muezzin* intoned the familiar Arabic call, Suleyman came up and shoved him away from the microphone.[42] According to my fictive brothers, Suleyman spoke in the odd stress pattern shown below (stressed syllables are underlined):

Example 10. Suleyman's assertion of clerical authority.

āmi āz<u>ān</u>   di-<u>bo</u>,   <u>ā</u>mi   nā<u>māz</u>   parā-<u>bo</u>!
I call.to.prayer   give-will, I   Islamic.worship   read-will

"<u>I</u> will <u>give</u> the call-to-<u>pray</u>er; <u>I</u> will <u>lead</u> wor<u>ship</u>!"

As the young men narrated this event to me, they re-created the strange singsong intonation in which Suleyman asserted his right to a leadership role. The prosodic contours of Suleyman's speech became salient to these local adolescents and then to me. Although—after meeting him and hearing him relate his troubles—my relationship with Suleyman took on a deep filial affection, it began out of my interest in local views of how madness was linked to marked speech. Whether or not my cousins' quotation was accurate, the Suleyman character they animated was linguistically egocentric, as they repeated the I in each line of his rather poetic utterance. Along with the singsong intonation, the pronoun adds to the color of the utterance by enhancing its rhythmic complexity while maintaining its balance.

Days later, the fictive brothers who had told me of Suleyman led me to his village, an hour's walk from ours. I found the old man immensely likable, and something about his intrapsychic struggle marked him as a sensitive and intelligent man. One could not help being struck by his extreme emotional volatility and by what seemed to me inappropriate affect; he passed rapidly from weeping to laughing, and the reasons were not always apparent. A month after that first meeting, a slightly different contingent escorted Faisal and me for a return visit. Later, Faisal and I made four more visits, without our fictive brothers. From what we had seen, they either laughed at him or reinforced the religious-ideological stance of those who kept Suleyman restrained. Our own presence and our interest in his symptoms were problematic enough; I felt it was an unethical imposition on him when we kept bringing along the *jubak* (adolescents).

Although Suleyman's "head" was "hot" for most of 1991–92 (when I first knew him) and there had been other periods in his life when he was—according to the Bangladeshi psychiatrist who later treated him—manic-depressive,[43] he had led what was regarded as a successful life overall. He was a high school graduate—far beyond the norm for his age-grade—and he had fathered four sons and a daughter. He variously attributed his *pāgalāmi* (madness) to his maternal grandmother's blood and to the incubus spirit that had haunted his grandmother and had later become intimate with Suleyman as a young man, causing dangerous semen discharges.[44]

Example 11. Suleyman's incubus.

S= Suleyman; F= Faisal.

(1) S   āmrā parī e āmār mā nānir parīr āsar āsrā āchilo.
         We [have been influenced by...]; my mother came under the influence of
         my maternal grandmother's parī.

F   ācchā.
         Oh?

(2) S   se (bij theke) āmi āmār māthār madhye *defect* āche.
         From that seed I—there is a defect *in my head.*

It is unusual for the Bangladeshis I know to utter the first-person subject pro-noun by mistake, but he does so in this false start in a sentence of self-diagnosis, contributing to the number of first-person pronouns in his speech.

At other times, Suleyman and his interlocutors pointed to the disappearance of his son in explaining his heated emotion.[45] If anyone mentioned that son in 1992, Suleyman wept disconsolately. Speaking of his other sons, by contrast, could bring on a violent outburst of rage, since they have cooperated with Suley-man's younger brother in shackling him. (For his elder brother, quite deaf at his advanced age, who does not participate in the shackling episodes, Suleyman has nothing but respect. During one visit, Suleyman declared that the elder brother was going to heaven and the younger brother to hell. This message had to be repeated even more loudly before the deaf brother finally heard it.) Some neigh-bors and kin apparently dropped by just to provoke him, even during our visits. They seemed entertained by his ineffectual raging. He would throw things at them, even semisacred objects like a bookstand that he used in reading sacred texts, but it was fairly easy to remain out of his range or outrun him. Violent self-defense seems to be an option for him but not for a woman like Latifa.

Suleyman was shackled to the posts of his house for most of 1991–92 to restrain his unpredictable behavior. During our February 9 visit, Suleyman showed us the wounds left on his wrists by the recently unlocked chains, com-plaining that the wounds itched. To consider this on a par with the itching caused, say, by scabies (endemic in Matlab) would be a serious mistake for several reasons. Suleyman's wounds point to conflict; perhaps the fact that his kinsmen treat such shackling as a necessary evil to which they do not want Suleyman to draw attention. The context of this particular complaint was that Suleyman had uttered words evidently considered profane and was rebuked by another man in the room. Suleyman reacted explosively to that rebuke. When he became a little calmer, he replied more directly to the "gag order" that was being placed on him.

Suleyman's attribution of some of his troubles to a *parī* reminds us of Fatima's permeable self, her vulnerability to things *ālgā* (loose). His frequent use of first-person indexicals, however, more closely parallels Latifa's speech than Fatima's. Suleyman's grab—through his behavior at the mosque and his frequent use of I and my—for symbols of an authority that had not been legiti-mately granted him bespeaks a kind of egocentrism that, like Latifa's, might have helped earn him his family's wrath. Before leaving Suleyman's case, I will add another piece of evidence to strengthen this impression.

In his two turns at talk, presented below, Suleyman utters three clauses.[46] In the first two, although the possessive pronoun *āmār* is not necessary for referential clarity, it is included. Only in line 3, where the nominative pronoun *āmi* would have been acceptable, does Suleyman choose to omit it (omission is represented by ø):

Example 12. Suleyman's food claims.

1S	*āmār* upajukto khānā dite pāre nā keo ?[47]	No one can give me suitable food.
	āmār chelerā …	My sons …
2F	hm	Hm.
3S	[ø] *śikkhito* TO!	[I am an] educated [person], after all!

Suleyman insisted that he required some special food worthy (*upajukto*) of him, because he is "educated" (*śikkhito to!*). But his claims go unheeded. The I is heard, but is considered too loud in its self-assertion to pass local tests of normalcy.

Personhood Emerging in Interacting Context

Bangla troubles talk confounds strong forms of relativism and universalism in the anthropology of personhood. Bangladeshis' complaints project personal experience and simultaneously help constitute interdependence. To the claims of Dumont, which essentialize South Asian selfhood as hierarchically embedded and starkly contrasting with its essentialized polar opposite—the autonomous Western self—troubles talk brings conflicting evidence. Bangladeshis do not simply wait for their hierarchical moral superiors to intuit their unexpressed needs, as Roland (1988) says of most Indians; at times they express them with angry explicitness. But it will not do to press Freudian drive theory or sociobiology into the service of universalistic claims that the bottom line of human behavior across all cultural and linguistic groups is aggressive self-assertion. Excluding the extreme cases of poverty and of cosmopolitan wealth, both of which disperse families, Bangladeshis do inhabit closely knit relational webs whose relevance pervades life-activities—working, fighting, loving, and being ill. In a way that seems related to changes brought about by an economy increasingly linked with world capitalist markets, finding oneself thus embedded in relational selfhood is suffocating for some contemporary Bangladeshis (such as Habib's brother Meherban, exasperated over the previously cited potato affair). But their words of trouble do not reject their milieu or express desires for forms of autonomy prevalent in, say, Los Angeles and spreading in South Asian cities. Rather, they combine assertion of self with attempts to optimize relationships of dependency and interdependence. In general, Bangladeshi men and women have fewer qualms about expressing dependency needs than do most American men and perhaps women as well.

But such broad characterizations miss the particulars of linguistic form in which troubles are presented, received, authorized, or delegitimated. Grappling with language like Shefali's—her de-quotative or projective I—might help Western readers transcend the taken-for-granted assumptions that one word is unproblematically owned by one speaker or that speech transparently reflects some inner center of being—the self. True, verbal play with the I by Shefali or the others represented in this chapter is an achievement of an agent. Yet, not all those recorded during my fieldwork have achieved the right to such an assertion, to the status of an agent whose I carries the ring of authority or at least stakes a claim to it. The construction of agency varies not only across cultures as commonly understood but also across status groups and activity settings (Desjarlais 1997).

The relativity of the rhetorics of selfhood is evident in a Bangladeshi tendency to find signs of madness in the very marks of individualism praised in the West. An anecdote related to me by a friend who is a psychiatrist in Dhaka illustrates how madness becomes a key sign in the semiotic network (cf. Good 1977, 1994) around Bengali selfhood. My friend had to visit a government office, where she met a bureaucrat who discovered she was a psychiatrist. Of interest to us is what the bureaucrat said: He offered his opinion that madness and visiting a psychiatrist were both forms of *bilāsitā* (luxurious self-indulgence).[48] South Asianists will recognize in this definition inverted echoes of *Homo Hierarchicus* (Dumont 1970)—the self as radically embedded in a hierarchical structure encompassing family and caste and relegating the individual to the cultural sidelines.

This statement should be compared with my other interview data from Matlab. First, the handful of people from whom I requested a list of illnesses did not include madness. When I asked one such person about it, he said it was *not* an illness at all. Others whom I asked about *pāgalāmi* described it in moral terms—as a failure of moral discernment (telling right from wrong) entailing neglect of one's moral place in the world (*dharma*, in Hindu and Buddhist worldviews), the responsibilities accompanying our particular gendered role. Further, the tuneful laments and prayers I heard Latifa and Suleyman perform were critiqued in wide-ranging interviews in Matlab as a means of drawing attention to oneself more than of praying with appropriate sincerity and humble reliance on God. It is in this light that we should understand the bureaucrat's typification of madness as self-indulgence.

The transcripts of Suleyman and Latifa's talk stand out in that they demonstrate a high frequency of first-person indexical usage in relation to all points in their discourse when such usage was possible. I recorded Suleyman in an interview in which half a dozen of his relatives and neighbors were present. My recording of Latifa's talk features her making a long uninterrupted lament, though she was similarly surrounded by kin (see table 4-1). Both Suleyman and Latifa are engaged with others who label them *pāgal* (mad). Suleyman's linguistic egocentricity would be seen by some of us (not just his family) as more than eccentric—in fact, as pathological. This egocentricity, linguistically constituted

as it is, approximates the folk meaning of the terms *ahaṅkār* or *āmitva* (selfish-
ness, egocentrism, arrogance)—and helps constitute the meaning of the term
pāgal.[49]

We have seen that self-invocations do occur with some regularity in Bangla
troubles talk. However, their frequency varies across speech genres. Note, for
example, that Suleyman and Latifa, whom I recorded during informal conversations (interviews of a sort) and in highly marked lament performances, used
more first-person pronouns in the lament than in conversational interviews—
almost three times as many in Latifa's case. What this says is that the rhetorics
of self-making (Battaglia 1995b) are, to some extent, genre-specific, though
Suleyman's numbers also make clear the interpersonal variation in the self-
invocations (cf. Hanks 1990: 124–131) whose extreme pole is locally thought to
index madness. Intracultural variation and variation across genres are thus great
enough to render essentializations of South Asian personhood obsolete.

The use of pronouns in discourse is specific to that discourse; conversational cohesion is maintained not only within the speech of one, but across turns
of talk by multiple participants, and in this process pronouns play a role. Certainly Bangladeshi practitioners open their turns in encounters with patients by
greeting them and simultaneously opening their interviews, always (in my corpus) using the polite/distant form of the second-person pronoun, *āpni*. They ask,
āpnār ki haiyeche? (What has happened to you?) But they tend to drop pronouns
after they have used them to establish the interactive frame of a polite and professional encounter that involves two persons and sometimes a mediating relative of the patient. Patients, likewise, might be expected to use more pronouns in
contextualizing their talk initially but to drop them later. As far from these
encounters as we are, it might seem unnecessary to us that "patients"—defined
here as anyone presenting a problem to a practitioner of healing—should specify
that they are indeed referring to their own body, head, heart, or what have you.
Still, it does seem to be a part of the encounter's agenda to reaffirm that a
schema like the following is in effect—"patient specifies for practitioner where
he or she is experiencing distress." But then, once they have clarified or individuated their acts of reference—once the referential frame is well established—
practitioner and patient turn to other matters, including more precise specifications far beyond affirming whose body-mind is suffering.

Information flow, however, is not the only thing managed in such encounters. The encounter is deeply interactive, each partner remaining attuned to the
linguistic usage of the other and to what that usage might index. Some patients
might be sensitive, for instance, to the point at which practitioners drop indexicals. If pronouns become unnecessary—not only because a frame is safely
established but also because Bangla accepts zero anaphora constructions—then
those pronouns that are used long after the frame is established stand out all the
more.

To invoke a case I present more completely in chapters 5 and 10 (examples
13 and 56), Yasmin's pronoun usage is not remarkable in raw frequency terms:
She used neither more nor fewer pronouns than most (table 4-1). Yasmin was

Table 4-1. First-person pronouns per potential occurrence across a variety of complaints.

Gender	Name	Type	Possible First-Person Pronouns	Actual	Actual/ Possible
F	Monuza (female patient)	Medical encounter	10	1	0
F	Fatima	Medical encounter	40	5	.13
F	Sufia	Med	6	1	.17
F	Yasmin	Med	73	15	.21
F	Irani (female patient)	Med	11	3	.27
F	Mumtaz (female patient)	Med	10	3	.30
M	Cha (teastall man)	Conversation	20	3	.15
F	Bonhi	Conversation	18	5	.27
M	Yasin Eid	invw/conv	14	3	.21
F	Latifa	Conversational interview	57	22	.39
M	Suleyman	Conversational interview	33	23	.69
M	Suleyman	lament	8	6	.75
F	Latifa	lament	37	33	.89

Cases are rank-ordered by frequency of possessives *within a given speech genre*.

seeing a traditional practitioner, an herbalist named Ali with Ayurvedic loyalties. Her brother accompanied her both to pay for his services and to shield her from excessive interaction with men, including Ali. In both Ali's and Yasmin's speech, we see a decrease in pronoun usage as the interview moves beyond its opening phase. Hence the first-person indexicals that Yasmin uses later are par-ticularly interesting. She uses them at points of high drama in her presentation. In one such instance she says "*My* life is ending." In the other she says, "Unless God saves *me* [... there is no hope]."

The first- and second-person pronouns—I and you—are most often indexes, though, as Urban points out, some are anaphoric. Having made a case for the importance (for theories of the self) of analyzing complaints and particularly pronouns in them, these indexes deserve center stage. In the next chapter I analyze pronouns in terms of their own semiotic function as indexes, and also describe some of the alternatives that speakers use. In short, the next chapter describes the use of pronouns as only one of several strategic options available to the speaker trying to locate, individuate, and specify a problem as well as manage relationships with interlocutors.

5

SELF AND INDEXICALS: LANGUAGE AND LOCUS OF CONTROL

Western common-sense links between first-person pronoun use and egocentric-ity, I have argued, need deconstructing. The "I" of discourse is not unifunctional. Still, what people think about language forms like pronouns cannot be ignored, since linguistic ideologies shape not only worldviews but also the evolution of discourse practice and linguistic structure (Silverstein 1979, 1985). In the United States today, neither parents, teachers, nor assertiveness trainers typically con-sider themselves ideologues. But, in order to introduce (for American readers at least) the theme of how linguistic indexing of "locus of control" is significant for comparative cultural analysis, I am asserting here that the American embrace of "I-language" is strongly ideological. An explicitly promulgated linguistic ideol-ogy trains American children, when they feel hurt, to "use their words" (not their fists), while assertiveness courses teach adults to "own their feelings" by using I-language, which the courses model in utterances such as "I feel hurt/angry/etc. when you do that." Such assertiveness training has recently spread to American elementary schools, in classes on conflict resolution for children being initiated as peer mediators. This movement encouraging I-language and the owning of one's feelings reflects an ideology of self as locus of control over "privately owned" words and affect. A different kind of person is constituted in Bangla ways of speaking or verbal culture—including the Bangla preference for experiencer-subject constructions in troubles talk, described previously—and dominant Bangla linguistic ideologies.

Although the notion of locus of control arose within behaviorist learning theory, the indexing of loci of pain, discomfort, or other medical symptoms—or political dissatisfaction—is accomplished through the same semiotic means used to index or protest locus of control. Thus, my expanded notion of locus of control incorporates domains claimed by both psychologists and students of ideology. I adopt the term "locus of control" for my purposes in theorizing the range of Bangla alternative modes for indexing self, symptoms, or interactional tensions often related to issues of control.

In 1966, Rotter proposed that individuals vary in their ascription of respon-sibility for the occurrence of reinforcement, some ascribing that responsibility internally to themselves, others ascribing it externally to powerful others or some forces beyond their control. Soon thereafter, others began to apply Rotter's model of internal-versus-external locus of control cross-culturally (Hsieh, Shybut, and Lotsof 1969). In many ways these studies are problematic from the viewpoint of current anthropological theory. They treat cultures as "things" of which one can be a member—things influencing socialization patterns—rather than as elements in a repertoire of identities that social actors deploy strate- gically across various contexts, which is my perspective.[1] Still, if we modify its problematic definition of culture and its tendency to reify personality, we can use the cross-cultural locus of control literature to explore intercultural and intracultural variability in socialization and thus the production of various ways of being a person in society. Sociolinguistic models can help us build on the underlying insight of claims in the locus of control literature, such as the claim that "individuals raised in a culture that values self-reliance and individualism are likely to be more internally oriented than those brought up in a different set of values" (Maqsud and Rouhani 1991: 108), while attempting to transcend the circularity inherent in such culturological claims. The cross-cultural locus of control literature alerts us to the possibility that ambition, assertiveness, and internal locus of control (referred to as "internality") are strongly and perhaps uniquely reflected in the persons produced in postindustrial Western societies. In contrast, the Hong Kong Chinese (Hamid 1994) and Batswana (southern Afri- can; Maqsud and Rouhani 1991) student populations locate control externally more often than do the Western subjects for whom psychological instruments measuring locus of control were originally developed.

The culturological approach to the cross-cultural variability of the self, evident in Dumont (1970), seems inappropriate for studying the variability of locus of control when we ask whether the internality of the Western individual varies with class differences. In Botswana, as in the West, a "significant positive association between [high] socioeconomic status and internal orientation" is evident (Maqsud and Rouhani 1991: 112). This is true despite the lack of a signi- ficant correlation between self-concept, self-image, or self-esteem and socio- economic class (but see Rohner and Chaki-Sircar 1988 for other evidence). Let us start, then, from the assumption that locus of control is linked with econo- mies, relations of production, and the dominant ideologies undergirding them. The production of selves in classes of persons who participate in capitalist economies anywhere in the world is arguably unified by capitalism itself. Thus, former peasants in Bolivia who are being incorporated into the capitalist sector through mining come to experience themselves as autonomous entities, separate from others to a degree never experienced by their peasant ancestors. Document- ing Bolivian women's resistance to capitalism as "the devil," Michael Taussig argues that the atomization of relations and of persons, the severing of the once inexorable bonds of person and product or of person and group, is the inevitable result of capitalist transformation: "Man is individualized, as are all things, and organic wholes are broken into their supposed material constituents" (1980: 30). Ideologies common in capitalist societies accordingly stress the autonomy of individuals, and some would argue that the function of these ideologies is to mystify or obscure the degree to which the real locus of control lies beyond the individual—in the political economy, in the dominant mode of production.

Some studies of culture and the self leave room for intracultural or class-based variation in locus of control and relevant ideologies. Psychological anthropologist Hollan (1991, 1992) finds a significant gap between publicly affirmed cultural ideals of selfhood and relationality and subjugated discourses of self, affect, and relationships—an argument acknowledged by some psychologists.[2] Thus, in societies in which dominant, discursively expressed ideologies affirm the need to subordinate personal ambitions to the integrity of groups, psychobehavioral measures might well reflect dominant ideologies arising out of the political economic base—ideologies which, at best, *selectively* reflect personal consciousness or subjectivity. Individuals who might be actively nurturing personal ambitions, and hoping to achieve them through their interactions with others, might nonetheless deny, particularly in public, any personal responsibility for attaining what behavioral psychologists call "reinforcement." In India, just that sort of gap has been described by Mines (1988) and Derné (1995). Mines stresses how aging gradually opens doors for the expression of ambition, while Derné stresses how film, fantasy, and private interviews remain the homes for affirmation of what locus of control theory calls internality (ambition, personal rebellion, selfish desire, and hope founded on one's own actions).

In exhortations designed to make one speak in such a way as to obviously "own" one's "feelings," we see an ideology and construction of self quite at home in capitalist social formations. By contrast, Bangla ways of speaking documented here index an ideology touching on personhood, as well as on the material base of existence, an ideology that differs significantly from the capitalist emphasis on ownership. What I will stress here is the linguistic construction of particular attributions of locus of control. When I cite utterances in which a speaker's body parts are not explicitly "possessed" by that speaker, or in which a speaker avoids declaring what she herself desires, I am documenting a situated Bangla dispreference for locating control internally. The particular range of, and values assigned to, the words, grammar, and other discursive resources available to troubles tellers constitute the person/actor in that role, and project his or her locus of control.

Avoiding the First Person in Troubles Talk:
South Asian Immigrants and British Natives

My pronoun-based approach to cross-cultural differences in the presentation of self is not unprecedented. Research by Gumperz and Roberts (1991) in the United Kingdom has explored differences in linguistic self-presentation between South Asians and English natives; the relative frequency of first-person indexicals in the speech of the two populations plays an important role in their comparative analysis. Nouns and pronouns in oblique or nonsubject cases are used in Bangla constructions in which the English speaker expects the nominative case.

This tendency reflects—and helps to socialize—some Bangla speakers' external locus of control.

Gumperz and Roberts's comparative study was carried out at certain institutions serving clients from Asian and native backgrounds. At one such institution, they recorded a Bangladeshi man saying, "Considerable trouble is befalling me" (1991: 64; a literal translation of a Bangla original). The authors' comparison of Asian and non-Asian speech in such encounters revealed a tendency for Asian clients to include more passives (p. 65) and for native Britons to use more tokens of the pronoun I:

> The Asian clients' mode of presentation ... contrasts sharply with ... [that of] the British clients. The latter, as a rule, begin their interviews with a general introductory statement of what they have come for, a statement that explicitly identifies a problem for the counselor to deal with. In their accounts, they cast themselves as actors who are affected by the actions of other actors, and ... they are often quite explicit about how they feel about what happened. While the British clients personalize their situation, highlighting the 'I', the Asians present themselves as victims of circumstances and organize their accounts around the facts of what happened to them. (67)

> English clients ... represent themselves in personalized terms as agents who are affected by the institution's or its representative's actions. The difference between the two ways of perceiving the situation is reflected in pronoun usage. Note the prevalence of 'I' and the high incidence of transitive verbs in the English-English encounters. In the Asian-Asian encounters, we find an equivalently high number of passive constructions. (69)

Note also that not all first-person pronouns are equally avoided in the Asian-Asian encounters. The authors' translation transcript includes (1991: 70) a token of the pronoun me (indexing self as object or experiencer, not agent). Their findings parallel mine in ways that become evident below.

Pronominal Indexes and Alternatives: Just How
Revealing Are Self-Indexes?

What is meant by the claim that pronouns or other linguistic forms index a self? Clarifying that matter will help us see the significance of the range of indexicals beyond first-person pronouns available to Bangladeshi troubles tellers.

Social scientists have used (and sometimes abused) linguistics in many ways. The claim was made by earlier generations of anthropologists that the presence of first-person indexicals in every human language is solid evidence of a universal thing called a self or the sense of self, a phenomenon that purportedly exists outside of language, but this does not do justice to the complexity of the linguistic data. The naiveté of the claim becomes evident when we realize that indexicals gravitate toward two poles—the relatively presupposing and the relatively entailing or creative (Silverstein 1976, 1981).

Presupposing indexes point to some contextual fact that can be confirmed by recourse to nonlinguistic evidence. Thus, when a Dyirbal speaker in Australia

shifts into a "mother-in-law" register, use of the register presupposes the presence of someone related to the speaker in a certain way. It is possible that a
bystander who knows the speaker and his or her kin ties might look around and
identify the person for whose sake the speaker has shifted. On the other hand, if
three people speak a language that distinguishes two categories of "we"-ness—
inclusive and exclusive—the third person hearing the first two speakers switch
from the inclusive to the exclusive might well infer that he or she has been
suddenly left out, but cannot necessarily use anything in the environment to
explain that inference. The same phenomenon occurred when my ex-wife and I
used to shift into Bangla to share some private matter in the presence of our two
daughters—and they could be counted on to remind us that it is rude to do that!
Such use of language makes or breaks relationships, rather than being dictated
by them. The facts that those "we" pronouns entail have no necessary existence
outside the act of speaking. In fact, every conversational use of I and you is,
arguably, equally creative. Shefali's "I of discourse" conjures up a self.
However, particularly when she invokes the decentered I spoken by the spirit in
reported speech outside a trance-possession event, that invocation does not point
to a self (spirit or otherwise) whose presence can be confirmed outside the
reported speech.

Contrary to Western linguistic ideologies, then, we cannot take pronominal
indexes as pointers to an objectified self. Nor, perhaps, do the nonpronominal
indexes of rural Bangladeshi women locate or refer to troubles. What indexes
can do, however, is anchor a speaker's troubles to a body part or a self that
emerges in interaction. And, the talk that indexes those simplex troubles can also
point to metalevel troubles—troubles with the troubles talk.

The argument that the indexing of self in some way is salient for Bangla
speakers is on solid ground, particularly with this modification in our understanding of indexing and indexicality.

Literacy, Education, and the Self in Suffering

To paraphrase what someone told my Bangladeshi psychiatrist friend: The
virtuoso's elaboration of selfhood appears in Bangladesh to be a self-indulgent
luxury, *bilāsitā*. To explore one's subjectivity, to engage in introspection, to
reflect on the self and create a narrative autobiography with subjective depth—in
short, to "experience"—is arguably not a given of the human condition but
rather the product of specific historical-cultural circumstances (Desjarlais 1997).
It is not only Dumont's (1970) twin individualists—the Western person and the
Hindu ascetic—who may become psychological virtuosos in today's South
Asian societies. Duranti and Ochs (1986) describe how Western pedagogy—in
contrast to traditional Samoan patterns of interaction and socialization—spot-
lights individual achievement and indeed creates a milieu of individualism. Thus
literacy, wrongly associated *eo ipso* with certain forms of cognitive and cultural
complexity, may yet be associated with Westernization to the extent that schooling for literacy reflects or spreads Western individualism. An unschooled

woman of rural Bangladesh, like Fatima, probably has not received praise for individual achievements. She might become an assertive individual without training; but she cannot be compared with educated Bangladeshi women—particularly those who attend foreign-oriented urban schools—who have been *trained* to compete and to achieve as individuals. Indeed, an uneducated rural woman with a complaint has difficulty getting a patient and sympathetic hearing for her oral presentation. One of her literate sisters, the late activist and author Jahanara Imam (1986, 1990, 1991), has published works of nonfiction and an autobiography. In Imam's accounts of her own *Life with Cancer*, no one interrupts her complaints or those of others, whereas complaints by females in my sample are consistently interrupted. Illiterate women might have a knowledge of highly elaborated languages of pain and distress, but male hearers would scarcely allow themselves to perceive that from women's short self-disclosures. The poetry of selfhood can only shine out of small cracks in their metaphorical (thatched hut) cells. In contrast, readers of Imam's Bangla autobiography find not only page after page of descriptions of various types and stages of pain, but also reflections on the I of the author (1991: 34–35).

Strategies of Indexicality

As Gumperz and Roberts remind us, "there is not a one to one relationship between language as linguistic structure and rhetorical strategy" (1991: 71). It is important to see whether or not a troubles teller uses a pronoun such as I or my, and also to explore the ways in which such pronouns are successfully avoided, or—to privilege the pronouns less—to explore alternatives to the use of first-person indexicals in actual discourse. So, for example, in locating for herbalist Ali the particular tingling pain that she was experiencing in "her" head, Yasmin used no possessive pronouns (like my) but, rather, used the distal demonstrative *ay* (that) to ensure referential specificity:

Example 13. Yasmin refers to her head as "that" head—*ay māt[h]ā*

91Y   ay māt[h]ā-o laiyā sinsine b[h]āgechāge laiye jāy.
        The tingling pain in *that* head splits it in half.

Bangla Grammar's Flexibility in Relation to English and German

In most sentences in Bangla and other pro-drop languages, the overt expression of subject pronouns (for example, I) is completely optional. They are not needed to disambiguate a reference, since subject agreement (agreement for person and status, at least) is marked on the verb. So, one alternative to the use of lexical pronouns is to rely exclusively on verb suffixes. Agreement marking is required on all finite verbs. The optionality of realized subject noun phrases, together with verb marking for status but not for number of subjects, potentiates exploitable ambiguities.[3] It is easy in Bangla to underspecify subject referents for number, whether the subject is first, second, or third person. The absence of all indexicals, as in what traditional grammarians called impersonal constructions, typifies troubles talk. *Bhālo lāge nā* ([0-subject] good feel not) is the prototypical troubles utterance. It should be remembered, however, that this impersonality characterizes the surface form alone. Utterance context, which includes gestures and full noun phrases to refer to body parts and so forth, can personalize syntactically impersonal constructions deployed in troubles talk.

Bangla in Relation to English and German

First and second-person pronouns are indexical signs whose referents are context dependent and not semantically abstractable. English-speaking patients who present their complaints to physicians use them commonly in such forms as, "I feel ..." or "I've got a ... right here in my ..." or, "it makes me ..." Speakers of other languages—German as well as Bangla—resort to other linguistic forms in some of these constructions, such as definite articles (for example, *the* arm, *the* head) where English speakers might frequently use "my."

Definite articles have been analyzed as anaphors in English, typically accompanying nouns to mark them as old information. For instance, after delimiting reference to a certain house that might remain topical in a conversation, one speaker might refer to it thereafter as "the house," or later as "it." It is possible that such an anaphoric function is served (in languages like German and Bangla in which body parts are typically individuated by articles rather than possessives) by replacing a whole noun phrase (for example, "my arm") with a simple German article or a Bangla demonstrative.

The optionality of overt possessive pronouns in indexing ownership of body parts makes such a referential practice *marked*.[4] The unmarked background— here, the most common ways in which a speech community delimits reference to some self in troubles talk—is significant for its own sake. Such discourse habits as foregrounding or backgrounding the self in certain contexts must be assumed to have Whorfian effects on speakers' ways of perceiving their troubles and the worlds in which selves move. But there seems even more reason to expect that the most important effect of such backgrounds is to make exceptions—including the striking repetitions of I, me, and my (*āmi, āmāre, āmār*) in Latifa's lament— more salient.

Monuza was a patient at a clinic run by a nongovernmental aid organization (NGO) in Matlab. In only 1 of the 10 clauses of her speech in which a first person indexical would have been grammatical was such an indexical realized. That pronoun was the nominative form *āmi*. Thus in none of the four noun phrases that referred to her head as the locus of her symptoms did she use the possessive pronoun *āmār*. Instead, she used the definite article, a suffix in Bangla—[noun]-*ṭā*. In the other clause in which a possessive pronoun would have been acceptable, an experiencer-subject or dative-subject construction, the unrealized (optional) subject pronoun renders the surface grammar of the clause impersonal. Suleyman's and Latifa's lament transcripts provide counterexamples, texts in

which first-person indexicals are used in most clauses where they are grammatically possible (see table 4-1).

Use of Alternative Indexicals in Fatima's
Encounter with the Exorcist

I have shown how the Bangla article, /ṭi/, or /ṭā/ can replace first-person indexicals. It is useful to examine the speech of a single speaker—the transcript, for
example, of Fatima's encounter with an exorcist—to see a wide range of alternatives in practice, including demonstratives, quantifiers (especially the equiva-
lents of "whole" and "all," universal quantifiers), first person *plural* pronouns,
and a deictic adverbial of manner corresponding to "thus." The transcript excerpt
(example 14) begins with a question-and-answer exchange that is conventional
for ethnomedical encounters in Bangladesh. Boldface indicates points in the
conversation involving problems that I discuss later.[5] Fatima's indexicals and
anaphors are underlined, as are their English counterparts, but only when the
latter are necessary in the gloss but do not represent any Bangla segment. The
possible occurrences of first-person indexes, the actual occurrences, and alternative types are noted in the columns at the right.

Example 14. Fatima's referential practice.

F = Fatima; J = Jahangir; w = one of several sisters-in-law living together in Fatima's
compound and participating in the interview; E = ethnographer

Indexicals and Alternatives

ø = Absence of a possible first-person pronoun, that absence being associated with
impersonal constructions (only in the event that none of the following alternatives fills
this empty slot)
P = First-person pronoun or participant indexical (in odd form)
D = Demonstrative; DD = distal demonstrative; PD = proximal demonstrative
A = Definite article
Q = Quantifier, especially the "universal quantifier"
PL = First-person plural indexical
M = Deictic adverbial of manner (*eman*)
G = Grammaticalized trace of the pronoun (-*m*- as morpheme, derived from *āmi*)
P = Possible first-person pronouns, A = actual pronouns used, and Al = alternatives used

ID	Fatima (and those speaking for her)	Interlocutors (Jahangir et al.)	P	A	Al
1J		keman lāglo ār ekhan keman lāge purā *history*-ṭā kan. /pu/. *How did it feel, and now how does it feel. Tell the whole history. whole/*			
2F	/partham/ māse sāt tārikhe ø jvar [h]ai[ye]che. *The seventh day of the first month [I had] a fever.*		1	0	ø
3J		oṭā balte habe nā, ei tārikherṭā balen. *Telling that is unnecessary. Tell [the story of] this time.*			

4w | ei to, ei tārikheṛtā. *That's it, this the [one on] this time.*

5F | typh[oid]-er jvar tan ei ataṅgo bodh [h]aiyā geche. *From a typhoid fever, this limb went limp.* | 1 | 0 | PD

6F | kāil bodh [h]aiyā an^6 māthāṭā ei sārā āguner lulār matan [h]aile. *For a time it was limp. Now the head, this whole, [feels] like fire and smoke.* | 1 | 0 | A, PD, Q

7F | ār gharṭā ṭhagarmagar kairā jeno āur^7 upar paṛe. *And the house shakes as if it will fall on me.* | 1 | 1 | P

8J | gharṭā. *The house.*

9F | gharṭā. ei bāṛiṭā. satkanā bāṛiṭā. *The house. This compound. The (whole) compound.* | 1 | 0 | PD

10F | ār jeman hārintā śarīr kāippā jhinjhināiyā ei māthāṭā asthir [h]aiyā *And [it is] like the whole body trembles, tingles. This head gets unsteady* | 2 | 0 | Q, PD, 2A

11F | jeman ay niyāṣthār lage jeman āmār /damṭā/ bāṛiyā jāy gā. *like (????) (the breath) goes out [of me].* | 1 | 1 | DD

12w | ø /damṭā/ *(the breath)* | 1 | 0 | ø

13F | embā ālgi diyā d[h]airā rākhi. jadii jeman āmāgo fuber ay gharṭā (jeman āmār upare pare gharṭā). *I hold (it) up like this. If—like (the house will fall on me).* | 1 | 1 | PL, DD, A

14x | embe ālgi diyā d[h]airā? *Holding [it] up like this?*

15J | e ei bā. *like this, or this.*

16J | /anno kathā balen/. *Tell me [the] other story/stories.*

17w | kat[h]ā kan ki āre. *[To one of the other sisters-in-law?] Why do you speak?*

18J | tārpar? *Then?*

19F | her par/e/. *After /that/* | 0 | 0

20J | /āpnār/ ki abasthā lāglo? *How did your [V] situation evolve?*

21F | ø ki ra[ka]m lāge. *What it felt like, ...* | 1 | 0 | ø

22F | hārintā śa[r]īllā kāippā jeman āi śa[r]illā ka ø ekkebāre ki ra[ka]m je lāge, *The [whole?] body trembling like— my body completely—how it felt ...* | 2 | 0 | Q, DD? (P?) A ø

23F | ø kono ār kait[e p]āri nā. *I can't tell you anything else.* | 1 | 0 | ø

24F ø kait[e p]āri nā ki ra[ka]m   2   0   ø
je lāge. *I can't tell how it felt*.

25F ei jānalātā fikkā ...8 *This window [x;...*   0   0

26F ø ajñān [h]aiyā/ jāi. *I go unconscious.*   1   0   ø

27w /ajñān [h]aiyā/. */going unconscious.../*
...

41F a[k]hane sārā māthātā sārā māthātā eśar   2   0   2Q
nāmāzer par (diyā *or*theke)   2A
Now the whole head, the whole head,
after evening prayer time

42F ekṭā g[h]arṭā thagarmagar (ikar makar) kairā   1   0   A
ekṭā (ekṭu) iyā karbo ār āpnār śeṣ rāitre-/
One house shakes ... (??) then at
night's end—/

43J /tā [ha]ile gharṭā eman kare je—kise
kare—/ *Then the house does something—*
how does it do this?

44J āpni ei dharaner kichu bujhte (baste)
pāren nā ki. *Do you understand any*
such [reasons] or anything?

45F nā ø bujhāy nāi.9 e samay-e āmi to i   3   2   ø
and[h]o [h]aiyā jāi gā āmāre to ḍābārālāy.10
No (no one has explained it to me). At
that time I go blind and it pushes me down.

46J āmner ḍābāiyālāy? *It pushes you down?*

47F [h]ā *Yeah.*

48w [h]ā *Yeah.*

49J ācchā tā haile ki ālgār kichu āsarai
mane karen āpnārā nā ki?
Hmm, so then do you all think that
something loose is possessing [her]?

50w āche. *There is.*   0   0

51J ālgār kono ās/arai/
There's something loose /possessing/

52F /ālgā/ tanay nā ø śarīl durbal tani eiṭā   2   0   ø, G
kaitā m pāri /nā/. /*"Loose thing"/ or*
from bodily weakness, that I couldn't /say/.

53J /āicchā/.
/*Hmmm/.*

54F nā ay typh[oid]- ār jvarer ø /māṭ[h]ā.   2   0   DD, ø
Or that typhoid fever [in the] /head/ ...

55w /her thoṛ,/11 ki[s]er thoṛ kane kay.
What garbage! What a bunch of
garbage she utters!

56w jeṭā kas kāme kais. *What you*
[sT]12 say, make it useful!

57w eiṭā to kāme lāgbo nā. *There's no*
use to this.

58J		āmnerā keo kichu bailen nā e[kha]ni emne. *recording* hait[e]āche. *None of you should speak at all;* *right now recording is going on (.5 seconds).* [13]		
59J		hyā̃, tārpar giyā, tā ekhan to āpne sustho. *Yes, after that ... now you are well.*		
60F	hā. *Yes.*		0	0
61F	ei sandhyār pare ø e man lāge. *After sundown it feels like ...*		1	0 M, ø
62F	ø era[ka]m lāge. *It feels this way ...*		1	0 M, ø
63F	ø durbal śarīle /er t[h]e[ke]o a[k]hane/.[14] *weak in the body /now more than/ ...*		1	0 ø
64J		/tā haile/ to e sabe ālgār kichu nā āmār mane hay. /*So then/ this all has nothing to do with spirits, it seems to me.*		
65J		hay to durbaler t[h]eke emni lāge. *Maybe it's from weakness that you feel this way.*		
66F	lāgē hā̃. *Yes, [I do] feel [something]*		1	0
67w	/hā̃. *Yes*			
68J		ār ālgār kono laksman āmner nāi. *There is no sign of spirits in you*		
69w		nā—/. *No*		
70F	khāitā m lāitā m /pāri nā/. *I can't eat /or anything/.*		1	0 2G
71J		/ei to/ ālgār kono laksman ø nāi to. 0? 0 *That's [something else]. There's no sign of spirits.*		
72J		haito je d[h]araner āmnerā *idea* karen, hm? *Maybe the* idea *you all were thinking?*		
73J		ei d[h]araner kono kichu nāi to āmnerā āmio to dek[h]te pārlām. *There's nothing like that that you and I have been able to see.*		
74w		nā nā. *No, no.*		
75J		hay durbaler t[h]eke e sab kichu dharen nā. *Take it as forms of weakness.*		
76w	dharen nā[15] śarīlṭā kāpe /jadi. *Take—the body trembles. If/*			
77J		/āmrā/ jā bhābchilām hay to amun kichu /nā. *[To the ethnographer]: There's nothing here like what we thought.*		
78E		buj[he]chi . *I understand.*		
79J		buj[he]chen? *You [V] understand?*		
80w		dekhe dekhe. *He sees, he sees.*		
81J		he. *Yes*		

82F	śarīl ṭā sārāi jhimjhimā durbal, khāitā m lāitā m pāri nā. *The whole body tingles, and it's* *weak. I can't eat or anything.*		2	0	A Q 2G
83F	ḍāktārer ṭehā [16] ø cālāitā m pāri nā to cikitsā ø karum ki diyā. *I can't manage money for a doctor:* *How could I pay for treatment?*		2	0	2ø G
84J		hā tā[ha] ile ayguli haito āpnār bhālo bhālo jinis khāite haibo je. *Yes, so you* *probably should eat really good things.*			
85J		vitamin kichu khāite haibo tā [ha] ile ṭhik [h] aiyā jāibo. *You have to take* *some vitamins, then you'll get well.*			
86J		eiṭā, āmāre bal[e]chilo Rām ay Nur Mohāmmāder Mā āsār janno. *This, Nur Muhammad's mother told* *me to come.*			
87J		jār janno āmi ār āsi ār ki ... se śuinnā bailla /hm/. *That's why I came. She* *passed on a message. Hm.*			
88w		/okay/. OK			
89J		*okay, off*. OK. [Turn the recorder] off.			
Total			40	5	

ø = 15, A = 7, Q = 6, G = 6, PD = 4, DD = 3 or 4, M = 2, PL = 1, P = 1 or 2

Fatima's Referential Repertoire

Among the more interesting alternatives to the use of fully realized personal pronouns in the transcript excerpt above is what seems to be a reduced or grammaticalized form thereof (Hopper 1996). At least in the Chandpur/Comilla area, the multiword sequence infinitive—first-person pronoun—modal seems to be undergoing grammaticalization. That is, the pronoun as a free lexeme is becoming a bound morpheme. Line 52, *kaite [ā]m[i] pāri nā* (or *kaitām pāri nā*) is an example, as are lines 82 and 83. These grammaticalized or reduced pronominals can usefully be lumped with the idiosyncratic forms that seem to be pronominal (in lines 7 and 22) and with the one first-person plural possessive ("our" in line 13).

Fatima's most frequently chosen alternative to using first-person indexicals is to use nothing at all (ø). Where she does use alternative means of referential individuation, most of them are definite articles and universal quantifiers. The article *ṭā* (often pronounced *ḍā* in Matlab) bound as a suffix to *māthā* (head) four times, and *hārin* (Fatima's realization of *sārā*, a universal quantifier)[17] is used twice. Only when suffixed to *śarīr*, ([body]; often realized as *śaīllā*, as explained in the appendix) does the article perform its individuating function alone; in every other case other elements join in delimiting the reference.

Fatima's drawing on the universal quantifier in these is noteworthy, particularly in light of the affect-linked function ascribed to it, at least in English (Labov 1984; Ochs and Schieffelin 1989). Impressionistically, "all" and "whole" figure largely in underlining noun phrases in English complaints (for example, "all night long," "this whole side of my body"). [18] In the lines where she uses the quantifier—6, 10, 22, 41, and 82—it adds affective intensity to the reference, reminding the exorcist and other participants that her referential practice was no abstract exercise. This affective dimension adds "blood" to the "flesh" of what is, in other ways as well, an *embodied* practice.

Yet "embodiment *cannot* be treated from the perspective of an isolated speaker" (Hanks 1990: 133). This is true not only of the interactional deployment of first-person indexicals and affect-laden quantifiers but also of demonstratives and deictic adverbials of manner. Both types of index are ambiguous enough to demand the hearer's visual and mental attention. When Fatima says *ei atarigo* (in line 5)—assumedly with an accompanying gesture—she solicits her hearers' gaze to disambiguate her reference. [19]

In lines 21–24, Fatima seems to have difficulty giving linguistic form to her experience. "What it felt like, ... how (*ki ram*) it felt, ... I can't tell ..." It is tempting to read lines 61–62 as though they merely exemplify an inability to achieve referential clarity: "After sundown it feels like, ... it feels this way (*eman*), ... weak in the body ..."

The acts of reference attempted by the use of deictic adverbials of manner, *eman* and *ki ra[ka]m* (a rhetorical question functioning adverbially), is indeed unclear when we limit our attention to line 21 or line 61. In lines 22 and 63, however, Fatima goes on, by recourse to symbols more than indexes, to give semantic expression to her experience. Like Goffman's speaker who claims "I'm speechless," but is obviously not so in at least one voice; Fatima's utterance plays with several I's (1981: 148). While one could read Fatima's word *eman* as an indicator of the degree to which her reference was autistically trapped within her own mind, her deictic adverbials are better taken as facing outward rather than inward. Her underspecified indexes may in fact function as autoindexical signs. In drawing attention to themselves, these signs invite other participants to scaffold Fatima's narrative (Vygotsky 1978), to help her coconstruct the experience, offering a blank slate, as it were, for them to fill in, rather than one taken up with fully individuated referential forms. [20]

Sansom (1982) argues that, by surrendering the right to narrate one's illness to one's chief caregiver, Australian Aboriginals create a reciprocity of symbolic goods. Even this sort of reciprocity reminds us of the central place of exchange and circulation in social life (Urban 1996). Fatima's incomplete forms of reference are yet another way in which sociality is invited. Where my account differs from Sansom's, however, is in adding the recognition that "difference"—particularly gender asymmetry in such systems of exchange, be it of words, encouraging questions (Fishman 1983), semantic gaps, or silence—cannot be understood apart from considerations of domination and resistance. That is, to the extent that

"gappiness" is a tactic to which women like Fatima (in contrast with her dominant sisters-in-law, the male exorcist, or the urban Bangladeshi elite) are restricted, "difference" takes on particular meaning in relation to, not in contrast
to, dominance (Gal 1989).

Latifa's Contrasting Indexical Repertoire

Latifa, introduced previously, is the young woman whom her brothers forcibly
removed from her husband's home. With a different sort of force, Latifa drew
attention to her words as she continued lamenting her divorce, several years after
the fact, during her visit to my field home/her maternal uncles' compound. My
field assistant, Faisal, spoke on several occasions with Latifa, always surrounded
by others who lived in our compound; on several occasions we tape recorded our
informal interview. The following excerpt from such an interview helps us better
understand both how Latifa described her situation and how even Faisal's questions might have put Latifa on the defensive. The excerpt also contains evidence
of the difficulty of deciding, on strictly linguistic grounds, in which lines a first-
person pronoun is noticeably absent. Latifa's first-person pronominals are
underlined, and English pronouns not reflecting a Bangla original are in
brackets. In the first excerpt, Latifa is giving a long answer to an open-ended
question by Faisal.

Example 15. Latifa's monologue (addressed to Faisal).

P = potential first-person pronouns; A = actual pronouns

Line		Gloss	P	A
1	hego sāte b[h]ālo iyā kairā <u>āmi</u> āstām śeṣ bārer matan	Doing (x) well, <u>I</u> came with them for what was to be the last time.	1	1
2	tārā <u>āmāre</u> ki ānando (xxx)	What joy they [gave?] <u>me</u> ...	1	1
3	<u>āmār</u> doṣ āchilo <u>āmi</u> hego lage buijj[h]ā caltām	<u>My</u> "fault" was that <u>I</u> [began to] get along with them.	2	2
4	hego lage iyā kairā caltām	[I began to] adjust with them.	1	0
5	tārā eiḍāre (xxx) karlo kaiyā	It's because they did this; that is,		
6	emun āguner b[h]itare tārā hāt dilo kaiya	because they put [their] hand into this sort of fire that [unfinished]...		
7	jeːi de[k]hi āguner b[h]it[a]re <u>āmrā</u> hāt dei	As [I] see it, when <u>we</u> put our hand into fire,	1 pl	1 pl
8	āgune jvalbo	the fire will burn [it].		

In this passage, Latifa describes the "joy" that she felt when she began to
"adjust" to living with her in-laws, in contrast with the pain brought by her
brothers' intervention, putting their hands "into fire." Here, fire may call to mind
a cooking fire, an image she might associate with life with her husband. In such
a scene, a fire is not a threat but a blessing—unless and until someone puts his
hands into it.

P = potential first-person pronouns; A = actual pronouns

Line		Gloss	P	A
9	ke sārā ksman a[k]han ke jvalteche	Who is getting burned all the time?		
10	ke ki kartāche	Who does (what ???).		
11	kintu āmi je ki āgun jvali, jvali eiṭā to tārā buj[h]e nā	But they do not understand the fire that is burning me.	1	1
12	heo jadi mānuṣer matan mānuṣ [h]ay to	If they would act like human beings—		
13	tāi nā—tārā bujhto eiguli	right?—they would understand these things.	?	?

Whereas in the metaphorical situation, it would be only he who puts his hand into the fire who gets burned, Latifa points out that it was she who was burned when her brothers thrust their hands into her domestic life. In the preceding excerpt, Latifa used first-person indexicals in 8 of the 10 positions where they were possible. In the following lines, italicization marks both code-mixing and (lines 25, 29) words that become keys to Latifa's discursive self-construction.

14	āmār kono bācchā kācchā haiyā gechilo gā?	Did I have children? [No]	1	1
15	biyā [h]ai [ye]che āṛāi batsarer matan	The marriage happened about two and a half years ago	1	0
16	āi[ye]chi ājkā dui batsar. (2)	Since then [I] have come along for two years.	1	0
17	*Matric. pass* karār pare parei biyā haiyā geche gā	The marriage occurred right after I *passed* my *"Matric."* [10th grade]	2	0
18	tārā mane kar[e]che je	They [my brothers] thought,		
19	"āmrā māgnā biyā diyā [f]ālāi[ye]chi	"We have arranged a great marriage!		
20	ekhan āmrā jā:i icchā tāi: karte pārbo (5) •hh	Now we can do as we please!"		
21	tārā je āmār ei alpo bayasei gāi di[ye]che = kailjār b[h]it[a]re	Here I am of so few years, and [yet] they have given me such pain in my "liver"	2	1
22	(a[k]han eiḍā) ke b[h]og kartāche	Now who is experiencing/ suffering this?		
23	ke kartāche (1)	Who is experiencing/suffering it?		
24	(ki) āmār mato meyere tārā ekṭuku kairā rākhbo	They will keep a girl like me (on a short leash??)	1	1
25	ø *pāgal* bānāiyā rākhbo •hh	They will drive me *mad* and keep [me that way]!	1	0
26	āmār jibaner ki mulyo āche =	What is my life worth?	1	1
27	= āmi ki karte āichilām duniyāte	What did I come into the world to do?	1	1
28	āmār lekhāpaṛā ki (dar āche)	My education? What (fear is there??)	1	1
29	(xxx) āmi *kaṣto* kar[e]chilām (ki juddho karte)	I *worked hard/suffered* [in school?] (for what struggle?)	1	1

30	āmi ṭāwner kāche thākte pārlām nā	I never got to live in any town.	1	0
31	iyā karte pārlām nā	[I] never got to do whatever.	1	1
32	ei iyā āmār āchilo nā.	I never had whatever.	1	1

In the above excerpt, Latifa uses the first-person indexical in 9 out of 16 possible positions. The first-person figure (Goffman 1981) of her narrative is mostly a "me," a sufferer. Latifa projects the locus of control over her life as somewhere outside herself—namely, in her brothers' hands, particularly as they "keep her *pāgal*" (mad, line 25). The moral agency of the self projected in line 29 is, however, more than a "me-self."

Quite a bit later in the tape-recorded conversation with Faisal, Latifa addresses different themes, and seems resistant to speaking her own mind in any explicit way. Latifa's words are italicized to set them apart from Faisal's:

Example 16. Latifa talks to Faisal (continued).

P = potential first-person indexicals; A = actual first-person indexicals

Line		Gloss	P	A
1F	keno āpni ki ābār jāite cān ekhan dulābhāiyer aikhāne?	Why do you want to return now to "our brother-in-law's" place over there?		
2L	*ei ekṭā māinṣer (xxxxx)*	*This is people's ...*	0	0
3L	*tārā ei d[h]araner kāirjo kalāp kar[e]che (xxxxx)*	*They have done this sort of thing (??)*	0	0
4L	*firāiyā nite āi[ye]chilo jor kairā ānche*	*[My brothers] came and brought [me] back forcibly*	1	0
5L	*svāmir b[h]āt khāite dei nāi tārā jor kairā ānche.*	*They wouldn't let [me] eat [my] husband's rice; they brought me back forcibly.*	2	0
6F	se jadi ekhan nei tā[ha]ile āpni ābār jāben?	If he [your former husband] were to take you [back] now, would you go [back] again?		

In line 6, Faisal puts a hypothetical question to Latifa. But, as is evident below, she resists speaking about her own desires; she resists constituting her situation as one in which the self and desire are at stake (Wikan 1990). "Owning her feelings" is not Latifa's ideology.

7L	*nā Faisāl bhāi jeyi kāj kairā āi[ye]chi nibo nā (xxxxx).*	*No, brother Faisal, the deeds I did before leaving—he won't take me now.*	1	0
8F	nā, jadi ney, jāben āpni?	No, if he took you, would you go?		
9L	*(xxx)*	*(xxx)*		
10F	ācchaỹ tār ki kono doṣ chilo?	Well, did he have any faults?		
11F	māne se āpnār sāthe khārāp byabahār karto?	That is, did he treat you badly?		

12L	*(xxx)*	*(xxx)*		
13F	ji. ay bāṛir keo kono khārāp byabahār karto āpnār sāthe?	Yes, did anyone in his household treat you badly?		
14w2	(xxx) āi[s]yā par[e]che	[Someone has] come.		
15F	ji.	Yes.		
16L	herā <u>āmār</u> sāt[h]e khārāp byabahār kare nāi	*They didn't treat me badly.*	1	1
17L	<u>āmār</u> bāp b[h]āi-e kar[e]che, <u>āmi</u> kar[e]chi (xxxxxx)	*My father and brothers—and I— did [treat someone badly]*	2	2

Faisal was pursuing a line of questioning here that was based on what he had heard from others—namely that Latifa had complained about being mis-treated and that that was why her brothers had intervened. But Latifa wanted to present the situation as being quite the opposite: She (presenting herself as a moral agent this time) and her natal family had mistreated her in-laws. As every-one in the kin group had said, her brothers (or their agents) had beaten up her husband, publicly humiliated him, and caused him to pay to a middleman money fixed by a prenuptial agreement. (The middleman "ate" the money.) But, as Faisal continued to ask her about what he had heard, Latifa finally admitted to having sent word of mistreatment to her natal family:

18	(xxx)	(xxx)		
19F	to eḍi je keno karlo mā ni tārā khārāp byabahār	Why did (3rd person) … that is, treat [someone] badly		
20F	āpni ki āge āisā	Had you previously, uh …		
21F	āpnār bāp-b[h]āi-er kāche kai[ye]chen	told your father and brothers		
22F	je hei bāṛir lokjan āpnār sāthe khārāp byabahār kare bā kichu	that people in that household were treating you badly or anything?		
23F	āpni ka[k]hano kai[ye]chen nāliś kar[e]chen tāder nāme kakhano /āpā/	Had you at any time spoken ill of them, sister?		
24F	/a/ āge kai[ye]chen nā ki /ācchā/	/Uh/ had you said something previously? / Oh		
25L	/kai[ye]ch i/ kai[ye]chi	*/I had / /I had/*	2	0
26F?	to kai[ye]chen ki janyo takhan khārāp byabahār karto.	So, why did you say that they treated [you] badly?		
27L	<u>āmi</u> kai[ye]chi ār giyā d[h]aren a[k]han (xxx)	*I said it, and uh, for example, now…*	1	1
28L	kaile herā māni iyā b[h]itare ni[ye]che gā	*When I did say it, that is, they [her brothers?] took me "inside."*	2	0
29L	rāger b[h]itare ni[ye]che gā/ āchi/	*They took me "inside [their] anger." / I am-/*	2	0
30F	/ācchā /	/Oh/		
31F	/o āpni rāg/ (xxxxxx) rāg kairā kan /nāi/,	Oh, in anger, /you/—it wasn't out of anger [at your in-laws] that you said it.		
32L	/anek kathā (xxxxxx) / (xxxxxx).	/Many words (xxx)/ (xxxxxx)		
33F	ār tārā mā ni ei bhābe ksmepā jāibo	That they would get this upset—		

34F	seiḍāo āpni cān nāi nā ki nā cāi[ye]ch en.	you didn't want that, or did you?
35w?	ā[s]e [ek]hāne ā[s]e (xxxxxx) ekṭā (xxxxxx)	Someone is coming. Someone is coming.

Before they had yet another scare that someone was coming to disrupt the talk of the younger generation (see line 35), Faisal and Latifa were moving toward clarifying the events that had led to her divorce. Faisal interpreted Latifa's reference to her brothers' "taking [her words] in anger" as Latifa's way of indicating that they had misinterpreted her words, that they became angry when she had not intended that. Latifa let this interpretation stand. After a boy in the room hurt himself and was taken care of (in lines 36–40, which are omitted), Faisal wanted to know more:

41F	āpni kato dur lekhāparā kar[e]chen āpā	How far did you go in school, sister?		
42F	kato dur lekhāparā kar[e]chen	How far did you go in school?		
43L	Matric. pass *kar[e]chi*	*I passed my Matric.*	1	0
44F	*Matric. pass* kar[e]chen nā?	You passed Matric, eh?		
45F	ācchā keo jadi āpnār okhāne jāwār byabasthā kare	Uh, if someone arranged for you to go "there" [to your husband's home?],		
46F	āpni jāiben ekhan?	would you go now?		
47L	*eiḍā āmnego byāpār.*	*That's your [plural] affair.*	0	0
48F	nā āpni jāiben ki nā	No, would you go or not?		
49L	*eiḍā mānuṣe dckhbo jei b[h]ābe b[h]ālo [h] aibo.*	*People will judge that according to whatever they think best.*		

Faisal's interest in Latifa's education is relevant to the discussion of marriage and divorce not only because Latifa had raised the matter earlier, but also because one's educational attainments help determine the economics of marital arrangements (Rozario 1992). But he returns quickly to his attempt to get Latifa to assert herself and her own wishes rather than her fate. She resists, instead indexing an appropriate sort of deference, her willingness to conform to her family's wishes. But Faisal does not give up:

50F	mānuṣe bhālo to māni	"[Whatever] people [think] best"... I acknowledge [that's important].		
51F	āpnār bāp-bhāi-erā bhālo mane kare āpni bāṛi [te] thāken	Your father and brothers think it best that you remain in their home,		
52F	ay svāmir kathā ār nā balen	that you speak no more of that husband.		
53F	tārā heiḍā b[h]ālo mane kare	They think that is best.		
54F	a[k]han āpni konṭā bhālo mane karen	Now what do you think is best?		
55F	seiṭā ki āpni bhālo mane karen?	Do you think that is best?		
56L	*āmi mane kari je mil kairā dite pārle b[h]ālo ai*	*I think it best if they can reconcile [us] and give [me back to him].*	2	1

57F	mil kairā dite (xxx)	Reconcile and give ...	
58L	sāgarer bau bā[r]it[e].	*To the house of ("Ocean's" wife??)*	
59L	*mā-e kailo to jā[y] gā sampatti beiccā āinnā ṭākā diyā jāibo*	*Mother said land could be sold and the money given [for my re-marriage].*	1 0
60F	ei je ābbā baltāche jāiben āpnāder bāṛi jāiben nā ki	Your father is saying you shall go, go to your [plural] household, or what?	
61F	āpnār mā-e nā ki bailā	Your mother, I guess, said	
62F	geche jāygā ṭāygā bikri kairā ṭākā diyā dibe	land could be sold and she would give [you] the money.	
63?	(xxxxx)	(xxxxx)	

Responding to Faisal's urging, Latifa finally declared her hope and revealed what she said her *mother* had promised her: the sort of dowry necessary, presumably to renew her marriage with her ex-husband. (She was holding out for this in 1992 and was still demanding it in 1996). Faisal misspoke, putting this promise in the mouth of Latifa's *father*. It was a sensible mistake, but Latifa almost never spoke of her father while I was present. (He died in 1995, between my two periods of fieldwork.) In the following excerpt, several women ask Latifa questions:

64w?	en to beḍi jā - de[k]hāi[ye]che pachando-i kare nā	The girl—what she showed was that she didn't like [whom?].
65w?	mā - mā - bābā bhāi ṭāi kāroi dekhte pāre nā	Mother—mother, father, brothers— she can't stand any of them.
66w?	hei bāṛir kat[h]ā kaile ar jvar āse	Any mention of that household and she "gets a fever."
67F	ai je māre ṭāre /atyācār kare/	Well, (3rd person) beats [her], /tortures her/.
68w?	/hã/	/Yeah/
69w?	te gelei "ām̲ār (a[s]hen) śikal diyā bāindā	[She says], "If I go back (3rd person) binds me in chains.
70w?	jadi āisā pare gelei (ā[s]hen) bān[d]bo ni"	If [I] return, they will surely bind [me]."
71w?	(xxx) jāy nā eto din parjanto heo jāy nāi / ekhan jāy/	She doesn't go. It's been so long. /Now [3rd person subject] goes/
72F	/ācchā /	/Hm/.
73w?	(jāy) nā jāito ei śanto lāge nā onāre? nā /mane /[h]ay/	(She didn't go; if she went would it be a relief? /Apparently not.)/
74F	/ācchā/	/Oh./
75w?	ābār ekṭu kãn[d]le ṭānle	But if [subject unspecified] cries or keens,
76w?	b[h]āi-erā d[h]airā jei mārā māre b[h]āi-eo māre sab	those brothers grab and beat [Latifa]
77F	āpni bāṛi thekā jān ken[o] āpā	Why do you go out of your [own family's] compound?
78F	ay je ber haiye āschen ki janyo?	Why is it that you have come out?

One of Latifa's female cousins spoke up, pointing out the scandalous fact that Latifa can't stand her own natal family, but agreeing with Faisal that their beating her explains her animosity. Her cousins' discomfort with the moral dilemma of Latifa's situation is evident in line 73: "If she went [home], would it be a relief? Apparently not." The hope that Latifa could return to a harmonious life at her natal home was seductive to her cousins, to Faisal, and to me, but was simultaneously a cause of further discomfort as we knew it was unrealistic and unattractive to Latifa:

79L	*(firi mato)* <u>*ām*</u> *ār (bhāi kãnde) /(xxxx)/*	*(Shall [I] go back?) (If I do anything like that), <u>my</u> (brother cries) /(xxxx)/*	1	1
80F	/ji /	/Yes./		
81L	<u>*āmi*</u> *ghare thākum kemane jei kām kar[e]ch e orā t[h]ā[k] hā to jāy nā.*	*How could <u>I</u> stay at home? What they did makes it impossible to stay.*	1	1
82L	*je dini khun kar[e] che, kāro mukh cāitām nā pāri*	*Since the day they "murdered" [me, i.e. my marriage] [I] can't look at their face*	1	0
83w?	*je dine khun kar[e]che*	*(Since the day they "committed murder")*		
84L	*(dine)*	*That's it (xxx).*	0	0
85L	*mukh cehārā sāmne to (1) (pāi or pāp) (6)*	*It feels (like sin?) to be in their presence.*	1	0
86F	*ei janyo ber haiye āschen*	*That's why you've left?*		
87w?	*(xxx)*	*(xxxx)*		
88F	*āpni rojā thāken*	*Do you keep the fast?*		
89L	*(fāi or pāpi) to*	*([I] am a sinner, you know!)*[21]	1	0
90F	*nāmāz paren pāc wākto? (7)*	*Do you pray five times [daily]?*		
91L	*((nonverbal response?? Neg. head nod??))*	*[I can't.]*	1?	0?
92F	*nāmāz paren nā ei je pāp hay nā āpā?*	*You don't pray—isn't that sin, sister?*		
93L	*nā jato pāp kartāchi nā ((very breathy, quavery voice))*	*No, as much sin as I'm doing, you know?*	1	0
94L	<u>*ām*</u> *i nā pāp karile to*	<u>*I*</u>*'ve already committed sin(s).*	1	0
95L	*nā nāmāz pairā ki lābh [h]aibo?*	*Now what good will it do to pray?*	1	0
96L	*jei pāp kar[e]chi*	*The sin(s) I've committed ...*	1	0
97L	*e (pāp i to) kartāchi (2.5)*	*I'm committing more (sins) ...*	1	0
98L	*(āh mutto mutto nā)*	*(From then (?)) ...*		
99L	*kono iyā maton*	*(until now) ...*		
100F	*o, āpni ekhan-o ekhan-o pāp kartechen bujhen (5)*	*Oh, you feel like you are still sinning.*		
101L	*pāp kariyā (*<u>*ām*</u>*i iyā hait[e]āchi.)*	*[I] have sinned until <u>I</u> have become all*	1	1
102L	*pāp (er ceye ghure āi[s]ye)*	*(I have come around to the ultimate?) sin*	1	0

103F	ji?	What?		
104L	*pāp (er ceye ghure āi[ye]chi??)*	*(I have come around to the ultimate?) sin*	1	0
105F	(xxx)	(xxx)		
106L	*pāp nā haile niyā re i (dārun) to kājo hai[ye]c he*	*If there were no sin, this [prayer] might accomplish something (great).*	2	0
Total			57	23

If Faisal's tone seems moralistic, the reason could be that he shares with Latifa and her cousins a moral outlook informed by Islam—or at least he accepts that framework for village discourse. It might also be that Faisal's seeming accusations—"Why don't you return home, as you should?" and "Why don't you pray, as you should?"—are attempts to bait Latifa. They could be invitations for her to take an even more assertive stance against even the bedrock Matlab values that, one could argue, have resulted in her abuse. But she took no revolutionary stance; rather, she accepted Faisal's accusations and characterized her sin as unforgivable—though this, too, might be an invitation for others to exonerate her, just as Faisal's words might not be what they seem. She does not say what sin it was that preceded her failure to say her daily prayers. We can gather, however, that she is again expressing remorse over having complained about her marital life, or over her share of her family's corporate guilt in ending the marriage and beating up her ex-husband.

Latifa thus continued to generally resist Faisal's invitations to self-assertion.

Does Latifa Embrace or Avoid Self-Indexing?

In the excerpts transcribed above, Latifa used first-person indexicals in 23 out of the 57 clauses in which they could have occurred, particularly clauses in which the pro-drop potential of the Bangla language allows verbs to carry the first-person subject while the pronoun drops out—which occurred in 40 percent of possible contexts.

But to thus restrict our definition of contexts from which the I has been suppressed, to utterances whose verbs make a clear first-person reference, is to obscure some of the play of self/other or individuation/relationality evident in lines 1–9 and 45–56. As he did later with one of our fictive brothers who carried Latifa out of our compound when they could no longer tolerate her lamenting, Faisal pressed Latifa to take a personal stance, to offer her own evaluation of possible (or, in the case of our fictive brother, past) courses of action. Our fictive brother, when similarly pressed, said he thought the forced return of Latifa to her brothers had been wrong in a sense, though justified in terms of saving the reputation of his whole extended family, that reputation having suffered during Latifa's wandering lamentations. Crucially, both Latifa and her cousin resisted Faisal for quite a while before putting her wishes on record.

This delayed manifestation of an individual's opinion has its parallel in an extremely common South Asian custom: When offered food at someone's home, only those willing to risk being seen as greedy will accept the first offer, even if they are quite hungry. The offer, instead, must be parried. A polite host will persist until, typically, on the fourth offer, the guest acquiesces and both are regarded as having successfully performed a display of politeness. Rather than concluding that the interviewing techniques of Faisal, who was educated at Dhaka University, reflected the methodological individualism of his Western-influenced social science training more than his own village upbringing, it is just as valid to discern in the interaction of Faisal and Latifa a routine that parallels the rules of food politeness. Faisal offered Latifa the chance to savor a rare moment of self-expression. It was incumbent on her to resist, but only to a point. Eventually, negotiations of all sorts—including those seen in this "dance of desire"—can lead to the point where parties put their wishes on the table (cf. Rosaldo 1972).

At 40 percent of possible occurrences, Latifa's use of overt first-person indexicals is quite high for conversational speech (see Table 4-1). This we can attribute to Latifa's resocialization through schooling, which several of the women whose pronoun counts are represented in that table never had, or had much less of. Still, the transcript of Latifa's tuneful weeping provides a much stronger contrast with the speech of Fatima and of other relatively I-less speakers. In her lament (described in chapter 4, example 6), for instance, we find one line repeated seven times:

> <u>ām</u>āre nā khuno go kar[e]che, bun go bun.
> *Me have they killed, sister, O sister!*

Hearing Latifa's (now digitized) voicing of this idiom led my Bangladeshi consultant in Arizona to ask me, "Had they beaten her?" The idiom of murder is conventionally used by smaller people when they are being beaten by larger people. The image of death, however, invoked elsewhere in Latifa's lament through idioms that are derived from Islamic eschatology (the Field of Hāśar/ Judgment Day), brings to mind Foucault's (1965: 196) analysis of a modern European construction of individuality. "Generally speaking, the experience of individuality in modern culture is bound up with that of death." In her lament, Latifa invoked her teachers' view of her grief-stricken, death-like form:

| 8L | i-*school*-er-o sir-erā kay •hh
bun go o o bun •hh | *The teachers at the* school *say,*
sister, O sister, |
| 9L | "he māyāre kemte heman k[h]uno
go karlo" •hh
bun go bun o o. •hh | *"How they have murdered that*
girl!"
sister, O, O. |

Since Latifa positions herself as a modern woman through her appeal to the voice of education (line 8), we confront the possibility that for her, as for Foucault's modern European, a new vision of death constitutes a modern individuality. The lament refrain—"They have murdered"—is linked with the subjective, individuated first-person pronoun—me—in a single verb phrase. But, when we look at Latifa's discourse style in her talk with Faisal as well as her lament, the visions of fire and death are also linked with pervasive linguistic indexes of subjectivity—linked, more profoundly, at the level of discourse where language constitutes worldview. Such pronoun use is not characteristic of the Indo-Aryan lament genre in general, nor of the unmarked troubles telling speech of Latifa's female neighbors (analogous to Latifa's talk with Faisal). The only close counterpart is the speech of Suleyman who, like Latifa, was labeled "mad."

In both her conversation with Faisal and her tuneful weeping, utterances in which Latifa uses the words I or my typically project a narrative figure who is passive—the more so when the subject is sin, evidently, since the frequency of first person pronouns drops during her discussion of that topic. Thus she has her cake and eats it, too; she confesses to being a sinner at some level, but exactly by associating her I with the category of "sinner." Her narrative I is stuck in a genre of victimization, and she is unable to find a genre or position from which she can create a new identity with broader dialogical possibilities (Crapanzano 1996). "Passive" derives from the Latin term *passus*, "has suffered." Even the I that is repeated throughout Latifa's discourse indexes a self whose locus of control is external. The point is not that Latifa's locus of control is *exceptionally* external. Rather, I caution readers against overinterpreting the frequency of first-person indexicals, particularly me and my, in her discourse. The projection of the me-self as victim, through first-person tokens, is evident in Latifa's discourse as it is in that of South Asians in England studied by Gumperz and Roberts (1991).

Indexicals and Alternatives as Tactics

A link between speech and self-construction is suggested as we read Gumperz and Roberts's (1991) findings on the rhetorical strategies typically chosen by South Asians in their corpus. Indeed there is a tendency for some speakers in my corpus as well to choose agency-suppressing, pronoun-avoiding constructions. Put differently, they choose nonindexical forms of reference, or indexes (such as demonstratives) that do not explicitly invoke the self. In anchoring their forms of reference to shared symbols (in Peirce's sense of arbitrary conventionality) rather than to self-pointing indexicals, we can even argue that these particular speakers adopt a sociocentric, as opposed to an egocentric, referential strategy. Note, however, that nonindexical forms of reference are not chosen by all the speakers in my corpus, by any means. In fact, Monuza and Fatima represent an extreme end of a continuum, and they happen also to fall at the bottom of the status hierarchy. As poor peasant women they are excluded from the corridors, or open fields,[22] of power—that is, from conflict-resolution meetings and other public sites of local political activity. The fact that it is these two whose recorded speech includes the fewest pronoun choices out of all possible occurrences confirms a link between the self, reference forms, and power.

Hanks describes the distribution of rights to practice reference in various ways in a Mayan community. A social stratification by age helps distribute those rights. Thus an elder male he describes has the right not only to use I but also, in fact, to incorporate "his" laborers within his I. This contrasts sharply with the constraints on pronoun use felt by less powerful Mayan actors (1990: 124–131). We can call the elder's I both egocentric and encompassing. Dumont rightly associates encompassing with hierarchy. Here, however, we do not have a structuralist analysis of abstract categories in which higher levels of inclusive-ness entail an encompassing of lower categories. Rather, a superordinate actor's I asymmetrically encompasses the I's of his subordinates.

In my corpus of Bangladeshi speech the pattern is a bit different. Roughly, we hear egocentric and encompassing forms of reference in the troubles talk of the very secure or the eccentric, while those whose ground of reference is shakier tend to use sociocentric forms. Do the former possess all the discursive power? Importantly, there is at least potential power in the sociocentric tendency of some troubles tellers, like Fatima, to leave semantic spaces which inter-locutors feel compelled to fill. If interlocutors are thereby drawn into a shared web of meaning and experience—into intersubjectivity—then the teller has found a recipient for her troubles. If Fatima's ways of specifying her troubles seem to index an external locus of control more than body parts, that is not only because it is quite true that outside forces control much of her life, but also because her indexing of external control is a creative index in Silverstein's (1976) sense and is thus, paradoxically, powerful.

Still, the distinction between this and other forms of power should not be lost. Fatima's is the power of the disempowered. De Certeau (1984) distin-guishes between strategies and tactics, with the former requiring a fulcrum from which to exercise force, a status with solidity, a figurative social space from which to plan. Desjarlais (1997) links this with a trickster's motto from a slave saying that he gleaned from James Scott: " 'De bukrah [whites] hab scheme, en de nigger hab trick ...' Strategians scheme; tacticians trick" (Scott 1990: 163). Fatima tricks us into making meaning with her. Those labeled mad, like Latifa and Suleyman, approach power differentials head-on and, in doing so, approxi-mate a strategizing stance, approaching an ability to scheme. If a woman like Shefali, through possession/empowerment by a *parī* spirit, is able to find a fulcrum, or de Certeau's "fixed position" from which to exert force—a position unthreatened by the powers-that-be in her husband's compound, and achieve and maintain a domestic situation in which she has some status, we must say that she schemes and strategizes. But the true Matlab strategists, with secure political spaces from which to speak, are those found speaking at conflict-resolution meetings (Wilce 1996), rather than taking their troubles to pharmacies or to the homes of exorcists. They are not alone in possessing power in Bangladesh. But their secure grip on power—their secure and legitimated occupancy of a public space—conditions language use that differs from that of people like Shefali, Latifa, or Suleyman, who must remain tacticians.

6

LEARNING TO TELL TROUBLES: SOCIALIZATION OF CRYING AND TROUBLES TELLING

Every society seems to have a model, an ideal trajectory, of human development. A culturally ideologized and idealized locus of control—internal, external, or fluid—helps constitute developmental goals. The troubles telling "I" of Bangladeshi men emerges over developmental time, first socialized in the relatively special attention received by little boys; the narrative "I" of women as lamenters grows from a different developmental path. As is true of all such cultural models, the relationship between model and behavior seems natural to insiders, while outsiders who glimpse the model view it as constructed or imposed upon reality. A vision of how children acquire communicative competence is part of such models.

Bangladeshis hearing one another's distress signals evince a profound ambivalence—ambivalence around the values of interdependence, interpersonal autonomy, and dependence on Allah. These competing values shape the norms and patterns of troubles telling in Bangladesh. How are such patterns acquired? Telling troubles is treated in Bangladesh as a primarily self-assertive behavior. Self-assertion is recognized in many societies as a survival need. Once it stops crying, a hungry baby is doomed; according to the Bangla proverb, "If/when a baby stops crying, it gets no milk."

Vygotskian Models of Sociolinguistic Development

A developmental perspective envisions behaviors within trajectories—culturally prescribed paths of growth—in which children acquire competence in such domains as acceptable ways of crying and complaining. This process reaches beyond childhood. During my residence in the Rahman compound, the everyday behavior of children (cultural novices) and adult-child interactions frequently engaged my attention. Children do not need to be taught to cry, but caregivers give explicit attention to shaping a range of novice behaviors—from crying to verbalizing distress. Caregivers' reactions to children's crying in Bangladesh constitutes this crying as resistance; and where there is resistance, there is

104

conflict. Caregivers' attempts to distract children achieve limited success. As children mature, the values surrounding crying as a sign-vehicle,[1] and the particular occasions and goals of crying, continue to be themes in interpersonal conflict—as seen in the recordings I made in the field, as well as in Bangla literature. Caregivers construe the experience of suffering, or at least its discursive expression, as a right to which persons have limited access. Still, the ideology that attempts to govern the expression of discontent is only one force in a field of conflict.

The view of learning, language acquisition, and child development from which I work is Vygotsky's model, as extended by language socialization theorists Ochs and Schieffelin (1984). Children acquire language and culture together; they acquire cultural norms through involvement in language routines, and those routines and other uses of language also expose them to subtly encoded social structures and conventions (Ochs 1988; Schieffelin and Ochs 1986; Schieffelin 1990). Vygotsky's vision of cognitive development has been aptly labeled "sociohistorical." Humans are genetically predisposed to learn language and engage in other typically human activities. Still, rather than privileging these innate predispositions, it is axiomatic for Vygotskians that the categories of thought and expression are gradually internalized as novices (such as children and second language learners) participate in social activity. Affect, pain, distress, and other inner states presumably indexed in troubles talk—and the ways in which we attend to those inner states—are, to a significant extent, culturally situated. We acquire locally appropriate patterns of attending to bodily sensation as one type of culturally mediated experience largely through participating in locally normative forms of semiotic expression. As Vološinov argued, expression organizes experience (1973: 86).

We all seek out affective information from each other's linguistic, facial and other signals; particularly children and novices must attend closely to such signals. As participants in interaction, adults as well as children must attend to such cues—the sending and receiving of which can be called the social-referencing approach to affect—in order to participate meaningfully. In the clearest sort of developmental example of the social-referencing of affect, a child near the edge of a precipice sees the expression of fear on a caregiver's face and is likely to learn from it, to internalize fear. Developmental psychologists Bretherton and Beeghly (1982) have demonstrated that the American children they studied impute or ascribe affect to self and others by at least the age of 28 months. Included in what they label "affect" are states, such as pain and hunger, for which children acquire and use labels. The social-referencing model of affect learning invites linkage with modes of expression—novices do not learn to impute affect apart from its expression—and also invites application far beyond American children.

Distress and illness are socially constructed in that the experiences indexed by local terms for states of dysphoria and unwellness have meaning only in the moral universes that create these categories—the cultures that create labels for various forms of dis-ease. But how do we learn to feel and experience in ways that seem to fit these labels, these cultural schemata? Kleinman argues that if we are to understand how and why a category like "neurasthenia" continues to be invoked in China, we must investigate "family relations, and the socialization process and child and adult development: the learned daily life pattern of communicating distress and seeking help" (1986: 152). Neurasthenia is a useful example simply because it reminds English-speaking readers that the categories in which persons express distress vary across time (the diagnosis was once common in the West) and cultural space.

Although socialization theories might imply that every member of a given society follows the same progression of stages (the same developmental trajectory), that is not necessarily the case. Some novice behaviors are not expected to persevere into adult repertoires; they are not part of a trajectory.[2] Nor is socialization a one-way process turning biological individuals into encultured persons in absolutely predictable ways. Such a model construes actors as passive, "oversocialized" social dopes (Wrong 1961). By contrast, a language-socialization model of development stresses the active role of novices in the socialization process and lends itself to a less uniform vision of the goal of socialization. Since culture is not a "thing" at all—and, still less, one that is equally distributed in the heads of participants—we can expect children and adults to engage in conflict as they follow different strategies and harbor divergent ideologies supporting those diverse strategies.

Children learn language and culture together in activity contexts. That is, the structures (such as adjacency pairs) evident in linguistic interaction are acquired in and with lessons in the expression-experience of illness and distress. The involvement of a child, Taqbir (described below), in Wittgensteinian "language games" exemplifies that fact.

An Example of Troubles-Talk Socialization: Enticing Taqbir to Complain

The most explicit example of caregivers who shaped novice distress behaviors that I observed occurred when an adult male caregiver habitually engaged his nephew Taqbir in a complaint routine. I am unacquainted with its history, but I would guess that at some point the boy might have responded spontaneously, with a violent negative shaking of his head, to the inquiry, "Don't you feel good?" Or perhaps the almost-two-year-old had started to enjoy giving verbal and nonverbal "no's." At any rate, the elicitation routine[3] went like this:

Example 17. Taqbir's preverbal complaint.

Uncle—Taqbir! ay Taqbir! śarīr bhālo nā?
          Taqbir, hey Taqbir! Isn't your body [feeling] good?
Taqbir—((vigorously shakes his head))

The genius of this and other such routines lies in their subtle modeling. Word order in bipolar (yes-no) questions in Bangla is no different from the word order of statements. Thus, at some later date Taqbir, by simply removing the end-rising intonation of the sequence he has heard, can utter a well-formed complaint:

śarīr bhālo nā ([My] body [does] not [feel] good.)

Crying and Development

Episodes of crying as well as speaking drew my attention. When I heard crying in the Rahman compound, I would note its duration and location, who was involved, and any ensuing interaction. Many of those occasions involved the household of Aesha Begum. She and her children hovered somewhere above a state of hunger and illness in the midst of a more prosperous joint family. Her two oldest sons sent part of their salaries home whenever they could, and her husband's brothers and I periodically contributed food to her household.

My interest in children's crying is guided by a sense that it prefigures, or is developmentally homologous with, troubles telling. Children cry at those moments when adults might tell troubles, and sometimes tears accompany forms of expression that appear only later in a child's development. Moreover, caregivers' responses to children's tears play an important role in the socialization of affect and illness behavior; their responses shape the novice's developing habits of expression and experience. I expected to find patterns of the language socialization of affect comparable with Kaluli practice.

Schieffelin (1990) describes how the Kaluli seek to move their children's innate tendency to use "soft" language and tears toward the "hardness" of self-assertion and demands. Kaluli adults regard children as soft and pitiable; thus they need to be hardened, partly through acquiring *to halaido* (hard words). Hard words are grammatically well formed. Kaluli caregivers neither leave their emergence to chance nor wait to hear what infants are trying to say; rather, they model proper utterances. On the other hand, hardness also denotes assertiveness, while the natural state of infants is believed to be soft. What Schieffelin calls "appeal" (which we might gloss as whining) is viewed as part of the soft words regarded as natural to a child's earliest speech. What children need to learn is to press assertive demands upon those who are obligated to them by kinship or ties of reciprocity. Mere crying and most songs are soft, but laments and demands are hard.

The direction of such locally construed processes ("hardening," for the Kaluli) and the entailed ideology contrast with analogues in other cultures.[4] Still, it is not surprising that in Bangla discourse we find moral values linked with notions of development, notions of the desirable linked with the necessary. Such values cluster about polarities such as passivity and self-assertion, tears and anger.

Anthropologists often view age and gender differences in terms of role specialization. Specialization by age and gender is indeed a human universal. But both adults and children cry in Bangladesh. And while insiders and novice observers note that gender differences in Bangla affect expression, some adult men also cry. My "grandfather" Ahmed suffered from what he called a "heart" condition that caused chronic insomnia. After sleepless nights, I often heard Ahmed weeping loudly. His behavior, however, was not typical of most adults. In fact, crying seems to be less accepted beyond the age of 10 or so. During my stay, Habibur Rahman's granddaughter Khaleja lived with her grandparents, far from her parental home, in order to attend the nearby school and be able to help her maternal grandmother with cooking and cleaning. Khaleja was then 13. One night as Faisal and I ate dinner in Habib's house, as we always did, Faisal whispered to me that Khaleja was crying on the bed next to our table. He asked her what was wrong; someone told him that she had a headache. "*Bakā meye* [foolish girl]" he said; "no one cries over a headache."

Thus, crying is a complex sign; despite its biological side, it takes on meaning in human groups as a culturally constituted sign. Insofar as crying is a sign to others, its meaning seems to change over the course of life. This is particularly true insofar as crying indexes social relationships. People expect children to cry, and usually tolerate children's tears more than Faisal tolerated Khaleja's; caregivers often respond to a crying child with food, an embrace, or a gentle touch. Children's tears are congruent with their dependent status. By contrast, while even Ahmed Dada's tears also seem to index his need for help (for example for his descendants to bring him home remedies), he is neither decrepit nor resource-poor and his tears do not represent the same sort of dependency as a baby's tears do.

Calling on Mother: An Ambiguous Sign

Because South Asians—Muslims, in particular—are ambivalent toward dependence, interdependence, and autonomy, mothers themselves become ambiguous signs. Colonialism wounded South Asia; British insults to Hindus and Muslims, coupled with their praise of India's "martial races," gave birth to complex nationalist responses centering around gender, power, and autonomy (Nandy 1983). In Bangladeshi as well as Indian discursive self-construction, "mother" was constituted as an ambiguous sign. In Bangladesh today one hears people quoting the prophetic Hadith (traditions passed down from the Prophet and his companions). In answer to the question, "To whom do I owe the most respect?" the Prophet replied, "Your mother." His answer remained the same when pressed to declare the second and third persons deserving respect. "Father" was listed fourth. Perhaps for the very reason that mothers are valued in this way (as well as in infantile fantasy, according to Kakar [1978]), they are also feared and placed in symbolic opposition to Allah.

Hindu mother goddesses underwent successive transformations in reaction to colonial attacks on the masculinity of India, arising, in nationalist discourse, to lead the people in the inevitable battle with the colonizers.[5] Although this bespeaks a need to remake mother ideals in the image of something less passive and benign, Muslims have an even more profound ambiguity toward mothers as icons. Despite the exaltation of mothers in the Hadith and the tendency for adults in distress to call out *māgo!* (Oh mother!), there is a limit to proper dependence on mothers. Bangladeshi children learn, according to the evidence I present below, both to call on mother and to relativize that dependency in relation to the one who created both self and mother.

Bengali infants and toddlers who coo, babble, cry, or articulate find warm responses from adult and sibling caregivers. Bangladesh seems to be rather more like white middle-class American than Samoan or Kaluli culture, in that compe-tent Bengalis negotiate the meaning of preverbal children's sounds and moves. My older "sister" Samia came periodically to visit her family—her father (Habi-bur Rahman), her mother (Rani), and her daughter (Khaleja), whom she had sent to live with and help her parents. When Samia visited, she brought along her younger children. During one such visit, I recorded Samia and her 14-month-old daughter, Petuli. After Petuli had been crying for about 5 minutes, Samia asked her, "What? What happened?"—which construed the infant's crying as a mes-sage. This projection of intentionality onto infants aligns Bangladeshi caregivers with white middle-class American caregivers who also treat infants—at least those above 10 months or so—as signal-sending creatures possessing intention-ality and capable of engaging adults in pseudoconversation (Ochs and Schief-felin 1984).

More significant is the tendency for caregivers to hear kin terms in the bab-bling of babies.[6] Again, my data come from caregivers interacting with Petuli. For a short time in January 1992, during one of Samia's visits, a woman from Dhaka University assisted me in fieldwork. On that occasion, she approached Samia, showed an interest in Petuli's speech, and recorded Samia's interaction with Petuli.[7] Samia tried to get Petuli to call out for her. Then Samia and others, evidently hoping Petuli would imitate them, made the local versions of chicken sounds or chicken *calling* sounds, *coi coi coi*, but to no avail: Petuli would not talk on cue. Perhaps what transpired next—Petuli calling, *āmmā āmmā āmmā!!!*—was the result of Samia's manipulation. Samia is heard on the audio recording saying, "Give me [something]." Since I frequently saw adults tease children by asking them to give them some desirable object (typically food), often persisting until the child became angry or cried, I assume that that is what Samia did to Petuli. Note in example 18 how Samia echoes the stress patterns in her baby's speech, confining her echoes mostly to the single word Petuli uses, but "scaffolding," or building onto Petuli's performance, as a good pedagogue does:

Example 18. Caregivers make Petuli call for her mother.

P = Petuli; S = Samia

2S	ām mā	Mom my!
3P	ām mā	Mo mmy!
4S	o ām mā	O Mommy!
5P	ām mā:.	Mom my!
6S	ām mā, āmmāre!	Mom my! Mommy, hey!

7P	ām ma.	Mom my!
8S	o āpā opār. āpār ḍāk dāo.	Oh, sister is over there. Call your sister.
9?	ka "āpā," ka "āpā, māch den."	Say, "Sister!" Say, "Sister, give me fish!"

This stretch of mother-child talk exemplifies the sort of routines discussed in the language socialization literature, although it blurs the typological boundaries heuristically laid out by Ochs and Schieffelin (1984). They predict that the interactions that occur around infants and children in any given society will be typified as either child-centered or situation-centered, depending on the expected direction of accommodation. In the former, caregivers mimic whatever they imagine children to be "saying," while in the latter, they model the very utterance forms that would be appropriate for the child to use in a given situation, encouraging the child to adapt to the situation as defined by adults. In the preceding transcript, Samia repeats Petuli's utterance. She does so, however, on the basis of a kind of selective principle. She reinforces Petuli for calling her mother. Middle-class white caregivers in Ochs and Schieffelin's typology would grant even infants the right to generate unique utterances often connected with literacy activities (for example, pictures in books). By contrast, Samia and her cocaregivers (especially in line 9) selectively reward a particular utterance by Petuli, betraying the principle guiding their selective attention—"Learn to use kin terms!" But the utterance in the elicitation routine—"Say, 'Sister, give me fish!' "—also models a certain stance toward one's sister.[8] The stance modeled is an assertive sort of dependence; Petuli was taught to make demands of her older sister.

Overall, despite Samia's repetition of one of Petuli's utterances, the modeling seen particularly in lines 8 and 9 of the transcript places Bangladeshi socialization techniques toward the situation-centered pole in the Ochs and Schieffelin typology. When carrying children, Bangladeshis typically face them outwards—another characteristic of the situation-centered style of language socialization. The posture itself communicates something similar to the metamessage of the modeled utterance—children are to look outward, beyond mother (if that is who is carrying them), to receive from the extended family the verbal and visual cues on which they should model their emerging linguistic and kinesic habits.

Juxtaposing these naturally occurring data with an excerpt from the very popular, award-winning novel by Abu Ishaque (1955), later made into an even more popular film—*Surya-dighal bāṛi* (Sun-crossed [Inauspiciously aligned] homestead)—reveals a gendered twist. Even the talk surrounding Petuli exemplifies the linguistic patterning of that mother-child bond toward which Bangladeshis are somewhat ambivalent. In the interaction transcribed above, Petuli's dependence on her mother during a moment of distress (provoked, perhaps, by her mother) takes shape in the call, *āmmā*! I referred earlier to male fear of, and reaction against that bond.[9] Cultural ambivalence toward mothers is observable in situations involving illness, an example of which I derive from Ishaque's novel. I treat the novel as something of an ethnographic source. Its protagonist is Jaygun, the abandoned wife of Karim Baksh and mother of Kasu. Karim Baksh attempts to alienate Kasu from Jaygun, but succeeds only in frightening the boy. This fright is eventually understood by the characters as precipitating a life-threatening bout of typhoid fever; it is common for Bangladeshis in Matlab today to take the consequences of *dar* (fear, magical fright) that seriously. At the onset of the fever, Kasu, like Petuli, calls out for his mother. The boy's father punishes him for calling his mother by subjecting him to exorcistic techniques such as making Kasu inhale through his nose the painful fumes of hot mustard. Kasu's fevered babbling draws his father's attention. In a state of delirium (example 19) Kasu calls out (he is indicated by S; his father, by F):

Example 19. Karim Baksh criticizes Kasu's calls for his mother.

1S	mā, mā, māgo mā.	"Mother! Mother! Mother, O mother!"
2F	Karim Bakś bale myāo myāo karas kæ?	Karim Baksh says, "Why are you 'miaowing'?"
3F	Āllāh Āllāh kar. Āllā-e raham karbo.	Call 'Allah, Allah.' God Himself will have mercy."

(Transliteration from Ishaque 1955: 116)

The point to note here is the way a sort of pun is put to service in the micropolitics of sex and religion. Kasu's father intentionally misconstrues his plaintive "Ma!" (Mother!) as the meow of a cat.[10] Although Kasu's cry for his mother was not nasalized, his father's re-presentation of it was; my transliteration includes this as a subscript comma under nasalized vowels. Dimock (1989) has described the role of nasalization in a system of Bangla sound symbolism to which I can attest—nasalization is iconic of irritating things. By echoing his son's speech with added nasalization, Karim Baksh was recasting it as being demanding in an immature way, irritating and animal like.

This strategy, however, immediately gives way to another: Karim Baksh changes his rhetorical strategy midstream and acts as if he had never made the pun involving *mā* and *miaow* but had acknowledged Kasu's call for his mother. Baksh contrasts that call with another call which Kasu *should* have made: He says Kasu called out, "Mother" (miaow-like though it might have been) when he should have called on God. Karim Baksh's order to "invoke God rather than mother" captures concisely a religio-ideological aspect of gender conflict that, as we can see, is linked with the practice of troubles telling. We have seen how language socialization (largely by females) encourages children to vocalize their distress by calling out for their mothers. Even adults in distress call out, *māgo!* (Oh, mother!)

While my own observations do not include precisely this sort of criticism of mother-invocation in times of distress, Ishaque's account parallels other critical metadiscourses I heard. Children who performed songs to pray for rain, and women who performed laments, elicited criticism. Although that criticism is itself complex, multivocal, and polysemous, mother-calling and religio-magical folktales share something in common to which Bangladeshi imāms object: They represent verbalizations of forms of dependency of which imāms disapprove.

Laments and mother-calling are practices associated with women, and practices over which the Islamic clergy has little control.

In Ishaque's novel, Kasu's signals of distress lead to an illness for which Karim Baksh seeks spiritual intervention after a fakir interprets it as a possession illness. The novel's account of an exorcism plays with nasalization, thus adding another example of nasalized dialogue that helps reveal the significance of nasal-ization as a sign-vehicle. Possession sickness is not treatable without trafficking in the world of possessing spirits, and therefore a sort of seance was held. In that seance, a possessing *bhut* (spirit) is understood to speak through one of the fakir's disciples. Vocalizations heard during such sessions—a bizarre strangling noise, *hæˌrehāˌyhm*[11]—are understood to be the spirit *jap [jawab] lawāy* ([pro-viding the "answer" or voice that enables the spirit to, literally] take speech). What marks this as a spirit's speech is its nasalization. Spirit speech, even in folk narration today, is nasalized; in a variety of contexts, I have heard South Asians assert that spirits speak nasally.[12] As noted, father Karim Baksh's characteri-zation of his son's call for his mother was also nasalized, and "cat-ified" (*myāˌo myāˌo*). By juxtaposing these two instances of markedly nasal speech, the novelist Ishaque creates for us a trope, a metonym or literary metasemiosis. By associating (through the diacritics of nasalization) the demanding voice of the spirit with the voice of the immature, dependent child calling for his mother, Ishaque places these two in the same domain of semiotic conflict—that of immature and illegitimate demands. (Mature, socially legitimated demands are not represented as nasalized.) The semiotic conflict centers on competing valuations of calling on mother and of the demanding stance or communicative style associated with *bhuts*. The ambivalence surrounding assertive human speech reappears in depictions of *bhuts* making their demands so assertively and openly (as do the spirits who speak through possessed brides [Blanchet 1984]). This ambivalence also carries over into a local model of the emergence of "hard talk" in human development.

A Local Model of the Acquisition of "Hard Talk"

Alongside the selective ideological embrace of hierarchy as abiding submission to God and to male authority within the extended family, the following words of my friend Jalu Miah clearly describe a countervailing local idea mirroring the Kaluli concept that persons must become harder with age. However, whereas the Kaluli embrace that necessity as a virtue, Jalu evinced ambivalence toward the inevitable developmental hardening of his son's speech. Despite the sadness I heard in Jalu's voice as he described this developmental trajectory, it is also apparent that he apparently considers it as necessary as an infant's crying.[13]

I became acquainted with Jalu Miah through other friends when I was looking for a family to live with. Jalu and his 6-year-old son, Khalil, saw me at work with my tape recorder. One day in a conversation, Jalu reported to me that Khalil had asked him to get him a cassette player "like Jim's." Jalu told his son, "Baba,[14] maybe when you get big and are in college we'll get you one [it's not a toy]." I laughed along with Jalu—partly in the embarrassed knowledge that he might be telling me this in the hope that I would give him my recorder! Jalu (in example 20, represented by J) continued (speaking to the ethnographer, E):

Example 20. Jalu's metadiscursive reflection on maturation.

1J	chaṭo bāccāder kathā śune miṣṭi lāge, hāsi āse .	Little children's speech sounds sweet; a smile comes [to the hearer].
2J	baṛo bāccāder kathā sei rakam thāke nā.	Older children's speech doesn't stay that way.
3E	baṛader kathā-e dukhyo āste pāre!	Sorrow can come at the words of older ones.
4J	hyā̃, baṛo bāccār kathā karkaś, choṭoder kathā miṣṭi.	Yes, older children's speech is hard; little children's speech is sweet.

Note the contrast Jalu made between *karkaś* and *miṣṭi*. While the speech of little ones gives listeners pleasure, the speech of older children (and assumedly adults) is *karkaś*, defined in Mitra's dictionary as "hard, strong, firm; violent; harsh, rude, shrill; rough, uneven; cruel, unkind; unfeeling; miserly; bold, daring" (1924: 249). Jalu's comment gives us the sense that some Bengalis view the expected transformation of speech linked with maturation (or at least with certain older stages of childhood) as somehow regrettable. It is his son's *request* (polite assertion) that Jalu calls sweet; assumedly neither *ghyānghyān* (whining, nagging) nor the demands of a petulant *bhut* would qualify as sweet. *Miṣṭi* thus contrasts with the irritating quality associated with *ghyānghyān* and entails a Bangla aesthetic metric, one that is relevant to complaints. Jalu's comments are related to the sound symbolism that Dimock (1989) and I find associated with nasalized, low front vowels. Jalu serves notice that what is manifest in actors' responses to troubles talk is, in part, their aesthetic sensibilities.[15]

Challenging Troubles Talk, Anger, and the Subjectivity of the Complainer

Caregivers have ample reason, it seems to me, to see some crying as resistant. Regarding the polysemy entailed in crying, psychologists since Freud have argued that grief cannot easily be separated from anger. Crying can index a number of affective states. Aesha's children would often lie in the dust of the compound's courtyard and cry for as long as 15 minutes, sometimes until the grief of quiet sobbing gave way to anger. During her crying marathon, one 2-year-old girl tried to hit her 5-year-old brother. During other episodes, the same two children might be seen anxiously, pleadingly reaching for their mother, who was too busy cooking to stop to meet their demands—or perhaps she was simply avoiding the demand, construing it as unreasonable. Other episodes involved tears that seemed designed to elicit a certain desired effect, although not necessarily consciously, but, perhaps, having evolved as a strategy that has worked in the past.

Another child, my 7-year-old "nephew" Rajib (Habibur Rahman's youngest daughter's son), was in my room on one of the occasional evenings when *ui pokā*, moth larvae, emerged from cocoons in great numbers. Like most children at most times of the day, he was barefoot. Still, he stomped on the emerging insects with gusto. But almost immediately, Rajib began to wail in a manner which, whatever else it did, succeeded as a self-indexing sign.

> Example 21. Rajib's insect bite.
>
> kāmṛāy ! iś !
> [They] sting! Ouch!

No written transcription adequately represents the controlled panic or self-indexing distress effect created by his jumping up and down and making his high-pitched utterance. Suspending the question of Rajib's sincerity, we can still treat this as a significant role *performance*, a performance of distress. It is through inhabiting such roles (before audiences more competent than I in shaping the performance in Bengali ways) that children learn to tell troubles in ways that fit into larger Bengali social dramas. When caregivers ignore such displays as the one Rajib produced until they reach a certain pitch of intensity, children learn to self-dramatize.

The tendency for Aesha or her older children to endure a toddler's crying for as long as 15 minutes, only to then capitulate by offering the desired object— usually food—seems to reinforce tantruming. If, indeed, 7-year-old Rajib did dramatize his distress during the insect-killing event for my sake, perhaps it was because he had learned that such expressions elicit nurturing responses from caregivers. Caregivers might even perceive his distress calls as relatively *miṣṭi* (sweet). An incident involving two of Aesha's children exemplifies the nurturing response: The toddler fell down and had hardly begun crying when her older sister came and picked her up. By contrast, in another household I once heard my "uncle" (Habibur Rahman's brother) Said raise his voice in a sharp rebuke or warning to a crying child. Adults who do not want to be bothered by crying might thereby stop it before it dragged on any longer.

Children in South Asia are sometimes teased to the point of tears. But we have also seen that sometimes people also ignore, tease, or insult children who are already crying. Teasing can provoke a child's anger, in such situations as when someone takes an object away and threatens not to return it. In one such case, the relatively mature 8-year-old female victim did not cry, speak, or strike out; but when her tormentor did finally return the borrowed item the "victim" ran all the way home. It is common even among adults to ask the one being teased:

> Example 22. Teasing about anger.
>
> rāg kar[e]cho?
> Have you done anger (become angry)? [16]

The question "Have you done anger?" seems to fill the same slot in teasing or other face-threatening interactions that an apology might; that is, after the offense is complete, the question (like an apology) coerces the offended party to say that all is well. Since an admission of anger threatens the face of both parties, a perfunctory denial is expected. To some extent, then, teasing routines train children to endure discomfort and maintain an unperturbed self-presentation. Such a self-presentation is also inculcated by analogous routines among Tamils (Trawick 1990a), Balinese (Wikan 1990), Japanese (Clancy 1986), and Eskimos (Briggs 1970). Although I have no large corpus of examples of teasing, my sense is that emotional equanimity is expected of, and discursively foisted on, Bangladeshi girls more than boys.

Teasing and insults must also affect children's self-image and their emerging concept of selfhood. I have argued that the valorization of lifelong dependency is socialized through routines relevant to troubles telling. That is, one of the predominant vectors in Bangla language socialization trains children to act out selfhood in hierarchically bonded relationships—that is, to act as relational selves of the sort described by Dumont (1970) or Kurtz (1992). Conceivably, the effect of insulting an assertive or tantruming child might be to constrain his or her sense of selfhood options by punishing egocentricity.

The actors in another minidrama occupied two different households: Saju is a 20-year-old daughter of Habibur Rahman's brother Said; Faizam is Aesha's 3-year-old son and one of the compound's most active criers. The following excerpt from my fieldnotes illustrates the extent to which Said's household has grown tired of the noise of Aesha's children:

> Faizam was crying for about 15 minutes. He was clinging, at one point, to Aesha's sari (hand on her bottom); then they went inside. Later Faizam ran out, put one arm on the ground, and lowered his body gently onto the dust. Aesha kept busy cooking. Moni (Faizam's little sister) cried out inside at one point and that stopped his crying for a while.[17] Then Saju walked up, said something to him, took her sandal off her (right?) foot, and put her foot on the small of his back gently. Aesha's crossing from her home to her cook-house seems to have precipitated Saju's removal of her foot and her walking away.

In most Asian countries, including Bangladesh, touching another human being with one's foot—even pointing the foot at another—is such a grave insult that even its approximation requires a polite repair. Saju's act went unnoticed by elders, but I doubt that its force was lost on little Faizam.

Whining, demanding children, even those who want to play outside, when told that the sun will give them *jvar* (inner heat, fever), may be called *pacā* (rotten, spoiled) by caregivers. To American readers, the label "spoiled" might not fit children making this particular demand. To a Bangladeshi caregiver, however, it conveys a broader sense of children who have not learned to limit their demands. Often, they say this directly to the child. In fact, some caregivers attempt to get children to call themselves "spoiled."

Taqbir's mother is a nurse at an ICDDR,B clinic. His caregivers often called the 16-month-old boy "spoiled." He himself once told me that he was *pacā*. One day I saw the boy in the arms of his *ayah* (nanny, cook)—the place he generally wished to stay to find comfort. On that day, despite being thus cradled, he began to cry. She responded,

Example 23. Teasing Taqbir.

Tāqbir bhālo nā,	Taqbir is no good.
bhālo hale eto kānnākāṭi karto nā.	If he were good, he wouldn't cry so.
[Later ...]	
Tāqbir pacā. pacā nā?	Taqbir is spoiled. Spoiled, no?

On other occasions when Taqbir cried, his father would say, *mārum* (I'll hit [you]). Significantly, I never saw him actually hit his son. And when I did see elders strike children, it did not follow warnings. This fits a pattern of unfulfilled threats (and promises) that must diminish the sense in children's minds that words are potent, and reinforce their sense that the world is unpredictable and cannot be managed by mere speech. It might even be argued that calling children "spoiled" performs the same function. That is, the combination of relatively nurturing actions with harsh words sends the message that the child should "attend to what I do, not what I say." The very fact that Bengalis have an expression—*kathār kathā* (words of words)—for empty words might indicate that antilogocentrism appears in Bengali linguistic ideologies.[18] But ideologies such as these are not unmediated realities, any more than a society becomes free of poverty by claiming to be so. That harsh words do affect children is illustrated in the case of 7-year-old Rajib. He was in the care of his mother's brother, Tuslim (22 years old), one day when both came into my room. Rajib was whining, wanting Tuslim to let him play outdoors. Tuslim said to us both, "He's a little one; he'll get *jvar* [fever]," which seems, in this context, to refer to a magical, humoral, dangerous hotness.

Example 24. Criticism of childish risk-taking.

T—choṭo mānuṣ to, jvar āisā parbe.	[He's a] little person! "Fever" will fall on him.
tui pacā. ekdam pacā. pacā nā, Jim bhāi?	You are spoiled. [Isn't he] spoiled, Jim brother?

At that point Tuslim left. My fieldnote entry says, "Rajib wouldn't stay with me, though he stroked my arm. (Looking for what? Nurture after the abandonment and put-downs?) He left, and was soon crying. Tuslim laughed."

Resuming the theme of how caregivers' challenges to children's complaints serve to shape the form and quality of their complaining, I note one more pervasive form of challenge—dismissals typically resembling the following:

nā nā, kichu nā, kichu hay ni.
No, no, it's nothing; nothing has happened.

In late February 1992 I was standing on the steps of the ICDDR,B hospital in Matlab. The daughter of a staff person fell down, hurting her nose or fore-head. The child cried. Adults' responses followed:

Example 25. Injury on the hospital steps.

Caregiver	Another Adult Standing By
Nā nā, kichu nā. bhāṅe ni.	*Concrete* bheṅe geche.
No, no, nothing happened.	*The* concrete *has broken [not your nose].*
[Your nose] hasn't broken.	

Adult complainers receive such *śāntanā* ([words of] comfort) but they begin hearing it as children. From early in their troubles telling careers, Bangladeshis learn that others can be expected to dismiss concern, to discount the seriousness of a complaint.[19] The adults' responses to the crying of the child at the Matlab hospital are echoed in the ideal Bengali pattern of response to adult patients very concerned about their own condition. Biomedically oriented Bangladeshi practi-tioners whom I interviewed said they try to defuse patients' worries by discount-ing their statements of concern. I asked whether politeness dictates that kin and practitioner alike say *iś* (ouch, gee, my, dear) upon hearing of another's suffer-ing. No, they replied. On the contrary, they believe that for the caregiver to show concern is counterproductive. Affirming the patient's experience through any kind of reflecting or echoing strategies, thought by some Americans to indicate empathy, might simply alarm the patient. As a rare exception, they said that frightening patients does have its place—specifically to induce compliance in those who are complacent about taking the necessary steps to improve their prognosis. In the typical situation, however, revealing the whole medical truth to a patient would lead to what is seen as excessive worry; instead, reassurance is called for.

Affirmation of a sufferer as an autonomous locus of experience is not an accepted form of caring in South Asia, outside of cinematic fantasy (Derné 1995). Caring does not and should not constitute the Bangladeshi person as an individual or authoritative subject. Rather, persons experience caring in the context of hierarchical dependency. Socialization practices involving language and crying reinforce dependency, reproducing persons oriented toward hier-archy. On the other hand, children have been exposed, traditionally, not only to the crying of their peers but also to adults' laments and to songs, incorporating a degree of protest, sung by women during the *gāye halud* part of the wedding ceremony (Raheja and Gold 1994). They also hear the nasalized, stridently assertive voices (Bakhtin 1981) of spirits in folktales and in the voices of the possessed. Thus, a range of discursive resources constitutes the Bengali world inherited by children, a world more nuanced than Dumont realized. Bengali Muslim children cannot and need not look to the *sanyasin*, or renouncer, as their model for resistance, rejection, or individuation (Dumont 1970). They know that no totalizing vision of their world is adequate (Trawick 1990b); nor does that world require of them a total surrender of intrapsychic autonomy (Ewing 1991).

Rather, it suggests that there is a time and a particular voice for assertion, this voice (Bakhtin 1981) being often nasalized.

The historical dimension to the complexity of this social and communicative order, however, is a story of challenge and one that seems at present to foreshadow the silencing of some voices and genres, perhaps to be replaced by others. Tuneful weeping, along with spirits, spirit stories, and possession, are commonly experienced by fewer and fewer children. These modes of resistant or assertive communication might be replaced by others, perhaps hybrids of Bangladeshi and global cultural forms. Children of mothers active in the Grameen Bank (Khan 1994) might well learn militant chants, and learn to associate them with women. Other children seem to be growing up in environments from which traditional genres of complaint and resistance have all but disappeared, without a clear sign of what communicative forms will become vehicles for working through cultural tensions.

7

ICONS AND ICONIC INDEXES:
COMPLAINT PRACTICES AND LOCAL VIEWS

Peircean semiotics entails a set of tools quite useful in understanding phenomena of interest not only to medical anthropologists but also, more importantly, to the actors engaged in the situations reflected in my transcripts. For, using the vocal qualities they use means not only manipulating symbols in Peirce's sense of the term but also physically engaging listeners and forming a vocal icon of a nonvocal state, such as misery. The creaky voice (described and graphically depicted later in this chapter) may be a sign conventionally understood to resemble a particular sort of low-energy state (Brown and Levinson 1986: 119, 267, 268). But to understand its use in troubles talk, we must also see it as a sort of vocal gesture indexically linked with other gestures, some visible, some audible. The sum of these gestures seems to represent a category like suffering, physical depression, or weakness. Put simply, using the creaky voice or the other sign-vehicles I highlight later may be a familiar signal. Still, conventions do not abstractly govern behavior (Bourdieu 1977b). Hence, over and above the conventionality of the vocal gestures described later, their availability and local social history condition the significance of their use. This semiotic fact potentiates something even more interesting—the ability of actors to invoke, play with, and deviate from convention.

To understand a communicative phenomenon like troubles telling, we must attend to several facts simultaneously: First, speech, including troubles talk, is a *social practice*. But, second, interactions such as troubles talk also draw on *linguistic structure* as a storehouse of conventions. Third, troubles tellings are also *semiotic* events in which speech is only one of several sign systems in play. And fourth, people who engage in, or listen to, complaining have *commonsense impressions*—metonymic, reflexive, local-shorthand views of local practices—that have an indirect relationship to the linguistic and interactive structures observable in actual practice. These four dimensions of troubles telling determine the significance of complaint interactions, their manifold reality as practices structured linguistically and in other semiotic modes and objectified through common-sense impressions. They reflect the hierarchical structure of semiosis. Everyday practices are built from small semiotic systems but are also carried

119

into a reflexive, higher level as actors epitomize (Basso 1979)—mimic, critique, or otherwise typify (Schutz 1970)—those practices. Phonologic and syntactic aspects of complaints that are not always evident in local practice—but which, at least in one case, are made salient in commonsense impressions—aptly illustrate the four dimensions of significance.

Iconicity is the first of Peirce's three relations between signs and their referents. In contrast with indexicality and symbolicity, iconicity entails resemblance. My focus on iconicity, or iconism, is motivated by the observation that certain elements of language appear to insiders as natural, direct imitations or reflections of a given reality, and, therefore, as exceptions to the analyst's claim that sign-meaning links are arbitrary. Because they appear necessary or natural, they can play a particularly subtle role in shaping consciousness and ideology; that is, they are prime sites of "naturalization," whereby culture appears as nature (Parmentier 1994). In some cases the power of signs to shape cognition and ideology is a function of their taken-for-granted-ness (the inverse of their degree of consciousness; Hill 1995b). In other cases that I recorded, sign-vehicles that help constitute the troubles telling, such as creaky voice and grammatical parallelism, escape what Giddens (1979) calls "discursive consciousness" and are thus, by definition, less likely to be cited, reported, or imitated (Hymes 1981). Thus troubles recipients might immediately (in both the temporal sense and the sense of directness—the apparent lack of symbolic mediation) take creakiness as a vocal sign of weakness or misery. By contrast, it seems, at first glance, less surprising that those who heard Manwara Bibi's complaint (cited below) seemed to miss the subliminal levels of grammatical parallelism largely responsible for poetic effect (Jakobson 1987). The exclusion of such data from awareness makes possible the perpetuation of discourses on gender claiming that women's speech is halting and inappropriate. Thus in both positive and negative senses (by the inclusion of the unconscious sign-vehicle with all the other data processed in interpreting a total communicative event, or by its exclusion), that which remains unconscious has profound effects on the perceptions of speakers. Iconicities—perceived similarities between sign-vehicles and their objects—are likely to be taken for granted, and thus to fall into the category of those signs that have the subtlest effects on discourse and play the subtlest role in it.

It is by no means automatic, however, that a given sign-vehicle becomes an icon to users. Icons are not essentially or necessarily iconic. In fact, Gal and Irvine (1995) make iconicity one of three semiotic processes inherent in those ideologies of linguistic differences that index social identity. Often, however, such indexes appear to insiders or outsiders to be icons. Texans, for example, may see their slow drawl as an icon of their willingness to take time with people and may see the speed of New Yorkers' speech as an icon of their essential unsociability.[1] This sort of iconicity—in conjunction with the processes of recursiveness and erasure, as described by Gal and Irvine[2]—sustains folk and academic views of language and discourse practice. Such linguistic-ideological processes exemplify the semiotic reduction of diversity, ideological synecdoches in which parts stand for wholes, or, in phenomenological terms, "typifications" (Schutz 1970).

Less controversial forms of linguistic iconicity, recognized by all linguists, are onomatopoeia and sound symbolism.[3] Only recently have analyses of sound symbolism begun to include a discourse-pragmatics dimension. For example, Nuckolls's studies (1992, 1996) exploring the engrossing role of sound symbolism in lowland Ecuadorian Quechua narratives is exemplary in this regard. By contrast, much of the early work on sound symbolism was relatively disconnected from discourse usage. Still, the early work is useful here in that South Asian examples figure prominently therein. In fact, onomatopoeia (along with other lexical processes often treated as iconic—echo formation and reduplication) has been treated as a diagnostic feature of South Asia as a linguistic area.[4] It is my aim to situate Bangla iconicity in social interaction.

Complaint Iconicities

Three paralinguistic features typify Bangla complaints,[5] although their relationship to local practice is only probabilistic. These are qualities of the voice—creakiness, nasalization, and the crying voice—in which troubles talk takes shape *as both talk and sound*. Both creaky voice, particularly when it is whispery, and crying voice can be used to signal distress. Nasalization is used metalinguistically in characterizing complaints—making commonsense, pejorative typifications of troubles talk.

As linguistic forms, complaints are indeed multifunctional sign complexes. Complaints are multifunctional because they refer to some trouble but can also serve as indirect requests or even accusations. I call them sign complexes because a person often produces a complaint by exploiting several semiotic modalities simultaneously. From a semiotic perspective, they typically combine indexical and symbolic elements, but the iconic function is salient, too, as the three vocal qualities illustrate. Complaint signals include nonlinguistic vocalizations and nonverbal acoustic signs—sighs, crying, and gestures. Some of these are closely linked with particular linguistic elements. For instance, Bengalis use the word *kapāl* (forehead) as a metonym for the concept of fate, as they believe that one's fate is written there. To utter this word or simply to touch the forehead with one's hand, means "My fate is bad," or "This is happening because of my bad fate." Complaining involves a semiotic complex linking bodies, representations of inner experience, moral evaluations, and social relationships.

All three vocal qualities—creakiness, nasalization of vowels, and the crying voice—can appear in speech contexts other than complaints, and thus their association with complaints is only probabilistic. Understanding is a challenge faced by participants as well as analysts. For either, paralinguistic signals can have value. Their diagnostic value requires the interpreter to recognize patterns of cooccurrence involving semantic features as well. However, nasalization of vowels appears to be an icon of immature, naughty, irritating, loose, or transgressive speech. In fact, nasalization of the [æ] vowel can evoke an unpleasantness that may or may not be associated with human speech. (This explains the strikingly negative connotations of hangtang foreigner talk—again, nasalized nonsense talk full of low front vowels and aimed at foreigners—as described in chapter 1.)

Conventional Creaks

My interest in complaint speech was originally sparked by my listening closely to a recording of a dinner conversation in a Bangla-speaking home in Los Angeles. In verbalizing the pain she was experiencing, Bonhi's voice in that conversation became a whispery creak.[6] The Los Angeles Bangla-speaking dinner group consisted of Bonhi, her husband, and the husband's sister. Quite unexpectedly during dinner, Bonhi drew the others' attention to the pervasive physical pain she was experiencing. Brown and Levinson (1986: 199, 267, 268) propose that the whispery creak is associated universally with misery or commiseration; the acoustic character of the creak reflects a very low level of vocal energy, iconic of misery. Brown and Levinson's claim arises from their fieldwork in Dravidian and Mayan languages. Further evidence of the universality of this link between the creaky voice and suffering comes from the Amazonian Shokleng, among whom the creaky voice is found in everyday speech but is the typical or unmarked vocal quality in ritual wailing (Urban 1985: 311).

It is useful to compare two Bangla examples, both to indicate that the creaky voice is not isolated and to demonstrate that it is not deterministically gendered. These involve two troubles tellers, Bonhi and Ahmed, worlds apart in many ways but united by a common language and a creaky-voiced complaint. Bonhi, a Hindu woman from the cosmopolitan city of Calcutta, was studying in the United States when I recorded her, while Ahmed has scarcely ever left rural Matlab. The circumstances of recording their complaints should also be compared. Both complaints were in progress while I was absent. In Bonhi's case, the whole recording took place in my absence. The loud complaints of Ahmed, toward whom I felt a great deal of filial respect, seemed to call for my presence as his audience on the day before I left the field, in 1992. Bonhi lived in Los Angeles, and I recorded her and her family as they ate together. Thus it was not speech, let alone her complaint, that defined the social event—it was dinner, a speech situation, not an event defined by speech per se. When I heard Ahmed crying out in pain and went to be with him and to say good-bye, I created a speech event—though not the complaint that largely filled it. In neither of these events, however, are complaints as predictable and defining as they are in, say, encounters between Sonargaon bazaar pharmacists and those who come to tell their problems and receive a prescription.

Bonhi used a creaky voice in her complaint, but that vocal quality did not characterize her speech in the rest of the conversation. Indeed, the creaky voice is one mark of her shift into a "troubles register." In contrast, Ahmed uses a creaky voice throughout the recording. While Bonhi's creaky voice coincides quite closely with some key complaint words (but by no means all such words), the duration of Ahmed's complaint stretched the creak across a greater variety of words. And while Bonhi referred to diffuse bodily pain, Ahmed located his pain specifically in his abdomen.[7]

In 1992, Ahmed generally presented himself as timid, powerless, and dis-heartened in the face of social change and personal distress.[8] He spent many sleepless nights, and considers this a symptom of *hrid rog* ("heart" illness). Also, he identifies with his forebears, who had been so driven to despair by a kind of madness/sleeplessness that two in his immediate family committed suicide. Those who sleep lightly tell of Ahmed's wailing and pacing through the night. I myself observed it during the day. On my last day in the compound in 1992— the second Eid (feast day) of the Muslim year—Ahmed was unable to celebrate. He spent much of the day weeping on his bed, suffering from pain that his nephew Meherban ascribed to an exacerbation of a chronic parasitic infestation.

In the following discussion I refer to acoustic phonetics and provide wave-form pictures of creaky vowels. The purpose of this technical discussion is to provide visible evidence of the phenomenon. Transcripts *can* represent prosodic and paralinguistic vocal features (that respectively vary continuously [e.g., loud-ness] and discontinuously [e.g., nasality, creakiness], as noted by Crystal 1971), but waveforms make these patterns visible in a more powerful way.

Spectrograms and waveforms are icons, although unlike the iconicities of everyday vocal qualities or grammar, their social significance is limited to *academic* discourses in which they are embedded. Waveforms display amplitude (intensity, loudness) rather than frequency, and an account of creaky vowels must attend to both horizontal and vertical dimensions of the waveform. The vertical dimension is an icon of the voice's energy level. Louder sounds make higher waves. A low-energy creaky voice, particularly when it is whispery, produces short, low, weak waves. Still, sounds that are simply loud or soft vary in the same vertical dimension; hence one needs another parameter in determining the smoothness or creakiness of a vowel in a waveform. Spe-cifically, one asks about the regularity of variations in intensity over time— across the horizontal dimension. In a waveform of speech, the smoothness of a vowel appears as regularity or smooth periodicity between peaks of amplitude. Creakiness appears as irregularity in peaks, the absence of a regularly repeating pattern.

The waveforms in figure 7-1 display Bonhi's voicings of the word "pain." Bonhi's husband has just asked her whether she is in pain. Bonhi's creaky voice, by comparison not only with his voicing of "pain" but also with her typical voice, lacks energy. At different moments in the same dinner conversation, Bonhi produced two tokens of the /æ/ vowel, whose waveforms are displayed in the figure. Note the higher energy in the smooth voice that produced the /æ/ in *gastric*, in contrast with the low vocal energy in the creaky /æ/ of *byathā* (pain). Adding the horizontal dimension, the smooth vowel in /gastric/ displays itself in regular periodicity, while the creaky vowel of /byathā// displays an irregular pattern. (Compare the waveforms of Ahmed's creaky voice in figure 7-2.)

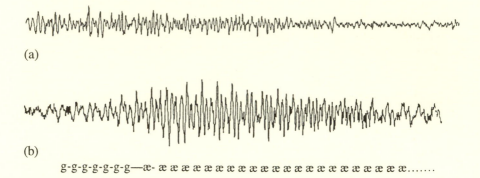

g-g-g-g-g-g-g—æ- æ.......

Figure 7-1. Waveforms of Bonhi's speech: (a) Bonhi's creaky *bya(thā)*; (b) Bonhi's clear *ga(stric)*.

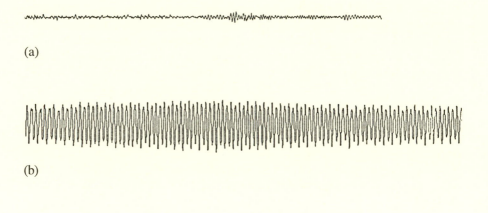

Figure 7-2. (a) Ahmed's *koljādā*; (b) Ahmed's "sung" /o/ vowel; (c) Ahmed's creaked /o/ vowel.

In my interviews with Bonhi, on our repeated viewing of the videotape of her troubles presentation, she herself described her purpose in using the creaky voice as *nāṭak* (dramatization). I present Bonhi's words alongside those of Ahmed here; despite the gaps in age, class, religion, and geography between them, their complaints show interesting similarities:

Example 26. Ahmed's and Bonhi's complaints compared.

Ahmed	Bonhi
ä:: byathā:, byathā:: bya:thā	sārā gā::ye byathā, nā?
Oh the pain, pain, pain!	*[There is] pain in the whole body, no?*
samasto kal[e]jä, samasto (śarir) byathā.	
The whole liver, the whole (body's) pain!	

The logic of the creaky voice as an icon of low energy or misery might well be globally distributed. However, there is a particular Bangla grammar of emotion in which universal quantifiers such as *samasto, sārā* (whole, all)[9] cooccur with lengthened vowels in key words such as *byathā* (pain) and *gā::ye* (body), and with creaky voice (marked with the special typeface). Together, these phonological features of some troubles talk utterances redundantly index dramatic intensity, *total* misery.

There is a set of Bangla metalinguistic terms for paralinguistic features—for wept speech and troubles talk, in particular. Speech distorted by crying is called *kọkiye balā*. The phrase needs parsing—*kọkāno* denotes "grunting, groaning, moaning" (Mitra 1924: 319) or "sobbing." The form cited is a verbal noun—a gerund—derived from the noun *kọk*, itself an example of Bangla sound symbolism (Dimock 1989). *Kọk* onomatopoetically or iconically represents the noise made by gulping or moaning. Adding a causative suffix to the noun produces the verb *kọkāno* (to produce the sound *kọk*). The verbal adjective or participial derivative *kọkiye*, in the phrase *kọkiye balā*, modifies speech. That is the term that local participants at a seminar at the Modern Language Institute of Dhaka University used to describe features of *bilāp* (tuneful, wept speech). According to my California Bangladeshi consultant Faisal, the referential range of *kọkiye balā* includes, at its periphery, the creaky voice. He says its core characteristics are the unique intonational patterns that define moaning and groaning in English and *bilāp* in Bangla, and the vocal breaks we call sobbing.

Nasalization

Bangla metalanguage also includes the phrase *nāke balā* (speaking nasally). Nasalized speech often serves a function in commonsense impressions of complaints, capturing, focalizing, or in some cases inventing a dimension of practice that is not always apparent to an etic eye. Bangla speakers sometimes use this feature to epitomize (Basso 1979) speech styles deemed to be irritating. Just as an exaggerated nasalization of speech in New York may serve to frame a representation of others' speech as insincere (Paul Kroskrity, personal communication, 1990), nasalization plays a significant role in common-sense representations of complaints in Bangla discourse.[10] I have not heard full-scale imitations of speech in which nasalization figures noticeably, but nasalization is conventionalized in words for nagging and whining.

Nasalization is associated with two forms of Bangla metacommunication related to complaining—namely, *ghyānghyān* and the speech of *bhut* (primal spirits), associated with women, impurity, the land, and Hinduism (Blanchet 1984). A standard dictionary consulted by native speakers of Bangla defines *ghyānghyān* as "an irritating nasalized cry or request" (Biswas, Dasgupta, and Bhattacharyya 1984: 216, translation mine). The English gloss "whine" will do. Biswas and his colleagues rightly assume that nasalization is *stylistically* significant. It is not phonemic in the spoken Bangla of Matlab, despite the ability of Bangla orthography to represent it. Holding in abeyance the question of the relationship between the speech of spirits and everyday human complaining or whining, I remind the reader that spirits also speak nasally. I have two electronically recorded instances of spirit speech; both represent the conventionally patterned performances of possession-mediums, rather than the spontaneous instances of possession that also occur.

My video recording of a trance session involving one possession-medium reveals nasalization of vowels and a rabbitlike wiggling of the nose as the most salient indications of the spirit's presence and its control over the medium's face and tongue. The male possession-medium receives, on behalf of the spirit, substantial sums of money for its diagnostic and prescribing activities. Although he is harassed by the local authorities, who consider him a con artist, the man's altered persona is solidly established with his clientele, legitimated in part by the visual and audible sign of nasalization.

Peirce/Piercing Our Consciousness: Nasalization As Sound Symbolism and Acoustic Power

Dimock (1989: 52) explores sound symbolism in Bangla, arguing that onomatopoeias are icons believed to represent some referent more directly than less marked forms of language. Although he does not cite the speech of the spirit in Ishaque's novel (discussed previously), he puts the spirit's speech in the context of symbolism that is attached to the nasalized vowel [æ].

> All symbolic forms with [æ] as the base vowel indicate something decidedly unpleasant, either in the nature of the thing indicated or in its effect upon the speaker. Thus, [*kæṭkæṭ*] indicates a color or combination of colors that is extremely harsh, or a shrewish, loud-voiced woman; [*ṭæktæk*], something annoying or vexing; [*pæcpæc*], thick, distasteful mud or dirt; [*pænpæn*], a child wheedling or crying for a long time, etc. The effect of any of these forms can be heightened by nasalization. (Dimock 1989: 66)

Dimock's analysis is empirically supported by my research. My fictive brother Tuslim, mystified by my recording of quotidian speech and interaction, laughingly described my corpus to his family as a bunch of children "doing *kæ kæ.*" I do not believe this onomatopoeia requires translation. The effect of his remark is to sum up all natural speech—particularly the complaints he knew were my focus—as irritating whinings.

Nasalization can act as an index of yet another, seemingly very different, way of speaking—reciting the Qur'an and calling Muslims to prayer (Nelson 1985). In fact, the nasality expected in these speech acts is lexicalized, in meta-discourse guiding practitioners, as *ghunnah, iqlāb,* or *ixfā'.* Nelson writes that "one of the most obvious characteristics of Qur'anic recitation is its nasal qual-ity. This is not to be attributed to custom, aesthetics, or natural voice quality ... but to the rules of [recitation, which are called] *tajwīd.* The effect of *gunnah* [and of related vocal practices] ... is to prolong the duration as well as to change timbre" of each sound, particularly vowels (1985: 22).

What I propose is that complaints, children, spirits—and even, at a different level, calls to prayer—share a common phonetic index in Bangla because they are somehow structurally homologous in a sound aesthetic that is both Bangla-deshi and unconscious (Sapir 1927). What might this aesthetic be, and what is its integrating value? Calls to prayer, children, and spirits share an ability to trans-gress the privacy of the ear and consciousness, to enter, to share and yet not share the listener-interlocutor's identity. Monsur Musa, Director General of the Bangla Academy (the Bangladeshi government's official language organization), affirms that whenever a jinn, *bhut,* or *rāksmos* (three sorts of spirits) are ani-mated in the folktale performances of grandparents, their voices are nasalized (Musa: personal communication, July, 1996). It could be no accident that Abu Ishaque's novelistic portrayal of the jinn/*bhut's* voice shares this trait with a 1992 performance by a male Bangladeshi Muslim possession-medium. Nor is this unrelated to the agreement among a number of Matlab and Dhaka inter-viewees in 1996 that a nasalized vowel is disagreeable relative to an oral vowel. In sum, it is no accident that the call to prayer (whose nasalization is prescribed by tradition), the whining of children, the persistent demands of the jinn in Ishaque's novel, and the Bangla lexemic representations of complaining, nag-ging, whining, and insistent crying (*ghyānghyān, pyānpyān*) all achieve their autoindexical, or attention-getting, function by a combination of nasalization and other homologous phonetic features (William Beeman, personal communication, 1995).

Icons of Crying in Laments

Urban has analyzed the sociocultural significance of ritual wailing among the Amazonian Shokleng, and, more generally, discovered the importance of speech styles that exploit iconicity:

> Speech styles are ... complex "icons." [By using marked values from everyday speech], they invite comparison between the functions of those values and the function of the speech style itself. That is, by virtue of similarity at the sign vehicle level, speech styles serve to relate together diverse parts of the linguistico-cultural system, bring them to bear on a single context-subject

matter.... Speech styles are indeed culturally constituted signals, ... they play a role in the creation and transmission of culture, and ... they make possible the "semiotic mediation" by means of which the world, and, in this case, especially the culture itself, is brought into intellectual and emotional focus. (1985: 327-8)

Urban later (1988) wrote that Shokleng ritual wailing iconically invokes the natural crying signal, but does so in a socially acceptable transformation. Rather than letting the affect control the individual, the "use of the meta-signal thus reflects a kind of socialization of the affect" (1988: 397).

Like the *ghām khādi* of Paxtun women "performing grief" (Grima 1992), grief performances in Matlab partake of both the ritualized and the improvised dimensions of genre described by Sawyer (1996). As in Urban's part of the Amazon region, Matlab lamentation exploits *icons* of crying. Why not simply call it crying? What makes it iconic of crying, one step removed from the original? The performance of grief transcribed below is a special sort of wailing or ritual crying. Latifa's tears move her to song. She sobs as she sings her sorrow; in fact, sobs mark the end of each line of Latifa's words in the transcript. Still, the singer displays her craft in the creative generation of lyrics within a pattern of rhythm and melody. Urban (1988: 397), writing of Amazonian ritual wailing but attaining a level of ethnological generality, points out a dynamic tension in each performance, a tension between standardization for the sake of communication, on the one hand, and the pull of uniqueness, the individuation of the experience on the other. That is the tension one hears in the tapes of Latifa, noticeable in the transcript if one imagines each of Latifa's lines closing with a sob (represented by •*hh*).

Throughout Latifa's melodic utterances one hears reminders of crying. Her tears flow and her voice chokes, and when her throat is open in song one still hears tension in the throat. That is an icon of crying. While this is far more ritualized than everyday crying—note the tunefulness, the textuality, the repetitive patterns of words (and tune)—it maintains a direct resemblance, an iconic relationship with everyday crying.

Iconicities at the Levels of Morphosyntax and Discourse in Troubles Talk

Some grammatical structures are iconic, creating concrete *syntactic* formalisms that parallel the *semantic* structures they represent (Haiman 1985). Bangla verb phrases that use reduplication to portray the semantics of reciprocal action are good examples (Wilce 1996). Since subject noun phrases are optionally realized in Bangla, their realization—even, or particularly, when they fill the role of semantic experiencer and are marked in the possessive case—is another iconic grammatical process, one that figures largely in the linguistic structure of Bangla complaints. Performing what is optional is an icon of intentionality or emphasis. In fact, the experiencer-subject construction is even more clearly iconic, at least for Bangla speakers, of a nonagentive model of action. An agentless construction is well suited to express the frequent sense that illness has no visible causative agent.

In his 1985 treatment of natural syntax in relation to iconicity, Haiman explores symmetries between certain patterns of perception and grammatical form. There is just such a congruence in Bangla between the perception of suffering as something beyond human volition and what Klaiman (1981) calls the grammar of nonvolitionality. The syntactic structure of troubles talk stereotypically uses the experiencer-subject construction. Given the semantics of nonvolitionality associated with this and allied constructions (Klaiman 1981), the experiencer-subject's function in Bangla might thus be compared with the pragmatics of the passive construction in Japanese, where the use of such syntax connotes suffering. The nonvolitionality of illness is a given. Yet, while the most common English way of describing an illness experience masks the experiencer's lack of control through verbs such as "feel" that metaphorize experience as action, Bangla manifests a preference for stative verbs and experiencer subjects. Transitive verbs are normally disfavored. Experiencer-subject constructions are syntactic icons of a Bengali sense that sufferers are victims more than agents.

Laments include more examples of syntactic iconicity, however, than the pervasive experiencer-subject structure that characterizes even everyday troubles talk. Latifa's wept speech actually contains multiple levels of iconism. Some of these are common to spoken Bangla, including reduplicated forms (Wilce 1996) such as that in line 2L:

2L āmāre ni deśe deśe [p]hirāy go bun •hh   They take me [from] land to land,
     bun go o o bun •hh   sister, O sister.

In her line 2, Latifa's repetition of deśe deśe diagrammatically depicts (Wilce 1996) her enforced journeys in multiple "lands," as her brothers sent her away to her in-laws during her marriage, then dragged her back to their home after her divorce.

12L je [ś]hunete hay to go •hh   *Whoever hears, perhaps,*
      śarīlerpaśam kāṛā kāṛā diyā go   *their skins crawl with gooseflesh,*
      jāy gā •hh
      bun go bun •hh   *sister, O sister.*

In line 12 the Bangla phrase *śarīler paśam kāṛā kāṛā diyā go jāy gā* (their skins crawl with gooseflesh) turns on the verb phrase *paśam kāṛā* (flesh standing up). The reduplication of the verb *kāṛā* (to stand, be upright) is not strictly necessary but adds intensity.[11]

Discourse Iconicity: Icons of Overcoming

Beyond these grammatical icons, iconism is seen at the level of discourse and poesy in Latifa's performances and in those of other sufferers. When linguistic form itself—at a level above the sound or poetic line (that is, the verse-and-stanza structure of poetic language)—reflects something of the author's mind, the author's genius, that is what Friedrich calls "the master trope," whose scope extends "over the whole poem or conversation that partly constitute[s] its gestalt" (1986: 40). Such a trope is an icon of creativity and cognitive organization, terms by which we evaluate everyday practices as well as linguistic structure as deployed in practice. This master trope is evident in Latifa's lament. The repetition of the vocative refrain, "Sister, O sister" and of the line, "They have murdered me!" adds not only intensity but also textuality. Latifa's entextualization (Bauman and Briggs 1990) of her performance not only renders it accessible to being received as verbal art but also makes it vulnerable to an immediate, local critique. Her kin focused on the very parallelism (repetitiveness) of her tuneful speech in dismissing it.

A striking example of the master trope at work in prosaic speech is Manwara Bibi's illness narrative, spoken to me and my field assistants—an icon of her clear thinking about illness. The neatly outlined narrative reflects a knowledge of the expression of illness that is routinized through years of experience. I do not claim, any more than Lévi-Strauss did in relation to myths, that the structure of her words indicates conscious crafting. Still, that structure, as laid out below, does show craft. Her narrative organization reflects habits of speech practice, interaction, and thought. It is a map—and maps are prototypical icons—that reveals her intelligent involvement as a healer with many patients. It is an icon of Manwara Bibi's strength of personality, the force reflected in her initiation dream and her subsequent healing practice, the force that enabled her to move outside her family home and, thus, for a rural Bangladeshi woman, to live an exceptional life. Manwara Bibi is the only person in Bangladesh to have told me of her initiation as a healer. She said, on one of my visits to her home, that she had been given a dream in which she was called to practice healing—though not of a shamanic sort, from what I could tell. In the dream she saw a book of cures, which she somehow internalized. Her experience of the call and of receiving this book, no doubt, continues to empower her.

The structure of this narrative struck me from the time I transcribed it. I have discussed it with several Bengali consultants and must admit that none of them—all male, unfortunately—saw evidence in the narrative that indicated the sort of intelligent design that I see. On the other hand, one such consultant strongly denied that the 4-4 structure (4 problems, then 4 solutions) was intentional: How could this illiterate woman achieve such literate structuring? He was denying that she could have *guciye baleche* (spoken in [such] a well-organized manner).

Example 27. Manwara Bibi's illness narrative and its logical structure.

1   Problem 1   jeno partham[12] āmār ekṭā sardir bhāb āchilo ār ki.
                  It was like, at first, the feeling of a cold or something came over me.

2   Problem 2   sardir bhāber tanay jeno-i ei jvar [h]ailo.
                  From that feeling of a cold, it was like a fever came.

3	Problem 3	jvarer tanay jeno-i māthā dharā [h]ailo. *From the fever came a headache.*
4	Problem 4	hei māt[h]ā dharār tanay ābār madhye madhye bahe piḍete ghāy. *After the headache came periodic low back pain.*
5	Summary of problems	to ei khāi[ye]chi lai[ye]chi cal[e]chi āijjā kay din dhairā, āijjā. *So, I'm just eating and coping for these past few days.*
6		ha, āijjā āsṭro din dhairā ār caltām pāri nā.[13] *Yes, it's been eight days that I can't get around.*
7		to a[k]hane khātār tale [s]huiyā rai[ye]chi ār ki. *So I've been lying on my bed or whatever.*
8		ei mane dharle khāi, nā khāile [s]hetā-e pairā (upare?) thā[k]hi. *So if it occurs to me I eat, and if I don't eat I just stay on it [my bed].*
…		
9	Solution 1	jā-i hok, ei futerā āinnā *capsule* di[ye]che, *Anyway, these sons [of mine] brought me capsules,*
10	Solution 2	futerā[14] āinnā *tablet* di[ye]che. eiḍi khāitāchi, *My sons brought me tablets. I'm eating those.*
11	Solution 3	gāo gasal dhawā dhawā-e, ay garam pāni kare. *I'm taking medicinal baths in hot water.*
12	Solution 4	ei garam pāni khāi. *I drink hot water.*
13	Summary of care	ta embe tālāś ṭālāś kartāche. *That's how they are taking care of me.*
14		ei bhāber tanay āmi [ekh]ane caltām āchi ār ki. *That's how I'm coping, or whatever.*

Manwara's narrative structure is an icon of her own habits of thought and speech and of her exceptional assertiveness. But the narrative does not reflect an autonomous individual. Manwara is about 50, quite old for a poor woman. What gives Manwara comfort and enables her to cope is the care of her sons. Her sat-isfaction derives from the respect and concern that her sons offer; her happiness depends on their care. About this dependence we should note two things. First, it is a presentation of self in Goffman's sense (1959). We do not know, from this self-presentation, how she experiences her self as such, how she conceives of her self, or what secret frustrations or ambitions toward greater interpersonal auton-omy she might harbor. Herein lies a second caveat: We should follow Ewing in distinguishing intrapsychic autonomy from interpersonal autonomy. The former entails an "ability to maintain enduring mental representations of sources of self-esteem" (1991: 132), the capacity to draw on memories and other forms of internal representation to nurture the sense of well-being. Manwara Bibi's self-presentation would cause us to believe that she feels loved, which is particularly important to her when she is ill.

Manwara's balancing of four remedies against her four symptoms, and the ending of her narrative on the optimistic note, "They are taking care of me, and that's how I'm coping," are what I call icons of overcoming. The attitudes toward women and their speech commonly expressed in the Sonargaon area are that they should remain in their husband's homes and that they are incapable of being articulate. Built up over years of resistance to the first attitude limiting her to the domestic sphere, Manwara's habits of speaking about and dealing confidently with illness overcome the second bias. Moreover, the structure of her narrative is an icon of her work to overcome her present symptoms, an icon of hope and of the comfort she is already receiving in the attentions of her sons.

Iconic Linkages: Posture, Gestures, Language, Thought, Culture

Complaints are semiotic events in which multiple sign systems are in play. Apart from physiological signs such as the pulse (the subject of some pioneering works on "the science of signs"—semiotics—written by sixteenth-century physicians), persons use the various sign systems at their disposal to describe troubles. When one feels that the trouble is located in a specific part of the body, one often uses gestures to draw attention to that part.

Thus gestures may not be merely icons that *resemble* the state of affairs they represent, as they are indexes, signs that point to, or focus attention on, something not necessarily similar in form to themselves. There is nothing imitative of pain per se about the gesture of pointing to one's headache with one's palm or finger. Gestures are by nature indexical signs, but some physical signs that appear gestural partake of the symptom (such as pain or fever) and are in that sense iconic. Think of the grimaces or the stretching motions brought on by the flu. Consider movements, in response to discomfort, that are superficially like spasms, but which—unlike involuntary twitches and spasms—fall under our control.

Figure 7-3. Bonhi pointing to her pain.

Bonhi's head, neck, and arm movements work in tandem with her creaky voice to graphically display that pain to which her words refer (see figure 7-3). Both visibly and audibly, indexically and iconically, she represents her discomfort to her family.

Bangla grammar of nonvolitionality is symmetrical with, or iconic of, the concept of pain, injury, illness, distress, or suffering as lying beyond human will.[15] This grammatical tendency is not merely reflective of a cultural concept. Habitual usage not only reflects but also sustains or even produces shared forms of thought.

Just as the grammar of nonvolitionality helps to both mark complaints and channel thought in a nonvolitional direction, sound symbolism can also play an active, and not merely reflective, role in relation to cultural schemata. Conventionalized linguistic forms become resources for strategic use.[16] As I learned in many hours of interviews with her, Bonhi had no convenient metalanguage to describe her creaky voice, but she had an embodied, aesthetic, pragmatic sense that this vocal quality was useful in dramatizing her condition. That usefulness arises not only out of a natural iconicity between low vocal energy and the suffering Bonhi was communicating, but also out of a presumed conventionality. Admittedly, I have only two recorded examples of the creaky voice. If, however, those two cases do represent a conventional form of semiosis, the availability or local social history of the convention conditions the meaning of each use and also potentiates more abstract communicative play through deviance from conventions.

8

TROUBLES TALK AND SOCIAL CONFLICT

Troubles talk is semiotically structured, but semiotic processes are always social processes. The means by which signs (e.g., troubles talk and its particulars) are construed is not immanent in the signs themselves, nor even in histories of how such signs have been construed, but rather, are emergent in performance. To use the rubric of "performance" in relation to troubles telling is to acknowledge, with Good (1994), Desjarlais (1992), and others, that illness narratives, laments, and other forms of troubles telling should be approached as aesthetic objects— no less controversial than the objects of art funded by the National Endowment for the Arts over which recent American culture wars have been fought.

During my fieldwork in 1991–92, I made not only audio and video record- ings but also careful notes—approaching a verbatim record—of 101 everyday complaints recorded on paper only. These lend themselves to tracing pervasive pragmatic patterns. The lack of comparative evidence from other societies is unfortunate. I do not intend to claim uniqueness for the Bangladeshi discourses represented here, nor, in relation to the patterns discussed below, can I say what they might share with troubles talk outside Bangladesh.

Naturally, given my intention to focus my fieldwork on troubles talk, my attention was riveted whenever anyone happened to complain spontaneously in my presence. Such spontaneous troubles talk could not be mechanically re- corded; but I did commit many linguistic and social features to memory and did write a verbatim entry in my fieldnotes within hours of the event. While tran- scripts of troubles talk in medical encounters or in recorded home interactions provide accuracy in detail, my analysis of the 101 complaints illumines everyday social relationships as the former cannot. I put questions to this corpus that isolated transcripts cannot answer. Some of the key questions are, How, and with whom, do rural Bangladeshis draw attention to their needs through troubles telling? And what response does this elicit? Patterns described in this and other chapters answer to these questions and offer an on-the-ground view of enacted personhood in South Asia.

What kind of data and what sorts of complaints are these? I recorded the sex and name of the person telling the trouble, name(s) of listener(s) and their relationship to the speaker, and the setting. Regarding the speaker-listener relationship, whenever it was a hierarchical one due to clear social-structural reasons of age or kinship, that is noted; in other cases no clear hierarchy obtains. (As noted in chapter 4, there is a positive correlation in this corpus between hierarchy and uttering the optional pronominal subject of the complaint. Complaints to a superordinate were more likely to realize first-person indexicals.) Setting and relationship determine whether I considered complaints to be *work related*—that is, having the potential of leading to a recognized inability to work (UBINIG 1989; Kleinman 1986: 152).[1] Some complaints were evoked (by a "how are you" question); others were volunteered. I also characterize the troubles content in relation to the (admittedly problematic) categories of "somatic" and "psychosocial." As I committed these encounters to memory, I paid particular attention to the overt "sympathy" level of the response. I treated both reflective echoing (explained later in this chapter) and attentive silence as marks of sympathy but categorized teasing and laughter as unsympathetic.[2]

If a speaker seems to initiate troubles talk out of the blue—in contrast with waiting for the elicitation of troubles by a polite or phatic question (Malinowski 1923)—might that index egocentric self-assertion? About 58 percent of the total complaints were volunteered. That figure, however, varied markedly according to the setting of the troubles talk, the listener's status, and work-disability relevance. About two-thirds of the complaints in Dhaka and in rural homes and offices were volunteered—but only one-third of *street* complaints. There is a slightly increased probability (63 versus 57 percent) that a speaker will volunteer a complaint when the listener is clearly his or her superior or elder. Those in my sample volunteered complaints when their shared activity context was work and when the listener was not working as hard as the speaker. They complained to employers, supervisors, or rich foreigners—perhaps in hopes of getting relief from overwork, or perhaps simply to vent negative feelings about the situation. Of the non-disability-related complaints, only 50 percent were speaker-initiated; but in cases where relief might be gained by complaining, 69 percent of complaints were speaker-initiated. I would not expect these Bangladeshi patterns to be unique by any means. Patterns of communicating distress and seeking help, though learned, are perhaps universally learned in contexts where work disability and relations of dependence and nurture are potentially relevant, as Kleinman implies (1986: 152–156; see also UBINIG 1989). The sensitivity of the initiative variable to setting undercuts the hypothetical link between speaker initiation and autonomous self-assertion.

Yet, more troubles were volunteered than elicited overall—evidence that troubles tellers are self-aware and are willing to bring attention to themselves even in a position of vulnerability. Complaints that I coded as "volunteered" include a few in which the speaker took the initiative by vaguely indicating that something was the matter, though not disclosing the problem itself.

Some 64 of the 101 complaints thematized bodily discomfort, but the predominance of somatic themes was not consistent across physical settings. Psychosocial complaints were more frequent in Dhaka and on the streets of the Sonargaon bazaar than in rural domestic settings. The emergence of a psychologizing kind of subjectivity in a modernizing city like Dhaka is to be expected

(Kleinman and Kleinman 1985: 434, 435). The rural, market-town street is a male domain, and males' complaints, overall, had a slightly higher probability of being somatic and publicly verbalized. A different set of factors explains why psychosocial and vague/sweeping complaints are higher on the streets than in our rural compound. First, the street sample is self-selected—acutely ill persons will not be walking the streets. Second, psychosocial news is news that may invite telling in public settings more than in domestic and work settings, where companions' intimate awareness of other's dissatisfactions—or a strong sense of the risks inherent in expressing them—would tend to limit nonsomatic complaints.

It seems possible that the type of trouble that needs to be told has an effect of its own on whether or not it is volunteered; in fact, 65 percent of psychosocial complaints were volunteered, versus 36 percent of somatic complaints.[3] The concerned attention of friends and family can assuage psychosocial distress. Psychosocial complaints, to the extent that they subtly indicate blame or seek to change relationships, must be expressed—even if indirectly—to have an effect. Admittedly, these benefits do not depend on initiating the topic of distress or well-being, but they increase one's motivation to speak—enough to overcome the barrier met when no one asks.

Teasing and Sympathy

Teasing might have a religious pedigree that helps relativize our approbation of sympathy. On two occasions in Dhaka, I accompanied the father of a longtime friend on his visits to his *pīr*—a Sufi Muslim preceptor or spiritual guide. Some Bangladeshi *pīr*s receive offerings fit for a king or a god; the well-known Pir of Atrashi counts among his millions of followers the former Bangladeshi president, General H. M. Ershad. My "uncle's" *pīr*, Baba, is neither as popular as that of Atrashi nor as removed from everyday life or discourse. He enjoys rhetorical swordplay with a group of four intelligent friends and/or disciples. All but one are over 60. These intelligent men believe Baba's claim to be 110 years old, despite his appearing only 50-something. And when they mention aches, pains, or weakness, they do not flinch when he laughs at them. He says, "I am over a hundred and strong as an ox; you are mere boys, and you complain of this and that!" After having a laugh at their expense, he suggests paternally that one eat more honey and that another play more golf on "Ershad's" course.[4]

Teasing and laughing are responses countenanced only within intimate relationships, or in relation to madmen on the streets. Siblings and cousins in Habibur Rahman's compound sometimes responded to each other that way, but did not always take the teasing as well as Baba's followers did. Teasing does not pass over great social distances or upward leaps of status. "Go ahead and die" is said to younger siblings, not elders or strangers. Male complainers in my corpus are more likely to receive such rude responses—from male interlocutors—than are females. In the 32 encounters in this corpus in which sympathy or derision were relevant responses, the 20 responses to male complaints were split evenly between sympathy and teasing. But 8 of 12 responses to females' complaints were sympathetic.

How do we explain this finding that females are more likely to receive a sympathetic hearing? It seems to confound my more anecdotal experiences with males who tease females, as they teased Latifa. We should look at the participant structure of the marked interactions. The women in my sample receive sympathy not from husbands or brothers but from sons—on whose support their future welfare depends—or from fictive sisters. In half the cases where women's complaints met with teasing, it was men who teased them. Of the remaining two cases, one victim of the teasing is Latifa—the brunt of everyone's criticism—and the other was teased for expressing a superstitious view of her illness in the presence of educated people. Male complainers are teased by other males, not by females. This might indicate a tough style of male-male communication analogous to that seen among white American middle-class males, contrasting with a more nurturing style predominant among females.

As a rich foreigner and the guest of Habibur Rahman, I was distant and powerful, even though a fictive kinsman. Brown and Levinson (1986), in their cross-linguistic study of politeness phenomena, found two constructs helpful in explaining who tends to receive demonstrations of politeness—the powerful and the distant. Consistent with their theory, responses to me—across gaps of wealth, power, and cultural identity—maximized politeness. One group of children expressed their best wishes:

Example 28. Sympathetic best wishes from children.

inśĀllāh   bhālo haiye jāben
God willing, you will get better.

When my fictive sister Amina and her 7-year-old son Rajib echoed my complaints, they were communicating empathy. One day my back was hurting badly. I got down to stretch it, then got up and said:

Example 29. A child's reflective echoing of an adult's pain.

Jim: khub byathā kare   It hurts a lot.
Rajib: byathā anek?   It hurts a lot?

By responding deferentially to both the form and the significance of my complaint, Rajib showed me a double courtesy. Put differently, his sympathy and respect were indexed by his echoing of my keyword. His mother Amina tended to offer echo complaints of her own instead of echo questions, deferring somewhat less than her son. Sometimes her troubles telling, in response to mine, involved a very different trouble; still, her habit seems homologous to Rajib's and also appropriate as an adult display of empathy. Amina's display can also be regarded as a polite way to preserve my "positive face," which Brown and Levinson (1986: 61) define as recognition and appreciation of oneself by interactants. Amina, in narrating illness events like mine, demonstrated that kind of recognition. She took my words and experiences seriously. At the same time, she gained my attentive regard for her illness narratives, thus attending to her own "face needs."

Echo complaints establish solidarity between the troubles teller and recipient. Recipients offer their own experiences partly to reassure the teller. Offering explanatory models accomplishes the same end. Folk disease etiologies can reassure the sick just as much as the authoritative diagnoses and explanations offered by practitioners can. Of the 16 overtly sympathetic responses I recorded, at least two of them included this form of reassurance through explanation. The same function is served by an act of verbal self-comfort; thus, in some cases, troubles tellers moved on to account for their own troubles, offering a causal explanation. In the number of these self-accounts that are admissions of missteps, excesses, or imbalances in one's lifestyle, we see the priority that people sometimes place on the assigning of meaning to illness. A hunger for meaning sometimes outweighs even the need to preserve one's face.

Discourse Structure in Complaint Interactions

Like Mills's (1959) "vocabularies of action," *accounts* are explanations of one's actions and motivations, means through which one manages one's social identity by reframing the relationship between one's behavior and societal norms (Fisher and Groce 1990: 227, 228). In several events in my corpus, troubles account for failures. Bengalis might call these *ajuhāt* (excuses), but that would predetermine their validity. In one of my more productive sociolinguistic interviews, I asked Jalu Miah about a few transcribed complaints. Since I wanted him both to respond to the form of the troubles talk and ascribe a gender and status to anonymous speaker-authors of decontextualized utterances, I gave him as few contextual clues as possible. Jalu ascribed the first complaint to a woman—for an interesting reason. Although it was I who had decontextualized it, he said that a woman must have uttered it, because only a woman would speak out of the blue like that. He went on to explain himself, giving me a hypothetical counter-example of males who make sense by speaking in context. This is mostly my paraphrasing of what he said; the two English words he used are shown in italics:

> Example 30. "Singing a reference" or "ground" as contextually appropriate excuse.
>
> Two adolescent boys are working in the fields. One is tired of working. But, unlike the woman who speaks without context, the boy *gāibe* (will sing) a *reference* or *ground*."

I don't know why Jalu introduced these two English words into the middle of his Bangla narrative. But in conjunction with the Bangla word *gāibe*, according to another consultant, "reference" and "ground" take on a derogatory flavor—more of an "excuse" than a mere "account" or "reason."[5] Jalu could have used the standard Bangla phrase *ajuhāt dibe/dekhābe* (will give an "excuse," or literally, a hand-washing). *Ajuhāt*, although a standard urban lexeme, is familiar in rural areas, too. Jalu's circumlocution was perhaps for art's sake; it was certainly evocative. So adolescent boys did not escape his representation with much more of their dignity than did women.

One account-complaint I overheard is particularly telling: I happened to be standing in the market area once when I overheard Habibur Rahman talking with another man. Habib evidently owed him money. He was saying:

Example 31. A complaint is offered to account for a social failure.

āmār śarīr beśi bhālo nā, ṭhānḍā sardi lāgche.
My body is not very well; I've had a cold and sniffles.

ṭākā āmi dimu[6] ni. e[k]han kintu ṭākā nāi.
I surely will give [back] the money, but right now [I have] no money.

In the transcribed encounter, the complaint functions like a cartoon line, "You wouldn't hit a guy with glasses, would you?" Habib's complaint strategically projects a weak and vulnerable self. It is no more surprising than a friend, in any society, who says—as one Bangladeshi did to me, "I haven't yet done what I promised to do for you; I'm still sick."

The preceding examples evoke temporary disability. Although masked by indirection, the contextual evocation is strong. Searle's classic treatment of indirect speech acts (1975) argues that speech acts such as making requests build upon certain logical conditions. He calls these "felicity conditions" because in the case of their nonfulfillment, the speech act will be infelicitous, inappropriate, or nonsensical. Having a need is a felicity condition for making a request, as is the listener's ability to do something about it. In explaining how speech acts can be made *indirectly*, Searle claims that to draw attention to the fulfillment of conditions for a particular speech act is to perform the act. Performing the speech act *indirectly* preserves face for both the speaker and his audience; it is a politeness strategy seen around the world (Brown and Levinson 1986). When my field assistant Faisal said, "My ear is killing me," after two hours of listening to a data tape using headphones, he was fulfilling the conditions necessary for making a request. That is, a request for a break makes sense only when a break is needed, as it obviously was then.

Jalu's invented scenario distills local practices and ideologies related to complaints. Bengalis recognize that people present accounts or excuses, depending on one's perspective. I predict that accusations of malingering and excuse-making would be more frequent in work-related contexts, where what is at stake is obvious to participants, as in the complaint/account in Jalu's scenario. There is a tendency in that direction in my findings; while sympathetic responses predominate in settings of leisure, there is a slight excess of critical responses over sympathetic responses to potential requests for "time off."

Work settings certainly include the household economy. In fact, a study in rural Bangladesh by Hashemi and Schuler (1992) indicates a systematic tendency to label women's complaints as "malingering." In most rural Bangladeshi households, women's work is within the compound. Hashemi found that rural women who *do* work for wages have an advantage over their counterparts when their illness complaints meet with disbelief. Their wages allow them to purchase medicines themselves, thereby avoiding confrontations over male-controlled funds.

From Vagueness to Clarity—Sighing and Verbalizing

Most of the complaints in my corpus move from vagueness toward specificity over the course of a complaint encounter, and from nonlinguistic vocal signs—serving self-indexing or preparatory functions—to verbalization. Sighs I heard often developed into verbal complaints in at least some settings. The sequence is linked with the dramatic-intensity range described below, and both have strong relations to gender. In fact, the gendered distribution of the nonverbal and the verbal is such that women may often be "allotted" only the sigh.

It is characteristic of linguistic *anaphora* for fuller, more explicit references to be followed by telegraphic "proreference" forms such as "it." Only by pointing back to their antecedents do such forms make sense. But speakers in my corpus also used the inverse strategy, building from vague hints toward specificity. Wordless sighs may index troubles, and troubles talk may begin with sighs as hints of words to come. Women—banned from speaking in domains defined as public—are sometimes confined to such nonverbal channels for venting their weary frustration, despair, or anger, though men as well as women sigh. Sighs take on meaning through their activity setting. Hard-working people sigh, sometimes as a preface to a verbal complaint about aches and pains. But Bangladeshis (and Americans) sigh particularly when they know they have an audience. Sighing, that is, is a social and communicative act, not a transparent revelation of a psychobiological state.

It was almost two hours later than usual one night, around 9:30, when Habibur Rahman returned from the bazaar to eat dinner. His wife, whose duty is to save the best portion and feed him whenever he arrives, sighed noticeably just after he entered. A bicycle rickshaw puller sighed as he let his passenger off. At 3:30 a.m.—just after his brother, Meherban the *Imām*, had broadcast from the mosque the call to rise and eat before sunrise when the day of fasting would begin—Habib sighed loudly. A beggar who walked into Habib's compound one day alternated between sighing and loudly exclaiming *mā go!* (O mother!) as he awaited food donations.

What stands out about sighing in Bangladesh is how the panhuman behavior is culturally canalized—Muslims tend to say "Allahu Allah" while sighing. Habib, his wife, the rickshaw puller, and the beggar all sighed thus. Breathing the name of God is an ancient Sufi practice; such *dhikr*—ideally entailing the recitation of the Arabic Qur'an—may, at least in Bangladesh, actually consist only of loud cries of "ĀllāHU" during inhaling (Āllā-) and exhaling (HU).[7] Thus sighing God's name in mundane settings is an invocation in the ancient sense of calling the divine to one's here and now, though this does not efface the plain-tive weariness typical of all sighs. Wordless sighs contrast somewhat with sighs of "Allah." Insofar as they can point to despair and frustrations that are relatively suppressed, often by a hegemonic kind of theology, wordless sighs are hidden transcripts (Scott 1990) more than their invocational counterparts are. Both an old man, who has been told that his patron will no longer lend him money, and a young female health worker, faced with evidence that AIDS will spread rapidly if Bangladeshi pharmacies continue washing needles in cold water and reusing them, sighed *wordlessly.*

Some sighs, perhaps those intended as hints, are supplemented by verbal specifications of a complaint. Discourse creates context. Contexts include topics; topics are one of many levels at which discourse tends to maintain cohesion over time. Settings vary as to the range of topics, genres, and speech-event types that tend to occur there. Institutional settings tend to restrict the types and topics of discourse; institutions manage, discipline, support, and maintain discourse and other social activity in a specialized domain. Medicine is one such institution. The snippets of medical interviews that follow represent both Bangladeshi "tra-ditional medicine" and biomedicine. The latter cases illustrate that biomedicine is far from a monolithic phenomenon with a single institutional structure. None-theless, Bangladeshi clinics oriented to biomedicine—and particularly those funded by Western donors—represent global material-and-discursive trends, and there are similarities in the styles by which some outposts of biomedicine in Bangladesh and in the West manage human life and discourse (Wilce 1994, 1995, 1997).

Compared with domestic settings, less conversational work needs to be done in medical settings to raise and maintain medical topics. The man who steps into Heykal Daktar's pharmacy from the dusty brick path in the Sonargaon bazaar needs only to declare what kind of health problem he has. (Rural *ḍāktārs* see patients in their private drugstores.) In fact, he might simply say, "Give me some aspirin." Or if he only stands there looking sick, the doctor will ask him what is wrong. But if he should wish to chat, he must rely on either his familiar face or his conversational efforts to maintain his right to sit there taking up limited bench space at the *ḍāktār*'s pharmacy/office.

In everyday settings, then, people *work* to take the floor and to introduce a complaint as a topic and keep the floor. Bangla speakers often make distress topical in the impersonal grammar of the experiencer-subject. Typically, they say *bhālo lāge nā* ([I/it do/does] not feel/seem good). If they are not careful to make that statement after a sufficient break or pause, hearers may read it as an assessment or evaluation of the previously current topic. That is, the ambivalent Bangla phrase may be heard as "[*that* does] not seem good." To be safer, one says *śarir bhālo nā* (body good [is] not) or *man bhālo nā* (mind/mood good [is] not). If a man approached a pharmacy and performed the same recognized con-versational move to initiate a complaint, those present would consider it odd if he did not introduce details immediately. In everyday social settings, by contrast, building context requires more talk.

Building a troubles context slowly might minimize some risks. A person—particularly a woman (as Hashemi and Schuler argued, 1992)—who is seen as too quick to complain might be rebuked and then might develop a reputation that would further harm her chances of getting necessary medical attention. A gendered ideology of language passed on to me by a male Calcutta immigrant in Los Angeles says that women should suffer without words (if not without sighs). The material reality behind that is that they must save their talk for the times it counts most; when resources are scarce, women's complaints will be discounted. Such factors help us understand why my "field mother" Rani rarely verbalized her complaints to men but often sighed aloud in their presence. And for the men in my corpus, hints or nonverbal indications of trouble often preceded specific verbalized complaints.

As environments for troubles telling, everyday social settings have advantages and disadvantages over busy medical institutions. On the one hand, everyday social settings allow narrative elaboration. Long narratives are an accepted feature of talk at meal times or over tea in a teastall. In fact, because of their value as entertainment and social glue, narratives play a role in *defining* everyday settings as such, overshadowing the smaller role played by complaints. The instrumental function of language—e.g., requests for relief or medicine—is somewhat effaced by its expressive and negotiative functions. Consider the following example. My colleague Faisal sat in a teastall one day, tape recorder in hand. In the recorded conversation, a man of about 60 began a story at around 10:00 A.M. He seized the floor with what speech writers call a "hook" to grab interest, announcing that he had just walked some 10 miles, starting at 3:00 a.m. It seems he heard something, got out of bed and went outside, and discovered his cow was missing. He chased it, with neighbors betraying the secrets of the cow's route all along the way, from 3 until 10 A.M. His long list of place names was strung together through predicate chaining—the end of one predicate would be repeated to form the topic-onset of the next sentence. The final destination mentioned was *bāṛit[e]* (at home), with the cow safely in tow. At that point someone—probably the proprietor of the teastall/restaurant—interrupted him to tell him there was flatbread ready to eat. But the old man was not quite finished and resisted that change of topic. The upshot of the night's walk remained to be told by him; the presence of flatbread could not interrupt the painful end of the story of the night walker (designated as W; T designates a voice probably belonging to the teastall proprietor):

Example 32. A teastall complaint.

W—pāwḍi āmār dhairā geche	My legs are all cramped.
[h]āṭte āri nā āmār tal pāwṭi dhare jāy.	I can't walk, the soles of my feet are all cramped up.
T—khāwā dāwā khā i[ye]chen ni.	Have you eaten yet?
W—hā?	What?
T—khāwā dāwā khā i[ye]chen ni.	Have you eaten yet?

The outcome of the all-night walk was that the soles of his feet were "all cramped up." But he himself had to tell it, and not leave it to his audience's imagination, because his discomfort was not hunger, as they had guessed.

The story ended and the conversation moved on. That is the nature of every-day social interaction. The discomfort was not serious enough to warrant further talk. When he had another turn at talk, the narrator shifted from his all-night walk to other stories. His friends had not laughed or teased him. They had displayed concern for his well-being by asking whether he had eaten—which is certainly a primary concern reflected in the traditional phatic words of greeting in other Asian societies.[8]

From Nonverbal Underplaying to Self-Dramatization

While complaints at home tend to move from the nonlinguistic to the verbally specific, complaints' dramatic intensity does not necessarily vary predictably over time. As I have mentioned, female actors in the complaint company may be allotted less dramatic roles than male actors, or they may be sanctioned for their dramatizations. Such was Latifa's fate, whereas my "grandfather" Ahmed frequently moaned and wept all night and all day. The only sanction he faced was increasing apathy.

Women who model their behavior after the ideal of silent suffering underplay their complaints. They express distress only in sighs, if at all. Others overplay their complaints. In example 21, I described how Habib's 7-year-old grandson Rajib dramatized the pain inflicted by some harmless larvae; he did so against the backdrop of a general pattern in which children learn that only by dramatizing their distress will they gain their mother's attention. Some Bangladeshi sufferers express a longing for death. April 9, 1991 was the first time I heard a Bangladeshi predict her own death; she seemed to be objectively judging her chances of surviving a tumor. The woman was Buji ("older sister," a common way of addressing one's grandmother), the stepmother of Habibur Rahman's cousin Bokul. For days I had heard rumors that she had two very large tumors, one where each hip bone protruded, and that they were feared to be cancerous. During those days I'm sure I heard the voice of a woman moaning rhythmically and melodically, stirring memories of Latifa's *bilāp*, although Latifa had left a week earlier. Everyone I asked denied having heard it. Finally, one evening after eating my dinner, I visited Bokul's house. It was a hot, wind-less night, and the heat and fumes coming from Bokul's kerosene lantern made things worse. He invited me to sit down and have some of the dinner he was still eating, which I politely declined. His wife and his son Salam were there. Buji sat apart from us, to one side of the single-room house.

I said, "I've come to see how Buji is." My words hung in the air through some 30 seconds of silence. Evidently, Buji had not been the center of attention before my entry, and the family had been—at least momentarily—in something like a state of denial. I had changed that. Buji sighed, "Allah" and something like, *kono śānti nāi* (I have no relief/peace). Salam was fanning me—a gesture of hospitality. I asked him to give me the fan, and I began fanning Buji. But this caused a problem—I think that my fanning sent hot kerosene fumes toward her, although what Buji soon complained about was the light that was bothering her eyes. After the lantern was moved from a spot between us to a new spot across the room, I resumed my fanning. It was a frustratingly insignificant gesture, but I could do nothing else. A little later, Buji said:

Example 33. Relief for Buji only in death.

kono śānti pāi nā,   mare jābo
I find no relief;   *I will die.*

Hearing this, Salam and I exchanged awkward glances. No one gave her *śāntanā*, the culturally expected comfort that denies pain, exhorting the sufferer to make her *man* (heartmind) strong against it. Exhortations to forget, to be strong, to steel oneself are conventionally offered to people in distress. But instead of offering Buji *śāntanā*, her stepson and daughter-in-law expressed remorse about their failure to seek treatment for her over the long period of months or years since the tumors had first appeared.

The next day I returned to visit Buji, and had this conversation:

Example 34. Buji's death wish.

J—kāje byasto?
Are you busy working?

B—nā, kāje byasto nā.   mairā jāi. [9]
No, I'm not busy.   *I [want to] die.*

B—owṣadh-bari ānte pāri nā, ṭākār laygge.
I can't [have anyone buy and] bring [home] medicines, for [want of] money.

The grammatical difference between the two days' utterances—*mare jābo* (on April 9) and *mare jāi* (on April 10)—involves tense and mood. Expressing a *belief* or fear that death is imminent, the first is future and indicative. The second utterance is nominally in the present tense, but exemplifies how that tense can be used—in irrealis, subjunctive, or optative constructions—to express a *wish*. We can compare it with the Bangla idiom used when announcing plans to enter or leave someone's social space—*āsi*. Such a verb, in other words, means "I am going" (or, "dying"), but here it *proposes* an act; it warns of an imminent plan.

Buji's *mare jāi* proposes (a desire) to escape her misery. But it probably also solicits something. If it seeks permission to die, the request is likely an ostensible one, in which the speaker's intent is no more directly related to her literal words than is an obviously insincere invitation to an event (Isaacs and Clark 1990). Buji sought something more concrete. It is hard to escape the interpretation that her words are an indirect request. On the one hand, her words imply that she would rather die than be a burden to her family. But she hoped that someone would do what, in fact, her family eventually *did* do—namely, expend

enough resources at least to send her for ostensibly free treatment at the government hospital in Matlab.[10] What is literally a death wish aims to elicit not agreement but support for life and treatment, although it does so indirectly. Buji probably counted on her family to follow Bangla norms and offer *śāntanā*. Naturally,
though, in doing so she took the risk that in their silence, or in their refusal to
underwrite medical treatment, her family might agree with her death wish.

I was so taken aback by her statements about death that I later questioned
Salam and Huda who were copresent with me on at least one of the two occasions. At first, the children reported her speech thus:

> Example 35. Children's echoing of Buji's talk of death.

> bāctām nā,   mārā jetām.
> I won't live, I'm going to die.

In Matlab speech, *bāctām (nā)* carries a future indicative sense (though in standard urban speech it is either past-habitual or present-subjunctive). It is a local
semantic equivalent of Buji's words on the first night, *bācbo nā*, replacing Buji's
slightly more standard idiom with a rural equivalent. But then Salam and Huda
confirmed that on the second day Buji had said *mare jāi*. Just as everyone I had
asked denied having heard Buji's wailing, I believe that the children's tendency
to avoid even repeating Buji's *mare jāi* reflects anxiety about the despair conveyed both by the wailing and by the stark grammar of death wishes.

Perhaps this Bengali practice of self-dramatization is salient enough to be
parodied in local stories similar to, but more pointed than, Jalu's tale of "singing
references" (Example 30). For the events described here, another explanation is
closer at hand. In the weeks following my first conversations with Buji, I believe
my inquiries about her health and her words of despair set off a round of imitations in the compound. That is my interpretation of the self-effacing humor in
the following scenes.[11]

On one occasion, I was bathing at the compound's well when Salam (S) and
Huda (H)—who had been present on April 9 during my first visit to Buji—came
up to me (J). Salam said:

> Example 36. Adolescents playing with the theme of death.

S1	mare gelām!	I have died.
J2	mare gelā? keno?	You [T] have died? Why [do you say that]?
S3	nāk bandho. sardi.	My nose is stopped. [I have a] cold.
S4	śvās nāwan cale nā.	It's impossible to breathe.
H4	mare jāk. tāi nā, Jim bhāi	Let him die. Right, brother Jim?
S5	Huda ḍākāt, tāi ei rakam bale, tāi	Huda is a robber, that's why he talks
S6	nā Jim bhāi?	like that. Right, brother Jim?

On another occasion, when I myself had a bad cold, I experimented with the
newly popular phrase. Rani (who is Buji's sister-in-law) just smiled and said
nothing as she walked away. But the nearby children who had heard me assured
me, "God willing, you won't die but will get better!" These children revealed

some anxiety over the mention of death even in their joking flirtations with the subject: in their substitution of a simple past indicative verb phrase—*mare gelām*—for the optative *mare jāi* (I want to die / let me die), which Buji used on the second day; and in their speedy offer of assurance that death would not take me.

Some gender distinctions break down with advancing age in South Asia, though habits may endure. Thus an elderly woman like Buji is given the latitude to cry or to wish for death, while a young woman like Latifa is not. Actually, my transcripts do not indicate a biological, or even a clear cultural, propensity for women to be more emotionally expressive than men, although it may be true that women perform *bilāp* (melodic, texted weeping) and *bāramāsyo* (an evidently extinct calendrical lament-genre of poetry) more often than men. Men are allowed great freedom to vocalize their somatic distress, to moan, or to complain dramatically. Perhaps only because of their general permission to speak in public, they may complain expansively and with intensity in public—but in unmarked styles rather than texted weeping.

Weeping and death wishes may cooccur. I am sure Buji performed *bilāp*. Ahmed also wept, but his texted lament lacked melody. Buji uttered her death wish in unmarked speech during my visits, and I do not know whether her publicly denied weeping also included such words. I recorded Ahmed's wept speech, including his statement:

> mairā   jāi gā
> I [want to] die!

Though Buji and Ahmed used similar words of despair, the history of suicide among Ahmed's ancestors and his own history of acute psychological disturbance remind us that texts always have dynamic contexts and reflect "what is at stake" (Wikan 1990). Intertextual relations (Bauman and Briggs 1990), in this case the relations between complaints and play-complaints uttered days or months apart, shape how discourse is received. This is as true of the self-dramatizations of sufferers as it is of religious dramas (Briggs and Bauman 1992: 152). In this case, Ahmed's kin hear in his words the echoes of relatives who have committed suicide after months of lamenting the condition he describes as heart illness.

Although I have taken pains to stress that self-dramatization is not exclusively Bengali women's behavior, the use of the tag question in Bonhi's complaint (example 26, chapter 7) fulfills the stereotypes of women's speech mentioned by male Bangla speakers (Indian linguist Probal Dasgupta, personal communication, 1993) and mentioned in relation to English, by Lakoff (1975). Lakoff argued that tag questions epitomize a stance that is unaggressive and thus polite at best—weak at worst. Levinson wrote, rather more neutrally, that tag questions typically function to draw one speaker's turn to an end and open up the floor to, or even select, the next speaker, manifesting a polite commitment to the interactive nature of talk (1983: 47). Eckert and McConnell-Ginet cite evidence that women's tag questions are powerful in their own way (1992: 478). Bonhi's tag (*nā?*) invites a supportive response; it is a rational and effective instrument for attaining her goal. Ahmed's *kọkāno* (moaning) speech also solicits the hearer's sympathy; but, assuming that the stereotypical gender association of tag questions is at least widespread, if not accurate, Ahmed's avoidance of tag questions might be due to their association with a female "voice" (Bakhtin 1981).

In the middle of April 1991, I asked nurses and doctors at the ICDDR,B clinic in Sonargaon about their clinical experiences, practices, or strategies in the face of patients' expressions of despair. My inquiries led them to speculate about two very different pragmatic functions. They said practitioners at times hear patients say something like this:

> Example 37. Clinical coping with patients' attitudes.
>
> > Mare jāit[e]āchi, bācbo nā.
> > I am dying; I will not survive.

Such patients, the clinicians say, just want more medicine. But other sufferers say:

> > Āllāh keno āmāke niye jācche nā
> > Why isn't God taking me?

In the words of the CRL staff, the latter are expressing

> maner dukkho. marte icchā kartāche. kaṣṭo sahyo hacche nā.
> mental pain. They want to die. [Their] suffering is becoming intolerable.

Regardless, the clinical recommendation is the same: The practitioner, far from empathizing, should exhort the patient to give up despair and make the *man* (heartmind) strong or firm. Only in those cases in which the clinician aims to change a complacent patient's behavior and induce compliance with treatment will he or she project a poor prognosis.

In sum, within constraints of gender and age, patients dramatize their suffering to mobilize or motivate positive responses from family or practitioners. Old women like Buji, young adults, and old men sometimes present their complaints with dramatic intensity.

Complaint Conflicts: Sympathy and Cash
As Limited Resources

Complaint interactions are often conflictual in their very nature. That fact is part of the *discursive consciousness* of the people around the Sonargaon bazaar; they talk about complaint interactions as conflicts. But native awareness of discourse practices and structure varies with the salience of the matter in question (Silverstein 1981). While people are discursively aware of the fraternal conflicts over the economic resources indirectly requested through complaints, the second sort of conflict presented below remains outside their awareness. As conversation analysis has long pointed out, the intricate, dancelike structure of conversation—it often breaks down in interethnic encounters (Gumperz 1982; Scollon and Scollon 1982) and many instances of doctor-patient communication (Mishler 1984; Todd and Fisher 1993)—is something that people achieve routinely but cannot describe. This everyday achievement, and even the nature of most failures to achieve conversational coordination, remain part of practical consciousness (Giddens 1984). I turn first to conflicts of which people do speak and, second, to structural tensions in interaction that remain outside their awareness.

In an informal interview I conducted at a teastall one afternoon, the men gathered there forcefully brought home to me the fact that health complaints at home both reflect and instigate conflict. They incite conflict because they represent indirect requests that the family's resources be spent on treatment. A prototypical scenario, as depicted in the teastall interview, involves a younger brother voicing his complaint-as-subtle-request to an older brother. And in fact, before the interview occurred, I had already witnessed two such fraternal interactions. When I first moved into Habibur Rahman's compound, Buji's stepson Bokul showed me the layout of the Baghmar village. As we walked, he described the families living in each compound. His younger brother Milon met us on the path, as he was going toward home and we were walking the other way. After passing us he mentioned offhandedly that his stomach was upset (M= Milon; B= Bokul):

> Example 38. Fraternal complaint interaction number 1: Stomach upset.
>
> Complaint:
>
> | 1M | dupure bhāt khāi[ye]chi ḍāl diye. | At lunch I ate rice with lentils. |
> | 2M | ekhan peṭ [p]hāpā [p]hāpā lāgtāche. | Now my stomach feels swollen up. |
> | 3M | bhamir bhāb hait[e]āche. | There is a "vomity" feeling. |
>
> Response:
>
> | 4B | āmi ki kaitām (kartām)? | What could I say (do)? |
> | 5B | ḍāktārke dekhān. | Show [yourself to] a doctor. |

If we follow the folk analysis offered by the teastall crowd, we take complaints as indirect requests for support or even for money to pay for treatment. In their model, a troubles recipient like Bokul might try to evade the implicit request. But Bokul did not avoid the implicit need for treatment. He brought it to light himself, perhaps as a preemptive strike, and then parried the request for help by leaving the matter of a doctor's visit—and fees—to Milon.

In other cases the brother in the role of complaint recipient, or patron, ignored the other's complaint. One night, Habib and his younger brother, the *Imām* Meherban, sat and talked with me in my room. Habib was talking about his current worry—a pump, one of his primary sources of cash income, needed repair. Meherban interrupted, trying to present his own concern to his elder brother. He said:

Example 39. Fraternal complaint interaction number 2: Interruption and pain.

> M—keman jeno ābār byathā karte ārambho kar[e]che āj.
> Somehow it has begun to hurt again today.

Habib ignored Meherban's attempt to change the topic and kept on talking about his pump—in effect, ensuring the flow of income before he would consider any expenditure.

Other complaints issuing out of fraternal contexts directly invoke relational tension. Around lunchtime, I heard Meherban's usually gentle voice being raised in a somewhat agitated discussion with Habib's wife. The words I caught clearly in his harangue were these:

> Example 40. Fraternal complaint interaction number 3: No peace.
>
> M—kono ra[k]hamer śānti nāi.
> There is no sort of peace. 12

My fieldnotes continue this story:

> Meherban came to my room after dark and I asked him what he had been so upset about. He told me … how he'd stored last year's potatoes in Matlab as seed for this year. Without permission, his younger brother Durim had sold some of those potatoes in the meantime. Meherban said if he'd known his stock of seed potatoes was half gone, he wouldn't have begun to plant this year. Habib knew, but hadn't told him. When Meherban found out, he told Habib he didn't want to plant this year, but Habib had insisted for some reason.13 Meherban went along. Now he says Habib sold or gave away the fertilizer he had expected to use after being talked into planting! It was that event, he said, which touched off his complaint to the "first lady" of the compound (*bāṛir bow*).

Meherban continued (in the gloss of "his" Bangla words written from my memory), now making me his audience:

> From next year I will never again do farm work.
> I want to stay in quietness [literally, live quietly].
> I want [literally, it seems good] to stay somewhat separate.
> I myself know what I must find to satisfy my heartmind.
> He [Habib] doesn't know.

My fieldnotes include this commentary on Meherban's words:

> His frustration seems to illustrate the risks involved in the weak boundaries between [items of] "personal" property if not between persons. This [frustration may be] inherent in living in an extended family—or [in] any intentional community? At any rate, Meherban wants to be more aloof, independent, etc.

If Meherban had known then that several months later, Habib would turn to him and request a sizable loan …

Amina: A Contained Conflict over Access to the Floor

Complaints evoke responses—expressions of concern, laughter, and criticism are all possible. Yet complaints may still be ignored, or others may offer their own complaints. Whereas the echo complaints discussed earlier represent polite offers of empathy, example 41 strikes me as a competition for attention—"[Look at] me, too." Example 4 (in chapter 4) presented an excerpt from the following speech event. In the scene depicted here, Amina and her son Rajib are visiting her parents, Habibur Rahman and Rani. Indeed, hardly a day passed without such a visit: during dinner in Habib's house, Amina and Rajib were frequent guests; the walk from Amina's postmarital virilocal home—her husband's home—took only five minutes. On one such night I recorded the dinner conversation. Amina was recovering from a cold and had a lingering cough. After one racking coughing episode, she complained that her head beat like a drum when she coughed. No one responded. Then she and her son Rajib jockeyed for the floor. On that night we ate together, and that was somewhat unusual, indicating that Amina's husband was probably away from home and that her in-laws did not miss her help much that night. Amina had flulike symptoms during March, and the current Islamic month of daylight fasting was not easy for her.

Example 41. Amina's complaint, Scene 1: Headache.

A = Amina; ?f = unidentifiable female speaker; R = Rajib, Amina's son (Habib and Rani's grandson); M = Amina's mother (Rani); F = Amina's father (Habib); CAPS indicate speakers' emphasis (louder segments)

A	((loud and deep chest cough))	
4A	iś i kāś dile u	Ouch—when I cough
5A	kapālḍā ṭan ṭane[14] othe.	I have a pounding pain in my forehead.
7M	ki? (5) ki āche=	What?! (5) What is it?

Amina is warmly welcomed in her natal home. In her husband's home she is daughter-in-law and worker, and even during visits with her mother, Amina helps with cooking. But in that setting consanguinity—and pride they take in her good marriage, her son, and her earnings as a community health worker—brings in special treatment. She takes the luxury of resting when she feels bad, a privilege that few rural Bengali mothers-in-law give.[15]

In the above lines Amina's cough, interpreted in her subsequent complaint, became the topic of conversation for a time. The cough and her description of the related pain in her head seemed to rivet everyone's attention. Both Amina's niece Khaleja and her mother responded with questions demonstrating concern. Then attention shifted—at least in part—toward a need to shut the window; as this was intended, presumably, to prevent an unhealthful draft from reaching Amina, the topic was still related to Amina's illness. After that shift, her health passed from the topical focus for a few minutes. But later came this exchange:

Example 42. Amina's complaint, Scene 2: Interrupted by her son's cries.

70F	yā /Āllāh/ [16]	Oh God.
71A	/rojā/ ((laughs)) [17]	Fasting—
72A	rojā thāikkā āmār pāwṭi āijjā	Keeping the fast, my leg today
73A	eman bhār [h] ai [ye] che ba[s]iyā thāikkā. (.8)	got so heavy.
74A	pāwṭi ekkebāre e ra[ka]m ((pots banging))	The leg got completely like this.
75A	e ra [ka] mi āch[e].	It's like this.
76M	beśi kare (xx) mes den x kay "NĀ:: !	[I say,] "Put a lot of ointment on it." [She] says, "NO:: !
77M	kon kon pā re." ((banging))	on (which which?) leg?"
78R	ā:::h::. (jathā xxxx)	Ugh!
	[	
79A	Nix	Nix
80A	Nix āche, āmāder?	Do we have any Nix?
	[	
81R	a:::h	a:::h
82A	(x) Nix (xx) ānche.	(?) [Did anyone] bring Nix [home]?
83R	N::H! (1) pāyṭā [18] culkāitāche [19]	NNNH! The leg is itching!
84?f	/(fāni or āpni) KAI [YE] CHILĀ[m] ./ (xx)	/I (or You) SAID .../
85R	/āmi satyi kare kai [ye] chi./ (.4)	/I said it truly. / (.4)
86?f	/āmi kai [ye] chilām je (xxxx) JVAR/	/I said (something about) FEVER/
87R	/a:::::::::::::::::::::::::::::::::::::/	Ow::::::::::::::::::::::::::::::::::::/
88R	(.5) ā::!	Ow!!
89A	((banging pots)) hm?	Hm?
90R	ā::h	Ow!
91?f	(a un ges ?)	(??)
92F	hm?	Hm?
93R	ekkāre peṭ bharā :::	[My] tummy [is] completely stu::::ffed.

In line 72, Amina's physical state returns to the topical foreground. Her words presuppose the rigors of her religious duty, the Muslim fast. I have heard Bangladeshi Muslims speak glowingly of the spiritual depths they attain and the solidarity they enjoy with all those who keep the fast of Ramadan. Others complain, even while mentioning that complaining about the fast is frowned upon; so their complaints are offered to intimates if at all.

New topics—fasting and leg pain—did not completely displace the topic of Amina's flulike symptoms. Although a complete transcription of some of the above lines has proven impossible, it seems that Amina's mother, M, is chiding her in lines 76, 77, and perhaps 86 (the speaker there not being positively identifiable). The words that are clear mark M's discourse as reported speech of the "I told you so" variety. A woman (Amina's mother again?) evidently reports a past conversation about *fever* (line 86) in which Amina rejected her advice (line 76). Now Amina requests medicine, but for her leg pain. She hopes the item has already been purchased. And in a prosperous peasant household like theirs, an item like a jar of Nix (a locally available vapor rub like Vick's) might well be on hand, even though other commonly used but more expensive and perishable medicines such as acetaminophen would not be stored but, rather, would be purchased as the need arose.

From the above transcript we do not learn whether Amina found Nix or any other ointment (line 76). Nor do these lines display quite the same unconditional support from her mother that was evident in lines 1–7 in example 41. And the timing of 7-year-old Rajib's words makes the discomfort of his *pāyḍā* (the leg) a competing claim on Rani's attention. Amina's leg trouble was still in the conversational foreground when suddenly Rajib sought to place *his* leg there, so to speak.

Along with Rajib's entry into the fray came another round of reported speech. Again, overlapping segments of conversation render the tape impossible to transcribe with complete confidence. I therefore restrict my arguments to features distinctly audible. *Kai[ye] chi*, a perfect tense–aspectual realization of the verb *kawā* (say, speak) is repeated in lines 84, 85, and 86. Evidently, Amina and her mother are carrying on the discussion of the advice her mother had given her. But Rajib evidently misunderstands this metacomment as a challenge to his sincerity (*satatā*), which he affirms in line 85 (*satyi ...*). His protest—like Jalu Miah's story about "singing references" (see example 30)—indexes a local discourse about "malingering," about the possibility of questioning the integrity of a complainer or at least a given complaint.

Troubles talk not only proceeds along recognized semiotic paths (such as that from sighing to words) but also helps constitute social structure—filial and sibling relationships and those between borrowers and lenders, women and men, and ethnographer-guests and their hosts.

Dialectics

Social structure is not just reflected, but is produced and contingently reproduced, in the kinds of interaction presented here (Giddens 1984: 179). Pervasive forms of gender hierarchy and gender segregation structure complaint interactions. Because of predictable patterns of segregation, the setting (e.g., rural streets versus the home) influences the gendered participant structure of a given complaint. My corpus reveals interesting patterns in the interactions between gender or setting on the one hand and troubles content and tone of response on the other. Ethnographic detail helps explain the patterns that do emerge, patterns better described as situational rather than pervasive, as emergent rather than determined. In some cases the power of interaction itself to reproduce social relations, or at least shape behaviors at one point in the history of a relationship, came into focus. Here I refer to responses in which politeness reproduces status and social distance. When complaints account for social failures or request help, they not only reproduce patron-client relationships, but also maximize what a client stands to gain therein. Strains on marital bonds, like Latifa's, and on fraternal bonds like that of Habib and Meherban, give rise to troubles. Bengalis do not often explicitly distinguish between the *śānti* (peace, relief, comfort) of fraternal harmony and that of relief from pain.

In a dialectic that is more subtle than essentialist dichotomizations of Western and South Asian selfhood allow us to grasp, Bangladeshi selves-in-interaction—troubles tellers—reach to create and re-create bonds in which their sense of self is embedded. And yet, the manipulation of resources and persons entailed in many complaint interactions points to a negotiative selfhood as familiar to American used-car lots as it is to South Asian bazaars.

9

INTERACTING WITH PRACTITIONERS

Until this point, I have privileged patients' perspectives. Now I must devote some attention to practitioners, their work, and their styles, not only to clarify various Matlab models of the medical interview but also to guard against the tendency to problematize only patients' words and leave unexamined the acts of practitioners. I begin with a domestic scene and shift to institutional settings such as bazaar pharmacies. Changes in the participant structure of complaint interactions accompany such shifts; since public space is men's space, men speak for women at pharmacies.

At the practitioner's shop, interaction proceeds along predictable lines. Homeopaths and Ayurvedic herbalists share common interview procedures with their allopathic *ḍākṭār* colleagues. Their questioning strategies are comparable to those of American physicians, but contrast with the practices of Bangladeshi diviners. While Ayurvedic and biomedical practice share an empirical orientation, diviners reveal problems and only then do they ask patients to confirm their pronouncements. In dialogical/empirical forms of medical practice in Matlab, patients are dominated by "guardians," who accompany them, and by practitioners. Practitioners' power is evident in three ways: They control the interview's topical flow, they manage the creation of meaning and the assigning of labels, and in extreme cases they control the social-situational definition of social actors by effectively ignoring a patient's words and personhood. Despite the differences in practice and medical theory, spiritual healers and diviners share with their empirically oriented colleagues a tendency to dominate patients. I refer to the facility with which they label patients *durbal* (weak). This I experienced most vividly when two practitioners unexpectedly cast me in the patient role. My reflexive analysis of the experience links up with my observations of patients labeled *durbal* by self or practitioner.

The reader may find my treatment of practitioners biased. Therefore, a word about my stance toward this important institution of Bengali culture is appropriate here. I have great respect for the Bangladeshi practitioners I know; I value my friendship with some. I find the gentleness of some exceptional in either a Bangladeshi or an American context. On the other hand, I believe there must be truth in grandfather Ahmed's impression that the departure of Hindu homeopaths and Ayurvedic doctors from Bangladesh in the years since 1947 has hurt the quality of therapeutic care available in rural areas.

Whereas a long anthropological tradition portrays healing rituals as means of social reintegration, I focus on the problematics of medicine, on the conflicts they leave unresolved, on the sense in which they do not heal social wounds but paper over and maintain them (Steedly 1988). This focus is admittedly partial. I sense that some cases of possession and exorcism are venues for remarkable forms of expression by women and means by which some tensions are indeed resolved and relations mended, if only temporarily.[1] These positive cases eluded me, while the encounters I did observe and record seemed inconclusive at best, and antitherapeutic at worst.

It is not individual practitioners who are implicitly critiqued here, but institutionalized medical relations. Practitioners who are at all professional are granted expert status by definition. Their knowledge and words are valued above those of patients, at least when it comes to conclusions involving etiology, prognosis, and prescription. But, just as the natural dominance of parents has pathological forms that compromise the health of the family system and of children (Parsons 1987), so it is with medicine. When practitioners' interruptions prevent the effective disclosure of symptoms, their dominance ceases to have therapeutic value, at least in systems requiring such disclosures from patients. In my opinion, any persuasive or placebo effect of practitioners' charismatic authority (Frank 1963) would in such cases be outweighed by its destructive effects.

To put dominance in context, expectations of hierarchy pervade relationships in South Asia; such expectations affect medical relationships. Still, even in Hindu India, subordinates expect to receive thoughtful and empathic consideration of even their unspoken needs in return for the honor they give superordinates (Roland 1988: 220). Islam in Bangladesh and elsewhere espouses an egalitarian ideology. Thus, while it is true that Bangladeshi patients might be willing to grant doctors more authority than a Western egalitarian ethos would countenance, literary and conversational references to practitioners' violations of the public trust manifest strong notions of reciprocity.[2] Concentration of medical knowledge has not reached high levels in the region; knowledge loosely reflecting the ancient Ayurvedic medical texts is widely shared.

Thus medicine is not alone in reflecting the problematics of power. It often merely reproduces broader relations of dominance. When medical encounters do reproduce gender hierarchy, the results can be disastrous. In a case involving the typical male bias in the triaging of health care in rural Bangladesh, Azahar, who combines Qur'anic exorcism with the prescription of allopathic medications, had made a woman and her baby wait for two hours until he finished treating all of his male patients. When he brought in the woman from the back room—where women wait for him to avoid men's gazes—he and I were shocked to see her emaciated baby. He urged her to immediately take the baby to the nutritional rehabilitation unit of the ICDDR,B's nearby hospital, and I put her on a rickshaw and escorted her there myself. Azahar's advice was good—but he should have given it two hours earlier. The biased triage probably cost the baby's life. In less visible ways, the filtering of all women's complaints through the voices of male guardians (discussed in this chapter) is equally destructive (Sansom's [1982] Australian case notwithstanding). At the very least, it must frequently result in inaccurate diagnosis and mistreatment. A further ground for my sense that Bangladeshi practitioners exercise an aggressive dominance over their patients is my own experience as a patient, particularly my experience of being labeled *durbal* (weak). I do not assume that Bangladeshis find practitioners' dominance offensive in the same way that I do. But even when they show no discursive awareness of their own resistance, some patients do in practice resist medical dominance. Latifa is one patient who experienced treatment itself as abuse. A final caveat: Bangladeshi curative practices reflect a hierarchy that might once have been less destructive. Had I done fieldwork there in a different era, I might well have found a healthier sort of social equilibrium like that envisioned in Parsons's (1987) model of the therapeutic relationship. Inegalitarian relations have, perhaps, become increasingly destructive as foreign models of medical interaction are being imported and as egalitarian ideologies—both Islamic and modernist—have largely failed to modify them. As it is, patients' expectations of egalitarianism are on the rise while practitioners' behavior reflects old and new forms of elitism. Latifa's story exemplifies this pattern.

Illness and Healing: Bangladeshi Models

Practitioners—even diviners—typically refer to those who visit them as *rogī*. Where practitioners differ is in their conceptualizations of and pragmatic responses to *rog* (illness). In this pluralistic system, clients choose the medical tradition best suited to handle a problem as they conceive it. Regardless of the type of treatment they finally get—if any—rural patients conventionally tend to link illness with the cosmos as it is ingested, offended, or otherwise experienced. Many foods have a humoral heating or cooling effect; ingesting them in excess or at the wrong time can upset the body's own balance. Because spirits and living saints—like the lords of Bengal's semifeudal past and all the voices warning women to stay out of public view—are easily offended, people may attribute symptoms of madness to an offended saint or spirit. Finally, diffuse symptoms may be attributed to ill winds and other *ālgā* (loose) things, and the attribution of illness to *ālgā* typically connotes a violation of group norms. Women who are bold enough to venture beyond safe domestic places may be metaphorically "struck" by loose things and loose winds (Blanchet 1984; and see discussion of *ālgā* following example 9, chapter 4).

On occasion, Women do practice healing in Muslim villages and even on the fringes of bazaars like Sonargaon, though their practice is not commercialized. Older women, in particular, practice noncommercial forms of healing, and they seem to do so in almost every compound in Matlab. I had expected that if I found any women practitioners in Bangladesh (and I did), they would conduct "kinder, gentler" consultations than men. That is not the case, and the reason lies in the changing organization of health care in rural Bangladesh. Thus this chapter concludes with a discussion of the social organization of medicine at the local, national, and global levels and of how political economy shapes medicine as well as gender.

Even if we view them as individuals with relatively unique narratives and communicative styles, patients do not communicate in a vacuum but rather, with interlocutors in diverse and stratified contexts. Interlocutors may elicit some complaints—by asking, "How are you?"—and yet may criticize others. Animating such criticisms are folk notions of the language of humans and spirits, as well as literary traditions that include sophisticated and explicit metadiscursive reflections. I take much of what people say about their own and others' speech as ideological. Ideologies refract practice. Thus folk discourse about complaints in Matlab or in Los Angeles is at least one step removed from the speech of patients, let alone their putative aims in complaining. Contrary to what Fabrega (1990: 662) claims for South Asian medicine in his discussion of the cultural specificity of notions surrounding somatization, Bangladeshis do sometimes question the sincerity of particular complaints and impugn the piety of troubles tellers. Examples are documented by Hashemi and Schuler (1992) as well as in this chapter.

In early 1992 old friends in Dhaka told me a story about an adult male relative (L) who had loaned a friend of his the equivalent of $1,500—far more than the average annual income there. I was not surprised to hear that the borrower failed to repay it. L started to visit the debtor (D) every day to ask for his money; even his sympathetic relatives called this "*birakto* (bothering) the debtor." According to my friends, D consulted a *kabirāj*-sorcerer to drive L mad and make him forget the debt. When L did lose his mind, his family sought help through another *kabirāj*. My friends told me how "their" *kabirāj*, a woman, had divined the cause of L's problem without having any normal access to the story of the debt. And she cured him. "Had the debt been repaid?" I asked. They said, "No, L 'forgot' about the debt—but at least he is well again." Bangladeshis describing their visits to healers do not typically mention harmony among neighbors as the desired end, but rather, the restoration of their loved ones. Still, some cures do restore relationships. In the case at hand the result was as much to the liking of D as it was to L's family. Had I pressed L's family, they might have expressed regret that the "restoration" did not include his money, but in telling me L's story, they stressed the return of his sanity as a credit to the practitioner. Certainly, their current satisfaction contrasts with L's pre-*kabirāj* dissatisfaction with his state of affairs and his obsession (as it was locally perceived) with recovering his money.

I bring up this story and stress the multiple perspectives even within this patient's family in order to introduce two questions. The first is that of the commensurability of Bangladeshi encounters I describe with those described in the medical sociolinguistics literature. It is possible to question the validity of considering both sets of encounters under one "medical" rubric. But the cross-cultural similarities are strong. Bangladeshis visit allopathic practitioners for largely the same reasons people visit doctors in industrialized countries—

perhaps to be tested and to receive diagnoses, but certainly to be cured of acute diseases or treated for injuries. Admittedly, Bangladeshis present other practitioners—homeopaths, herbalists, exorcists, diviners and possession-mediums, to name some—with a wider variety of troubles, many of which they would never present to allopaths. *Kabirāji* medicine in Matlab encompasses almost all those varieties of practice. Sick or lost animals, rebellious children, marital problems, or dizziness and confusion might move one to seek out a *kabirāj*. Westerners in various eras have presented problems like those to curers, priests, psychiatrists, and family therapists. Once we grant that medicine has symbolic *and* pragmatic functions in the West and in Bangladesh, the commensurability question loses urgency.

The second question is related to the first: Do Bangladeshi healers treat persons or groups? I raise the question because of Turner's (1964) influence and because of the social dimensions of the case cited above and those described below. Turner claims that returning patients to wholeness may be secondary, or at best, an entailment of the primary function of healing—restoring the equilibrium of social groups. Applied to my data, this may mean one of two things: first, satisfying the kin who arrange and pay for treatment, or second, restoring the patient(s) to harmony with them (and, perhaps, the family to its status in the community). It seems to me that the second outcome is not so common as Turner believed, which has important ramifications. "In more complex social environments ... class-stratified societies, and so forth—there can be no ... a priori assumptions of the therapeutic value, or even the existence, of social and cultural coherence" (Steedly 1988: 841); yet it is social coherence that, according to Turner, healing rituals create. In the illness stories I present, tensions remain between troubles tellers and others even while healing encounters attempt to reaffirm the solidarity between them.

Tracing the movement of a trouble from being mentioned off-the-cuff at home to being presented to a practitioner reveals the alterations to participant structure inherent in that movement. At home—to the extent that it is speech, and not a raw symptom like obvious coughing, that motivates a family to take a woman to a practitioner—a woman can sometimes speak for herself. But when she visits a practitioner in *his* natural setting—which, as public space, is by definition not women's space—a guardian must accompany and often *speak for* her. A postmenopausal mother, or more typically a husband, brother, or father acts as "client" (Bhattacharyya 1986), mediator, or the patient's interpreter (Hasselkus 1992). Such mediation presents problems for both patients and, sometimes, client-mediators; the complexities of participant structures in Bangladeshi illness and healing events require further comment.

Almost all women's visits to practitioners in rural Bangladesh are mediated. In fact, privacy is not expected when the patient is a woman—nor in any psychiatric cases, as Bhattacharyya (1986) reports from West Bengal. Thus, in some cases involving men and in almost all cases involving women, triangles emerge in which a client (a parent, husband, or brother) mediates between practitioner and patient. Although male guardians may have no greater communicative competence than women patients—and are less comfortable in relation to women's bodies than are female guardians (Margaret Leppard, personal communication, 1996)—they often serve as interpreters for the two parties. One sees the translator role of guardians most clearly when they re-present the practitioner's questions to the patient in the intimate idiom of rural Bangla. By intimate forms, I mean not only phonology and grammar that typify rural Matlab Bangla and thus signal solidarity, but also intimate pronouns.[3] Such a grammar indexes extremes in either solidarity or status/power asymmetry. It contrasts with the grammar of face and distance-maintaining constructions used by male practitioners in addressing patients and clients. This intimate language variety constructs a circle of solidarity which, by definition, encompasses kin and excludes practitioners. It imports into the institutional setting a domestic form of interaction; asymmetrical use of intimate pronouns by guardians and the very act of interpreting for women reproduce their domestic status. Bengali women are constructed—partly through speech events like this—as dependent persons, socially and physically weak. Yet, if they are aware of this at all, neither men nor women patients openly resist it; at least one woman hesitated to describe her own symptoms in front of her mother until her mother insisted that she do so. The benign face of protection perpetuates female patients' disenfranchisement, the situation in which others speak for them; we must look in the cracks of discourse for signs of resistance.

The devoicing of women in medical settings is relative. Women who have just delivered babies in the government hospital in Chandpur (the central city of the district in which Matlab is located) are intensely defended by guardians against direct questions by medical staff. By contrast, when both women and men accompany such a woman and the doctors must explain obstetrical procedures, men may become befuddled while the women interact with more confidence. Women in guardian roles play an active role in negotiating treatment decisions. The domain of childbearing is theirs, after all. Still, only men can serve as final *legal* authorities when difficult medical decisions must be made. Their legal responsibility over matters in which they feel quite incompetent places them in what Bangladeshis call a "false position."[4]

Unfortunately, although some of my case studies are longitudinal, the only patient for whom I have recordings both at home and in a medical setting is Buji, whose age places her beyond the need for *parda* and male supervision. I refer to Buji's case and others below.

One of the few spontaneous domestic complaints I was able to record mechanically took place in my field home over dinner. Again I refer to Amina's troubles talk (A = Amina; M = her mother):

Example 43. Amina's complaint at her parents' home, revisited.

1A	((coughs)) iś i kās dile u	Ouch! When I cough
2 A	kapālḍā ṭan ṭane othe.	I have a pounding pain in my forehead.
...		
4 M	KI?! (5) ki āche=	What?! (5) What is it?

No one spoke for Amina here, any more than they could cough for her. She coughed, then complained that the cough made her head ache. My host family tacitly acknowledged the speaker's subjective authority in such events—only she felt the pain; only she could speak authoritatively of it. She offered the initial information and she herself fielded questions about her state. On occasions like this, her interlocutors might offer advice or show concern. Sometimes, noticing symptoms, they can even be said to speak for the complainer. But example 43 exemplifies the role of kin-audiences—listening and asking questions to clarify and show concern. Thus, domestic complaint interactions involve two proto-typical roles—troubles teller and troubles recipient (Jefferson 1981). But if either of Amina's parents, or even her younger brother, were to take her to see Heykal Daktar in town, Amina's visit would probably proceed as Yasmin's or Sufia's did (see example 44).

From Home to Practitioners' Shops

Bangladeshis speak of "showing" practitioners—that is, presenting themselves and showing the problem. Some 9 months before the 50-year-old woman Yas-min "showed the *kabirāj*" in November 1991, she had fallen from the rafters of her home and evidently broken her clavicle. She had already visited many other practitioners and a government hospital, which had taken an x-ray. Yasmin had had several conditions diagnosed, including ulcers and cancer. Her husband's resources exhausted, she had turned to her brother. He had brought her to Ali and would pay Ali's bill. As for *kabirāj* Ali, ICDDR,B staff had pointed me to him in November, and the day of Yasmin's visit to him was the first of three times I spoke with him and observed his practice. Ali's practice—relying on the pulse for diagnosis, conceiving of disease causation in humoral terms, and coun-tering humorally "hot" and "cold" imbalances with dietary interventions—bears an allegiance to Ayurvedic medicine. But his contemporary environment is com-petitive, dominated by cosmopolitan biomedicine. Thus, much of his therapeutic banter with patients like Yasmin aims to assure them, and visitors like me, that his medicine works. He swears that his patent remedies—herbal preparations in what seem to be brown molasses balls 1–2 centimeters in diameter—are the only cures in the world for cancer, gangrene, and *bārzin*.[5] By November, Yasmin was experiencing sleeplessness and digestive failure. She had "showed" the female doctor at the government hospital in Chandpur, too, who had diagnosed the lump in Yasmin's shoulder as a tumor. In the spring of 1992 she died.[6]

Heykal and I had friendly chats almost every time I walked through the So-nargaon bazaar. I observed and made video and audio recordings of a number of his clinical interviews. Unlike Ali, Heykal is a *hāture ḍākṭār*—that is, a "doctor" with an orientation toward cosmopolitan/allopathic medicine, whose training is completely apprenticeship based. Heykal happens to have a high school educa-tion (which, in Bangladesh, means through 10th grade); if anything sets him apart from his neighbors and perhaps even most *hāture ḍākṭār*, it is his public schooling—not formal medical training. Like most *hāture ḍākṭār*, Heykal's simple chamber is located in his own private pharmacy.[7]

In January 1992, Heykal Daktar treated 25-year-old Sufia. She and her family had walked a few miles to see him, and they told Heykal of her lower abdominal pain and of a lump, perhaps in Sufia's uterus. She and her mother conarrated the history, viewing the lump as a residual from her miscarriage. Two months after that consultation, I visited Sufia at her parental home, along with a male and a female field assistant. We played portions of the audio recording of that consultation and asked about her current state and the history of the problem, and about how she and her mother had felt about the interview. Like Heykal, we could not avoid the mediation of her parents; unlike the *ḍākṭār*, we could not fulfill their expectation that we would also provide medical help. Sufia's family told us that her husband had sent her back to her parents after the miscarriage and her later failure to achieve a successful pregnancy and birth.[8] Her family also linked the lump with spirits offended by some behavioral slight— probably by Sufia. Neither issue had come up in their consultation with Heykal. After that visit to her parental home I saw Sufia on one other occasion—in the Sonargaon bazaar, evidently shopping, probably with a guardian nearby.

The juxtaposition of excerpts from transcripts reveals a structural similarity, a shared factor setting these encounters off from domestic complaints. While Amina and others who initiate complaint interactions at home speak for themselves, guardians accompany and speak for Yasmin and Sufia during medical interviews.

Example 44. Clients translating for patients in medical interviews.

A = Ali Kabirāj; Y = Yasmin; SM = Sufia's mother; B = Yasmin's brother; H = Heykal Daktar

Ali K. and Yasmin's Brother	Heykal D. and Sufia's Mother
Practitioner's question:	
1A āpnār ki asubaidā bartamāne dekhā geche? *What sickness has now appeared in you?*	
2A seṭā āpni kan *You tell [me] that.*	
	Practitioner's question:
3A asubidhā. *The problem...*	3H ei ki asubidhā āpnār? *What is your problem here?*
Brother passes the question to patient.	Mother passes the question to patient.
4B ka kon hān theikā tor ki [h]ai[ye]che ka— *Tell what happened from what [in sequence].*	4SM kabi nā? *Won't you [sT] speak?*

Yasmin and Sufia saw different sorts of practitioners. What they do have in common is the mediation of family members who speak for them and interpret for the doctor, as exemplified in lines 4B and 2SM, respectively. That mediating role is reflected in the form and function of the client's speech. In both cases displayed above, clients interpret, translate, or reframe practitioners' questions. Yasmin's brother's idiom is a markedly nonstandard one in comparison with the practitioner's speech (though Ali's first pronunciation of *asubidhā* is also non-standard); we can consider it a translation of Ali's words into an idiom more familiar to Yasmin. And in both cases clients alter pronominal reference from the respectful or distant V used by the practitioners to the demeaning or intimate sub-T.

Insofar as practitioners' language is foreign to their patients—a problem common to many cosmopolitan doctors in South Asia (Hasan 1979; but cf. Sachs 1989)—clients perform a valuable service when their translations are accurate and raise the comfort level of the patient.[9] There are two problems with such a sanguine view of clients as interpreters. The problems reflect two views of patients' communicative competence. First, consider the phenomenon of interpretation in relation to the patient's competence in the realm of *speech reception* (comprehension). A translation is superfluous when a traditional practitioner's speech is close to that of his neighbors, male and female. To interpret construes the young woman patient as one who needs help, not only as a patient but also as a communicator. The second point is related, taking the woman patient's *speech production* as its point of departure. In some cases family members seem to collude in frustrating the efforts of patients to exercise autonomy in explaining their experience to practitioners, even to an exorcist, as in Fatima's case.

One of the rare cases I know of in which a practitioner rejected a mediator involved a tragic clash among parties caring for a dying boy. The ICDDR,B field demography worker assigned to the Sonargaon area informed Faisal and me of a death—a life event within his purview. A 10-year-old boy, Loqman, had died of severe diarrhea. The accompanying blood probably indicated shigellosis. But my ICDDR,B demographer colleague (responsible for entering records for all births and deaths in the area) reported the case to me because of the imputed cause:

Example 45. Why Loqman died.

bhut-e	thāpar mārche.
ghost-ERGATIVE	blow struck
A ghost struck [him].	

The colleague knew me well enough to know this would arouse my interest. Still, Faisal and I waited another day before going to the boy's house. We expressed our condolences. As the family told us what had happened to the boy in their own words—which strongly contrasted with my colleague's report—we shared their grief all the more. They told me how they had taken the boy to a series of practitioners—homeopaths, Heykal Daktar, and another allopathic clinic. They never mentioned having consulted any spiritualist sort of *kabirāj*; in fact, when we asked, they explicitly denied that and said they did not believe Loqman's illness had resulted from a blow struck by a ghost. The blow they described—to their pride—had been delivered by staff at the last clinic, which we shall call the Modern Clinic.

Loqman's family hovered above hunger. Hence his mother could not afford the luxury of *pardā* but worked hard outside all day while the boy's paternal grandmother took care of the children. It was Loqman's grandmother who had taken him to Heykal and to the Modern Clinic. That one or more adults should accompany the sick boy is, of course, the norm at that clinic and throughout Bangladesh. After all he had had severe diarrhea and was losing blood before and after admission. But for some reason, according to Loqman's mother's account, the staff there acted as if only parents were appropriate guardians. Assuming that such was indeed the attitude taken that day, I can only speculate on the reason. Perhaps the Modern Clinic's staff had imbibed some sort of nuclear model of the family from their Western patrons and program administrators. Whatever the explanation, the English gloss of Loqman's mother's story conveys a sense of what is at stake in mediating medical treatment.

Example 46. Modern clinic rejects Loqman's grandmother.

The man insulted my mother-in-law (crying). I told them my mother-in-law has raised him (*lālan pālan kar[e]che*). I am nothing but a wet-nurse. They told my mother-in-law, "*beṭi saro.*" ("Hey, old woman, get out.") They pushed her. We cried.

Practitioners in extremis—for example, those who know that their patient will die and that they might be blamed—may make client-caregivers into scapegoats. I bracket this whole series of events, although each of the various stories I heard has truth in it. What is clear from the family's story is the personal involvement of clients in medical interactions and the potential costs of the mediator role, although the risks are normally low and outweighed by benefits. Put in the coldest terms, while in the exceptional case mediators lose face, their authority is typically enhanced as practitioners attend to *their* accounts with as much seriousness as patients' self-reports.

I have already lamented my lack of longitudinal data on individuals recorded across a variety of settings, particularly home and clinic. The exception is Buji's case, which I introduced in the previous chapter. Buji was, on most days (barring the darkest times of morbid hopelessness), an exceptionally engaging woman. Not only at the hospital to which her family finally took her, but also at home, her communicative style—full of saucy, spirited teasing—stood out in my experience. She was living with her stepsons in Habib's compound and was worried about two tumors that had appeared on her waist earlier that spring (1992). I recorded her as she spoke with her junior coresidents, with another grandson (Latifa's brother, a *ḍākṭār*, who actually attempted to surgically remove her tumors himself), and with staff at the Matlab government hospital. When I visited her at the hospital, she had been there about three weeks. A government doctor there had removed one tumor soon after she was admitted, and then she stayed on, awaiting the removal of her second tumor. Present with Buji during my videotaping at the hospital were her sister and niece. I recorded two encounters that Buji had with the male hospital staff. In the first, an orderly, or attendant, asked her how she was. To do so, he cut off the talk of Buji's sister, treating it as irrelevant.

Minutes after she spoke with the orderly, someone told Buji she could see the doctor. She had to walk downstairs from her hospital bed to his office and wait while he attended to several others. Finally, he turned directly to Buji to announce that she was to go home with her wound well dressed and a prescription in hand, to recover completely, and then return for the second operation. Her sister and niece joined her in voicing mild objections to the plan. When Buji asked, "Must I come back this far again?" I think she was expressing a preference to stay and finish treatment as quickly as possible. What is salient about the four-party interaction—the doctor with Buji's party of three—was the confidence of the women and how the doctor unpretentiously entered into their joking. They told him he was heartless. He laughed, but went on to explain the need for the first wound to heal. They negotiated a date for her return. Then the doctor asked Buji who her companions were, thus drawing attention to what otherwise passes as normal, the presence of kin-clients when a woman visits the doctor. Buji answered, and the consultation ended.

As Buji's troubles talk moved to the hospital, her communication became somewhat more instrumental. Both in her utterances and in those of her practitioners, activity-centered topics pertaining to treatment replaced her diffuse expressions of despair. As the cast of interlocutors changed, Buji's focus changed from death wishes (described in the previous chapter) to the date of her next surgery. The change reflects both the participant structure of the speech events and the way treatment at the hospital seemed to invest the future with a positive importance in her perspective.

Troubles talk may follow a predictable trajectory as it crosses contexts. It is generally at home that persons first utter complaints, some of which will be referred to practitioners. They generally speak for themselves, and those who control family finances evaluate the seriousness of the illness—typically weighing most heavily its effect on the patient's ability to work. (None of these steps is purely objective. Since patients know their ability to work is being observed, conscious or unconscious manipulation of the sick role is a possibility.) Family members accompany those patients who are construed as incompetent or needing protection, help, or supervision. In such cases they play the mediating role of client. Adult men who visit practitioners generally go alone—if they are conscious. In most cases where the patient is a man—in the absence of researchers like myself or apprentice practitioners like the 18-year-old boys who help Heykal Daktar—no client mediates the interview or speaks for them. Institutional settings move communication from an affective-expressive to an instrumental mode. But as participants accompany women from home to hospital, modes of communication may move with them.

Comparing Practitioners' Interview Styles

An extremely broad range of practitioner types makes Bangladesh a *locus classicus* of medical pluralism. Many distinct types of practice fall under the Matlab term *kabirāji*. The *kabirāj* is, loosely, a traditional healer. But his or her lore may include herbal treatment, Ayurveda, and spiritual therapy (chiefly exorcism). And the *kabirāj* is only one among many types of practitioners, even in Matlab, where the term covers several categories lexically distinguished in other parts of Bangladesh. My hypothesis is that the homogeneity in the ways that these diverse Matlab practitioners interview patients is a recent phenomenon with a cause linked with changes in the political economy. The commercialization of healing coincides with the hegemony of interview models that reflect their technological and foreign origin in biomedicine. Thus, despite the pluralism in concepts of the body and disease and in approaches to treatment, I find little divergence, among a rather broad range of practitioners, in interview style. My sense is that *kabirāj* consultations have conformed with the increasingly dominant model of the biomedical interview (as have Tahitian ethnomedical encounters; Clark 1993). Still, I will point out small linguistic differences corresponding with the divergent systems of medicine. Waitzkin (1991) describes what American M.D.s are trained to get (quickly!) from their patients: a chief complaint, the present illness, past history, family history, social history, review of the body's systems, a physical examination, and the planning of other investigations, such as what tests are to be ordered. All these lead to a diagnosis and therapeutic plan.

These conventional interview-examination categories address domains of information that the doctor should discover. Yet transcripts like the following present not domains of information or motivations to seek it, but questions and answers in real interactions. Still, we can see in the medical consultations transcribed here that both sorts of practitioners do ask introductory questions that elicit "chief complaints" and "present illnesses." Though Ali's herbal remedies reflect the influence of Ayurveda, and Heykal's medicines and his practice are cosmopolitan-allopathic, their questions are remarkably similar. (Punctuation in this transcript, as in others, reflects intonation, not grammar.)

Example 47. Practitioners with divergent theories but similar questions.

A = Ali; H = Heykal; Y = Yasmin; M = mother.

Ali Kabirāj		Heykal Dāktār	
1A	āpnār ki asubidhā bartamāne dekhā geche. *What sickness has now appeared in you.*	3H	(Repeating earlier answer and going on) biś paciś batsar, ei ki asubidhā āpnār.

		[She's] 20–25 years ... <u>what's</u> <u>your</u> <u>problem</u> here.
2-3A	seṭā āpni kan. asubidhā. *You tell [me] that. The problem...*	5H ki asubidhā balun. *Tell [me], What [is the]* *problem.*
	(After a gap, the patient eventually says...)	(After a gap, the client eventually says...)
11Y	(nāiyer gol di[ye]che xxxx) cakkar (dāne hetāre) ba[s]iyā rai[ye]che. (1). *A mass sits just underneath the* *navel*	10M lāge (nān) cāgār[10] matan ār ki. (2). *It seems like a mass or* *something.*

Both *ḍākṭār* and *kabirāj* ask their patients an open-ended question that elicits information relevant to two categories—the chief complaint and the present illness. Any distinction between those would seem irrelevant to their practices. The Hindu *ḍākṭār* Krishna's opening question differs little from that of his Muslim neighbor/competitor Heykal—or from Ali's. Any noticeable difference in the example is stylistic.

Example 48. Two practitioners: Meandering informality versus fluent competence.

	Ali Kabirāj	Krishna Daktar
1A	āpnār ki asubidhā bartamāne dekhā geche? **What sickness has now appeared** **in you?**	
2K	seṭā āpni kan. *You tell (me) that.*	1K ki, asubidhāṭā ki, kan. *What. What is the problem. Tell me.*
3K	asubidhā. *The problem...*	

The stylistic difference between the *ḍākṭārs* and *kabirāj*—one congruent with my observation of many interviews conducted by the *ḍākṭārs* and several by Ali—is that the *ḍākṭārs* move more rapidly toward the information sought. This fits the pattern I have observed, that cosmopolitan practitioners see more patients per day, and spend much less time with each, than do *kabirāj*. Thus the relative fluency of both Krishna and Heykal—completing in one abrupt utterance what the relatively less direct Ali repeats and stretches over three lines—bespeaks their more hurried and competent self-presentation. Ali has time and takes it, and his relatively meandering and nonstandard speech creates little distance between himself and his patients.

Again comparing Ali's questions with those of Krishna Daktar, we find a nearly identical concern to take a history. But differences in linguistic form correspond with differences in social status and theoretical orientation. It is typical for exorcists and other traditional practitioners in South Asia to resemble their neighbors and clients in language and education even if their ritual or socio-economic status differs (Hasan 1979: 181; Kapferer 1991). The difference to which I called attention above was a matter of fluency or, perhaps more accurately, directness—a trait associated with both impoliteness and modernity in a number of speech communities (Rosaldo 1972; Brown and Levinson 1986). Another dimension of contrast is standardization—conformity to a standard variety of language promulgated in the national media. Ali's speech typifies the informal register of Matlab Bangla—for example, the eliding of medial consonants like /t/. Phonological and grammatical similarities between Ali's speech and that of his clients help create solidarity, whereas the slightly more standardized speech of the *ḍākṭār* helps maintain a social distance between relatively educated practitioners and their patients. Practitioners' speech is not homogeneous. Thus the question asked by Ali is less standard than that of his more cosmopolitan counterpart, Krishna (example 49).

Example 49. Two practitioners' questions.

Kabirāj Ali (A) and his Patient, Yasmin (Y)	Krishna Daktar (K) and his Client, Sufia's Mother (M)
22Y buk pāt, / *liver*/... *Chest (or, breast),* /liver.../	13K śowan (4) kato din jābat byathāḍā *Lie down. (4). How long has* *the pain been [going on].*
23A /ācchā/ eḍā kay din jābat e? /*OK,*/ *how* long *have you* *had this in all?*	(1.5)
24Y āj e na mās, hacche *It's been nine months* *today.*	14M āijke das bāro din geche ei rog *(1.5) [Counting back from] today,* *10–12 days of this sickness have* *passed.*

Krishna's speech is relatively careful, complete, explicit, and in conformity with the Calcutta-Dhaka grammatical standard. Such speech would not typify Matlab patients. The distance between the speech of practitioners and that of patients varies, partly because the degree of explicitness in practitioners' speech styles varies. Note that this explicitness ought not be confused with wordiness, indirection, or expansive informality—quite the contrary. Example 50, a display of the history-eliciting questions of the three practitioners, shows a continuum of explicitness, or specificity; as you read from left to right, specificity increases—as does sociolinguistic distance from the patient.

Example 50. Explicitness in three practitioners' questions.

Ali Kabirāj	Heykal Daktar	Krishna Daktar
/ācchā/ eḍā kay din jābat e? /*OK*/, *how long has* this *been going on?*	kato din ei abasthā *How long [has] this* situation *[been in* *existence]?*	kato -din jābat byathā-dā *How long [has]* this pain *been going on?*

Krishna's reference to pain is more explicit than Heykal's mention of "this situation," which in turn is more explicit than Ali's "this." But, rather than taking the class status of these men as determining their speech styles, we can simply take explicitness as a strategy for projecting technical competence and maintaining professional distance. Such a strategy reflects a postmodern situation, a sort of medical pluralism in which modernist-cosmopolitan biomedical discourses exert an influence even on *kabirāji* practice.

As I begin to examine the power or dominance that practitioners exercise over their patients, I should note the relevance of the differences just described. It may be the case that the expert knowledge of any practitioner makes him or her dominant over the patient. But there are important variations in styles of practice. The crisp, measured, rational competence of the biomedical practitioners constructs one sort of authority with links to the global market and to cosmopolitan biomedicine. While power is equally manifested in traditional healing practices, it takes quite a different form there. Traditional practitioners, maintaining at least a show of reliance on the authority of ancient ideas with once-unchallenged currency, treat clients more gently. Their interruptions are judicious. Their ability to impress lies less in flashy efficacy than in links to a whole cultural system that still carries much weight in Matlab.

Outside the Dialogical Pattern: Divination

The consultations described in this section cannot be called interviews in any sense comparable to the biomedical interview, as they reflect epistemologies that differ markedly from empiricism. I will describe divination first, then turn to palmistry, and finally, to the spiritual preceptorship of a fakir.

As I have pointed out, there are relatively slight differences between the interviewing approaches of the empirical-dialogical practitioners. This reflects an increasing similarity at an ideological level. In the framework established by Sudhir Kakar (1991: 31), who divides forms of medicine less along modern-traditional lines than along the crosscutting fissure between the empirical and the "arational," even the Ayurvedic practice of Ali is a form of rational, empirical medicine, even "bio" medicine. Cosmopolitan biomedicine, as well as other empiricist forms of medicine *seeks accounts from patients*. Not so with the diviner Delwar Kari. Though a patient or a client may take physical ailments to a diviner, as to a *ḍāktār*, the diviner does not ask about symptoms—he *announces* them. Delwar may give *owṣadh* (medications) or *tābiz* (from the Arabic word *ta'wiz*, amulets)—but only after uncovering the roots of the personal problem in the social and spiritual world.

I observed or recorded a dozen divinations on four occasions by Delwar Kari, whose practice is located quite far from Sonargaon but is close to the town of Matlab. The title *kārī/qārī* bestows an air of Islamic respectability by indicating (with an uncertain degree of truth) an ability to recite the Qur'an faultlessly—but also knowledge of Islamic lore. The ritual use of the signs of literacy, such as the ink of copied Qur'anic verses and the letters of personal names and the number values to which they conventionally correspond, is common to the divination and exorcism practiced in other Muslim societies. Delwar Kari's pro-cedure is stereotyped to the point of rigidity. His clients come into his chambers. He asks them to state the name of the *rogī* (patient), then he asks the patient's mother's name.[11] These names he transforms into their numerological values. Comparing those with a paradigm of values and symptoms, he divines the prob-lem and its underlying cause. Problems may be mood shifts or diarrhea, but the cause is always the same. Whoever presents a problem is told that someone has conspired against the client or the *rogī*, planting a series of *tābiz* against them. (*Tābiz* refers both to protective amulets and to items and acts used in sorcery.) Delwar thus divines the presence of aggressive, harmful *tābiz*.

The two columns in the following example contrast the practitioners' inter-active styles, demonstrating that—despite superficial similarities—the diviner's and the *ḍāktār's* questions seek totally different sorts of information. The diviner wants only two names. On the basis of the names, the *śarīlerabasthā* (body's state) is divined and announced. The return to a questioning mode in Delwar's line 4.29 bears no functional relation to Heykal's question in his line 5.

Example 51. The place of questions in divination and in empirical medicine.

Delwar Kari, Diviner (Case 4)		Heykal Daktar	
4.2D	āmnār nām karbo? *Shall I do your name?*	1H	bayas kato? *How old [is the patient]?*
4.5D	āmnār mā [e]r nām? *Your mother's name?*	3H	[Repeating parents' answer and going on] biś paciś batsar, ei ki asubidhā āpnār? *[She's] 20-25 years—what's your problem here?*
	((*A gap of several minutes, during which the name–numerological divination is calculated...*))	5H	ki asubidhā balun. *Tell [me] what [is the] problem.*
	[*The revelatory "diagnosis" begins with the following line:*]		(*S's mother speaks in 6–9...then*)
4.10D	Shahinā-ke ei tin bār jāduṭanā karā hay. *Shahina has been cursed several times.*	10M	lāge (nān) cāgār matan ār ki. (2). *It feels like a mass or something.*
4.29D	āpnār śarīlerabasthā ki ei? *Is this your physical condition?*		

A glance at the first lines (4.2D and 1H) indicates that both consultations begin with questions from the practitioner. But whereas Heykal's question serves biomedical information-gathering purposes regarding reproductive functioning, Delwar's question elicits the names of the patient and the patient's mother for the sake of his numerological divination. While Delwar *divines* the problem, Heykal *asks* what it is in line 5. And while Heykal's client and patient disclose the problem to him, Delwar assumes his revelations are accurate. Only after his formalized declaration does he ask the client—who is typically not the patient—for confirmation of that accuracy (line 4.29D).

What about taking a history? The diviner effectively dispenses with that. There are always temporal references in the divinatory formula. In fact, in one of the dozen cases of Delwar's divination that I recorded, perhaps when his guard slipped, he (D) let a client (the patient's mother, M) fill in some missing information during a pointed pause. By contrast, the authority of Krishna Daktar does not consist of any divinatory gift but, rather, in his ability to manipulate the discourse and the material of bioscience. When there is a need for Krishna (K) to know more than his patient (P) tells him in line 14, the *ḍāktār* can only ask a follow-up question (line 15K).

Example 52. Declaration versus information-gathering in divination and empirical medicine.

Delwar Kari (case 6)		Krishna Daktar	
6.5D	e byāpāre bigato *This matter [began]*	13K	śowan (4). kato din jābat byathāḍā? Lie down. (4) How long in all [have you had] the pain?
6.6M	pāc mās *five months*	14P	(1.5) āijke daś bāro din (1.5) [It has been] twelve days [as of] today.
6.7D	[Kari divines extra timing details of which the client is unaware] pāc mās cār din āg theke *Five months, four days ago.*	15K	āge chilo? *Has this happened before?*

Example 52 makes apparent the contrasting theories of knowledge, the ideologies of medical discourse held by the two practitioners. Line 6.6M, the point at which the client (the patient's mother, M) fills in a temporal detail, is a glitch rather than an acknowledged part of the divinatory method. Granted, Delwar paused slightly—perhaps this was an invitation to fill in the gaps in his revealed knowledge, but an invitation he could easily deny in a pinch. By contrast, Krishna's patient's statement in line 14P was overtly solicited.

If we conceive of therapeutic modalities along a continuum in which "talking cures" (Showalter 1985: 156), or logotherapies, form one pole, diviners represent the opposite extreme. As practiced by the three men I have observed, divination involves a silent manipulation of objects or numbers. Although religious divination is always semiotic in nature,[12] it is usually embedded in interaction, and is sometimes interpretable as a form of interactive psychotherapy.[13] The logic of divination necessitates a distancing from human intention and intervention (DuBois 1987).

Those who seek Delwar Kari must know, by his reputation, that he will construe their presenting complaint as a *durghaṭanā* (misfortune) resulting from *jādutana* (sorcery). The attribution of illness and other problems to object-intrusion, witchcraft, and sorcery is widespread enough to be called universal (Wallace 1966: 114). Tensions in a community find expression in witchcraft and sorcery beliefs in Bangladesh and elsewhere. South Asian societies as diverse as ethnic Tibetans in Nepal (Desjarlais 1992: 53) and Bengalis in Bangladesh share a common idiom for describing sorcery attacks: *bān* (arrows). Bengalis are said to attack each other by <u>striking</u> or stabbing with arrows (*bān* <u>*mārā*</u>). A sorcerer's *tābiz* finds its way into strategic places, as Delwar's divination ritual reveals. Delwar's large clientele indicates that the willingness to attribute hostile inten-tions to one's neighbors is very widespread in Matlab. His divinations turn up conspiratorial sorcery by small mixed-sex groups, some with fair skin—a desirable attribute that might arouse jealousy or even be associated with aggressive self-pride. Sorcery follows enmity. It may result from conflict over signs of wealth and may aim to disrupt an impending marriage or destroy one's reputa-tion. It attacks the psychosocial balance of individuals and creates disharmony in families. While *jādutanā* is distinct from the threat of things *ālgā*—"loose" things like jinns and the evil eye—the former can exacerbate problems caused by the latter, and Delwar often mentions both.

To the extent that the client sitting with Delwar in fact refrains from reveal-ing the problem, his divinations are projections, sensitive readings of personal and societal cues. Actually Delwar's clients interrupt if he errs, and in various ways they participate in the declaring of his findings, as when the patient's mother revealed a temporal detail. But in comparison with the patients of other practitioners, they are passive. Clients expect those who manage spiritual realms—for example, Delwar Kari, Bozlu Pagla (presented below), or a possession-medium like Shefali—to have supernatural access to knowledge. They have the ability to lay bare the secrets of one's domestic and personal life. What this tradition grants them, in contrast with empiricism, is the right to assign labels without reference to idiosyncratic history, personality, or behavior. Delwar no doubt draws on an encyclopedic knowledge of the people of his area and tailors his pronouncements to them. It is precisely because the natural paths of knowledge to which he has access are, however, kept from conscious view (Wilce 1996, 1997) that his stereotyped divinatory diagnoses are authoritative in constructing social reality.

Most of this diviner's patients—that is, those who fall victim to sorcery—are women, though most of the clients who present their troubles are men. Women patients, if told they are somatically weak, will confirm the diagnosis, which he invites all his clients to do. Hence, divination is one among many ideological avenues through which Bangladeshi women are represented as weak, through which their structural weakness is naturalized. Delwar also attributes nervousness and indecisiveness to females. But such forms of *durbalatā* (weak-ness) do not preclude the appearance of dark faces (*kālo mukh*) indicative of hot, angry heartminds or mentalities (*garam man-mānasikatā*). The three symptoms that Delwar ascribes to every patient in my sample are a burning sensation (*jvālā porā*), pain (*byathā*), and a *mejāj* (mood, temper) that *garam haiyā othe* (literally, "becoming hot, rises up"). Anyone can have a hot temper. But it was one of his nonpresent female patients—all between the ages of 15 and 35—whose mood swings (literally, "two faces in one month—one dark, one clear") he construed as a symptom. That would seem to imply either that women are expected to moderate their emotional expressions or that their failure to do so is more salient than men's.

Since all of the 12 divinations I watched Delwar perform followed causal scripts or schemata (Nuckolls 1992) and thus tended to repeat themselves,[14] I present his schematic structure, in the second column, along with the text and the gloss. Column 2 categories in brackets describe speech acts that were a part of Delwar's other divinations but not of this one. For instance, the column 2 entry beside line 2.14 indicates the absence of a frequent item in his disclosures—the influence of something *ālgā* (loose) in addition to the influence of the several *tābiz*. Column 2 categories that are underlined are unusual or unique to one divination. Capitalized words are louder, or vocally stressed.

Example 53. A complete transcript of a consultation with Delwar Kari.

Line	Interactive Move/Content	Text	Gloss
2.1	rogī̃ s address	Matlab thānā-e, Durgapur grāme,	In the Matlab village of Durgapur
2.2	name and sex	Mansurā Khātuner ekṭi meye	Mansura Khatun has a daughter
2.3C	repair	Salfinā, Salfinā khātun.	Salfina, Salfina Khatun.
2.4K	self-repair	ei to. Salfinā khātun, arufe Putul.	Yes, that. Salfina khātun, called "Putul."
2.5	False start [15]	ei meyer-o,	This girl has also—
2.6	Opening summary: x has been cursed	ei meyeṭike-o kayekbār jādutanā karā hay.	This girl has been cursed several times.
2.7	History/duration	bartamāne, duy mās āge,	Two months ago—
2.8	Response and [identification of sorcerers]	tāhār bibāho bandho rākhār janno,	in order to put a stop to her marriage [plans]—
2.9	Sorcerers' motivation [Spirit factors]	śatrutā mulak,	out of enmity
2.10	Total number of tābiz	pāṇcṭi tābij karā hay.	five tābiz were placed.
2.11	First set of tābiz: [Location in inanimate matter]	ekṭā tābij āche?	One tābiz is [there (location unspecified)]?
2.12	2d set: fed to victim	ār ekṭā tābiz tāke khāwāno haiyāche?	Another tābiz was fed to her.
2.13	3d set: sent by breath	ār ekṭā tābij furā diyāchen?	[A respect-marked 3d person] blew another tābiz [sending it on the wind]?
2.14	4th set: fed to dog [Non-tābiz (ālgā)]	ār duyṭi tābij KUKURKE khāwāno hay.	And two tābiz were fed to the dog.

2.15	Symptoms: set one: burning sensation	ihār dārā-e, tār jvālā poṛā-o kare?	Hence it feels like she is burning?
2.16	Set two: pain	chinchiniyā kare byathā kare?	It hurts like prickling pain,
2.17	Set three: "Heated" mood	mejāj garam haiye oṭhe?	the mood rises up hot?—
2.18	Idiosyncratic, non-specific, psychological symptoms, psycho-social deviance	eki māse cehārā duy rakam haiyā jāy.	In one month her countenance turns two ways.
2.19	(elaborating 2.18)	ekbār kālo hay? ābār pariṣkār hay.	Once it is black, then it is white/clear.
2.20	Sorcerers' motive	bibāho bandho rākhār janno ei durghaṭanā karen.	[A respect-marked 3d person] brought about this misfortune to stop [her] marriage.
2.21	Duration (repeated)	ei ghaṭanā duy mās āge Durgāpur grāme,	This event [occurred] two months ago in the village of Durgāpur.
2.22	Victim's Islamic name and mother's name	Mansurā Khātuner beṭi Salfinā Khātun	It was done to Mansura Khatun's daughter Salfina khātun,
2.23	Victim's nickname	arufe Putule Putulke karā haiyāche.	(also known as Putul).

In the two lines below, Delwar (D) breaks the divination frame with his client (C), asking him a question:

224D	Confirmation-Question	ṭhik ni ho?	Right, isn't it?
225C	Confirmation-Response	hm	Mhm.

Line 2.17 is common to all of Delwar's divinations. But line 2.18 fills the "slot" in Delwar's script reserved for idiosyncratic features—in this case, the problem of emotional lability. Other than her gender, I know nothing about her, nor do I know whether Delwar was acquainted with her. So I don't know why he makes the attribution to this patient. Practitioners like Delwar play as much of a reflective and constructive role in the conceptualization of persons, selves, and bodies as they do in the nosological, or diagnostic, system of Bengali ethno-medicine. Delwar's power shows in his sensitive invocation of subvariants within his schema. Not everyone who visits him hears the same presentation. One slot in particular within his schematic declarations is filled with variable symptoms—if not idiosyncratic, at least varying in a patterned way from divina-tion to divination. In this slot he aggregates symptoms with psychosocial roots into constellations comparable to syndromes in Western medicine. The set of problems ascribed to one woman patient—tingling pain in the abdomen (perhaps referring to twitching or even cramping), somatic weakness, arm and leg twitches, disturbed eating and elimination, and nervousness along with the symptoms Delwar always recites—parallels the "neurasthenia" of earlier

European and contemporary Chinese sufferers (Kleinman 1986). Contrast that with what Delwar divined for a male: Delwar uncovered how he tended to misconstrue kind words ("If you say something nice, he takes it the opposite way"); the patient's abdominal pain was not said to tingle. (Perhaps the tingling he divines in female abdomens is linked with the Bangladeshi male tendency to project sexual desire onto women.)

Divination, then, contrasts sharply with styles of practice that do not hide their dialogical nature. Dialogue, specifically the contribution of clients in the declaration of illness, is a repressed reality within divination. Given the minimal role allotted to clients, interruption and other assertions of power by the practitioner are irrelevant within divinatory practice. Nonetheless, divination certainly occasions powerful moments in the social construction of persons. Divination performs that function by projecting symptoms onto patients. Divination is not alone in that regard. Spiritual preceptors, palm readers, and astrologers also project *durbalatā* (weakness) onto their clientele.

Astro-Palmists, Saints, and Other Esoteric Healers

My analysis of divination encounters uncovers patterns in the social construction of weakness. Besides diviners, Bangladesh has other practitioners whose concepts of troubles and therapy appeal to forces beyond the natural sciences. Like diviners, they claim to have esoteric sorts of knowledge linking the cosmos and the heart. And such claims of knowledge class their work, along with psychiatry, as "tinkering trades" (Goffman 1961) whose privileged access to the mind makes them vulnerable to the criticism that they "make people crazy" (as Karim's father [see the front matter] said of many fakirs, "saints," and spiritual "healers" in Bangladesh). In what follows, I consider the relative truths of that and less-jaundiced perspectives on these Bangladeshi therapies.

Compared to diviners, palm readers, astrologers, exorcists, and fakirs are a bit more dialogical in style. On some of the evenings I spent in Dhaka after arriving in Bangladesh in October 1991, I saw two shops that displayed intriguing signs showing a raised human palm. Having read Pugh's (1983) analysis of astrology in India as a therapeutic modality, I thought it worthwhile to investigate. The sign on one of the Dhaka shops reads, "Professor Hawlader, *jyotiṣī*" (astrologer; *jyotiṣī* in Bangladesh almost invariably practice palmistry as well as astrology).[16] So, inside the shop, the professor says to me, "Let me see your palm." I stretch my right hand across the table compliantly. He manipulates my palm, squeezing it in various ways to make certain lines prominent. This goes on for about two minutes. "You have a very unstable mind, flexible, constantly changing. This means you have a lot of anxiety all the time. You're never quite sure ... But you have a very creative mind. This line here is your mental creativity. And [looking at which line on my palm?] you are adaptable, very able to mix with people in different situations."

I have referred to divination as a cross between projection and sensitive

observation. So, too, with astro-palmistry, though I would stress here the element of projection. Whatever validity there might have been in his declaration of
my instability, the professor needs to impute some sort of weakness to me as
part of creating the need for his services. That is all the more evident in my
interaction with another practitioner, Bozlu. I consider Bozlu, like the agnostic
Hawlader, a soul doctor and counselor; but—unlike Hawlader—Bozlu is certainly a believer.

During my first days in the Matlab area, the ICDDR,B staff helped me meet
a variety of *kabirāj* and other traditional practitioners. Among them was Bozlu,
who was known as a *fakir*—a spiritual preceptor—or *pāgalā* (ecstatic, "divinely
mad"; McDaniel 1989). He has attracted disciples, and the public presents him
with their illnesses—or weaknesses—on occasion. Actually, few people seek
treatment from him; like Professor Hawlader, he blends palmistry and astrology
with the selling of gems for their value in a kind of "fate therapy." Both men—
the "professor," through a book describing his methods, and Bozlu in an interview with me—foregrounded the role of gems. The *Pāgalā* said that selling them
is his primary livelihood, as it is for other such fakirs.

Bozlu was responsible for my most intense experience in the Bengali
"patient" role. It is through him that I have gained the most insight into the
sensibilities (Desjarlais 1992) evoked by labeling a patient *durbal*. I have mentioned how Delwar ascribes weakness (nervousness, indecisiveness) to women
patients. In the case of diviners, exorcists, and holy men like Jahangir, Delwar,
and Bozlu, whose diagnoses are sometimes made without the explicit disclosure
of symptoms by their patients, the constructedness of "weakness" becomes
salient (Wilce 1997).

One of the first things Bozlu mentioned to me during our initial meeting in
October 1991 was his chronic cough. Like other noncommercial healers I met,
Bozlu is a "wounded healer"; he apparently has severe asthma. He says no medicines touch his cough; nevertheless, he notes that, "We have a *tarikā* [in Arabic,
a *tariqā*, "path," such as one of the Sufi orders and its lore] and through its spiritual procedures, I get some relief. That's my only medicine."[17]

I had been asking him questions, particularly about his *tarikā*, when he
turned the tables on me—the first of many times he did so. The questioner's role
is, after all, a powerful one; questioners control conversational topic (Paget
1993). After seeking permission to ask me something, Bozlu queried whether I
knew what might lie ahead on my path. And, more important, did I have the
absolute confidence that I could face it? It was not until I was about to leave that
he revealed the full import of the question. But gradually it became clear that he
claimed a spiritual-mental resource that I did not have, that I was ill-prepared to
face certain contingencies. He mentioned that I was *durbal* (weak) in some
sense. Linking that diagnosis with his particular version of Sufi concepts of
personhood and its ideal path of spiritual development, Bozlu the following
comments:

Example 54. The healer Bozlu compares himself with the ethnographer.

B = Bozlu; J = Jim

B—āmi āmār mājhe āchi.	I am within myself [self-contained?]
āpni āpnār mājhe nan.	You are not within yourself.
J—āmi āmār mājhe nā ? āmi kothāy ?	I'm not within myself? Where am I?
B—āpni pratyeker maddhye āchen.	You are within everyone else.
Ph.D. śeṣ kare āpni takhan āpñar	When you finish your Ph.D., then you
mājhe haben.	will be within yourself.
ekhan kintu āpni anner buddhite āchen.	But now you are within others' wisdom.
Professor-rā, ICDDR,B , āmār theke...	Your professors, ICDDR,B, me ...
anner kāche āpnāke bikri karechen.	You have sold yourself to others'
	wisdom.

I was embarrassed; it was hard to deny his insight—or his aggressive directness! It was only the second time we had ever met. (All of my Dhaka friends to whom I later mentioned Bozlu's words expressed some indignant surprise at the invidiousness of his comparison. Seeing how his comments had rankled me, perhaps my friends and surrogate parents in Dhaka simply wanted to offer me support.)

More and more of what Bozlu meant about my weakness and unpreparedness for future disasters leaked out as our meeting drew to a close. The asthmatic Bozlu explained, "If you breathe from the lungs, you'll have no strength. But if you breathe from your diaphragm, then strength will reside in your body." We left his house and walked together to the riverside, from where I would take a country boat to my temporary room at the ICDDR,B hospital's guesthouse. Outside the stall where we shared one last cup of tea, he took my right hand in his firmly and closed his eyes for about 45 seconds. To facilitate my comparison between his words and those of Hawladar (cited above), I have juxtaposed them here:

Example 55. Attribution of weakness by two esoteric practitioners.

Astro-Palmist (Hawlader)	Fakir (Bozlu)
	Ah, … I can perceive that your body
	is good, healthy…
You have a very unstable mind,	but you are weak in the heartmind.
flexible, constantly changing.	Because of this heartmind's weakness,
This means you have a lot of anxiety	sometimes the body also trembles.
all the time.	If you had strength in your heartmind,
You're never quite sure...	no bodily *pīṛā* could remain.

Among other definitions for *pīṛā*, Mitra's dictionary lists "pain, distress, affliction, sorrow, suffering; a disease, sickness, illness, an ailment" (1924: 968). Such a polysemous term is an apt one for the fakir's nondualistic conception of trouble in the heartmind and body—the *durbalatā* in my social status, perceptible in my palm.

Before I got on a country boat along with a few others to cross to Matlab on the other shore, Bozlu explained more of what it was that he had to offer his disciples. He did so by using me as an example of those who need his path: "When you are at ICDDR,B, you are well, you are at peace. But if you went out on the road and were in an accident, wouldn't you lose consciousness?" Unperturbed by the thought of becoming *ajñān* (phonetically, *Og:æn*, unconscious), I said, "Yes, so?" He said, "I have the authority to resist becoming *senseless* (here he used English). I asked, "Even in an accident?" "Yes," he said, "I have that authority. That is actually my best secret, that is my work." I led him on: "With medicine?" "No." "By *dhikr* (a breathing-chanting technique)?" I wondered. "That's only one part of it. You have to work at it."

Obviously this was esoteric knowledge he wasn't about to reveal immediately. But I was getting an idea of what he had to offer people, so I sought confirmation of my new understanding: "So it seems many have this fear that they might lose their *jñāna* [phonetically, *gæn*] and they come to you?" "They do." I found it remarkable that people would have such a fear of losing consciousness that even after severe trauma, they would seek to retain conscious control of self even at the risk of enduring greater pain. This must represent an important value as well as an important culturally conditioned phobia. Valuing the control of self is part of the aesthetics of everyday life in northern South Asia (Desjarlais 1992: 76–78). That value motivates Bozlu's neighbors to come and sit at his feet, to learn the esoteric disciplines, to keep unconsciousness at bay at all costs.

Now, looking back at the encounters with Bozlu and Hawlader, I wonder how accurate my impression was that they were waging a campaign against my self-confidence. What if I *am* deficient in terms of the defense mechanisms that Bengalis construct to control themselves and handle negative affect? Men explicitly say that women are not capable of controlling themselves. When I met the "professor" and the "*pāgalā*," I was indeed emotionally vulnerable. My homesickness, my depression, my grief for what I had temporarily lost—all these were evident. Perhaps rather than just wanting to feel one up on me, they were noticing a lowering of my defenses, indirectly warning me that I was not strong in the way Bengalis make themselves strong, that from their perspective I was risking evil results by continuing to feel sad (Wikan 1990).

Whatever truth there may be in this interpretation, I still believe that Bozlu and Hawlader treated me as they treat clients. Whether we consider their actions as designed to reveal to me areas of my *durbalatā* or, in effect, to *create* it by disturbing my sense of equilibrium, they must strive to create in others the need for their services. This exemplifies their active role in the reproduction of Bengali concepts of the self and in the self-awareness and self-monitoring of Bengalis.

Global and Local Factors in the Sociology of
Bangladeshi Medicine

Channels of cosmopolitan influence on rural biomedicine in Bangladesh are
multiplex. Preventive and maternal-child health programs are often funded from
abroad. That is the case in what I have called the Modern Clinic in Sonargaon,
part of an organization whose top-level management personnel were, in 1992–
96, expatriates in Bangladesh. People in mid-level management—Bangladeshis
and expatriates—all have foreign Ph.D.s. But more significant than the national
origin of staff and funding is the bioscientific model under which they operate—
one that gives mixed results. On the one hand, the Modern Clinic's backers have
spawned research and interventions from which many individuals—including
myself—and organizations have benefited in terms of health and scientific
understanding. On the other hand, the very strengths of the model contribute to
its flawed bedside manner, as seen at the Modern Clinic in Sonargaon. The fault
lies with the model and the culture-specific hierarchies into which it plays, not
with the staff.

Due to the range of problems they treat and to their worldview and methods,
other healing practices in Matlab would scarcely be recognized as medicine by
American physicians. Nevertheless, I have shown here the existence of striking
parallels between disparate modes of practice—in interview style. I attribute the
convergence to two factors: shared goals and diffusion-assimilation. Along with
other classical forms of medicine, as practiced in Egypt, Greece, and early
Islamicate cities (Hodgson 1974), Ayurveda shares a fundamental empiricism
aimed at deducing materialistic causality from empirical signs or symptoms. Although modern Western medicine has recent historic roots in the Enlightenment,
the empiricisms of these medicines are homologous. Cosmopolitan biomedicine
penetrated all of South Asia with the help of British policies in the colonial era,
and its hegemony continues to grow, with pharmaceuticals as its vanguard.
Closely following it are interview methods facilitating a rapid decision as to
which of the new drugs to sell the patient. The prestige and governmental support enjoyed by biomedicine warrants the interpretation that even its particular
form of empiricism—manifested in its interview style—has influenced indige-
nous practices. But the argument from similarity of goals is more parsimonious.
Patterns of hierarchy that predate but are, admittedly, given new shape by European influence also impact medical practices. I have highlighted the mediating
role that kinsmen play in women's visits to practitioners, as well as practitioners' control over the "floor," over interpretive and labeling processes, and
ultimately over the constitution of patients as person-subjects or nonpersons/
objects. Whatever the roots of these patterns and their relation to dominant
modes of subsistence,[18] the results are clear—women and the mentally disturbed
(such as Farhad, example 58, chapter 10) lose the right to construct their own
accounts.[19] Vulnerable persons thus become vulnerable to further loss of
personhood.

If I subsume gender organization and the distribution of health and healing under the political economy, it is not because I follow a crassly materialist social theory. I do not believe that a reified thing called "the political economy" sits atop a pyramid of influence with complaint behavior at the bottom. Rather, I follow Bourdieu (1977) and Urban (1996) in describing social and linguistic relations as exchanges, while maintaining a dialectic focus on culturally specific relations between the material basis of those exchanges and their ideological representation. For instance, Bangladeshi household economies traffic in forms of symbolic capital akin to the "currency" that Bourdieu finds in North Africa—family honor epitomized by women's shame and their submission to men's control. Therefore, it is of great importance for the Bangladeshi rural middle classes—the landless poor cannot afford *parda*—that not even sickness occasions any exercise of autonomy by women, such as an opportunity to represent their own lives and complaints to a male doctor in the bazaar. A violation of this would constitute a squandering of symbolic capital. It would translate into material loss for a family through the later need to pay a higher dowry when giving its women in marriage than would otherwise have been the case. Hence complaints and rights of self-representation fit into a give-and-take that also includes commodities.

Sociolinguistic Links, Discourse Levels,
and Styles of Practice

Phonology and lexical choices (e.g., pronoun use) in complaints are sensitive to sociolinguistic contexts. But we also see evidence of the sensitivity of troubles tellers to changing contexts of situation at higher levels of discourse, such as shifts from an affective to a predominantly instrumental mode. It is here, beyond the sentence level, that the most socially significant patterning of linguistic usage is seen. We find telling sociolinguistic links in discourse patterns involving multiple turns at talk and in the unfolding of complete illness narratives. So I have dwelt on how complaints move toward increasing specificity, and how context is related to the tone of communication; the next chapter highlights how practitioners and guardians interrupt patients. This ought not be misconstrued as an affirmation that context is a given (Goodwin and Heritage 1990: 284, 285). In most cases, it is true, pharmacy- or hospital-based activities dominated by *ḍākṭār*s unfold predictably. Thus, talk is instrumental, the body is treated atomistically as a repository of so many separate sick or healthy organs, and psychosocial factors are as out of place as are speech forms like weeping or yelling. But, just as physicians who disclose their own experiences with pain or disabilities create a therapeutic intersubjectivity with their patients (Toombs 1992) and positively affect patient satisfaction (Putnam and Stiles 1993), so assertive patients can change, rather than reproduce the hierarchical model of the practitioner-patient relationship, transforming the context. To some extent, Buji and her sisters, by teasing Buji's doctor and laughing with him, created a context that more closely resembled family conversation than the common model of Bangladeshi medical consultations.

It is in these higher-level discourse patterns that I find evidence of the role of complaint interactions in the social construction and reproduction of emotional bonds and relations of power. Struggling to get by and to get better, troubles tellers in such interactions do the best they can. Far from being passive participants in hierarchies or being unmotivated by their personal troubles, Bangladeshi individuals do what they can to optimize such relationships, to make even their weakness a strength. And, even at moments when healers seem most clearly to participate in the cultural construction of women and others as weak, their therapies are not Machiavellian ploys. Rather, as I argued vis-à-vis Bozlu Pagla in this chapter, the labeling and treating of weakness reproduces modes of affect control or suppression, and the healer's conscience is probably clear when they help the weak to recover their guard (Wilce 1997).

In most of this book I intentionally maintain a patient-centered focus, but I have stepped out of that frame in this chapter for several reasons. First, "institutionalized" healing lies just outside, and helps define, everyday interactions. That is, actors know that everyday troubles reports may move families to resort to practitioners. Such knowledge is among the factors that make everyday complaining the occasion of conflict—the potential for resource expenditures makes elders skeptical of complaints as potential requests. Buji's troubles talk, for example, moved from its domestic stage—in which her expressions of despair speak in part to the knowledge that her illness may necessitate expenditures—to a hospital.

Second, institutional settings for troubles talk are sites for its most systematic development. Complaints at pharmacies are frequent, ordered, and even stereotyped. Third, it is in such interactions that we also find the most systematic evidence of the challenges that troubles tellers face. The next chapter documents moves (especially interruptive moves) that are sometimes made by troubles recipients at home but are clearest in the more hierarchical relationship between patients and practitioners. In relating to female patients, practitioners play a role analogous to that of male guardians. But practitioner dominance is more consistent than that of guardian-clients, who—like Loqman's family—may also be subjected to a practitioner's power display.

This chapter organizes styles of practice dichotomously, comparing those that elicit a patient history with those, like divination and palm reading, that ostensibly discover and present to the patient his or her history by nonlinguistic means. The latter sorts of practice can and do claim a hoary tradition within and outside South Asia. Delwar Kari follows a script that attributes most problems to sorcery and thus "uncovers" (and constructs) the social tensions in which Bengalis live. In problematizing mood changes and anger—particularly for women, who constitute the majority of the patients whose cases clients bring him—Delwar also reproduces cultural models of emotion and gender that help make a *sustained* critique of medical relations by female patients "unthinkable" (Bourdieu 1977b: 170). This helps us understand the reaction to Latifa's performances. Yet it is true that even those spiritual practitioners who rendered me *durbal* did so in good faith (p. 173), probably seeing themselves as shoring up those whose defenses have grown thin. Still, the fact that we find evidence of dominant behavior in these nondialogical therapies seems to require an explanation of medical dominance that goes beyond discursive form. It is not the sex of the practitioners but rather cultural models of gender and power relations—as well as global influences—that explain how male (or female) practitioners are allowed to threaten patients' face with impunity.[20]

A social structure may outlive the individuals who enact it, but they are not mere pawns in it. In the next chapter, I will turn to patients' resistance—through metacomplaints—to the structure of complaint interactions.

10

METACOMPLAINTS: CONFLICT, RESISTANCE, AND METACOMMUNICATION

Months after falling from the rafters above her single-room house, Yasmin came to Ali, the Ayurvedic *kabirāj*. About five minutes into the consultation, Yasmin turned to a new facet of her trouble, asserting, "I hadn't told you that; I haven't told the half of it!" A bit later as Yasmin began to express despair, Ali cut her off. Before she could finish saying, "My life is beginning to come undone," he stepped in to ask, "Then your appetite and thirst are weak?"

One finds in Bangladeshi medical encounters a pattern in which the right to tell one's own troubles is contested and accommodation between patients and their interlocutors is tenuous. The transcripts analyzed in this chapter illustrate Briggs's claim that "discourse is not simply *talk about* conflict and accommodation—it *embodies* them" (1992: 356). Illness interactions reflect and construct relations between patients, kin, and practitioners in their sociocultural context. This chapter makes three specific and interrelated points. First, illness interactions in the rural Matlab area of Bangladesh are often adversarial, as they can be in Western countries. Patients' talk disturbs and moves others. It may point to conflict external to the medical situation as much as it points to symptoms. But medical encounters themselves always involve negotiation and often fail to resolve discord. Conflict internal to Matlab medical encounters centers not only on explanatory models of the illness but also on the right to speak (cf. Lazarus 1988). Both kin and practitioners often prevent the sick person from telling what the trouble is, and patients sometimes resist such limitations, albeit nonconfrontationally, via "metacomplaints." Even if the patient *can* express the problem, fresh contention arises over its implications. Conflicts that appear specific to a given case or set of actors reflect broader patterns of social relations in Bangladesh and also the global flow of ideas, products, and power.

The second point is that critical sociolinguistic analyses of medical relationships, particularly practitioner-patient communication, should be extended to traditional medical settings in poor countries. Some explorations of Western medical encounters have focused on the conversational enactment of power, but fine-grained discourse analysis has been consistently missing from the ethnography of non-Western medical encounters.[1] Few besides Frake (1964) have applied linguistic tools to non-Western medical events. This division of the world and of academic labor creates the impression that only Western patients speak powerfully and that only non-Western practitioners act symbolically. I describe here how Matlab patients clash with *kabirājes*, but especially with family members and *ḍāktārs*, the local practitioners of biomedicine. Although some traditional practitioners in Matlab allow patients more time to develop their stories than their biomedical counterparts do, *kabirāj* Ali cut off his patient Yasmin at the most sensitive point of her narration. Thus we find cases across a spectrum of Bangladeshi medical encounters in which patients struggle to find their voices or make them heard.

Third, I stress that Bangladeshi patients—like other Bangladeshis—are not passive before powerful individuals (practitioners, males, etc.), but rather, engage them, challenging or setting limits on their dominance. Through their complaints ("Something is wrong") and metacomplaints ("I can't tell you my troubles"), some patients bring social contradictions to light. "Patients," both in functionalist grammar and in medical encounters, are objects of the actions of "agents." Patients may indeed be dominated in the social relations of medicine, but they take active roles in conflict nonetheless. This chapter's account of the agency of patients in Bangladesh contributes to the literature on "resistance in everyday social relations in South Asia" (Haynes and Prakash 1992).

Four transcripts illustrate these arguments. The fact that three of the four selected patients are women reflects their overrepresentation in the ranks of the silenced, the interrupted, and the misconstrued. The four persons saw three practitioners, and kin participated in three of the recorded encounters. All four had trouble with their troubles talk. In their encounters and in several others analyzed previously in this book, someone—not necessarily the patient—called attention to a snag in the communication of another, primary-level trouble or complaint. Two of these four patients make what I call metacomplaints, pointing to a higher-level trouble with their troubles-telling encounter. Like fissures appearing after an earthquake, communicative troubles betray social-structural fault lines. Although defensive and repressive reactions from listeners may inhibit a full expression of their illness narrations, they do not always silence sufferers but in fact may occasion metacomplaints. Metacomplaints, exemplifying the reflexive capacities of actors and of language itself, construct theoretical understandings of medical encounters useful to participants and to us.

Presenting primary-level complaints to practitioners appears high on the "job description" of patients. I use the term "patients" here for two reasons. First, the four persons selected were called *rogī* (patients) because of varying combinations of self-description, reputation, and treatment-seeking behavior. But second, I use the term here to deliberately invoke its use in biomedicine's understanding of clinical encounters. There has been much discussion—at least among social scientists of medicine and psychiatry—of how patients' complaints correspond with illness and disease (Good and Good 1981; Ware 1992; Waitzkin 1991). Biomedicine treats pathologies as objective entities and complaints as one audible sign along the road to diagnosis to be balanced by objective—often *visible*—test results. Physicians do not assume a simple correspondence between presenting complaints and the pathology to be diagnosed; this is especially true of psychiatrists. There is, nonetheless, a naive realism inherent in biomedicine's reification of complaints as well as disease entities. When complaining is objec- tified as complaints/symptoms, troubles telling as an interactive process is lost to view.

The three women and one man discussed here were referred to as *rogī* (patients). Two of them voice metacomplaints of the "I can't tell" variety. In one case a doctor dismisses his patient's complaint, and in the last we see the kind of conflict of interpretations that motivates metacomplaints. Metacomplaints, as comments on the conversation at hand, simultaneously index the social situation. The four interactions are heterogeneous in form and focus; problems and block- ages vary with the lives in which they are embedded. Yet the patients all face one common obstacle to voicing their complaints: suppression, typically through interruption. In three of the four situations, it is a male who interrupts. Practi- tioners and kin typically interrupt patients, though sometimes patients also inter- rupt practitioners. In each event, participants contest the right to represent illness and its social context.

I now present four persons' encounters with practitioners, with Farhad's story being the only one introduced for the first time in this chapter: *Fatima* is a middle-aged woman for whom an exorcist was called to treat transient losses of speech and consciousness. *Yasmin* is a middle-aged woman with a painful lump above her breast. *Sufia* is a young woman who sees a doctor for complications following a miscarriage. *Farhad* is a young man complaining of diarrhea, who is dismissed by the doctor as "brainless."

Fatima's encounter (example 14, chapter 5) and Yasmin's and Sufia's en- counters (related below), are arranged in three columns. In the first column, line numbers are given and speakers are identified by the first letter of their names. The next two columns present speakers' utterances, with the second column being assigned to the patient and the third to her interlocutors—particularly, the practitioner. In Fatima's encounter, line 1J actually indicates the 25th line of a transcript, the rest of which is available in my files; J designates the exorcist, Jahangir. The second column contains not only the patient's words but also the words of those who speak for her or "duet" with her (Falk 1979). The columns thus become a means of representing roles played. In this manner I visually distinguish speakers who at least momentarily speak on the patient's behalf from those who are clearly not taking her role—including some who, at other times, did so. Jahangir's role as interviewer-exorcist sets him apart as the prototypical "other" for Fatima, and I therefore place all of his utterances in the third column. Some actors play alternating roles, and their comments are therefore placed in different columns according to the stance exhibited in a particular turn at talk.

Fatima, Her Sisters-in-Law, and an Exorcist

Fatima was introduced in chapters 4 and 5 as the woman periodically beset by a *bobā* (a spirit of speechlessness); she was a self compromised by "something loose." The complete transcript of her abortive exorcism interview with Jahangir revealed the linguistic alternatives to pronominal self-indexing that characterizes Fatima's symptom narration (see example 9 in chapter 4 and example 14 in chapter 5).

Within the cacophony typifying a multiparty conversation, Fatima tries to present a coherent view of her mysterious symptoms. Fatima's sisters-in-law sometimes supportively "duet with" her, but they also interrupt her with ridicule. In that sense, we cannot hold Fatima solely responsible for not being able to speak—note her frequent metacomplaining refrain, *kait[e] ām[i] [p]āri nā* (I can't say). Nor can we map subjection-domination directly onto female and male or patient and practitioner. We may take Fatima's metacomment, "I can't tell you anything more" (example 14, line 23) not only as an attempt to involve others in the coconstruction of her talk, as I argued in chapter 5, but also as a protest conveyed (albeit indirectly) to her superiors—the wives of her husband's elder brothers. Jahangir usually presents himself as concerned only with Fatima's version, resisting the attempts of the other women to play a role in the interview he is conducting; thus his elicitation of their opinions (line 49) comes as something of a surprise. But at several points, Jahangir invites Fatima to continue her story. At times she begins to speak fluently, but then—as if struggling to create a new language for her embodied distress (Scarry 1985)—she bogs down in the attempt. She tries to say something about her "whole body" (see example 14, lines 6, 10, 22, 41). But beyond the verb *kāippā* (trembling; line 10), she is at a loss to predicate much about her *state*. She lets line 21 dangle with the indirect question, "How I feel …"—which, I have argued, might invite "scaffolding," help in constructing her narrative. In line 26, she says she "can't say" what happens, because she loses consciousness[2]—as if her inability to describe her experience somehow needs to be justified.

When Fatima repeats the theme "I can't say" in line 52, it indicates that she is unable to decide which of two diagnoses fits her better. A contingent diagnosis of spirit illness brought the exorcist to the scene, but now she proposes another—*durbalatā*. Although what is labeled "weakness" in Matlab may refer to social vulnerability or inadvisable emotional transparency (see chapter 9), Fatima offers it—and Jahangir accepts it—as a materialist alternative to the hypothesis of *ālgār āsar* (the influence of something loose or wild). It has the advantage of limiting the problem to a tangible domain such as nutrition but the disadvantage of calling for a long-term increase in consumption beyond Fatima's means (see line 85). Jahangir's nutritional advice in fact fails to come to grips with her family's economic status. Her husband, still alive in 1992, was selling his labor by the day, and her son cannot help her. Stratification within the compound renders Fatima's status marginal. Her sisters-in-law seemed vigorous and assertive beside her.[3]

The other diagnosis floated in this conversation—"loose/wild influence"—captures the mysteriousness of Fatima's incompletely described experience. In the local schema, the "influence" diagnosis calls for exorcism, which might have seemed more within Fatima's reach than long-term nutritional change.[4] But in line 52, she displayed ambivalence toward talk of "loose" things; reasons for this emerged in follow-up interviews. Among the symptoms that Jahangir failed to elicit were episodes of speechlessness that lasted for days at a time. It is the story of this symptom that helps us understand why Fatima was disappointed when the exorcist left her with the diagnosis of "weakness" and the suggestion that she eat better. Her ambivalence toward the two diagnoses reflected her feelings toward the moral implications of *ālgā* and the economic implications of anemia.

Moral implications include more than the fact that spirits attack women who violate *pardā*. The talk of *ālgā*/spirits brought to mind what Fatima associated with the world of spirits—a very particular transgression and a lost opportunity. She and her family regard her speechlessness—and perhaps her dizziness and other somatic symptoms—as the results of violating a taboo on disclosing her secret visitor, apparently a spirit. Because she told of him, her spirit-*ālim* (Muslim cleric) became a *bobā*, a spirit of speechlessness.

Fatima was not experiencing mutism at the times of my visits in 1991–92 (whereas they were again reported, along with fainting, in 1996), but even in 1992 her family considered her physical symptoms to be part of the yet unre-solved spirit-sickness. Of the four speakers presented in this chapter, Fatima performs the most complex metacommunication. The life history she conarrates with her sisters-in-law is peppered with the words "can't say";[5] chiefly, she can't say which diagnosis—something loose or weakness due to a poor diet—is the more likely. *Kawā* (speaking; more often here, *not* speaking) appears at three levels in that story. First, the *ālim* forbade her to speak of him. Then, when she told her secret, her experience of him/it was transformed. Finally, as *bobā*, his influence upon her prevented her from saying anything. This can be construed as the revenge of the *ālim*. The *ālim-bobā* can also be interpreted as the idiom in which Fatima indicates the gender of the power that silences her again and again. Once burned (punished for speaking about her spirit-*ālim* visitor), she is twice cautious about speaking. For Fatima, speaking—particularly in reference to her own condition and its ambiguous relationship to the realm of the mysteri-ous—has become problematic. Her own self-reports to the exorcist and eth-nographer are as weak as her own words indicate—"I can't say ..."

Yasmin, Her Brother, and the Herbalist Ali

I said at the outset of this chapter that I would reveal asymmetries of power and knowledge in practitioner-patient relations. I indicated there that American medical sociology has provided linguistic evidence of such asymmetries and that I would provide homologous evidence. Even when real asymmetries of power are at work, patients are agents rather than victims to be blamed or excused (Todd 1993; Todd Fisher 1993). Yet, as other medical sociolinguists have found, I also find evidence of domination in the asymmetrical control of conversational topic by practitioners. Yasmin's case exemplifies these tendencies.

By the time 50-year-old Yasmin showed Ali the lump near her clavicle in November 1991, she had suffered for at least nine months, "showing" a variety

of practitioners. Now she sat in Ali's little shop. She complained of pain radiat-
ing from the clavicle through one whole side of her body and also of insomnia
and a complete loss of appetite. But such a summary fails—as did Ali's feedback—to capture the force and lived significance of each symptom exposition
(Putnam and Stiles 1993; Good 1994) and the difficulty of the dialogue through
which each symptom emerged (Gumperz 1982; West 1984).

In their consultation in November of 1991, Ali first asked Yasmin to tell
him her problem. As if she hasn't understood his question, her brother "trans-
lates" it, urging her, with intimate/condescending second-person forms, to narrate the problem. She then begins to describe her pains in detail (in lines 1–47),
but her brother steps in and adds details on the root or *usilā* ([source of] the
influence) of the problem (lines 48–64).[6] When Ali asks about her pain (line 67),
who else but Yasmin can put it into words (Scarry 1985)?

In the following interchange, Yasmin tries to move from the instrumental to
the affective, to change the topic to express her anxiety about her worsening
condition. Perhaps it was important to her to share that anxiety. In the transcript,
kabirāj Ali cuts her off from developing her theme.

Example 56. Yasmin's metacomplaint.

Y = Yasmin, client; A = Ali, practitioner; B = Yasmin's brother

Line	Yasmin	Yasmin's Interlocutors
65Y	rāit /kairā/ *At night–*	
66B		/ei fulā di[ye]che/ āḍḍiḍa[7] bhāiṅā geche, bhāiṅā geche. *This swelled up; the bone's broken,* *it's broken.*
67A		ācchā, eiḍār bhit[a]re byathā-bedanā āche kichu ? *Mhm, is there any pain inside this place?*
68Y	ha, rāt din. *Yes—night and day!*	
69Y	**ghum jāite pāri nā, (a[k]han)** **kai ni to, ardhek kathā kai nei.** *I can't get to sleep—I haven't* *told you yet, I haven't told* *the half of it.*	

In lines 70–90, Yasmin distinguishes several aspects of her pain and explains
why it keeps her from sleeping. She summarizes her desperate state in lines 91–
94, to which Ali's response (line 95) seems to be an anxious return to procedures
that comfort him rather than his patient:

91Y ay māt[h]āo laiyā sinsine bāge
sāge laiye jāy.
The tingling pain in that[8] head
splits it in half.

92Y   an ār śānti nāi kono ra[k]hami.
       There is no longer any sort of
       relief [or "peace"].

93x   ((someone coughs))

94Y   **eḍār laiggāo śānti nāi heḍār**
       laiggā śānti /nāi/.
       There is no relief from this, no
       relief from this.

95A   to āpner jibbāḍā ekṭu de[k]hān āmāre (5).
                                           So, please [V] show me your tongue. (5)

In lines 96–105 the two discuss Yasmin's problems with digestion and elimination. Just as she concluded her turn in 91–94 with a general statement of her
despair, so line 110 gives Yasmin's interpretation of the seriousness of her
trouble with food, expressed in 107–109.

106A   ācchā khāwā dāwā-e āmnār
                                           asubidhā kare ki ?
                                           Hmm, does eating cause you
                                           trouble?

107Y   asubidhā āche nā? buk tirāś lāge nā ?
       Isn't there trouble? Isn't my
       chest/throat dry?

108Y   āndājer upare jāni dugā dugā diyā ṭheillā
       bahe ṭheillā.
       By guessing [how much I can tolerate]
       I force down little bites.

109Y   bhār kairā ṭheillā ṭheillā khāwā (the[k]he
       barābaillā).
       I shove it right down [my own throat].

110Y   **āmār to jiban-o mocon[9] ārambho**
       /[h]ailo/.
       My life is beginning to come undone.

111A   **/khidā tiśnā/ kam?**
                                           Your appetite and thirst are
                                           weak?

112Y   khidā ekk[eb]āre nāi. *I have no*
       appetite at all.

Yasmin herself eloquently characterizes her struggle to tell the whole story:
"I haven't told the half of it yet!" (line 69).[10] She has had at least spotty opportunities to speak in lines 1–68, but line 69 bespeaks Yasmin's anxiety that she
might not finish her story. It exemplifies the balance of indirection and assertiveness that is Yasmin's adaptation to her conversational environment. It is a
metacomment that leaves unstated the reason she has not been able to "tell half
of it"—her interlocutors won't let her. For them to take a turn at talk while she is
pausing is one thing. But—before and after line 69—Yasmin's brother and the
herbalist interrupt her as she is responding to a question, listing things, and beginning an important theme.

Their most striking interruption follows her disturbing and perceptive remark in line 110: "My life has begun to come undone." Before she could finish
uttering those words, Ali stepped in to ask, "Then your appetite and thirst are
weak?" (line 111). With that, he shifted the mode of conversation from the
affective—Yasmin's choice—back to the instrumental by returning to one of his
routine questions. To be fair, Ali's question in line 111 was a tentative summary
of Yasmin's words, and in line 112 she confirms he has the gist. But his summary ("no appetite?") misses Yasmin's affective tone and trivializes her life-
and-death struggle. It is true that concern over her appetite loss is widespread in
the household context, as well as in that of folk medicine (Nichter 1981: 382).
Moreover, practitioners and other listeners expressed to me in interviews the
belief that they have an obligation not to empathize with, but to fight, feelings of
despair.

It is also true that a practitioner, even one who has as few patients as Ali
seems to have, cannot let one go on talking forever. The day of Yasmin's visit,
he spent about 30 minutes with her even when there was another woman in the
same room waiting for a follow-up consultation. Cutting off the development of
some themes in an illness narrative is the prerogative of the practitioner, and
which topic he cuts off might reflect his sense of a relative lack of competence
in that area. But the interruptions here reveal a pattern that compromises the
narrative authority of the patient. And, though Ali may well have had the most
benign and culturally legitimate of motives, the very fact that Yasmin keeps on
trying to tell her own story indicates that Ali's interruption of her journey into
despair is unwelcome. In a purely individualistic psychological model, Yasmin
should be allowed to journey to the *other side* of her despair. That model would
be foreign to Matlab, as well as to some forms of psychotherapy in the United
States that countenance interruptions "to preempt the clients from verbally
painting themselves into an unhelpful corner" (Gale 1991: 43). This particular
interruption of Yasmin is one of the sites at which Bangla medical discourse
contributes to the construction of Bengali persons. Ali indeed halts a flight into
subjectivity and psychologizing discourse. As a cultural value this cannot be
judged. On the other hand, insofar as Yasmin's words were an alarm signal just
months before she died, Ali failed her by ignoring it.

Thus, two desires, two situated notions of therapeutic speech, clash here.
The patient is keen to express a fear that she is dying, while the healer believes
he must ward off all signs of despair. Yasmin's brother's willingness to spend
time and money for her must be recognized. And the motivation of the practitioner and kin for suppressing Yasmin's words is, if at all conscious, benign. But
there is no doubt that, at some level, Yasmin's eloquent representation of her
inner world threatens the world crafted by men like her brother and the herbalist.
They cut off the rhetorical line she is pursuing before the threat can take mature
form.

My Bangla-speaking consultants regard the clarity, volume, and sheer
persistence of Yasmin's speech as remarkably assertive for a Bengali woman.
Probably it was her persistence that had persuaded her brother to spend a little

more money to see Ali that day, rather than give up after hearing the grim diagnosis of several other practitioners. Perhaps that persistence extended her life a little, even when social and medical constraints—mediated by verbal interaction—conspired against it.

Sufia's Visit to Heykal

As with Ali and Jahangir, I also met Heykal early in my fieldwork. But since Heykal's shop was on the path I walked almost daily, I had much more contact with him throughout my stay in Matlab than with the other two practitioners. Beyond observing and recording a number of his clinical interviews, such as that with Sufia, I enjoyed many cups of tea with the *ḍāktār*.

Kabirājes like Ali and most *hātuṛe ḍāktārs* practice in pharmacies that they own and run. But whereas Ali prepares his own remedies, almost all of Heykal's medicines are manufactured by multinational pharmaceutical companies in Bangladesh, running the gamut of items available in the West. More than other Muslim practitioners in the Sonargaon bazaar, Heykal displays his piety openly in his clothing and speech. Still, patients do not bring him problems like prolonged grief, mutism, or forms of deviance, which they regard as spirit-caused and thus within the domain of the *kabirāj*. As a *ḍāktār*, Heykal's orientation is toward cosmopolitan/allopathic medicine; he values a scientific way of knowing. Relative to a *kabirāj*, he gives patients less time to answer open-ended questions. He is friendly but businesslike. We can thus compare Heykal to the traders, shopkeepers, and other small businessmen on Java whom Geertz (1968) observed to be the most active partisans of rationalizing, scripturalist, modernist Islam in Indonesia in the 1950s and 1960s.

We can also compare Heykal's style with the style of biomedical practitioners of biomedicine in other societies; he is a "nice doctor" (Davis 1993) who may be the interrupter or the one interrupted, one who *sometimes* pursues patient's themes in his questions (Mishler 1984). But as in Mishler's depiction of doctor-patient interactions in America, Heykal's agenda of questions takes on such a life of its own that both the patient's concerns and the family's get lost. Moreover, Heykal's response to Sufia's symptom account challenges her authorial power to describe her own experience.

Sufia and her mother conarrated the history, linking the lump with the aftermath of a miscarriage. The consultation transcribed here opened with Sufia's mother and Heykal Daktar urging her to recite her medical history. But Sufia's attempts to tell her own story fail, and her mother takes up the task in line 10.

Example 57. Sufia, her mother, and Heykal: Negotiating the reality of a lump.

Sufia and Her Mother	Heykal Daktar
3H	ei ki asubidhā āpnār?
	What is your [V] problem here?
4M kabi nā?	
Won't you [sT] speak?	

5H   ki asubidhā balun.
                                    Tell [V], What's the problem.

6S   /prathamḍā/
     The start?

     ...   ...

10M **lāge** (nān) **cāgār matan** ār ki. (2).
     It feels like a mass or something.

11M ai je e āpnāder sāthe nā jato owṣadh-
     baṛi nilām nā?[11]
     *Remember how many pills we got
     from you all?*

12M ei māyār leggāyi ni[ye]chilām. e bāccā
     (huynnā) chilo,
     *It was for this girl we got them. She
     was pregnant,*

13M tārpar ei bāccā (1)
     then the fetus–

14M mane karen *her labor* de[k]hā geche.
     –imagine delivery [miscarriage] started.

15M tārparerḍā āsteyi eiḍā
     Then gradually it–

16H   sairā geche. kakhan se sar[e]che?=
                                    *–fell away [miscarried]. When did it
                                    fall away?*

17M =eiḍār cā[k]hāḍā raiyeche pare.[12]
     This mass stayed behind afterward.

18H   ka māser bāccā naṣto [h]aiyā gelogā
                                    *A fetus of how many months was
                                    spoiled?*

19M chay māse
     Six months.

When Heykal asks when the baby "rotted" or was "spoiled" (naṣto) and
Sufia's mother answers inaccurately, she cuts in on her mother's narrative to
correct the month and tell the remainder of the story herself—so far as Heykal
will allow:

20S cā:r māser. cāir māser.
     Four months. Four months.

21M cā:r māser.
     Four months.

22H   cār māse naṣto [h]ai yā gechegā
                                    /eḍā ki/
                                    *It got spoiled at four months;
                                    /what is that/*

23S **/cā:r/ mās *cā:r mās* bhālo chilo.**
     **/Four/ months, ... For four months
     it was fine.**

24?   ki? *What?*

25S   cār mās par *After four months*

26   /thekei er pare/ *from that point on*

27M   /ekṭa rog hailo/ *an illness started.*

28S   ekṭa rog haiyā ...
       The illness which started–

29H   ki /hailo/? *What [kind of illness]*
                                                started?

30S   /ek/ deṛ mās ekṭā peḍ[13] byathā
       There was abdominal pain for one
       to one and a half months.

31H   ācchā tārpar? *Uh huh; then?*

32S   eiḍār theikkā ek deṛ mās rakto geche.
       From this, bleeding lasted one to one
       and a half months.

33S   rakto jāwār par peḍete cā[k]hār mato iyā geche.
       After the bleeding, something like a mass
       formed in the abdomen.

34S   erpar ([ekh]ane) mās mās jāit[e]āche.
       After that, now the blood passes monthly.

35S   (2) /e[k]han/. /Now/

36H   /e[k]han ki/ jāit[e]āche?
                                                /Now is/ [blood] passing?

37H   ekhan rakto (kono beśi) geche?
                                                Now is there irregular bleeding?

38S   nā a[k]han mās mās jāy.
       No, now it passes monthly.

39H   ekhan mās mās jāy?
                                                Now it passes monthly?

41   mās mās balte oḍā ṭhik āche,
                                                Because it's monthly, things are OK.

42   eto /(śakto) problem nāi/.
                                                It's /not that hard a problem/.

43S   /āmār peḍer maddhye cā[k]hār matani
       /In my abdomen/ there is like a mass.

44S   (sui) āger cā[k]hār matan cā[k]hā.
       (?) The old mass-like lump.

45H   āger mato cākā haiyā geche nā?
                                                Like before, a mass has formed,
                                                eh?

46S   ha. *Yes.*

47H   *(xx)*

48S   hei āgerṭāi *It is the old mass.*

49H   buj[he]chi *I understand.*

Between lines 49 and 62, Heykal asks Sufia more questions about how well her
menstrual blood flows, whether it "breaks up" normally. She says it does. He
then asks her about the mass:

63H   ekhan ki peḍe cākā **anubhab**
                                                        kart[e]āchen?
                                                        *Do you [V] **sense** a mass in your
                                                        abdomen now?*

64S   hm, peḍe cā[k]hā āche.
       *Yes, there **is** a mass in [the]
       abdomen.*

65H   cākā **anubhab** kart[e]ā/chen/.
                                                        *You [V] are **sensing** a mass.*

66S   /hā/. *Yes.*

We find two points of conflict in Sufia's encounter with Heykal—first over her pregnancy, and then over the lump. In the opening lines of the transcript, Sufia defers to her mother's recounting of events. Heykal pursues the chronology with Sufia's mother, focusing on the miscarriage. Sufia's mother seems to avoid the blunt Bangla verb phrases that Heykal (perhaps insensitively) supplies when he finishes her sentence, saying, in line 16H, *sar[e]che* (fell away) and, in line 18H, *naṣto [h]aiyā gelogā* (got spoiled). These are phrases women do not hesitate to use among themselves, but they might well resent a male doctor using them (Margaret Leppard, personal communication, 1996).[14]

In lines 19–20, Sufia corrects her mother's mistake (it happened at four, not six gestational months), and with this, she finds her voice and her mother's role recedes to the background. Heykal's use of the word *naṣto* was like a red flag for Sufia. Evidently unwilling to let the man thus dismiss her reproductive career— for her marriage and economic security depended upon a successful performance here—Sufia herself steps in to construct the event more positively, stressing that for four months the pregnancy had progressed well.

Both women stress the *cākā* (mass, lump) in Sufia's lower abdomen (lines 10 and 33). At first Heykal ignores them. There are marks of intensity when Sufia tries to return Heykal's attention to the lump in line 43. Her use of the possessive pronoun *āmār* (my)—an exception to the avoidance of indexicals discussed in chapter 5—and her interruption of the practitioner's questioning agenda (Mishler 1984) add an assertive tone to the utterance. Heykal's first acknowledgment of the lump in line 45 is a wooden echo. The interaction tension reaches a climax in lines 63–65 when Heykal rephrases Sufia's statement with the complex verb of perception, *anubhab kar* (sensing, subjectively feeling), thus devaluing her account. Although Heykal utters even these lines in a friendly or sympathetic tone, we cannot fail, any more than Sufia did, to miss his repetition of that verb phrase in lines 63 and 65. Nor can we overlook Sufia's assertive response in line 64 in which she insistently substitutes *āche* (the existential/ assertorial verb "there is") for *anubhab kar*. To paraphrase her, Sufia says, "It's not, as you say, a subjective experience; there *is* a mass in my abdomen." As in the conflict over her pregnancy, Sufia resists the "voice of medicine" (Mishler 1984). But, like Heykal's performance, hers is less confrontational in volume and voice quality than it is at the lexical-grammatical level; the conflict thus remains below the surface. Finally, deferring to Sufia and to the family's collective insistence that he take the lump seriously, Heykal performs an external abdominal examination.[15]

At both points of conflict, Sufia asserts her competence—her power to nourish a fetus, if only for four months, and to verbalize the state of her own reproductive organs ("there *is* a lump"). But such assertiveness is radically constrained. In my interview at her home, no member of Sufia's family blamed her husband for sending her away—or Heykal for dragging his feet before doing the examination. As for Heykal, despite his gentle manner and his economic interest in treating the problems Sufia presents, his words reproduce the local and bioscientific delegitimation of women's voices. As the next case shows, this tendency to question patients' narrative authority extends beyond cases like Sufia's.

Heykal Dismisses Farhad's Complaint

By manipulating words and selective attentions, a Matlab practitioner may determine who, among those who visit him, becomes a speaking subject and who remains the object of his gaze, discourse, or derision. Because of the inherent asymmetry in the practitioner-patient relationship, such authority to construct persons can never belong to the patient. In that sense labeling is the exclusive privilege of the practitioner. Forms of this privilege vary across practices and institutional sites in Matlab—a dialogical reality may underlie the appearance of the practitioner's diagnostic privilege in exorcism, divination, or even Ali's herbalism—but the match between interview practice and the ideology of practitioner privilege is close in Heykal's interaction with Farhad. In this encounter, two practitioners objectify their patient (more than his illness) in a particularly unilateral way.

Farhad is a 30-year-old man; the only time I saw him was during the event transcribed here. What I say about that event owes to my knowledge of Heykal and to his interaction with Farhad, as I recorded it. Heykal evidently knew Farhad; he acted as if Farhad were so insane (*pāgal*) that no one need attend to what he says. I have no way to assess that claim, but it clearly placed Farhad beyond the possibility of receiving medical attention for his complaints. Interestingly, Heykal has told me that he provides antipsychotic injections to other patients under the distant supervision of a psychiatrist; he is capable of treating madness as a professional. Perhaps Heykal reacted to Farhad as he did because his training is minimal and pharmacologically oriented; his ability to treat psychiatric patients is limited to a dispensing role. Heykal's behavior toward the young man—chuckling and making clearly audible remarks about him to others—was no better and no worse than the common treatment of the publicly mad that I observed on many occasions in Matlab.

Heykal was busy in his inner chamber when Farhad first appeared. Other patients and pedestrians were copresent when Heykal's apprentice invited Farhad to speak.

Example 58. Heykal Daktar dismisses Farhad's troubles talk.

F = Farhad (patient); A = Apprentice (doctor's apprentice); H = Heykal Daktar

ID	Farhad	Apprentice
1A		ki haiyeche kaiben to. *Tell what happened.*
2F	peṭṭā biṣ kare ār ki. *The stomach hurts or whatever.*	
3A		hā̃. *Yes.*
4F	ār pāikhānār sāthe ekṭu hāw (o jāy). *And a little mucous passes with [my] stools.*	
5A		hāw o jāy? *Mucous passes, too?*
6F	sinsine bed[a]nā kare (e ra[k]ham). *[It] tingles and hurts (like this).*	
7A		āmāśā haiyeche? *Do you have diarrhea?* [16]
8F	ki jāni. *What do I know?*	
...		
50H		*brainless* to! *Really brainless!*
52H		ar kathā (.8)—kathāi *valueless.* *His talk (.8)—his whole talk is valueless.*

The transcript opens with the apprentice's smirking invitation for Farhad to present his symptoms. Farhad took the opportunity and presented his complaint (lines 2, 4, and 6). In mock seriousness, the apprentice (in lines 3 and 5) echoed Farhad's words and then (in line 7) asked if he had *āmāśā* (dysentery with blood). Assuming that the term always indicates bloody stools, the practitioner could rightly expect the patient to know if he had *āmāśā*. But Farhad replies, *ki jāni* (What do I know?). Perhaps he simply has not noticed blood; at the very least, his words represent a plea of ignorance before medical authority. They may also represent an indirect request, like Fatima's, for the kind of dialogical scaffolding (Vygotsky 1978)—the practitioner reminding Farhad what signs distinguish *āmāśā* from other enteric conditions—that would enable a confirmation of the diagnosis. Finally, the words may betray Farhad's awareness that his listeners are scarcely hiding their scorn for him.

When Heykal himself emerged from his inner chamber, he noticed Farhad waiting but did not speak to him. Like his apprentice, the *ḍākṭār* laughed at his patient. I still expected Heykal to begin a medical interview. Instead, he turned to me and made gestures indicating that Farhad was mentally ill, then said to me:

<u>Heykal</u>

50H   *brainless* to!
                                    Really brainless!

52H   ar kathā (.8) kathāi *valueless.*
                                    His talk, his whole talk is valueless.

When Heykal not only ignored, but also belittled, his expectant patient, it left me feeling very uncomfortable. At the same time, the *ḍākṭār*'s behavior bears an affinity to a hermeneutic model of medicine. This response to Farhad evinces a belief that complaints do not always mean what they say, and that the manifest content of the speech of the "brainless" (the mad) can or should be ignored. Assuming for a moment that Farhad was both mad and physically ill, how could he convince anyone that he needed help? How could his requests be taken seriously? I don't know the sources of Heykal's concepts of madness. Given that his formal schooling is minimal, I suspect that Heykal draws in part on ethnopsychiatric folk knowledge. But there is also a fascinating parallel between his praxis and that of psychiatrists in industrialized countries who treat vague or excessive symptom expression as a sign of a somatization disorder (see chapter 1). Heykal assumes the right to question his patient's attribution of distress to a bodily symptom. But unlike his Western counterparts in biomedicine, Heykal does not pursue the somatization diagnosis further by prescribing any psychopharmaceuticals, despite the fact that he sells them to other patients. He simply waits for Farhad to leave. Farhad, in contrast to Sufia, offers little resistance to Heykal's dismissal. He smiles, as people in rural Bangladesh do when they are shamed.

My point has nothing to do with my friend Heykal personally. Rather, I offer the commonalties of his interaction with Sufia and Farhad—the delegitimating of their presentations of self and symptoms—as evidence of general tendencies. What I am addressing is the tendency for patients to clash with practitioners or kin over their self-representations, as well as over explanatory models for their current state, and the tendency for some to resist the authority of the practitioner, especially via metacomplaints. Medical discourse is at least indirectly about conflict as well as illness and treatment.

A tabular presentation facilitates our grasp of the common patterns revealed by the interactions of Fatima, Yasmin, Sufia, and Farhad with their practitioners (see table 10-1).

Microconflict and the Indexing of Macrotroubles

This chapter has described events in the lives of four *rogīs* in Matlab, stressing conflictual aspects of their medical interactions. It is not the case that all instances of overlap in medical conversation always entail an interruption of the patient, or that sympathy is never offered to Matlab patients—any more than it is true that Western practitioners universally ignore or delegitimate their patients' words. But even in situations in which patients are allowed to present relatively

Table 10-1. A comparison of metacomplaint encounters.

	Fatima	Yasmin	Sufia	Farhad
1. Sex, approximate age	F (45)	F (50)	F (20)	M (30)
2. Event setting	Home	Chambers	Chambers	Chambers
3. Medical trouble	Dizziness, fainting	Tumor	Abdominal mass/lump	Diarrhea
4. Metacommunication	Patient—"I can't say how it feels"	Patient—"I haven't told you half…"	Practitioner–Reinterpretive paraphrasing	Practitioner—"his words are *valueless*"
5. Form(s) of blockage/inhibition	Confusion, interruption, ridicule	Interruption	Struggle for discursive/epistemological authority	
6. Practitioner	Exorcist-*kabirāj*	Herbalist/Ayurvedic *kabirāj*	Biomedical *ḍāktār*	Biomedical *ḍāktār*
7. Supernatural agency invoked	Male spirit silencing her	—	Spirit as cause of her lump, not mentioned to practitioner	—
8. Social label	*māthā-byārāmi*	*rogī*	*rogī*	Practitioner says, *"brainless"*
9. Outcome	Inconclusive, conflicting diagnoses	Died 6 months later	No improvement	No improvement

long illness narratives, practitioners and kin in Matlab do not just add to, or coconstruct, but also disrupt those narratives. Within certain relationships it is not unusual to interrupt, challenge, or laugh at troubles stories. So Matlab illness interactions are often adversarial. Patients and their interlocutors compete for the right to speak; they dispute illness meanings. In cases like Yasmin's, listeners might interrupt sufferers to halt a downward spiral of despair. But it is not' always easy to separate such benevolent motives from others, such as the need of listeners—including practitioners—to reduce their own anxiety. Those needs may conflict with the patient's; by interrupting Yasmin, Ali prevented her from putting her own narrative closure on her story of growing despair. And in any case the reshaping of complaints, the troubling of troubles talk, is one of the discursive means sustaining Matlab's hierarchies of power.

Despite the particularity of local meanings of illness and the pluralistic con-text of health and healing in Bangladesh, analogies exist with Western biomedi-cine. Although divergent ideologies of language and hierarchy tend to mask the similarities, I find them not only in the forms of practitioner dominance but also in the responses of patients. Practitioners cut off the development of important themes when they interrupt patients' narratives. And the hermeneutics of diag-nosis can delegitimate patients' words, challenging their authority as self-aware subjects. Biomedical practitioners in Bangladesh and in Western societies share a reductionist empiricism that can alienate patients. If Heykal's verbal chal-lenges to his patients resemble the American medical delegitimation of chronic pain, the resemblance owes to the empiricism common to both. Regardless of his level of training, Heykal owes allegiance to a scientific materialism that equates the "medically invisible" with the "imaginary" (Ware 1992: 356).

Practitioners in Matlab tend to dominate patients in ways unnecessary to the construction of a healer's charisma or to a placebo response to that charismatic authority. Like their American counterparts, they tend to have an agenda of questions and procedural routines that leads them to miss patients' deepest con-cerns (Paget 1993: 124). Despite the differences in theoretical orientation and technology between herbalist Ali and an American doctor, the discursive control exercised by both practitioners deprives their female patients of an effective voice. Controlling topic through questioning strategies may make resistance less thinkable if it succeeds at surrounding some patients with the comfort of a known hierarchical structure. But as I measure patients' responses in Matlab—not by explicit reflections in interviews with me but by their immediate re-sponses to interruptions during medical consultations—such asymmetrical control often provokes the discontent it aims to suppress.

Conflicts—at home or in treatment settings—arise not out of any ill will directed against *rogī*s but out of the inherent threat that illness and complaints pose to tranquillity and the social order. Yasmin's expression of despair, and her brother's references to the exhausting of family finances to pay practitioners, foreshadowed her impending death. Sufia's husband sent her away because of her miscarriage. Interlocutors muffle Fatima's complaints and Farhad's with commands, interruptions, and ridicule. Fatima's case reminds us that the problem lies more with pervasive cultural patterns of communication—in which the speech of the powerless is cut off—than with practitioners as individuals. It was her senior sisters-in-law, and *not* the exorcist, who radically compromised her fluency. Indeed, some modes of therapy in Matlab seem relatively conducive to patients' telling their stories of illness. Despite the problematics of Ali's consultation with Yasmin, he allowed her to develop her themes with a great deal more freedom than Heykal did. It is not the bedside manner of *ḍāktār*-pharmacists but their strong *medications* that attract customers. Their busyness, together with their empiricist orientation, make them the greater threat to a patient as poet, as author of her life, and as expert in her own subjectivity.

As real as it is, domination by kin or practitioners does not render patients altogether voiceless or powerless to resist. Patients do at times resist others' attempts to stifle or delegitimate their complaints. Yasmin and Fatima strive against great odds to keep control of discourse topic long enough to clearly present their stories. First Sufia's mother and then Sufia herself struggle for several conversational turns to frame Sufia's problems in their own terms. They try to paint Sufia's reproductive abilities with a soft brush even when Heykal speaks more bluntly about her miscarriage. And when Heykal tries to put a verb of subjective uncertainty in Sufia's mouth, she voices at least one strong affirmation that she knows her own body, before acquiescing to his authority.

The three women's challenges to practitioners and kin are indirect. We see no frontal attack on accepted norms of communication. Each patient struggles to assert limited rights or to incrementally increase control in the interactions in which self and illness are constructed. They try to present themselves in the best possible light and restore a sense of well being, transcending their status as patients in both the grammatical and institutional senses, asserting agency by raising their voices. That form of social action is a necessary prerequisite to changing patterns of social practice and, specifically, to humanizing the practice of medicine in Matlab. When a patient's act of pointing to a broader problem is itself treated as a symptom, as was the case with Farhad—and with Latifa (whom I revisit in the next two chapters)—the dialogue is severely restricted.

11

THE PRAGMATICS OF MADNESS: PERFORMANCE AND RESISTANCE

> What is my illness that I should take medicines? By calling me "mad"
> they prevent me from speaking!—Latifa

Sophocles said, "Whom the gods would destroy they first make mad."[1] Could it be that kin and neighbors, at times, do something similar? The key task of this chapter is to show the link between a series of laments and the fact that the kin who heard them labeled the performer mad, thereby undermining her "footing."[2] There are few published transcripts of the speech of those understood to be mad in Third World countries, let alone accounts of local evaluations. To that end, along with the text of the lament as it was embedded in multiparty talk, I also describe here the response of a Bangladeshi academic seminar to my recordings and transcripts. While kin denied the artfulness of the lament, the seminar was happy to assign it a genre label and romanticize it as folklore. Although the performer's kin exercised power brutally at times, it also works in subtler ways.

> Power is more than an authoritative voice in decision-making; its strongest
> form may well be the ability to define social reality, to impose visions of the
> world. Such visions are inscribed in language and enacted in interaction.
> Although women's everyday talk and women's 'voice' and consciousness as
> evidenced in expressive genres have been studied quite separately... both can
> be understood as strategic responses, often of resistance, to dominant, hege-
> monic cultural forms. Often the form is a culturally defined opposite, as well as
> the ideology. Thus attention to linguistic detail, context of performance and the
> nature of the dominant forms is essential. (Gal 1989: 27)

As Gal and Latifa herself attest, we see power most clearly in the selectivity of language ideologies—namely, in both familial and academic reactions to the speech of people like Latifa.

In common with others in the Western academic tradition, medical anthropologists have tended to take language—even the complaints of patients—as an unproblematic tool, a transparent medium for accurate reference (Kuipers 1989: 102; cf. Good 1994; Das 1996). Both medical and anthropological interviews are typically treated not as performances creating (contested) contexts of their own

(Briggs 1984: 23–25; 1986), but as opportunities in which free agents are able to intend and achieve reference to presupposed medical realities. Medical anthropology has tended to speak of healing realities, illnesses, and diseases as socially constituted in some vague sense, whereas linguistic-anthropological studies can show them to be entities produced by the very discursive forms in which they are expressed (Kuipers 1989). The denotative-referentialist ideology of language pervading Western academia as well as popular discourses (what Good [1994] calls the empiricist philosophy of language) ignores its performative, culturally constitutive potential.

In contrast, I will argue here that examining the interactive nature of a lament performance by Latifa points toward a more adequate account of the processes whereby persons are labeled "mad" in Bangladesh and elsewhere.

What linguists call performativity is the creative and entailing (versus the reality-presupposing) aspect of language, the power of speech acts to constitute social reality.[3] "Where practice approaches break definitively with speech act theory is in their insistence that performative effectiveness does not depend upon the preexistence of conventional speech act types. Instead, it is an emergent feature of practices" (Hanks 1996: 236). In fact, merely to claim that Latifa's speech performatively/effectively constitutes her as mad would be to agree with her family. A practice view, on the other hand, uncovers the interactivity in which performance is generated, labels attached and contested, and realities officialized.

Performance theory has informed neither medical anthropology's analyses of routine medical encounters nor its reflections on its own methods, particularly its reliance on interviews not balanced by naturalistic observation. Whereas denotative referentialism presumes that one form is as good as another for conveying the form-neutral content of speech, performance inherently involves "an assumption of accountability to an audience for *the way in which communication is carried out*" (Bauman 1975, emphasis added). Thus a text-centered, purely formalist account of texted weeping as verbal art will be inadequate. Nor are the intentions and referential acts of agents, such as those described here, always the most relevant dimensions for analysis. The lament reinscribed here abundantly manifests the indexical-entailing power of speech-in-interaction functioning quite apart from individual intent.

This performance approach facilitates reconsideration of the link between art and madness, bringing linguistic-anthropological theory to bear on the verbal-art performance of one who is called mad in Bangladesh to argue that her performance and the madness label are both dialogically constructed (Vološinov 1973; Bakhtin 1981). I find Vološinov's (1973) vision of the intrinsic dialogism of "the word" and his insistence that these words are ideological formations useful starting points in the analysis of Latifa's interaction with her kin. The object of ideologies is often language itself; Latifa, her kin, those who later listen to her taped lament, and medical anthropologists—each of these work from within distinctive, limiting, and (in this Foucauldian sense) productive ideologies of language.

Contexts and contextual effects of performance are never neutrally produced or labeled, but are themselves contested (Lindstrom 1992). A woman's
verbal framing of her marriage (and, metacommunicatively, her framing of her
lament on its destruction) differs from men's contextualizations of those same
events. In attending to Latifa's tuneful speech as interactively emergent and
ideologically relevant performance rather than innocent reference, I am responding to a call from Kleinman, Rhodes, and others to "shift our perception of
boundaries" and focus on suffering rather than illness (Rhodes 1990: 172; cf.
Kleinman, Das, and Lock 1996). Insofar as it resonates with Foucauldian
approaches currently in use, medical and psychological anthropology will find
much of this congenial, while its distinctly un-Foucauldian attentiveness to
formal analysis may be refreshing and challenging. An interpretive account of
Latifa's performance will help us feel our way toward a new medical-linguistic
anthropology.[4]

Latifa and Her Family

I have already introduced Latifa. It bears mentioning here that from what I
know, her relations with her parents, two sisters, and two brothers were not
under stress before her marriage. When I met her, Latifa's father did not appear
in person alongside her (as did her mother), nor was he mentioned in her conversation—an unexplained absence. During her 1992 visit to Habibur Rahman's
compound, Latifa's maternal cousins referred to her quite openly as *pāgal* (mad,
insane), a label connoting condemnation of speech and behavior on moral,
aesthetic, and pragmatic grounds. We know all too little about how many people
are labeled mad in Bangladeshi villages, nor is it safe to presume that all of them
are mentally ill. Significant epistemological questions would remain even if
there were any studies of psychiatric morbidity in rural Bangladesh. But the
issue of the prevalence of symptoms like prolonged weeping or sleep disorders
like Ahmed's ("psychiatric" symptoms in biomedical discourse) is relevant to
Latifa's maternal uncles in a very particular sense; not only do some members of
their compound quite openly speak of an inherited tendency toward what they
variously describe as head problems, heart problems, and insanity, but others
(including Aesha, introduced early in this book) resist being included in that
group of sufferers. By contrast with her cousins openly calling her mad, when I
visited Latifa's patrilineal home compound in 1996, her father's kin spoke of her
as greatly improved, though admitting that she was still grieving (*dukkho kare*)
over her ex-husband. They seemed bent on avoiding the label *pāgal*.
     The differing evaluations of Latifa by maternal cousins and paternal kin
partly reflect their differing stakes. Those who feel morally obligated to arrange
a new marriage for Latifa—her father's kin—have striven to protect her by arranging treatment (as I saw in 1992) and by resisting stigma (in 1996). But they
had other pressing concerns, too, including the marital fate of their own sisters
and daughters—and, thus, concerns that Latifa would tarnish their collective
reputation. The two men who physically dragged Latifa out of the compound,

ending her 1992 visit, were soon to seal their sisters' marital negotiations. One of those two men was Latifa's maternal cousin, the other a neighbor. Both arranged marriages for their sisters within months of Latifa's 1992 visit. Bangladeshi marital negotiations involve reciprocal judgments of family status or symbolic capital. That status is measured in part by the degree to which the families succeed in keeping their women from wandering or otherwise violating *pardā* (gender segregation rules). Any evidence that a family was harboring, or even encouraging, mad ravings in violation of *pardā* would make it difficult for them to arrange marriages for their sisters or daughters, even if those young women were not the ones accused of mad behavior.

So when Latifa's cousins called her mad, it was a way of attending to several culturally freighted indexes upon which many Bangladeshis would agree: (a) Latifa wandered about, violating *pardā*; (b) she wouldn't stop expressing herself, transgressing local aesthetic limits on the quantity and nature of speech; (c) she used many grammatically unnecessary first-person pronouns (see line 13 of example 60, below, and Table 4-1); and (d) her mode of expression was often tuneful.

Regarding the first and second criteria, my adopted family cited this proverb to characterize the uncontrolled speech of the mad:

> Example 59. Proverbial linkage of goats and madness.
>
> chāgal-e ki na khāy, pāgal-e ki nā kay?
> What wouldn't a goat eat; and what wouldn't the mad say?

Both goats and the so-called mad ignore humanly accepted limits. But underlying all of the indexes of madness is a deviant attraction of attention to self. In labeling Latifa mad, her cousins did not invent a notion of madness—there is widespread agreement in conceptualizing madness as deviant egocentricity, and as either a sort of willfulness or part of a syndrome in which one's *māthā* (head) is made *garam* (hot) by emotional words and actions that are under conscious control. Nor did Latifa's cousins act with conscious malice toward her; rather, their collective self-interest prompted action, either in keeping her from becoming crazy or at least in distancing themselves from behavior that brought disrepute on the family.

During Latifa's visit, I interviewed her, one of her brothers, and some of her cousins about her divorce, her so-called transgressions, their use of the label *pāgal,* and her treatment. Also, as part of the audience, I recorded several of her appeals, including the nighttime appeal to Latifa's great aunt (addressed as *bun,* "sister"), discussed below. In making these appeals, her rhetorical tool was lamentation.

Family and neighbors recognize that there is something wrong with Latifa. So might we, but what is it? And, for us, the objectivity of this "recognition" is problematized by our desire to listen to Latifa—we don't listen to the insane—as well as by our reading of Foucault and Goffman. Consider these problematics— the ambiguity of my dual position as anthropologist and "brother," the power of

Latifa's weeping, and the anger it stirred in others. Consider my obligation to relate to Latifa's brothers (whom she still calls "robbers and thugs," which is to say they exercise power illegitimately), to her cousins, and to Latifa, when, at the same time, I wanted to join her in denouncing and resisting them. Such complexities have made her ongoing story the greatest emotional and moral challenge of my field experience. It was tempting for me to believe that Latifa was not *pāgal*-mad but just plain mad-as-hell, though my 1996 visit raised fresh questions about her psychological state. How can Latifa keep hoping to be reunited with a man whom she now knows was remarried and divorced again, and who is not interested in reconciling with her? To me, such hope seems remarkably tragic; to at least some members of her extended family, it seems abnormal. Like others called *pāgal*, Latifa objects to the medicalization of her life complaints (see the epigraph that begins this chapter).[5] Still, she was subjected to involuntary countertreatment for love magic and is caught in a treatment system from which there seems no escape.

The dialogue I interpret here entails Latifa bemoaning how her brothers "murdered" her by ending her marriage, while her kin speak of faith in Allah, and of a new marriage. But to pretend that all of the interactive give-and-take may be reduced to this textual content, and to attribute that content to each actor's communicative intentions, would be to reproduce the personalist-intentionalist bias in Western ideologies of language,[6] as well as the referential-ist bias in medical anthropology. In fact, Latifa's performance is constituted by the *interaction* between an ideology of gendered language as spun out by her relatives' saying that she is mad even while she is singing, and Latifa's presentation of self and the implicit ideology of language she deploys in resistant dialogue with them.

Social and economic conditions in Bangladesh have parallels throughout India and Pakistan. Research on North Indian song and lament genres (e.g., Raheja and Gold 1994) cannot be reviewed here, but one parallel from a region of India adjoining Bangladesh is worth citing to contextualize my presentation. Tiwary ethnographically situates performances of wept speech, including griev-ances, in Hindu villages of Bihar, just west of Bangladesh. The parallels with Latifa's situation are striking:

> For such a weeping session there is even a term in Bhojpuri and Magahi; it is /*bhēt*/, which may be glossed as 'meeting (some one).'... Every statement ends with a refrain which is made up of the term of address which the girl uses for her weeping partner: ... aunt ..., father's sister ..., sister ..., grandmother ..., mother. (Tiwary 1978: 25)

> Women comment on each other's ability to move people deeply by their weep-ing. [Grievances are often aimed] at the menfolk. [The performer] may go on a kind of hunger strike, shun food and water, and weep at regular intervals until her grievances are fully met and she is satisfied ... The topic is usually her grievance against the person with whom she has quarreled and the suffering that has been her lot since her entry into this family [here Tiwary presumes the accused to be her husband's family rather than her brothers as in Latifa's lament] ... She may convey not only her complaints through the wept

statements; she usually voices her threats too. The message is intended for all concerned to pay heed to her sad plight. It is quite effective, especially if she keeps it up for many days. (p. 26)

Parallels between these Bihari laments and Latifa's performance include their duration over several days, the particular females addressed by kin terms, the male targets, the admixture of complaints and threats, and the immediate on-site evaluation of the performance. It is through laments like Latifa's that people from Afghanistan and Pakistan (Grima 1992) to India and Bangladesh aestheticize suffering. The significance of parallels adduced here will become clearer after I have presented and commented on the transcript of Latifa's performance.

A final parallel useful in framing my discussion of Latifa's crisis comes from Das's description of the Punjabi gendered division of labor in mourning the dead (a division of labor that is reversed when the occasion for mourning is violence against women). Note, in her analysis, the play of public and private expression, male and female, the expressible and the inexpressible, death and discourse:

> The experience of loss in the flow of everyday life makes the voices of women "public" in the process of [funerary] mourning. In the genre of lamentation, women have control both through their bodies and through their language— grief is articulated through the body, for instance, by infliction of grievous hurt on oneself, "objectifying" and making present the inner state, and is finally given a home in language. (Das 1996: 68)

> The excess of speech in the [funerary] mourning laments and the theatrical infliction of harm on the body by the women stands in stark contrast to the behavior of men. In the course of everyday life men dominate the public domain in terms of the control over speech, but in the case of death they become mute ... Thus, if women perform the task of bearing witness to the grief and the loss that Death [not some culpable person] has inflicted (otherwise people will say was it a dog or cat that died, one woman told me), it is men who must ritually create all the conditions so that the [wandering spirits of the] dead can find a home ... All this [discursive ordering of grieving] is reversed when the normal flow of life is seen as disrupted by the violence of men. (p. 81, 82)

> [In those reversed situations, the order of discourse is best described as] men moulding the silences of the women with their words. (p. 88)

Das's account indicates, among other things, that attitudes toward lament, at least in funerary contexts, are informed by concepts whose scope includes much of South Asia, regardless of religion.

Latifa's Texted Weeping and the Surrounding Conversation

The transcript presented here represents an event in March 1992—one nighttime lament in the series that Latifa performed during her visit to my field home. Interspersed with my commentary, the transcribed lines are arranged in two ways:

1. The opening lines, relatively uncluttered by nonfocal talk,[7] are displayed in three columns. On the left is a line number and the speaker's initial. A transcription of the Bangla is given in the middle column. On the right is a

translation. Any comments made by ratified audience members and bystanders are underlined to set them off from Latifa's lines, and italics marks code-mixing. Typographical lines in Latifa's performance represent oral lines punctuated by the sobs (transcribed as •hh) that remind us that we deal here with her cries of grief and outrage.

2. In certain passages (e.g., lines 53–67) where inside and outside talk link, or where the sideplay is particularly useful in explicating Latifa's story, I have selectively represented bystanders' talk along with the lament. In such passages, the outsiders' talk is in the middle column and Latifa's words are on the right, with the translations of each found in the same column with the Bangla original. This arrangement helps me highlight the intricate ways that reality was inter-actively constructed during the focal event.[8]

Participants

L = Latifa
B = Bun/Buji, Latifa's "sister," to whom she addressed the lament. The term is used here, and commonly, to address (but never refer to) Latifa's "grand-mother," the wife of her mother's uncle.
A = Amina, Latifa's slightly older married female cousin, daughter of Rani
S = Samabedanā,[9] Latifa's female cousin, 14 years old at the time
D = Musa's brother Dulal, Latifa's same-age cousin
F = Faisal, my field assistant
R = Rani, Latifa's mother's cousin, my "field mother," Amina's mother
MM = Musa's mother, an aunt with an identifiable voice
Other numbered K's are other aunts (*khālā*, mother's sisters) standing outside.
M = Musa, Latifa's older male cousin
J = Jim Wilce
x = unidentified speaker

Seated on her "sister's" bed (see Figure 4-3), Latifa sang to her while others outside the house participated in their own satellite conversations orbiting Lati-fa's central performance. The sister sat there, too; she listened, exhorted Latifa to keep faith in God, and begged her to *try* the magical remedies they had bought from a learned Muslim man. Standing inside, beside the bed, two of Latifa's male cousins laughed about how loudly and melodically she cried. (Interviews I did in 1996 revealed how men in Matlab appeal to Islamic prohibitions on women doing *anything* loudly.) Other cousins and aunts were standing outside in the courtyard with Faisal and me; this position aptly represents my status as an outside observer, despite being a fictive brother or uncle (etc.) to the others. Near us, several aunts and two female cousins quoted the increasingly scandal-ous gossip about Latifa's performances. They debated her sincerity, truthfulness, and sanity (see lines 91–96).

On that night Latifa moved from speech to texted weeping to unmarked speech. Latifa crafted her lament musically and poetically, making effective use of such rhetorical devices as reported speech, religious metaphor, and somatic imagery. Still, Latifa as author produced this text interactively—in a close dialogue with her audience (Duranti and Brenneis 1986; Vološinov 1973: 86; Hill 1995a).

Example 60. Latifa's performance.

1L	ki aśānti karlo go bun •hh	What havoc they wreaked,
	bun go bun •hh	sister, O sister!
2L	āmāre ni deśe deśe [p]hirāigo bun •hh	They took me from land to land,
	bun go o o bun •hh	sister, O sister.

The first lines I recorded of Latifa's lament (in progress when I turned on my tape recorder) introduce three parties to a conflict: (a) an unspecified third-person referent (known only through the agreement-marking on the verbs in lines 1 and 2), probably referring primarily to her brothers, whom she held responsible for the havoc (literally, lack of peace) in her life; (b) *āmāre* ("me") in line 2 (Latifa's self-reference); and (c) her "sister."

Latifa bemoans the way they jerked her about, first by arranging her marriage outside her village in another "land" (a reference to village exogamy), then by forcibly returning her to her own land. Line 2 is the first of many tokens of the first-person singular pronoun in this recording. This *āmāre* serves as an encompassing, or chiastic, marker for the wept speech,[10] appearing in its first and last lines (compare lines 2, 106, and 114). In line 2 we can also perceive a response to criticism that she has done too much traveling of late outside her natal home; Latifa says, in so many words, "*They* moved me!"[11] When we hear this sort of dialogue within one utterance, we are listening as Vološinov or Bakhtin would.[12]

Latifa marshals other "voices" (Bakhtin 1981; cf. Vološinov 1973), co-opting others' words for her own use, recontextualizing and thereby defusing a quoted accusation by responding immediately in her own terms:

3L	āmi ni "kāro bārit jāwnā mānuṣ" •hh	"A person who goes to others' homes,"
	āchilām bun •hh	[they said] I was, sister,
	bun go o o bun •hh	sister, O, O sister.
4L	kono mān[u]ṣe tay āmāre kono din de[k]he nāi •hh	Yet no person ever saw me, sister, O, O sister.
	bun go o o bun •hh	

The dialogization of Latifa's voice adds a decentering counterweight to the individuation implicit in her remarkable use of pronouns.

To underline the musicality of her performance, I present here a musical transcription of lines 3–4, which starts on the tonic in the first musical staff, moves to the subdominant (the fourth degree above the tonic) in the third staff, and then cadences back on the tonic in the fourth staff (see figure 11-1).

Figure 11-1. Musical transcript of line 3 of Latifa's *bilāp*.

Beyond the quoted speech mentioned above, Latifa's use of reported speech is even more obviously put to strategic use in the next instance, line 5. There, Latifa symbolically expands her sympathetic audience by animating characters who—seeing the signs of her suffering—look on her with shock:

5L	man[u]ṣe dekhle nā i āmāre •hh	If people [do] see me [now],
	kay "āpner ki o go [h]ai [ye]che" •hh	they ask, "What on earth happened to you?"
	bun go o o bun.	sister, O sister.
6L	āmār śâr̃il dekhle man[u]ṣe	If they see my body,[13]
	[s]hirbā diyā •hh	people shiver,
	uḍe[14] •hh bun o o o go •hh	sister, O sister.

The shock expressed by these newly introduced characters adds to the on-the-ground interaction voices in solidarity with Latifa, reflecting a perception of her treatment at the hands of her brothers as a scandal. (If her physically copresent audience held such a perception, only one adolescent girl, Samabedanā, voiced it, saying, "Only the one feeling the sorrow can understand it ... We only laugh!" This overlaps Latifa's line 34, below.) Latifa thereby projects (performatively constitutes) the sympathetic audience that is lacking on the ground—the flip side of how her audience shapes her text and its replays (recontextualizations), construing her speech as symptom.

Latifa uses body imagery to portray the depth of her grief. Her reference to bodily signs of misery does more than warrant treating this as a story that is somehow medical—it anchors her utterances in material reality.[15] Latifa alludes to her anorexic appearance in line 5. That emaciated appearance was due in part to protest fasting. In the everyday semiotics of the popular medical sector in South Asia, women (and to some extent men) experiencing *kaṣto* (hardship, stress) resort to a variety of idioms of distress, such as the refusal of food (Nichter 1981).

A later line (36) mentions damage to Latifa's *kalejā* (liver)—an idiom that approximates a "broken heart," but also resonates with esoteric spiritual discourses.[16] She holds her brothers responsible:

36L	/āmār kal[e]jāt/ kemte ghāi-o go dilo •hh	How they have hurt my liver,
	bun go o o bun •hh	sister, O sister!

Since on occasion they chained and beat her, liver damage here might well be more than a figure of speech. Using somatic images is, at first glance, a strategic retreat to her brothers' medicalization of her anger; but Latifa's symbolic use of her body is powerful in its own right. It was a vision of Latifa's embodied grief that shocked the figures (teachers and others) she animated in line 5.

7L	hārā-e kay bārā-e kay •hh	(Family and outsiders) say,
	bun go a bun •hh	sister, O sister,
8L	i-*school*-er-o *sir*-erā kay •hh	The *sirs* [teachers] at the *school* say,
	bun go o o bun •hh	sister, O sister,

9L   "he māyāre[17] kemte heman k[h]uno   "How they have murdered that
      go karlo " •hh bun go bun /o o. •hh/   girl!" sister /o o/.

10B   /(erā) kaibo jāi (gā or bā) (onerā)/   /They will say (whatever [they
                                                   say])./

11L   je [s]hunete h ay hirbā diyā uḍe go •hh   Whoever hears of it, perhaps,
      bun go o o[18] bun. •hh   shivers, sister, O sister.

12L   je [s]hunete h ay to go •hh   Whoever hears, perhaps,
      śa[r]iler paśam kāṛā kāṛā diyā go   their skins crawl with gooseflesh,
      jāy gā •hh bun go bun. •hh   sister, O sister.

13L   āmi e āgun kemte sahyo go karum •hh   How can I bear this fire,
      bun go a: a: bun •hh   sister, O sister?

14L   dhum rānāy āmāre bujhāibā •hh   Tell me—will the smoke (not sear)
      bun go o o bun. •hh   me? sister, O sister.

Latifa's invocation in lines 8–9 of the voice of secular education—the voices of her teachers saying they don't recognize her grief-stricken form—is telling, and not only because she had been a high achiever in school, which is itself evidence that, long before her marriage, Latifa manifested a degree of self-assertion fairly unusual in women. Schooling represents partial liberation from domesticity in rural South Asian villages. Relatively educated women in South Asian villages may try to "renegotiate their roles as wives and mothers so as to perpetuate the greater autonomy experienced in school" (LeVine et al. 1993: 282). Latifa's excellence in school, however, and her animation of the voices of her teachers, seem to have brought her more hostility than respect.

Latifa's exploitation of the theme of "fire" (in lines 13–14 and 42–43) was discussed in chapter 4.

15- 16L   āmāre nā khun-o go kar[e]che •hh   They have murdered me,[19]

In lines 15–16 we hear Latifa introduce what will be a refrain in the remainder of her performance; Latifa resistantly insists on indexing her individuated experience of injustice, literally, "Me they have murdered." The very pronouns divide her from her brothers, her family. Frequent use of first-person singular pronouns pervades the lament, yet it characterizes neither Bangladeshi laments in general (Mukundaram 1589) nor the conversational complaints of Latifa's female neighbors. In fact, the frequency of first-person pronouns in Latifa's lament markedly exceeds that of the other troubles tellers in my corpus (Table 5). The only close counterpart is the speech of a man, Suleyman, who, like Latifa, was labeled mad. Insistent indexing of self is a sign of madness to Latifa's community. Latifa continues:

17-18L   bun go: o: o: bun. bun •hh   sister, O, O sister, sister
19L   = āmāre nā khun-o go kar[e]che •hh   Me they have murdered,
20L   bun go o o bun •hh   sister, O sister.
21L   āmāre nā khun-o go kar[e]che •hh   Me they have murdered,

22L	bun go bun •hh	sister, O sister.
23-24L	āmāre nā khun o go kar[e]che •hh =	Me they have murdered,
25B	=Āllā::h=	God! =
26L	= bun go o bun •hh	= sister, O sister.
27L	āmi to kato bhālo pāi[ye]chi go bun •hh	I—what a fine thing I had found,
28L	bun go bun •hh	sister, O sister!
29L	āmāre nā khun-o go kar[e]che •hh bun go bun •hh	Me they have murdered, sister, O sister.
30-31L	āmāre nā khun-o go kar[e]che •hh bun go bun •hh	Me they have murdered, sister, O sister.
32L	āmāre nā khun-o go kar[e]che •hh	Me they have murdered,
33?	((sharp sudden vocalization like a shout))[20]	
34L	bun go bun •hh	sister, O sister

Latifa repeats the theme of her murder, portraying her days with her husband (line 27) as an interlude of peace in her otherwise miserable life. In the sideplay conversation taking place outside—words simultaneous with her lines 19–34—Faisal and I heard two divergent evaluations of Latifa. Musa, her male cousin, said, "She has no shame, crying thus for her husband."

To pretend that performances of verbal art take place in a social vacuum in which only individual intent matters, that the audience plays no role in shaping such performance, entails a serious failure of method. Audiences are coperformers (Duranti and Brenneis 1986). Latifa's concentric audiences spoke during her performance—sometimes timing their utterances to coincide with her sobbing inhalations but often overlapping her sung-wept speech. What was significant about this was the way that Latifa, in the midst of her performance, interacted with these other speakers, both inside and outside the house. God's name was not far from Latifa's lips; she invoked Mabud (the Lord) in other performances that were less interactive (or interrupted, depending on one's perspective) than this one. On that particular night, however, Latifa seemed to take up God's name from her "sister," Buji (who urged her to do so in line 35)—echoing Buji's invocation, though with less optimism than the older woman projects.

35B?	Āllāhi to / (bharasā)./	God is [one's only reliable] hope.
36L	/āmār kal[e]jāt/ kemte ghāi-o go dilo •hh bun go o o bun •hh	How they have hurt my liver, sister, O sister!
37L	Āllāh t ay āmār laiggā nāi-o go •hh nāi o o o go •hh	God is not with me, no, sister. [*Or:* There is no God with me ...]
38L	Āllāh t ay āmār laiggā nāi-o go •hh	God is not with me [There is no God with me]
39-40L	nāi o o o go •hh	no, sister.
41L	āmāre nā kiyā karlo •hh bun o go •hh	What they have done to me, sister, O sister!

Latifa declares her "abjection" (Kristeva 1982) or abandonment by the divine.
The extent to which this expression of abjection represents an angry resistance to
her family's Panglossian response to her laments, resistance to the hegemony of
a theology that leaves little room for laments and lamenters, is not clear. The fact
that the old man Suleyman's similarly constructed lament (below) elicits a
rebuke motivates further investigation into the element of resistance in Bangladeshi laments. Suleyman, like Latifa, expresses abjection in a theological idiom;
theirs is a theology formulated in resistance to another theology.[21]

Suleyman	āmār bhāgye	In my fate...
Relative	(śunen. ei rakam karen nā.)	Listen—don't do like that!
Suleyman	ei::::: nāi je Āllāh.	... there is no God [for me].[22]

Latifa goes on to link her brothers forcibly removing her from her husband's
home with the Judgment Day:

42L	hāśarer-o māḍer matan kairā go •hh ānlo go bun •hh bun go bun •hh	The fire of judgment day they've brought down, sister— sister, O sister.
43L	hāśarer-o māḍer matan kairā go bun o go •hh	It's like the day of judgment, sister, O.
44L	āijā jadi erā diyā lāy to •hh	Today, if they took [me] back,
45L	bun o bun •hh	sister, O sister—
46-47L	tārā kẹ āmāre e jor kairā ānche •hh	Why have they forcibly brought me away,
48L	bun o o o o go •hh	sister, O sister?
49-50L	āmi to ei bār[i]t kām kairā khāile to go bun •hh	If I could earn [my] food in this home, O sister,
51L	āmi śāntite thāktām •hh	I would be in peace
52L	bun o bun •hh	sister, O sister.

Latifa projects her desire to live anywhere but with her brothers—at either her
husband's home or the home of her uncles.

Still singing, she is addressed in line 54 by her female cousin Amina, one of
those standing with me outside. Amina's theme (Latifa's need to come in and
eat) was, in turn, taken up by her mother, Rani (R).

	Outside	Inside
53		tārā āmāre āinnā *By removing me,*
	R—he Latifā. (ā[s]ibā nā?)	eṭā go kar[e]che •hh
54	Hey Latifa! Aren't you coming [to eat?]?	*oh, how much* [23] *they have done*
55	R—bhāt khāy (nā bale). (They say?) she hasn't eaten.	bun ā ā ā •hh *sister, O, O!*
56		•hh

57 R—he karbo (he karbo bhāt ānbe nāi)
   She'll do this and that but she won't eat.   ((coughs))=

58 R—tār ekṭu:: bhāt bale khāi[ye]che.   =tārā-e āmāre ki ār
   They say she's only eaten a tiny bit.[24]   *To me they*

59 R—kāillā ābār dekhlā he meye āi[ye]che.   •hh
   You saw again yesterday when this
   girl came.[25]

60 āijā kon bārit geche sārā din   jabār[26] go karlo •hh
   (byabasthā kare)   *have done violence.*
   All day today, to whose compound did
   she go (and eat?)

61–62   bun go o bun •hh
                                                   sister, O sister!

63–67   tārā-e āmāre ki āre (ānteo) jabār
                                                   mārlo •hh
                                                   bun go bun •hh
                                                   They have done violence to me,
                                                   sister, O sister.

In lines 59–60, and again in lines 63–67, Latifa evidently compares her treatment at the hands of her brothers with the sacrifice of animals (see note 26). Speaking simultaneously with Latifa, Amina and her mother seem to express concern for her, hungry as she must be. Yet the undertone of moral disapproval and shame is evident. Like line 99 ("They say she moved around all day"), lines 59 and 60 must be interpreted in the light of the local version of *pardā* rules prohibiting marriageable women from moving about freely. Latifa's violations of *pardā* pro-vide her family with one index of her madness.

68-71L āmāre ni gharer bāhir karlo   They have cast me from the
        go bun o o •hh   house, sister,

72-73L bun go a a •hh   sister—sister, O.

72-75L āmāre ni gharer bāhir karlo   They have cast me from the
        bun •hh   house,

76-78L bun go o o •hh ((long sob)) o o   sister—sister, O ((long sob)) O O

79-80L āmi khodār kāche jā caī[ye]chilām   What I had asked of God [in
        go (bā) •hh   prayer],

81-82L jā [h]aito go pāi[ye]chilām   Perhaps [I] received.
        o o a go •hh

Precisely who cast Latifa out is not clear from either these lines or other conversations with her; she never mentioned it after lines 68–71. In lines 79 and 80, Latifa portrays her marriage as an answer to her prayer, the blessing of God. It is noteworthy, though, that she uses the Persian word *khodā* for God, rather than the Arabic Allah, which has recently come to be preferred (and sometimes imposed) by Islamists in Bangladesh.

What Latifa said next is striking. A more explicitly resistant piece of meta-communication—a questioning of the social order and communicative structure determining her existence—could hardly be imagined:

83L	*āmāre diye pāgal kaiyā* kaite dilo nā go •hh	By *calling me "mad,"* they prevented me from speaking!
84L	*āmāre kemte khun-o go kairā laiyā go nā •hh bun go bun* [27]	Why have they taken and murdered me, sister, O sister?

Latifa objects not only to the physical coercion her brothers exercised in pulling her from her husband's home, but also to the "order of discourse" (Foucault 1980: 133; Lindstrom 1992: 105) imposed on her and on those who might speak for her. It is one thing to read Goffman, Bateson, [28] Laing, or Foucault describing the silencing of those labeled mad, and quite another to hear Latifa herself challenging the label and the silencing it effects. In line 83 Latifa literally says, "Me, *calling*, 'mad' (or, because they *label* me mad), they would not permit to speak." Latifa's underlined verb of speaking indexes the arbitrariness, the constructedness of her diagnosis. Her utterance, double-voiced in Bakhtin's sense, quotes their diagnosis while simultaneously and radically recontextualizing it. Latifa thereby renders the label just a label, not a fact. Compare Latifa's line 281 (uttered in the unmarked, conversational style that re-emerged as she stopped weeping):

281 L	*kāhinī* (*or* kai nāi) maraner abasthā kairā [fe]lāi[ye]che pāgal bānāiyā [fe]lāi[ye]che,	The story [of how] (*or* I have not told how) they have brought me to death's door, and made me crazy.

Latifa blames her family—particularly her brothers—for rendering her mad. To the extent that she *is* upset, it *is* their fault. But she is not only upset; she says they have "brought me to death's door." Her misery is embodied and her very survival threatened.

I noted earlier that the way Latifa picked up the name of God from her interlocutor's lips exemplifies the interactivity of the lament. Now we see the synchronous interconnection— or, more accurately, the blurring of the distinction—between the speech inside (Latifa) and outside the house (sideplay among overhearers rather than validated addressees) exemplified in the way that Latifa's cousin Amina picks up her mention of *pāgal* (line 83) and throws it back at her, but without the verb of speaking, *kaiyā*:

85A	he Latifa, cup karas nā? Hey, Latifa, won't you shut up?	•hh
86	A [to others outside with her]— cheḍir māthā āro pāgal hai beśi. The girl's head will get even crazier.	

87 K3—māthā-e māthā (bipad āche)   āmāre kemne (x x x x) hailo o o
                                        o go •hh
   <u>(There is that danger) to her head.</u> *How has [it] happened to me, O,*
                                        O, oh!

88 K1—māthā-e to   āmāre kemne (x x x x) hailo o o
                                        o go,
   <u>in her head</u>   *How has [it] happened to me*

89   *O, O, oh!*

Whereas Latifa's double-voiced line 83 hedges—holding the label *pāgal* at arm's length—no such skeptical distancing is heard in Amina's affirmation that Latifa's crying makes her even crazier. Thus, in the space of one line, Amina shifted from a conversational voice engaging Latifa as a person (a socially rec-ognized and responsible actor) to what Bakhtin calls the authoritative voice, here serving to objectify Latifa and her situation. The folk-scientific authoritative voice in lines 86 and 87 echoes the directive authority of line 85, where Amina issues a command to shut up.[29] Amina's statement is neither conditional nor personal; rather, it claims authority impersonally. Amina's voice imposed a diagnosis, locating Latifa's *pāgalāmi* (madness) in her head. Crucially, the logic of lines 85–87—blaming her madness on her refusal to shut up, her persistence in wept speech—justifies attempts to silence her. Silencing Latifa is of a piece with subjecting her to discipline,[30] and to the treatment her family wanted her to receive at the hands of the *imām* of a nearby mosque—the treatment she was evidently successfully avoiding by moving about somewhat secretly during the day. Amina's location-objectification of the problem within Latifa's head is echoed by Latifa's aunts after line 90.

90 F—ki hai[ye]che cāci?   •hh
   <u>What happened?</u>

91 MM—kay mān[u]ṣe kay śaṅ karo.   āmāre kemte
   <u>[They] say, people say, "You [Latifa]</u> *Me, how...*
   <u>are joking."</u>

92 MM—kay śaṅ karo ḍaṅ karo   khun-o o go kairā
   <u>They say, "You're joking, you're</u> *they have murdered!*
   <u>pretending."</u>

93 MM—eḍi kay hudā-e.[31]   () nāi-o go •hh
   <u>They/she thus speak(s) emptily.</u> *There is no ...*

94 MM—tabu-o māthā to eḍi kay   o o o o go •hh
   huḍā, nā e ḍikḍā-o.
   <u>Still, (the head ... people/Latifa</u>
   <u>speak emptily, or "also in this direction.")</u>

95   (x x x) bujhi nā go bun
                                        I don't understand, sister...

96 K2—jeḍi kay, ṭhiki kay.
   <u>What (she/they) says (say) is true.</u>

97 K3—tārā je (āche, kemne āche
kemne je eti k ay-i)
(That [her brothers] brought her home,
how they brought her ... all that

98   āmāre
                                                      me...

99 MM—emni sārā din-i k ay ghur[e]che
They say she moved around all day.

100 (xxxx jāmāi et dure)
Her ex-husband's place is so far.

101   (Buji) go o o o
                                                      Grandmother-sister, O, O, O.

102 K2—jāmāi (rākhbo etā tānsiyāre [*or*
tānche ār ki] xxx)
Her ex-husband (might take her back—
that is what draws her so).

103 K3—māre dare
[Someone] beats [her].

104   (xxx) Buji (xx).
                                                      Grandmother-sister ...

Latifa's remarkably isolated word "me" in line 98 conveys a sense of the me-self as victim. Still, it is obvious in the excerpt above that Latifa's verbal intensity was waning. During that relatively wordless time in Latifa's keening, my field assistant Faisal (F) listened to an account of the situation from those standing outside with us. Their account alternated between an overt evaluation of the legitimacy of Latifa's acts and a retracing of her story's narrative thread in answer to Faisal's questions. Direct answers to Faisal's query in line 90—"What happened?"—at times gave way to a debate over the legitimacy of Latifa's symptoms. Line 96 acts as a hinge; in declaring at least some of the claims and counterclaims to be true, one of the aunts seemed to open up the talk for people to contribute whatever they knew as truth with regard to Latifa. This debate has complex implications for Latifa. On the one hand, Musa's mother,[32] in line 92 (They say, "You're joking, you're pretending") casts doubt on the authoritativeness of Amina's reference to Latifa's "head" problem. Yet it is not quite her own voice in which Musa's mother puts distance between herself and the certainty. Rather, she cites others' voices—"people say"—introducing these new voices into the discourse just as Latifa did in her lament. Her own stance toward these borrowed voices is not clear; line 91 is laced with ambiguity, so that we are unsure whether it is the people whose words are "empty" or Latifa who is "empty" according to rumor. Likewise, the aunt in line 96 (what she/they says/say is true) never clarifies *whose* claims she means to affirm.[33] The rumors cited by the three aunts (K2, K3, MM) cast doubt on Latifa's morality, since autonomous wandering violates *pardā*.[34] The upshot of this is that the aunts raise the possibility that Latifa, rather than being mad, might in fact be a manipulator. That status change cuts both ways, ascribing more agency to the young woman while at the same time impugning her character.[35]

In line 106 we see that Latifa repeats the charge that they have hurt her liver; she is in pain! Perhaps precisely because hearing that pain is so disconcerting, Faisal continues to receive the aunts' account of just how Latifa continues to be so drawn to her former husband, rather than silently listening to her lament:

Outside	Inside
105 F—ke tābij utthān kar[e]che (eke)? <u>Who put magical charms in her courtyard?</u>	
106	āmār kail[e]jāt kemne *To my liver*
107 K1—jāmāi tābij kar[e]che ār ki. <u>[Her ex-]husband did the magic or whatever.</u>	
108	gāi o go dilo *What pain they gave!*
109 bhālo-r janno kar[e]che ār ki. <u>He did it for good [motives] or whatever.</u>	
110	dilo o o o go *... gave [pain] o o oh!*
111 A—pahelā pahelā or svāmire dekhte pāre nāi etā to ektā. <u>At the very start of their marriage,</u> <u>she couldn't stand her husband;</u> <u>that's one [reason].</u>	
112 A—takhan jāmāi anek kichu pānir madhye <u>Then the husband began putting lots of</u> <u>different things in water.</u>	
113 A—rāikkhā-dāikkā meyere khāwā i[ye]che. <u>Putting them there, he fed it to the girl.</u>	
114	hāy hāy. āmāre ki karlo. *Woe, woe! What did they* *do to me!* [Unmarked speech; weeping has ceased]

Is the weeping, her ongoing attraction to her ex-husband, to be explained by love magic? Latifa's kin believe so; they are convinced that, while they were still married, he planted various charms in such a way that they would secure for him Latifa's abiding affection.[36] Such charms now appear to Latifa's natal family— to interpret their model in Kristeva's (1982) terms—as a polluting remainder of this man.

Latifa's lament was winding down by line 114 and returning to the first-person indexing of self-as-victim with which she began the taped portion of her lament. Lines 110–113 foreshadow the shift from tuneful weeping into the unmarked speech style that finally emerges in that line. The icons of weeping

(Urban 1988) that had so clearly punctuated her song/speech began to fall away. They were replaced first by the onomatopoeic interjection, *hāy hāy* (line 114), which represents crying without necessarily performing it. Gradually, even such response cries (Goffman 1981) gave way to what Latifa's interlocutors regarded as rationality. There follows about two minutes of tape in which the recorder picked up only the speech of those outside and a few snippets of the post-lament conversation of those inside, including Latifa, all speaking more quietly than they had during her lament. After the passing of much inaudible taped speech, we hear the elderly "sister" and addressee of the lament speak:

141B   (āmrā jes) ceṣṭā karbo (Āllāh-e.)   (We will try, by God)

When Latifa's "sister" responded to the long, indirect plea, she voiced the commitment I heard several times during Latifa's visit—to pay the dowry and other expenses of a new marriage. But she is not caving in to Latifa's demands to be reunited with her former husband; in fact, the "sister" also raised the issue of the *owṣadh* they wished Latifa would try, the Islamically sanctioned remedies that she had been throwing away or somehow avoiding. To this Latifa responds in what appears to be anger:

143L	āmār ki asukh je āmi owṣadh byabahār kartām?	What is my illness that I should take medicines?
144L	āmār ki.	What [illness] do I have?
145L	āmāre xxx biye dibo. jā (xx) biye kartām.	They'll give me in marriage [again]. The marriage I would enter [is with]
146	[Woman? Girl?] (asukh nā)	(Not sick)
147	[Boy?] to owsadh felāitāche ::: !	She is discarding her medicines/ amulets!

The child in line 147 carries on a theme heard in the strip of talk extending from before line 143 to after line 147—Latifa's noncompliance. Latifa, however, does, in practice, what Kuipers (1989: 102) recommends—she rejects compliance as the measure of the effectiveness of medical communication. To reject the compliance benchmark is to reject an ideology of language common to medicine and medical anthropology: that language is a neutral tool for accurate denotative reference. When language is used appropriately in the medical domain, according to this ideology, words adequately reflect nonlinguistic facts. In actuality, neither Latifa nor her family takes discourse this way. Rather than reflecting facts about her inner state, Latifa's cousin Amina says that her linguistic performance is responsible for creating or exacerbating the danger to her head (lines 86 and 87). Latifa, on the other hand, implicitly calls for a recognition of her right to perform speech acts more commonly associated with male students in Dhaka than with ex-wives in Matlab—making protests and demands.

Latifa complains of being shackled at home—*aṭkāiyā rākhā*—in lines 152–169 (not included here). Rather than being sympathetic, one woman in the house tells her that locking her up that way is good. There is talk of arranging a new marriage. A male cousin says he will look for another *ālim* (Islamic teacher), and the girl Samabedanā—again in sympathy with Latifa, who had evidently objected (even while the marriage was being arranged) to her former husband's facial hair—says she will look for a clean-shaven *ālim* (something of an oxymoron). Several laugh at that. The next voice heard turns the humor on Latifa:

168 M	nā- kāndār sur (balo) dekhi to bādbār.	The tune of your weeping (you say?) is (bad?)
169M	bākibār (svar) ekhan diben. (1)	Now put a (better?) voice to it.
170 L	*(hunde dibo e[kha]n dā ek)* *ṭiṭkāri māren.*[37]	*You ridicule me.*

Here (line 168) is on-the-ground performance criticism—Musa says he didn't like the tune she used in her crying. Here Musa is acknowledging the tunefulness or musicality of Latifa's performance, albeit critically. Though we might call this art criticism informed by an empowered language ideology, to Latifa it was *ṭiṭkāri mārā* ([hitting with] teasing, or ridicule).

The two sometimes intertwining conversations continue inside and outside the house. Samabedanā hears Amina tell the story of another person who cried tunefully. Then, again shifting the topic more explicitly to Latifa, Samabedanā says Latifa's crying was *madhur* (honeyed). Soon thereafter, Samabedanā herself begins to hum—evidently inspired and touched by her older cousin's melody, as one might be after listening to a tragic aria as part of an opera.

About five minutes later, Latifa—speaking now in unmarked intonation contours but still metaphorically, and with marked rhetorical force—introduces the image of "defective seed" into the discourse (lines 250–264, not shown here). Soon it becomes clear that she is condemning her whole clan, which includes her hosts. Paradoxically to us, the image shifts from seed to "blood," and Latifa's male cousins seem to praise her demeaning attack:

264 M	ei ei daśtā kathār madhye ektā kai[ye]che	In all these "ten" words, she has [finally] said something.
265 D?	ektā kathā kaili re	You [sT] really said something there!
276L	e rakter nā ? ḍā [k]hāiter bun ḍā[k] hāiter māyā.	*Doesn't it inhere in this "blood"? [I am] the sister of a robber, the daughter of a robber.*
277M	hā	Yes! [touché!]
278L	*ei baṅśer sab kichu.*	*Everything in [everyone in] this lineage!*
280 D	hā. jñan to kay (x) Latifā pāgal (āche *or* hai[ye]che) brains thik āche ekhano *out* h ay nā[i].	Yes, her conscious self-control (was missing?) but she is not chronically insane; her brains are okay, they haven't gone *out*.

Latifa's *jñan*, her "conscious self-control"—so precious to Bozlu and his followers (chapter 9)—had been only temporarily lacking; hence she had violated norms so as to index madness; by moving about, singing her words, and persevering in self-assertion, grief, and rage. Perhaps taking encouragement from their seeming praise for her direct critique, Latifa goes on to call her male kin a gang of thugs, but her male cousins respond with the equivalent of "touché!" One of my Bangladeshi consultants in Arizona interpreted this by recourse to a story of his own. He remembered how, during his school days in Bangladesh, his friends would often put him up to certain deviant behavior, only to withdraw and be entertained by the spectacle of his being caught and punished alone. As he became wise to this, he told them he would not serve their need to be entertained. To the extent that Latifa's experience is like that of my consultant, the younger men in Latifa's audience were egging her on to set her up for the violent disciplinary treatment she was to receive within days of the transcribed event.

That violent suppression of her lamenting, and the prevention of my witnessing the scene, were foreshadowed by what Latifa's same-age male cousin Musa said (overlapping Latifa's lines 26 and 27 and not displayed earlier) as he stood in the courtyard: "She's crying for her husband, she has no shame, ... no modesty." Later, Amina spoke bluntly: "Hey Latifa, won't you shut up?" (line 85). While in words like those we find coercion, at a later stage in the interaction between Latifa and her kin (lines 264–280) we see an ideological dimension working more subtly than does explicit coercion. We see it when Latifa's critics seem to use praise (as in line 264) to reinforce the return of sanity as indexed by her return to conversational speech. When she shifted to a conversational speech style (which they seemed to cast as a rational—as opposed to a tuneful, versified—rhetoric), they suddenly acknowledged her wit and praised her acerbic attacks on the patriline. One male cousin could then pronounce her sane—her brains had not left her, after all (line 280). So, by direct and indirect verbal threats and through odd praise, Latifa's kin tried to shift her from tuneful weeping to a less impassioned genre. In this small incident, the pull exerted by Latifa's cousins in the direction of rationality (Wilce 1998) points to much larger forces that would "disenchant" the world or "rationalize" it (Weber 1958), and that also have begun to split off madness from sanity (Foucault 1973).

When tolerance of Latifa's weeping in her maternal uncles' home and in the neighborhood did finally give out, two or three men grabbed her hands and feet and dragged her out of their courtyard. They escorted her back to her natal home quite late at night. Another cousin ordered me away from this awful scene and back into my room. As they left the courtyard, they dismissed her now more urgent wailing as *purān kāndā-i* (old crying). Their use of the unmarked term *kāndā* (used for any kind of crying), coupled with *purān* (old), indicated the end of their patience with her expressions of grief. To dismiss Latifa's aesthetic and rhetorical achievement, as her uncle did, by deriding her tune, exemplifies the principles of selectivity inherent in a particular ideology of language and gender,

one which might even be said to breed the violence I was prevented from witnessing.[38]

When I last spoke with Latifa's brothers in April 1992, they confirmed that
they had chained her inside the house when she returned, to keep her from wandering. I saw Latifa that May, too, and naively asked whether she felt better. She
responded bitterly:

> L—What sickness do I have? Am I sick?
> J—I see you're smiling.
> L—I smile for peoples' sake.[39]

She explained that she was afraid that if she wailed they would beat her again,
returning her to a kind of domestic incarceration. But her brothers could not
have chained her with impunity without the ideological work done by their
characterizations of her verbal art as inappropriate ranting that indexes (and was
likely to exacerbate) her madness.

Genre and Language Ideologies

Before we can analyze the coming together of gender and this particular speech
genre in the face of death or injustice—events prototypically motivating South
Asian laments—we must problematize "genre." How are events—instances of
speech—categorized, and how, in turn, do those categories come to take on their
own significance? As Hanks (1996) argues, "genre" is a good place to start if we
want to analyze the routinization and the ideologization of practices, including
communication. If we aim to put Latifa's speech acts in broader context(s), linking them with similar communicative forms is a good first step. To do so, we
must recognize the existence of marked and unmarked forms of troubles telling.

My investigation of genre arose out of my painful involvement with Latifa.
Latifa's sorrows disturbed far more than the routine of my fieldwork—I cannot
resolve the turmoil, concern, tension, self-doubt, and soul-searching that she
touched off. As inadequate as these responses sometimes seem, the best that I
have been able to do is to accept her request that Faisal visit her ex-husband, and
to understand and represent in this work what Latifa was doing. My interpretive
journey has led me to speak with some four dozen people about this event and
others with which it might be compared. Insights gleaned from these conversations are reflected throughout this book. It was fairly early in those conversations
that I first perceived a link between Latifa's performances and "literary" genres.
That insight came from Professor Mansur Musa and others at Dhaka University
in April 1992. I have struggled, however, not to privilege the labels assigned by
academics and to continue to listen to Latifa's kin and other ordinary people in
Matlab. Keep in mind that, at the time of her lamentations, no one present used
any term but *kāndā*, the unmarked word for crying, to describe Latifa's weeping,
unless perhaps they added a descriptor to acknowledge that it was *sur diye*

(tuneful)—and then deride the tune! In fact, no one present during her laments invoked *any* label for a marked genre, as did the seminar audience for whom I played the audiotapes of performances by Latifa and Suleyman.[40] After I had returned to Los Angeles in 1992, I played the audio recording of Suleyman's tuneful weeping—"There is no God for me!" (blasphemy in the ears of some)— for a Bangladeshi man living there. Perhaps it was the conventionalized association between women and *bilāp* that led him to call Suleyman's taped song a *jārī gān*, or religious dirge. At any rate, my inquiries into genre and values have uncovered more discord than consensus.

Less controversy surrounds the labeling of unmarked, conversational troubles talk. Whether visiting practitioners, preparing to do so, or simply inviting a recognition of pain, what Bangladeshis say people do is "talk about (or reveal, show) problems."[41] Children and adults may also *kānnākāṭi karā* (do weeping), or simply *kāndā* (crying). These speech genres (Bakhtin 1986) are not only less controversial, but they practically pass unnoticed, relative to other, more salient genres of verbal art.[42] Yet, the fact that Latifa's audience was able to characterize her textual production as *kāndā* (crying) shows that the boundaries between these marked and unmarked genres is not only vague but ideologically constituted. In contrast with unmarked conversational complaints, laments are marked speech forms that must be even more markedly socialized. Bengalis recognize several genres of stylized crying, including the *bāramāsyo* (calendrical laments) discussed previously; *marsiyā*, or *jārī gān* (dirges), sung in commemoration of the martyrdom of *Imām* Husein (Dunham 1997); and *bilāp* and *āhājārī* ([secular] laments and violent [secular] weeping). More than everyday forms of speech or crying, these lament genres are performances—audiences will thus attend to the "how" as well as the "what." Whereas the *bāramāsyo* is, at least to Bangla scholars, a valued genre of written and oral literature, everyday expressions from crying to griping are not. It is the combination of speech, song, and tears that sets contemporary oral laments apart. These marked performances are salient enough to become objects of on-the-spot folk literary criticism, for laments are aesthetic constructions, rendered so partly by their very tendency to be evaluated.

Bāramāsyo lyrics follow a specific formula; *bilāp*, by contrast, refers more inclusively to stylized weeping or ritual crying. The sobbing solo performer, often a woman, "sings" her sorrow. People perform *bilāp* at times of loss and bereavement. Rural people often perform *bilāp* when a close relative dies, and *bilāp* may also be performed either by a bride leaving her natal family for that of her husband or by the family members left behind. A woman who performs *bilāp* at those moments meets approval and understanding, not scorn. But people draw on such genres on atypical occasions, too, including economic distress or an unwanted divorce, as in Latifa's case. Then they risk censure to evoke the genre's affective associations. Sometimes wept appeals "work." Latifa's performance should be understood in light of the potential of the *bilāp* to elicit a supportive response from the audience.[43]

Still, genres are not fixed, given, or neutral entities, but rather—as typifications of practices (Schutz 1970)—they are fluid because they are constantly renegotiated and manipulated for ongoing sociopolitical purposes. Briggs and Bauman (1992) have demonstrated political dimensions of the act of genre-labeling, stressing how such labels construe family resemblances between texts or performances rather than objectively reflecting essential textual structure. Latifa's local audiences—regardless of the range of genre terms available to them—assigned a label to her performances as it suited their purposes. Bangla lament genres correspond to Latifa's transcribed performance in complex ways—no performance simply reproduces a genre template. Also, labels for an oral text may be "thrown" or coolly chosen, either process being fraught with ideology. Bangla speakers can play both with family resemblances and with gaps between old and new texts, between genres and instantiations/perform-ances. Such gaps are intrinsic to the performance as an aesthetic process.

Given the gappiness and ideological exploitability of the genre-performance relationship discussed here, I argue that Bangladeshi ideologies of gendered speech shape laments and responses. Bengali evaluations of laments and of silence have other South Asian parallels. The point of the genre analysis is that, despite the way Latifa's kin wish to use the evidence of prolonged weeping to label her as an individual, her performance is part of a cultural tradition as well as a particular social conflict in which labels are weapons.[44] Such weapons are deployed in "context contests" (Lindstrom 1992), in legitimacy struggles, and in contesting "madness"—topics for the next chapter.

12

LEGITIMACY, ILLEGITIMACY, AND MADNESS IN BANGLADESH

Matlab people have a proverbial saying they use when someone speaks in a loud, uncontrolled manner: *pāgal-e ki nā kay* (What won't the mad say!). The proverb does not specify just what it is that the mad *do* say; it does not provide the benchmarks of eccentricity. Egocentricity in speech is surely one of those. The notion of *pāgalāmi* in Bangladesh (glossed as "madness" and thoroughly described [in its West Bengal form] by Bhattacharyya 1986) occupies an important place in local discourses about selfhood.

Both Latifa and Suleyman are referred to as mad, and both wept-sung-spoke their sorrows. Their exceptionally frequent use of first-person pronouns including "I" was noted. Both were forcibly restrained and shackled. Judging from the way his "figure" (Goffman 1981) was animated by the boys in my compound, Suleyman was deemed linguistically egocentric partly for his dynamic intonational contours and his repeated use of "I." In the boys' representation of Suleyman's speech, the pronoun also enhances the rhythm and balance of the lines he ostensibly uttered. Yet the *āmitva* (egocentricity) of Suleyman's and Latifa's speech constituted a large part of their offense. Our understanding of how this connects with power relations in broad terms benefits from recent theorizations of legitimacy.

The linguistic anthropologist Laura Graham draws on the work of historian Michael Warner (1990) to lay out two principles or paths to follow to achieve legitimacy—the principle of negativity or the principle of notability. Warner describes how Benjamin Franklin, for example, had to assert individual leadership in a climate in which "the negation of self in public discourse [was] a condition of legitimacy" (Graham 1993: 720). Graham finds that the Xavante take the Warner's "principle of negativity" to its logical extreme. The Xavante achieve legitimacy through a public rhetorical negation of self.

The eccentric, or decentered, is excluded from legitimacy in many polities. Bourdieu's comments on legitimation are embedded in an important theoretical statement on the relationship of discourse to social order:

> To give an account of discourse, we need to know the conditions governing the constitution of the group within which it functions: the science of discourse

must take into account not only the symbolic power relations within the group concerned, which mean that some persons are *not in a position to speak* (e.g., women) or must *win* their audience, whereas others effortlessly command attention, but also the laws of production of the group itself, which cause certain categories to be absent (or represented only by a spokesman). These hidden conditions are decisive for understanding what can and cannot be said in a group. Thus we can state the characteristics which legitimate discourse must fulfill, the tacit presuppositions of its efficacy: it is uttered by a legitimate speaker, i.e., by the appropriate person, as opposed to the impostor (religious language/priest, poetry/poet, etc.); it is uttered in a legitimate situation, i.e., on the appropriate market (as opposed to insane discourse, e.g., a surrealist poem read in the Stock Exchange)[1] and addressed to legitimate receivers; it is formulated in the legitimate phonological and syntactic forms (what linguists call grammaticalness), except when transgressing these norms is part of the legitimate definition of the legitimate producer. (1977: 650; italics in original)

Suleyman made a grab1 for legitimacy at the mosque, staking a loud claim on an authority that was not legitimately his. He thereby became the prototypical impostor. His speech was taken as "insane discourse," to use Bourdieu's phrase. It was the contextual appropriateness, and not the grammaticality or coherence, of Suleyman's utterance that was in question. Returning to the Warner-Graham notion, it is the principle of negativity that constitutes legitimacy for the *muezzin* (the one who gives the call to prayer) in rural Bangladesh—their calls are valued for repeating the sacred Arabic words in a standardized chant form, not for idiosyncratic signatures, detectable though those may be. To say that Suleyman's taking of the mike was illegitimate because it violated the principle of negativity is to call it egocentric. Self-assertions of legitimacy via the notability strategy are, at least in Matlab mosques, dismissed as egocentric to the point of insanity. Only those who have already, through a history of small achievements, won a standing—those who are "in a *position* to speak" (to revert to Bourdieu)—have the right to speak in this context.

Outside of recognized discourses—socially recognized frames which, far from being neutral, empower some to speak while silencing others (Foucault calls these frames "disciplines")—are areas of silence or taboo. Foucauldian disciplines are domains of knowledge "confirming which statements are true, which are false, and which are inaudible." Lindstrom, in his account of Tannese "context contests" on Vanuatu, argues that there are the island "procedures [that] establish areas of taboo or 'silence' by making certain kinds of talk appear inauthentic, mad, irrational, or false" (1992: 104). Suleyman violated such disciplinary bounds, making a selfish (*āmitva*-ish) claim to an authority not sustainable by a Bangladeshi discipline, staking his claim on his own notability. It is in the light of such violations that we must understand Suleyman's domestic incarceration, which gave rise to his most pathetic laments. The talk transcribed below involves me (J) trying to become better acquainted with Suleyman (S) in February 1992. (B = Suleyman's daughter):

Example 61. Suleyman claims a throne.

0J	to kitāb- ki kitāb partāchen cācā?	So, you're reading a holy book, Uncle?
...		
1S	hām bādśā hai TO!	We are Emperor!
2J	ācchā.	Oh.
3S	bādśā hai.	We are Emperor.
4J	hā, bādśā nā?	Yes, Emperor, eh?
5S	°bādśā hai.°	We are Emperor.[2]
...		
10S	āmi pāgal bādśā hudā arsā hudā hudā.	I am the Mad Emperor, Emperor without portfolio, empty, empty.[3]
11S	(āṅgo āmi) (otālā or potāḍā) [h]ai [ye]chi āmi.	(Our,[4] I) am (all-in-all?)
12J	hm.	Hmm.
13S	(ayḍār bodā gay āhammak / garto [h]ai [ye]chi./)	I'm no better than an asshole.
14B?	((shocked, rebuking tone)) /hmmm!/	Oooh!
15W2	(Another female voice, much higher)—(cup!)	Quiet!
16?	hm. (eita keman kathā). ā.	Hm. (What kind of talk is this!) Ah!
...		
25A	kat[h]ā kam kan!	Speak few words!
26S	/HE!/	Hey!
27A	/hā/ kat[h]ā kam kan.	Yes, speak few words.

Transcript lines 1–10 above present Suleyman's declaration, "We are/ I am the (Mad) Emperor." In declaring himself Emperor, Suleyman goes beyond his normally Urdu-mixed Bangla into Urdu grammar—a "breakthrough into performance" of the voice of the Emperor (Hymes 1981). Speaking from the Mughal past, the Emperor's voice sounds appropriately Persianized (which is precisely the aural effect of Urdu on Bengali ears). Suleyman not only chooses an Urdu pronoun for his self-designation, but chooses the appropriate, royal "we" in line 1. This code-switch into Urdu renders his speech style and his claim marked, altered, ludic.

When I visited Suleyman in 1991–92 and heard his claim to be the *Pāgal Bādśa*—and heard his neighbors and nephews silence his "obscene" complaints (line 13) about the fact that he was not treated in a way befitting an educated man, let alone an emperor (cf. example 13)—I was witnessing a struggle for legitimacy. In everyday terms, legitimacy is respect. Refracted though they may have been through the locally constituted frame of madness, Suleyman's laments cry out for respect. Was he truly mad? Suleyman was grossly unhappy with his own life, at least at many moments in 1992. In 1996 he and his wife declared that his 1992 verbal expressions, which I regard as at least poetic and perhaps prophetically insightful, were symptomatic of a pathologically selfish perspective that he now renounces. Mental illness may, to Western biopsychiatrists, be clearly inscribed on the genes and their neurochemical products; but such faith in objective diagnosis is difficult to sustain from the position of a Suleyman—or of a Latifa, who said in 1992, "What illness do I have that I should take cures?"[5]

Just as Suleyman's words, uttered in chains (and at home), cannot be understood apart from incidents like that at the mosque which led his relatives to chain him, Latifa's texted weeping cannot be understood apart from the venues of legal argument from which she was excluded. For days and perhaps years (ever since the public meeting which had cut her off from her husband, declaring them divorced), Latifa had attempted to argue her case. No women are permitted to attend the sort of public meeting at which her marital fate was decided.[6] Latifa's melodic animations of the victim-plaintiff's role in her uncles' (and, at other times unrecorded, her brothers') homes were attempts to create an alternative venue for conflict resolution. Her song itself created such a virtual venue, invoking her former teachers as members of the jury. In her song, she also disputed her family's accusation that she had violated *parda* by leaving her home, showing her face to outsiders. Whether or not some of her lament performances were in neighbors' homes, and not only in relatives' homes, Latifa was not able to present her case in any forum that was unambiguously public. The question here again is one of the right to speak—in this case, to complain. But it was not only the act of communicating itself, but also the form and themes of Latifa's communication that were challenged. Songs with poetic structure are, after all, legitimately performed by poets, as Bourdieu says—or by Hindi film stars!—but not by "the girl next door" who is subject to the rules of *parda*.

Rural South Asian women live uniquely constrained lives. Their talk of troubles, or of anything else, will naturally point to the experience of self-and-other formed within these constraints. Structural constraint is, however, not the only force producing relational selves; generic traditions also play a role. The old man, Suleyman, bewailed the disappearance of his son. But it is not typically *filial* relationships that are thematized in laments, nor do men typically perform them. Women's laments, through centuries of *baramasyo* (Vaudeville 1986) and in Matlab today, thematize the loss of key supportive men—husbands and brothers. Latifa bewails the loss of her husband and the unjust treatment that she has received at the hands of her brothers. To her, too, it seems that God has turned away.

Troubles Talk, Gender, and Resistance

How can we arrive at a broader, situated understanding of troubles talk, particularly of laments like Latifa's interactive production, and of the competing evaluations of both narrative event (the lament) and narrated events (the tragedy bewailed) that typify laments? To answer that, we must look for cultural values (e.g., surrounding gender) commonly invoked in such matters and in discursive acts of resistance, for institutionalized forms of discourse production and reception as they are reflected in the politics of genres, and for the working of ideologies of language. These are not distinct entities but concentric circles of the context in which events like Latifa's weeping take place and which that event also helped shape—aspects of that single process that Giddens (1984) calls "structuration." Interactive performances such as Latifa's and Suleyman's reflect—and also contribute to the reproduction of—structures of knowledge and practice in Bangladesh. Both of their laments were performances not only of "lament" but also of "doing 'engaging in conflict' "—conflict over "diagnosis" of passionate speech/a heated head; over differently positioned evaluations of events; and, in Latifa's case, over norms of gender and marriage. The dialectic of control (Giddens 1984: 16) is evident throughout Latifa's interactions with her kin. The dialectic was not absolutely predetermined by one party's intentions or even its resources. Her brothers—not present on the night I recorded Latifa, but effectively controlling resources at home, such as locks and chains—have consistently met with enough resistance from Latifa that their designs for therapy (including arranging a new marriage) were frustrated from 1990 until at least 1996.

Resistance is gendered, and women have carved out their own spaces and discursive-actional strategies for resistance. In many societies women perform laments to resist a variety of powers—those of shamans (Briggs 1992b) or of other men who start wars (Caraveli 1986) that kill their kin; of religious authorities (Das 1996), particularly insofar as they monopolize death, its meanings, and its rituals (Caraveli 1986; Seremetakis 1990); or, generally, of those who control women's lives, sexuality, and economic security. Laments, in short, are frequently vehicles of social protest for women. As such, they are perceived as threats to the social order, and have, in various times and places, been associated ("strategically," as it were, by male authorities) with madness. Yet such a metapragmatic characterization (Crapanzano 1990) is not uncontested; "the poetic expression of grief is perceived by the lamenters themselves not only as an emotional outburst but as a means of mediating that emotion and thereby avoiding the excesses of madness that death might otherwise provoke" (Holst-Warhaft 1992: 28).

Particular discourses of value surround gender, sexuality, and marriage in Bangladesh and South Asia in general, discourses that are not monologues but contestations. In 1992, Latifa's brothers portrayed their responses to Latifa as generously beneficent, and her cousins betrayed only the slightest amount of self-doubt over their participation in returning her violently to them. In justifying their intervention to end her marriage, the brothers cited the reports that Latifa had sent to the effect that her husband's family was mistreating her. The fact that she changed her mind again about her marital situation after they "rescued" her only supports men's claims that women like Latifa make trouble. It might well appear to them that she is playing a cynical game with her benefactors, never satisfied with what they arrange for her, always looking for ways to make them look bad.[7] The divorce was publicly recognized. No lamenting of a socially legitimated divorce (two years old by the time of the 1992 lament) could be countenanced within a local ideology of emotion, for in that ideology, crying is idealized only when directed toward God, or for the men of one's house, or as part of a validated collective ritual. Finally, the extended family's *marjādā* (respect) was being compromised by Latifa's flaunting of gender restrictions, and her individual needs had to be subjugated to the greater needs of the kin group.[8]

Gender is mapped onto Bangla speech in nonobvious ways. Folk models cast women's speech as halting despite what seems to me Latifa's objective superiority, vis-à-vis the men who ridiculed her, in ethnopoetic skill. Latifa's live audience seemed unaware of how laughing at the men's jibes at her empowered the men at her expense; in that environment, counterdiscourses could only mount *indirect* challenges. Keep in mind how men in Matlab sometimes ascribed pragmatic incompetence—e.g., speaking out of context, to women; Jalu argued that only males consistently make sense by maintaining a clear context (see Example 30). The essentializations of gender and of speech as a production of autonomous individual strategists go hand in hand in this ideology. An interactionist analysis of Latifa's madness helps to deconstruct both essentializations.

Scott, in exploring the nature of resistance to power, addresses gender hierarchy in passing: "Public transcripts" spoken by the powerless often seem submissive, if sometimes ironically so, whereas "hidden transcripts" celebrate visions of rebellion. Yet "the frontier between the public and the hidden transcripts is a zone of constant struggle between dominant and subordinate—not a solid wall" (1990: 14). Songs and even grumblings as alternatives to open complaining or protest (p. 154) are among the texts that press against the "frontier." Latifa's and Suleyman's interactions with powerful family members resulted in a breach of the wall. Scott asks why groups such as women (here, Latifa's female kin) would fail to show solidarity with any act of resistance to male control over their sexuality (in marriage and divorce) and to their free movement in space (which, to Bangladeshi men, indexes sexual freedom, the violation of *pardā*).[9] Yet, although he finds the notion of "false consciousness" extremely problematic, Scott (1990: 82) also admits that a durable hegemony becomes possible when a large group—like women—has before it the possibility of achieving higher status (as mothers and mothers-in-law) at the end of a long road of submission (to men and, as "brides," to their mothers-in-law).[10] In the case of gender relations in Bangladesh, therefore, the prevailing virtue becomes one of patient acceptance. If Latifa's life story typifies the contemporary Bangladeshi rural scene, it reminds us that historic shifts in expectations nurtured in school may result primarily in isolated cases of frustrated and tragic resistance, just as women's changing consciousness provoked a medicalization of feminist activism in nineteenth-century Europe (Showalter 1985).

Forms of lament in Bihar (Tiwary 1978), and Das's (1996) study of the silence as well as narratives surrounding death and communal violence in Delhi, can serve as a larger context for Bangladeshi performances. Das's theorization of gender and grieving helps us interpret many things—particularly the angry reaction to Latifa's performance. Latifa's experience of violence is analogous to

Punjabi women's experience of the violence perpetrated by their own men; thus
it falls into a category of reversed experiences not normally inscribed in lament.
Violence committed by men against daughters, sisters, and wives may be intended to uphold the family virtue and honor (Das 1996: 77), but it is not
memorialized in *bilāp*, as were the heroic deaths of their men in battles in both
Vedic and colonial eras (Das 1996: 82, 83). Adapting the words of Das (1996:
68), it is not only women's voices that lamenting makes public, but also, in
Latifa's song, the violent deeds of her brothers. For a bride to weep when she
returns to her natal family (rather than when she leaves home) is a particularly
provocative reversal. True, Bangladeshi Muslim gender values do condemn
publicizing the female voice in loud crying; but the norm reversal and publicizing of her brothers' deeds—in a season when her kin were concerned with
making marital arrangements for yet other sisters—would have given ample
reason to suppress her songs even if she had whispered them.

Language Ideologies

My previous discussion of genre labels laid the groundwork for understanding
conflicts fought with words and over words (including troubles talk and metacomplaints), but is nonetheless concerned with action, power, and ideology. The
rubric of language ideologies helps unite those concerns, and is particularly
compatible with a theory of practice that emphasizes the role of reflexive action
in the dialectic of structuration. Language ideologies are "beliefs about language
articulated by the users as a rationalization or justification of perceived language
structure and use" (Silverstein 1979: 193), and play a role in the evolution of any
language (Silverstein 1981, 1985). Recent linguistic ideological analyses relate
observable features of language use (including verbal art) to power relations, and
emphasize heterogeneity in both language and reflections on it. When we bring
this approach to the study of folklore and performance, we find the links between power and genre (traced by Briggs and Bauman 1992) to be mediated by
ideologies of language. This approach helps us interpret troubles talk, and
particularly laments, by prompting us to take genres as ideological (not neutral)
framing devices wielded as control gambits by people with differing interests
and access to power.

    Cousins and neighbors of Latifa and Suleyman—via the particular ideologi-
cal selectivity evident in audience reflections upon their performances and the
madness frame they attempted to impose on them—were thereby able to accomplish their domestic incarceration. It is not that the two sets of kin and neighbors
had that as their goal or were malicious by nature; their interests simply lay in
keeping them both at home and saving their collective reputations.

    In my 1996 fieldwork I asked dozens of men and a few urban women what
people do at times of loss, eliciting descriptions of, and labels for, various kinds
of weeping as well as evaluations of various genres of tuneful language.[11]
Matlab men typically identified *bilāp* with the tuneful, texted weeping that
typically accompanies death and some points in wedding ceremonies. When I

asked where the tunes come from, people agreed that they come from the heart. And, although I heard echoes of other voices and opinions between the lines, people told me that weeping loudly and tunefully is bad. Almost all mentioned at least one Islamic reason to condemn loud weeping (though one man said that he hopes his children—especially his daughters—*will* weep loudly when he dies). Islam, they say, prohibits loud wailing at the death of one of God's servants. They also say that Islam prohibits women from making their voices heard beyond the limits of their family circle, and certainly *bilāp* violates that restriction. But a connection—a link between *bilāp* and Bengali tradition on the one hand, and modernity, Islam, and Weberian rationalization on the other—came to light when people told me that weeping among *urbanized* Bangladeshis is silent (interiorized, privatized, and demystified, in contrast with its aestheticization in rural traditions).[12]

Some voices in Matlab find in the very tunefulness of *bilāp* and related acts the sin of drawing attention to oneself (perhaps in the guise of praying).[13] This tendency to draw attention to the self was identified by another consultant as characteristic of madness as a luxury (*bilāsitā*) or a game.[14] It is no accident that many genres in which *women* once more freely expressed themselves are now under attack, that genres giving free range to women's verbal competence are being forgotten. When folk models of language and gender ascribe anonymous samples of ungrammatical, confusing, or faltering speech to women—and such models must have influenced the hearing given Latifa's performance and, indeed, prevented it from getting a full hearing—they reproduce gender hierarchy.[15]

Criticism (in the technical sense) of performances like those of Suleyman and Latifa is not confined to Matlab; this becomes a tale of (at least) two audiences, *several* receptions. Weeks after Faisal and I recorded Latifa and Suleyman singing-weeping, I played the audio recordings to a seminar at Dhaka University's Institute of Modern Languages. The academic audience readily labeled them *bilāp*; they linked Latifa's bewailing of her beloved with the pining of Radha for Krishna, inscribed in Bangla literary tradition. Why was their approach so very different from that of the on-site audiences? Apart from the gap between being face-to-face with Latifa and Suleyman and hearing them on tape, Dhaka academics nurture a secular vision of Bengal that romanticizes folklore, a vision poles apart from that of reformist Islam (Geertz 1968). Although my readers might well sympathize with the Dhaka academics' response—invoking genre labels that add dignity to Latifa's and Suleyman's verbal actions—we must see both responses to their performances as ideological. Both rural and academic ideologies of gender reflect the disempowerment of women—reflect it and simultaneously *mask* how it is socially and linguistically accomplished. Latifa framed her performance as a plea for justice, constructed with a view toward aesthetic and rhetorical punch; her cousins represented it as just another example of the dangerous sort of behavior that maintains a prolonged cycle of madness. The seminar framed the two recordings as rustic and romanticized offshoots of a valued literary tradition, but also as examples of the supposedly "direct" expression of emotion they associate with women and the mad (see note 18).

It is significant that a major objection of Latifa's kin to her weeping performances was that she did not restrict herself to the approved setting—"her" household (broadly defined to include that of her mother's brothers)—or to the behavioral component of domesticity metonymically associated with it. Thus, the response of Latifa's kin exemplifies something that Silverstein (1992: 320) writes about language ideologies. He points to "the special position of certain institutional sites of social practice as both object and modality of ideologization"—sites that serve both as ideal objects and as channels of ideologizing. Such sites are tropes, metonyms that transcend topography and include the events and speech styles associated with social spaces like the kiva (Kroskrity 1992).[16] The *bāṛi* (home, compound) is just such a metonymic site for the actors in Latifa's drama.

Sites are linked with ideological positions and with positions in structures of power. Performances and critiques flow out of such positions. If it is easy to demonstrate the positionedness of the live criticism of Latifa, it is also easy to position the response of those Bangladeshis for whom I played the tapes in Dhaka and the United States—their cosmopolitan evaluations are also ideological. We recognize, along with the Dhaka academics, the artistry of both performers—and, perhaps, identify with the "antitheology" of both (see Ewing 1994)—and so, particularly if we misconstrue ourselves as objective, the partiality of the live domestic audience stands out. It was my playing of the tape-recorded performance of Suleyman, a *man* (the same tape that my Los Angeles consultant called a *jārī gān*), that elicited the label *bilāp* from participants in my Dhaka seminar. Yet, despite the unreflective ease with which the seminar labeled a man's taped performance a *bilāp*, one of the professors who so labeled the man's song made laments out to be exclusively woman's work in his mention of *bilāp*. In his sociolinguistic monograph, Humayun—touching briefly on lament—betrays the selectivity typifying ideology in failing to note that men like Suleyman as well as women lament. His description of women "dragging the words [of *bilāp*] almost like songs" (1985: 40) fails to do justice to their poetic, rhetorical, and musical structure.[17] Moreover, to claim as he does that these songs reveal immediate feelings (p. 40 and my seminar transcript)[18] reproduces an association of women with emotion. Like the rural claim that *bilāp* tunes come straight from the heart, the Dhaka academic voice denies the social context, literary tradition, and rational (if interactive) agency that produce laments. Humayun and the other seminar participants thereby continued a process of "rationalization" entailing attacks on improvised, passionate forms of cultural expression, one that began in colonial Bengal (Banerjee 1989). In Bangladesh—by no means isolated from global forces—genres of eloquent protest are thus troubled by metadiscursive currents running through both rural and academic life.

13

TROUBLES TALK AND ITS TROUBLING
(AND TROUBLED) ELOQUENCE

This book has explored two sides of "eloquence in trouble"—first, the eloquence people seem to discover in producing troubles talk; and second, the degree to which genres like lament are themselves in trouble. (Both sides of the picture are represented in Table 13-1, which summarizes the discursive features and ideological links manifested in selected examples from earlier chapters.) Why should they be in trouble? We should hesitate before ascribing "genre troubles" to fundamentalism simplistically conceived. Islamic prohibitions on women speaking loudly can only be invoked indirectly as motivations for Latifa's cousins' violent efforts to stop her performances, to finally remove her and her weeping from their compound. But, whatever the motivation, kin closed ranks in 1992 to impose a particular interpretation of Latifa, her speech, and her self-projections. The framing of speech, like the labeling of illness and disease, affects illness careers but also rhetorical careers. To frame is to exercise power, mediated by linguistic ideologies; such exercises of power are never unilateral. Latifa and others do not passively accept labels like "mad" but, rather, actively participate in the discourses in which labels are negotiated. What the preceding chapters have documented, therefore, are manifestations of performativity as discursive power ascribable to Latifa in her resistance, but particularly to the more dominant authors of her life story.

For those who write about women in South Asia, it is a struggle to adequately represent their agency—especially when women's agency may be manifested in the way that they take pain inside themselves and *actively* hide it (Das 1996). It is equally challenging to represent both the violence that some women have experienced and the cultural and ideological contexts in which they and their men understand it. Without romanticizing their lives or writing them out of the silence which might be their chosen mode of communication, we owe those Bangladeshi women who do voice their sorrows a good listening. It is right to recognize in many speech genres of women and of subalterns in general—and particularly in laments—transcripts of resistance, some of them not so hidden (Scott 1990). At the same time, the troubles talk that this book presents also resists us, pushes back against any efforts to co-opt it for any one theoretical

Table 13-1. Some communicative features and social-semiotic phenomena evident in the discourse analyzed in the book.

Chapter	Feature	Broader discursive category	Social-semiotic phenomenon/principle illustrated
1	*dukkha-kaṣṭer kathā*	Bangla label for troubles telling	Presence or absence of a *single lexeme* label for a phenomenon says little about its local reality
4, 8	*āmi, āmār* (I, my)	Pronominal indexes	(4) Wide personal variation found in frequency of such indexes, and variation across Bangla genres; (8) sociolinguistic variation found in frequency of pronoun use; sensitivity to audience and setting
5	a) *māthā-ṭā* (head-the)	Non-indexical self-reference	"External locus of control" fits non-market economy and concomitantly appropriate constructions of self
	b) *emun lāge* (feels "like this")	Nonspecific reference	Nonspecific reference can entail a request for interactive scaffolding
6	*karkaś* (hard speech)	Term in local model of children's linguistic-pragmatic development	Ambivalence uncovered even toward what is regarded as a necessary trajectory in the local model
7	Creaky voice, nasalization	Phonation qualities	Projected, in typifications of troubles talk varieties, as iconic of weakness and tendency to irritate; iconicity and indexicality meet in these features
8	Explicitness in troubles talk	Discourse structures in domestic social contexts	Typically increases over the life of "a complaint" as first expressive resorts "fail"
9	a) Explicitness in practitioner's questions	Discourse structures in medical practitioners' interviews	Varies with practitioner's healing tradition and level of formal education
	b) Divination	Local genre of healing discourse	Diviner takes over troubles telling from client; patient is absent
10	Interruption by practitioner	Conversation's structure, turn-taking	Similar tendency to interrupt patients in both the United States and Bangladesh
11	a) *bilāp*	a) Bangla genre label	A structural relationship abetween bilāp and pāglāmi uncovered by comparing strategies underlying deployment/withholding of labels for speech genres and for persons
	b) *pāglāmi*	b) Label for "madness"	
12	Self-assertion	Social distribution of rights to speak meaningfully	When speakers overstep their bounds in following the "principle of notability," speech designed to redress grievances becomes a confirmation of illegitimacy

project, be it "critical" or "hermeneutic" (Brown 1996). The experiences in-scribed in bodies—like those of Suleyman (wounded where chains cut into his arms), of Latifa ("withered" partly from protest fasting), and of Fatima (via symptoms that escape words)—and transcribed in troubles talk, continue to defy resolution and thus bear strong affinity with other sorts of aesthetic objects (Desjarlais 1992; Good 1994).[1] The very duration of grieving by these three per-sons—Latifa's and Fatima's extending into my most recent period of fieldwork in 1996—exemplifies the way that life itself seems to resist them, and the way their stories parallel complex and multivocal fiction. That is, their stories (trou-bles narratives) neither resolve conflict without complication nor present them-selves univocally, any more than would a Dostoyevsky or a Faulkner novel.

Latifa's experience resists *my* desire to see closure. My discomfort with this story, which resists resolution, arises particularly out of my sense that, even in local terms, Latifa suffered an injustice, and that her grievance has not—and perhaps never can be—redressed. It also arises from my sense of the moral ambiguity of being involved, yet failing to help. Her story has thus become for me a key symbol of the complexity of my field relationships. Latifa, I sense, feels that my field assistant betrayed *her* hope that some words we could speak with her ex-husband's family would effect a reconciliation. The resistance of Latifa's narratized life to reduction, resolution, and closure; the acoustic, musi-cal, poetic, and rhetorical codes informing her tuneful, texted weeping; and the dancelike intricacies of interactivity in the production of each performance—all these point to their dual nature as social actions and aesthetic objects. If their aesthetic quality contains something of the nightmarish and much of the contro-versial, that is exceptional in neither illness narratives (Good 1994) nor the broader range of aesthetic production.

Speech-in-use functions at many levels; transferring information about language-external realities is only one of these, but it happens to be the most salient function for many Westerners. Yet speaking, singing, or silence also *create* realities—particularly social, affective, and conceptual realities. At times, the attempt to create new conceptual and political realities through speech is rather explicit. Latifa's 1992 performances enacted her resistance to her broth-ers' power, to their label, and to magico-religious treatment. They constituted her attempt to alter her relationships, to escape from that treatment, and to per-suade her more distant kin to try to reunite her with her ex-husband. The meta-complaints of Fatima and Yasmin, and the tenacious struggle of Sufia to define her own bodily experience, represent a similar resistance to the interactive routines constituting their medical encounters and their social positions. At least to those whose understanding of persons transcends the utilitarian and the mechanical, illness, healing, and the discourses that surround them are painful but nonetheless aesthetic realities in which persons and groups have much at stake (Wikan 1990, Good 1994).[2]

To affirm that Latifa, Fatima, and Yasmin were subjected to universal forms of male domination[3] does not excuse us from interrogating the particular Bangla-deshi diagnostic processes that reproduce male dominance, nor from exploring

the tragic potential in therapies for inflicting harm on patients in any society
(Showalter 1985; Astbury 1996). To do so requires us to examine performances
and performativity in the light of linguistic ideologies. Audience evaluations of
tune and structure in Suleyman's and Latifa's laments helped constitute the
performance as verbal art, albeit in a backhanded way. The author-performers
contributed to this constitutive process by regimenting their productions according to recognizable norms and thereby framing the production as something
whose form as well as content invited comment. But those very interactive
processes by which performances are anchored to a social and historical genre
context render the performance susceptible to decontextualization and objectification. "Performance puts the act of speaking on display—objectifies it ... By
its very nature, then, performance potentiates decontextualization" (Bauman and
Briggs 1990: 73). That is, the "indexes of performance" that draw attention to
Latifa's very signs (words, symmetric versification, tune, tears whose aesthetic
function semioticians describe as self-indexing) lend themselves to becoming
objects of commentary. In a paradoxical and tragic way, then, the very achievements of Latifa and Suleyman, their dialogical performances, rendered their
words and lives more vulnerable to the objectification entailed in labeling—they
became "mad." The more Latifa resorted to the only form of protest available to
her, the more easily others could point to such performances as self-indulgent or
somehow defective in form, and thereby marginalize the performer. This effect
only appears to be a natural diagnostic inference derived directly from texts
when viewed from a vantage point like that of kin and neighbors; it is, however,
a culturally specific typification reflecting ideologies of language.

Ideologies filter every reception of linguistic performance. They limit audiences' perceptions; we all attend selectively to features of such discourse. The
aesthetic criteria informing familial criticism of performances include norms of
setting, occasion, emotion, music, and rhetoric. Latifa's kin held her guilty of
violating these norms when she prolonged her grief, immodestly displayed passion, performed for neighbors, sang per se, and favored a poetic rhetoric over
cool rationality. We hear in their derision echoes of broader discourses of
religious "reformism" that reject most Bengali folk practices, especially those
that are somehow female-centered (Mannan 1966: 171). A language-ideology
perspective on the event in the village (as well as the seminar, see note 18 in the
previous chapter) highlights tensions between performances and models, as in
models of men's and women's language. So mystifying are the ideological links
between women and the home (and between male bards and public audiences)—
and so powerful is their anger at Latifa's lament per se, not to speak of her
inversion of lament norms—that Latifa's kin could not *hear* her art. As little as
the academic seminar might have in common with the rural response to Latifa's
bilāp, they both helped construct women as weak, inarticulate, and emotional.
But Suleyman's case equally highlights how parties in ethnomedical encounters
invoke shared ideological representations to preserve family reputation at the
expense of one suffering member.

Admittedly, my own embrace of the Dhaka label *bilāp* betrays my partiality, my readiness to consider even Latifa's so-called transgressions (acts that shocked some) to be aesthetic achievements—acts constituting the surprises, problematizations, or complications without which narrative fails to be compelling.[4] Latifa transgressed cultural spaces, times, and generic forms. Ultimately, it was her movement and her verbalizations outside domestic boundaries that her brothers cited as the reasons for her punishment. Even this violation, however, can be seen as a ludic act. Latifa's performances in outlawed places reflect, on a topographic level, a violation of norms analogous to that entailed in the content of her text. At the levels of site and of what is utterable, she defies the boundaries of performance. Her melodic text maintains just enough contact with tradition to move listeners[5] like Samabedanā. And, finally, Latifa's song achieves an aesthetic level in its multivocality (Bakhtin 1981; Good 1994), juxtaposing two sets of symbols and two uses of the same set—Islamic symbols commonly invoked in Matlab to support the repression of such women, which, along with a second set of symbols (surrounding education), Latifa uses to justify her discursive self-assertions.[6]

Treating so-called illnesses like Suleyman's and Latifa's as essentially performative helps us grasp complex stories like theirs; to dwell on the dialogical production of madness through these performances (which were themselves thoroughly dialogical at levels of synchrony and diachrony, in form as well as outcome), is to open territory I hope more medical anthropologists will pursue. The argument that labels influence illness careers is not new; still, few studies have explored *how* labels are produced or how conflicts arise in making them stick. What is quite new is my call for research in psychiatric discourse to link two sorts of labeling practice; I argue that characterizations of and labels for *persons/conditions* are often linked with characterizations of and labels for *speech genres*, ways of speaking.[7] Without blaming the victim—this apparent risk in my performance-centered approach is blocked, I believe, by the uncovering of multiple layers of interactivity—I have shown how kin used the very performance through which Latifa sought to resist the label "mad" to reinforce that label. The dialogical nature of the performance itself and its various entextualizations (Bauman and Briggs 1990)—the echoes, replayings, and evaluations of "Latifa's" (co-authored) performance by a series of voices including our own—is crucial to an adequate portrayal of labeling performances, genres, persons, and psychiatric conditions.

A critical ethnopoetics of power, linguistic form, and metadiscursive characterizations with their links to gender and ritual helps to deconstruct the referentialism pervading psychiatric and academic ideologies of language. As we do fine-grained analyses of domestic discourses leading up to and out of the diagnostic process, we uncover tensions, conflict, negotiation, interactivity, *and a linkage of "egocentric" oratorical elaboration with madness* (see Boddy 1994: 422, 423; Abu Lughod 1985: 257).[8] The fact that this last link is now being made in Matlab seems to bear witness to the encroachment of a new form of civilization (in the sense intended by Foucault 1973) on Bangladesh; it might bear witness, that is, to the point in Bangladeshi history when madness is excluded from legitimate discourse. To exclude such transcripts of discourse from psychiatric anthropology entails the risk that we shall overlook the moments at which South Asian inclusivism (Dumont 1970; Tambiah 1990) is displaced—though *Homo hierarchicus* might well live on, in a new form, to the extent that self-assertion continues to be labeled "self-indulgent luxury" or "madness." In any case, such historically decisive moments are heavily laden with linguistic performativity and ideologies—not innocent reference to innocent facts.

The Politics of Troubles Talk: Objectifying
Pain, Opening up the Body Politic

This book has explored the semiotics, social psychology, interactional dynamics, and politics of Bangla troubles telling. Although we might distinguish these three dimensions for analytic purposes, they are, as I have shown, inseparable in practice. Bangla troubles talk helps to fashion the experience of trouble, constituting troubles encounters as variably useful, comforting, and supportive, or frustrating and conflictual. The discursive resources at hand—conventions of turn-taking and interpretation (chapter 10) as well as grammar (chapters 4 and 5) and phonation (chapter 7)—help interlocutors produce Bangla troubles. Readers will recognize, too, a kinship between these Bangla troubles and troubles that are "Englishly experienced." The semiotics informing my analysis opens various ways of viewing that paradox. First, consider iconicity. Iconic sign relations seduce us into feeling that they are in every sense natural, and relations that any social system projects as natural are projected as iconic. But the relationship between the Bangla language and Bangla ways of managing trouble appears natural only if one looks out unreflectively from within Bangla communicative practices or within a shallow sort of Whorfianism. The shades or tones of troubles-experience that result from telling them in Bangla is particular to the forms of Bangla discourse explored in this book, and yet transcends them because of the conventions of reflexivity built into those very discourses. The more one attends to Bangla troubles talk, the more both the conventionality and improvisational playfulness of genres touching on troubles become evident. What also becomes clear is the tendency not only for scholars local and foreign but also participants in troubles talk to objectify, represent, synthesize, and generally entextualize that talk (Mannheim and Tedlock 1995; Silverstein and Urban 1996). Whatever we feel about such objectification, its pervasiveness is undeniable, and contains a better potential than that which is most often in focus. Metacomplaints and other such reflections on troubles talk carry the humanizing potential typifying creative semiosis. Sometimes even patients who "can't tell" their problems manage to indicate where broader problems lie, and, in doing so, make possible a progression of critical transforming discourses.

At several points in this book, I have discussed the relationship between complaints which do and do not have another agent as their target and topic. If the former could be labeled "state-of-being complaints," the latter are "accusations." The distinction is not only analytic or etic but corresponds with Bangla categories (*nāliś, abhijhog* [accusation]; *dukkha-kaṣṭer kathā* [troubles talk]) as well. It breaks down, however, when a description of one's pain is the ground of an accusation. Chapters 10–12 make obvious the need to reunite what for analytic purposes I have sundered.

In this context it is useful to make explicit the links between the individual body, the social body, and the body politic (Lock and Scheper-Hughes 1990: 50). What this study has contributed to such integrating visions is a portrayal of complex homologies between somatic, psychosocial, and political complaints. If somatic complaints index problems in the individual body, political protests—however inchoate they may be, appearing even in the form of metacomplaints—can invoke problems in the body politic in quite somatic terms (Wilce 1996). The space between these various bodies is mediated by metaphors like emotion (p. 69) and illness.

Anthropologists and postmodern literary critics have recently become more vocal in addressing links between their respective disciplines and human rights, including the right to remain free from torture (Messer 1993; Johnson 1993). Making such links seems particularly appropriate for those of us who study speech as a social and hence a political phenomenon. Political troubles talk (protest) is a common target for violent repression. But the expression of psychological and physical pain is also political—not only does willfully inflicted pain bring the topic to the courtroom or to Amnesty International's attention, but the provision of care is also a resource whose distribution is political. Only when one's pain becomes known publicly, and its source addressed, can this politics of pain have a benign resolution. It is not the cathartic benefit of verbalizing a pain complaint that Elaine Scarry sees:

> When physical pain is transformed into an objectified state, it (or at least some of its aversiveness) is eliminated. A great deal, then, is at stake in the attempt to invent linguistic structures that will reach and accommodate this area of experience normally so inaccessible to language; the human attempt to reverse the de-objectifying work of pain by forcing pain itself into avenues of objectification is a project laden with practical and ethical consequences. (1985: 5, 6)

> The language of agency [e.g., "this pain is like someone hitting me with a hammer"] has on the one hand a radically benign potential and on the other hand a radically sadistic one ... The torturer and the state at war use that language to create the illusion of power. (p. 13)

> The particular perceptual confusion sponsored by the language of agency is the conflation of pain with power. (p. 18)

The process of expressing pain is one of creation, one that is morally urgent since the invisibility of pain makes sufferers politically impotent. Since regimes of torture rely on euphemizing it as "information gathering," and since war and torture can only be glamorized by imaginally separating them from the reality of the pain they inflict, verbally objectifying pain or disclosing its source is a creative political act (Scarry 1985: 11–23). "Moral rightness ... tends to lie with the most articulate" (p. 201), with those who succeed in marshaling linguistic and interactional resources to make their complaints effective. But to define successful complaints in those terms is to make clear how much they entail particular political environments.

If the concept of human rights is to have universal value in policy discourse, it should be made clear that the social and rhetorical self whose rights we affirm is the social and rhetorical self, not the autonomous self, the atom of Western liberal political theory. "You are permitted to deconstruct the so-called 'liberal' self, as the political atom of all kinds of contractualist political theories. The further task then presents itself, that of reconstructing the self as *ipse* [the self capable, In Ricoeur's words, of *"keeping one's word"*] ... Such a capable subject is worthy of esteem and respect. And that may be deemed sufficient to make sense of the concept of a subject of rights" (Ricoeur 1993: 105, 109). This subject—that is, the true subject of human rights—does not exist on its own, but in social interaction, as Wayne Booth argues.

> What is essential about that self is not found primarily in its differences from others but in its freedom to pursue a story line, a life plot, a drama carved out of all the possibilities every society provides: the amount of overlap with other story lines matters not a whit. (p. 89)
>
> [In torture] the torturer is still plotting *his* life story—and making it dreadfully worse by the minute. The tortured one is, by contrast, no longer able to plot ... His plot, as 'self-determined,' has been destroyed. (1993: 93, 94)

It is thus not her reductive status as a political atom, but her ability to narrate, which—in this postmodern reconsideration—makes "the person" a legitimate subject of human rights. And it is this discursive foundation of the social-individual life that requires us to treat troubles telling in relation to a renewed conceptualization of human rights.

Again, I am not arguing that the right to tell one's own troubles is universal per se. Remember the Aboriginal Australians of the Darwin fringe camps whose troubles telling rights were transferred to those most responsible for treating their illness and thus restoring their tongues after serious illness had been "talkin' through them" (Sansom 1982). Narrative is always coconstructed with an audience (Duranti and Brenneis 1986), and we can consider the Darwin camp dwellers as embracing one extreme of that reality. What I am arguing is that, however people might conceive of themselves in relation to others (including conarrators) and to their troubles narratives, their ability to assume locally construed authorial roles is central to their human agency.

Inflicting pain and silencing victims is not justified by national political leaders in Bangladesh. In response to national women's movements, laws have been passed intending to protect women from such abuses as acid-throwing—a periodically epidemic phenomenon in South Asia in which a jilted man disfigures the woman he cannot possess. Faced, in their clinical practice, with other sorts of pain, some younger members of the Bangladeshi psychiatric elite have taken an activist turn, exposing widespread and hitherto *unspoken* abuses against children and psychiatric patients. The violence endured by Suleyman and Latifa occurs throughout rural Bangladesh, as it did until recently in the West (and, some would argue, still does in the form of frontal lobotomization and renewed practice of electroshock therapy). One Bangladeshi psychiatrist, on the basis of her own clinical experience, says that a common treatment for insane women is to tie them to a tree at midday and beat them. To the extent that such violence functionally serves to suppress incipient protest, we must see it as linked to the rights of women and men to freely construct a self-narrative. Beyond the right to narrate— free from torture and violence—one's own existence, the right of freedom of speech is enshrined in the Bangladeshi constitution and common discourse—in the oft-heard request [*āmāke*] *kathā balte den* (let me speak).

In 1993 Islamic militancy brought Bangladesh into the spotlight of the world press and of human rights activists. That fall, one militant group in Bangladesh issued a *fātwā* (religious sentence or ruling) calling for the death of Taslima Nasrin, whose fiction inscribed a pressing social problem. Nasrin's novel portrays a Hindu family torn asunder in the communal tensions following the destruction of the Ayodhya mosque in India. Nasrin's attention to this problem offended the sentiments of hard-line Islamists. This case has obvious parallels to that of Salman Rushdie. Nasrin now lives in dreary exile in Europe. In reaction to world outcry in 1993, two trends were visible. First, the Bangladesh government provided Nasrin with police protection, although they took no action against the instigators of the threats. Second, paranoia was inflamed in certain sections of the Bangladeshi Muslim population claiming that the human rights outcry arose out of a plot by the Indian government against Bangladesh's sovereignty (Thikana Bangla Weekly 1993).[9] It is not difficult to see at work in the Taslima Nasrin flap another body metaphor—the body politic comes to regard a member as outside itself and perceives all that lies outside as a threat (cf. Das 1996, and Lock and Scheper-Hughes 1990: 65). Despite the delicacy of such matters, national and international activism can appropriately speak for the rights of women, the mentally ill, and religious and ethnic minorities. It is hoped that this book strengthens the hands of activists and legal reformers, particularly within Bangladesh, who will ensure the fair enforcement of current statutes protecting women and men.

The Bangladeshi elites engaging in activism on behalf of currently inexpressible pains are mostly secular-modernist in outlook. If nothing else, this book has made it clear that the implicit ideologies of expression held by Dhaka academics, psychiatrists, and Matlab lamenters (e.g., stances toward lamenting) are not uncontested. The economic dependency of women has prevented them from seeking medical care on their own and has rendered them vulnerable to being ignored or divorced for presenting complaints and seeking care through their husbands. Community development aimed at ending this dependency is crucial to ensuring the efficacy of their complaints. But activists' work on behalf of women and other vulnerable populations will ensure that patient resistance pays off, that eloquence is no longer endangered, and that patients or sufferers as objects of complaints will at least be given the chance to be subjects.

Coda

The work of becoming human together, and of producing humane societies, makes use of the same discursive resources constituting Bangla troubles talk. The work of narrating a life, trouble and all, involves the self in many forms (as a "figure" in, as well as a "principal" or author of the narration, to name but two Goffmanian self forms) as well as audiences. It is equally urgent for families, communities, and nations to find narrative strategies that satisfy not only their own needs but also those of neighbors. In fact, the metatroubles plaguing troubles telling in Bangladesh or anywhere should be seen as a microcosm of the crisis of "self" confronting nations. In Iran, for instance, revivals of traditional discursive rituals of grief "may, paradoxically, pose a fundamental crisis for institutions and ideology"—including the very religious institutions receiving new ideological support from the state (Good and Good 1988: 60).[10] The same analogy can be drawn between troubles surrounding Bangla troubles talk and the troubles of the former Yugoslavia; ethnic strife there has largely hinged upon the narrative construction of grief and historic grievances. By contrast, the national hopes pinned on Truth Commissions in South Africa, Chile, Argentina, or Guatemala entail hopes that judicially mediated encounters unearthing violent troubles can become truth encounters that establish justice and peace.

It has not been easy for the new nation of Bangladesh to discover a discourse in which to establish national goals transcending the mutually conflicting interests of various elites (Alam 1995). Although I am not as sanguine about any literal hope arising out of the event as is Alam, I share his sense that the 1992 movement led by Jahanara Imam to confront the atrocities of 1971 is a trope for a more open public discourse in Bangladesh. Like Truth Commissions elsewhere, Imam's People's Court or the writings of Taslima Nasrin can be characterized as forms of national troubles talk striving toward new and humane forms of national self-production. If these forms of discourse are threatened along with Matlabi traditions of *sāhir*, *bilāp*, and even the everyday *dukkha-kaṣṭer kathā* of Aesha, the loss is not only to troubles tellers but to the community as a whole.

TRANSCRIBING MATLAB SPEECH

Table 1 explains correspondences between Bangla orthography, Bagchi's (1996) transliteration, and the phonetics of Matlab speech. My numbering of the Bangla symbols indicates a conflation under one number of those symbols whose differ- ence was realized in Sanskrit but is not realized in spoken Bangla, at least in Matlab. What I have tried to do throughout the book is to make a compromise between a transliteration recognizable to the scholarly community (Bagchi 1996) and a transcription that attempts to faithfully represent what I actually heard people say. Because this book might be used as one of the few published sources on Matlab speech, I want those who use it to be able to accurately recover that speech from my transcripts.

Following Ferguson (1959) in his analysis of diglossia, I refer to "standard" Bengali as H (high), while eschewing the implied value judgment. It is simplest, but admittedly problematic, to portray rural phonetics as a realized form of an underlying H system; again, I eschew the implied value judgment.

Vowels

First, note that I follow Indological transliteration conventions rather than using IPA phonetic symbols in representing both vowels and consonants (compare Bagchi 1996). Thus the vowel represented by the phonetic symbol /a/ is repre- sented herein by ā (see table).

[a] ----->ā

Again following Indological convention, I use the symbol /a/ to represent the Bangla descendent of Sanksrit's short /a/, which is phonetically realized as [O] (see Table).

a -----> e or [æ] in some contexts:
    H āpnār -----> [apner]
    or āpnār -----> [amner] (p----->m only in this word, as far as I know)

e -----> i (sometimes)
    theke -----> [tiki] (sometimes)

e -----> ā (sometimes)
    meye -----> [maya]

Table 1. The orthography of standard Bengali, its transliteration and its phonetic transcription

	Bangla Symbol	Transliteration	Pronunciation	Examples as in in my transcripts with phonetic representation where it diverges
1.	u	a	1. O as in law. 2. Closed o with no diphthongal glide. Due to a phonological vowel-raising rule, it is pronounced as [o] when it immediately precedes the high vowels [i] and [u], such as Latifa—[pronounced Lotifa (underlining for my expository purposes only)]. Since u is the "assumed vowel" in the Bangla syllabary, it is understood to follow consonants even where it is not written. In word final position, for instance in first-person future verbs, this assumed vowel is realized as [o].	1. fal [fOl] 2. jābo 3. byāthā [bætha][1] 4. dalān-ǿ
	u	a	3. Low front vowel, æ, as in apple.	
	u	a	4. Silent, omitted in word-final position except in poetic recitation style.	
2.	uh	ā	Low central vowel as in father, or low front vowel as in fan.	mathā āmerikā [æmerika] byāpak [bæpOk]
3.	o/e	i	Tense high front vowel as in chlorine	ei/ ki
4.	E/O	ī	In rural speech, identical to o	parī
5.	x	u	High rounded back vowel as in ruminate	ghum
6.	≈	ū	In rural speech, identical to x	
7.	n/g	l, e	Lax front vowel, tensed before high vowels as in [petuk]	pet [pEt] petuk [petuk]
8.	N	ay*	(ai in Bagchi) diphthong as in boy	aytā [Oyta]
9.	U	o	Tense mid back vowel as in open, but with no diphthongal glide	jābo, otā
10.	U'	ow	Tense mid back vowel with strong off-glide, as in "oh wow!"	owṣadh
11.	Z/V	n*	Voiced velar nasal as in song (Bagchi transliterates Z as ṃ but the distinction is not realized in contemporary speech)	bhānā [bhaNa]
12.	´	[V]*	Nasalization (stylistic, not phonemic in spoken rural speech); corresponds to French nasalized vowels, e.g. bon	hyāre-hāy-hum [hære hay hum]

			Description	Example
13.	s	k	Unaspirated voiceless velar stop as in "ski"	keman [kœmOn]
14.	S	kh	Aspirated voiceless velar stop as in cat	khāwā
15.	w	g	Unaspirated voiced velar stop as in go	goṭā
16.	W	gh	Aspirated voiced velar stop (does not occur in English)	ghyānghyān
17.	T	c	Unaspirated voiceless palatal affricate something like church	cokh, culkāy
18.	t	ch	Aspirated voiceless affricate as in chin, sometimes realized as [s]	āchen [asen]
19.	m	j	Unaspirated voiced palatal affricate as in jump	jāti
20.	M	jh	Aspirated voiced palatal affricate	jhimjhim
21.	nÅ	ñ	Not produced in Matlab speech	
22.	y	ṭ	Unaspirated retroflexed voiceless stop something like Ashton	ṭoṭ, ṭākā
23.	Y	ṭh	Aspirated retroflexed voiceless stop something like time	ṭhikānā
24.	X	ḍ	Unaspirated voiced retroflexed stop something like day	ḍal
25.	K	ṛ	Ultra-retroflexed front-flapped sonorant (contrast minimally with #40 in rural speech)	bāṛāno
26.	C	ḍh	Aspirated voiced retroflexed stop (does not occur in English)	ḍhākā
27.	L	ṇ	In spoken Bangla, identical with #32 in rural speech	citraṇ
28.	j	t	Unaspirated voiceless dental stop	tantane
29.	J	th	Aspirated voiceless dental stop	thānā
30.	r	d	Unaspirated voiced dental stop	dalagato
31.	R	dh	Aspirated voiced dental stop (does not occur in English)	dhān, krodh
32.	l	n	Voiced alveolar nasal as in nose	naṣṭo
33.	b	p	Unaspirated voiceless bilabial stop something like spot	pān
34.	B	f*	(ph in Bagchi) voiceless labiodental fricative something like fish	fal [fOl]
35.	f	1. b	Unaspirated voiced bilabial stop as in boy	balte [bOlte]
and	f	2. as subscript	a) Geminates the consonant to which it is subscripted, or	āmitvo [amittO]
			b) Has no phonetic realization	jvar [jOr]
				svāmi [Sami]
36.	F	bh	Aspirated voiced bilabial stop (does not occur in English); sometimes approximates English /v/ as in love	bhālo, lobh
37.	p	m	Voiced bilabial nasal as in man	mukh
38.	I	j*	(ẏ in Bagchi) unaspirated voiced palatal affricate as in joke	jābo
39.	i	y	Voiced semivowel as in lawyer	meẏe

245

Table 1. (ctd.)

Bangla Symbol	Trans-litera-ation	Pronunciation	Examples as in in my transcripts with phonetic representation where it diverges
40. k	r	Lingual flap similar to initial /r/ in Spanish	rāg, erā, jār
41. c	l	High-tongued liquid as in leap	likhen, bellāl
42. v	ś	Palatal sibilant as in shine	śānti [Santi]
43. D	ṣ	Alveolar sibilant something like shine	kaṣṭo [kOSto]
44. d	s	Pronounced as [S] in most words but as [s] before non-retroflex coronals ([t], [n], [r], and [l]) and in loanwords	saṅge [SONge] sālām [salam]
45. z	h	Hello	hok
46. :		The "visarga" is often transliterated as "h" but, since its effect on pronunciation is to geminate the following consonant, I represent it by doubling that consonant.	dukkho [dukkʰo]

Conjuncts whose pronunciation is not obvious in the conventional transliteration:

47. P	kṣ	The ṣ geminates and aspirates the k	bhikṣuk [bʰikkʰuk]
48. Pπ	kṣm	The m is not phonetically realized; see above	lakṣmi [lokkʰi]
49. ¶	jñ	Unaspirated voiced velar stop as in go	jñān [gæn]

1. Here and throughout the book, h following stop consonants represents aspiration [pʰ, tʰ, ṭʰ, kʰ, bʰ, dʰ, ḍʰ, gʰ].
* = Departure from Bagchi

246

Simplification of vowel clusters. It is quite common for the cluster occurring in perfective verbs — stem+i+yā+suffix— to be reduced to [i], though I have typically represented such forms as shown below to indicate the unsimplified version of the cluster:

iyā-----> i

Thus, ha-iyā-che-----> [hOise] (represented in transcripts as hai[ye]che) [Note that in the urban *calti* or HCB (high colloquial Bengali, Chatterjee 1986) the older long forms of verbs are simplified in a slightly different way:

ha-iye-che-----> [hOcc^{h}e]]

Consonants

There is some tendency in Matlab, perhaps from Assamese influence not far to the east, to replace stops with fricatives, as in:

s -----> [h]
sometimes k -----> [h], as in:
    theke -----> [tEhE], ṭākā -----> [ṭehā], cākā -----> [caha]
sometimes t -----> [h], particularly in the distal pronominal deictics
    (he/they, over there):
tār -----> [her], tārā -----> [hera]
h -----> [ø], as in
    haiyā-----> [Oya]
ch -----> [s]
    āche -----> [ase], and ācchā -----> [as:a]

In what seems to be hypercorrection, the reverse sometimes happens (s -----> ch):

āssālāmu āleykum ----->[acchalamu aleykum]
ṭ ----->[ḍ]

This is not consistent, but is most noticeable in the definite article suffix:

    -ṭā -----> [-ḍa]
Aspiration -----> [0]

The contrast between aspirated and unaspirated stops, both voiced and voiceless, tends to be lost.

    theke -----> [tEhE]

Morphophonemics

Participles seem close to H *suddho* Bangla (HSB, diglossic written form; see Chatterjee 1986), in which participles are formed as root-*iyā*. Matlab participles tend to metathesize the y of HSB iyā with the root of the verb and geminate the last consonant of the root:

śuniyā -----> [Suynna], baliyā (HCB bale)-----> [bOylla]

Similar examples of metathesis and gemination. A similar pronunciation pattern is seen in the word śarīr (body). Like H participles, the H form has a consonant followed by i. Matlab pronunciation, however, metathesizes the i and geminates the last consonant of the noun root (C_1 i -----> i C_1 C_1):

śarir ---> [SOil:a], pratham ----->[pOrthOm]
(Fatima; line 2F, example 14, chapter 5)

Infinitives follow HSB quite closely, ending in [-ite] and thus contrasting with the H colloquial where the rule for infinitives and participles requires drop-ping the formative i vowel. In Matlab, however, constructions requiring infini-tives are sometimes subject to transformation, particularly through elision, quite possibly reflecting the grammaticalization of the pronoun āmi.

1st.person.verb+infinitive+pārā (to be able) ----->infinitive-[m par]-
or, eliding several sounds, finite.verb+infinitive+pārā ----->infinitive-[ār]
āmi kai-te pār-i nā -----> [ami kOyta-m par-i na] *or* [kOy-t-ar-i na]

I draw special attention to such forms as possible instances of grammaticaliza-tion, e.g. in Fatima's line 52 in example 14, chapter 5.

Tense-aspect. In H karcho (sometimes [kOrcʰo])—signifies present-con-tinuous tense-aspect. In Matlab, both [kOrcʰo] and [kOrso] carry the perfective meaning borne by the standard karecho; i.e., Matlab speech elides the [e] in per-fective verbs.

Elision occurs in other contexts as well. Whole medial syllables may be elided:

rakam -----> [rOm].
I have represented this elision as: ra[ka]m.

Morpholexical/Lexical Variants. Plural morphemes such as the standard genitive.plural /-der/ are typically realized as [-go]:

tāder-----> [tago/hego], "their."

NOTES

Preface

1. The ICDDR,B was founded by the Southeast Asian Treaty Organization as the Cholera Research Laboratory (CRL) in 1960 in Dhaka, then the provincial capital of East Pakistan. Most of the funding and personnel were provided through USAID. Cholera continued to claim lives throughout the SEATO region, but East Pakistan was chosen because the disease was endemic there. In Dhaka, research and treatment were carried out in a facility shared with the government public health complex in the Mohakhali neighborhood. In 1963, a field station for conducting vaccine trials was established in Matlab, then part of the Comilla district. A simple "floating hospital" was established to serve the riverine countryside where cholera thrived. In 1966 they were joined in their public health efforts by the government, which established a health complex in Matlab. The floating hospital was eventually replaced by a stationary hospital in Matlab served by a fleet of speed-boat ambulances and ICDDR,B subcenters, including one in the bazaar or union town I call "Sonargaon," the subcenter where "Taqbir's" parents worked.

Chapter 1

1. Seremetakis argues that this is a valid position from which to view Maniate social life, particularly the life of Maniate women, since peering through "the optic offered by death" and funerary laments is precisely the strategy, "the central task, and the cognitive orientation assumed by Maniate women in their performance of death rites. To examine death in Inner Mani is to look at Maniat society through female eyes" (1991: 15).

2. The contributors to Fauveau (1994) do not claim to know the population of the whole district, though the study villages in Matlab in which ICDDR,B does demographic surveillance had over 300,000 people in 1988.

3. Administrative units in Bangladesh, from smallest to largest, are the village, union, *upajila*, and district. Beyond Chandpur and Matlab, place names and names of patients are fictitious. Unpublished surveys of practitioners, by name and type, are available from J. Chakraborty and M. Sarder, of the ICDDR,B (Matlab).

4. The Bangla pronunciation, *jāri*, represents the borrowed Persian term, *zāri*.

5. Matlab consultants tell me that *āhājārī* is even "more pathetic, heart-wrenching, and heart-felt" than *bilāp*.

6. The embankment is part of the Meghna-Dhonagoda Irrigation Project, a massive ecological intervention with mixed results (Huda, Huq, and Bhuiyan 1991; Cobb 1993).

7. Out of a sample of 200 women from my study villages who had visited the nearest ICDDR,B health clinic over two years, half were landless. Among those landless families is that of Fatima, described in several chapters of this book; it is no accident that this destitute woman is among the least confident of the troubles tellers described in the book.

8. The words of Latifa and Suleyman, much in focus in later chapters, exemplify "public transcripts" of resistance.

9. For a discussion of the heteroglossia, polysemy, and conflicts surrounding Muslim veiling, see Macleod (1991) and Ahmed (1992: 236, 242).

10. I refer to the language spoken in Matlab (and Dhaka, etc.) as Bangla and the people as Bengali, following the usage of contemporary Bengali intellectuals (Clint Seely, personal communication, 1995). There is no evidence to justify the claim that the language of Bangladesh is so distinct from that of the Indian state of Bengal as to deserve a different name. The traditional name designating the language, Bengali, has been used to describe all of the dialects together. It is not used to exclude the dialects used in Bangladesh, nor does my use of the term "Bangla" exclude the Calcutta dialect.

11. Persian is an Indo-European language, sharing common ancestry with the Indo-Aryan languages at some distant point in the past. Still, it is part of a different branch of the Indo-European family, and when Bangla or Hindu borrow from Persian, it is truly borrowing, not just a sort of family reunion.

12. "Indirection"— linguists' term verbal indirectness— is explored as a strategy of politeness by Brown and Levinson (1986). See also the typology of various forms of indirection provided by Brenneis (1988).

13. For a discussion of cross-cultural variation in greeting questions and their orientation to space and motion in the South Pacific, see Duranti (1992: 663).

14. The evident acceptability of "Where will it be gone?" gives lie to the linguists' rule that only transitive verbs may be passivized and thus illustrates how social factors sometimes overshadow purely grammatical ones in determining what is "good speech." Admittedly, the English translation is odd, but the Bangla sentence did not raise local eyebrows.

15. Indeed, though her ground-breaking study of dative subjects in Bengali was by no means about troubles talk per se, the dative subject examples that Klaiman (1981) lists include many that are related to troubles talk.

16. Grammatical subjects of verbs such as "see" in English are not semantic agents but experiencers, and verbs like "see" are stative rather than active.

17. In conversation analysis, routinized pairs of utterances such as questions or invitations and answers/responses are called "adjacency pairs."

18. The oral *bilāp* genre is paralleled by a centuries-old written tradition.

19. Those who have analyzed local taxonomic systems have often noted the absence of terms at certain levels of inclusivity. Hanks (1990) is a good example; he shows no concern over the absence of a Mayan term for "deixis" or "indexicals," the major focus of his investigation. Citing cognitive theory on category terms, Hanks argues that the basic level of categories available to an actor's consciousness is "neither the most inclusive ... nor the most specific ... term, but rather an intermediate level of inclusiveness somewhere between the two" (1990: 151). That is the case with Bangla complaints.

20. *Āllāh Āllāh karā* (literally, "do 'God, God'") is an expression widely used in Bangladesh for an individual prayer, a recitation, or other Islamic observances. It denotes the repetitive invocation of God.

21. On the pull exerted by Arizona Tewa "kiva speech," see Kroskrity 1992.

22. I stress that English is no less constraining on my analysis than is Bangla—hence the need for neologisms such as "state-of-being-complaints" and "troubles talk." It is difficult to resist the thought that the downplaying of agency in Bangla constrains cognitive habits when one is listening to stories of discouragement by foreign or highly Westernized public health workers who have failed to convince Matlab residents of the germ

theory of disease causation or of the efficacy of affordable sanitation and hygiene measures. It is also difficult to resist the sense that the two groups occupy different worlds, each disbelieving in the other, while the public health workers' form of ethnocentrism is more likely tinged with classism.

23. Ready-mades are chunks ready to be used—poetic lines (or even whole stanzas) or musical bars or longer melodic lines—that are available for "quotation" and recombination.

24. The ludic-critical role of such performances has parallels elsewhere in South Asia (see, for example, Trawick 1988; Raheja and Gold 1994).

25. For three other works explicitly describing patients as agents, see MacIntyre (1977), Sansom (1982), and Gear, Liendo, and Scott (1983).

26. This gloss for the Indo-Aryan *man* or *mon* follows the translation lead of Desjarlais (1992) in his sensitive treatment of the transformation of suffering in Nepal. A more processual term, *cintā-bhābanā*—heard in Dhaka more than Matlab—is quite literally rendered by Wikan's nondualizing gloss for the Balinese category "thought-feeling." My point in citing the Bangla term and its Balinese parallels is to provide further warrant for the nondualistic rendering of *man/mon* as "heartmind."

27. By "political economy of speech" I mean control over semiotic resources— unequally distributed rights and responsibilities of exchange, labeling, and "ownership" of words.

28. The pattern of doctor-patient interaction is linked with gender asymmetry. Ainsworth-Vaughn and others have found that female physicians in North America do not interrupt patients as frequently as do their male counterparts. But female kin or practitioners can and do interrupt men according to my Bangladeshi data, although females are interrupted more often, regardless of the sex of the interrupter. "Few features of language directly and exclusively index gender," because particular correlations are "non-exclusive" (Ochs 1992: 340). As is seen in the case of Farhad, it is not "women's language," but "powerless language" (O'Barr and Atkins 1980), that is typically silenced or cut off.

29. Many studies of cross-sex conversation find males controlling topics and interrupting females more than they themselves are interrupted (West and Zimmerman 1975, 1983; West 1984; Davis 1993), though other studies not only produce counterevidence but critique the method of West and Zimmerman (Murray 1985; Murray and Covelli 1988).

30. The very fact that *rudālī* is not found in any of my four Bangla dictionaries highlights the importance of my words: "There once was ..." The social category might be extinct; an alternative hypothesis is that, despite one Bengali's (Mr. Khan's) testimony, the class of persons might have been mostly confined to regions contiguous to Bengal.

31. This is not a deficit or any absolute absence—there is a rich psychological lexicon in Sanskritic Bangla, a lexicon on which psychological publications from Calcutta have drawn—but a relative unavailability in common speech, probably similar to the situation with European languages before Freud.

Chapter 2

1. In no way should the reader interpret this narrative as an objective indictment of the family of Habibur Rahman. He and his brothers told me, to the contrary, that they do bring Aesha food from the market almost daily. A community health worker says that Aesha *is* (not was) *pāgal* (mad, insane).

2. Bengalis can also speak of problems as *durghaṭanā* (misfortune). Obeyesekere describes the presentation of "misfortunes" (Sinhala *doṣa*, whose Bangla counterpart means "fault") to the spiritual practitioners involved in the *Cult of the Goddess of Pattini* (1984: 36–44). In Sri Lanka, as in Bangladesh, the domain of misfortunes that may be presented to such practitioners is broad indeed.

3. Aesha, and several others old enough to be my aunts or uncles, called me *cācā* (father's brother), a term of respectful distance. Everyone in the family addressed me by whatever kin term seemed appropriate to them; most of the elders used *cācā*, and most of those who were my age, or younger, used *bhāi* (brother).

4. "Our" or "my."

5. Here Aesha uses the pronoun *tui* (on the three levels of distance/honor, see the Transcription Conventions). It contrasts with the respect form, *āpni*, that Aesha Begum and I use for each other and that she uses for most men. The addressee of *tui* is evidently one or all of the children in the room.

6. Or, "a lot of different people say, ..."

7. She might mean either the *target* or the *source* of the comment is "good."

8. She is addressing a child of another house in the compound and, through her, the adults who regularly gossip about her.

9. That is, "survive the flood": the idiom reflects the frequency of flooding in Bangladesh.

Chapter 3

1. McKim Marriott's work (e.g., 1976), in contrast with the work of Louis Dumont, is explicitly concerned with varna-based variation in styles of selfhood and interpersonal engagement. But he describes it as an "ethnosociology," not an ethnopsychology, and limits his variationist attentions to the four *varna* groups of the Hindu caste system. Individual variation within each *varna* does not claim a place in Marriott's modeling of the self in India.

2. It is not altogether glib to remind my Western readers interested in the self that the nature of the *ātmā(n)*, or self/Self, was explored in India long before it was in Greece. I make no assumption that burning questions in ancient textual traditions are central in the thoughts and behavior of contemporary Hindus—let alone Muslim Bangladeshis. I cite the antiquity of the self problem in South Asia to indicate that this discourse was an ongoing one when Dumont's European predecessors first encountered India, or when interactionist theories of the self were emerging in the United States.

3. This "triangulation," in which the key point in the triangle is someone else who is said to love the speaker, should be compared with Takeo Doi's (1973) description of the Japanese concept *amae* (passive love).

4. The contrast with Tamils, and perhaps with other South Asians who feel that love should be nourished by hiding it (Trawick 1990) could not be stronger.

5. Understanding how Bangla conversation builds self and relationality simultaneously is aided by reference to Mead's work (1995b), ideas that underlie those of Goffman and of more recent linguistic anthropologists. Mead, describing how the self arises out of discourse as social interaction, finds a balance between two forms of the self: the ontologically prior "me" (self from the viewpoint of others who react to "me") and the derivative "I" (self as agent in relation to others, center of subjective experience viewing others). One hears the "me" or me-self projected loudly in self-reflexive statements by

Bangladeshi women and men. My concept of the me-self has more to do with loss of agency than did Mead's concept.

6. By this I mean that the self attached to territories could be conceived of as fluid, transpersonal, familial, or otherwise social.

7. Das (1996) describes the motivations of women who, though having experienced rape and the murder of their menfolk, veil their troubles.

8. On the distribution of rights to say "I," see Hanks (1990). For an analogous argument regarding "experience," see Desjarlais (1997).

9. For the history and utility of this relatively new research paradigm, see Silverstein (1979); Kroskrity, Schieffelin, and Woolard (1992); and Woolard and Schieffelin (1994).

Chapter 4

1. Whorf's (1956) classic example is the intersubjective, conventionalized, grammatically founded sense of time (which becomes subjective or internalized as speakers of Hopi or a European language grow up using those languages).

2. Interestingly, one of these troubles tellers was another American researcher who experienced an attack by an invisible but tangible choking force. A roommate from that locale intervened, and the ability to breathe was restored. To that researcher, local spirits became all too real.

3. Obvious parallels between the Bangla term *dar*, and *susto* (magical fright) as described in Latin American societies (Gillin 1948), have yet to be explored.

4. Here again, note the need in English for a qualified phrase such as "state complaint" to indicate complaints that refer primarily to internal states rather than making explicit accusations.

5. For a fascinating account of how even "one speaker's" sentence structure is emergent or interactively constituted, see Goodwin (1979).

6. See Hallowell (1955: 89) for a discussion of the significance of Boas's claim for a psychological universalism. More recently, scholars have treated pronouns as "shifters" (Silverstein 1976), or as keys to "participation frames" (Goffman 1981). Goffman (1981) and Hanks (1990) make strong cases against taking frame-relevant action or "referential practice"—including the practice of referring to or animating the character of a self—at face value. That is, the linguistic ability to animate a self ought not to be taken as evidence of an essentialized biological entity or a psychological center of experience (Silverstein, in press).

7. My transcript of a moot (old English for "open/folk court") contains a pointed example of this use of the Bangla pronoun *āmrā* (we; Wilce 1996).

8. This is the argument of William Hanks (1990: 7): "When speakers say 'Here it is', he or she unavoidably conveys something like, 'Hey, you and I stand in a certain relation to each other and to this object and this place, right now'."

9. The deictic *e* ("this") has no obvious referent. Compare Fatima's line 61 in example 14.

10. For a description of possession-mediumship in another South Asian context, see Nuckolls (1991).

11. *Dhikr*, the remembrance of Allah through the chanting of holy texts by Muslims—particularly Sufis—is sometimes associated with rhythmic movement (e.g., the whirling of the dervish [*darbeś*] saints), and thus with trance-mysticism, in a variety of Islamic civilizations.

12. The Persian *pari* is an Indo-European cognate of the English "fairy." There is something of a double standard in operation in light of the man Suleyman's relations with a *pari* functioning as an incubus, which is not the reason he is scandalous. It is Suleyman's public behavior that causes scandal. Although people know about his *pari*—formerly his grandmother's, now his by tragic inheritance—they do not gossip about that but, rather, about how he stole the microphone from the muezzin, and how he speaks in a singsong voice. For a psychoanalytic account of South Asian possession and incubus spirits, see Obeyesekere (1981).

13. My "uncle" is Shefali's husband. Faisal is asking here whether or not Shefali's husband had engaged the spirit in a sort of divinatory dialogue.

14. In Islamic Asia, including Afghanistan and perhaps Bangladesh, a similar concept of human existence and virtue seems to exist, linking suffering with saintliness and thus motivating a similar presentation of self (Grima 1991; Goffman 1959).

15. That is, an illness marking the spiritual initiation of a person into the role of shaman; see the story of Manwara Bibi in chapter 7.

16. Many an analyst of possession and possession cults (Kennedy 1967; Lewis 1975; Beals 1976; Blanchet 1984: 52, 53; McDaniel 1989) has considered such states functional for the group and, particularly in the case of women and other relatively disadvantaged individuals, a form of individual and corporate self-assertion tolerated where other forms are suppressed.

17. Urban also finds a kinship between semiotic and psychoanalytic theory in the context of the development of the self. We may view this development either ontogenetically or as a kind of interactive emergence; the self, in these two perspectives, develops over autobiographical time or develops/emerges in a given interactive event. Combining the two perspectives in a single model, discursive self-formation is a constant process.

18. "Egocentricity is a special case of sociocentricity, which is more basic" (Hanks 1990: 515).

19. I learned this only in 1996. Dowry murders—faked suicides of women killed by in-laws who retaliate for failure to provide a promised dowry—have become all too common in South Asian countries.

20. Latifa's brothers are not wealthy. I presume that the purpose of his calling my attention to the expenses they were incurring for this treatment (under a contract calling for 100 Taka per month over 10 months) was to demonstrate to me how generous their commitment was to their sister.

21. Latifa's brothers themselves told me how they had chained her. Latifa told us of the beatings.

22. The fact that they *expressed* willingness to fund her dowry and arrange another marriage for her indicates that, even to her brothers, finances were not the only obstacle preventing her from being reunited with her ex-husband. Still, Latifa's mother asked me for money for the dowry fund or to send her abroad (where she might find a wealthier man to marry, even without a dowry).

23. In typical usage, the proverb corresponds to "a bird in the hand," but the literal focus of the proverb on the significance of the mother's brother should not be overlooked.

24. The literal meaning of the title *kabirāj,* from which the adjective *kabirāji* derives, is "king of the verse" (the "verse" denoting sacred Sanskrit texts of Ayurveda, such as the Caraka Samita). The heterogeneous array of practitioners called *kabirāj* in Matlab may practice herbalist-Ayurvedic medicine, specialize in exorcism, or combine spiritualist-Islamic practices with the dispensing of allopathic remedies.

25. If this is true in any sense, it must be qualified; what her brothers say they want is that Latifa should agree to marry someone else. At any rate, it is clear that Latifa did not want to go on living with her brothers, nor did they want her to.

26. Unfortunately, I have not been able to ask Latifa directly about literary sources on which she might have consciously drawn. A contemporary Western woman, who testifies of finding liberation through the teachings of a South Asian Sufi master, quotes this proverb: "The path of love is like a bridge of hair across a chasm of fire" (Tweedie 1979).

27. I prefer "classical" to "Hindu." To speak of "Hindu" authors is to take the risk of anachronism and essentializing labels for communal groups whose boundaries hardened much later.

28. In actuality, it is as likely to have been a genre in which a female figure served as a slate onto which male poets projected desire. See Selby (1996).

29. *Hashr*, in Arabic, "gathering," is used as a technical term in Muslim theology for the final gathering of all humans and jinns on Judgment Day (Gardet 1980: 236). Though I translated line 42 as referring to the "fire of judgment," that is its connotation only. Fire is what people think of when they think of *Hashr*.

30. Here I invoke the socially significant but linguistically arbitrary designation of certain linguistic varieties as standard or high ones, and particularly Ferguson's notion of "diglossia" as an emic polarity of "hi" and "lo" variants (1959), widely agreed to characterize linguistic variation within the Bangla language community as well as others.

31. From the vantage point of the Calcutta standard, Matlab colloquial Bangla adds the vowel /w/ to the noun root. To both is added a suffix—the definite article, /-ṭi/.

32. Klaiman labels the /-e/ suffix on pā-e "locative," but that suffix is multifunctional. It also reflects the time when Bangla—like other North Indian languages—had an ergative-absolutive case system. Thus, /-e/ serves to stress the agency of noun phrases whose agency is either divine and thus extraordinary, or else lower on a Bangla animacy hierarchy (e.g., insects or snakes that bite humans, or *bhut*-spirits cited in example 45). This ergative /-e/ appears throughout the examples in this book, e.g. in 17L and 59L of example 16 in chapter 5, and in the proverb cited in example 59 (chapter 11). The *pā-e* example from Klaiman (1980) is exceptional in that its final /-e/ marks what is, in the sample sentence, an experiencer subject—not an agent.

33. Indirect and nonmonetary means of reimbursing exorcists have been mentioned by other observers, such that some can make a living thereby (Islam 1985: 145).

34. A complete transcript is found in example 14 in chapter 5.

35. A Bangladeshi consultant living in Arizona told me that he had once had the power to see the future in dreams, but lost it when he told others about the dream. He says that when Allah gives special gifts like this, they may be lost if the recipient talks about it.

There is a parallel in the Greek classics, as cited by Kierkegaard: "When Amor leaves Psyche, he says to her: You will bear a child who will be divine if you remain silent but will be human if you betray the secret" (Apuleis, *The Golden Ass*, as cited by Kierkegaard 1983: 88).

36. One might compare this Bangladeshi experience with reports of night terrors from other parts of the world (Hufford 1982). Further interpretive work on this phenomenon is needed. The *bobā* experience can be explored as a rejection of normative discourse patterns, a dramatization of the message "I can't speak freely," or a retreat to a preobjective and preverbal developmental stage (Csordas 1990).

37. I do not deny that the stories of Fatima's involvement with spirits had moral connotations. My point here is only that the shorthand label her sisters-in-law most frequently gave her condition lacked the pejorative moral connotations of *pāgal*.

The hopelessness entailed in labeling Fatima's condition a *māthār byārām* arises from its connotation that the illness is endogenous, rather than an acute attack by a passing spirit (Bhattacharyya 1986).

38. Whereas the Qur'an mentions the pleasures that these female beings will provide to (heterosexual) male believers in paradise, Shefali's invocation of *parī* evinces something more like solidarity.

39. This correlation is clear only in an interpretive sense; the idea that such connotations would be available to all Bangla speakers, or even females among them, is far beyond what I claim.

40. Naturally, Fatima's case is not a mirror image of Shefali's. While we could say of Fatima that her bouts of speechlessness constitute her central complaint, that would not do justice to her whole experience. During the transcribed encounter between Fatima and the exorcist, her primary complaint was a distressing kind of experience for which she was not finding ready words. *That* constitutes Fatima's metacomplaint, a concept I define in chapter 10.

41. Suleyman had given his daughter in marriage to a son of Habibur Rahman's brother.

42. Funds from Middle Eastern countries have provided amplification systems to most of the thousands of mosques that dot the Bangladeshi countryside.

43. Suleyman and several others who called themselves *pāgal* (mad) or burdened with *hrid rog* (heart sickness) had given me generous time and honest reflections on their pain. I felt I owed them something. Thus I arranged for Dr. Rizwana Quaderi, a British-trained psychiatrist at the Institute for Post-Graduate Medical Research Hospital in Dhaka, to visit Matlab for a field clinic. I made arrangements for the several people I was seeing to attend this clinic. Dr. Quaderi met some and invited one to her hospital, where she gave her a prescription of oral antipsychotics and administered an antipsychotic injection; these brought about a marked and positive change in the young woman's condition. Suleyman and Ahmed were unable to attend the field clinic. It was only on the basis of my description that Dr. Quaderi diagnosed Suleyman. However, a colleague of Dr. Quaderi in Dhaka saw and treated Suleyman in 1995 in my absence. Suleyman and his wife feel that he has completely recovered, although he suffers some confusion that they interpret as an evidently permanent side effect of the medicine he took that year.

44. On anxiety over loss of semen (*dhātu*, regarded throughout South Asia as the possession of females as well as males), see, inter alia, Obeyesekere (1976, 1978).

45. The son went to Pakistan seven years ago so that he could earn money to send home. He wrote a few letters the first year, but has not communicated at all for six years.

46. The third lacked a verb, which is not always diagnostic of clause status in Bangla or in other languages requiring no copula.

47. In keeping with transcription conventions of conversation analysis, this question mark does not designate a syntactic question, but only a rising intonation.

48. Ali, Moniruzzaman, and Tareq (1994: 561) define *bilāsitā* as "luxury, foppishness; high living, love of pleasure; self-indulgence; wantonness; dissipation; playfulness; life of pleasure; self-gratification."

While there is validity in seeing structural-functionalist cultural reasons to label the assertive or self-indulgent as mad in Bangladesh or India—and there is nothing inherently less humane about such a diagnostic criterion—more recent examinations of healing

(Steedly 1988) persuade me to notice "healing" events that actually deepen division and distress. At any rate, I concur with the following statement: "It is simply unacceptable that, in the closing days of the twentieth century, in so many countries the chronically mentally ill [let alone persons like Latifa, whose diagnosis is disputable] are still abandoned in conditions of ... brutality" (Department of Social Medicine 1995), in which we must include chaining and beating.

49. Note that both *āmitva* and *ahaṅkār* derive from forms of "I"—*āmitva* is a straightforward derivative of the everyday Bangla pronoun *āmi*, and *ahaṅkār* derives from the Sanskrit first-person nominative pronoun.

Chapter 5

1. The "identity repertoire" perspective on ethnicity(ies) is highly compatible with, and has received much recent impetus from, sociolinguistic research. See, for example, Kroskrity (1993) and Rampton (1995).

2. As Hamid (1994) admits, what is measured in psychological-behavioral studies of locus of control (and self-monitoring as a close correlate) may be *"the cultural value placed on* the monitoring of self-other expressive behaviour rather than any fundamental difference in a manifest self-presentation style" (p. 366; emphasis added).

3. Compare English ambiguities such as the purportedly generic "he" and the role of pronouns like "you" in gender socialization in White middle-class American families (Ochs 1992), and Japanese syntactic ambiguities by which mothers use impersonal constructions when giving children directives, and thereby background their individual agency (Clancy 1986).

4. The claim holds only for varieties of Bangla such as that spoken in Matlab. In written or relatively standardized spoken Bangla, the realization of the overt pronominal form is common enough to make the absence of such possessives the marked case.

5. Such problems include seeming vagueness, metacomplaints, disagreements, and interruptions.

6. Here [*an*] could be a phonetic realization of /*ekhan*/ (now) or, more idiosyncratically, of /*āmār*/ (my).

7. Here [*āur*] seems to be a phonetic realization of /*āmār*/ and has been coded as such.

8. For consistency, the demonstrative and article have been underlined here, but they are not counted in the total since they do not seem likely to have been replaceable by a first-person pronoun.

9. Whereas Jahangir asked if they understood (*bujh*) the symptoms in a certain way, Fatima's uptake of that same lexeme, *bujh*, is altered. Rendering it a causative, *bujh-ā*, she makes herself the potential patient or object of explaining, rather than the agent of understanding. In either case, the ø marks the absence of the pronoun that could have served as either subject or object of either verb and would in either case have preceded it.

10. Fatima says *ḍābārālāy*, or *ḍubāiyā phelāy* (submerges [me], pushes [me] under). Since she is talking about something that happens inside her dry house, I have translated this as "pushes me down."

11. *Ṭhor* means the "spathe of a plaintain tree," or a "mere trifle; nothing" (vulgar connotations; Ali, Moniruzzman, and Tareq 1994: 285).

12. The markedly intimate or demeaning form *tui* is the implicit pronominal form with which the imperative [*kas*] agrees. It is the lowest-ranking option in the respect paradigm.

13. By rebuking Fatima's kinswomen for ridiculing and interrupting her, Jahangir is simultaneously helping Fatima, upholding what he imagines to be my standards for a recorded interview, and reproducing gender hierarchy (he, a man, is telling women to shut up). This is an embarrassing instance of the ethical ambiguities inherent in post-colonial field relationships.

14. *Ahane* seems to be a common Matlab realization of / *ekhan*/ (now).

15. Jahangir's *dharen nā* in line 75 could also be heard as *dharan* (form/example of). In either case, the women's use of *dharen* (take [for example]) immediately following Jahangir's is a sign of attunement (Becker 1988; Trix 1993) via format tying (Goodwin and Goodwin 1987).

16. That is, *ṭākā* (money).

17. *Hārin-ṭā* (realized once in this transcript as *hālinṭā*) seems to be an idiosyncratic phonological variant of *sārā-ṭā* ("whole-the," all). One idiosyncratic aspect of Fatima's use of the Bangla universal quantifier *sārā*, when she uses that word instead of *hālinṭā*, is its placement (line 6F):

"an māthāṭā ei sārā āguner lulār matan [h]aile."
(Now the head, this whole, [feels] like fire and smoke)

We could interpret this instance of *sārā* as postpositive to *māthā*, or as an ellipsis, a false start on a new noun phrase never uttered. The second case (*śailṭā sārāi*, line 82F) seems to confirm the first postpositive interpretation. Since the normal order of elements in Bangla noun phrases is adjective-noun, this example of the quantifier following the noun is unusual.

18. The use of the universal quantifier in such affect-laden phrases fits Labov's (1984) characterization of its link with affective intensification.

19. For a demonstration of how self-repair or restarting sentences can serve to solicit gaze, see Goodwin (1979).

20. For an analogous phenomenon, see Scollon and Scollon (1982: 19): "Instead of showing your qualities ... you reduce them somewhat ... so that the other speaker can boast for you. This is a kind of lure that is cast out in order to make your conversational partner do some of the work of displaying your abilities. You understate your case and your partner then builds it up." Gendered differences in pause length might explain how it is that male practitioners seem naturally to be able to interrupt patients like Yasmin (Gal 1989).

21. This is an evasive analog of the English saying "What you see is what you get."

22. Political meetings (Wilce 1996) are held in open fields, not in closed corridors. Still, they manage to exclude women, since open, public spaces are precisely those from which women are excluded in Bangladesh.

Chapter 6

1. In Peircean semiotics, sign relations are generated between signs per se (sign-vehicles) and their objects, grounds, and interpretants (i.e., the more developed signs created in the minds of persons perceiving the sign-vehicles). Sign-vehicles are the material bases—in sound or some other medium—of the perceptible cues that signal something to someone.

2. The fact that I heard the proverb, "If/when a baby stops crying, it gets no milk," as a justification of demands presented by adults is remarkable in relation to what Kurtz (1992) claims about the way caregivers' attention-cum-frustration responses to children's crying encourages them to give up selfish demands.

3. See Schieffelin and Ochs (1986). The routine under discussion, though not as common as those they describe, parallels more common elicitation routines at the heart of language socialization.

4. For instance, Samoan children are "born assertive" and must learn respect (Ochs and Schieffelin 1984).

5. For the dark side of this discourse and its ongoing effects on women, see Das 1996.

6. Kurtz (1992) makes the learning of kin terms the most explicit agenda of language socialization in North India, noting that a child's correct use of a kin term may occasion an exception to the taboo on praising children overtly.

7. My assistant's interest skews the data, but not irredeemably. While her interest might have provoked an atypical degree of linguistic self-consciousness, the content of the language was filled in by Samia and her kin as they saw fit—namely, address-routines, that is, eliciting kin terms.

8. The stance being modeled is reminiscent of that which is tragically presented in the myth of "The Boy Who Had No *Āde*," as interpreted by Schieffelin and Ochs (1986) and by Feld (1990).

9. This male fear is seen even more clearly in the culturally constituted necessity of painful male initiation ceremonies among the Sambia of Papua New Guinea, in which adolescent boys are radically separated from their mothers (Herdt 1987).

10. The Bangla representation of the sound of a cat is nearly identical to its English counterpart. After hearing catcalls on the streets, I asked friends what this seeming insult might signify. I learned that cats represent some sort of sexual transgression—perhaps having sex in a standing position—that Bangladeshis associate with foreigners.

11. Transliteration and translation are mine. Nasalization is marked in the standard way in the original Bangla orthography, and with a subscripted comma here. In 1984, as I studied Ishaque's (1955) novel with a tutor in Bangladesh, I asked about the significance of these nonsense syllables. Their only significance, he replied, lies in the nasalization of the vowels; the words are semantically empty. Spirits, he explained, are widely believed to speak through the nose—an opinion I have since heard repeated in other contexts.

12. These include an ethnographic presentation arising from encounters with spirits in Bihar, India (Schmalz 1996) as well as accounts at the Bangla Academy (staff, personal communication, June 1996) of how Bangladeshi storytellers animate spirit characters.

13. Although both Kaluli and Bangla speakers view the emergence of hard talk as a developmental necessity, if Jalu Miah is typical, Bangladeshis do not celebrate it as unambiguously as do Kalulis.

14. Adults affectionately address boys as *bābā* (literally, father), and girls as *mā* (literally, mother). The effect might be to model for the child-recipient the language he or she ought to use with parents, a practice comparable to using the V form of the second-person pronoun toward children.

15. For this insight, I am indebted to Desjarlais (1992) and to Good (1994), but I am applying it, among other things, to Bangla sound symbolism.

16. The question connotes, "Have I succeeded yet in making you angry?" The tense-aspectual status of the verb *karso* is ambiguous because of the homophony of two forms. In standard Bangla, *karcho*, sometimes pronounced *karso*, is present-continuous. In rural Bangla, *karso* is the equivalent of the standard form *karecho*, and is perfective. In Matlab the perfective tense-aspective meaning can safely be ascribed to this form.

17. Did he stop out of curiosity as to what response might be pending?

18. For parallel evidence from India, see Kurtz (1992: 74, 130, 132). English speakers manifest linguistic ideologies similar to what I am calling antilogocentrism in Bangla when they dismiss a promise or other speech act as "just words."

19. One of my Bangladeshi "fathers" since 1983, Mr. K., Karim's father, rejects that generalization. Perhaps it fits the traditional rural form of showing *samabedanā* (sympathy) more than it fits the urban form.

Chapter 7

1. This, at least, is conveyed by many interviewed on the video *American Tongues,* produced by the Center for Applied Linguistics, Washington, D.C.

2. Recursiveness and erasure are processes whereby differences salient at one level of a relationship are (in the former case) recursively projected onto other levels of that relationship, and whereby (in the latter case) those differences are erased. See Gal and Irvine (1995).

3. Whereas onomatopoeia refers to lexical elements, I use the term "sound symbolism" in a more general sense. Sound symbolism can entail single sounds or relations between poetic lines; I use "onomatopoeia" in the common sense, to refer to whole and single words designed to imitate their referents. Sound symbolism includes onomatopoeia. Sound symbolisms are typically language specific, often entailing linguistic imitations of the sounds of natural phenomena, animals, or persons but sometimes less explicit associations between a certain sound and a value or affective meaning.

4. See Apte (1968), Bhaskararao (1977), Emeneau (1969), Masica (1991), and Wilce (1996). A recent study of reduplication by Abbi (1992) marks an increase in the scope of these South Asian studies of lexical semantics.

5. "Paralinguistic" here refers to suprasegmental linguistic phenomena (Crystal 1971), not to gestures and other visible semiotic signals.

6. It was Ian Maddieson, in the phonetics laboratory at UCLA's Department of Linguistics, who, after listening to the tape, labeled this voice quality. Professor Maddieson has, since then, offered comments on spectrograms and waveforms of Bonhi's and Ahmed's vowels. I am indebted to Ian and the laboratory staff, as well as to UCLA's Department of Anthropology, which funded my Los Angeles pilot study of Bangla discourse.

7. More intensive analyses of these two transcripts might pursue two hypotheses. The first would take Bonhi's and Ahmed's different degrees of specificity at face value, indicative perhaps of a fever or flu-like pain in Bonhi's case and, according to Ahmed's kin, parasites in his case. The other hypothesis would be that Bonhi, who told me later that she was attempting to dramatize a need for relief from some of her work at home, used this general reference as the sort of blank slate to which I referred earlier, a means of involving listeners in her account, a trick in the sense of the South Carolina trickster cited by Scott (1990; see also my chapter 5). The trick corresponds to de Certeau's "tactics" (versus "strategies"). The lack of specificity in Bonhi's complaint reflects and reproduces the weakness of her position—indeed, the lack of a proper place of her own from which the higher leverage of de Certeau's strategies would be possible (1984: xix). I am indebted to Desjarlais (1997) for this theoretical link.

8. In 1996 he was manic and aggressive, returning to the state of *pāglāmi* (madness) in which my field family, in 1991–92, had told me he had once suffered.

9. "Universal" here refers not to all cultures but to the logic of intensity or quantification (Labov 1984).

10. According to Professor Clint Seely of the University of Chicago, stage representations of elderly people also have them speak in a nasal voice (personal communication, 1995). Could older people be stereotypically associated with a certain vocal style and a tendency to complain, just as the speech acts of crying and whining are associated with children? One anecdote supports the hypothesis: I once asked an old man at a teastall how he was. He replied, "In poor health. *What do you expect* of an old man?" On other occasions people told me—evincing surprise that I needed to be told—that old people can be expected to spend their time crying and *Āllāh Āllāh karā* ("doing 'God, God'").

11. That intensification is typical of the function of reduplicated forms throughout South Asia (Abbi 1992; Wilce 1996).

12. On metathesis, which this realization of the word *partham* (*pratham*, first) represents, see the appendix.

13. *Caltām̐ pāri nā* (compare the standard *āmi calte pāri nā*, or perhaps, *calte āmi pāri nā*). As argued in chapter 5, this form represents an incipient grammaticalization of the pronoun /*āmi*/, that is, its reduction to the bound suffix /-m/. See also *caltām̐ āchi* in line 14.

14. *Futerā*, i.e. *putro-rā* (sons).

15. A concept of disease that puts it under human control can be a pernicious thing, as Susan Sontag has argued regarding cancer and self-healing (1977–78: 40).

16. At least one individual I know exploited the nasalization stereotype. The man, mentioned in chapter 6, quit his factory job and moved back to his village home to practice a form of possession-mediumship in which diagnosing and prescribing were central. His mediumship was marked not only by audible nasalization but also by the further focalization of the nose through constant twitching. His nose twitched thus only during his periods of trance possession. In arguing that this healer exploited a stereotype, I am not necessarily presuming that his practice was a sham or that he never *experienced* possession but only acted the role effectively. I am simply arguing that the form of the trance behavior can only be understood in a cultural context in which nasalization is indexically associated with spirits, children, and assertive demands.

Chapter 8

1. I intend, of course, to include women's and men's domestic labor under the "work" rubric, and to invoke the notion of a sick role (Parsons 1987).

2. Teasing might well "hide" but still index love (Kurtz 1992; Trawick 1990; Wikan 1990). I deny, however, that Latifa's cousins; and brothers' *ṭiṭkāri* (teasing) of her (see my discussion of Latifa's lament, line 170, in chapter 11)—as just one example of teasing—has strong cultural justification. Neither Latifa nor her family has ever represented their behavior to me as an ideal of love.

3. Although mine is a nonrandom "opportunity sample," the chi-square text of the correlation between "speaker initiative" and both "audience" (speaking to one's superior) and "disability-relevance" approached significance ($p < .075$). Pennebaker finds evidence that his research subjects experience endogenous health benefits when they self-disclose life trauma under controlled conditions. These conditions were intensive journal writing (Pennebaker, Kiecolt-Glaser, and Glaser 1988) and, in the case of Holocaust survivors, video archiving (Pennebaker, Barger, and Tiebout 1989). Benefits were marked for those disclosing trauma for the first time. Having the flu is not one of those topics, nor does Pennebaker argue that complaining about the flu helps to cure it.

4. I discussed the teasing of children in chapter 6. It is common for disciples to call

Muslim *pirs* and Hindu *gurus* "Baba," which means "Daddy," so it is not surprising that patterns like teasing should be shared in relationships that Bengalis treat as analogous (caregiver-child and preceptor-disciple). For a sensitive treatment of the relationship between Hindu women and their gurus, see Roy (1975), who experienced profound sympathy from her guru. One can assume, however, that his expressions of sympathy followed local sensibilities.

5. Jalu seems to mean that boys would make up a "ground" on which to excuse non–compliance with some directive, "referring" that noncompliance to some cause.

6. *Di-m-u*: a typical nonstandard realization of the standard form *di-b-o* (give-will-I).

7. On loud *dhikr*, see Schimmel (1975: 176), chapter 4 on Shefali, and particularly chapter 4, note 11.

8. Cantonese speakers traditionally greet each other by asking, "Have you eaten rice yet?"

9. It is possible that Buji said, not *mairā jāi* (I [want to] die), but *mare jāitāsi* (I am dying).

10. Such institutions all too often fail to provide the promised treatment without payment for every individual item or act of service.

11. This self-effacing humor" entails exaggerated complaining that *invites others* to deflate it. The benign examples cited here contrast with the despair evinced by Suleyman's confused references to himself alternately as emperor and asshole (see example 60).

12. The Rolling Stones' words, "I can't get no satisfaction," offer an equally good gloss.

13. I imagine that Habib was offering words that he considered *śāntanā* (hortatory encouragement or comfort), discussed earlier.

14. *Ṭan ṭane* (pounding, throbbing) is both onomatopoeic (imagistic) and reduplicated (diagrammatic), thus doubly iconic (Wilce 1996). Amina's voice here sounds strained and high, weak.

15. The privilege is rarely given, unless their "brides"—new daughters-in-law— become possessed. Spirits "strike" young, recently married women in Matlab more frequently than any other category of persons. In the two cases I saw (and in those described by Blanchet 1984), the possessed woman received special attention, and special dispensation to break taboos of various sorts.

16. *Yā Āllāh* is an invocation like those combined with sighs, discussed elsewhere in this chapter.

17. Does the laughter index Amina's embarrassment at interrupting her father?

18. It is unclear whether Rajib says *pāyḍā*, *pāwḍā*, or *pācā* (gluteus, bottom).

19. Rajib speaks here in a pinched voice, like that of C, his maternal grandmother.

Chapter 9

1. I refer to cases of which I heard secondary accounts but which always seemed to escape my view. But I am also referring to Shefali's case, example 5.

2. Ishaque (1955) is only one of a number of Bangla literary representations of practitioners who do and do not keep the public trust.

3. See my discussion of the three levels of respect/intimacy encoded in Bangla second-person indexicals in the front matter. It is the third, most intimate level—*tui*, or "subT"—that guardians use with female patients in some of the transcripts presented here.

4. My impressions of the Chandpur government hospital's delivery ward are exclusively from medical anthropologist Margaret Leppard (personal communication, 1996).

5. As far as my field assistant Faisal and I could tell, the diagnostic category *bārzin* is also Ali's discovery.

6. Despite foot searches in the vicinity where she was reported to live, and searches through the archives of the ICDDR,B's surveillance system—the archives that had motivated me to choose Matlab as a field site—our efforts to locate Yasmin between November and April failed. In April Faisal and I finally discovered her records at the ICDDR,B—only to learn that she had died.

7. Fatima's exorcist Jahangir and Yasmin's herbalist Ali share with *hātuṛe ḍāktārs* like Heykal an apprenticeship training. According to a folk etymology, *hātuṛe ḍāktār* is picking up the "hammer" (*hātur*) and using it. Dictionaries do not seem to support this etymology, citing only the connotations of "quackery." Whereas in Dhaka, owner, pharmacist, and physician are often three distinct individuals, in the Matlab area they are more commonly one.

8. Rural Bangladeshi men tend to divorce a wife who shows any sort of problem in having children or even one who bears children but no sons.

9. Compare with this the American study by Hasselkus (1992).

10. *Cāgār*, that is, *cākā-r* (lump-genitive).

11. Delwar thus draws on an important cultural theme honoring mothers. A cult of motherhood thrives in patriarchal Bengal (Bagchi 1990) and even draws on Islamic discourse to support it. This might well be because, as Byron Good was told by a diviner/"prayer writer" in Iran, "You can never really know who the father is" (1977: 44).

A traditional saying attributed to the Prophet (a Hadith) is often quoted in Bangladesh. A man asked the Prophet what person in his life deserved the most honor. "Your mother," he answered. "And after my mother?" "Your mother," he repeated. "And then?" "Your mother" came a third time. "After my mother," asked the inquirer, "whom should I honor next?" Finally the Prophet answered, "Your father."

12. "Religious divination is always practiced in the context of a mythological belief in a doctrine of signs" (Wallace 1966: 108).

13. This was clearly the case in the interactive style of Indian astrologers studied by Pugh (1983).

14. The appendix to Wilce (1994) contains a chart comparing all the transcribed consultations of Delwar in my recorded corpus and exemplifying both the formulaicity of his divinations and his improvisations (Sawyer 1996) on the formula.

15. I call 2.5 a false start because line 2.6 shows it to be a grammatical error that Delwar self-corrected. Whereas he had meant to open the summary with a passive construction in which the victim as its topic appears in a sentence-initial position in the objective case appropriate to the passive, he mistakenly used the genitive case. Rural speech substitutes the genitive in other slots which are occupied by objective-case nouns in standard speech. Perhaps this habit of usage led to Delwar's mistake.

16. The stars are connected with the fate written on one's palm. It is not perfectly clear to me on what basis Hawladar is called a "professor," though he has written a book on his specialty.

17. My account of Bozlu's words reflects fieldnotes taken during the event without the benefit of a mechanical recording.

18. Veiling practices spread along with intensive agriculture (Boserup 1970). On the construction of patients as nonpersons/objects, see the discussion of Farhad's case, example 58, chapter 10.

19. A more complete interpretation of these phenomena is found in Wilce (1997).

20. On face, see Brown and Levinson 1986. Practitioners' sex can usefully be distinguished from the gender role that they play and from their class status. One of the most abrasive and insulting practitioners of medicine whom I recorded in Bangladesh is a woman. All of her patients are poor women, who are separated from her by a great class gap. In other social contexts, and particularly when she is with men, she is quite polite, though she retains a uniquely forceful manner.

Chapter 10

1. Exceptions include Brown (1988), Roseman (1991), and Desjarlais (1992).

2. Or, "becomes exhausted." Margaret Leppard (personal communication, 1996), a medical anthropologist and midwife working with women in the same Chandpur district, says the term often has this figurative sense.

3. Even if we accept a portrayal of the whole compound as an impoverished environment that compromises health, it is always the case within such environments that "some are for social, psychological, and biological reasons at enhanced risk" (Kleinman 1986: 182).

4. Fatima's evidently poor nutritional status indicates that we cannot rule out anemia as an explanation for her reference to an experience of being *durbal*. Still, the application of that label to women in Bangladeshi discourse is a facile one, reflecting and constituting a gender ideology. Weakness is a polysemous social construction of women's or men's experience, as explored in chapter 9 (and see Wilce 1997). As for a Matlab notion of anemia, my sense is that government nutrition-education campaigns have been grafted onto local knowledge systems, resulting in popular awareness of a condition owing to poor nutrition and conceived of as a lack of blood. I believe that the relatively cosmopolitan exorcist had such a concept in mind when he told Fatima she should eat better.

5. In fact, the distribution of the verb *pār* (can) among the participants in the original exorcism consultation is revealing. It is used eight times—twice by *kabirāj* Jahangir, and six times by Fatima. Whereas all six of Fatima's usages are accompanied by *nā* (negating the verb, thus expressing in_ability_), Jahangir never says *pāri nā* or construes the outcome of this consultation to reflect an inability on his part. My later encounters with him were friendly; he seems unaware that his clients feel that Fatima's problem is unresolved. Moreover, he always answered my questions about his further exorcism activities with an embarrassed smile and a statement to the effect that no one had called on him recently.

6. *Usilā,* from the Arabic word *wasīla* (Hilali and Haq 1967: 1), means "ways and means, instrumentality." Actually, Yasmin's brother seems rather to invoke the idea of *silsilā* (root, line of transmission) with its Sufi sectarian resonances.

7. *Aḍ:iḍā* or *aḍi-ṭā* is a realization of the standard Bangla *hāṛ-ṭā* (the bone). Note the lack of a first-person possessive here, a phenomenon explored in chapter 5.

8. "That" head, not "my" head. See the discussion surrounding line 22, example 14, in chapter 5.

9. *Jiban-o* (life-also) is to be distinguished from *jibāno* (little organism, germ)—a concept rarely invoked in ethnomedical discourse. *Mocon*, here translated as "come undone," denotes "a setting free … act of unfastening, untying" (Mitra 1924: 983). In Bangladesh, Faisal understood Yasmin to say *muchon* (wiping out, erasure), and Asad (my Los Angeles consultant) thought she was mispronouncing *mucṛāno*. It was originally Faisal's transcription that led me to believe that Ali was cutting off Yasmin's most

poignant expression of despair. Asad, contemplating the possibility that Yasmin was saying *mucrāno* (knotting, cramping), argued that this entailed her development of the abdominal-pain theme, whereas the more existential comment did not. But, unable to deny that she says it is her *jïban* (life) that is subjected to *mocon/mucrān/muchon*, he is willing to allow that she has extended the discourse beyond Ali's question. The admitted lack of unanimity among my Bangla-speaking consultants aside, it is clear to them and to me that Ali does not allow her to develop this point, one that is important to her.

10. Gumperz (1982: 183) presents an account of an interethnic interview in which a man from India and a woman from the United Kingdom repeatedly fail to come to terms. The man tries to explain his view of the problems evident in his job history. To her attempt to reflect what she thought he was saying—"You can't get a job"—he replies, "No this is not actually the situation, I have not completely explained my position." The parallel between his words and Yasmin's—"I haven't told the half of it"—indicates a style of metacommunicative protest that, though not unique to South Asians, may be in widespread use there.

11. Sufia's mother is alluding here to an earlier visit to Heykal that I had not observed.

12. The = signs at the end of line 16 and at the beginning of line 17 indicate that the two utterances are "latched," with only a minimal pause between them. They are almost, but not quite, overlapping utterances. Line 16 itself is a sort of interruption in which Heykal completes the sentence that Sufia's mother was unwilling to complete. Thus her utterance in line 17, closely following Heykal's insertion, continues where she left off but jumps over the sensitive matter of the miscarriage itself.

13. *Peḍ*, that is, *peṭ* (abdomen).

14. Margaret Leppard cites women who say that their lives are "spoiled" or "finished" (words that recall not only Sufia's words but also Yasmin's) when they must have a hysterectomy or be incapacitated from continuing with the heavier work of mothering and other domestic tasks. Women's roles in domestic production and reproduction are, she argues, central to their identities, and it is that fact to which these despairing words testify.

15. Upon hearing of Heykal's use of *anubhab* in this situation, one informant opined that it was Heykal whose approach was too subjective; he said the *ḍāktār* should have ordered an x-ray to remove any doubt left by his palpation of Sufia's abdomen. For a parallel case of a male practitioner casting a woman's perception as subjective, followed by the woman's affirmation "it *is* such-and-such," see chapter 5, example 14, lines 49–50.

16. In the folk taxonomy of enteric conditions, *āmāśā* refers to diarrhea with blood, and never to cholera. The ICDDR,B glosses *āmāśā* as "shigellosis."

Chapter 11

1. Major parts of this chapter appeared in *Culture, Medicine, and Psychiatry* (volume 22, number 1, pages 1–54).

2. I am remetaphorizing Goffman's (1981) trope. By "footing," Goffman meant "participants' alignment, or set, or stance, or posture, or projected self."

3. The concept of performativity has evolved in recent linguistic anthropology—from Austin's (1962) notion that we "do things with words." Austin coined the term "performative" for certain erba dicendi ("verbs of speaking" or reporting speech), like "I christen …," that appear to bring about the realities they describe. Recent critiques of speech-act theory stress that personal intentions may not decide which acts are being

performed or which realities are officially brought into existence in speech interaction. Individuals do not necessarily "do things with words." Often, words themselves are taken by agents-in-interaction as doing things. For an excellent, critical, anthropological review of speech act theory and the philosophy of language in this century, see Lee (1997).

Hanks stresses that performativity itself is locally perceived and constituted (as does Parmentier 1994), and that the speaker of a "performative verb," to whom "the words appear to have the 'magical' effect of creating as a socially binding reality the event that they literally describe, ... is simultaneously defining himself or his current situation and being defined by it" (Hanks 1996: 206). Cf. Das (1996: 70).

4. Good (1994) and Desjarlais (1997) start to map out this ground.

5. In comparison with the societies that Foucault describes, the process of medicalizing madness is not as far along in Bangladesh.

6. I provide evidence later in the book illustrating how linguistic ideologies function, (a) embodying diverse situated perspectives; (b) reflecting the positioned interests of those invoking them; (c) being expressed at varying levels of awareness (dominant ideologies are the most implicit and assumed); (d) playing a role in identity formation—in the effacing of differences of power and status and in the imagining of solidarities; and (e) filtering perceptions of communicative and social practice (my interpretive reflections on personal communication by Paul Kroskrity, reflecting a School of American Research Seminar on Language Ideologies, April 1994).

7. By "nonfocal" talk, I mean sideplay by nonratified participants and byplay between ratified and nonratified participants, in Goffman's (1981) terms.

8. In those passages, the juxtaposition of the columns represents the simultaneity of the outside and inside discourse. Any overlap (marked within / /) or latching (marked with =) is between speakers in a single column, left or right.

9. This pseudonym means "shared pain," or "sympathy."

10. Schematically, the rhetorical structure called *chiasmus* (crossing-over) may be represented as an "abc-cba" pattern. One could say that the "a"—here the Bangla pronominal form *āmāre*—encompasses or marks the boundaries of many poetically well-formed texts from that region (Wilce 1989).

11. This interpretive insight derives from John Runnion and the 1995 Seminar in Verbal Art at Northern Arizona University.

12. "In point of fact, word [every word?] is a two-sided act. It is determined equally by whose word it is and for whom it is meant. As word, it is precisely *the product of the reciprocal relationship between speaker and listener, addresser and addressee*" (Vološinov 1973: 86).

13. Latifa's reference to *āmār śail* makes her body a sign more explicitly than would a pronoun ("me"). One of my male consultants in Matlab used the English "body" rather than Bangla *śarir, śarīl, śail* when speaking of his mother's strict observance of *pardā*— "She kept her '*body*' covered."

14. *Uḍe*, that is, *oṭhe* (rises, stands up).

15. Embodiment (Csordas 1990) is a reality she might try to shape discursively, but one which, like the chains her brothers placed on her, resists her.

16. *Kalejā* (liver) figures largely in a Bangladeshi discourse with which I began to be acquainted in 1996, one referred to as *deho tattva* (body theory). Further investigation of this discursive tradition ought to pursue what Good (1994) calls a "civilizational" level of inquiry, linking contemporary Bangladeshi invocations of the liver with major documents in the Islamic medical traditions, such as Ibn Sina's writings. Good (1977) traces the understandings of the heart and liver in a contemporary Iranian community to Ibn Sina; the

liver, in this tradition, is "the seat of the natural faculty and the baser human appetites" (Good 1977: 36). Younger social scientists working for the ICDDR,B—particularly Md. Habibur Rahman—alerted me to *deho tattva* as a Sufi-influenced model of the body. Habib affirmed that, in that discourse, the liver (rather than the heart) is the seat of the emotions (personal communication, 1996).

17. *Māyā* in rural Bangla (cf. standard Bangla *meye*, "girl, daughter") is homophonous with the Sanskrit term *māyā* (deception) but context distinguishes the two.

18. Pharyngealized phonation; that is, one hears in her lament a tightening of her voice—one of the icons of crying discussed in chapter 7. It is represented here by the outline typeface

19. *Khun*, the noun "murder, kill," is often found in combination with the auxiliary *karā* (do), the phrase being glossed "do murder / commit murder." *khun-o* means "murder-even."

20. This might have been a shout of rebuke, or possibly a dog's bark.

21. This theology verges on blasphemy, although it is not quite as explicitly blasphemous as Punjabi laments can become (Das 1996: 80). Yet, it has strong religious precedents as in Psalm 22. As Scarry (1985) claims about the Hebrew experience of God, Latifa's experience of Allah is juxtaposed with—or perhaps constituted within—the experience of bodily pain, as a sign of the presence (in the Hebrew case) or the absence (as Latifa claims) of God inscribed on her body.

22. Taken together, Suleyman's two lines could also mean, "God is not fated to be on my side." Compare Latifa's lines 37 and 38.

23. That is, "How much [damage]?"

24. That is, ever since she arrived a week ago?

25. That is, how late she returned from her wanderings.

26. Phonetically, Latifa seems clearly to produce *jabār*, but this leaves my Bangla-speaking consultants confused—there is no such Bangla word. Latifa evidently meant to produce one of the following: *jabar* (Arabic *jabr*, violence); *jabar* (Persian *zabar*, above, strong [overpower]); or *jabāi* or *jabeho* (Arabic *ḍabḥ*, Persian *zabḥ*, [ritual animal] sacrifice). What seems clear is her intent to evoke an image of violence and also male domination (only men are allowed to be present and to officiate in Muslim sacrifices—relevant here if *jabāi* is the intended form).

27. The sob marking the end of this line is transcribed as line 85, since it is overlapped by the speech of Amina represented there.

28. Note that, by questioning the fairness of the communicative system in which she is embedded (Wilce 1995), Latifa breaks out of the taboo on metacommentary that Bateson (1956) considered the third, most entrapping element of a schizophrenogenic double bind.

29. In Bakhtin's (1981) formulation, authoritative discourse "demands that we acknowledge it; ... we encounter it with its authority already fused to it. The authoritative word is located in a distanced zone" (p. 342).

Amina's location of the danger in (or her specification of the danger *to*) Latifa's head bears comment. Local discourse describes the head of the mad as heated, evoking humoral concepts of hot and cold and a notion that strong passion creates heat, which disturbs the balance of the embodied heartmind (*man*) or head. See discussion of Suleyman in chapter 4.

30. My use of the term "discipline" here intentionally evokes Foucault (1977). Latifa's brother (D) visited "our" home some time after she had been dragged away and returned to his surveillance. When I (J) asked about her, he brought up the subject of

keeping her chained up so "that her body might get well, ... that the *utsrinkal kāj* [undisciplined, indiscreet acts] that she now does might return to normal."

J—"What falls under *utsrinkal?*"

D—*Utsrinkal*, that is, that she [does not] stay in our limited situation, [nor] stay in our house; that is, [she should] not go out.

31. Musa's mother is either continuing to report others' speech—"They [gossips] make empty claims against Latifa's sanity," or her own opinion of Latifa's speech—"She [Latifa] speaks incoherently." The difference turns partly on the meaning of *hudā* (empty/emptily). For another emotional context that the word *hudā* helps significantly to constitute, compare example 61, chapter 12.

32. Referring to "Musa's mother" as such—teknonymy—reflects local practice.

33. As Clancy (1986) notes for Japanese, Bangla speakers are able to exploit the systematic potential for ambiguity inherent in the language's lack of insistence that a subject be overtly present in a given utterance. The women outside Latifa's house could therefore have intentionally exploited this ambiguity, rather than committing themselves on the politically dicey issue of whose word to affirm.

34. After her lament, Latifa directly challenged those norms as a hypocritical attempt to equate veiling or isolation with morality, asking, "If I did anything wrong, wouldn't it be found out? What difference does it make if I move about from land to land?"

35. I was struck in 1996 by the tendency of Matlab residents to consider madness or deviance to be *willful*, sometimes doubting that the person in question was "mad" at all. There appears to be less distance between calling someone a manipulator and calling her "mad," if we keep two things in mind. First, madness may be *treated* with folk medicine but is not regarded as an illness like others; that is, it is not medicalized to the extent that insanity is in the West. Second, both forms of attribution—madness and willful deviance—can, in contemporary Bangladeshi discourse, index an underlying ascription of an excess or a deformation of self or ego.

36. In 1996, Faisal interviewed a diviner/spirit-medium whose divinatory proclamations typically center on charms planted by the client's nearby enemies—neighbors who were otherwise frustrated in their schemes to gain love or wealth and who thus had to resort to sorcery against the client. In treating these problems, if he cannot find those charms himself, he tells people that he sends a jinn to unearth them and bring them to his desk. The diviner told Faisal that he actually keeps a set of charms in a muddy state so that he can display them as the result of such searches underneath people's courtyards.

37. Latifa says, "You ridicule me," perhaps referring to their talk of arranging a new marriage for her when she wants her old one restored. In short, Latifa is reacting to the teasing not of her voice but of her marriage, and specifically to their proposal that she marry another *ālim*. According to one Bangladeshi consultant in the United States, she is characterizing their words according to the proverb *khāte gā-e nun-e chitāno*, "rubbing salt into [her] wounds."

Hunde dibo e[khā]n dā ek (line 170) could be Latifa's phonetic realization of *śunte dibo*, "I will give you a 'banknote' [noteworthy insult?] to listen to [since you ridicule me]!" However, another possible hearing is *digun undā khārāiyā* (doubly, standing it up?), which would pertain to the intensity of their ridicule as she experiences it.

38. As Latifa was being picked up and carried by several young men moving her from my field home to her father's home some 10 miles away, I tried to emerge from the house but was forbidden by those of her male cousins who stayed behind.

39. *Mānuṣer janne hāsi.*

40. Can we attribute Latifa's relative's ridicule to defensive anxiety? Personal anxiety here is a microcosm of ideological defensiveness (Eagleton 1991), in this case overdetermining the denial of Latifa's message and craft.

41. That is, they engage in speech acts called *dukkho-kaṣṭer kathā balā* (speaking words of grief and hardship [see chapter 2]), *asubidhā[r kathā] balā/ kawā* (speaking words of trouble), or *asubidhā prakāś karā* (giving expression to trouble).

42. Verbal art genres in Bangla are marked in at least two senses—they are lexicalized (given single-word lexical labels and thus recognized and subjected to evaluative scrutiny) and they are relatively objectified. This objectification entails an exaggeration of certain poetic tendencies in all speech, and an exaggerated reflexivity. That is, verbal art by definition (Bauman and Briggs 1990) puts speaking itself on display and thus points to itself—is self-indexing.

43. See Tiwary (1978: 26). Bangladeshi evidence of their pragmatic "effectiveness" comes from Doreen Indra, who describes how a weeping destitute woman sometimes plants herself outside the home of a prosperous kinsman and laments until he allows her a place on his land (personal communication, November, 1992). "Effectiveness" is in quotes, however, to remind us that such performances are not necessarily instrumentalist or rational-pragmatic. To view communication as primarily instrumentalist is in itself an ideology of language to which I do not subscribe. Though I might describe genres as weapons in performers' hands, I do not mean thereby to neglect the role of jouissance, the joy of language as sensate object (Kristeva 1993)—also relevant to its use in acts of resistance.

44. The lament, that is, is part of a communicative practice which, though it must be conceived as flexible and dynamic, is a tradition that speakers recognize and work and play with.

One motive for my return in 1996 was to discover whether the anger of Latifa's kin explained not only their overall desire to stop the weeping but also, specifically, their generic characterization of it and the label they had assigned it. For Latifa's kin to have highlighted the performance as such and its links with traditions (traditions not only valued as literature but also indexing the relatively open gender relations of another era), by using labels like *bāramāsya* or *bilāp* would have placed Latifa's kin in a relationship with Latifa—and with expressivity as an aesthetic and ideology as well as a practice— very different from that which they actually occupy. I confirmed in 1996 that Latifa's uncles recognize the word *bilāp*; still, the fact that they spontaneously used only *kāndā* (crying) during our 1996 conversation about Latifa, and about tuneful weeping in general, indicates that the label *kāndā* was not intended as a spiteful denial of the classier label, *bilāp*. Thus, although they did reject Latifa's 1992 "art," that rejection was expressed not as much through the label they gave it as through the larger orders of discourse in which they framed it (Lindstrom 1992). At the same time, Latifa's family *treated* her performance as quite distinct, as if, without invoking one of the marked genres by name, they still recognized the family resemblance between her performance and those genres that are markedly distinct from "plain old" (*purān*) crying or talking. Lexical labels are not the only cues that actors use to engage in metalinguistic characterization.

What I had most wanted to do was to speak with Latifa herself, tell her what I had learned from her, and reflect with her on the events of 1992 and her life since then. That was not possible, however, since she would not talk with us while her family was present. Latifa finally decided to speak with us only after we had left her brothers' and mother's house; she caught up with us on the path back to the boat we had rented for the day. Yet, when she was actually close enough to speak with us, she seemed to play hide-and-seek with us. Faisal feels that she wanted very much to ask us to pay another visit to her husband, but was so uncomfortable while speaking with men outside her home that she could not do so. She and her mother did not come to meet us the following day at my old field home, as they had promised to do, and thus we had to content ourselves there with simply asking Latifa's uncles about the events and about the categories in which they understood her performance.

Chapter 12

1. Contrary to what Bourdieu says, insane discourse can achieve a kind of legitimacy in a certain kind of social setting. Corin describes how some persons in Montreal recognize the religious discourse of one nonhospitalized schizophrenic man there—paralleling that of Suleyman presented in this chapter—as legitimizing his claim to be "the Pope of the Church of Universal Reason" (1990: 179).

2. In lines 3 and 5, the first-person verb, without an explicit subject, could equally well support a singular pronominal subject, "I," but the (Urdu code-mixed) explicit pronominal subject line 1, *hām,* means "we."

3. The gloss "Emperor without portfolio" is from Los Angeles–based consultant Asadul, who says both *hudā* and *arsā* (empty) derive from Urdu and are analogous to the Bangla term *khāli* in rural usage, though the terms otherwise have very different glosses in Urdu usage. As used in Bangla, *hudā* connotes "without anything else," as in *āmi hudā bhāt khaichi,* "I ate rice without anything else" (as opposed to *āmi ḍāl diyā bhāt khāi[ye] chi,* "I ate rice with lentils").

4. It sounds as if Suleyman says, "*āngo, āmi*" in line 11—"our ... I"—probably a self-corrected error.

5. On madness versus mental illness, see Fisher (1985).

6. A different conflict-resolution meeting is described in Wilce (1996).

7. This represents an amalgamation of the words of several men, including two local doctors not personally acquainted with Latifa, but speaking generally about educated women, and one psychoanalytically trained American anthropologist. But it is also my attempt to sympathetically present Latifa's brothers' perspective. The question of ending men's roles in "arranging women's lives" never arises.

8. *Marjādā* could also be glossed as "symbolic capital" (Bourdieu 1972). Still, we ought not presume that such cultural values as family reputation are unproblematically accepted by all Bangladeshis as relevant to these events. If only because of the way I narrated it, this story has elicited strong disapproval of her family's handling of the situation from a number of persons across a range of social classes in Matlab and Dhaka.

9. Why did Latifa's aunts and even her same-age female cousins seem to take the side of their fathers and brothers against her? The question is naive, given the broad dependence of these women on men. Still, given the historic changes that Latifa, her school successes, and her more direct complaint actually exemplify, we should ask whether and where women might nurture a consciousness of injustice and solidarity in resistance to it. See Scott (1990: 119).

10. Jeffery (1979: 172–175) describes another impediment to solidarity resistance: women in *pirzāde* families—whose economic role and status as official custodians of a Pir's (saint's) tomb makes *parda* and submissiveness affordable—would lose much in a revolution that would place them on a par with destitute women, who currently show much less submissiveness toward men than do the *pirzāde* women.

11. Although I had enough time in 1991–92 to facilitate informal conversations with

women, my efforts to speak with women in 1996 were frustrated by their male guardians in the homes I visited and their general absence from public domains.

12. Another reason for stifling *bilāp* was often cited: in the context of mourning the dead, the corpse itself will suffer if its relatives *bilāp*. Given the fact that this anxiety is felt in other South and Southeast Asian societies (Das 1996; Wikan 1990), I attribute it to civilizational traditions apart from Islam.

13. To help Western readers cross the *Verstehen* gap, I might mention that even St. Augustine had profound misgivings about church music (or, at least, certain forms of it), for similar reasons.

By the time I revisited him in 1996, Suleyman had recovered from his earlier head troubles, and now agreed with his wife that the tunefulness of his earlier protests against his treatment (for which no one had a genre label) was literally wrong-headed. His despair, they agree, was part of the general illness that he now defines as an inability to tell right from wrong (and, I gather, to trust the ideologized order of things; cf. Wikan 1990). Despite his change of perspective on those matters, Suleyman in 1996 denied that it was right, good, or therapeutic for anyone to chain or beat him, or others they call mad.

14. This is only one explanation of madness, of course. It has, however, something in common with another common causal explanation—possession by spirits called *bhut* or jinn. Both involve stretching, changing, or violating norms of selfhood. For an excellent discussion of a range of explanations for madness in West Bengal, India, see Bhattacharyya (1986).

15. I am not arguing that Latifa's was an exemplary or beautiful *bilāp*, or denying the validity of the "performance criticism" offered by her kin. I am arguing that contemporary ideologies of language and gender, influenced by models from both the Middle East and First World media, cannot valorize women's troubles talk, nor can they perceive therein even the level of aesthetics that Good sees in illness narratives in general, and that I have pointed out specifically in Latifa's even more marked (tuneful, poetic) production.

16. Kivas are underground pits for ritual observances among Pueblo peoples of the U.S. Southwest.

17. The passage deserves to be quoted as a whole: "There is a style of lamentation called /bilap/, among women. In /bilap/ women *drag* the words almost like songs. They express their *immediate feelings* either in prose or in rhymed words. The tune is fixed. Bilaps are made on two occasions: (i) when a woman leaves her father's house after marriage and (ii) after somebody's death" (Humayun 1985: 40, emphasis added). "Dragging the words" is an unfortunate calque (excessively literal translation) of the Bangla verb *ṭānā* that is used to describe not true song but singsong, accented, drawled, or otherwise marked speech. Also problematic is the attribution of fixity to the tunes used by Latifa and other lament performers, which are clearly more a product of jazzlike improvisation than rote reproduction.

18. The language of one unidentified seminar participant stresses a particular immediate feeling—the sense of helplessness. Such a focus on feelings further problematizes the unilateral association of laments with women.

This is an excerpt from a transcript of an Institute of Modern Languages/Dhaka University seminar:

takhan ego defense mechanism tayri kare.	*Ego defense mechanisms form.*
māne eṭā geche (ār) mānasik je ekṭā asahāyatā	*[In crises] they vanish. A sense of helplessness*
bodh se gāner mādhyame prakāś pāe.	*is felt. It finds melodic expression.*
(sutā galāe)	

je bhābe tā- ābeg-guli pra—	*The tone in which ābeg [normally] find express—*
emotion guli prakāś karto-	*emotions find expression,*
setā-i (baiśeś) prakāś kare ār ki.	*[the tunefulness] expresses them uniquely.*
eṭāke regression bale ....*	*That's called regression ...*

What the Bangladeshi Freudian said (above) makes sense within some genres of our own academic discourse. But that in itself is part of what we must consider problematic. The ideology of language (more broadly, of semiosis) reflected by the Dhaka academics (in their publications as well as in the seminar) is one, influenced by Western folk and academic models, that objectifies emotion and treats expressive modalities as conduits or containers (Reddy 1993) that carry emotion-objects to the outside world in an unproblematic way.

Chapter 13

1. Indeed, Desjarlais (1992) argues that the aesthetic sense pervades experiences of illness and healing and not only their narrative representation.

2. Although the romanticization of illnesses such as tuberculosis might have been more common in nineteenth-century Europe than in our era (Sontag 1977–78), symbolic expressions of pain and suffering can appear, even to more recent observers, as supreme human achievements (Scarry 1985).

3. Latifa is not alone in being subjected to regimes of discipline and treatment from which she finds no escape. For hegemonic Western cultural links between conceptions of madness and of women, see Showalter (1985) and Astbury (1996). For Indian countercultural associations of women's ecstatic ("mad") religious expressions, see McDaniel (1989) and Allen and Mukherjee (1982).

4. See Brooks and Warren (1949: 312), Good (1994: chapter 7), and Wilson (1993).

5. For an account of lament-song moving hearers to tears, see Feld (1990).

6. Extending Bateson's (1972) arguments regarding art, play, and fantasy provides a theoretical warrant for a general, if not a universal, connection between verbal play/art and reflexive toying with (if not always breaking of) conventions. There is no play without paradox, which always strains norms of interpretation even if it reproduces them at some level.

7. This linkage is carried out in practice but has not always informed the metatheories of medicine, psychiatry, or medical anthropology. I acknowledge, however, that my argument echoes Crapanzano's (1990) with regard to metapragmatic ascription and the self.

8. The problem with Abu-Lughod's (1986) otherwise persuasive argument that "idiosyncratic," seemingly non-socialized and unconventional expressions of sentiment are labeled mad and deprived of honor among Bedouins is that it fails to problematize genres and evaluative norms as processes. When she writes, "Those who express strong sentiments of attachment and vulnerability in the culturally approved way can still claim to embody the cultural ideals" (p. 257), she objectifies "the culturally approved way" as if it were neutral.

9. I do not believe that the dismissal of human rights issues such as torture as a merely Western concern merits response. Nor do I wish to be read as denying that human rights are honored by Islam, in contemporary Islamist theological-political discourse, or even, perhaps, by Islamist regimes. There is some tension between secular human rights

discourses and a variety of religious institutions. Opposition to the affirmation that "women's reproductive rights are human rights" has at least been portrayed in the media as arising from the Vatican and from Catholic and Islamic national representatives to recent global conferences on women. This stance does not necessarily entail opposition to any particular exercise of protest speech. Muslim men in Matlab, however, make a woman's leadership of the governing party and women's marches in Dhaka a metonym of Bangladesh's need for Islamist reform. Leila Ahmed affirms the attempt of the early pioneers of Islamic law to institute justice; though they inherited customs that adversely affected women, their attempt was to moderate those customs. She says, "In contrast, their descendants, today reinstituting the laws devised in other ages and other societies, are choosing to eschew, when it comes to women, contemporary understandings of the meanings of justice and human rights" (1992: 242). If Islamist regimes "defer" the issue of justice for women, as Ahmed argues (1992: 243), they are not alone. Nor is such a deferral part of a monolithic tendency, as if there were one Islamism or fundamentalism. The late-1996 declaration by the state of Iran that the emerging Taliban government in Afghanistan violated the spirit of Islam by denying women the right to be employed illustrates the heterogeneity of Islamist polities.

10. Good and Good (1988) have described the traditional transformative role played by the *ta'zieh* (a display of grief in Shi'a Islam commemorating martyrdom) as a ritual of transcendence, but also have documented the co-opting of *ta'zieh* by the revolutionary Iranian state, transforming it from a mode of resistance into a state symbol.

REFERENCES

Abbi, Anvita. 1992. *Reduplication in South Asian languages: An areal, typological and historical study*. New Delhi: Allied Publishers.

Abu-Lughod, Lila. 1986. *Veiled sentiments: Honor and poetry in a Bedouin society*. Berkeley: University of California Press.

Ahmed, Leila. 1992. *Women and gender in Islam: Historical roots of a modern debate*. New Haven, CT: Yale University Press.

Ainsworth-Vaughn, Nancy. 1992. Topic transitions in physician-patient interview: Power, gender, and discourse change. *Language in Society* 21: 409–426.

Alam, S. M. Shamsul. 1995. *The state, class formation, and development in Bangladesh*. Lanham, MD: University Press of America.

Ali, Mohammad, Mohammad Moniruzzaman, and Jahangir Tareq, editors. 1994. *Bangla Academy Bengali-English dictionary*. Dhaka: Bangla Academy

Allen, Michael and S. N. Mukherjee. 1982. *Women in India and Nepal*. Canberra: Australian National University Press.

Appadurai, Arjun. 1986. Is homo hierarchicus? *American Ethnologist* 13: 745–761.

———. 1990. Topographies of the self: Praise and emotion in Hindu India. In *Language and the politics of emotion*, edited by Lila Abu-Lughod and Catherine Lutz, pp. 92–112. Cambridge: Cambridge University Press.

Apte, Mahadev. 1968. *Reduplication, echo formation and onomatopoeia in Marathi*. Deccan College Building Centenary and Silver Jubilee Series No. 38. Poona: Deccan College.

Astbury, Jill. 1996. *Crazy for you: The making of women's madness*. Melbourne: Oxford University Press.

Austin, J. L. 1962. *How to do things with words*. 2nd ed. Cambridge: Harvard University Press.

Bagchi, Jasodhara. 1990. Representing nationalism: Ideology of motherhood in colonial Bengal. *Economic and Political Weekly* 25(42): 65–71.

Bagchi, Tista. 1996. Bengali writing. In *The world's writing systems*, edited by Peter T. Daniels and William Bright, pp. 393–402. New York: Oxford University Press.

Bakhtin, Mikhail M. 1981. *The dialogic imagination*. Edited by M. Holquist. Austin: University of Texas Press.

———. 1986. *Speech genres and other late essays*. Austin: University of Texas Press.

Banerjee, Sumanta. 1989. Marginalization of women's popular culture in nineteenth century Bengal. In *Recasting women: Essays in colonial history*, edited by Kumkum Sangari and Sudesh Vaid, pp. 127–179. New Delhi: Kali for Women.

Basso, Keith. 1979. *Portraits of the Whiteman*. New York: Cambridge University Press.

Bateson, Gregory. 1958. *Naven*. 2nd ed. Stanford: Stanford University Press.

———. 1972. Toward a theory of schizophrenia. In *Steps to an ecology of mind*, pp. 201–227. Scranton, PA: Chandler.

275

Battaglia, Debbora. 1995a. Problematizing the self: A thematic introduction. In *Rhetorics of self-making*, edited by D. Battaglia, pp. 1–15. Berkeley: University of California Press.

———, editor. 1995b. *Rhetorics of self-making*. Berkeley: University of California Press.

Bauman, Richard. 1975. Verbal art as performance. *American Anthropologist* 77: 290–311.

Bauman, Richard, and Charles Briggs. 1990. Poetics and performance as critical perspectives on language and social life. *Annual Review of Anthropology* 19: 59–88.

Beals, Alan R. 1976. Strategies of resort to curers in South India. In *Asian medical systems*, edited by Charles Leslie. Berkeley: University of California Press.

Becker, Alton L. 1988. Attunement: An essay on philology and logophilia. In *On the ethnography of communication: The legacy of Sapir. Essays in honor of Harry Hoijer 1984 by J. H. Hill, D. Tedlock, and A. L. Becker*, edited by Paul V. Kroskrity. Other Realities, Vol. 8. Los Angeles: UCLA Department of Anthropology.

Benveniste, Emile. 1971. *Problems in general linguistics*. Translated by Mary Elizabeth Meek. Coral Gables: University of Miami Press.

Berry, Diane S., and James W. Pennebaker. 1993. Nonverbal and verbal emotional expression and health. *Psychotherapy and Psychosomatics* 59: 11–19.

Bhaskararao, Peri. 1977. *Reduplication and onomatopoeia in Telegu*. Minor Series, No. 3, Centre of Advanced Study in Linguistics, University of Poona. Poona: Deccan College.

Bhattacharyya, Deborah. 1986. *Pāgalāmi: Ethnopsychiatric knowledge in Bengal*. Foreign and Comparative Studies—South Asian Series, No. 11. Syracuse, NY: Maxwell School of Citizenship and Public Affairs.

Biswas, Saylendra, Sasibhusan Dasgupta, and Sridinescandra Bhattacharyya, editors. 1984. *Saṁsad Bāṅgālā Abidhān (Samsad Bangla dictionary)*. Calcutta: Sahitya Samsad.

Blanchet, Thérèse. 1984. *Women, pollution and marginality: Meanings and rituals of birth in rural Bangladesh*. Dhaka: Dhaka University Press.

Boas, Franz. 1995. [1911] Introduction to the Handbook of American Indian Languages. In *Language, culture, and society: A book of readings*, edited by Ben G. Blount, pp. 9–28. Prospect Heights, IL: Waveland.

Boddy, Janice. 1994. Spirit possession revisited. *Annual Reviews of Anthropology* 23: 407–434.

Booth, Wayne C. 1993. Individualism and the mystery of the social self; or, Does amnesty have a leg to stand on? In *Freedom and interpretation (The Oxford Amnesty Lectures 1992)*, edited by Barbara Johnson, pp. 69–102. New York: Basic Books.

Boserup, Ester. 1970. *Women's role in economic development*. London: St. Martin's.

Bourdieu, Pierre. 1977a. The economics of linguistic exchanges. *Social Science Information* 16: 645–668.

———. 1977b. *Outline of a theory of practice*. Cambridge: Cambridge University Press.

Brenneis, Donald. 1988. Talk and transformation. *Man* (n.s.) 22: 499–510.

Bretherton, Inge, and Marjorie Beeghly. 1982. Talking about internal states: The acquisition of an explicit theory of mind. *Developmental Psychology* 18: 906–921.

Briggs, Charles. 1984. Learning how to ask: Native metacommunicative competence and the incompetence of field workers. *Language in Society* 13: 1–28.

———. 1986. *Learning how to ask: A sociolinguistic appraisal of the role of the interview in social science research*. Cambridge: Cambridge University Press.

———. 1992a. "Since I am a woman, I will chastise my relatives": Gender, reported speech, and the (re)production of social relations in Warao ritual wailing. *American Ethnologist* 19(2): 337–361.

———. 1992b. Linguistic ideologies and the naturalization of power in Warao discourse. In *Language ideologies* (special issue edited by Paul Kroskrity, Bambi Schieffelin, and Katherine Woolard). *Pragmatics* 2: 387–404.

———. 1993. Personal sentiments and polyphonic voices in Warao women's ritual wailing: Music and poetics in a critical and collective discourse. *American Anthropologist* 95(4): 929–957.

Briggs, Charles, and Richard Bauman. 1992. Genre, intertextuality, and social power. *Journal of Linguistic Anthropology* 2(2): 131–172.

Briggs, Jean. 1970. *Never in anger: Portrait of an Eskimo family*. Cambridge: Harvard University Press.

Brooks, Cleanth, and Robert Penn Warren. 1949. *Modern rhetoric*. 4th ed. New York: Harcourt, Brace.

Brown, Michael Fobes. 1988. Shamanism and its discontents. *Medical Anthropology Quarterly* 2: 102–120.

———. 1996. Resisting resistance. *American Anthropologist* 98(4): 729–734.

Brown, Penelope, and Stephen Levinson. 1986. *Politeness: Some universals in language usage*. Studies in Interactional Sociolinguistics 4. Cambridge: Cambridge University Press.

Brown, Roger, and Albert Gilman. 1960. The pronouns of power and solidarity. In *Style in language*, edited by Thomas A. Sebeok, pp. 253–276. Cambridge: MIT Press.

Capwell, Charles. 1986. *The music of the Bauls of Bengal*. Kent: Kent State University Press.

Caraveli, Ana. 1986. The bitter wounding: The lament as social protest in rural Greece. In *Gender and power in rural Greece*, edited by Jill Dubisch. Princeton, NJ: Princeton University Press.

Caudill, William, and David W. Plath. 1974. Who sleeps by whom? Parent-child involvement in urban Japanese families. In *Culture and personality: Contemporary readings*, edited by Robert LeVine, pp. 125–154. Chicago: Aldine.

Cavell, Marcia. 1987. The self and some related issues: A philosophical perspective. *Psychoanalysis and Contemporary Thought* 10: 3–27.

Certeau, Michel de. 1984. *The practice of everyday life*. Translated by Steven Rendall. Berkeley, CA: University of California Press.

Chatterji, Suniti Kumar. 1934. *The origin and development of the Bengali language*, Vol. I. London: George Allen and Unwin.

Chatterjee, Suhas. 1986. Diglossia in Bengali. In *South Asian languages: Structure, convergence and diglossia*, edited by Bh. Krishnamurti, Colin P. Masica, and Anjana Sinha, pp. 294–302. Delhi: Motilal Banarsidass.

Chodorow, Nancy. 1974. Family structure and feminine personality. In *Women, culture and society*, edited by Michele Z. Rosaldo and Louise Lamphere, pp. 43–66. Stanford, CA: Stanford University Press.

Clancy, Patricia. 1986. The acquisition of communicative style in Japanese. In *Language socialization across cultures*, edited by Bambi B. Schieffelin and Elinor Ochs, pp. 251–272. London: Cambridge University Press.

Clark, Sheila Seiler. 1993. Anxiety, cultural identity, and solidarity: A Tahitian ethnomedical encounter. *Ethos* 21(2): 180–204.

Cobb, Charles E. 1993. Bangladesh: When the water comes. *National Geographic* 183: 118–134.

Comaroff, Jean. 1985. *Body of power, spirit of resistance*. Chicago: University of Chicago Press.

Compact Oxford English Dictionary. 1991. Oxford: Clarendon Press.

Comrie, Bernard. 1981. *Language universals and linguistic typology: Syntax and morphology*. Chicago: University of Chicago Press.

Corin, Ellen E. 1990. Facts and meaning in psychiatry. An anthropological approach to the lifeworld of schizophrenics. *Culture, Medicine, and Psychiatry* 14: 153–188.

Crapanzano, Vincent. 1990. On self characterization. In *Cultural psychology: Essays on comparative human development*, edited by James W. Stigler, Richard A. Shweder, and G. Herdt, pp. 401–426. Cambridge: Cambridge University Press.

———. 1996. "Self"-centering narratives. In *Natural histories of discourse*, edited by Michael Silverstein and Greg Urban, pp. 106–130. Chicago: University of Chicago Press.

Crystal, David. 1971. Prosodic and paralinguistic correlates of social categories. In *Social anthropology and language*, edited by Edwin Ardener. London: Tavistock.

———. 1991. *A dictionary of linguistics and phonetics*. 3rd ed. Oxford: Basil Blackwell.

Csordas, Thomas. 1988. Elements of charismatic persuasion and healing. *Medical Anthropology Quarterly* 2: 121–142.

———. 1990. 1988 Stirling Award Essay: Embodiment as a paradigm for anthropology. *Ethos* 18: 5–17.

Daniel, Valentine. 1984. *Fluid signs: Being a person the Tamil way*. Berkeley: University of California Press.

Das, Veena. 1986. The work of mourning: Death in a Punjabi family. In *The cultural transition: Human experience and social transformation in the Third World and Japan*, edited by Merry I. White and Susan Pollak. Boston: Routledge and Kegan Paul.

———. 1990. Our work to cry, your work to listen. In *Communities, riots, and survivors*, edited by Veena Das, pp. 345–398. Delhi: Oxford University Press.

———. 1996. Language and the body: Transactions in the construction of pain. *Daedalus* 125(1): 67–91.

Davis, Kathy. 1993. Nice doctors and invisible patients: The problem of power in feminist common sense. In *The social organization of doctor-patient communication*, edited by Alexandra Dundas Todd and Sue Fisher, pp. 243–265. 2nd ed. Norwood, NJ: Ablex.

Department of Social Medicine, Harvard Medical School. 1995. *World mental health: Problems and priorities in low-income countries: Executive summary*.

Derné, Steve. 1995. *Culture in action: Family life, emotion, and male dominance in Banaras, India*. Ithaca, NY: SUNY Press/Cornell University Press.

Desjarlais, Robert R. 1992. *Body and emotion: The aesthetics of illness and healing in the Nepal Himalayas*. Philadelphia: University of Pennsylvania Press.

———. 1997. *Shelter blues: Homelessness and sanity in a Boston shelter*. Philadelphia: University of Pennsylvania Press.

Devi, Mahasweta. 1994. The funeral wailer. In *Women, outcastes, peasants, and rebels: A selection of Bengali short stories*, edited and translated by Kalpana Bardhan, pp. 206–228. Berkeley: University of California Press.

Dimock, Edward C. 1989. Symbolic forms in Bengali. *The sound of silent guns and other essays*, pp. 52–61. Delhi: Oxford University Press.

Doi, Takeo. 1973. *The anatomy of dependence*. Tokyo: Kodansha International (distributed by Harper and Row, New York).

DuBois, John W. 1987. Meaning without intention: Lessons from divination. *International Pragmatics Association Papers in Pragmatics* 1: 80–122.

Dumont, Louis. 1970. *Homo hierarchicus*. Chicago: University of Chicago Press.

Dunham, Mary Frances. 1997. *Jarigan: Muslim epic songs of Bangladesh*. Dhaka: University Press Ltd.

Duranti, Alessandro. 1992. Language and bodies in social space: Samoan greetings. *American Anthropologist* 94: 657–691.

Duranti, Alessandro, and Donald Brenneis, editors. 1986. The audience as co-author (special issue of *Text* 6/3).

Duranti, Alessandro, and Eleanor Ochs. 1986. Literacy instruction in a Samoan village. In *The acquisition of literacy: Ethnographic perspectives*, edited by Bambi Schieffelin and Perry Gilmore. Norwood, NJ: Ablex.

Eagleton, Terry. 1991. *Ideology: An introduction*. London: Verso.

Eckert, Penelope, and Sally McConnell-Ginet. 1992. Think practically and look locally: Language and gender as community-based practice. *Annual Review of Anthropology* 21: 461–490.

Edelsky, Carole. 1981. Who's got the floor? *Language in Society* 10: 383–421.

Emeneau, Murray. 1969. Onomatopoeics in the Indian linguistic area. *Language* 45(2): 274–299.

Ewing, Katherine P. 1990. The illusion of wholeness: Culture, self and the experience of inconsistency. *Ethos* 18(3): 251–278.

———. 1991. Can psychoanalytic theories explain the Pakistani woman? Intrapsychic autonomy and interpersonal engagement in the extended family. *Ethos* 19(2): 131–160.

———. 1994. Dreams from a saint: Anthropological atheism and the temptation to believe. *American Anthropologist* 96(3): 571–583.

Fabrega, Horacio, Jr. 1990. The concept of somatization as a cultural and historical product of Western medicine. *Psychosomatic Medicine* 52: 664.

Falk, Jane. 1979. The conversational duet. Unpublished Ph.D. diss., Princeton University.

Fauveau, Vincent, editor. 1994. *Matlab: Women, children, and health*. Dhaka: International Centre for Diarrhoeal Disease Research, Bangladesh.

Feierman, Steven. 1985. Struggles for control: The social roots of health and healing in modern Africa. *African Studies Review* 29(2–3): 73–146.

Feld, Steven. 1990. *Sound and sentiment: Birds, weeping, poetics, and song in Kaluli expression*. 2nd ed. Philadelphia: University of Pennsylvania Press.

Feld, Steven, and Aaron Fox. 1994. Music and language. *Annual Review of Anthropology* 23: 25–53.

Feldman, Shelley. 1983. The use of private health care providers in rural Bangladesh: A response to Claquin. *Social Science and Medicine* 17(23): 1887–1896.

Ferguson, Charles A. 1959. Diglossia. *Word* 15: 325–340.

Finkler, Kaja. 1991. *Physicians at work, patients in pain: Biomedical practice and patient response in Mexico*. Boulder: Westview.

Fisher, Lawrence E. 1985. *Colonial madness: Mental health in the Barbadian social order*. New Brunswick, NJ: Rutgers University Press.

Fisher, Sue, and Susan B. Groce. 1990. Accounting practices in medical interviews. *Language in Society* 19: 225–250.

Fishman, Pamela M. 1983. Interaction: The work that women do. In *Language, gender, and society*, edited by Barre Thorne, Cheris Kramarae, and Nancy Henley, pp. 89–101. Rowley, MA: Newbury House.

Foucault, Michel. 1965. *The birth of the clinic: An archaeology of medical perception.* New York: Vintage.

———. 1973. *Madness and civilization: A history of insanity in the age of reason.* New York: Vintage.

———. 1977. *Discipline and punish: The birth of the prison.* Translated by Alan Sheridan. New York: Vintage.

———. 1980. *Power/knowledge: Selected interviews and other writings*, edited by Colin Gordon. New York: Pantheon.

———. 1985. The order of discourse. In *Untying the text: A post-structuralist reader*, edited by Robert Young, pp. 48–78. Boston: Routledge and Kegan Paul.

Frake, Charles. 1964. The diagnosis of disease among the Subanun of Mindanao. In *Language in culture and society*, edited by Dell Hymes, pp. 193–211. New York: Harper and Row.

Frank, Jerome D. 1963. *Persuasion and healing: A comparative study of psychotherapy.* New York: Schocken.

Friedrich, Paul. 1986. *The language parallax: Linguistic relativism and poetic indeterminacy.* Austin: University of Texas Press.

Fuller, Christopher John. 1992. *The camphor flame: Popular Hinduism and society in India.* Princeton, NJ: Princeton University Press.

Gaines, Atwood, and Paul Farmer. 1986. Visible saints: Social cynosures and dysphoria in the Mediterranean tradition. *Culture, Medicine and Psychiatry* 10: 295–330.

Gal, Susan. 1989. Between speech and silence: The problematics of research on language and gender. *Papers in Pragmatics* 3(1): 1–38.

Gal, Susan, and Judith T. Irvine. 1995. The boundaries of language and disciplines: How ideologies construct difference. *Social Research* 62 (4): 967–1001.

Gale, Jerry Edward. 1991. *Conversation analysis of therapeutic discourse: The pursuit of a therapeutic agenda.* Advances in Discourse Processes, Vol. 41. Norwood, NJ: Ablex.

Gardet, Louis. 1980. Ḳiyāma. *The Encyclopaedia of Islam,* Volume V. Fascicules 81–82: 235–238. Leiden: E. J. Brill.

Gear, Maria Carmen, Ernesto Cesar Liendo, and Lila Lee Scott. 1983. *Patients and agents: Transference-countertransference in therapy.* New York: Jason Aronson.

Geertz, Clifford. 1968. *Islam observed: Religious development in Morocco and Indonesia.* Chicago: University of Chicago Press.

———. 1984. "From the native's point of view": On the nature of anthropological understanding. In *Culture theory: Essays on mind, self, and emotion*, edited by Richard A. Shweder and Robert A. LeVine, pp. 123–136. Cambridge: Cambridge University Press.

Giddens, Anthony. 1979. *Central problems in social theory: Action, structure and contradiction in social analysis.* Berkeley: University of California Press.

———. 1984. *The constitution of society: Outline of the theory of structuration.* Cambridge: Polity / Basil Blackwell.

Gillin, John. 1948. Magical fright. *Psychiatry* 11(4): 387–400.

Goffman, Erving. 1959. *The presentation of self in everyday life.* Woodstock, NY: Overlook Press.

————. 1961. *Asylums: Essays on the social situation of mental patients and other inmates*. New York: Doubleday Anchor.

————. 1963. *Stigma: Notes on the management of spoiled identity*. Englewood Cliffs, NJ: Prentice Hall.

————. 1974. *Frame analysis: An essay on the organization of experience*. Cambridge: Harvard University Press.

————. 1981. *Forms of talk*. Philadelphia: University of Pennsylvania Press.

Good, Byron J. 1977. The heart of what's the matter: The semantics of illness in Iran. *Culture, Medicine, and Psychiatry* 1: 25–58.

————. 1994. *Medicine, rationality, and experience: An anthropological perspective*. The Lewis Henry Morgan Lectures 1990. Cambridge: Cambridge University Press.

Good, Mary-Jo Delvecchio, and Byron Good. 1981. The meaning of symptoms: A cultural hermeneutic model for clinical practice. In *The relevance of social science for medicine*, edited by Leon Eisenberg and Arthur Kleinman, pp. 253–279. Dordrecht: D. Reidel.

————. 1988. Ritual, the state, and the transformation of emotional discourse in Iranian society. *Culture, Medicine, and Psychiatry* 12: 48–63.

Goodwin, Charles. 1979. The interactive construction of a sentence in natural conversation. In *Everyday language*, edited by George Psathas, pp. 97–121. New York: Irvington.

Goodwin, Charles, and Marjorie H. Goodwin. 1987. Children's arguing. In *Language, gender, and sex in comparative perspective*, edited by Susan U. Philips, Susan Steele, and Christine Tanz. Cambridge: Cambridge University Press.

Goodwin, Charles, and John Heritage. 1990. Conversation analysis. *Annual Review of Anthropology* 19: 283–307.

Graham, Laura. 1993. A public sphere in Amazonia? The depersonalized collaborative construction of discourse in Xavante. *American Ethnologist* 20(4): 717–741.

Grima, Benedict. 1991. The role of suffering in women's performances of *paxto*. In *Gender, genre, and power in South Asian expressive traditions*, edited by Arjun Appadurai, Frank Korom, and Margaret Mills, pp. 81–101. Philadelphia: University of Pennsylvania Press.

————.1992. *The performance of emotion among Paxtun women*. Modern Middle East Series No. 17. Austin: University of Texas Press.

Gumperz, John. 1982. *Discourse strategies*. Cambridge: Cambridge University Press.

Gumperz, John, and Celia Roberts. 1991. Understanding in intercultural encounters. In *The pragmatics of international and intercultural communication*, edited by Jan Blommaert and Jef Verschueren, pp. 51–90. Amsterdam: John Benjamins.

Habte, Demissie, editor. 1990. *Annotated bibliography of ICDDR,B studies in Matlab, Bangladesh*. Dhaka: International Centre for Diarrheal Disease Research.

Haiman, John. 1985. *Natural syntax: Iconicity and erosion*. Cambridge Studies in Linguistics No. 44. Cambridge: Cambridge University Press.

Hallowell, Alfred Irving. 1955. The self and its behavioral environment. *Culture and experience*, pp. 75–110. Philadelphia: University of Pennsylvania Press.

Hamid, P. Nicholas. 1994. Self-monitoring, locus of control, and social encounters of Chinese and New Zealand students. *Journal of Cross-Cultural Psychology* 25(3): 353–368.

Hanks, William F. 1990. *Referential practice: Language and lived space among the Maya*. Chicago: University of Chicago Press.

————. 1996. *Language and communicative practices*. Critical Essays in Anthropology, No. 1. Boulder: Westview.

Harris, Grace Gredys. 1989. Concepts of individual, self, and person in description and analysis. *American Anthropologist* 91: 599–612.

Hasan, Kamil A. 1979. *Medical sociology of rural India*. Ajmer: Sachin.

Hashemi, Syed M., and Sidney R. Schuler. 1992. Disparate responses to men's and women's health: Evidence from rural Bangladesh. Paper presented at the 91st annual meeting of the American Anthropological Association, San Francisco.

Hasselkus, Betty Risteen. 1992. The family caregiver as interpreter in the geriatric medical interview. *Medical Anthropology Quarterly* 6: 288–304.

Haynes, Douglas, and Gyan Prakash, editors. 1992. *Contesting power: Resistance and everyday social relations in South Asia*. Berkeley: University of California Press.

Herdt, Gilbert. 1987. *The Sambia: Ritual and gender in New Guinea*. New York: Holt, Rinehart and Winston.

Herzfeld, Michael. 1993. In defiance of destiny: The management of time and gender at a Cretan funeral. *American Ethnologist* 20(2): 241–255.

Hilali, Shaikh Ghulam Maqsud, and Muhammad Enamul Haq. 1967. *Perso-Arabic elements in Bengali*. Dhaka: Central Board for Development of Bengali.

Hill, Jane H. 1995a. The voices of Don Gabriel: Responsibility and self in a modern Mexicano narrative. In *The dialogic emergence of culture*, edited by Dennis Tedlock and Bruce Mannheim, pp. 97–147. Urbana: University of Illinois Press.

————. 1995b. Mock Spanish: A site for the indexical reproduction of racism in American English. http://www.cs.uchicago.edu/l-c/archives/subs/.

Hodgson, Marshall G. S. 1974. *The venture of Islam: Conscience and history in a world civilization*. Chicago: University of Chicago Press.

Hollan, Douglas. 1991. Emotion work and the value of emotional equanimity among the Toraja. *Ethnology* 31(1): 45–56.

————. 1992. Cross-cultural differences in the self. *Journal of Anthropological Research* 48(4): 283–300.

Holland, Dorothy, and Naomi Quinn, editors. 1987. *Cultural models in language and thought*. Cambridge: Cambridge University Press.

Holst-Warhaft, Gail. 1992. *Dangerous voices: Women's laments and Greek literature*. London: Routledge.

Hoopes, James, editor. 1991. *Peirce on signs: Writings on semiotic by Charles Sanders Peirce*. Chapel Hill: University of North Carolina Press.

Hopper, Paul J. 1996. Some recent trends in grammaticalization. *Annual Review of Anthropology* 25: 217–236.

Hsieh, T. T., J. Shybut, and E. J. Lotsof. 1969. Internal versus external control and ethnic membership: A cross-cultural comparison. *Journal of Consulting and Clinical Psychology* 33: 122–124.

Huda, A., Muhammad Huq, and A. I. Bhuiyan. 1991. The Bangladesh Meghna-Dhonagoda irrigation project. *Public Administration and Development* 11: 215–218.

Hufford, David. 1982. *The terror that comes in the night: An experience-centered study of supernatural assault traditions*. Publications of the American Folklore Society, n.s., Vol. 7. Philadelphia: University of Pennsylvania Press.

Humayun, Rajib. 1985. *Sociolinguistic and descriptive study of Sandvipi: A Bangla dialect*. Dhaka: University Press.

Hymes, Dell. 1981. *In vain I tried to tell you: Essays in Native American ethnopoetics*. Philadelphia: University of Pennsylvania Press.

Imam, Jahanara. 1986. *Ekattarer dingulee (The days of '71)*. Dhaka: Sandhani Prakasani.

————.1990. *Of blood and fire: The untold story of Bangladesh's war of independence*. Translated by Mustafizur Rahman. Dhaka: Academic Publishers.

————. 1991. *Kænsārer sāthe basabās (Living with cancer)*. Dhaka: Afsar Brothers.

Irvine, Judith. 1989. When talk isn't cheap: Language and political economy. *American Ethnologist* 16: 248–267.

Isaacs, Ellen A., and Herbert H. Clark. 1990. Ostensible invitations. *Language in Society* 19(4): 493–510.

Ishaque, Abu. 1955. *Surya-dighal bāṛi (Sun-crossed homestead)*. Dhaka: Nowroj Kitabi-stan.

Islam, Mahmuda. 1985. *Women, health, and culture: A study of beliefs and practices connected with female diseases in a Bangladesh village*. Dhaka: Women for Women.

Jakobson, Roman. 1987. Subliminal verbal patterning in poetry. In *Language in litera-ture*, pp. 250–261. Cambridge: Harvard University Press.

Jeffery, Patricia. 1979. *Frogs in a well: Indian women in Purdah*. London: Zed Press.

Jefferson, Gail. 1980. On "trouble-premonitory" response to inquiry. *Sociological Inquiry* 50(3–4): 153–185.

————. 1981. The rejection of advice: Managing the problematic convergence of a "troubles-telling" and a "service encounter." *Journal of Pragmatics* 5: 399–422.

————. 1984a. On stepwise transition from talk about a trouble to inappropriately next-positioned matters. In *Structures of social action: Studies in conversation analysis*, edited by J. Maxwell Atkinson and John Heritage, pp. 191–222. Cambridge: Cam-bridge University Press.

————. 1984b. On the organization of laughter in talk about troubles. In *Structures of social action: Studies in conversation analysis*, edited by J. Maxwell Atkinson and John Heritage, pp. 346–369. Cambridge: Cambridge University Press.

Johnson, Barbara, editor. 1993. *Freedom and interpretation: The Oxford Amnesty lec-tures, 1992*. New York: Basic Books.

Kaeppler, Adrienne. 1993. Poetics and politics of Tongan laments and eulogies. *Ameri-can Ethnologist* 20(3): 474–501.

Kakar, Sudhir. 1978. *The inner world: A psychoanalytic study of childhood and society in India*. New Delhi: Oxford University Press.

————. 1991. *Shamans, mystics and doctors: A psychological inquiry into India and its healing traditions*. Chicago: University of Chicago Press (by arrangement with Alfred A. Knopf).

Kapferer, Bruce. 1991. *A celebration of demons: Exorcism and the aesthetics of healing in Sri Lanka*. 2nd ed. Oxford and Washington, D.C.: Berg and Smithsonian Institu-tion.

Kennedy, John G. 1967. Nubian Zar ceremonies as psychotherapy. *Human Organization* 26(4): 185–194.

Khan, Sharmin. 1994. Banking on women: Credit and community construction in rural Bangladesh. Paper presented at the 1994 meetings of the American Anthropological Association, Atlanta, GA.

Khare, Ravindra S. 1984. *The untouchable as himself: Ideology, identity and pragmatism among the Lucknow Chamars*. Cambridge: Cambridge University Press.

Kierkegaard, Søren. 1983. *Fear and trembling/Repetition (Kierkegaard's Writings, 6)*, edited and translated by Howard V. Hong and Edna H. Hong. Princeton, NJ: Prince-ton University Press.

Kirmayer, Laurence J. 1984. Culture, affect and somatization, parts 1 and 2. *Transcul-tural Psychiatric Research Review* 21(3): 159–188; (4): 237–262.

Klaiman, Miriam H. 1980. Bengali dative subjects. *Lingua* 51: 275–295.

———. 1981. *Volitionality and subject in Bengali: A study of semantic parameters in grammatical processes.* Bloomington: Indiana University Linguistics Club.

Kleinman, Arthur. 1986. *The social origins of distress and disease.* New Haven, CT: Yale University Press.

———. 1992. Pain and resistance: The delegitimation and relegitimation of local worlds. In *Pain as human experience: An anthropological perspective*, edited by Mary-Jo DelVecchio Good et al., pp. 169–197. Berkeley: University of California Press.

Kleinman, Arthur, and Joan Kleinman. 1985. Somatization: The interconnections in Chinese society among culture, depressive experiences, and the meanings of pain. In *Culture and depression*, edited by Arthur Kleinman and Byron Good, pp. 429–490. Berkeley: University of California Press.

Kleinman, Arthur, Veena Das, and Margaret Lock, editors. 1996. Social suffering. Special issue of *Daedalus* 125(1).

Koss-Chioino, Joan. 1992. *Women as healers, women as patients: Mental health care and traditional healing in Puerto Rico.* Boulder: Westview.

Kristeva, Julia. 1982. *Powers of horror: An essay on abjection.* Translated by Leon S. Roudiez. New York: Columbia University Press.

———. 1993. The speaking subject is not innocent. In *Freedom and interpretation*, edited by Barbara Johnson, pp. 147–174. New York: Basic Books.

Kroskrity, Paul V. 1992. Arizona Tewa Kiva speech as a manifestation of linguistic ideology. *Pragmatics* 2(3): 297–309.

———. 1993. *Language, history, and identity: Ethnolinguistic studies of the Arizona Tewa.* Tucson: University of Arizona Press.

Kroskrity, Paul, Bambi Schieffelin, and Kathryn Woolard, editors. 1992. *Language ideologies.* Special issue of *Pragmatics* 2(3).

Kuipers, Joel C. 1989. "Medical discourse" in anthropological context: Views of language and power. *Medical Anthropology Quarterly* 3(2): 99–123.

Kurtz, Stanley N. 1992. *All the mothers are one: Hindu India and the cultural reshaping of psychoanalysis.* New York: Columbia University Press.

Labov, William. 1972. *Sociolinguistic patterns.* Philadelphia: University of Pennsylvania Press.

———. 1984. Intensity. In *Georgetown University round table on languages and linguistics,* edited by Deborah Schiffrin, pp. 43–70. Washington, D.C.: Georgetown University Press.

Lakoff, Robin. 1975. *Language and woman's place.* New York: Harper and Row.

Lazarus, Ellen S. 1988. Theoretical considerations for the study of the doctor-patient relationship: Implications of a perinatal study. *Medical Anthropology Quarterly* 1: 34–58.

Lee, Benjamin. 1997. Talking heads: Language, metalanguage, and the semiotics of subjectivity. Durham: Duke University Press.

LeVine, Robert A., Sarah E. LeVine, Amy Richman, F. Medardo Tapia Uribe, and Clara Sunderland Correa. 1993. Schooling and survival: The impact of maternal education on health and reproduction in the Third World. In *Health and social change*, edited by Lincoln Chen, Arthur Kleinman, and Norma Ware, pp. 257–284. Boston: Department of Population and International Health, Harvard School of Public Health / Harvard University Press.

Levinson, Stephen C. 1983. *Pragmatics*. Cambridge: Cambridge University Press.

Levy, Robert. 1973. *The Tahitians: Mind and experience in the Society Islands*. Chicago: University of Chicago Press.

Lewis, Ioan M. 1975. *Ecstatic religion: An anthropological study of spirit possession and shamanism*. Harmondsworth: Penguin.

Lex, Barbara. 1979. The neurobiology of ritual trance. In *The spectrum of ritual: A biogenetic structural analysis*, edited by Eugene G. d'Aquili, Charles D. Laughlin, Jr., and John McManus. New York: Columbia University Press.

Li, Charles N. 1976. *Subject and topic*. New York: Academic Press.

Lindstrom, Lamont. 1992. Context contests: Debatable truth statements on Tanna (Vanuatu). In *Rethinking context: Language as an interactive phenomenon*, edited by Alessandro Duranti and Charles Goodwin, pp. 101–124. Studies in the Social and Cultural Foundations of Language No. 11. Cambridge: Cambridge University Press.

Lock, Margaret, and Nancy Scheper-Hughes. 1990. A critical-interpretive approach in medical anthropology: Rituals and routines of discipline and dissent. In *Medical anthropology: Contemporary theory and method*, edited by Thomas M. Johnson and Carolyn F. Sargent, pp. 47–72. New York: Praeger.

MacIntyre, Alasdair C. 1977. Patients as agents. In *Philosophical medical ethics*, edited by Stuart F. Spicker and Hugo Tristam Englehardt, pp. 197–212. Boston: D. Reidel.

Macleod, Arlene Elowe. 1991. *Accommodating protest: Working women, the new veiling, and change in Cairo*. New York: Columbia University Press.

Malinowski, Bronislaw. 1923. The problem of meaning in primitive languages. In *The meaning of meaning*, edited by Charles K. Ogden and Ivor Armstrong Richards, pp. 296–336. New York: Harcourt, Brace.

Maloney, Clarence. 1988. *Behaviour and poverty in Bangladesh*. Dhaka: Dhaka University Press.

Mannan, Qazi Abdul. 1966. *The emergence and development of dobhāṣi literature in Bengal (up to 1855 A. D.)*. Dacca: Department of Bengali and Sanskrit: University of Dacca.

Mannheim, Bruce, and Dennis Tedlock. 1995. Introduction. In *The dialogic emergence of culture*, edited by Dennis Tedlock and Bruce Mannheim, pp. 1–32. Urbana: University of Illinois Press.

Maqsud, Muhammad, and Sepideh Rouhani. 1991. Relationships between socioeconomic status, locus of control, self-concept, and academic achievement of Batswana adolescents. *Journal of Youth and Adolescence* 20(1): 107–114.

Marriott, McKim. 1976. Hindu transactions: Diversity without dualism. In *Transaction and meaning: Directions in the anthropology of exchange and symbolic behavior*, edited by Bruce Kapferer, pp. 109–142. Philadelphia: Institute for the Study of Human Issues.

Masica, Colin P. 1991. *The Indo-Aryan languages*. Cambridge: Cambridge University Press.

McDaniel, June. 1989. *The madness of the saints: Ecstatic religion in Bengal*. Chicago: University of Chicago Press.

Mead, George H. 1995a. The problem of society: How we become selves. In *Language, culture, and society: A book of readings*, edited by Ben G. Blount, pp. 85–94. Prospect Heights, IL: Waveland.

———.1995b. The relation of mind to response and environment. In *Language, culture, and society: A book of readings*, edited by Ben G. Blount, pp. 95–101. Prospect Heights, IL: Waveland.

Mertz, Elizabeth, and Richard Parmentier, editors. 1985. *Semiotic mediation: Socio-cultural and psychological perspectives.* Orlando: Academic Press.

Messer, Ellen. 1993. Anthropology and human rights. *Annual Review of Anthropology* 22: 221–249.

Mills, C. Wright. 1959. *The sociological imagination.* New York: Oxford University Press.

Mines, Mattison. 1988. Conceptualizing the person: Hierarchical society and individual autonomy in India. *American Anthropologist* 90(3): 568–579.

Mishler, Elliot G. 1984. *The discourse of medicine: Dialectics of medical interviews.* Norwood, NJ: Ablex.

Mitra, Subal Chandra. 1924. *The student's Bengali-English dictionary.* 2nd ed. Calcutta: New Bengal.

Mukundaram, Kabikankan. 1589. *Candimangal.*

Murray, Stephen O. 1985. Toward a model of members' methods for recognizing interruptions. *Language in Society* 14(1): 31–40.

Murray, Stephen O., and Lucille H. Covelli. 1988. Women and men speaking at the same time. *Journal of Pragmatics* 12(1): 103–111.

Nandy, Ashis. 1983. *The intimate enemy: Loss and recovery of self under colonialism.* Delhi: Oxford University Press.

Nelson, Kristina. 1985. *The art of reciting the Qur'an.* Modern Middle East Series No. 11. Austin: University of Texas Press.

Nichter, Mark. 1981. Idioms of distress: Alternatives in the expression of psychosocial distress: A case study from South India. *Culture, Medicine, and Psychiatry* 5: 379–408.

Nuckolls, Janis. 1992. Sound symbolic involvement. *Journal of Linguistic Anthropology* 2(1): 51–80.

———. 1996. *Sounds like life: Sound-symbolic grammar, performance, and cognition in Pastaza Quechua.* Oxford Studies in Anthropological Linguistics No. 2. New York: Oxford University Press.

O'Barr, William M., and Bowman K. Atkins. 1980. "Women's language" or "powerless language"? In *Women and language in literature and society,* edited by Sally McConnell-Ginet et al., pp. 93–110. New York: Praeger.

Obeyesekere, Gananath. 1975. Sorcery, premeditated murder, and the canalization of aggression in Sri Lanka. *Ethnology* 14: 1–23.

———. 1976. The impact of Ayurvedic ideas on the culture and the individual in Sri Lanka. In *Asian medical systems,* edited by Charles Leslie. Berkeley: University of California Press.

———. 1978. Illness, culture, and meaning: Some comments on the nature of traditional medicine. In *Culture and healing in Asian societies: Anthropological, psychiatric and public health studies,* edited by Arthur Kleinman, Peter Kunstadter, Edmund R. Alexander, and J. L. Gate. Cambridge, MA: Schenkman.

———. 1984. *Medusa's hair: An essay on personal symbols and religious experience.* Chicago: University of Chicago Press.

Ochs, Elinor. 1988. *Culture and language development: Language acquisition and language socialization in a Samoan village.* Studies of the Social and Cultural Foundations of Language No. 6. Cambridge: Cambridge University Press.

———. 1992. Indexing gender. In *Rethinking context: Language as an interactive phenomenon,* edited by Alessandro Duranti and Charles Goodwin, pp. 335–358. Studies in the Social and Cultural Foundations of Language No. 11. Cambridge: Cambridge University Press.

Ochs, Elinor, and Lisa Capps. 1996. Narrating the self. *Annual Review of Anthropology* 25: 19–43.

Ochs, Elinor, and Bambi Schieffelin. 1984. Language acquisition and socialization: Three developmental stories and their implications. In *Culture theory: Essays on mind, self, and emotion*, edited by Richard Shweder and Robert LeVine, pp. 276–320. New York: Cambridge University Press.

———. 1989. Language has a heart. In *The Pragmatics of Affect. Text* 9(1): 7–25.

Paget, Marianne A. 1993. On the work of talk: Studies in misunderstandings. In *The social organization of doctor-patient communication*, edited by Alexandra Dundas Todd and Sue Fisher, pp. 107–126. 2nd ed. Washington, D.C.: Center for Applied Linguistics.

Papanek, Hanna. 1990. To each less than she needs, from each more than she can do: Allocations, entitlements and value. In *Persistent inequalities: Women and world development*, edited by Irene Tinker, pp. 162–184. New York: Oxford University Press.

Parmentier, Richard J. 1994. *Signs in society: Studies in semiotic anthropology*. Bloomington: Indiana University Press.

Parsons, Talcott. 1987. Illness and the role of the physician: A sociological perspective. In *Encounters between patients and doctors: An anthology*, edited by John D. Stoeckle, pp. 147–156. Cambridge: MIT Press.

Peirce, Charles Sanders. 1991. [1868] Questions concerning certain faculties claimed for man. In *Peirce on signs: Writings on semiotic by Charles Sanders Peirce*, edited by James Hoopes, pp. 34–53. Chapel Hill: University of North Carolina Press.

Pennebaker, James W. 1990. *Opening up: The healing powers of confiding in others*. New York: W. Morrow.

———. 1993. Social mechanisms of constraint. In *Handbook of mental control*, edited by Daniel M. Wegner and James W. Pennebaker, pp. 200–219. Engelwood Cliffs, NJ: Prentice Hall.

Pennebaker, James W., Steven D. Barger, and John Tiebout.

———. 1989. Disclosure of traumas and health among Holocaust survivors. *Psychosomatic Medicine* 51: 577–589.

Pennebaker, James W., Janice Kiecolt-Glaser, and Ronald Glaser. 1988. Disclosure of traumas and immune function: Health implications for psychotherapy. *Journal of Consulting and Clinical Psychology* 56(2): 239–245.

Pinker, Steven. 1994. *The language instinct*. New York: W. Morrow.

Population Crisis Committee. 1988. *Country rankings of the status of women: Poor, powerless, and pregnant*. Briefing Paper 20. Washington, D.C.: Population Crisis Committee.

Prindle, Carol. 1988. Occupation and orthopraxy in Bengali Muslim rank. In *Sharī'at, ambiguity, and change: Moral principles in tension in South Asian Islam*, edited by Katherine P. Ewing, pp. 259–287. Berkeley: University of California Press.

Pugh, Judith. 1983. Astrological counseling in contemporary India. *Culture, Medicine, and Psychiatry* 7(3): 279–299.

Putnam, Samuel M., and William B. Stiles. 1993. Verbal exchanges in medical interviews: Implications and innovations. *Social Science and Medicine* 36: 1597–1604.

Radcliffe-Brown, Alfred Reginald. 1964. *The Andaman Islanders*. New York: The Free Press.

Raheja, Gloria Goodwin. 1988. *The poison in the gift: ritual, prestation, and the dominant caste in a north Indian village*. Chicago: University of Chicago Press.

Raheja, Gloria Goodwin, and Ann Grodzins Gold. 1994. *Listen to the heron's words: Reimagining gender and kinship in North India.* Berkeley: University of California Press.

Rahman, Makhlisur. 1986. *Tradition, development, and the individual: A study of conflicts and supports to family planning in rural Bangladesh*, edited by P. Kane and L. Ruzicka. Department of Demography: Asian Population Change Series No. 1. Canberra: Australian National University.

Rampton, Ben. 1995. *Crossing: Language and ethnicity among adolescents.* Real Language Series. London: Longman.

Reddy, Michael. 1993. The conduit metaphor: A case of frame conflict in our language about language. In *Metaphor and thought*, edited by Andrew Ortony, pp. 164–201. Cambridge: Cambridge University Press.

Reiser, Stanley. 1978. *Medicine and the reign of technology.* Cambridge: Cambridge University Press.

Rhodes, Lorna Amarasingham. 1990. Studying biomedicine as a cultural system. In *Medical anthropology: Contemporary theory and method*, edited by Thomas M. Johnson and Carolyn F. Sargent, pp. 159–173. New York: Praeger.

Ricoeur, Paul. 1993. Self as *ipse*. In *Freedom and interpretation: The Oxford Amnesty lectures, 1992*, edited by Barbara Johnson, pp. 103–120. New York: Basic Books.

Rohner, Ronald P., and Manjusri Chaki-Sircar. 1988. *Women and children in a Bengali village.* Hanover: University Press of New England.

Roland, Alan. 1988. *In search of self in India and Japan: Toward a cross-cultural psychology.* Princeton, NJ: Princeton University Press.

Roseman, Marina. 1991. *Healing sounds from the Malaysian rainforest: Temiar music and medicine.* Berkeley: University of California Press.

Rotter, J. B. 1966. Generalized expectancies for internal versus external control of reinforcement. *Psychological Monographs*, 80 (1, Whole No. 609).

Rosaldo, Michelle Z. 1972. I have nothing to hide: The language of Ilongot oratory. *Language in Society* 2: 193–223.

Roy, Manisha. 1975. *Bengali women.* Chicago: University of Chicago Press.

Rozario, Santi. 1992. *Purity and communal boundaries: Women and social change in a Bangladeshi village.* Women in Asia Publication Series. London: Zed Books.

Sachs, Lisbeth. 1989. Misunderstanding as therapy: Doctors, patients and medicines in a rural clinic in Sri Lanka. *Culture, Medicine, and Psychiatry* 13: 355–349.

Sansom, Basil. 1982. The sick who do not speak. In *Semantic Anthropology*, edited by David J. Parkin, pp. 183–196. London: Academic Press.

Sapir, Edward. 1927. The unconscious patterning of behavior in society. In *Selected writings of Edward Sapir in language, culture, and personality*, edited by David G. Mandelbaum, pp. 544–559. Berkeley: University of California Press.

Sawyer, Keith. 1996. The semiotics of improvisation: The pragmatics of musical and verbal performance. *Semiotica* 108(3/4): 269–306.

Scarry, Elaine. 1985. *The body in pain: The making and unmaking of the world.* New York: Oxford University Press.

Scheper-Hughes, Nancy, and Margaret Lock. 1987. The mindful body: A prolegomenon to future work in medical anthropology. *Work in Medical Anthropology Quarterly* 1(1): 6–41.

Schieffelin, Bambi B. 1990. *The give and take of everyday life: Language socialization of Kaluli children.* Cambridge: Cambridge University Press.

Schieffelin, Bambi B., and Ochs, Elinor. 1986. Language socialization. *Annual Review of Anthropology* 15: 163–191.

Schimmel, Annemarie. 1975. *Mystical dimensions of Islam*. Chapel Hill: University of North Carolina Press.

Schmalz, Mathew N. 1996. A slave for Jesus: Portrait of an Indian charismatic healer. Paper presented at the Panel, Narrative and Identity in South Asian Religions, 25th anniversary conference on South Asia, Madison, WI.

Schutz, Alfred. 1970. *On phenomenology and social relations*, edited and translated by Helmut Wagner. Chicago: University of Chicago Press.

Scollon, Ron, and Suzanne Scollon. 1982. *Narrative, literacy, and face in interethnic communication.* Norwood, NJ: Ablex.

Scott, James C. 1990. *Domination and the arts of resistance: Hidden transcripts*. New Haven, CT: Yale University Press.

Searle, John. 1975. Indirect speech acts. In *Syntax and semantics 3: Speech acts*, edited by Peter Cole and Jerry Morgan, pp. 59–82. New York: Academic Press.

Seremetakis, C. Nadia. 1990. The ethics of antiphony: The social construction of pain, gender, and power in the southern Peleponnese. *Ethos* 18(4): 481–511.

———. 1991. *The last word: Women, death, and divination in Inner Mani*. Chicago: University of Chicago Press.

Selby, Martha Ann. 1996. Desire for meaning: Providing contexts for *Prākrit gāthās*. *Journal of Asian Studies* 55: 81–93.

Showalter, Elaine. 1985. *The female malady: Women, madness, and English culture 1830–1980*. New York: Pantheon.

Shweder, Richard A., and Edmund J. Bourne. 1984. Does the concept of the person vary cross-culturally? In *Culture theory: Essays on mind, self, and emotion*, edited by Richard A. Shweder and Robert A. LeVine, pp. 158–199. Cambridge: Cambridge University Press.

Silverstein, Michael. 1976. Shifters, linguistic categories, and cultural description. *Meaning in anthropology,* edited by Keith Basso and Henry A. Selby. Albuquerque: SOAR / University of New Mexico Press.

———. 1979. Language structure and linguistic ideology. In *The elements: A parasession on linguistic units and levels,* edited by Paul R. Cline, William Hanks, and Carol Hofbauer, pp. 193–247. Chicago: Chicago Linguistic Society.

———. 1981. The limits of awareness. Working Papers in Sociolinguistics 84. Austin: Southwest Educational Development Laboratory.

———. 1985. Language and the culture of gender: At the intersection of structure, usage, and ideology. In *Semiotic mediation: Sociocultural and psychological perspectives,* edited by Elizabeth Mertz and Richard Parmentier, pp. 219–259. Orlando: Academic Press.

———. 1992. The uses and utility of ideology: Some reflections. In *Language ideologies*. Special issue of *Pragmatics* (2), edited by Paul Kroskrity, Bambi Schieffelin, and Kathryn Woolard, pp. 387–404.

———. 1996. Indexical order and the dialectics of sociolinguistic life. In *SALSA III (Proceedings of the Third Annual Symposium about Language and Society)*, edited by Risako Ide, Rebecca Parker, and Yukako Sunaoshi, pp. 266–295. Texas Linguistic Forum Vol. 36.

———. In press. Whorfianism and the linguistic imagination of nationality. In *Language ideologies*, edited by Paul Kroskrity. Santa Fe: School of American Research.

Silverstein, Michael and Greg Urban, editors. 1996. *Natural histories of discourse*. Chicago: University of Chicago Press.

Singer, Milton. 1994. Semiotic anthropology. In *Encyclopedia of language and linguistics*, edited by William Bright, pp. 3795–3799. New York: Oxford University Press.

Sontag, Susan. 1977–78. *Illness as metaphor*. New York: Farrar, Strauss and Giroux.

Spiro, Melford. 1993. Is the Western conception of the self "peculiar" within the context of the world cultures? *Ethos* 21(2): 107–153.

Spivak, Gayatri Chakravorty. 1994. Can the subaltern speak? In *Colonial discourse and post-colonial theory: A reader,* edited by Patrick Williams and Laura Chrisman, pp. 66–111. New York: Columbia University Press.

Steedly, Mary Margaret. 1988. Severing the bonds of love: A case study in soul loss. *Social Science and Medicine* 27(8): 841–856.

Tambiah, Stanley J. 1990. *Magic, science, religion and the scope of rationality*. Cambridge: Harvard University Press.

Tannen, Deborah. 1979. *Processes and consequences of conversational style*. Ann Arbor, MI: University Microfilms.

Taussig, Michael. 1980. *The devil and commodity fetishism*. Chapel Hill: University of North Carolina Press.

Ṭhikānā Bangla Weekly. 1993. Tārā-o ki cān Bāṅlādeśer śimānto muce felte? (Do they also want to erase the borders of Bangladesh?). New York. September 11, page 1.

Tiwary, Kapil Muni. 1978. Tuneful weeping: A mode of communication. *Frontiers* 3(3): 24–27.

Todd, Alexandra Dundas. 1993. Exploring women's experiences: Power and resistance in medical discourse. In *The social organization of doctor-patient communication*, 2nd ed., edited by Alexandra Dundas Todd and Sue Fisher, pp. 267–285. Norwood, NJ: Ablex.

Todd, Alexandra Dundas, and Sue Fisher, editors. 1993. *The social organization of doctor-patient communication*. 2nd ed. Norwood, NJ: Ablex.

Toombs, Kay. 1992. *The meaning of illness: A phenomenological account of the different perspectives of physician and patient*. Dordrecht: Kluwer.

Trawick, Margaret. 1988. Spirits and voices in Tamil songs. *American Ethnologist* 15: 193–215.

———. 1990a. *Notes on love in a Tamil family*. Berkeley: University of California Press.

———. 1990b. Untouchability and the fear of death in a Tamil song. In *Language and the politics of emotion*, edited by Catherine A. Lutz and Lila Abu-Lughod, pp. 186–206. Cambridge: Cambridge University Press.

Trix, Frances. 1993. *Spiritual discourse: Learning with an Islamic master*. Conduct and Communication. Philadelphia: University of Pennsylvania Press.

Turner, Victor W. 1964. An Ndembu doctor in practice. In *Magic, faith, and healing: Studies in primitive psychiatry today*, edited by Ari Kiev. New York: Free Press.

Tweedie, Irina. 1979. *Chasm of fire: A woman's experience of liberation through the teachings of a Sufi master*. Tisbury, England: Element Books.

UBINIG. 1989. *Illness behaviour: Experiences from six villages in Bangladesh*. Dhaka: UBINIG Project.

Urban, Greg. 1985. The semiotics of two speech styles in Shokleng. In *Semiotic mediation: Sociocultural and psychological perspectives*, edited by Elizabeth Mertz and Richard Parmentier, pp. 311–329. Orlando: Academic Press.

———. 1988. Ritual wailing in Amerindian Brazil. *American Anthropologist* 90: 385–400.

————. 1989. The "I" of discourse. In *Semiotics, self, and society*, edited by Benjamin Lee and Greg Urban. Approaches to Semiotics 84. Berlin: Mouton de Gruyter.

————. 1996. *Metaphysical community: The interplay of the senses and the intellect*. Austin: University of Texas Press.

Vaudeville, Charlotte. 1986. *Bārahmāsā in Indian literatures: Songs of the twelve months in Indo-Aryan literatures*. Delhi: Motilal Banarsidass.

Vološinov, Valentin Nikolaevitch. 1973. *Marxism and the philosophy of language*. Translated by Ladislav Matejka and Irwin R. Titunik. Cambridge: Harvard University Press.

Vygotsky, Lev Semenovitch. 1978. *Mind in society: The development of higher psychological processes*, edited by Michael Cole et al. Cambridge: Harvard University Press.

Wadley, Susan S. 1983. The rains of estrangement: Understanding the Hindu yearly cycle. *Contributions to Indian Sociology* 17(1): 51–85.

Waitzkin, Howard. 1991. *The politics of medical encounters*. New Haven, CT: Yale University Press.

Wallace, Anthony F. C. 1961. The psychic unity of human groups. *Culture and Personality*. New York: Random House.

————. 1966. *Religion: An anthropological view*. New York: Random House.

Ware, Norma. 1992. Suffering and the social construction of illness: The delegitimation of illness experience in chronic fatigue syndrome. *Medical Anthropology Quarterly* 6: 347–361.

Warner, Michael. 1990. *Letters of the republic: Publication and the public sphere in eighteenth-century America*. Cambridge: Harvard University Press.

Weber, Max. 1958. *The Protestant ethic and the spirit of capitalism*. Translated by Talcott Parsons. New York: Scribners.

Werbner, Pnina. 1996. The making of Muslim dissent: Hybridized discourses, lay preachers, and radical rhetoric among British Pakistanis. *American Ethnologist* 23(1): 102–122.

West, Candace. 1984. *Routine complications: Troubles with talk between doctors and patients*. Bloomington: Indiana University Press.

West, Candace, and Don H. Zimmerman. 1975. Sex roles, interruptions and silences in conversation. In *Language and sex: Difference and dominance*, edited by Barre Thorne and Nancy Henley. Rowley, MA: Newbury House.

————. 1983. Small insults: A study of interruptions in cross-sex conversations between unacquainted persons. In *Language, gender, and society*, edited by Barre Thorne, Cheris Kramarae, and Nancy Henley, pp. 102–117. Rowley, MA: Newbury House.

Whorf, Benjamin Lee. 1956. The relation of habitual thought and behavior to language. In *Language, thought, and reality: Selected writings of Benjamin Lee Whorf*, edited by John B. Carroll, pp. 65–86. New York: Wiley.

Wikan, Unni. 1990. *Managing turbulent hearts: A Balinese formula for living*. Chicago: University of Chicago Press.

Wilce, James M. 1989. Analysis of a Paharia folktale: The jackal story. *Anthropology UCLA* 16(1): 35–59.

————. 1994. Repressed eloquence: Health communication in Matlab, Bangladesh. Unpublished Ph.D. diss., University of California, Los Angeles.

————. 1995. "I can't tell you all my troubles": Conflict, resistance, and metacommunication in Bangladeshi illness interactions. *American Ethnologist* 22(4): 927–952.

————. 1996. Reciprocity in imagining community: The play of tropes in a rural Bangladeshi moot. *Journal of Linguistic Anthropology* 6(2): 188–222.

————. 1997. Discourse, power, and the diagnosis of weakness: Encountering practitioners in Bangladesh. *Medical Anthropology Quarterly* 11 (3): 352–374.

————. 1998 Lamenting Death, or the death of lament? The politics of lament and religion in Bangladesh and beyond. *SALSA V* (Proceedings of the Fifth Annual Symposium about Language and Society), University of Texas, Austin, 1997. Mani Chandrika Chalasani, Jennifer A. Grocer, and Peter C. Haney, editors. Texas Linguistic Forum 39: 235–247.

Wilson, Elizabeth. 1993. Is transgression transgressive? In *Activating theory: Lesbian, gay, bisexual politics*, edited by Joseph Bristow and Angelina Wilson, pp. 107–117. London: Lawrence and Wishart.

Woolard, Kathryn, and Bambi Schieffelin. 1994. Language ideology. *Annual Review of Anthropology* 23: 55–82.

Wrong, Dennis. 1961. The oversocialized conception of man in modern sociology. *American Sociological Review* 26(2): 183–193.

Zola, Irving. 1992. Self, identity, and the naming question: Reflections on the language of disability. *Social Science and Medicine* 36(2): 167–173.

INDEX AND GLOSSARY

Nematode Ecology and Plant Disease

Frontispiece. (top) Stone-fruit orchards near Nuriootpa in South Australia. Patterns of variable tree growth are associated with changes in soil type. The soil is basically sand over clay with low fertility and subject to waterlogging. Various pathogens including *Meloidogyne javanica* occur in the orchards. (bottom) An almond orchard on red-brown soil at Willunga in South Australia. Sodium toxicity, waterlogging, pests and disease are possible factors influencing tree growth. The pattern of variable growth is associated with soil type and age of tree. Vines in the top left corner are also affected. (Reproduced by permission of J. R. Harris, C.S.I.R.Q. Division of Soils).

Nematode Ecology and Plant Disease

H. R. Wallace

Professor of Plant Pathology
Waite Agricultural Research Institute
University of Adelaide
South Australia

Edward Arnold   London
Crane, Russak   New York

First published 1973
by Edward Arnold (Publishers) Limited

Published in the United States by:
Crane, Russak & Company, Inc.
52 Vanderbilt Avenue
New York, N.Y. 10017

Library of Congress Catalog No. 73-90720
ISBN 0-8448-0271-9

Printed in Great Britain by
Alden & Mowbray Ltd
at the Alden Press, Oxford

Preface

My previous book, *The Biology of Plant Parasitic Nematodes*, was published in 1963 and is now out of print. Since 1963 there have been marked advances in our knowledge of plant nematodes, so marked in fact that a revision of the book by simply adding new references and inserting extra information seemed impracticable. The subject has evolved too much for that; new and important aspects have arisen, other topics thought to be important ten years ago now seem less important and, furthermore, my ideas on many aspects of plant nematology have also evolved (hopefully in the right direction). Thus the changes required in a new edition of *The Biology of Plant Parasitic Nematodes* would have been too great to justify their publication under this title. In surveying the progress in nematology over the last few years, it seems to me that there is now an abundance of information on subjects that could usefully form a framework for discussion of the ecology of nematodes and the diseases they cause in plants. This book differs from its predecessor in covering a wider field of enquiry. Frequent reference is made to papers in medical science, parasitology, plant pathology and ecology, and no attempt has been made to review completely the plant nematological field in any topic. Instead, references have been selected that help to illustrate or support an argument or some facet of information. In spite of these changes, this book still contains most of the original topics, hence it should continue to serve as a text book for students, as well as providing thought for research workers and those involved in the vital jobs of diagnosis and control of disease in plants.

I am grateful for helpful criticism from my colleagues in the Plant Pathology Department and elsewhere at the Waite Agricultural Research Institute. I am also indebted to Miss T. Siekmann for typing and secretarial help, to Mrs. L. Wichman who prepared the figures, to Mr. Brian Palk who photographed them and to Miss F. Teare for assistance in checking the script. Thanks are also due to Mr. J. Harris of the CSIRO Division of Soils for the aerial photograph shown on the cover.

1973   H.R.W.

Contents

1 Introduction

In examining crops in different parts of the world I have frequently been impressed with the way in which colleagues readily recognize the association between disease symptoms and a causal pathogen. As with the medical practitioner there is some satisfaction in putting a name to a disease, indeed there seems to be a sense of obligation to do just that. If, however, we consider the whole crop and ask why some areas have more diseased plants than others and whether some factor, other than the pathogen, is influencing plant growth, the answers are usually speculative and imprecise. The cause of indecision of course lies in the ecological complexity of the crop system, with its numerous interacting factors.

The textbooks do not help much either. There is plenty of information on the biology of nematodes, their relationships with plants, the symptoms of diseased plants and methods by which nematodes can be controlled. Such information is invaluable when we know that a particular problem is caused chiefly by nematodes but how often is a diseased crop sampled to establish this conclusion? Very infrequently, I suggest. There are, of course, situations where devastation in a crop is obviously associated with the presence of some nematode and recommendations for their control are justified. However, even here the ecologically-minded nematologist may ask himself whether some other environmental component had not predisposed the crop to such devastation and whether control of this other hidden factor might not be more efficient and economical. Furthermore, it is likely that in terms of yield, losses from devastated parts of a crop may be much less than the total losses in the much wider area of apparently healthy plants. There is, therefore, a need for information on the etiology of disease in the field to establish the main causes. If this is not done, nematologists will continue to implicate nematodes as important causes in situations where they may be only one of numerous contributory factors. More importantly, however, nematodes may be dismissed or overlooked in a failing crop because of inadequate analysis of the situation and lack of problem definition. Statements in textbooks and papers on the major importance of nematodes in agriculture seem to be based less on facts than on a desire to promote the subject and to justify research on nematodes. This is not to say that nematodes are not important, in fact they may very well turn out to be more important than we imagine at present; but such conclusions can only be established from experiment, not on affirmations based on logic or faith.

The problem of dealing with ecological complexity is a theme which runs through most of the following chapters. It is a problem that pervades many topics from the physiology of the individual diseased plant to the ecology of the diseased crop. It is also a practical problem because the success of any attempt to control disease in which nematodes are involved depends largely on its solution.

There are two ways of writing about nematology or any other organism-orientated subject. All the known facts about nematodes can be collated and presented as a series of topics on different aspects of nematode biology: or the subject can be considered in wider terms in which comparisons are made with other organisms and information from other fields is culled for useful pointers that might provide fresh ideas about nematodes and the diseases they cause. I have chosen the second alternative because, in my opinion, the major problems in nematology and plant protection generally, demand information from other disciplines if they are to be solved.

Both ways of writing about nematology have their advantages and disadvantages. The first method, although thorough, is perhaps too specialized; the second way on the other hand lays itself open to criticisms of superficiality and over generalization. However, there is so much useful information to be gained from areas outside nematology that the attempt seems worthwhile. It is perhaps significant that those papers that seem to have made a major contribution to nematology (as judged by the frequency to which they are referred) have come from authors who have adopted a wider outlook on the problem. The paper of Harris and Crofton (1957) on structure and function in nematodes echoes D'Arcy Thompson's earlier conclusions and the several papers of Seinhorst on nematode populations are based on the entomological work of Nicolson. Until Seinhorst put forward his ideas, the topic of nematode populations was replete with data but lacked much useful theory.

At a recent seminar on etiology of plant diseases an entomologist remarked that he had the feeling of having heard it all before as he listened to the discussion and arguments on procedures for coping with numerous variables in the field, with the efficacy of models and the relative attributes of different statistical analyses. That the entomologists and ecologists went through these stages several years ago leaves one with the notion, that in a subject like plant nematology, there is an inevitable evolution in the learning process, an ontogeny of thought that must be completed before we reach the required level of competence to handle such problems as the etiology of disease in crops. Hopefully, the nematologists will be able to capitalize on the progress made by ecologists in other fields and so accelerate their own progress. It is clear from the papers of Norton (1971) and Ferris (1971) and their colleagues for example, that the big jump into factorial analysis from the more common descriptive associations between nematodes and plant disease has already been made. And the model of Jones *et al.* (1967) indicates how problems in multifactorial systems might be tackled. Even in these areas, however, the statistical analysts hold the reins, eventually the nematologists will take command and specify clearly the problem he wants solved and how the data might be analysed.

Plant nematology is a practical subject and most research in that field is concerned directly or indirectly with the search for ways in which nematodes and disease might be controlled. It might be argued that all research on nematodes is useful because there is no knowing when some apparently useless piece of information may become significant in a new context. Few would disagree with this view, however it seems to me that nematologists should also be doing research on aspects that are contributing directly to the problem of disease control. By direct contribution I mean research that is done to answer specific questions that arise from the analysis of factors causing disease in a crop. Thus the exercises of problem definition by systems analysis and simulation or modelling demand information that can only be gained by biochemical, physiological and ecological experiment.

What I have tried to do in this book is to write a story about nematodes and disease in plants using some information from medical science, parasitology, plant pathology and ecology to support my arguments. The objective is to contribute to a better understanding of how plant diseases associated with nematodes might be controlled. To do this, we need to know how the nematode damages the plant and the relationship between the numbers of nematodes and disease. Disease is a property of the plant, hence it is inevitable that the plant or the crop should, as a recipient of nematode damage, receive a great deal of attention. Consequently, how well the plant tolerates damage and how it resists attack are important aspects because in disease these attributes appear to be inadequate to restrain the nematodes.

The question of deciding how important nematodes are in a disease situation is left to the end of the story. Here it takes a practical turn and the question of analysing ecological systems is considered followed by an appraisal of the problem of what to do about disease in crops. No simple answers are offered, rather the suggestion is made that more consideration should be given to strategy i.e. how existing methods of control might be used more effectively.

Finally, whatever approach we take to achieve the goal of controlling disease associated with plant nematodes, knowledge of the nematodes themselves as well as the plants which they parasitize, will increase the chance of success. Expertize in the modern methods of systems analysis and simulation, although invaluable, has less impact in my opinion, if there is not someone in the team who has a thorough understanding of what 'makes nematodes tick'. In other words there must always be room for the specialist who studies different aspects of the biology of plant nematodes.

References

HARRIS, J.E. and CROFTON, H.D. (1957). Structure and function in the nematodes: internal pressure and cuticular structure in *Ascaris*. *J. exp. Biol.*, **34**, 116.

FERRIS, V.R., FERRIS, J.M., BERNARD, R.L. and PROBST, A.H. (1971). Community structure of plant-parasitic nematodes related to soil types in Illinois and Indiana soybean fields. *J. Nematology*, **3**, 399.

JONES, F.G.W., PARROTT, D.M. and ROSS, G.J.S. (1967). The population genetics of the potato cyst-nematode *Heterodera rostochiensis*; mathematical models to simulate the effects of growing eelworm-resistant potatoes, bred from *Solanum tuberosum* ssp. *andigena*. *Ann. appl. Biol.*, **60**, 151.

NORTON, D.C., FREDERICK, L.R., PONCHILLIA, P.E. and NYHAN, J.W. (1971). Correlations of nematodes and soil properties in soybean fields. *J. Nematology*, **3**, 154.

2 Nematodes as parasites and pathogens

The extraction of food from one organism, the host, by another organism, the parasite, inevitably entails some disturbance of the host's integrity. The disturbance is something foreign and unusual that changes the existing order of things and upsets the stability of the host. If the disturbance persists it may produce a series of events that create different and more drastic disturbances which we call the symptoms of disease. Under these circumstances the nematode becomes a pathogen as well as a parasite.

Something should be said about the terms 'parasite' and 'pathogen'. I take the view that a pathogen is some factor (not necessarily a parasite or even living) that causes or contributes to disease. What I mean by disease is discussed in Chapter 9. Thus, whether a parasite is also a pathogen depends entirely on the host's response to disturbance by the parasite. An individual parasitic nematode may only become a pathogen when there are sufficient numbers of individuals of the same species in the same plant to cause disease. Or, a population of parasitic nematodes may only become pathogenic when the host's ability to resist or tolerate disturbance is inadequate. Many of the parasites mentioned in later chapters are potential pathogens. Whether they realize this potential however, depends on factors outside the individual parasite; such factors may be considered as environmental components in the ecological web of host and parasite. Accordingly, I only refer to pathogens when disease is evident. It should also be mentioned that not all pathogens are parasites; root-feeding insects and root-browsing nematodes may not be parasites, but they may certainly cause disease, hence they are pathogens.

Clarification of the terms 'parasite' and 'pathogen' may prevent ambiguity at a later stage; it also raises the idea, that in looking for ways of controlling disease caused by nematodes, we might achieve this objective by turning a pathogenic population into a parasitic one, either by reducing its numbers, or by modifying the environment in such a way that the plant can tolerate disturbance from the nematodes and so maintain its health.

5

In summary, the term 'pathogen' is not particularly useful as it requires too much qualification to make its meaning clear; hence, I shall use it as little as possible.

How the nematode causes disturbance

PENETRATION

Initial disturbance to the plant occurs when the nematode arrives at the plant surface. In soil there is frequently an exploratory phase when the lips are pressed against the root surface and numerous cells are probed with the stylet. Such behaviour suggests that the nematode is responding to stimuli, possibly tactile or chemical, that determine where feeding or penetration will occur. Consequently some cells may be punctured by the nematode's stylet in the early stages of infection causing some superficial damage. Such behaviour is reminiscent of the exploratory probings of the aphid's proboscis on a leaf or the mosquito's stylet on skin.

The stylet may also be used in a rasping action in the same way that some trematodes remove tissues from the gut wall of the host thereby causing extensive lesions. *Trichodorus viruliferus*, for example, rasps the epidermis and hypodermis of the host root causing a superficial but characteristic browning (Pitcher and Flegg, 1965).

The nematode, having selected a cell or an area on the root, its activities become more purposeful; the stylet is thrust rapidly backwards and forwards through the cell wall and the first major disturbance occurs. There is no evidence that there is any 'softening' of the cell walls by nematode secretions prior to penetration as occurs with some fungi. The penetration of powdery mildew germ tubes into the epidermal cells of barley, for example, consists of two processes: (1) a digestion of the cuticle and cellulose portion of the epidermal wall by enzymes apparently secreted from the infection peg, (2) mechanical pushing of the infection peg through the cell walls (Edwards and Allen, 1970).

To indicate the general mode of penetration and some of the differences in behaviour between nematode species let us look at a few examples.

Second stage larvae of *Meloidogyne naasi* aggregate round root tips, occasionally thrusting their stylets against epidermal cells in the regions of cell differentiation and elongation. Once a point is selected, the larva presses its lips against the cell wall and thrusts the stylet rhythmically until the cell wall is punctured. The same rhythmical process of stylet activity is used whenever the larva encounters a cell wall as it moves into the root (Siddiqui, 1971).

A similar story is presented by Clark (1967) in her description of *Nacobbus serendipiticus* feeding in tomato roots. To penetrate the root, the second stage larvae press their lips against the cell wall and move over the surface, the spear being thrust occasionally. Eventually a point is selected where the spear is thrust rhythmically until the cell wall is pierced. The head then moves slowly sideways, with continued spear thrusting, so that the hole in the cell wall becomes large enough for the larva to enter. Inside the root the larvae move intracellularly, penetrating the end and side walls of cells and causing much damage.

Telotylenchus loofi makes tentative jabs at the root surface of sorghum without puncturing cell walls. When a spot is found that is favourable for feeding a series of thrusts at a rate of two per sec is made with the stylet until the epidermal cell is punctured. The lip region is closely pressed against the plant epidermal cell and feeding starts immediately following puncturing of the cell (Tikyani and Khera, 1969).

The rupture of cell walls of the plant host appears to be a similar process for many nematode species, even those that feed on fungal hyphae. Studies on fungal feeders, however, have contributed two useful items of information: (1) In *Aphelenchus avenae* (Fisher and Evans, 1967) and *Aphelenchoides bicaudatus* (Siddiqui and Taylor, 1969) there was no evidence that suction between the nematode's lips and the hyphal surface was a prerequisite for feeding, (2) it is possible that stylet action is a response which occurs only when the greater part of the lip surface is stimulated by resistance from an immovable surface; thus labial papillae and not amphids may be involved in the process of penetration (Fisher and Evans, 1967). Perhaps the same events occur when some nematodes feed on roots.

Xiphinema and *Longidorus*, because of their longer stylets, might be expected to behave differently from the nematodes mentioned so far. A detailed description comes from Cohn (1970) and, initially at least, the story is familiar. *Xiphinema* probe the surface with quick jabs of their stylets and feeding then begins with the nematodes pressing their lip region against the epidermis and inserting the stylet into the root tissue. The tip of the stylet often reaches the stele when the diameter of the root is sufficiently small. It takes about 8 min to insert the stylet whereas feeding periods last several hours and in some cases up to 3 days. *Longidorus africanus*, on the other hand, has short feeding periods up to 15 min. Depth of penetration and diameter of root influence the amount of damage caused by the feeding of *Xiphinema*. Disturbance to the root system appears to depend on the accessibility of the vascular tissues, hence shallow penetration (Fisher and Raski, 1967) and large diameter roots (Pitcher and Posnette, 1963) prevent the stylet reaching these particular tissues and damage is slight. On thin roots or root tips, however, penetration of the stylet to the stele occurs and disturbance is obvious in the form of swellings, galling and reduced root growth.

Structures like mandibles of insects, chelicerae of ticks and the hooks of hookworm larvae are particularly destructive in their action; whole groups of cells and tissues of the host or prey are destroyed. Mouthparts which are more needle-like, on the other hand, are less destructive because they penetrate a very small area. *Xiphinema* and *Longidorus* probably cause little damage while actually penetrating the root of the host plant; it is the subsequent feeding activities that create the major disturbance to the host's physiology. The same can be said of the tabanid flies and mosquitoes which have sucking mouthparts formed of small stiletto-like needles that are driven down into the skin of the vertebrate host. The insect that most resembles *Xiphnemia* and *Longidorus* however is the aphid which inserts the tips of its stylets into the phloem sieve tubes of the host plant. The sap being under considerable pressure is forced up the food channel; thus the aphid exerts no suction to ingest the sap. Whether *Xiphinema* and *Longidorus* feed in the same way as aphids is not known, but it can be argued that if these nematodes do insert their stylets into phloem sieve tubes then pressure within the plant cells will tend to force the sap up the stylet. However, unlike aphids which have separate food and salivary channels, *Xiphinema* and *Longidorus* have one channel down the stylet which must serve both processes. Hence it might be concluded that if the nematode is to secrete enzymes or other salivary substances into the sieve tubes during feeding, it must exert sufficient pressure to overcome that of the plant.

Another nematode worth considering is *Tylenchulus semipenetrans* which causes disturbance in the host plant in a somewhat different way from other nematodes because of its mode of penetration. The second stage larvae penetrate the root with the anterior part of their bodies. Three moults then occur and the young adult females penetrate deeper into the cortex breaking one cortical cell after another before becoming sedentary. At this stage the female can only move its head to feed on the cells around it (Schneider and Baines, 1964). The body of the female is constricted at irregular intervals that probably correspond to the pressure of the plant cells (Cohn, 1964). The disturbance here is caused by growth of the nematode into the tissues whereby a tunnel is formed, and by feeding on the cells in the localized area at the end of the tunnel (Cohn, 1965).

In some ways the penetration of *T. semipenetrans* into the root resembles penetration by some parasitic fungi. The fungal hypha in contact with the plant increases locally in size and flattens to form an appressorium which anchors the fungus to the root. A pointed structure, the infection peg, then develops and penetrates the cuticle. After penetration the threadlike infection peg then expands to form a hypha, and enzymes are secreted that dissolve cell walls thus facilitating further incursion into the host plant. There is some similarity between the nematode's stylet and the fungal infection peg; the mode of invasion in *T. semipenetrans* by growth rather than movement is also similar. Hence it is worth asking whether the nematode, like the fungus, secretes enzymes to facilitate penetration and thereby causes further disturbance in the host. We might go even further and enquire whether the nematode secretes similar enzymes; after all, the barriers to penetration that lie in the chemical composition of the cell walls of the plant are the same for both organisms. We shall discuss the disturbing influence of nematode secretions in a later section, but before doing so let us examine the feeding process in more detail because this is likely to be a major source of disturbance.

FEEDING

The simplest type of feeding is seen in *Aphelenchus avenae* which feeds on fungi. After the fungal wall is penetrated the contents of the cell are sucked out; there is no injection of secretions (Fisher and Evans, 1967). *Aphelenchoides bicaudatus* behaves similarly (Siddiqui and Taylor, 1969). Some fungi also absorb the plant cell contents directly but frequently the contents are degraded by the parasite's secretions first. Similarly, the fungus-feeding nematode, *Ditylenchus destructor*, injects digestive substances into the host over a short period prior to the longer period of ingestion. Secretions flow from the dorsal gland through the lumen of the spear and into the fungus cell following penetration by the spear. Ingestion of cellular contents begins with rhythmic pulsations of the cardia and adjacent portions of the intestine (Anderson, 1964). Doncaster (1966) describes ingestion by the same nematode as involving pulsation of the posterior pharynx assisted by occasional pumping of the median bulb.

The introduction of secretions into the host cell during salivation probably contributes to extra-oral digestion prior to ingestion. The duration of salivation may be the longest phase of the feeding process, as in *Trichodorus similis* (Wyss, 1971) in which a relatively short time is required for ingestion. The various phases of the feeding process may not be so clear-cut however; in *Hemicycliophora similis*, for example, the pumping of the oesophageal bulb caused some fluids to flow back and forth between the host cell and the oesophagus. Saliva was produced continuously and was presumably mixed with the cell contents (Klinkenberg, 1963).

Thus, as well as disturbance by mechanical damage during penetration and feeding there is the additional influence of saliva, secretions or enzymes. It is therefore important to know their identity and function.

SECRETIONS AND EXCRETIONS

Parasitic fungi release numerous substances into the host as they extract nutrients. Enzymes break down cell walls and degrade the cell contents and, as a result, toxic metabolites are formed usually by the plant which may damage the protoplasts of the host's cells, or change the osmotic relations of the cells and the permeability of the cell walls. Growth-promoting substances resembling those produced by plants may be introduced into the host. Alternatively, parasitic fungi may secrete substances that stimulate the production of plant growth substances or inactivate their inhibitors.

Information about nematode secretions is less well documented, although there are numerous suggestions that parasitic nematodes probably produce enzymes of one kind or another. However, the suggestions are largely based on data concerning internal enzymes and growth substances of nematodes and observations on changes that occur in the plant host after infection. Moreover, it is not always clear whether the experimental procedures excluded microbial contamination, whether methods to sterilize nematodes interfered with secretion, or if lysis of nematodes in suspension produced enzymes. The problem of isolating and identifying nematode secretions is partly one of obtaining enough material. It may also be related to nematode behaviour because if, as Bird (1966) suggests, the freeliving stages do not exude either enzymes or plant growth regulators in any quantity until they receive stimuli from the plant, then it may be unrealistic to incubate nematodes in solution and expect them to secrete enzymes. Although Bird has no evidence to support this hypothesis other than inability to detect growth-promoting substances in *Meloidogyne*, the idea is sound. After all, it would be wasteful, to say the least, for a nematode to continue secreting enzymes in the absence of a substrate in the host plant. So the evidence that nematodes secrete enzymes for particular tasks like cell wall degradation and extra-oral digestion is sparse and unreliable. The same can be said of the animal parasitic nematodes. Although histochemical studies indicate that these parasites secrete enzymes during penetration of the host's skin, there is little evidence of their identity. In fact, knowledge of the mechanisms involved in the penetration of host tissues and cells by parasites of animals is superficial (Lewert, 1958).

The host may not be just a passive substrate on which the nematodes' secretions act; instead, nematodes may have developed systems for directing the host's metabolism (Dropkin, 1969), or for initiating physiological processes that achieve the same objective without the direct injection of an enzyme. For example, *Ditylenchus dipsaci*, a parasite frequently associated with host cell separation, possesses a large amount of pectinase, and Riedel and Mai (1971) suggest that the different symptoms produced in different host plants by populations of *D. dipsaci* may be caused by different pectolytic enzymes associated with these populations. Krusberg (1967), on the other hand, while not denying that pectin-degrading enzymes enable *D. dipsaci* to attack higher plant tissues, suggests that separation of cell walls is probably not a function of nematode pectinases but is the result of some kind of plant growth regulator. Again, it is possible that the granular exudation which adult female *M. javanica* inject from the dorsal oesophageal gland into host cells, may contain material capable of synthesizing enzymes only when placed in the cytoplasm of the host (Bird, 1968).

The recovery of growth-regulating substances from nematodes (Yu and Viglierchio, 1964; Viglierchio and Yu, 1968; Cutler and Krusberg, 1968) does not necessarily indicate that these substances are synthesized by the nematode and secreted through the stylet during the feeding process; they may simply be ingested following other physiological processes. Webster (1967) suggests that the secretion of proteolytic enzymes by nematodes into plants releases IAA and gibberellins which are bound to proteins. Or, as Myers and Krusberg (1965) indicate, amino acids that initiate gall formation may be discharged, a process involving the production of growth-promoting substances by the plant. Such an hypothesis is attractive because there is good evidence that nematodes discharge many kinds of substances and not just from the stylet. The stimulation of host tissues at the posterior end of nematodes, for example, suggests that excretory products may provide the stimulus (Endo and Veech, 1969), and studies on the permeability of the nematode body wall certainly do not rule out the possibility that ions are readily released (Marks *et al.*, 1968). The most convincing evidence, however, comes from experiments where substances released into solution by nematodes have been identified. Thus larvae of *Heterodera glycines* emitted five amino acids: alanine, aspartic acid, glutamic acid, glycine and serine. Adults released γ-aminobutyric acid, histidine, phenylalanine and proline (Aist and Riggs, 1969). A detailed list of compounds released by *Ditylenchus triformis*, *D. dipsaci*, *D. myceliophagus*, *Meloidogyne incognita* larvae and *Pratylenchus penetrans* includes amino acids, amines, ammonia, proteins, 1,2 dicarboxylic acids, aldehydes and organic acids (Myers and Krusberg, 1965). Exudates released from female *Meloidogyne javanica* were shown to consist of basic proteins containing carbohydrates. The basic proteins were histone-like in nature and were derived from the breakdown of granules in the ampulla of the dorsal oesophageal gland (Bird, 1968).

The fact that nematodes secrete substances into the plant that can, theoretically at least, initiate the kinds of physiological changes that we recognize as symptoms of disease, and that such changes as hyperplasia and increased metabolism can occur at the posterior end of nematodes (Endo and Veech, 1969), suggests that we should not put too much emphasis on the secretion of enzymes and growth substances via the stylet. The excretions and exudates, by their quantity and quality, may be sufficient to initiate many of the characteristic symptoms of nematode infection. Fluorescent antibody techniques have shown that antigenic material exudes from the excretory pores and, to a lesser extent, from the stylet of larvae and adults of *Meloidogyne javanica*. The gelatinous matrix exuded from the adult female also has antigenic properties (Bird, 1964). So it appears that the nematode may be emitting several substances in different quantities as it feeds on the host tissues. If this is so, then this kind of disturbance is not necessarily related to feeding but to other normal excretory and secretory functions of the nematode. In other words, nematodes in close proximity to a plant may cause disturbance by just being there and performing their normal physiological processes including excretion.

It might be argued that the well-defined and characteristic formation of syncytia in plants, infected with nematodes like *Meloidogyne* and *Heterodera*, demands a more specific influence by the nematode than the release of excretions and exudates, or the secretion of non-enzymic substances through the stylet. But such an argument denies the active participation of the plant in the process. Dropkin (1969) sums up the situation by suggesting that the response of plants to infection with these nematodes is not passive but is an active participation in a process initiated by the nematode. The entomologists face a similar problem with the galls produced by some plant bugs. One school suggests that a specific substance in the saliva of the insects is responsible for the galls. Another argues that the chemical stimulus is nonspecific and that the insect, because of its behavioural characteristics, stimulates the production of complex galls by applying stimulatory substances in definite places and at particular concentrations (Miles, 1968). What the nematode secretes that stimulates and maintains syncytia is yet to be elucidated.

One further item of disturbance associated with feeding should not be overlooked. Just as internal parasites, like liver flukes, may aggravate disease in animals by permitting bacteria from the intestine to enter blood vessels, so may nematodes allow other parasites to infect a plant. Wounds on roots of sugar beet seedlings caused by *Heterodera schachtii* permit the penetration and establishment of the fungus *Rhizoctonia solani* without the formation of the usual infection structures (Polychronopoulos *et al.*, 1969). Secondary microbial invasion of tomato plants infected with larvae of *Meloidogyne incognita* caused 75 and 48% reduction in weight of foliage and roots respectively. Under aseptic conditions, the same number of larvae caused only 37% reduction of foliage and an increased root weight of 50% (Mayol and Bergeson, 1970). *Radopholus similis* may create in the plant cortex a food base for weak unspecialized fungal parasites and thereby produce more damage (Blake, 1966). Larvae of *Nacobbus serendipiticus* move intracellularly in tomato roots penetrating end and side walls of cells which then become infected with bacteria (Clark, 1967). As a source of disturbance micro-organisms may be an important factor especially where cell destruction is extensive during penetration and migration in the root, but how important and widespread it is appears to be largely unknown.

MIGRATION THROUGH TISSUES

Some species of nematode disturb only a few cells during feeding or penetration and if such activities result only in the death of the cells the overall damage to the plant is likely to be small. On the other hand, there are some nematodes that move through the tissues feeding on cells as they go and leaving tunnels and cavities behind them. Between these two extremes there is a series of species that cause such mechanical damage to varying degrees.

The true ectoparasites, such as *Xiphinema* and *Longidorus*, damage the plant by penetrating and feeding on cells with the stylet. There are also some species, like *Nacobbus serendipiticus*, whose larvae feed either on the surface of the root or enter the root to feed. Internal feeding, unlike surface feeding, stimulated gall production (Clark, 1967). Similarly *Hoplolaimus coronatus* may feed endo- or ectoparasitically on cotton roots (Krusberg and Sasser, 1956). *Telotylenchus loofi* has no specific region for feeding; root hairs, rootlets, main roots and the root cap are all attacked. Some individuals embedded the head and body up to the oesophageal region in the tissues of the main root while feeding (Tikyani and Khera, 1969). Similarly *Scutellonema brachyurum* (Nong and Weber, 1965) and *Hoplolaimus indicus* (Gupta and Atwal, 1971) feed on the cortical tissues of *Amaryllis* and tomato roots, respectively, by embedding the anterior part of the body in the root. *Trichodorus christiei* sometimes penetrate to half a body length as they force apart the loosely adhering cells at the root cap (Russell and Perry, 1966). Finally, there are those nematodes that completely enter the root and once inside migrate through the tissues either inter- or intracellularly. *Helicotylenchus multicinctus*, for example, may migrate for distances up to 75 cm from the pseudostem of bananas (Strich-Harari *et al.*, 1966). The burrowing nematode, *Radopholus similis*, forms tunnels and cavities by lysis of cells as the nematodes progress through the root cortex (Blake, 1966). Damage of this kind is extensive but the plant may suffer less disturbance if only cortical cells are destroyed. The fact that large numbers of *Pratylenchus* spp. can occur in roots, without causing any appreciable reduction in rate of growth of the plant, is probably because the nematodes feed on cortical cells and leave the vascular tissues undamaged. Wyss (1970) remarks on such an event in his description of the mass parasitism of strawberry roots by *Pratylenchus penetrans*. These observations are reminiscent of the parasitism by nematodes of some insects, in which the whole body cavity is apparently occupied by the nematodes and yet the insect remains alive.

Which tissues are disturbed by the nematode is therefore important and, in general, damage or disturbance of cells in the stele or in the region of the root tip are likely to have the most influence on the plant. Newly hatched larvae of *Xiphinema* that fed on the outer cortical cells well back from the root tip produced no symptoms, whereas, when they migrated to the root tip to feed shortly before moulting, small galls were produced on the roots (Fisher and Raski, 1967). The feeding site of *Tylenchulus semipenetrans* is located in the cortex rather than in the phloem or phloem parenchyma where *Rotylenchulus*, *Nacobbus*, *Meloidogyne* and *Heterodera* feed (Van Gundy and Kirkpatrick, 1964), and may explain why *T. semipenetrans* is possibly a less damaging parasite.

In nematodes like *Heterodera* and *Meloidogyne*, migration through the cortex, and feeding on syncytial cells of the stele, cause two kinds of disturbance. In potato roots, for example, second stage larvae of *Heterodera rostochiensis* cause necroses by travelling a certain distance through the cortex. As a result, the growth rate of roots is reduced. Shortly after penetration, the larvae become sedentary and induce changes in the vascular bundle to form syncytia or giant cells. Plant metabolites are channeled to the syncytia, and vessels are obstructed (Seinhorst and den Ouden, 1971). Although both types of disturbance cause disease in the plant the first is destructive; necrosis of the cells is a one-way affair with the cells as a passive substrate to the mechanical and chemical activities of the nematode. With syncytial formation, however, there is an interaction and interdependence between the cells and the nematode; the plant cells are not passive but respond to the nematode in such a way that it can continue to extract nutrients from them without killing them. Dropkin (1969) has attached the useful labels of 'destructive' and 'adaptive' cellular changes to these two reactions.

Conclusions

The incursion of the nematode, wholly or in part, into a plant host causes disturbance in the cells in the immediate vicinity of the nematode. The extent of the disturbance is determined by (1) where the disturbance occurs, whether it is in vascular or non-vascular tissues, (2) the nature of the disturbance, whether it is mechanical or chemical, (3) the frequency of the disturbance—whether a nematode feeds rapidly or slowly, on a few or many cells during its life, (4) the degree of invasion by secondary organisms that aggravate the disturbance caused by the nematode alone, (5) the intensity of the disturbance—whether a nematode disturbs the plant simply by feeding on a few cells or destroys a large number of cells while tunnelling in the tissues.

The description of the nematode as a disturbing agent in plants is only part of the picture however. Whether disturbance at the cellular or tissue level sufficiently affects the whole plant to reduce its rate of growth, is influenced by other factors such as environment and the ability to tolerate damage or to counteract the disturbance. But these are topics we will consider later. The intensity of disturbance is also influenced by the numbers of nematodes that occur in a plant at any one time; this subject is of such importance that it deserves a chapter of its own.

References

AIST, S. and RIGGS, R.D. (1969). Amino acids from *Heterodera glycines*. *J. Nematology*, **1**, 254.

ANDERSON, R.V. (1964). Feeding of *Ditylenchus destructor*. *Phytopathology*, **54**, 1121.

BIRD, A.F. (1964). Serological studies on the plant parasitic nematode *Meloidogyne javanica*. *Expl Parasit.*, **15**, 350.

BIRD, A.F. (1966) Some observations on exudates from *Meloidogyne* larvae. *Nematologica*, **12**, 471.

BIRD, A.F. (1968) Changes associated with parasitism in nematodes 4. Cytochemical studies on the ampulla of the dorsal oesophageal gland of *Meloidogyne javanica* and on exudations from the buccal stylet. *J. Parasit.*, **54**, 879.

BLAKE, C.D. (1966). The histological changes in banana roots caused by *Radopholus similis* and *Helicotylenchus multicinctus*. *Nematologica*, **12**, 129.

CLARK, S.A. (1967). The development and life history of the false root-knot nematode, *Nacobbus serendipiticus*. *Nematologica*, **13**, 91.

COHN, E. (1964). Penetration of the citrus nematode in relation to root development. *Nematologica*, **10**, 594.

COHN, E. (1965). On the feeding and histopathology of the citrus nematode. *Nematologica*, 11, 47.

COHN, E. (1970). Observations on the feeding and symptomatology of *Xiphinema* and *Longidorus* on selected host roots. *J. Nematology*, 2, 167.

CUTLER, H.G. and KRUSBERG, L.R. (1968). Plant growth regulators in *Ditylenchus dipsaci*, *Ditylenchus triformis* and host tissues. *Plant and cell physiol.*, 9, 479.

DONCASTER, C.C. (1966). Nematode feeding mechanisms. 2. Observations on *Ditylenchus destructor* and *D. myceliophagus* feeding on *Botrytis cinerea*. *Nematologica*, 12, 417.

DROPKIN, V.H. (1969). Cellular responses of plants to nematode infections. *Ann. Rev. Phytopath.*, 7, 101.

EDWARDS, H.H. and ALLEN, P.J. (1970). A fine-structure study of the primary infection process during infection of barley by *Erysiphe graminis* f. sp. *hordei*. *Phytopathology*, 60, 1504.

ENDO, B.Y. and VEECH, J.A. (1969). The histochemical localization of oxidoreductive enzymes of soybeans infected with the root-knot nematode *Meloidogyne incognita acrita*. *Phytopathology*, 59, 418.

FISHER, J.M. and EVANS, A.A.F. (1967). Penetration and feeding by *Aphelenchus avenae*. *Nematologica*, 13, 425.

FISHER, J.M. and RASKI, D.J. (1967) Feeding of *Xiphinema index* and *X. diversicaudatum*. *Proc. helminth. Soc. Wash.*, 34, 68.

GUPTA, J.C. and ATWAL, A.S. (1971) Biology and ecology of *Hoplolaimus indicus* (Hoplolaiminae: Nematoda). I. The life stages and the feeding behaviour. *Nematologica*, 17, 69.

KLINKENBERG, C.H. (1963). Observations on the feeding habits of *Rotylenchus uniformis*, *Pratylenchus crenatus*, *P. penetrans*, *Tylenchorhynchus dubius* and *Hemicycliophora similis*. *Nematologica*, 9, 502.

KRUSBERG, L.R. (1967). Pectinases in *Ditylenchus dipsaci*. *Nematologica*, 13, 443.

KRUSBERG, L.R. and SASSER, J.N. (1956). Host-parasite relationships of the lance nematode in cotton roots. *Phytopathology*, 46, 505.

LEWERT, R.M. (1958). Invasiveness of helminth larvae. *Rice Inst. Pamphlet*, XLV (1). 97.

MARKS, C.F., THOMASON, I.J. and CASTRO, G.E. (1968). Dynamics of the permeation of nematodes by water, nematocides and other substances. *Expl Parasit.*, 22, 321.

MAYOL, P.S. and BERGESON, G.B. (1970). The role of secondary invaders in *Meloidogyne incognita* infection. *J. Nematology*, 2, 80.

MILES, P.W. (1968). Insect secretions in plants. *Ann. Rev. Phytopath.*, 6, 137.

MYERS, R.F. and KRUSBERG, L.R. (1965). Organic substances discharged by plant-parasitic nematodes. *Phytopathology*, **55**, 429.

NONG, L. and WEBER, G.F. (1965). Pathological effects of *Pratylenchus scribneri* and *Scutellonema brachyurum* on *Amaryllis*. *Phytopathology*, **55**, 228.

PITCHER, R.S. and FLEGG, J.J.M. (1965). Observation of root feeding by the nematode *Trichodorus viruliferus* Hooper. *Nature (London)*, **207**, 317.

PITCHER, R.S. and POSNETTE, A.F. (1963). Vascular feeding by *Xiphinema diversicaudatum*. *Nematologica*, **9**, 301.

POLYCHRONOPOULOS, A.G., HOUSTON, B.R., and LOWNSBERY, B.F. (1969). Penetration and development of *Rhizoctonia solani* in sugar beet seedlings infected with *Heterodera schachtii*. *Phytopathology*, **59**, 482.

RIEDEL, R.M. and MAI, W.F. (1971). Pectinases in aqueous extracts of *Ditylenchus dipsaci*. *J. Nematology*, **3**, 28.

RUSSELL, C.C. & PERRY, V.G. (1966). Parasitic habit of *Trichodorus christiei* on wheat. *Phytopathology*, **56**, 357.

SCHNEIDER, H. and BAINES, R.C. (1964). *Tylenchulus semipenetrans*: Parasitism and injury to orange tree roots. *Phytopathology*, **54**, 1202.

SEINHORST, J.W. and DEN OUDEN, H. (1971). The relation between density of *Heterodera rostochiensis* and growth and yield of two potato varieties. *Nematologica*, **17**, 347.

SIDDIQUI, I.A. (1971). Comparative penetration and development of *Meloidogyne naasi* in wheat and oat roots. *Nematologica*, **17**, 566.

SIDDIQUI, I.A. and TAYLOR, D.P. (1969). Feeding mechanisms of *Aphelenchoides bicaudatus* on three fungi and an alga. *Nematologica*, **15**, 503.

STRICH-HARARI, D., MINZ, G. and PELED, A. (1966). The spread of spiral nematodes in banana roots and their control. *Israel J. Agric. Res.*, **16**, 89.

TIKYANI, M.G. and KHERA, S. (1969). In vitro feeding of *Telotylenchus loofi* on great millet (*Sorghum vulgare*) roots. *Nematologica*, **15**, 291.

VAN GUNDY, S.D. and KIRKPATRICK, J.D. (1964). Nature of resistance in certain citrus rootstocks to citrus nematode. *Phytopathology*, **54**, 419.

VIGLIERCHIO, D.R. and YU, P.K. (1968). Plant growth substances and plant parasitic nematodes. 2. Host influence on auxin content. *Expl Parasit.*, **23**, 88.

WEBSTER, J.M. (1967). The influence of plant growth substances and their inhibitors on the host-parasite relationships of *Aphelenchoides ritzemabosi* in culture. *Nematologica*, **13**, 256.

WYSS, U. (1970). Parasitierungsvorgang und pathogenität wandernder wurzel-nematoden an *Fragaria vesca* var. *semperflorens*. *Nematologica*, **16**, 55.

WYSS, U. (1971). Der Mechanismus der nahrungsaufnahme bei *Trichodorus similis. Nematologica*, **17**, 508.

YU, P.K. and VIGLIERCHIO, D.R. (1964) Plant growth substances and parasitic nematodes I. Root knot nematodes and tomato. *Expl Parasit.*, **15**, 242.

3 Numbers of nematodes and disease

With all the damage caused by the insertion of stylets into cells, removal of cell contents, secretion and excretion of substances and burrowing within the root, it might be expected that a plant would show more intense symptoms of disease as the number of parasites feeding on it increased. And this is so, with some important qualifications. Most, if not all, plants and animals are probably infected by one or more species of parasite at any one time and yet the majority of them do not appear to be diseased. It looks as though the density of parasites has to reach a certain level before disease occurs or at least can be detected. The idea that a certain number of parasites is required to produce clinical signs of disease in animals is well known in parasitology for example. There are reports that at least 10 000 *Trichostrongylus colubriformis* are required to cause death in guinea pigs (Herlich, 1969), whereas 75 000 *Trichostrongylus axei* is the minimum number needed to produce clinical signs in lambs (Ross *et al.*, 1969) compared with 250 000 in adult sheep (Leland *et al.*, 1960). The expression, clinical signs, as used by the parasitologist is a vague term however, as it depends on the perceptive experience of the observer. Even where such criteria as weight, temperature and the volume of plasma and erythrocytes are used, the influence of low infection levels on the host may be difficult to detect, i.e. to show that they are significantly different at a statistical level of probability from uninfected controls. The problem lies in the inherent variability of these characters between individuals in animal populations.

In spite of these difficulties, however, there is sufficient evidence to indicate that animals may be able to support a particular number of parasites before their physiological functions are impaired to such a degree that symptoms of disease are apparent. The ability of the plant host to support such a population of parasites is called tolerance in plant nematology; it is a property of the plant and, if its characteristics are to be understood, we must examine the reactions between host and parasite and not just the relationships between inoculum level and plant yield. As Kalmus (1966) says '... looking at life as a biologist, implies looking at it in the search for "machinery" and not only for morphological detail or biochemical reactions'. Can plants tolerate a particular number of parasitic nematodes before they become diseased? And if so what 'machinery' is involved? This is one question we will try to answer.

Plant pathologists appear to take a somewhat different view of tolerance, for it is defined by the National Academy of Science as 'the ability of a host plant to survive and give satisfactory yields at a level of infection that causes economic loss to other varieties of the same host species' (Schafer, 1971). Such a definition implies that plants can be parasitized and still give satisfactory yields. Moreover, the definition recognizes that some varieties have this ability more than others. However, there is no mention of how tolerance might be achieved, for example, through the physiological activities of the plant to compensate for and regenerate lost tissues. Schafer (1971) clearly recognizes these properties however, because he states that tolerance may be due to compensatory growth, or that plants do not express the full capabilities of their metabolism in yield, rather a reservoir of unused yielding capacity absorbs the disease. Such views are in accordance with the tolerance concept in nematology although there seems to be a lack of data that indicate how these properties are reflected in the relationships between population density or numbers of propagules and growth of the host plant. Instead, there are many references to numbers of propagules and disease incidence or numbers of lesions which embrace the topic of inoculum potential. There are also references to disease intensity and yield as in the review by Large (1966), but we will refer to a paper by James *et al.* (1968) to indicate a plant pathological viewpoint. These authors showed that there was a linear relationship between disease caused by *Rhynchosporium secalis* on the upper two leaves of spring barley and yield. This correlation was justified by the fact that the top two leaves produce most of the carbohydrate for the grain. James and his co-workers point out that even if photosynthesis by the leaves is prevented by excluding light from them, ear photosynthesis can compensate for much of the loss in photosynthesis that results. Again, mention is made of the fact that 33% thinning of the barley stand followed by up to 40% defoliation of the remaining plants at the single shoot stage, did not significantly reduce yield. In some experiments, up to 66% thinning and 40% defoliation failed to cause significant losses in yield. The barley plant has ample ability indeed to tolerate damage, but with a parasite like *Rhynchosporium* that causes leaf blotch of barley, the effects of the disease might not be due to a simple loss of leaf area alone, but to some unknown physiological inhibitory process. As we shall see, the linear regression lines of James and his coworkers are similar to those showing the relationship between nematode numbers and yield in the field.

Neither the parasitologists nor the plant pathologists appear to have examined the problem of tolerance and tolerance level in a quantitative way, so we must look to plant nematology data for enlightenment.

The relationship between numbers of nematodes and plant growth

The influence of nematode numbers on plant growth and yield can often be expressed as a linear regression of growth or yield on log nematode numbers. It is possible that competition at high densities of nematodes for invasion and feeding sites reduces the yield reduction *per nematode* as the population increases; thus the curve tends to flatten at high densities, hence transforming nematode numbers to log numbers produces a linear relationship. However, the regression line of best fit depends on the variability of the data. Thus, in field experiments there is often a large variability in the associations between low nematode numbers and high yields and this is one reason why regressions can often be represented equally well by the equations $y = a - bx$ and $y = a - b \log x$ (Brown, 1969). In other situations a regression of log nematode numbers on yield may be statistically significant but some authors are not satisfied that this explains the true relationship. Jones *et al.* (1965), for example, found that the regression of weight of pea tops on the log of numbers of eggs of *Heterodera goettingiana* per g of soil gave good fits at two sites. However the pattern at another site suggested a sigmoid curve and this was confirmed to some extent when yields were expressed as percentages of an assumed maximum yield and changed to probits; a better fit to a straight line was thereby obtained, the correlation coefficient increasing from -0.68 to -0.80. Jones *et al.* (1967) further indicated that a sigmoid relationship probably existed between the log of the initial population of *Heterodera rostochiensis* (eggs per g of soil) and the yield of tubers from potatoes resistant to the nematode. Sykes and Winfield (1966) express similar doubts about the 'fundamental shape of the curve'. They found a good correlation between the weight of green produce of winter cauliflower and log numbers of eggs of *Heterodera cruciferae* per g of soil, and yet they suggest that the shape of the curve is likely to be sigmoid.

The validity of the relationship expressed by the sigmoid curve is therefore tenuous; in fact few have produced a non-linear regression line that gives a better fit than the regression of log numbers of nematodes on yield. There are plausible reasons why the relationship between nematode numbers and plant growth should be a sigmoid curve. Tammes (1961), for example, suggests that the relationship can be divided into three stages. In the first stage the injurious factor (nematodes) has hardly any influence on yield because of compensation. The second stage shows a yield loss correlated with increase of the injurious factor. In the third stage, the effect of the injurious factor is either a level of maximum possible injury (which may be zero yield) or the self-limiting effect of the injurious factor (e.g. competition for invasion and feeding sites). However, Tammes' descriptive

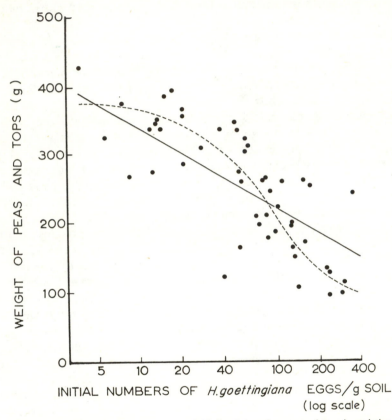

Fig. 1   The relationship between yield (weight of peas and tops) and the initial numbers of eggs. The solid line is a significant regression line fitted to the points: the sigmoid broken line is a curve fitted by eye. The experiment was done in microplots using the pea variety 'Big Ben'. (After Jones *et al.*, 1965)

model, plausible as it is, cannot tell us whether the sigmoid curve really exists in nature, this can only be established by subjecting data to statistical analyses that indicate whether, at low nematode numbers the yield is constant, or decreases only slightly compared with that at higher nematode numbers. In other words, is there a flat part to the curve initially? This is the major aspect of the problem because flattening of the curve at *high*

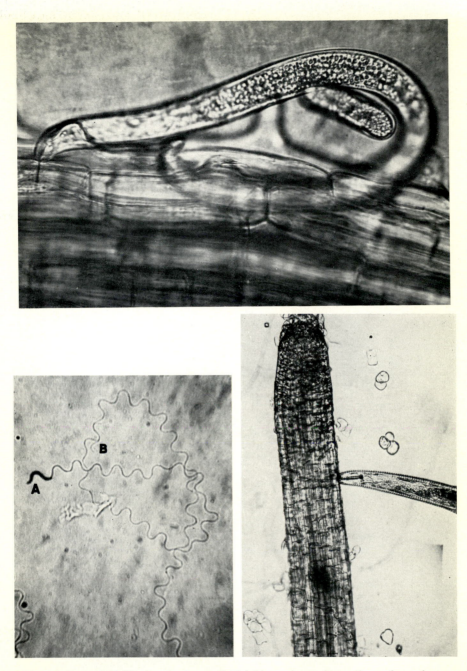

Plate 1 (lower left) Tracks of a larva of *Meloidgyne incognita* on the surface of agar. Length of larva ⅓ mm; A, nematode; B, track. (Sandstedt *et al., Nematologica,* 1961. E. J. Brill. Reproduced by permission)

Plate 2 (top) Female *Paratylenchus projectus* feeding on epidermal cell of tobacco root. One egg has been laid. (Reproduced by permission of Rhoades and Linford, 1961a)

Plate 3 (lower right) *Hemicycliophora similis* feeding on a root of *Vaccinium macrocarpon* showing penetration of mouth spear. (Zuckerman, *Nematologica,* 1961. E. J. Brill. Reproduced by permission)

numbers seems inevitable. After all, there must be a minimum yield which may be zero, and it is impossible to have less than zero even if numbers of nematodes continue to increase.

The Seinhorst hypotheses

As there appear to be no published data that establish unequivocally in statistical terms that yield remains fairly constant at low nematode numbers, it will be worthwhile to re-examine some published data. Fortunately, Seinhorst and his colleagues provide us with excellent material for this purpose; their experiments are well constructed and replicate values for treatments are frequently provided.

Before we do this, however, let us examine the hypotheses of Seinhorst, for he more than anyone else has made a valuable contribution to this aspect of plant nematology. Seinhorst (1961) made three points: (1) that in measuring yields of crops grown in the presence of nematodes, it is essential to cover a wide range of nematode numbers in the samples if amount of damage is to be predicted; (2) that the population level, at which destruction becomes noticeable, varies with the nematode species; (3) plants appear to have larger root systems than are necessary to give good top growth. At a later stage, in a search for a model that would adequately express these ideas, Seinhorst (1963) suggested that the competition curve of Nicholson (1933) was probably the best, especially when the ability of the plant to replace lost roots was included. Applying the Nicholson curve, Seinhorst indicated that yield was proportional to $c(1-a)^n$ where n = nematode density, $c(>1)$ and $a(0<a<1)$ are constants expressing the regenerative power of the plant and amount of damage done per nematode. The main idea behind the formula is that the effect per nematode on rate of growth per plant decreases with increase in nematode density because areas of root tissue damaged by individual nematodes increasingly overlap the higher the density. (There may be other reasons why the effect per nematode decreases, e.g. increased competition for limited feeding sites.)

Pursuing this line of argument, Seinhorst concluded that damage by a nematode (as measured by growth or yield), occurred only when its density exceeded the tolerance limit of the attacked plant. When the initial density of the nematode was lower than the tolerance limit, it only became damaging when its subsequent density on the attacked plant and under the given ecological conditions exceeded this limit. Thus *Heterodera trifolii* on white clover seedlings was not thought to be the cause of poor growth in this crop because the population density did not reach the tolerance level of the plant as established from pot experiments (Seinhorst and Sen,

1966). How far the tolerance levels in the pot experiments reflected the tolerance level in the field was not assessed however. Seinhorst (1963) pointed out that there may be some species of plant nematodes that never reach the tolerance level, even when the host is susceptible and when environmental conditions are most favourable. This will be a point worth remembering when we come to discuss the etiology of disease, because the presence of a parasitic nematode, even in considerable numbers, does not automatically make it a likely cause of failure in a crop. Thus little or no damage is caused to citrus trees by *Tylenchulus semipenetrans* when numbers in the roots are as high as 4000 per g (Cohn *et al.*, 1965). Despite a 56-fold increase in numbers of *Criconemoides curvatum* on hairy vetch, grown in pots, top weights of plants infected with this nematode were no different from uninfected controls (Malek and Jenkins, 1964).

Further application of the Nicholson equation gave Seinhorst (1965) a more comprehensive model. He used two ideas: (1) that plants may have more roots than they really need to support the amount of shoot they produce, thus the plants can sustain a certain amount of loss in roots. Thus, if there is no loss in shoots up to a nematode density Q, then the yield at nematode density P is given by the equation $y = z^{P-Q} = c_1 z^P$, where c_1 is a constant slightly larger than 1. (2) Most plants can replace lost parts and, if it is assumed that the capacity of replacement is proportional to the rate of growth, then the formula $y = z^P$ can be further modified to $y = c_2 z^P$ in which c_2 again is a constant slightly larger than 1. Combining the two formulae we get $y = c_2 c_1 z^P = c z^P = z^{P-T}$ in which y becomes 1 if $P = T$ because y is given by the ratio

$$\frac{O_P - O_{min}}{O_{max} - O_{min}}$$

where O_P = yield at nematode density P, O_{min} is the yield with no nematodes and O_{max} is the maximum yield reduction. Thus the yield at nematode density T (the tolerance level) is the same as the yield in the absence of nematodes or O_{min}. By giving different values to the constants c and z Seinhorst (1965, 1966) and Seinhorst and Kuniyasu (1969) claimed that this model agreed well with experimental data relating yield to nematode population density.

At this stage it should be pointed out that Seinhorst's model is based on several assumptions, e.g. that the 'average' nematode is the same at all densities, and whether a nematode attacks a plant or not, is not influenced by the presence or absence of other individuals attacking the same plant. The tolerance level concept is also an assumption which Seinhorst introduced at a later stage, but this assumption is somewhat different from the first two which are difficult to test. It is hard to visualize, for example, how an experiment might be devised to disprove the hypothesis that nematodes act independently of other nematodes when attacking a plant. Wallace (1966) suggested six ways in which invasion of tomato roots by *Meloidogyne javanica* might be influenced by the density of nematodes, thereby casting doubt on Seinhorst's assumption that nematodes act independently of each other during invasion. Similarly, Baxter and Blake (1967) in their studies on the invasion of wheat roots by *Pratylenchus thornei* showed that the distribution of nematodes in the root indicated that some parts of the root had a greater chance of being invaded than others. They concluded that their results were incompatible with Seinhorst's assumption of random distribution.

Seinhorst (1970) rejects such conclusions, however, because they do not indicate whether nematodes attract or repel each other when invading roots. Seinhorst states that non-random distribution may only indicate that the root system consists of portions with different attractiveness. Seinhorst is possibly correct and it still remains to be shown that nematodes do influence each others activities during invasion, not an easy task. If, in fact, the assumptions on which Seinhorst bases his model prove hard to test, then it is questionable whether the model is as useful and biologically realistic as Seinhorst claims. Perhaps quite different assumptions could give the same basic equation relating numbers and yield.

Most of Seinhorst's assumptions can be tested however, particularly the tolerance concept and the properties of the plant that give it a measure of tolerance to nematode damage. To do this we will use some of Seinhorst's own published data.

In Fig. 2, I have redrawn two of Seinhorst's graphs relating nematode numbers to plant weight as he gives them in his paper (Seinhorst and Kuniyasu, 1969). In these graphs, nematode numbers are expressed on a logarithmic scale. I have also plotted the same points for nematodes, arithmetically against plant weight, because I want to stress the fact that, although the original curves of Seinhorst do suggest that initially the curve is flat, this is largely an 'optical illusion'. Regression analyses of the data indicated that the relationship between weight of carrot leaves and nematode numbers was linear (Fig. 2b) whereas the regression of nematode numbers on root weight was quadratic (Fig. 2d). Furthermore, in Fig. 2d, the curvature is the opposite to that depicted in Fig. 2c. Regression analyses of other data were similar to those just described or else no statistically significant regression line could be fitted.

It can be concluded, therefore, that there is little experimental evidence to indicate that the curve of nematode numbers on yield is initially flat i.e. the damage *per nematode* is initially less than at higher nematode numbers. In fact the data supports the contrary hypothesis. Accordingly it is invalid to assess a tolerance level 'by eye' from graphs where log numbers of nematodes are plotted against yield. It might further be concluded that the Seinhorst hypotheses which assume the existence of a tolerance level have limited usefulness until further experiments are done to test this premise. Such experiments will not be easy because of the

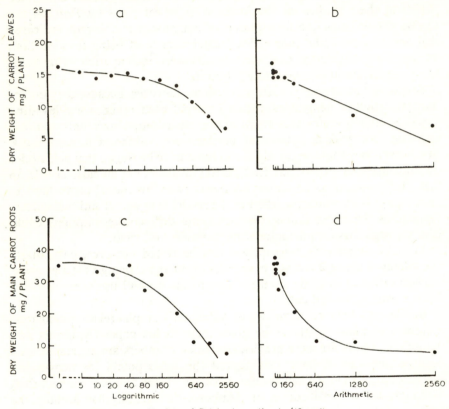

Fig. 2 Pot experiments showing the relationship between the initial density (logarithmic) of *Rotylenchus uniformis* and (a and b) the dry weight of carrot leaves and (c and d) the dry weight of main roots of carrots. (a) and (c) are after the original data of Seinhorst and Kuniyasu (1969); (b) and (d) are graphs of the same data as (a) and (c) respectively with nematode numbers expressed arithmetically.

large amount of variability in growth between individual plants. Even Seinhorst's experiments, meticulous as they are, have a low value of r^2 indicating that nematode numbers account for only a small part of the observed variability in growth between treatments. Seinhorst's experiments were not done to test the tolerance level hypothesis, rather this aspect was assumed and if true the arguments that follow seem valid. As Figs. 2b and 2d indicate, the points on the curve at low populations are too crowded to enable an unequivocal decision to be made about the validity of the tolerance level.

Oostenbrink (1966) stresses the importance of the rectilinear regression of log numbers of nematodes against yield and compares it with the dose-response curve used in animal toxicology. Oostenbrink expresses the view that at low densities the curve may be continuous with the linear regression line, or there may be a peak due to stimulation of growth at low numbers or flat because 'the plant can sustain a certain amount of damage or can compensate for it by regeneration'. At high densities the curve may also continue in a linear fashion to zero yield, or suddenly fall to zero when the plants die or the curve may become horizontal when the plants escape damage. In commenting on the way Seinhorst fitted sigmoid curves to data that were originally expressed as linear regressions, Oostenbrink sees no reason why the linear regressions should be replaced by the sigmoid and he produces data to show that most regressions of log nematode numbers and yield are in fact linear and that exceptions to this rule are rare.

There is little to argue about in Oostenbrink's conclusions and my previous remarks are more or less in agreement. It is possible that Seinhorst himself might find little to criticize in this particular aspect of the relationship between nematode numbers and plant yield. So who is right? Is Seinhorst's model false? There is no straight-forward answer because variability of data does not permit an unequivocal decision to be made about how good the hypothetical curves fit the observed data. And even if they did, they do not necessarily validate the model, other models with equally good fits might be produced, and even the same mathematical model might be produced with quite different assumptions. The point at issue is not whether theoretical curves give a good fit to observed data, but whether the initial assumptions on which the model is based are biologically realistic and near enough to the real thing. The purpose of the model is to produce a simple approximation to reality that helps us to reason and understand a complex system. The model does not provide us with conclusions but with ideas that we can use in further experiments.

The heuristic model, which makes precise statements leading to further experiments, seems to be the type proposed by Seinhorst and its validity must therefore be measured in terms of its usefulness. In my opinion Seinhorst's models have raised a multitude of new ideas and suggested many new lines of thought in plant nematology, so in this sense the models are valid. Of course they will be improved in time as some of the assumptions are disproved and replaced by better ones; the tolerance level concept is one aspect that needs further enquiry. Oostenbrink's curves are largely descriptive, and descriptions are not models because they throw no further light on the problem. However, in discussing the ends of the linear regression line Oostenbrink introduces some useful ideas based on existing information about tolerance. So Oostenbrink could be attributed with a 'conceptual model', one in which existing facts are built into a framework in a certain manner. The modern approach of systems simulation is concerned with the building of such conceptual models.

In spite of these criticisms and qualifications however, it can be concluded that tolerance is a useful concept that needs to be demonstrated by experiment in nematode-plant associations. The tolerance level idea, is much harder to accept, in fact there is no experimental evidence that supports it. Experiments are needed using a range of low population densities, a high degree of replication and plants selected for their uniformity. Without such precautions, there will probably be little chance of obtaining a result which gives an unequivocal answer to the question, 'is there such a thing as a tolerance level?' For the same reasons, there will be little likelihood of detecting a tolerance level, even if it exists, by sampling plants and nematodes in the field. Even pot experiments, however carefully controlled, will not yield data that will enable us to say 'at this level of nematodes, plant growth was increasingly inhibited as the numbers of nematodes increased; before that level growth was unaffected'. However we might find that there will be a section of the graph covering a range of nematode densities when the gradient of the curve changes from being somewhat flat to somewhat steep.

Even if tolerance levels or ranges exist in some nematode–plant associations, it is doubtful whether they can ever be reliably assessed in the field by simple visual inspection. To detect differences of 10 or even 20% yield within a crop is difficult, but to pick out those plants which are just beginning to show unthrifty growth and thereby estimate the tolerance level is practically impossible. Consequently, although severe effects of nematode damage may be readily observed in a crop, the transition from tolerance to intolerance is obscure.

For all these reasons doubt has been expressed about the usefulness of tolerance levels in ecological studies of plant nematodes (Wallace, 1971). Perhaps it would be more realistic to let the farmer decide what percent loss in yield he was willing to accept on economic grounds. The density of nematodes associated with this loss in yield could then be called the tolerance level. Such an approach has the advantage of being independent of the nature of the relationship between nematode numbers and yield, all that is required is a statistically significant regression line that fits the field data (Wallace, 1971). Such an approach might be useful in perennial crops such as fruit trees and vines where sampling for nematodes could provide the information that would help the grower or extension worker to decide whether control of nematodes was likely to be worthwhile.

Although there are serious reservations about tolerance level in ecology, there is little doubt that the concept of tolerance might be important in the physiology of the plant infected with nematodes.

The nature of tolerance

Plants have the ability to tolerate many kinds of disturbing influences without their growth being excessively impaired. Tolerance to heat, cold, drought and salinity exist in plants in varying degrees, largely as a result of their inherited characteristics. But the way a plant grows is not solely the consequence of inherited potentialities. There is a continual interaction between the specific kind of growth determined by the chromosomes and possibly in part by the inherited cytoplasm, and the environment in which the plant is situated (Bell, 1966). Thus it is likely that plants have the physiological capacity to 'absorb', to compensate and to repair damage. By these means they maintain their physiological efficiency and increase their chances of survival. Such properties in a plant are obviously desirable from the agriculturalist's viewpoint and, in selecting lines with resistance or tolerance to disease, it is useful to be able to recognize the characteristics of the tolerant plant. Thus, the ability to maintain normal rates of photosynthesis and, consequently, yielding ability in spite of infection by a parasite, is a helpful pointer (Scharen and Krupinsky, 1969). To achieve such ends, the plant may have to divert metabolites from one part of the plant to another, the diseased tissue may, in effect, become a sink. Thus in potatoes infected with *Phytophthora infestans*, there is an increased import by translocation of ^{14}C to mature infected leaves and a decreased export from these leaves suggesting that a metabolic sink is formed in the infected leaves which puts them in competition for solutes with uninfected organs (Garraway and Pelletier, 1966). In fact inhibition of some physiological activity like photosynthesis in infected tissue can be compensated, at least in part, by stimulation in organs at a distance from the infected leaf (Livne, 1964). Situations like this are common in plant pathology and indicate that the plant is equipped physiologically to maintain its stability in the face of the parasite's disturbing influence.

In addition, the plant (as Seinhorst has already indicated) may have excess roots and so be able to tolerate a certain amount of loss before affecting top growth. Understanding of this particular aspect of the plant's physiology is lacking, but it is known for example that grasses may lose half their roots and not be harmfully affected (Last, 1971). There are examples from the parasitology world too. Thus it has been shown that there is probably sufficient reserve capacity in the intestine of chickens infected with *Eimeria acervulina* to ensure that absorption of nutrients remains unchanged. As most of the damage to plants caused by nematodes occurs in the roots it is as well to ask how efficient roots are at replacing lost tissues and how much loss in roots a plant can sustain. According to Burström (1965) roots have four functions, anchorage, synthetic capacity, salt uptake and water uptake. Roots are so organized that the active centres are located in the interior around endodermis, pericycle and primary stele. The peripheral parts, epidermis and cortex occupying two-thirds of the sectional area are less important. Apart from allowing the invasion of microorganisms, superficial wounds are therefore of little importance. Plants can counteract the destruction of roots by the formation of adventitious roots which are produced by a hormonally regulated process induced by the loss of the primary root. Burström stresses the importance of reduced root systems on water uptake and transpiration. He suggests that root systems are not overabundant and mutilations of even limited range may seriously affect the plant especially under conditions where great demands are made on the roots.

One fact is clear, the plant is not likely to be a passive recipient of destruction by nematodes, it can actively repair damage and regenerate tissues through hormone regulation. Wound responses in the cortical tissues of roots infected with *Tylenchulus semipenetrans* (Schneider and Baines, 1964), increased nodular efficiency in soybeans infected with *H. glycines* (Lehman *et al.*, 1971) and the increase of root growth relative to shoot growth in potatoes infected with *Heterodera rostochiensis* (Seinhorst and den Ouden, 1971) are three examples which support this view. More convincing however, are the reports of increased plant growth at low nematode infections. This aspect is of importance because not only does it indicate the active nature of plant tolerance, but it throws more light on the tolerance level concept.

Stimulation of plants infected with nematodes

There are several records where nematode infection has apparently stimulated plant growth. Here are a few examples. Coursen and Jenkins (1958) showed that, in tall fescue infected with *Paratylenchus projectus*, the average number of tillers produced on plants inoculated with 1000, 5000 and 10 000 nematodes was 17, 16 and 29 compared with 13 in the uninfected controls. The top growth of sugar cane seedlings was higher with infection levels of 100 *Trichodorus christiei* than at 0, 500, or 1000 nematodes (Apt and Koike, 1962). Although these authors state that the only significant difference was between the 0 and 1000 nematode infection levels, it is quite possible that a statistically significant quadratic regression line could have been fitted to the data thereby indicating a peak response at 100 nematodes. Malek and Jenkins (1964) found that hairy vetch infected with *Criconemoides curvatum* grew faster than uninfected plants during the greater part of the study, and they suggest that, as a result of root proliferation, top growth may be stimulated by low numbers of nematodes and that growth is not retarded to any extent until numbers reach a very high level. The researches of Madamba and his colleagues (1965) indicated that the growth of peppers, peanuts and *Crotolaria* was stimulated by various species of *Meloidogyne*. Stimulation occurred primarily at the lower infection levels, at high inoculum levels growth was suppressed. The numbers of nematodes that gave maximum stimulation were different for different hosts. In this study, it was concluded that the production of lateral roots accounted for the increased weight of roots in stimulated plants, and they suggested that the pericycle, by assuming meristematic activity, caused lateral roots to be produced just above the root apices. The increased root growth gave added powers of water and mineral uptake. Doney and his coworkers (1971) observed a significant increase in petiole length in sugar beet plants 8 to 9 weeks after inoculation with *Heterodera schachtii* larvae. Similarly, the wild grass *Sporobolus poiretii* developed heavier top weight and produced more inflorescences when infected with *Aphelenchoides besseyi* than did uninfected plants (Marlatt and Perry, 1971). An initial inoculum density of 5000 *Trichodorus christiei* per seedling resulted in a significant increase in the number of secondary roots of tomato seedlings less than or equal to one cm in length and a significant decrease in roots longer than this. At the lowest initial density large numbers of secondary roots developed (Hogger, 1972).

From these examples it is evident that stimulation may be caused by nematodes with a wide variety of feeding habits, by foliar as well as soil nematodes. Furthermore stimulated growth may be apparent in leaves, roots, petioles, stems and inflorescences. Thus stimulation of the plant at low nematode numbers is a general and probably a common phenomenon.

The most plausible explanation for the stimulation of plants by nematodes is that there are two mutually independent effects on plants both depending on nematode density. Seinhorst (1968) proposed that these two effects were (1) growth stimulation which could be expressed by the formula $y = c - (c-1)e^{-KP}$ in which y = yield expressed as a proportion of the yield in the absence of nematodes, P = nematode density, c = ratio between yield at $P = \infty$ and $P = 0$ and K = a constant relative to growth stimulation per nematode. (2) Growth reduction according the equation $y = z^P$. Seinhorst suggests that the effects probably occur simultaneously, in which case, combining the two equations gives $y = [c - (c - 1)e^{-KP}]z^P$. Depending on the values of c and K, this equation gives yields which (1) at first increase with increase in nematode numbers and then decrease again, (2) remain more or less constant to a certain value of P then decrease or (3) decrease continuously. In a later paper Seinhorst and den Ouden (1971) applied the 'stimulation model' to account for marked increases in growth of potato haulms grown in soil containing *Heterodera*

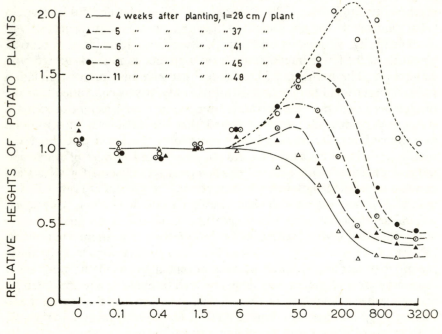

Fig. 3 Relative heights of potato plants var. 'Libertas' grown at a low nitrogen fertilizer level in relation to population density of *Heterodera rostochiensis*. (After Seinhorst and den Ouden, 1971)

rostochiensis and at a low nitrogen level. Haulms were considerably longer and a little heavier at high than at low nematode densities. Furthermore, the later the dates on which the haulms were measured, the taller the plants and the higher the nematode density at which maximum growth occurred (Figure 3). Such stimulation, Seinhorst suggests, could be explained by assuming that damage caused by invasion necrosis retarded the development of the plants and delayed the time of tuber formation without affecting the growth of the tubers. Consequently plant development was shifted partly to a period with longer days and higher temperatures resulting in taller plants.

Seinhorst's model indicates that the relationship between plant growth and nematode numbers may be any one of a series of curves depending on the intensity and kind of stimulatory process occurring in the plant in response to nematode disturbance, and on the intensity and kind of disturbance or damage caused by the nematode. The previous conclusion, that there is no reason to expect that all or even most relationships between plant growth and nematode numbers will be sigmoid, is therefore justified.

Although Seinhorst and den Ouden (1971) provides a cogent explanation for stimulation in potatoes infected with *H. rostochiensis* other than the 'growth hormone' hypothesis, it seems likely that, in fact, growth regulatory substances play a dominant part and over the next decade there will probably be an increasing amount of data indicating their importance in the physiology of the diseased plant. Studies on the relationship between numbers of *Meloidogyne javanica* in several host plants indicate the variety of responses and the apparent frequency with which stimulation occurs (Wallace, 1971). In this research the opposing influences of root destruction and metabolic sink formation on the one hand and root regeneration and growth hormone production on the other are imagined to work simultaneously. If the inhibitory processes predominate, yield or growth of plants is reduced, if the stimulating components predominate there is less or no growth reduction, and there may be an increase in growth if growth substances are produced in excess. This is not an unusual occurrence; organisms that react to a disturbance to maintain their stability or integrity frequently over-react or over-compensate. For example, bean leaves carrying a light infection of rust showed consistent stimulation during the flecking period when symptoms were first apparent (Livne, 1964). In other words the feed-back mechanism is not perfect. A root or shoot which is correcting its position as a consequence of displacement will always 'overshoot'. This leads to a renewed geotropic stimulus which will tend to bring the organ back again. There is thus a certain amount of oscillation about the vertical before the system becomes stabilized (Bell, 1966). The same may be true of plants infected with low nematode numbers, perhaps the growth hormone response overshoots to give stimulated growth. Equally likely is the possibility that at a later stage of growth stimulation may disappear as stability is achieved and the plant regulates its physiology to cope with the nematodes' disturbing influence.

We can conclude therefore that the relationship between plant growth and numbers of nematodes will vary with the species of nematode and host. The sigmoid curve, which might suggest the existence of a tolerance level, is in fact only one of a series of curves (Wallace, 1971) and it may occur only infrequently at that.

The regulation of nematode numbers

We have seen some indications that the plant responds to infection by nematodes by compensating for damage. The plant may also maintain its own stability by reducing the ability of nematodes to cause damage; this is called resistance and will be discussed at a later stage but it is worth noting here that resistance is an example of negative feedback in that the level of response of the plant in resisting the disturbance (nematode damage) is determined by the degree of the disturbance (numbers of nematodes). However, we might imagine that it would be beneficial to the nematode, i.e. increase its chance of survival, if there were negative feedback processes that regulated its numbers to the extent that it did not kill its host and thereby obliterate its source of food.

With one exception, this aspect of plant nematology has received little attention. It seems likely for example, that the numbers of nematodes invading a root might be influenced by the numbers that have already invaded. Do roots that are initially attractive to nematodes become less so as infection progresses, as suggested by Siddiqui (1971)? How much might rate of root growth and density of nematodes in the soil affect such a relationship? There is also the possibility that nematodes like *Heterodera* and *Meloidogyne*, that cannot locate a feeding site in the root because they are already occupied, might be stimulated to leave the root, rather than to wander through the tissues causing further damage. The size of females and their fecundity may decrease as populations increase. The number of adults of the animal parasitic nematode *Ostertagia ostertagi* increased in calves as the infection rate increased. However, the number of eggs in the faeces then fell and was associated with a decrease in size of females and lack of development of the vulval flap (Michel, 1969). Such density-dependent processes have not yet been studied seriously; the exception is sex ratio of nematodes in infected plants.

According to Wynne-Edwards (1965) animals have evolved means of regulating their own numbers by a homeostatic process with negative feedback so that each habitat in which an animal lives carries only that number of individuals for which there is food. Although such an idea can obviously be applied to nematodes feeding on roots, it would be difficult to devise an experiment that tested the hypothesis that nematode numbers were regulated to keep in harmony with the existing availability of food, to use the terminology of Wynne-Edwards. However we can accept the general idea and search for any regulatory processes of behaviour or physiology which might achieve that end. The relationship between sex ratio, population density and environment is one such process.

The sex ratio of the nematode *Nippostrongylus brasiliensis* in rats changes to give more males the greater the infection level. Female worms tend to be eliminated from the host in greater numbers than the males and the process appears to be achieved through an immunological response of the host (Sey, 1969). Triantaphyllou (1960) showed that the sex ratio of *Meloidogyne incognita* changes by other means. At low nematode densities in tomato roots, most larvae developed into females, whereas at high densities apical root galls were formed and most larvae became males. Triantaphyllou found that second stage female larvae could reverse their sex and continue development to adult males with two testes. Male intersexes and males with one testis were also found. Subsequent work by McClure and Viglierchio (1966) supported Triantaphyllou's findings. *M. incognita* were cultured on excized roots of cucumber and, even under conditions of extreme crowding, the sex ratio was only slightly altered, although the rate of development was severely reduced. The excized roots were in intimate contact with the agar medium which supplies their nutrient so they were not dependent on translocation of organic compounds from the shoot. Hence disturbances in the vascular system, which might occur in intact plants, would not occur in excized roots and lead to nutritional deficiencies. McClure and Viglierchio conclude that sucrose deficiency, caused by vascular disturbance and reduced translocation, might affect the sex ratio most. Davide and Triantaphyllou (1967a) consider that differential mortality is not the main cause of change in the sex ratio in *Meloidogyne* spp. and they interpret the problem in terms of the following alternative hypotheses: (1) Infective larvae are genetically fixed with respect to their sex, and sex expression is not affected by subsequent environmental influences during development; (2) The infective larvae may be genetically determined as males and females, and the two sexes may be in approximate equal numbers, but sex expression depends largely on environmental influences during development, so that genotypically male larvae give rise to adult female larvae. Davide and Triantaphyllou clearly favour the second hypothesis on the basis of their research, and their later work (Davide and Triantaphyllou, 1967b) indicates that the nutritional condition of the tomato plant may be the most important environmental factor determining sex. There is little doubt that as population density of *Meloidogyne* spp. increases the proportion of males increases and Trudgill (1967) showed that the same occurred with *Heterodera rostochiensis* in potatoes and he suggested that competition for giant cell sites was probably the determining factor (Fig. 4). This is really another way of saying that food is in short supply. Trudgill, in fact, suggests that only second stage larvae with giant cells of adequate size can become females and that the observed changes in sex ratio, without a change in the total number of nematodes, reflects a nutritional effect on sex determination. It might be gathered therefore that Trudgill supports Triantaphyllou and Davide's hypothesis on the masculinizing effect of environment (particularly nutrition) on sexual determination in which the females may undergo sex reversal to become males. In fact, Ross and Trudgill (1969) produced a model based on the hypothesis that the second stage larvae of *H. rostochiensis* arrive at their feeding sites within the host plant roots at random, and become female only when they have room to

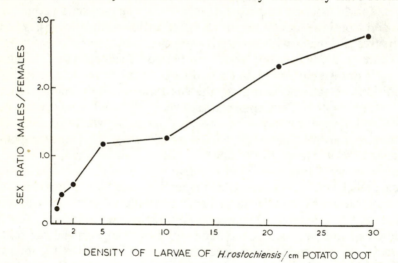

DENSITY OF LARVAE OF *H.rostochiensis*/cm POTATO ROOT

Fig. 4   The influence of density of larvae of *Heterodera rostochiensis* on the sex ratio of adults in potato roots. (From data of Trudgill, 1967)

produce a large enough group of giant cells. They further suggest that when larvae are many in a root few become female, competition for food is reduced and hence all females have sufficient food to become adult and produce eggs. The excess larvae that become males possibly require less food and so cause less damage to the host root system.

Trudgill's (1967) studies on the sex ratio of *Heterodera rostochiensis* involved counting the numbers of mature males and females. Such a procedure, as Johnson and Viglierchio (1969) point out (without however referring to Trudgill's paper), might not give the true sex ratio but may reflect differential development. Observations on *H. schachtii* in sugar beet indicated that females which had not developed beyond the third or fourth stage were common, whereas most males developed to maturity. Furthermore, sex reversal and intersexes were not observed in *H. schachtii*. Kerstan (1969) adopts a similar view because he concludes that changes in sex ratio of *H. schachtii* were caused by the selective death rate of female larvae, and that sex is predetermined before larvae penetrate the host plant root. Similarly, increased male to female ratios in *Heterodera glycines* were attributed to differential death rate of male and female larvae under conditions of food stress created by crowding (Koliopanos and Triantaphyllou, 1972). There is a further possibility mentioned by Davide and Trianta-phyllou (1967*a*) that the male and female second stage larvae differ in their ability to invade the plant. Thus sex ratio may be determined at the plant surface.

That there are changes in sex ratio there is little doubt, and the change appears, theoretically at least, to confer advantage to the nematode in that its numbers are regulated to reduce the damaging effect on the host of too many nematodes in a small volume of root. The processes whereby changes in sex ratio are achieved are still not fully understood. Perhaps different species have different methods. However, whatever the means the end result is the same. The two aspects of tolerance and regulation of nematode numbers both influence the growth of the plant. They also interact with each other in the process, for the ability of a nematode to regulate its own numbers within the host plant will inevitably influence the amount of disturbance to which the plant is subjected, and how much the plant will have to respond to tolerate the damage. Such interactions, complex as they are, form only a part of a whole system of interacting factors more of which will be described as the story proceeds.

References

APT, W.J. and KOIKE, H. (1962). Influence of the stubby-root nematode on growth of sugarcane in Hawaii. *Phytopathology*, **52**, 963.

BAXTER, R.I. and BLAKE, C.D. (1967). Invasion of wheat roots by *Pratylenchus thornei*. *Nature Lond.*, **215**, 1168.

BELL, P.R. (1966). Regulation of plant growth. In *Regulation and control in living systems*. Edited by H. Kalmus. Wiley, viii, 468 pp.

BROWN, E.B. (1969). Assessment of the damage caused to potatoes by potato cyst eelworm, *Heterodera rostochiensis* Woll. *Ann. appl. Biol.*, **63**, 493.

BURSTRÖM, H.G. (1965). The physiology of plant roots. In *Ecology of soil-borne plant pathogens*. Edited by Baker, K.F. and Snyder, W.C. University of California Press. 577 pp.

COHN, E., MINZ, G. and MONSELISE, S.P. (1965). The distribution, ecology and pathogenicity of the citrus nematode in Israel. *Israel. J. Agric. Res.*, **15**, 187.

COURSEN, B.W. and JENKINS, W.R. (1958). Host-parasite relationships of the pin-nematode, *Paratylenchus projectus* on tobacco and tall fescue. *Pl. Dis. Reptr.*, **42**, 865.

DAVIDE, R.G. and TRIANTAPHYLLOU, A.C. (1967a). Influence of the environment on development and sex differentiation of root-knot nematodes. 1. Effect of infection density, age of the host plant and soil temperature. *Nematologica*, **13**, 102.

DAVIDE, R.G. and TRIANTAPHYLLOU, A.C. (1967b). Influence of the environment on development and sex differentiation of root-knot nematodes. 2. Effect of host nutrition. *Nematologica*, **13**, 111.

DONEY, D.L., WHITNEY, E.D. and STEELE, A.E. (1971). Effect of *Heterodera schachtii* infection on sugarbeet leaf growth. *Phytopathology*, **61**, 40.

GARRAWAY, M.O. and PELLETIER, R.L. (1966) Distribution of C^{14} in the potato plant in relation to leaf infection by *Phytophthora infestans*. *Phytopathology*, **56**, 1184.

HERLICH, H. (1969). Dynamics of prepatent infections of guinea pigs with the ruminant parasite, *Trichostrongylus colubriformis. J. Parasit.*, **55**, 88.

HOGGER, C. (1972). Effect of *Trichodorus christiei* inoculum density and growing temperature on growth of tomato roots. *J. Nematology*, **4**, 66.

JAMES, W.C., JENKINS, J.E.E. and JEMMETT, J.L. (1968). The relationship between leaf blotch caused by *Rhynchosporium secalis* and losses in grain yield of spring barley. *Ann. appl. Biol.*, **62**, 273.

JOHNSON, R.N. and VIGLIERCHIO, D.R. (1969). Sugar beet nematode (*Heterodera schachtii*) reared on axenic *Beta vulgaris* root explants. *Nematologica*, **15**, 144.

JONES, F.G.W., MEATON, V.H., PARROTT, D.M. and SHEPHERD, A.M. (1965). Population studies on pea cyst-nematode *Heterodera goettingiana* Liebs. *Ann. appl. Biol.*, **55**, 13.

JONES, F.G.W., PARROTT, D.M. and WILLIAMS, T.D. (1967). The yield of potatoes resistant to *Heterodera rostochiensis* on infested land. *Nematologica*, **13**, 301.

KALMUS, H. (1966). Introduction. Control and regulation as interactions within systems. In *Regulation and control in living system* Edited by H. Kalmus. Wiley, viii, 468 pp.

KERSTAN, U. (1969). Die Beeinflussung des Geschlechterverhältnisses in der Gattung *Heterodera*. 2. Minimallebensraum—selektive absterberate der Geschlechter—Geschlechterverhältnis (*Heterodera schachtii.*). *Nematologica*, **15**, 210.

KOLIOPANOS, C.N. and TRIANTAPHYLLOU, A.C. (1972). Effect of infection density on sex ratio of *Heterodera glycines*. *Nematologica*, **18**, 131.

LARGE, E.C. (1966). Measuring plant disease. *Ann. Rev. Phytopath.*, **4,** 9.

LAST, F.T. (1971). The role of the host in the epidemiology of some non-foliar pathogens. *Ann. Rev. Phytopath.*, **9,** 341.

LEHMAN, P.S., HUISINGH, D. and BARKER, K.R. (1971). The influence of races of *Heterodera glycines* on nodulation and nitrogen-fixing capacity of soybean. *Phytopathology*, **61,** 1239.

LELAND, S.E., DRUDGE, J.H., WYANT, Z.N., and ELAM, G.W. (1960). Studies on *Trichostrongylus axei* (Cobbold, 1879). V. Some quantitative and pathologic aspects of experimental infections with a horse strain in sheep. *Am. J. vet. Res.*, **21,** 449.

LIVNE, A. (1964). Photosynthesis in healthy and rust-affected plants. *Pl. Physiol.*, **39,** 614.

MADAMBA, C.P., SASSER, J.N. and NELSON, L.A. (1965). Some characteristics of the effects of *Meloidogyne* spp. on unstable host crops. *North Carolina Ag. Exp. Stn. Tech. Bull.*, **169**.

MALEK, R.B. and JENKINS, W.R. (1964). Aspects of the host-parasite relation-ships of nematodes and hairy vetch. *New Jersey Agric. Exp. Stn. Bull.*, **813**.

MARLATT, R.B. and PERRY, V.G. (1971). Growth stimulation of *Sporobolus poiretii* by *Aphelenchoides besseyi*. *Phytopathology*, **61,** 740.

MCCLURE, M.A. and VIGLIERCHIO, D.R. (1966). The influence of host nutrition and intensity of infection on the sex ratio and development of *Meloidogyne incognita* in sterile agar cultures of excised cucumber roots. *Nematologica*, **12,** 248.

MICHEL, J.F. (1969). Some observations on the worm burdens of calves infected daily with *Ostertagia ostertagi*. *Parasitology*, **59,** 575.

NICHOLSON, A.J. (1933). The balance of animal populations. *J. Anim. Ecol.*, **2,** 132.

OOSTENBRINK, M. (1966). Major characteristics of the relation between nematodes and plants. *Meded. LandbHoogesch. Wageningen*, **66** (4), 1.

ROSS, J.G., PURCELL, D.A. and TODD, J.R. (1969). Experimental infections of lambs with *Trichostrongylus axei*. *Res. vet. Sci.*, **10,** 142.

ROSS, J.G.S., and TRUDGILL, D.L. (1969). The effect of population density on the sex ratio of *Heterodera rostochiensis*; a two dimensional model. *Nematologica*, **15,** 601.

SCHAFER, J.F. (1971). Tolerance to plant disease. *Ann. Rev. Phytopath.*, **9,** 235.

SCHAREN, A.L. and KRUPTINSKI, J.M. (1969). Effect of *Septoria nodorum* infection on CO_2 absorption and yield of wheat. *Phytopathology*, **59,** 1298.

SCHNEIDER, H. and BAINES, R.C. (1964). *Tylenchulus semipenetrans*: Parasitism and injury to orange tree roots. *Phytopathology*, **54,** 1202.

SEINHORST, J.W. (1961). Plant-nematode inter-relationships. *Ann. Rev. Microbiol.*, **15**, 177.

SEINHORST, J.W. (1963). Enkele aspecten van het onderzoek over planten-parasitaire aaltjes. *Meded. Dir. Tuinbouw.*, **26**, 349.

SEINHORST, J.W. (1965). The relation between nematode density and damage to plants. *Nematologica*, **11**, 137.

SEINHORST, J.W. (1966). *Longidorus elongatus* on *Fragaria vesca*. *Nematologica*, **12**, 275.

SEINHORST, J.W. (1968). A model for the relation between nematode density and yield of attacked plants including growth stimulation at low densities. *Comptes Rendus du Huitième Symposium International de Nematologie, Antibes*, **83**.

SEINHORST, J.W. (1970). Dynamics of populations of plant parasitic nematodes. *Ann. Rev. Phytopath.*, **8**, 131.

SEINHORST, J.W. and DEN OUDEN, H. (1971). The relation between density of *Heterodera rostochiensis* and growth and yield of two potato varieties. *Nematologica*, **17**, 347.

SEINHORST, J.W. and KUNIYASU, K. (1969). *Rotylenchus uniformis* (Thorne) on carrots. *Neth. J. Pl. Path.*, **75**, 205.

SEINHORST, J.W. and SEN, A.K. (1966). The population density of *Heterodera trifolii* in pastures in the Netherlands and its importance for the growth of white clover. *Neth. J. Pl. Path.*, **72**, 169.

SEY, O. (1969). The influence of size and duration of infection on changes in the sex ratio of *Nippostrongylus brasiliensis* populations in rats. *Parasit. Hung.*, **2**, 45.

SIDDIQUI, I.A. (1971). Comparative penetration and development of *Meloidogyne naasi* in wheat and oat roots. *Nematologica*, **17**, 566.

SYKES, B.B. and WINFIELD, A.L. (1966). Studies on brassica cyst nematode *Heterodera cruciferae*. *Nematologica*, **12**, 530.

TAMMES, P.M.L. (1961). Studies of yield losses 2. Injury as a limiting factor of yield. *T. Pl. ziekten.* **67**, 257.

TRIANTAPHYLLOU, A.C. (1960). Sex determination in *Meloidogyne incognita* Chitwood 1949 and intersexuality in *M. javanica* (Treub. 1885) Chitwood, 1949. *Ann. Inst. Phytopath. Benaki*. N.S., **3**, 12.

TRUDGILL, D.L. (1967). The effect of environment on sex determination in *Heterodera rostochiensis*. *Nematologica*, **13**, 263.

WALLACE, H.R. (1966). Factors influencing the infectivity of plant parasitic nematodes. *Proc. R. Soc. Lond.*, **B. 164**, 592.

WALLACE, H.R. (1971). The influence of the density of nematode populations on plants. *Nematologica*, **17**, 154.

WYNNE-EDWARDS, V.C. (1965). Self-regulating systems in populations of animals. *Science, N.Y.* **147**, 1543.

4   The plant responds to the nematode

Plants respond to the disturbance caused by nematodes in ways which often appear to have some useful function to the plant. We have already discussed one such response, the compensation for damage. Such responses are considered to be useful because their effects appear to give the plant an increased chance of survival; they could be called adaptations or characteristics which the plant has evolved that provide survival value. In this chapter we shall consider those types of response that maintain the physiological efficiency (or health) of the plant so that it can grow and reproduce in spite of the damaging effects of the nematodes. We shall discuss resistance in the next chapter. The problem here is, how do we attribute a function to some observed response? With resistance it is sometimes possible to show that a change in the host's physiology, such as the production of a metabolite, is the direct cause of the parasite's being unable to develop in the host. More frequently, however, we can only guess at the possible function of a response and of course it may have no function at all; it may merely be the consequence of some other process. The problem of cause and effect is very real here; we have to decide whether a response is initiated by the parasite and has survival value. Such responses may have the property of feedback, i.e. they influence the factor causing disturbance, the intensity of the response being a function of the intensity of the disturbance. Such responses with feedback are teleological (Sluckin, 1960) a word which arouses discomfort in many of us but in the present context seems perfectly justifiable. In fact this chapter may be called a teleological argument because I am proposing that many responses of the plant to nematode damage are 'purposeful' in that their function is to maintain the integrity, health and physiological efficiency of the plant and thereby increase its chance of survival. Such a property would arise through natural selection.

Obviously this is not a new idea but I think it is worth introducing for four reasons: (1) it provides a framework on which information about plant responses to nematodes can be built. It is much more useful to attempt some hypothetical synthesis of such facts than to merely catalogue the various events that are observed in diseased plants; (2) the hypothesis may raise questions that suggest new and interesting experiments; (3) it enables the subject of disease to be discussed in a somewhat different light; (4) it is a more interesting way of conveying information.

Before we consider the responses of plants to nematodes it will be worthwhile to examine some of the attitudes of plant pathologists and parasitologists to this subject.

Some ideas on the nature of the host's response

There are some responses which occur commonly in diseased plants. Photosynthesis is reduced, although it is important to note that whereas it may be inhibited in infected tissues (e.g. leaves of bean containing the bean rust, *Uromyces phaseoli*), it may be increased in non-infected leaves on the same plant. Increase in respiration usually follows infection by a parasite and is often quoted as an indication that the host is 'fighting' the parasite. Protein synthesis is often stimulated in infected plants to a level much greater than that required to maintain the parasite. New enzymes are often formed and the plant cells grow and divide. Polyphenoloxidase activity increases and new metabolites are formed which are toxic to many microbial parasites. The metabolism of growth regulators changes in various ways and the production of excess auxin is common. In response to restricted waterflow in the plant's vessels, transpiration is reduced. Consequently the stomates close, at least initially, there is a localized accumulation of ethylene and auxins and these in turn affect cell permeability and cause yellowing of foliage, epinasty or premature leaf abscission. In some infected plants nutrients accumulate at the site of infection, due in part to mobilization of materials from distant uninfected regions and possibly controlled by a cytokinin-like mechanism (Goodman *et al.*, 1967). In general, there is an enhanced synthetic activity of the host and parasite, associated with increase in respiration and soluble nucleotides (Heitefuss, 1966).

Even with this cursory glance at the plant's response to infection it is not difficult to imagine that the plant is doing something more than responding in a passive way to the parasite. The same can be said of animals infected with nematodes; here are three examples. Sheep infected with gastro-intestinal nematodes, and rats with *Nippostrongylus brasiliensis* and *Hymenolepis nana*, have many more globule leucocytes than in uninfected animals. There was no evidence of a relationship between the presence of the globule leucocytes and the immune response (Whur, 1966). Humans infected with the hookworm *Ancylostoma duodenale* have a reduced red cell and plasma volume corresponding to reduced body weight which presumably compensates for the reduced cell volume (Saif, 1968). The α-globulin in the serum of sheep infected with *Oesophagostomum columbianum* retains the same level as in uninfected sheep, a possible indication that compensatory synthesis of this protein is occurring to maintain osmotic pressure produced by loss of albumin. Loss of β_1-globulin and albumin on the other hand are probably a consequence of inflammation of the alimentary tract. Increases in β_2 and γ-globulin are attributed to an immunological response because previous work showed that large amounts of these proteins are transferred across the gut into the mucus and that antigen from the nematode larvae reduces their electrophoretic mobility (Dobson, 1967). In these three examples from the parasitology field, the authors not only recorded the physiological changes in infected animals, but also were thinking in terms of possible functions that such changes might have in benefiting the host either by compensation or resistance (the immunological response). Their view of the host is not one of passive acceptance of the parasite's damaging influence but an active physiological response that attempts to maintain health.

The plant, like the animal, responds to stimuli from the parasite to counter infection. As Beckman (1964) puts it, 'Host plants do not exist passively to serve as substrates for every exo-enzyme of every parasite, or as metabolic systems to be poisoned by the many toxic agents that could be produced by invading parasites. Infection results in a dynamic interaction between host and parasite in which resistance is the rule and susceptibility the exception'. A good example of this interaction between host and parasite is seen in the wilt fungi (Dimond, 1970). The parasites on entering the host occupy the xylem vessels which contain inorganic nutrients and low concentrations of amino-acids and sugars. The wilt fungi grow through the vessels thereby increasing resistance to flow of water. The parasites release metabolites which pollute the transpiration stream, thereby inducing the plant to release compounds of low molecular weight such as growth regulants, and larger molecules consisting of polysaccharides, glycopeptides and hydrolytic enzymes. *As the parasite invades, the host responds.* Respiratory activity increases and polyphenols and auxins accumulate in tissues in a series of interlinked reactions. Simultaneously gels and tyloses develop in vessels. Hyperauxiny induces the formation of tyloses in diseased plants and together with gums and gels they reduce the migration of spores within vessels and reduce the flow of water. In this graphic account of the interaction between the vascular wilt pathogen and the host the impression one receives is a cohesive story relating the various events in the web of interacting factors. Here, there are examples of cause and effect, of host responses that are beneficial, of consequences which have no direct influence on the plant's survival, and of resistance. More than anything, it is this type of detailed hypothesis that is required in nematode-plant interactions.

Perhaps it was the same view that led Dropkin (1969) to say that cellular reactions to *Ditylenchus dipsaci*, *Meloidogyne*, *Heterodera* and *Nacobbus* were not passive responses to enzymes emanating from the nematode, but rather suggest an active host participation in response to some controlling force from the parasite.

The responses of plants to parasites can be described at the biochemical, cellular or physiological level. Ideally such descriptions should include all three because they are obviously related in a cause and effect way. Uritani (1971) provides us with a story of the kinds of biochemical events that occur in an infected plant. As the parasite penetrates cells, protein changes occur in adjacent cells. Frequently there is an increase in respiration; an activation of phenylalanine ammonia-lyase activity; there is increased activity of mitochondria and an increase in the activity of some enzymes in the glycolytic and pentose phosphate pathways. Arising from these changes (or possibly initiating them) is a release of ethylene which may be responsible for primary and secondary protein changes; it may also act as a hormone by activating some specific sites of plant nuclear DNA. Uritani concludes that changes in protein after infection are related to defence action, because abnormal metabolites are produced in adjacent non-infected tissues. Such metabolites accumulate in infected tissues and are toxic to parasites and inhibit their grown and penetration. The pathway of abnormal metabolite production is accomplished by forming *de novo* some enzymes located in the pathway, in response to infection. Alternatively, enzymes already present may be activated.

The biochemical machinery appears to be reacting in a 'purposeful way' to infection; there are changes in the metabolic pathways to produce new substances that inhibit the parasite and inevitably there are by-products of these reactions that are mere consequences of these changes. These variations in the infected plant are regulated by the plant under the stimulus of the parasite. But this relationship may not be perfect, i.e. the by-products of defense reactions may be toxic to the plant or the plant's ability to regulate the various biochemical processes may be impaired or inadequate, and the result is physiological dysfunction; but we will pursue this aspect later when we discuss the nature of disease.

As well as releasing metabolites that are toxic to the parasite, the plant may repair damage and maintain the stability of its cell membranes. Wheeler and Hanchey (1968), for example, argue that membrane stability and self-repair may be crucial factors which determine resistance and susceptibility. Most plant and animal cells can repair wounded tissues, and Owens and Specht (1964) have suggested that tumour formation (including nematode-induced syncytia) might in fact be related to a wound-healing response in both self-limiting and autonomous tumours. The self-repair mechanism in livers infected by liver flukes, and the relation of inflammation to tissue repair in animals, reflect the inherent ability to heal wounds. Similarly, the ability of plants to repair damaged tissues is a well known phenomenon. The callus formed by the cambium at wounds has a protective as well as a repairing function. The growth substances auxin and traumatic acid are involved in the response. In woody tissues, where the growth of the fungal parasite is strongly inhibited, there is increased metabolism in cells adjoining those that are infected, cell division starts again, lignin is formed and a cork layer surrounds the infection site. In this way the infection may be localized by a rapid formation of barricade tissue and the infected site may even be sloughed off (Tomiyama, 1963). The sealing process, which involves gelation and hyperplasia, follows most vascular infections and provides defence against infection by many potential pathogens (Beckman, 1967). Similar responses occur in animals infected with nematodes. Bronskill (1962), for example, observed that juveniles of rhabditoid nematodes penetrate the blood, sinus and cardial epithelium of the proventriculus of mosquito larvae and then enter the host's body cavity where they complete their development. By 5 hours a thick capsule develops about many of the ensheathed immature adults.

So far we have seen that following infection a series of events occurs that initiates the formation of new metabolites, enzymes and reactions, some of which are related directly or indirectly to inhibition of the parasite, to repairing wounds and to isolating the parasite at the infection site. Such responses are beneficial to the plant and we might surmise that they are adaptations that have evolved through natural selection. Less clear-cut in their function, however, are those responses that maintain the physiological efficiency of the plant in the face of damage in some localized tissue. Thus it is possible to imagine that with all the increased metabolic activity occurring at the infection site, there is a drain on the plant's resources in other tissues. The infection site in fact becomes a metabolic sink. It seems feasible that the plant might have the ability to increase its rates of photosynthesis, respiration, transpiration and other activities to maintain its growth.

In fact, most descriptions of infected plants indicate the contrary, i.e. physiological activity is reduced. For example, Duniway and Slatyer (1971) show that the transpiration and photosynthesis of tomato leaves infected with *Fusarium oxysporum* are markedly reduced 15 days after inoculation. Ponderosa pine seedlings infected with the fungus *Verticicladiella wagenerii* showed dramatic decreases in net photosynthesis and transpiration one month after inoculation (Helms *et al.*, 1971). And there are many similar reports from observations with other hosts and parasites. However, potato leaves infected by *Phytophthora infestans* showed an increase in rate of photosynthesis (Farrell *et al.*, 1969) and, as the authors point out, the common factor to all the recorded instances of stimulated photosynthesis is that the increase was always noted in the early stages of infection or at low levels of infection or both. Yarwood (1967) comments that the limitation of increased photosynthesis to the early stages of infection supports Gäumann's idea that all infections are initially stimulatory and that like low dosages of poisons, low levels of an injurious infection may be stimulatory. It seems to me however, that increased rates of photosynthesis may be more prevalent at least in plants infected with obligate parasites than is at present indicated by the literature. If the metabolism of cells increases in the region of infection so that they act as metabolic sinks, then it is likely that photosynthetic rate will increase. This is a well known phenomenon in plant physiology. For example, King *et al.*, (1967) have shown that the rate of photosynthesis by the flag leaf of wheat can be extensively, rapidly and reversibly changed by varying the demand for assimilates from the leaf. The authors quote several examples where change in sink size by removal of plant parts has influenced photosynthesis. Their results with wheat showed that the photosynthetic rate of the flag leaf was reduced by removing the main sink, the ear, and restored to normal levels (i.e. increased) by the substitution of an alternative sink in the roots and young tillers. They suggest that levels of growth substance within the sink organ may affect its growth rate and thereby induce changes in photosynthetic rate by altering assimilate accumulation in the leaf.

The hypothesis that the degree of accumulation of assimilates in the leaf may be an internal factor which controls leaf photosynthesis has been reviewed by Neales and Incoll (1968). The most interesting aspect from the plant nematology viewpoint, however, is experiments like those of Thorne and Evans (1964), who showed that photosynthesis in leaves could be increased by providing a better sink in the roots for assimilates. The significance of the sink capacity hypothesis is emphasized by Watson (1968) who stresses the importance of sink capacity on the growth of organs that constitute yield and indirectly affect photosynthesis by a feedback mechanism. Thus substances in excess of sink capacity decrease photosynthesis and vice versa. Watson goes on further to say that the activities of growth substances at appropriate times and places, and their interactions with the supplies of nutrients and photosynthates, determine the development of the plant, the differentiation of its tissues, the correlative growth of different organs and the change with age in the form of the plant.

From this brief description of one aspect of the plant's physiology, the concept of the plant as an integrated system of self-regulatory processes clearly emerges. Into this homeostatic system an intruder in the form of a parasite enters the scene causing disturbance. In the case of photosynthesis it seems likely that the creation of sinks by parasites may very well produce increased leaf photosynthesis by the feedback mechanisms just described; unless, of course, the demands of the sinks created by the parasite are too excessive, or the destruction of plant tissues so severe, that sinks are actually destroyed, when photosynthesis might be expected to decrease. In other words, increased rates of photosynthesis may occur in infected plants that are maintaining their integrity and health through their physiological regulatory processes.

Now let us look at some of the plant responses to nematodes to see if they can be accommodated in the general picture I have just presented.

Responses to plant nematodes

To present a cohesive story of how the plant responds to nematode infection, I will begin with those basic responses that manifest themselves as biochemical changes and then proceed to physiological and morphological changes. The general picture is of a highly complex web of interacting processes where a change in one process causes a change in other processes which in themselves become the causes of other effects. At the centre of the web are molecular changes spreading out to the edges, so to speak, to give visual aspects like changes in the form of growth and coloration that we call symptoms. In our present state of knowledge we get only brief glimpses of the whole web; large sections are missing, the relation of one section to another is doubtful and of course the pattern of the web will vary with the species of nematode and host plant. Nevertheless I think it is worthwhile attempting such a synthesis because it may illustrate the main theme underlying the story, that some of the changes we observe are plant adaptations that help to keep the plant healthy.

BIOCHEMICAL RESPONSES

The importance of DNA as the carrier of genetic information in the plant cell, and its role along with RNA in protein synthesis need not be stressed. The experiments of Rubinstein and Owens (1964) on the synthesis of DNA and RNA in the syncytia of tomatoes infected with root knot nematodes, provide a useful starting point for the story. These authors studied the incorporation of tritium-labelled thymidine and uridine into root galls in tomatoes infected by *Meloidogyne incognita acrita*. Using micro-autoradiographic techniques, they observed the incorporation patterns during the ontogeny of the galls. With thymidine-treated plants microspectrophotometric measurements were made on DNA in feulgen stained nuclei. The results indicated that the developing syncytium is a region of intense RNA and DNA synthesis. DNA, unlike RNA, seemed to be dependent on a close association with the feeding nematode. In studies on the growth of syncytia in beans, tomato (Fig. 5) and cabbage infected with *M. javanica*, Bird (1972) also showed that syncytial and nuclear growth, and DNA content, increased until just before the developing nematode started to lay eggs. Furthermore, Owens and Specht (1966) comment that changes in amount of nucleic acids probably reflect changes in the regulatory and functional components of plant cells. One teleological explanation is that the nematode induces and controls the syncytium and its metabolism to obtain necessary nutrients without killing the plant. While not denying this possibility it seems equally likely however, that responses may have evolved in the plant that accommodate the parasite while enabling the plant to maintain its own health. In other words the synthesis of DNA and RNA is the result of an interaction between plant and nematode.

More DNA and RNA means that more amino acids are available for incorporation into proteins; it does not necessarily follow that there will be an increase in free amino acids in the infected plant, in fact they could decrease. Nevertheless, it is a common observation that in plants infected with nematodes, there is such an increase. The reason may lie in increased proteolytic activity that releases amino acids from proteins. Thus the total free amino acid content in leaves of grapefruit plants infected with *Radopholus similis* was 18 and 81% greater after 8 and 12 months respectively, compared with leaves from uninfected plants. Arginine formed a much greater proportion of the free amino acids in the infected plants. The presence of this amino acid is a characteristic of citrus trees under stress of various kinds (Hanks and Feldman, 1966). Total free and bound amino acids in alfalfa and peas infected with *Ditylenchus dipsaci* were greater than those in uninfected plants (Fig. 6). The levels of amino acids did not appear to be involved in the initiation of plant galling as their increase in galls appeared after galling was initiated (Howell and Krusberg, 1966). In the fibrous root of *Beta vulgaris* infected with *Heterodera schachtii* concentrations of total amino acids, aspartic acid, glutamic acid and glutamine were significantly increased (Doney *et al.*, 1971). There is little indication from these examples of increased amino acid production whether there is any function or 'purpose'. Does the production of arginine in the citrus plants infected with *R. similis* have any significance for example? There is room for further enquiry here. To indicate the sort of enquiry I mean, let us look at the experiments of Epstein and Cohn (1971). They measured the amino acids in the terminal root galls of *Bidens tripartita* and *Vitis vinifera* infected with *Longidorus africanus*. The galled root of *Bidens* contained 73% more cell-wall protein and 184% more free

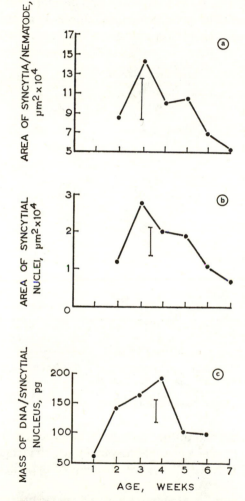

Fig. 5 The growth of syncytia induced in tomato roots by *Meloidogyne javanica*. (a) Growth of syncytia, (b) growth of syncytial nuclei, (c) mass of DNA per syncytial nucleus during growth of *M. javanica*. (After Bird, 1972)

amino acids. The major changes were a large increase in proline (1900%) and a decrease in aspartic acid (56%) compared with uninfected plants. The authors suggest that proline may play a role in the formation of xylem because this amino acid is immediately released by ruptured vascular bundles when an intact plant is wounded. Furthermore, the authors comment that as proline is a readily available storage compound in moisture deficient tissues and may accumulate from protein hydrolysis during drought and since proline is more soluble than other amino acids, its accumulation may enable osmotically bound water to increase. Thus

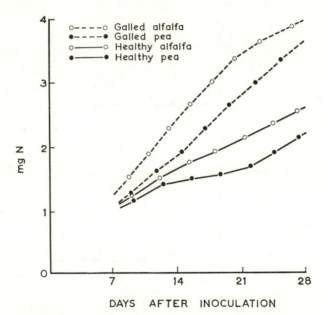

Fig. 6 Total nitrogen in healthy and in *Ditylenchus dipsaci*-galled alfalfa and pea shoot tissue collected 7, 14, 21 and 28 days after inoculation. Nitrogen expressed as mg per g dry weight. (After Howell and Krusberg, 1966)

water could be conserved during drought. The production of proline may therefore be thought of as a possible adaptation which increases the infected plant's chances of survival. These are the kinds of hypotheses that are well worth testing.

As proteins are built up of amino acids it is not surprising that they, too, usually increase in the infected plant. There are many references in the literature indicating that this happens. The proteins of most interest are enzymes. The syncytia that develop in soybean roots in response to infection by *Meloidogyne incognita acrita* contain oxido-reductive, hydrolytic and oxidative enzymes of increased activity (Veech and Endo, 1970). In the same host, infected with *Heterodera glycines*, certain host enzymes were localized near the nematode stylet during penetration and migration of the infective larvae (Endo and Veech, 1970). Increased enzyme activity was observed in syncytia during the early stages of disease development and, in susceptible hosts, high enzyme levels were demonstrated as the syncytia developed. In particular, glucose-6-phosphate dehydrogenase and 6-phospho-gluconate dehydrogenase, enzymes of the hexose monophosphate shunt pathway, appeared to increase in the syncytium. Enzymes of the major respiratory pathways also increased; malate dehydrogenase (tri-carboxylic acid cycle), a diaphorase (step between the TCA cycle and terminal oxidation), cytochrome oxidase (aerobic terminal oxidation) and ethanol and lactate dehydrogenases (anaerobic respiration). Any increase in the energy requirement of plant cells to tolerate, resist or accommodate the nematode, is therefore provided by the increase in the biochemical components that determine the rate of respiration. Kannan (1967) in fact concludes that the increased activity of dehydrogenases involved in the carbohydrate metabolism in galls on plants infected with *Meloidogyne incognita acrita*, might stimulate respiratory activity and indicate that the plant is combating the infection.

Plant growth is regulated by growth-promoting substances or hormones such as auxins, gibberellins, cytokinins and ethylene. Changes in the concentrations of these substances produce changes in the growth and form of tissues and organs in the plant.

Thus, auxins, which are normally synthesized in young leaves and shoot tips, promote extension growth. They have an important influence on changes in cell walls such as occur in hyperplastic tissues. Auxins also influence the permeability of cell walls, and may be involved in reactions with plant phenols in the presence of polyphenol oxidase to form quinones. Such reactions are recognized by the browning of cell contents or the necrotic response in cells that have been injured by many types of parasites, including nematodes. In addition, auxins are believed to influence respiration and RNA and protein synthesis in the plant. It is clear, therefore, that any changes in the concentration of auxin in plants infected with nematodes will lead to profound physiological changes. There are numerous reports of increased quantities of auxin within galls of plants initiated by *Meloidogyne* spp. Setty and Wheeler (1968), for example, examined roots of tomato plants with galls of *Meloidogyne* spp. and found that although the concentration of auxin was the same in infected and uninfected roots, the total amount in the roots of the infected plants was greater because they had heavier roots. Moreover, galled roots contained more bound auxin and more tryptophan (a precursor of auxins) hence the authors surmised that the nematode larvae hydrolysed the plant proteins to yield tryptophan which then reacted with the endogenous phenolic acids to produce auxin. It is possible that the formation of auxin-like compounds may be synthesized as the gall responds to nematode infection, because Bird (1962) found an ether-soluble growth-promoting substance, not present in adjacent tissues, in galls induced on tomato roots by *Meloidogyne javanica*. Increased auxin levels in *Meloidogyne* galls have also been reported by Yu and Viglierchio (1964) and Viglierchio and Yu (1968).

The endogenous plant growth regulator, ethylene, is known to be involved in such plant responses as epinasty, hypertrophy and hyperplasia, increase in respiration and stimulation of root formation. Thus, the intro-

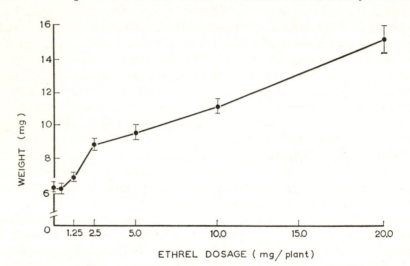

Fig. 7 The influence of the dosage level of ethrel on the weight of galls induced by *Meloidogyne javanica* in tomato roots. (After Orion and Minz, 1969)

duction of ethrel, a precursor of ethylene, was found to increase the fresh weight of plant galls induced in tomato by *Meloidogyne javanica* (Fig. 7). The increase in size of ethrel-treated galls was attributed to the proliferation of the parenchymal tissue and not through any influence on the nematode which developed normally. The results suggest that increase in gall size, the stimulus to form aerial roots and reduction in plant height, are related to the production of ethylene in the infected plant (Orion and Minz, 1969).

Cytokinins influence cell division but their activity depends on the presence of auxin. These growth regulators also influence the rate of senescence which they possibly do by influencing messenger RNA synthesis, thereby preventing the genes from being repressed and allowing the cells to continue their synthesis of both RNA and protein. Varghese and Kumari (1970) suggest that changes in the auxin-kinin ratio in roots of *Solanum melongena* infected with *Meloidogyne incognita acrita,* may be responsible for the acceleration of the physiological mechanism that determines root and shoot initiation and so accounts for the formation of adventitious roots in these infected plants. There were no measurements of growth regulators to support this idea, however. Krupasagar and Barker (1966), on the other hand, detected kinetin-like substances with a greater activity in tobacco roots infected with *Meloidogyne incognita* than in uninfected roots. In tobacco callus assays, extracts from galled roots had six times more cytokinin activity than extracts from normal roots.

There is some evidence, therefore, that changes in concentration of growth regulators occur following infection by nematodes. There are also indications that physiological responses are of the kind that might be expected from such changes. Furthermore, as Dropkin (1969) says, such changes suggest an active host participation in response to some controlling force from the parasite that stimulates the formation in its host of certain growth regulators which in turn regulate some of the observed changes. Some, at least, of these observed changes might promote survival of the plant by repairing damage, regenerating lost tissues, actively resisting the nematode or maintaining physiological performance.

STIMULATED METABOLIC ACTIVITY

Increases in amounts of nucleic acids, amino acids, proteins, enzymes and growth regulators in cells close to the nematode are indications or causes of increased metabolic activity. Autoradiography and wet combustion analysis of plant tissues showed a marked accumulation of ^{32}P-phosphates in galled roots of tomatoes infected with *Meloidogyne incognita*. The data suggest that the rise in metabolic activity as shown by the accumulation of phosphates may concentrate vital elements at the expense of the growing points (Ishibashi and Shimizu, 1970). In other words the galled tissues are acting as a metabolic sink. By using a split root technique, Bergeson (1966) demonstrated that excesses of nitrogen and potassium in the roots of tomatoes infected with *Meloidogyne incognita* were probably caused by transportation of these minerals from non-infected tissues to the infection sites. Such mobilization was so extensive that, in infected plants, roots on low nutrient supply had a higher concentration of nitrogen than those on full nutrient. In uninfected plants, on the other hand, the nitrogen in starved roots was about 68% of that in roots with full nutrient. Bergeson discounts the possibility that accumulation of minerals in infected roots is caused by their inability to translocate them to other parts of the plant.

This is further evidence, therefore, that infected tissues are metabolic sinks. But is the mobilization just described simply a process of redistribution of resources in the plant? If so, minerals may accumulate in the roots at the expense of the foliage as Bergeson suggests; or does the biochemical and physiological machinery in the foliage work faster to meet this new demand? We don't know, but I suggest that it is a distinct possibility and an hypothesis worth testing. There is no lack of evidence that infection sites have a higher metabolic activity if increases in enzyme activity (Kannan, 1967; Endo and Veech, 1969, 1970; Veech and Endo, 1969), cellular responses (Paulson and Webster, 1970; Owens and Specht, 1964) and DNA and RNA synthesis (Rubinstein and Owens, 1964) are any indication. What we need now are measurements on physiological processes that can be correlated with the biochemical changes. In this way we may get a better indication of the strands in the web of the plant's reaction to infection.

CHANGES IN CELL CONTENTS

Increase in size of the nucleus and nucleolus in plant cells is a common response to nematode infection. Endo (1971) refers to several such observations in syncytia associated with *Meloidogyne* and *Heterodera*. Similar changes have been observed in roots of bananas infected with *Radopholus similis* (Blake, 1966), in corn roots (1 to 3 mm behind the meristem areas) infected with *Tylenchus agricola* and *Tylenchorhynchus claytoni* (Deubert *et al.*, 1967), in orange roots infected with *Tylenchulus semipenetrans* (Schneider and Baines, 1964) and in tomato infected with *Dolichodorus heterocephalus* (Paracer *et al.*, 1967). Increase in nuclear volume may result from nuclear fusion or increased ploidy, as in syncytial nuclei, but it may also be an indication of active metabolism (Owens and Specht, 1964) or of an increased requirement by the cell for DNA (Rubinstein and Owens, 1964). Increase in density of cytoplasm and decrease in volume of vacuoles are also common. Corresponding increases in the concentrations of protein and RNA and in numbers of mitochondria, proplastids, Golgi bodies, and in the density of the endoplasmic reticulum in syncytia induced by *Meloidogyne javanica* in tomato roots (Bird, 1961), possibly indicate a high level of protein synthesis.

CHANGES IN PHYSIOLOGY

Information on the influence of nematodes at different population levels on such responses as respiration, translocation, photosynthesis, transpiration and nutrient uptake by whole plants, is sadly lacking. There are

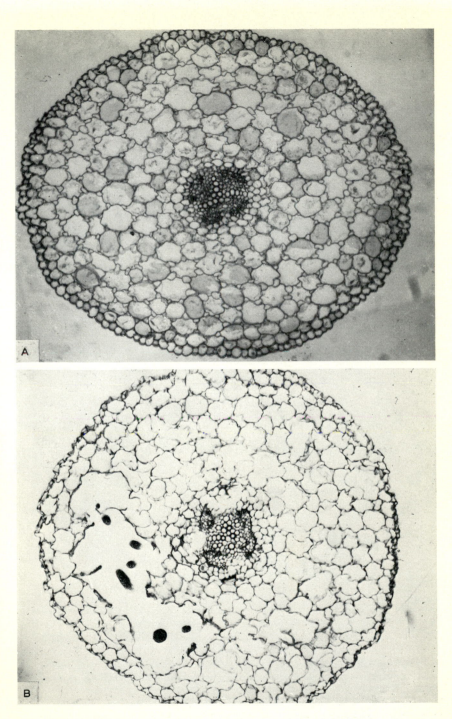

Plate 4 Transverse section of lucerne roots showing effects of *Ditylenchus dipsaci*. A, one week after inoculation—no apparent symptoms; B, four weeks after inoculation showing cell destruction with nematodes in the cavities. (Reproduced by permission of L. R. Krusberg)

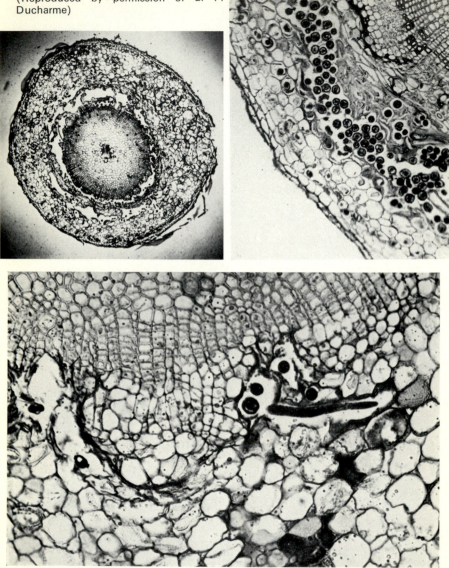

Plate 5 (right) Transverse section of a citrus rootlet containing a cavity formed by and filled with *Radopholus similis*. (Reproduced by permission of E. P. Ducharme)

Plate 6 (top left) Transverse section of a citrus root showing the stele girdled by a cavity formed by *Radopholus similis*. (Reproduced by permission of E. P. Ducharme)
Plate 7 (bottom) Transverse section of a citrus root infested with *Radopholus similis* showing hypertrophy and hyperplasia of pericycle. (Reproduced by permission of E. P. Ducharme)

observations on the differences between infected and non-infected plants in concentration of such elements as nitrogen, phosphorus, potassium, calcium and magnesium and deductions that absorption, translocation and accumulation of mineral constituents are changed following infection (Heald and Jenkins, 1964; Jenkins and Malek, 1966), but no direct measurements of these physiological aspects have been made. Sometimes the concentration of some elements increases in infected plants, while others decrease and the pattern of accumulation varies between plant species. In other words, this is a weak link in the argument that plants respond to infection by increasing their physiological activity. There is an obvious need for some research on the physiology of plants infected by nematodes at different population levels. Following previous arguments I would expect that at low infection levels most of these physiological processes would increase in activity but decrease at high infection levels, especially where there is a compatible nematode-plant association.

SYNCYTIA AND GALLS

Of all the aspects of plant response to nematodes none has received more attention than syncytium and gall formation in plants infected with *Meloidogyne, Heterodera* and *Nacobbus* (see reviews by Dropkin, 1969; Endo, 1971). The main feature of syncytia, apart from their characteristic ontogeny and unusual cellular contents, is their increase in metabolic activity. Syncytia are essential for the nematode if it is to develop and mature, consequently they can be considered as adaptive cellular changes (Dropkin, 1969). The nematode, according to this view, has presumably evolved particular secretions and types of behaviour that enable it to stimulate changes in cellular metabolism that are necessary for its own survival. However, it is also possible that the plant has evolved particular physiological properties that enable it to respond to the nematode stimulus in such a way that the disturbance created by the nematode is minimized, thus giving the plant a better chance to survive. We might even ask if the nematode confers some benefit on the plant it is parasitizing, such as *Rhizobium* or mycorrhizal fungi do to their hosts. After all, at low populations, *Meloidogyne* appears to stimulate growth (Wallace, 1971). Such speculations are probably difficult if not impossible to test experimentally but apart from being a good talking point they do influence the way we interpret observations on cellular responses. Thus there are several accounts in the literature that correlate syncytial ontogeny with nematode development, population increase, sex ratio and other characteristics of the nematode. Where syncytia are developed the plant is said to be susceptible, and susceptibility is measured in terms of the nematode's ability to reproduce.

Such experiments emphasize the significance of syncytia for the nematode's survival. There is somewhat less information correlating syncytial formation with the physiological performance of the plant. The kinds of questions that might be asked are: Can the production of enzymes and growth regulators in the syncytia be correlated with changes in the physiology and growth of the whole plant? Do such changes help to maintain the physiological stability of the infected plant? At what levels of nematode infection are syncytial responses correlated with dysfunction in the plant? These questions involve studies on the physiology of the infected plant as a system containing numerous interacting components of which the nematode is the initial stimulus or source of disturbance. This approach is one way to tackle the difficult problem of nematode—plant interactions. We shall refer to it later when we discuss the nature of disease.

Galling, i.e. hypertrophy and hyperplasia of cells that produce abnormal swellings, is probably a consequence of other plant responses. It may be one of those responses that does not contribute to the stability of the plant; at least it is difficult to put forward any hypothesis suggesting that the gall might benefit the plant. On the contrary, galls may be deleterious to the plant, a possible indication that the plant is overcompensating for nematode damage by producing auxins in excess. Once again the influence of galls on the physiology of the whole plant is not known.

WOUND RESPONSES

Plant responses that appear to localize an infection by surrounding it with a barrier of cells may be termed wound responses, a teleological term that implies that the response is beneficial to the plant. Thus Sembdner (1963) in describing the histopathological changes in tomato roots infected by *Heterodera rostochiensis* refers to hyperplastic responses as a wound periderm reaction. A similar response occurs in the cortex of citrus roots containing *Tylenchulus semipenetrans* (Van Gundy and Kirkpatrick, 1964). In edible ginger infected by *Meloidogyne incognita*, wound cork developed in differentiated rhizomes and lignified wall thickening of the pericycle and endodermis occurred in fleshy roots (Huang, 1966). Following infection by *Ditylenchus dipsaci* in a resistant variety of pea seedling, cork was formed in the periphery of the cortex, and reticulate secondary wall thickenings occurred in cortical cells adjacent to the cork (Hussey and Krusberg, 1968). Even the thick wall which develops round the syncytium initiated by *Meloidogyne* may be a self-limiting response (Owens and Bottino, 1966) and the formation of the syncytium may be related to wound healing (Owens and Specht, 1964). The statements attribute a self-preserving quality to the responses, but how do we know if they are justifiable conclusions ? It is difficult to imagine how we might test this conclusion with an experiment in which prevention of the wound or of self-limiting responses could lead to a conclusion that without them the plant is worse off. Nevertheless they are worthwhile statements because they do suggest that the plant has the adaptive ability to counteract nematode disturbance.

A further response to infection is the formation of tyloses in the xylem cells of the host. When *Hoplolaimus coronatus* feeds on cotton roots such structures appear round the feeding zone where they plug the xylem elements (Krusberg and Sasser, 1956). In coconut palm infected by *Rhadinaphelenchus cocophilus* (Blair and Darling, 1968) and in cabbage roots containing *Pratylenchus penetrans* (Acedo and Rohde, 1971) tyloses occur in response to infection. In these cases the response, which resembles that in plants infected with such fungi as *Fusarium* spp., is usually thought to be a cause of impedence to the translocation of water although with fungal infections it may have the beneficial effect of reducing the spread of spores throughout the plant.

CHANGES IN GROWTH AND FORM

We have now reached the extremities of the web of plant responses where changes are apparent in growth and form. Such symptoms of nematode infection are important because they are often associated with loss in yield. Stunting and reduced rate of growth, discoloration of foliage, twisted leaves and distorted shoots are all indicative of that lack of physiological stability that we call disease; they may be caused by any one of the changes in physiological function already described. Stunting and poor growth may be caused by reduced translocation, inadequate nutrient absorption, abnormal production of growth regulators, reduction in the numbers of roots, toxic metabolites and so on. If the physiology of diseased plants were studied in detail it would probably be found that any one symptom was the result of numerous interacting disturbances. Hence, even in the unlikely event where a nematode is the sole cause of a disease, it is difficult to diagnose the causal organism on symptoms alone, especially when damage occurs in the roots. With foliar and stem nematodes on the other hand, symptoms often indicate the species involved. Most of these changes are of no benefit to the plant and they may be debilitating, sometimes to the extent that the plant fails to mature and yield fruit; it may even die.

Some other changes may be beneficial however. Root proliferation, a common feature of many infections, may possibly indicate that the plant is responding to root destruction by excessive regeneration of new roots. Leaves of plants infected with *Meloidogyne* are often a darker green than those of uninfected plants. Infection with viruses sometimes produces the same effect. In such leaves, chlorophyll content may be enhanced and consequently photosynthesis may be increased, a possible indication that the plant is working harder to maintain growth in spite of a drain on its resources through the creation of metabolic sinks in the root syncytia. Change in leaf colour may also result from nutrient imbalance, so until experiments are done showing that the infected plant with discoloured leaves can maintain its reproductive capacity, we cannot claim that such changes support the hypothesis that the plant has homeostatic properties in relation to disturbance by nematodes.

Some conclusions

It is clear from the few examples I have quoted that several nematologists feel that many of the responses to infection are beneficial to the plant. Dropkin's 'adaptive response' is a good example. This does not mean, of course, that the nematode is any less important than the plant in its influence on the type of response. The ectoparasitic nematodes may be divided into two groups according to their adaptive ability. The first group, exemplified by *Dolichodorus* provokes extensive, localized reactions and might be termed a primary pathogen that has evolved specialized physiological adaptations such as enzyme systems. In the second group *Tylenchus* is an example of an ectoparasite that causes only slight host reactions and has fewer adaptations (Paracer *et al.*, 1967). In other words when plant responses are considered, we have to imagine a system containing two organisms, the plant and the nematode, each responding to stimuli from the other with adaptations that each has evolved. In such a system we could envisage a spectrum of nematode—plant associations starting with those with few adaptations to those with many. Such a spectrum would correspond to increasing compatibility between the two organisms. In studying complex systems of this kind we may have to resort to new research strategies, where we simulate the situation by flow diagrams that attempt to simplify the complexities of the system and which yet contain the essential quality of the organisms in real life, their homeostasis. We shall return to this aspect later when we discuss disease.

References

ACEDO, J.R. and ROHDE, R.A. (1971). Histochemical root pathology of *Brassica oleracea capitata* L. infected by *Pratylenchus penetrans* (Cobb)

Filipjev and Schuurmans Stekhoven (Nematoda: Tylenchida). *J. Nematology*, **3**, 62.

BECKMAN, C.H. (1964). Host responses to vascular infection. *Ann. Rev. Phytopath.*, **2**, 231.

BECKMAN, C.H. (1967). Respiratory response of radish varieties resistant and susceptible to vascular infection by *Fusarium oxysporum* f. *conglutinans*. *Phytopathology*, **57**, 699.

BERGESON, G.B. (1966). Mobilization of minerals to the infection site of root knot nematodes. *Phytopathology*, **56**, 1287.

BIRD, A.F. (1961). The ultrastructure and histochemistry of a nematode-induced giant cell. *J. biophys. biochem. Cytol.*, **11**, 701.

BIRD, A.F. (1962). The inducement of giant cells by *Meloidogyne javanica*. *Nematologica*, **8**, 1.

BIRD, A.F. (1972). Quantitative studies on the growth of syncytia induced in plants by root knot nematodes. *Int. J. Parasit.*, **2**, 157.

BLAIR, G.P. and DARLING, H.M. (1968). Red ring disease of the coconut palm, inoculation studies and histopathology. *Nematologica*, **14**, 395.

BLAKE, C.D. (1966). The histological changes in banana roots caused by *Radopholus similis* and *Helicotylenchus multicinctus*. *Nematologica*, **12**, 129.

BRONSKILL, J.F. (1962). Encapsulation of rhabditoid nematodes in mosquitoes. *Can. J. Zool.*, **40**, 1269.

DEUBERT, K.H., NORGREN, R.L., PARACER, S.M. and ZUCKERMAN, B.M. (1967). The influence of *Tylenchus agricola* and *Tylenchorhynchus claytoni* on corn roots under gnotobiotic conditions. *Nematologica*, **13**, 56.

DIMOND, A.E. (1970). Biophysics and biochemistry of the vascular wilt syndrome. *Ann. Rev. Phytopath.*, **8**, 301.

DOBSON, C. (1967). Pathological changes associated with *Oesophagostomum columbianum* infestations in sheep: serum protein changes after first infestation. *Aust. J. agric. Res.*, **18**, 821.

DONEY, D.L., WHITNEY, E.D. and STEELE, A.E. (1971). Effects of *Heterodera schachtii* infection on sugarbeet leaf growth. *Phytopathology*, **61**, 40.

DROPKIN, V.H. (1969). Cellular responses of plants to nematode infections. *Ann. Rev. Phytopath.*, **7**, 101.

DUNIWAY, J.M. and SLATYER, R.D. (1971). Gas exchange studies on the transpiration and photosynthesis of tomato leaves affected by *Fusarium oxysporum* f. sp. *lycopersici*. *Phytopathology*, **61**, 1377.

ENDO, B.Y. (1971). Nematode-induced syncytia (Giant cells). Host-parasite relationships of Heteroderidae. In *Plant parastic nematodes* Vol. 2. Edited by Zuckerman, B.M., Mai, W.F. and Rohde, R.A. Academic Press, xvi+347 pp.

ENDO, B.Y. and VEECH, J.A. (1969). The histochemical localization of oxidoreductive enzymes of soybeans infected with the root knot nematode *Meloidogyne incognita acrita*. *Phytopathology*, **59**, 418.

ENDO, B.Y. and VEECH, J.A. (1970). Morphology and histochemistry of soybean roots infected with *Heterodera glycines*. *Phytopathology*, **60**, 1493.

EPSTEIN, E. and COHN, E. (1971). Biochemical changes in terminal root galls caused by an ectoparasitic nematode, *Longidorus africanus*: amino acids. *J. Nematology*, **3**, 334.

FARRELL, G.M., PREECE, T.F. and WREN, M.J. (1969). Effects of infection by *Phytophthora infestans* (Mont.) de Bary on the stomata of potato leaves. *Ann. appl. Biol.*, **63**, 265.

GOODMAN, R.N., KIRALY, Z. and ZAITLIN, M. (1967). The biochemistry and physiology of infectious plant disease. D. Van Nostrand Co. Inc., ix + 354 pp.

HANKS, R.W. and FELDMAN, A.W. (1966). Quantitative changes in free and protein amino acids in leaves of healthy, *Radopholus similis*-infected and 'recovered' grapefruit seedlings. *Phytopathology*, **56**, 261.

HEALD, C.M. and JENKINS, W.R. (1964). Aspects of the host-parasite relationship of nematodes associated with woody ornamentals. *Phytopathology*, **54**, 718.

HEITEFUSS, R. (1966). Nucleic acid metabolism in obligate parasitism. *Ann. Rev. Phytopath.*, **4**, 221.

HELMS, J.A., COBB, F.W. and WHITNEY, H.S. (1971). Effect of infection by *Verticicladiella wagenerii* on the physiology of *Pinus ponderosa*. *Phytopathology*, **61**, 920.

HOWELL, R.K. and KRUSBERG, L.R. (1966). Changes in concentrations of nitrogen and free and bound amino acids in alfalfa and pea infected by *Ditylenchus dipsaci*. *Phytopathology*, **56**, 1170.

HUANG, C.S. (1966). Host-parasite relationships of the root knot nematode in edible ginger. *Phytopathology*, **56**, 755.

HUSSEY, R.S. and KRUSBERG, L.R. (1968). Histopathology of and oxidative enzyme patterns in Wando peas infected with two populations of *Ditylenchus dipsaci*. *Phytopathology*, **60**, 1818.

ISHIBASHI, N. and SHIMIZU, K. (1970). Gall formation by root-knot nematode *Meloidogyne incognita* (Kofoid and White, 1919) Chitwood, 1949, in the grafted tomato plants, and accumulation of phosphates in the gall tissues (Nematoda: Tylenchida). *Appl. Ent. Zool.*, **5**, 105.

JENKINS, W.R. and MALEK, R.B. (1966). Influence of nematodes on absorption and accumulation of nutrients in vetch. *Soil Sci.*, **101**, 46.

KANNAN, S. (1967). Activity of dehydrogenases in tomato root-knots infected with the root knot nematode. *Indian J. exp. Biol.*, **5**, 266.

KING, R.W., WARDLAW, I.F. and EVANS, L.T. (1967). Effect of assimilate utilization on photosynthetic rate in wheat. *Planta*, **77**, 261.

KRUPASAGAR, V. and BARKER, K.R. (1966). Increased cytokinin concentrations in tobacco infected with the root knot nematode *Meloidogyne incognita*. *Phytopathology*, **56**, 885, (Abstract).

KRUSBERG, L.R. and SASSER, J.N. (1956). Host-parasite relationships of the lance nematode in cotton roots. *Phytopathology*, **46**, 505.

NEALES, T.F. and INCOLL, L.D. (1968). The control of leaf photosynthesis rate by the level of assimilate concentration in the leaf: a review of the hypothesis. *Bot. Rev.*, **34**, 107.

ORION, D. and MINZ, G. (1969). The effect of ethrel (2 chloroethane phosphonic acid) on the pathogenicity of the root knot nematode, *Meloidogyne javanica*. *Nematologica*, **15**, 608.

OWENS, R.G. and BOTTINO, R.F. (1966). Changes in host cell wall composition induced by root-knot nematodes. *Contrib. Boyce Thompson Inst.*, **23**, 171.

OWENS, R.G. and SPECHT, H.N. (1964). Root knot histogenesis. *Contrib. Boyce Thompson Inst.*, **22**, 471.

OWENS, R.G. and SPECHT, H.N. (1966). Biochemical alterations induced in host tissues by root-knot nematodes. *Contrib. Boyce Thompson Inst.*, **23**, 181.

PARACER, S.M., WASEEM, M. and ZUCKERMAN, B.M. (1967). The biology and pathogenicity of the awl nematode, *Dolichodorus heterocephalus*. *Nematologica*, **13**, 517.

PAULSON, R.E. and WEBSTER, J.M. (1970). Giant cell formation in tomato roots caused by *Meloidogyne incognita* and *Meloidogyne hapla* (Nematoda) infection. A light and electron microscope study. *Canad. J. Bot.*, **48**, 271.

RUBINSTEIN, J.H. and OWENS, R.G. (1964). Thymidine and uridine incorporation in relation to the ontogeny of root-knot syncytia. *Contrib. Boyce Thompson Inst.*, **22**, 491.

SAIF, M. (1968). The blood volume changes in ancylostomiasis. Study with sodium radiochromate. *Z. Tropenmed. Parasitology*, **19**, 216.

SCHNEIDER, H. and BAINES, R.C. (1964). *Tylenchulus semipenetrans*: parasitism and injury to orange tree roots. *Phytopathology*, **54**, 1202.

SEMBDNER, G. (1963). Anatomie der *Heterodera rostochiensis*-gallen an Tomatenwurzeln. *Nematologica*, **9**, 55.

SETTY, K.G.H. and WHEELER, A.W. (1968). Growth substances in roots of tomato (*Lycopersicon esculentum* Mill.) infected with root-knot nematodes (*Meloidogyne* spp.) *Ann. appl. Biol.*, **61**, 495.

SLUCKIN, W. (1960). *Minds and Machines*. Penguin Books Ltd., 239 pp.

THORNE, G.N. and EVANS, A.F. (1964). Influence of tops and roots on net assimilation rate of sugar-beet and spinach beet and grafts between them. *Ann. Bot.*, **28**, 499.

TOMIYAMA, K. (1963). Physiology and biochemistry of disease resistance of plants. *Ann. Rev. Phytopath.*, **1**, 295.

URITANI, I. (1971). Protein changes in diseased plants. *Ann. Rev. Phytopath.*, **9**, 211.

VAN GUNDY, S.D. and KIRKPATRICK, J.D. (1964). Nature of resistance in certain citrus rootstocks to citrus nematode. *Phytopathology*, **54**, 419.

VARGHESE, T.M. and KUMARI, K. (1970). Meristem induction in *Solanum melongena* roots by *Meloidogyne incognita* var. *acrita*. *Nematologica*, **16**, 457.

VEECH, J.A. and ENDO, B.Y. (1969). The histochemical localization of several enzymes of soybeans infected with the root-knot nematode *Meloidogyne incognita acrita*. *J. Nem.*, **1**, 265.

VEECH, J.A. and ENDO, B.Y. (1970). Comparative morphology and enzyme histochemistry in root knot resistance and susceptible soybeans. *Phytopathology*, **60**, 896.

VIGLIERCHIO, D.R. and YU, P.K. (1968). Plant growth substances and plant parasitic nematodes. 2. Host influence on auxin content. *Expl Parasit.*, **23**, 88.

WALLACE, H.R. (1971). The influence of the density of nematode populations on plants. *Nematologica*, **17**, 154.

WATSON, D.J. (1968). A prospect of crop physiology. *Ann. appl. Biol.* **62**, 1.

WHEELER, H. and HANCHEY, P. (1968). Permeability phenomena in plant disease. *Ann. Rev. Phytopath.*, **6**, 331.

WHUR, P. (1966). Relationship of globule leucocytes to gastrointestinal nematodes in the sheep, and *Nippostrongylus brasiliensis* and *Hymenolepis nana* infections in rats. *J. comp. Path.*, **76**, 57.

YARWOOD, C.E. (1967). Response to parasites. *Ann. Rev. Plant Physiol.*, **18**, 419.

YU, P.K. and VIGLIERCHIO, D.R. (1964). Plant growth substances and parasitic nematodes. I. Root knot nematodes and tomato. *Expl Parasit.*, **15**, 242.

5　The resistance of the host to nematodes

The responses of the plant to disturbance by the nematode appear so far to be aimed at maintaining plant health without directly influencing the nematode itself. Responses that inhibit the parasite are collectively called resistance, which is measured in terms of the ability of the parasite to grow and reproduce on the host. Here for the first time is a clearcut teleological response; structures or physiological characteristics that occur in resistant but not in susceptible plants have the function of inhibiting the parasite to give the host a better chance of surviving. Resistance may therefore be considered as an adaptation that has evolved during the association of plant and parasite, although it is likely that some hosts are resistant to particular parasites even though they have never been in contact. In either event, how efficient the resistance of a plant is to a particular parasite is determined by the plant's genotype although, as we shall see later, environment may modify such efficiency.

Resistance as described by the animal parasitologists and the plant pathologists is of two kinds: (1) Passive, pre-existing resistance factors or natural resistance. (2) Active or provoked resistance. In the first type of resistance the defensive characteristics are already there waiting, so to speak, for the parasite to attack. The second type of resistance is more subtle, it comes into action only when the parasite invades the host, and generally speaking the intensity of the host's response is determined by the intensity of the parasite's disturbing influence, a good example of negative feedback.

As the plant pathologist and the nematologist share a common interest in plant health, and as the animal parasitologist is often concerned with parasitic nematodes, it will be worthwhile to survey briefly some of the attitudes to resistance contained in these two disciplines.

Attitudes to Resistance

NATURAL RESISTANCE

Resistance factors may operate even before the parasite reaches the

63

plant surface. Thus root exudates may inhibit germination of fungal spores, or they may selectively favour the reproduction of micro-organisms that inhibit potential pathogens. To invade the host the parasite must penetrate the animal's skin or the plant's epidermis and in these outer layers repellent and inhibitory substances may afford resistance. If invasion occurs through natural openings, there may be differences in the size of apertures (e.g. stomata) between different plant varieties that confer some degree of resistance. Within the plant other factors may oppose the parasite; such substances as phenols, quinones, alkaloids and glycosides may be inhibitory. In animals the body fluids may contain substances that inactivate enzymes released by the parasite; others, like peptides, fatty acids and lactic acid are toxic to parasites. Animals also possess cells called phagocytes that destroy old exhausted cells and foreign particles as well as parasites. Thus in animals and plants there is probably a range of non-specific substances that inhibit a wide range of invading parasites. The main problem in discussing natural resistance however, is the difficulty with which such ideas can be tested experimentally. It is a relatively simple matter to show a significant correlation between the presence of some compound, like an amino acid or a phenol, and resistance in the plant, but quite another to demonstrate that the compound is directly responsible for inhibiting the parasite. The same may be said about structural and anatomical differences between hosts. Experiments that modify these properties and at the same time show a change in resistance in the host may provide only part of the answer, but they are at least better than correlations with no attempt to establish cause and effect.

INDUCED RESISTANCE

The animal parasitologists call it acquired immunity. This type of resistance appears only after infection, and its nature is determined by the kind of infecting organism. The factors in the blood and tissues of the animal that inhibit the parasite are called antibodies and they occur in the globulin fraction of the serum as γ-globulins. Proteins and polysaccharides introduced into animals stimulate the production of antibodies; parasites elicit the same response. The substances which stimulate antibody production are antigens. The antibodies dissolve the invading parasites or cause them to aggregate or render them susceptible to phagocytosis or precipitate their secretions. Antigens are effective only when they are foreign to the animal into which they are introduced; thus enzymes and toxins released by parasites (including nematodes) in the host are antigenic and stimulate the production of antibodies. Although antibodies usually circulate in the animal's blood stream and are carried all over the body, some are produced in local regions, such as the uterus or in the mucous surface of the intestine, in response to local antigenic action. One type of immune response in animals, hypersensitivity, is worth mentioning because it occurs in plants too. In this reaction there is a rapid and violent response by the host which may inhibit the parasite by inducing changes in the host's tissues, such as swelling and fluid formation, that make feeding by the parasite more difficult. Localized necrosis may also occur leading to isolation of the infection. Hypersensitivity may also be detrimental to the host when the response is so exaggerated that it becomes an allergy.

Acquired immunity and the antigen–antibody reaction are characteristic of vertebrate animals. In invertebrates however, the body fluids do not resemble vertebrate serum, neither do they contain substances comparable to antibodies. Nevertheless, invertebrates respond to the incursion of foreign substances in their tissues by phagocytosis and by encapsulation. The phagocytes can distinguish between foreign bodies and their own substances and furthermore it is likely that the body fluids of many invertebrates contain a variety of substances that react with antigens. Such substances probably inhibit parasites and although they are not globulins and therefore not antibodies as found in the vertebrates, they appear to do the same kind of job.

Plants, like invertebrates, do not have antibodies. Nevertheless resistance to disease in plants is not simply a matter of toxins being present in the plant before infection, but of a type of metabolism that will respond to infection by producing such substances (Wood, 1967). There is some evidence that an immunological response may occur in plants, thus susceptibility may occur when parasite and host have a common antigen. When the host does not have the antigen that is present in the parasite, a resistant response occurs. Although no antibodies are formed, other substances may have the same function as in invertebrate animals. Thus, induced immunity or resistance in plants more closely resembles the non-specific resistance in animals following infection by various agents (Matta, 1971). Furthermore, it is possible that agglutinins in plants have evolved in response to the presence of plant parasites. The agglutinins may control the growth of plant parasites by inhibiting the polygalacturonases they secrete. In this respect, the plant agglutinins may be analogous to animal antibodies (Albersheim and Anderson, 1971). The argument, that lack of a circulatory system in plants precludes comparison with animals, omits the fact that in animals the immune response may be localized. Furthermore, there are similarities between vaccination in animals and acquired immunity in plants although the biochemical mechanisms may be different. For example, Weber and Stahmann (1966) inoculated the cut surfaces of sweet potato root tissue with non-pathogenic isolates of *Ceratocystis fimbriata* and induced a resistance or immunity to subsequent challenge by pathogenic isolates. As in animals, changes in protein synthesis were involved in the plant response.

There is no need to take the comparison between animals and plants any further; there is sufficient evidence to suggest that their responses to infection have enough similarities to justify the plant nematologist's interest in both areas of research. However, our main concern is with *plant* responses so let us look at some current views on the nature of induced resistance in plants to parasites other than nematodes.

Following infection there may be structural changes that inhibit the parasite. The chemical constituents of cell walls change and certain types of tissue may contain cells whose walls become suberized or lignified thus impeding the spread of the parasite. Resistance may also be associated with the absence or unavailability of an essential requirement, such as a nutrient, or with the absence from the host of a stimulus that initiates some behavioural response in the parasite, such as the formation of infection cushions in some fungi, or the attraction of zoospores to root tips.

Resistance may be achieved through the inactivation of toxins and enzymes released following invasion by the parasite, which is thereby prevented from obtaining nutrients or from degrading cell walls to obtain food. Phenolics are common enzyme inhibitors of this kind.

Substances toxic to parasites and produced in the host after infection result from those changes in host metabolism that were mentioned in the previous chapter. Such toxins may be absent in healthy plants, or occur only in very small concentrations, and superficially they appear to resemble the substances produced in animals by the antigenic response. There is often an increase in concentration of enzymes that catalyze reactions involving phenols and related compounds. For example, resistant plants may have increased polyphenoloxidase, peroxidase or catalase activity.

The production of common phenolics and other substances collectively termed phytoalexins, is an important feature of the resistant reaction. Such substances are not usually present, in resistant tissues, in concentrations high enough to inhibit infections, but a continuous flow of phenolics from adjacent tissues to the infection site concentrates them sufficiently to localize and inhibit the pathogen. A phytoalexin, according to the hypothesis of Cruickshank (1963), is a principle which inhibits the development of a fungus in a hypersensitive tissue when the host cells come into contact with parasite. The defensive reaction occurs in living cells only as a response to necrobiosis. Phytoalexins are non-specific in their toxicity towards fungi, although fungal species may be differentially sensitive to them. The basic response in resistant and susceptible hosts is similar but there is a marked difference in the speed of formation of the phytoalexin, being quicker in resistant tissues. The defensive response is confined to the tissue colonized by the fungus and its immediate neighbourhood and the sensitivity of the host that determines the speed of host reaction is specific and genotypically determined. Thus, susceptibility may be caused by the inability of the infecting fungus to stimulate the formation of phytoalexin, or it may be tolerant to the concentration of phytoalexin produced. How phytoalexins inhibit fungi is largely unknown but one at least, the phytoalexin of bean, phaseolin, may disrupt the plasma membrane of the fungus (*Rhizoctonia solani*) or affect some process needed for membrane function (Van Etten and Bateman, 1971).

Non-pathogens usually stimulate less phytoalexins than pathogens but are sensitive to the amounts that they do produce. Pathogens on the other hand usually stimulate relatively large amounts of phytoalexins, to which they are not sensitive. Thus, phytoalexins seem to protect a plant against all parasites except those specialized to itself, and explain why most plants are resistant to most pathogenic fungi (Garrett, 1970).

Hypersensitivity is associated with phytoalexin activity and we have already seen that animals have hypersensitive reactions too. In this reaction there is a rapid killing of host cells that limits the growth of the parasite producing a localized necrosis. The parasite may simply die of starvation but substances toxic to the parasite may also be produced. Although hypersensitivity in plants is usually correlated with necrosis, Wood (1967) points out that factors that confine a parasite within the plant tissues may be the same as those where death of the cell occurs; in other words, there is no logical reason why hypersensitivity should be confined to interactions culminating in the death of the cell. In animals at least cell necrosis is not a consistent feature of hypersensitivity.

In trying to visualize the general nature of the resistant response in plants, it is clear at the outset that there must be some kind of communication between plant and parasite. Whether this communication involves the DNA–RNA synthesis pathway, enzymes and enzyme precursors, or some other as yet undetermined systems, is unclear, but the end result is an orderly transmission of messages and effects from one organism to the other (Ehrlich and Ehrlich, 1971). Perhaps the concept of inducers is an indication of this initial interaction. Frank and Paxton (1971) showed that a glycoprotein in *Phytophthora megasperma* var. *sojae* induces phytoalexin production in soybeans. The authors suggest that the production of the inducer is the key reaction attributed to the resistance gene in soybeans. In resistant varieties the amount of inducer produced by the fungus is greatly increased, while in susceptible varieties there is no change in its amount. It is feasible that genes in the parasite direct, through their secretions (inducers), the synthesis of compounds which activate (de-repress) the genes in the host. The activated host genes, through changes in cell metabolism, then disintegrate the cellular organization of the host giving a hypersensitive reaction that destroys the symbiotic relationship between host and parasite (Hadwiger and Schwochan, 1969). The idea of enzymes being activated following infection is also supported by Kosuge (1969). Following this initial response (at the centre of the web of plant responses) a series of other changes occur that are associated with the resistance response and which we have discussed in the previous chapter. Protein changes (Uritani, 1971) and change in membrane permeability (Wheeler and Hanchey, 1968) may occur early in the course of events and lead to the production of abnormal metabolites (phytoalexins) that accumulate in infected areas and inhibit the parasite. Daly *et al.* (1970) have suggested another idea, that susceptibility rather than resistance is the inducible active property of the host. They propose that in cases of obligate parasitism, compatible relationships may require changes that provide a suitable metabolic environment for the parasite. In other words, the parasite induces changes in the host that provide for a compatible association, i.e. tolerance and susceptibility. It might be argued however, that the plant may have evolved the ability to respond, or not to respond, to inducers from the parasite. In any event it is likely that communication between parasite and host is a two-way business and it is not unreasonable to think that the plant has as much influence on the subsequent events as the parasite. (Perhaps the plant has an inducer that causes the parasite to produce an inducer that initiates the hypersensitive reaction and the production of phytoalexins.)

Resistance may be termed vertical or horizontal according to the nature of the interaction between varieties of the host and races of the parasite. Thus in vertical resistance there is a differential interaction between varieties of host and races of parasite; a variety is more resistant to some races of a parasite than others. In horizontal resistance there is no differential interaction, the resistance is evenly spread against all races of the parasite (van der Plank, 1968). Polygenic horizontal resistance is believed to be present to some extent in all species of host plants and is characterized by having little affinity with specific resistance which is recognized by hypersensitivity and a correspondence between the genes of host and parasite. It probably results from the presence in the plant of many different characters each of which may be independent. These could be concerned for example in rate of penetration of the leaf or production of fewer lesions (Watson, 1970). In fact the whole range of physiological characteristics that enables a plant to maintain its stability in the face of parasitic disturbance constitutes horizontal resistance. As van der Plank (1968) says, horizontal resistance is governed by genes that are not special resistance genes but are simply those that *occur ordinarily in healthy plants and regulate ordinary processes*. Differences in resistance between varieties can therefore be expected to be the rule.

Many of the plant responses to infection that inhibit the parasite are characteristic of vertical resistance (i.e. major genes are involved) in which resistance is clearly defined to give segregation of populations into distinct groups. Horizontal resistance, on the other hand, is polygenic and consequently less clear cut, because there are numerous processes of different impact and importance. Nevertheless, horizontal resistance is just as important as vertical resistance in spite of its somewhat vague nature.

At a later stage (Chapter 9) we shall discuss the concept of the plant as a self-regulating system that maintains its own stability and health in the face of environmental disturbance. Such an ability to maintain homeostasis includes, not only those activities called vertical resistance and the numerous ordinary processes referred to by van der Plank (1968) as constituting horizontal resistance, but also those processes called tolerance which have been discussed in the previous two chapters.

Resistance in plants to nematodes

The dual importance of the parasite and plant in resistance has already been emphasized. The situation may be summed up as follows. The nematode induces a host response by the nature of its secretions or mechanical damage; the plant responds to this disturbance in a variety of ways which either compensate for damage (thereby conferring tolerance on the plant) or which inhibit the nematode (resistance). Both of these responses can be considered as beneficial to the plant. There are also responses such as syncytial formation that appear to be beneficial to the nematode enabling it to obtain nutrients from the plant and so to develop and reproduce without causing so much dysfunction that the plant is killed. The relationship is not perfect, however, because when large numbers of nematodes invade the plant the cumulative effect of the damage, however small per individual nematode, may be sufficient to seriously impair the plant's normal functions. On the other hand, nematodes may have adaptations that enable them to regulate their own numbers in the plant and so avoid this situation—we have already seen that change in the sex ratio may contribute to this end. Account must also be taken of natural or preformed characteristics of the plant that inhibit the nematode and which are not the consequence of an induction–response process. The nematode may have adaptations to overcome these barriers too. Furthermore, many of these interactions may occur in the same confrontation between nematode and plant.

Resistance is clearly a complex business involving different kinds of host response and various nematode adaptations. We are in fact dealing with a system of numerous interacting factors that have evolved in this association between a parasite and its host. What we observe in the way of biochemical and histological changes in the host, and the effect of such changes on the nematode's survival and reproductive capacity, are only expressions of many preceding interactions. In the present state of our knowledge we can only study these expressions of resistance and speculate on the nature of the system that produces them.

Expressions of resistance

Plants sometimes have a natural resistance through substances that are toxic or inhibitory to nematodes. There are the well known inhibitory chemicals in roots of *Tagetes* and *Asparagus* that reduce the rate of hatch and invasion of some nematodes. The resistance factor may influence nematodes before they reach the plant; thus *Ditylenchus dipsaci* was less attracted to a resistant than to a susceptible variety of alfalfa (Griffin and Waite, 1971), possibly because the resistant plant released attractive chemicals in lesser quantity, or released a repellent substance as it appears to do in sweet potato. Jatala and Russell (1972) found that the rate of larval penetration of *Meloidogyne incognita* was significantly higher in susceptible than in resistant varieties of sweet potato. The longer the time prior to inoculation that the roots of susceptible plants were allowed to grow, the more larvae invaded the roots. With the resistant variety the opposite happened; numbers of nematodes fell as the length of time prior to inoculation increased (Fig. 8). The authors conclude that nematode-repellent exudates may be one of several factors in the resistance of sweet potato to *M. incognita*. In most plants however, resistance only occurs during or after penetration and may be the result of toxic substances within the tissues. Analysis of susceptible and resistant varieties of a species may indicate the presence of a chemical that occurs in greater concentration in the resistant variety. Giebel (1970), for example, prepared ethanol extracts from roots of 21 species of Solanaceae and determined the quantities of total phenols, mono- and polyphenols. He found that resistance to *Heterodera rostochiensis* was correlated with a high ratio of mono- to polyphenols. If the mechanism, whereby the balance of phenols inhibits the nematode, is elucidated by experiment, then we can conclude that there is a preformed or natural resistance to *H. rostochiensis* in some of the Solanaceae. In fact there are few cases where preformed substances are claimed to confer resistance in a plant and when such claims have been made they have usually only been correlations with little or no evidence that the substance is toxic to nematodes. It is therefore safe to assume that in most cases resistance is a complex physiological series of reactions from which numerous by-products may be produced that do not necessarily inhibit the nematode.

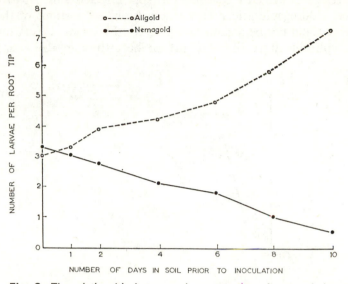

Fig. 8 The relationship between the penetration of two varieties of sweet potato by *Meloidogyne incognita* after 48 h exposure and the period the roots were in the soil prior to inoculation. (After Jatala and Russell, 1972)

Hypersensitivity

A frequent response to infection is a rapid browning of cells next to the nematode. Thus, in chrysanthemum leaves infected with *Aphelenchoides ritzemabosi*, browning is very rapid in certain varieties in which the nematode does not reproduce. Chlorogenic acid and isochlorogenic acid are the chief phenolic substrates and their oxidation and polymerization to form brown pigments following penetration of cells by the nematode's stylet, is therefore associated with resistance (Wallace, 1961a). The nematode's role in the response, and how reproduction is inhibited, are unknown however. There was no correlation between phenolic content or polyphenol oxidase concentration, and resistance, in the varieties of chrysanthemum tested, and Wallace (1961b) suggests that the absence of some nutritional factor, or a change in the physical surroundings of the nematode in the leaf, might make the plant resistant. These suggestions now seem implausible. De Maeseneer (1964) has suggested that perhaps the resistant chrysanthemum varieties contain more conjugated phenols, giving a higher concentration of free polyphenols through hydrolysis by the nematode's saliva at the point of penetration. To support this view De Maeseneer gives evidence that in *Ficus* spp. infected with *Aphelenchoides fragariae*, chlorogenic acid occurs in the browned portions of the leaves whereas it could not be demonstrated in healthy leaves. It was concluded that polyphenols were liberated in the host through the action of β-

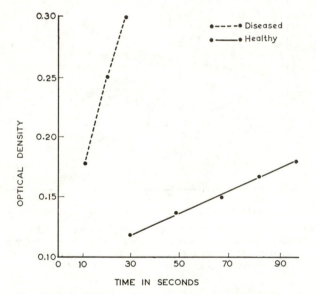

Fig. 9 Peroxidase activity of cabbage roots uninfected (healthy) and infected with *Pratylenchus penetrans*, 72 h after inoculation. Time-rate of optical density change in pyrogallol solution in the presence of H_2O_2 was measured at 420 nm. (After Acedo and Rohde, 1971)

glucosidase on conjugated phenols, as occurs in wilt disease in tomatoes. The presence of β-glucosidase was demonstrated in *A. fragariae*.

Other responses associated with the hypersensitive reaction include an increase in peroxidase activity (Fig. 9), pectic xylem plugs, an accumulation of oxidase-mediated polyphenols and an increase in polyphenols such as ferulic acid (Acedo and Rohde, 1971). High peroxidase activity in parenchymatous cells directly associated with nematode-induced cavities is reported by Hussey and Krusberg (1970). The hypersensitive reaction may sometimes be accompanied by formation of wound periderm and an accumulation of a suberin-like material (Van Gundy and Kirkpatrick,

1964). These are well known plant responses to parasitic fungi; in fact, it looks as though the nature of the hypersensitive reaction is the same for both fungi and nematodes. Furthermore, De Maeseneer's (1964) observation that chlorogenic acid occurs only in the diseased portions of *Ficus* leaves infected with *A. fragariae*, indicates that phytoalexin-like substances may be involved in resistance. Abawi and his colleagues (1971) have shown that phaseolin, a bean phytoalexin, can be isolated from aseptically-grown *Phaseolus vulgaris* seedlings infected with axenized *Pratylenchus penetrans.*

The fate of the nematode in the resistant plant

Although we do not know how nematodes are inhibited in resistant plants, there are many observations on how the nematode reacts. The ability of nematodes to orientate to the resistant host root may be less efficient (Griffin and Waite, 1971). The rate of invasion may be less; fewer larvae of *Meloidogyne naasi* penetrated resistant oat roots (Siddiqui, 1971) and in resistant varieties of sweet potato fewer larvae of *Meloidogyne hapla* invaded. If resistant and susceptible varieties are invaded in equal numbers the nematode larvae may be unable to develop in the resistant plant. In the roots of a resistant cantaloup, the development of larvae of *Meloidogyne incognita acrita* beyond the second stage is inhibited (Fassuliotis, 1970) and the same is true for *M. javanica* larvae in *Tagetes* spp. (Daulton and Curtis, 1963). In such situations, the nematode is unable to obtain nutrient from the host because the mechanism of nematode induction and host response is of a kind that denies the nematode access to the biochemical machinery of the plant. Hence we can say that there is a lack of recognition between nematode and plant. Reynolds and his co-workers (1970) showed that larvae of *Meloidogyne incognita acrita* invaded resistant and susceptible alfalfa roots in equal numbers. After three to four days, the number of larvae in resistant roots decreased sharply until after 7 days few remained in the roots and of those remaining none had developed (Fig. 10). The larvae left the resistant plants within a few days of penetration and, what is more, there was no evidence of a host response in the form of necrosis or syncytial formation. There may in fact be symptoms of a hypersensitive response other than the rapid necrotic reaction; the cytoplasm in the cells may become granular and plasmolyzed and the nuclei may change shape, as they do in resistant pea seedlings infected with *Ditylenchus dipsaci* (Hussey and Krusberg, 1968).

In some resistant plants, the nematode may be able to develop part of the way to maturity or in a population some may reach maturity while the others die or become males. Thus, in resistant cantaloup roots few larvae of *Meloidogyne incognita acrita* developed to the adult female stage. Resistance was associated with delayed development of larvae to adults and a shift toward maleness. Syncytia were formed but they were smaller and contained fewer cells than those in susceptible hosts (Fassuliotis, 1970). Similarly, resistance in potato varieties infected with different populations of *Heterodera rostochiensis* appears to be related to the size of the syncytia that are formed. Increasing resistance was expressed in the development of the nematode: (1) most larvae survived with the production of many

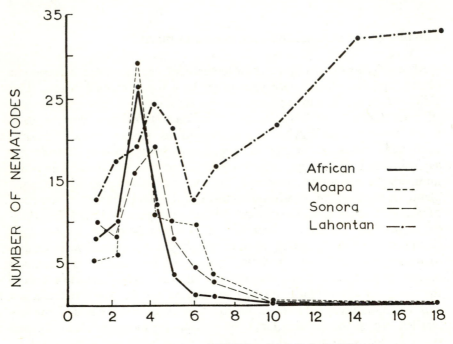

Fig. 10 The number of *Meloidogyne incognita acrita* within the roots of the resistant varieties of alfalfa, 'African', 'Moapa' and 'Sonora', and the susceptible variety 'Lahontan'. (After Reynolds *et al.*, 1970)

males and females, (2) most larvae survived but most became males, (3) most larvae died and of the survivors most became males (Trudgill and Parrott, 1969). On the other hand, inability to develop may be caused by abortion of the syncytia. Baldwin and Barker (1970), for example, suggest that the groups of empty syncytia in roots of resistant corn hybrids may be caused by frequent feeding on these cells but, more likely, it is caused by lack of feeding that sustains DNA synthesis. The low production of cysts by *Heterodera trifolii* on *Trifolium repens* is associated in part with syncytial abortion (Singh and Norton, 1970). In resistant soybeans infected with *Heterodera glycines*, syncytia were initiated and enzyme activity was slightly increased, but the syncytia eventually became necrotic and deteriorated, a response which, according to Endo and Veech (1970), is probably an active mechanism to limit the development of the syncytia thus preventing maturation of the nematodes.

There is little evidence that the fate of the nematode within the host is influenced by toxic substances released during the interaction between nematode and plant. However, Van Gundy and Kirkpatrick (1964) suggest that the roots of some resistant rootstocks of citrus may contain a substance that is toxic to nematodes. They are careful to point out however, that root-juice toxicity may not necessarily be an adjunct to resistance in spite of the fact that it is correlated with degree of resistance.

It is clear from these few examples that resistance to nematodes may take many forms and may affect the nematode at any stage of its life cycle.

Resistance and nematode populations

The main feature of resistance is its effect on the reproduction of the nematode. In breeding plants for resistance, and in assessing the relative resistance of plant varieties, the rate of reproduction is the basic criterion. There are immune plants on which a particular nematode cannot reproduce at all, and there are the susceptible ones on which it reproduces well. Between these extremes there is a spectrum of degree of resistance. We can compare the resistance of a particular variety of plant to different populations and races of a nematode species or to different species. Or we can compare the resistance of different plants to the same race of nematode. To make such comparisons the numbers of individuals produced by a known number of individuals in the original inoculum has to be assessed. The situation is clearly described by Jones *et al.* (1967), Seinhorst (1966, 1967) and in the review of Nusbaum and Barker (1971). In simple terms the relative resistance (or susceptibility) of a host can be assessed by the relationship between the initial (Pi) and final (Pf) densities of nematodes on a host plant. The straight line given by $Pf = Pi$ is called the maintenance line. When the curves relating Pf and Pi fall below this line then the plant is a non-host or a poor host: when the curve lies above the maintenance line the host is a good host, the degree of 'goodness' being determined by its distance above the maintenance line (Fig. 11). In other words if $Pf/Pi < 1$ the host is a poor one because the nematode population is decreasing, but if $Pf/Pi > 1$ the host is good because nematode numbers are increasing. The terms 'poor' and 'good' host are really expressions of resistance.

The population curve is the broad picture, the final outcome of all the events concerned in the relationship between the nematode and plant. Let us now consider the nature of resistance to see if we can get any glimpses of how the nematode-plant system might function.

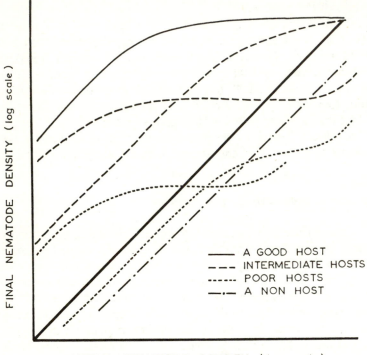

Fig. 11 The relation between initial and final densities in experiments with a nematode on a good host, intermediate hosts, poor hosts and a non host. (After Seinhorst, 1967)

The nature of resistance

First of all let us look at some opinions that have been expressed on how resistance might work. Webster (1969) states that nothing is known of the biochemical system controlled by the resistance genes in plants. However, he favours the hypothesis that a gene in the plant cell controls either the type of protein bound to a plant growth regulator or the occurrence of a particular enzyme in the plant. In a previous paper, for example, Webster (1967) suggested that the response in susceptible plants depends on the appropriate proteolytic enzymes breaking the specific peptide bonds, and so releasing tryptophane and gibberellic acid which produce an actively growing or modified tissue that provides the nematode with adequate nutrition. Presumably, the plant is resistant when any of the requirements in this causal chain is deficient.

In several papers Giebel and Wilski present a detailed hypothesis, more or less on the same lines as Webster, to explain resistance of potatoes to *Heterodera rostochiensis*. They first propose that resistance in potato depends on the presence of phenolic glucosides that are hydrolysed in resistant plants by β-glucosidases secreted by the nematode. Consequently, free polyphenols are released which cause necrosis. One biotype of the nematode secreted so little β-glucosidase that necrosis failed to occur,

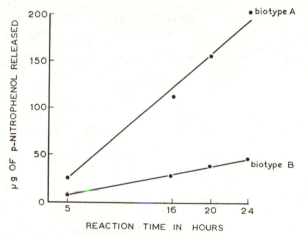

Fig. 12 β-glucosidase activity of 2000 larvae of *Hetero-dera rostochiensis* of biotypes A and B at pH 4.5. (After Wilski and Giebel, 1966)

whereas enzyme activity was much greater in another biotype and the necrotic response was evident (Wilski and Giebel, 1966. Fig. 12). Later experiments (Giebel and Wilski, 1970) indicated that the inhibition of destruction of IAA by phenolics was more pronounced in susceptible than in resistant potatoes. In both kinds of potato, β-glucosidase secreted by the nematode released IAA, kinetin and phenolic compounds from complexes. By the interaction of IAA oxidases and the phenolics, the IAA was destroyed. The difference in the rate of destruction between the resistant and susceptible varieties is attributed to differences in the kinds of phenolics and the activity of IAA oxidase. Consequently there is an increase of IAA in susceptible plants and a decrease in resistant plants. Whether syncytia or necrotic cells are formed is then determined by the balance between

IAA and kinetin; a preponderance of kinetin leads to a necrotic reaction. The hypothesis received further support by the demonstration that in resistant potatoes there is a higher ratio of mono- to polyphenols that inhibited IAA destruction only slightly, i.e. IAA decreased (Giebel, 1970).

At first sight the results of Dropkin and his colleagues (1969) are contradictory, for they found that by the exogenous application of kinetin they

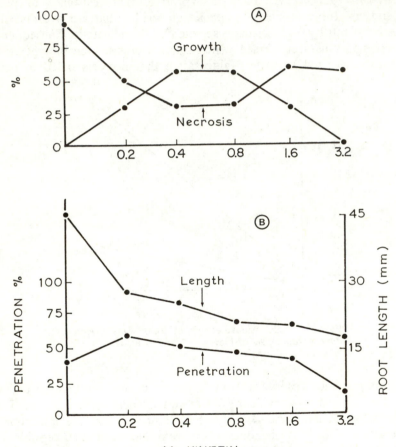

Fig. 13 The influence of kinetin on (A) larval growth and host cell necrosis and on (B) root length and larval penetration of roots. Twenty Y-91 tomato seedlings were incubated at 27 °C for 24 h on water-agar containing the appropriate kinetin concentrations. Fifteen larvae were added to each root, and the seedlings held at 27 °C for a further 4 days. Ordinate for growth (A) = (larvae showing growth/larvae within roots) × 100; Necrosis (A) = (larvae associated with necrosis/larvae within roots) × 100; Length B = root length in mm at end of experiments; Penetration (B) = (larvae within roots/larvae added) × 100. (After Dropkin et al., 1969)

could decrease the resistance of tomato to *Meloidogyne incognita* (Fig. 13). However, apart from the fact that Dropkin studied a different nematode and host plant, it is clear that the extent of reversal from resistance to susceptibility is dependent on cytokinin concentration, so without data to compare concentrations of cytokinins in both these experiments it is invalid to make comparisons. The chief message is that growth regulators are probably involved in the plant's response that gives resistance, that balances of growth regulators and phenolics may be important determinants of resistance, and that there are numerous biochemical reactions that precede and follow the visible necrotic response.

Discussion of the nature of resistance has so far only referred to hypersensitivity as a plant response that inhibits the nematode, but we have already seen that there is a whole spectrum of response from hypersensitivity to the highly adaptive response of syncytial formation in plants infected with *Meloidogyne* and *Heterodera*. To explain such interactions in biochemical terms is obviously beyond our comprehension at present. Furthermore, the question of specificity raises more problems. A plant which is resistant to one species may be susceptible to others. The soybean variety Peking is resistant to *Heterodera glycines* for example, but susceptible to *Pratylenchus brachyurus* and *P. zeae* (Endo, 1967). On the other hand soybean cultivars resistant to *Heterodera glycines* are also resistant to *Rotylenchulus reniformis*; presumably the same gene or linked genes are responsible for resistance to both species (Rebois *et al.*, 1970). Again, a few larvae of *Meloidogyne incognita* occasionally develop to maturity in roots of resistant tomato plants and do not incite the hypersensitive reaction. The reacting substances in the tomato are apparently not specific to the presence of all the nematodes but only to a portion of the population. Thus there appear to be two races each secreting a characteristic substance (Riggs and Winstead, 1959). In fact, there is probably a wealth of genetic diversity in both host and parasite that determines the parasite's fate (Dropkin and Webb, 1967) and, we might add, the plant's fate too. The polygenic nature of resistance in some plants to nematodes indicates the degree of complexity of the biochemical machinery with which plants are equipped to resist nematodes, e.g. in sugar beet infected with *Heterodera schachtii* (Curtis, 1970), in wild *Cucumis* (cantaloup) infected with *Meloidogyne incognita acrita* (Fassuliotis, 1970) and in *Nicotiana* infected with Osborne's cyst nematode (*Heterodera* sp.) (Baalaway and Fox, 1971). Furthermore, the possibility that nematode species may contain numerous biotypes, as in *Heterodera rostochiensis* (Jones and Pawelska, 1963), makes any explanation of the nature of resistance even more difficult. It is little wonder that van der Plank (1968) feels that the highly specific differential interactions between host and parasite that underlie vertical resistance are unlikely to be explained by such general host responses as hypersensitivity.

The problem of complexity was apparent in the discussions in previous chapters on tolerance, and physiological responses of the plant to infection, and we will meet it again when we consider the etiology of disease. However, it is not the purpose of the present discussion to present a depressing picture of insoluble complexity but rather to try and depict the degree of complexity and to suggest possible ways of dealing with it.

The best way I can depict the complexity of the plant's biochemical and physiological system is to imagine a hundred of those charts of metabolic pathways (that frequently adorn the biochemist's wall) joined together to form a complete picture of the plant's metabolic machinery. In the healthy uninfected plant, the machinery is busily working as essential chemicals enter the system and are manufactured into various other substances as the plant grows. At one point a foreign substance (such as a nematode secretion) enters the factory and immediately there are changes in the system; new substances are formed, alternative metabolic pathways are taken, the tempo of some processes increases, of others decreases, and these changes radiate outwards to influence every corner of the system. To make the picture more realistic we have to imagine that the nematode is also a metabolic factory of equal complexity and that the nematode and plant meet at several biochemical points. Changes in the plant's metabolic factory at the points of union with the nematode may be such as to inhibit further disturbance by the nematode, or the changes may enable materials to flow from the plant to the nematode as materials flow in the other direction. In some associations between nematode and plant the change in activity may be localized in a few metabolic pathways, in others it may reverberate through the whole system. The introduction of a further factor into the plant system (such as a cytokinin) may so alter the stream of metabolic events that the relationship between plant and nematode is altered (from resistance to susceptibility).

If the picture I have drawn is anything like nature we might expect that many of the changes we observe in infected plants are just consequences and not directly involved in resisting the nematode. Such consequences may be closely correlated with the resistance response, they may even be an essential part of it, but they may have no influence on the nematode's physiology. In fact, there is little evidence of how nematodes are inhibited in resistant plants. The substances formed by polymerization during the browning reaction may be toxic to nematodes but there is little evidence for this; the necrotic response described by Giebel and Wilski (1970) may be several biochemical reactions away from the point where the nematode is actually inhibited. Perhaps the closest we get to an example of this proximity between nematode and plant is the toxic glycoside released by the Mary Washington variety of asparagus that appears to inhibit the nematode by inhibiting its acetylcholinesterase (Rohde, 1960).

We can of course recognize and measure resistance, and study its genetics of inheritance, without understanding how it works. For this reason changes in the plant that are correlated with resistance, like the degree of necrosis or the increase in numbers of the nematode or the amount of a particular chemical such as a phytoalexin, are particularly useful.

One way in which the problem of complexity might be tackled is to study isolated parts of the system in the healthy and infected plant until a point is reached when we put the pieces together to form a whole like a jigsaw. But the analogy is false; the plant is not made up of discrete inter-locking pieces; it more closely resembles the web that we have mentioned already. The web is characterized by the multitude of interconnecting strands just as the plant's biochemical machinery is a web of chemical interactions, and unlike the jigsaw there are an unlimited number of ways in which the strands might conceivably be assembled. However, out of all these possible patterns there are very few that work in any way like the real thing. Let us assume that there is a large amount of information on the biochemical relationship of a nematode and its host. We can imagine how the two machines might work and interact, in fact we can express our ideas in the form of a diagram, a flow chart, which shows how the various components in the two systems operate. We might call this diagram a conceptual hypothesis because it expresses our ideas on relationships without much evidence to support them. To test the hypothesis we can use a computer to see how change in the input to the model influences the output, whether, for example, a given number of nematodes attacking a plant results in a particular yield from the host after the initial event of nematode invasion has set in motion trains of biochemical changes that traverse the metabolic web. By manipulation of the variables in the model supported by experimental data to ensure that such manipulations are biologically realistic, we eventually arrive at a model of the host-parasite system that works in a similar way to the system in real life. This approach to the understanding of complexity involves the subject of systems simulation and cybernetics, new subjects that have hardly touched plant nematology. This approach is attractive because there is new purpose in doing experiments in plant-parasite relations; experimental data can be used to formulate better conceptual hypotheses and at the same time incorporate more reliable relationships into the model. The concepts of tolerance and resistance become a natural property of the models through the feedforward and feedback loops that contribute to stability of the system. Furthermore the model, if it is not too complicated, can have an explanatory role and reduce complexity to a level which we can grasp.

References

ABAWI, G.S., VAN ETTEN, H.D. and MAI, W.F. (1971). Phaseollin production induced by *Pratylenchus penetrans* in *Phaseolus vulgaris*. *J. Nematology*, **3**, 301. (Abstract.)

ACEDO, J.R. and ROHDE, R.A. (1971). Histochemical root pathology of *Brassica oleracea capitata* L. infected by *Pratylenchus penetrans* (Cobb) Filipjev and Schuurmans Stekhoven (Nematoda: Tylenchidae) *J. Nematology*, **3**, 62.

ALBERSHEIM, P. and ANDERSON, A.J. (1971). Proteins from plant cell walls inhibit polygalacturonases secreted by plant pathogens. *Proc. Nat. Acad. Sci. U.S.A.*, **68**, 1815.

BAALAWAY, H.A. and FOX, J.A. (1971). Resistance of Osborne's cyst nematode in selected *Nicotiana* species. *J. Nematology*, **3**, 395.

BALDWIN, J.G. and BARKER, K.R. (1970). Histopathology of corn hybrids infected with root knot nematode *Meloidogyne incognita*. *Phytopathology*, **60**, 1195.

CRUICKSHANK, I.A.M. (1963). Phytoalexins. *Ann. Rev. Phytopath*, **1**, 351.

CURTIS, G.J. (1970). Resistance of sugar beet to the cyst-nematode *Heterodera schachtii* Schm. *Ann. appl. Biol.*, **66**, 169.

DALY, J.M., SEEVERS, P.M. and LUDDEN, P. (1970). Studies on wheat stem rust resistance controlled at the Sr 6 locus. 3. Ethylene and disease reaction. *Phytopathology*, **60**, 1648.

DAULTON, R.A.C. and CURTIS, R.F. (1963). The effects of *Tagetes* spp. on *Meloidogyne javanica* in Southern Rhodesia. *Nematologica*, **9**, 357.

DE MAESENEER, J. (1964). Leaf-browning of *Ficus* spp., new host plants of *Aphelenchoides fragariae* (Ritzema Bos.). *Nematologica*, **10**, 403.

DROPKIN, V.H., HELGESON, J.P. and UPPER, C.D. (1969). The hypersensitivity reaction of tomatoes resistant to *Meloidogyne incognita*: Reversal by cytokinins *J. Nematology*, **1**, 55.

DROPKIN, V.H. and WEBB, R.E. (1967). Resistance of axenic tomato seedlings to *Meloidogyne incognita acrita* and to *M. hapla*. *Phytopathology*, **57**, 584.

EHRLICH, M.A. and EHRLICH, H.G. (1971). Fine structure of the host-parasite interfaces in mycoparasitism. *Ann. Rev. Phytopath.*, **9**, 155.

ENDO, B.Y. (1967). Comparative population increase of *Pratylenchus brachyurus* and *P. zeae* in corn and soybean varieties Lee and Peking. *Phytopathology*, **57**, 118.

ENDO, B.Y. and VEECH, J.A. (1970). Morphology and histochemistry of soybean roots infected with *Heterodera glycines*. *Phytopathology*, **60**, 1493.

FASSULIOTIS, G. (1970). Resistance of *Cucumis* spp. to the root-knot nematode *Meloidogyne incognita*. *J. Nematology*, **2**, 174.

FRANK, J.A. and PAXTON, J.D. (1971). An inducer of soybean phytoalexin and its role in the resistance of soybeans to *Phytophthora* rot. *Phytopathology*, **61**, 954.

GARRETT, S.D. (1970). *Pathogenic root-infecting fungi*. Cambridge University Press, xi + 294 pp.

GIEBEL, J. (1970). Phenolic content in roots of some Solanaceae and its influence on IAA-oxidase activity as an indicator of resistance to *Heterodera rostochiensis*. *Nematologica*, **16**, 22.

GIEBEL, J. and WILSKI, A. (1970). The role of IAA-oxidase in potato resistance to *Heterodera rostochiensis*. *Proc. IX-th Int. Nemat. Symp. Warsaw Sept.* 1967, 524 pp.

GRIFFIN, G.D. and WAITE, W.W. (1971). Attraction of *Ditylenchus dipsaci* and *Meloidogyne hapla* by resistant and susceptible alfalfa seedlings. *J. Nematology*, **3**, 215.

HADWIGER, L.E. and SCHWOCHAN, M.E. (1969). Host resistance responses—an induction hypothesis. *Phytopathology*, **59**, 223.

HUSSEY, R.S. and KRUSBERG, L.R. (1968). Histopathology of resistant reactions in Alaska pea seedlings to two populations of *Ditylenchus dipsaci*. *Phytopathology*, **58**, 1305.

HUSSEY, R.S. and KRUSBERG, L.R. (1970). Histopathology of and oxidative enzyme patterns in Wando peas infected with two populations of *Ditylenchus dipsaci*. *Phytopathology*, **60**, 1818.

JATALA, P. and RUSSELL, C.C. (1972). Nature of sweet potato resistance to *Meloidogyne incognita* and the effects of temperature on parasitism. *J. Nematology*, **4**, 1.

JONES, F.G.W., PARROTT, D.M. and ROSS, G.J.S. (1967). The population genetics of the potato cyst-nematode, *Heterodera rostochiensis*: mathematical models to simulate the effects of growing eelworm-resistant potatoes bred from *Solanum tuberosum* ssp. *andigena*. *Ann. appl. Biol.*, **60**, 151.

JONES, F.G.W. and PAWELSKA, K. (1963). The behaviour of populations of potato-root eelworm (*Heterodera rostochiensis* Woll.) towards some resistant tuberous and other *Solanum* species. *Ann. appl. Biol.*, **51**, 277.

KOSUGE, T. (1969). The role of phenolics in host response to infection. *Ann. Rev. Phytopath.*, **7**, 195.

MATTA, A. (1971). Microbial penetration and immunization of uncongenial host plants. *Ann. Rev. Phytopath.*, **9**, 387.

NUSBAUM, C.J. and BARKER, K.R. (1971). Population dynamics. In *Plant Parasitic Nematodes*. Edited by B.M. Zuckerman, W.F. Mai and R.A. Rohde. Vol. 2. Academic Press, xvi + 347 pp.

REBOIS, R.V., EPPS, J.M. and HARTWIG, E.E. (1970). Correlation of resistance in soybeans to *Heterodera glycines* and *Rotylenchulus reniformis*. *Phytopathology*, **60,** 695.

REYNOLDS, H.W., CARTER, W.W. and O'BANNON, J.H. (1970). Symptomless resistance of alfalfa to *Meloidogyne incognita acrita*. *J. Nematology*, **2,** 131.

RIGGS, R.D. and WINSTEAD, N.N. (1959). Studies on resistance in tomato to root-knot nematodes and on the occurrence of pathogenic biotypes. *Phytopathology*, **49,** 716.

ROHDE, R.A. (1960). Acetylcholinesterase in plant-parasitic nematodes and an anticholinesterase from asparagus. *Proc. Helm. Soc. Wash.*, **27,** 121.

SEINHORST, J.W. (1966). The relationships between population increase and population density in plant parasitic nematodes. 1. Introduction and migratory nematodes. *Nematologica*, **12,** 157.

SEINHORST, J.W. (1967). The relationships between population increase and population density in plant parasitic nematodes. 3. Definition of the terms host, host status and resistance. 4. The influence of external conditions on the regulation of population density. *Nematologica*, **13,** 429.

SIDDIQUI, I.A. (1971). Comparative penetration and development of *Meloidogyne naasi* in wheat and oat roots. *Nematologica*, **17,** 566.

SINGH, N.D. and NORTON, D.C. (1970). Variability in host-parasite relationships of *Heterodera trifolii*. *Phytopathology*, **60,** 1834.

TRUDGILL, D.L. and PARROTT, D.M. (1969). The behaviour of nine populations of the potato cyst nematode *Heterodera rostochiensis* towards three resistant potato hybrids. *Nematologica*, **15,** 381.

URITANI, I. (1971). Protein changes in diseased plants. *Ann. Rev. Phytopathology*, **9,** 211.

VAN DER PLANK, J.E. (1968). *Disease resistance in plants*. Academic Press, x + 206 pp.

VAN ETTEN, H.D. and BATEMAN, D.F. (1971). Studies on the mode of action of the phytoalexin phaseolin. *Phytopathology*, **61,** 1363.

VAN GUNDY, S.D. and KIRKPATRICK, J.D. (1964). Nature of resistance in certain citrus rootstocks to citrus nematode. *Phytopathology*, **54,** 419.

WALLACE, H.R. (1961a). Browning of chrysanthemum leaves infested with *Aphelenchoides ritzemabosi*. *Nematologica*. **6,** 7.

WALLACE, H.R. (1961b). The nature of resistance in chrysanthemum varieties to *Aphelenchoides ritzemabosi*. *Nematologica*, **6,** 49.

WATSON, I.A. (1970). Changes in virulence and population shifts in plant pathogens. *Ann. Rev. Phytopath.*, **8,** 209.

WEBER, D.J. and STAHMANN, M.A. (1966). Induced immunity to *Ceratocystis* infection in sweetpotato root tissue. *Phytopathology*, **56,** 1066.

WEBSTER, J.M. (1967) The influence of plant-growth substances and their inhibitors on the host-parasite relationships of *Aphelenchoides ritzema-bosi* in culture. *Nematologica*, **13,** 256.

WEBSTER, J.M. (1969). The host-parasite relationships of plant-parasitic nematodes. *Adv. Parasitol.*, **7,** 1.

WHEELER, H. and HANCHEY, P. (1968). Permeability phenomena in plant disease. *Ann. Rev. Phytopath.*, **6,** 331.

WILSKI, A. and GIEBEL, J. (1966). β-glucosidase in *Heterodera rostochiensis* and its significance in resistance of potato to this nematode. *Nematologica*, **12,** 219.

WOOD, R.K.S. (1967). *Physiological plant pathology*. Blackwells Sci. Publ., xi + 570 pp.

6 The distribution and abundance of nematodes

The amount of disturbance in a host by parasites and the subsequent response of the host are influenced to a large extent by the distribution of the parasites in the host. Their occurrence in a particular organ or tissue and their concentration at particular sites may profoundly affect the course of disease. Outside the host, the distribution of parasites in the soil, air, water or other plants may determine which individuals in the host population become infected and which escape. Distribution of parasites is thus an important aspect of disease and even casual observation indicates that they are seldom distributed uniformly within or outside the host. Hence, we refer to intestinal worms, liver flukes, root-rot fungi, leaf and stem nematodes and so on; there are certain sites where they are particularly prominent and others often close by, where they seem to be absent.

This is not to say, however, that uniform distribution never occurs. The distribution of eggs in the *Heterodera* cyst may approach uniformity whereas the distribution of cysts on the host root may be non-uniform. Similarly, animals with strong territorial behaviour may have a fairly uniform distribution, although it may be non-uniform over a larger area. Non-uniform distribution may be of two general types, random and clumped, and of the two, clumped distribution is the most common in nature. Thus, it appears that where living organisms occur in space is not simply a question of chance, there are factors which influence their distribution. As organisms have particular requirements for resources and can only function efficiently between certain limits of the numerous environmental components, it is not surprising that they tend to have a patchy distribution, because the environmental components themselves are usually distributed in a non-uniform fashion. Furthermore, behavioural characteristics of organisms may lead to a patchy distribution where individuals attract each other or to a more uniform distribution when they repel each other and occupy a particular territory.

One way to determine the nature of the distribution of a parasite is to take many small samples of the area or volume under consideration and see

Plate 8 (above) Influence of *Ditylenchus dipsaci* on oats. Left hand plant un-infested; right hand plant infested, showing swelling of the shoot bases and increased tillering. (Reproduced by permission of Rothamsted Experimental Station)

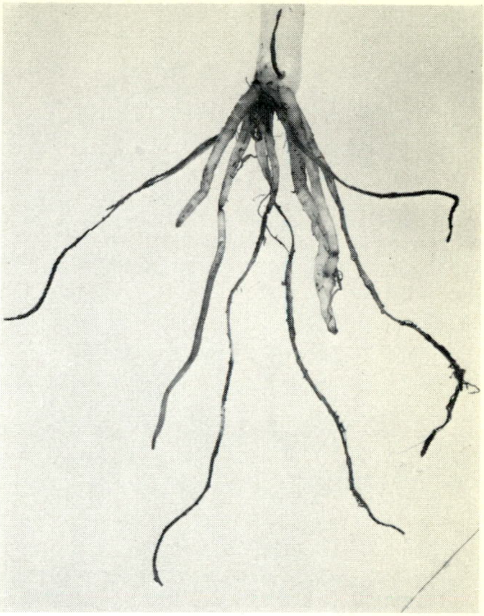

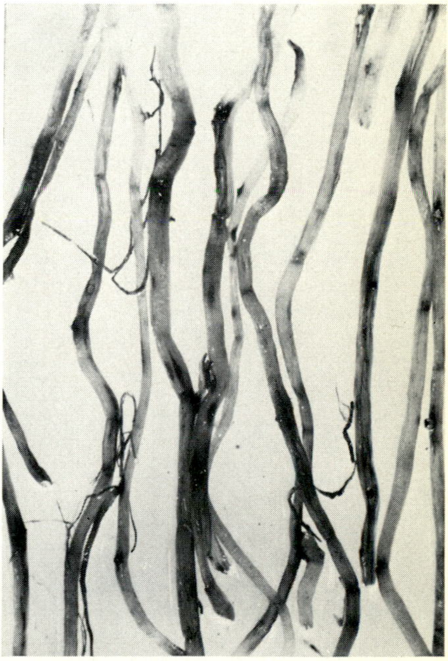

Plate 9 (top right) Destruction of roots of a young banana seedling by *Radopholus similis.* (Reproduced by permission of New South Wales Dept. of Agriculture)

Plate 10 (bottom right) Lesions on cotton roots caused by *Belonolaimus gracilis.* (Reproduced by permission of T. W. Graham)

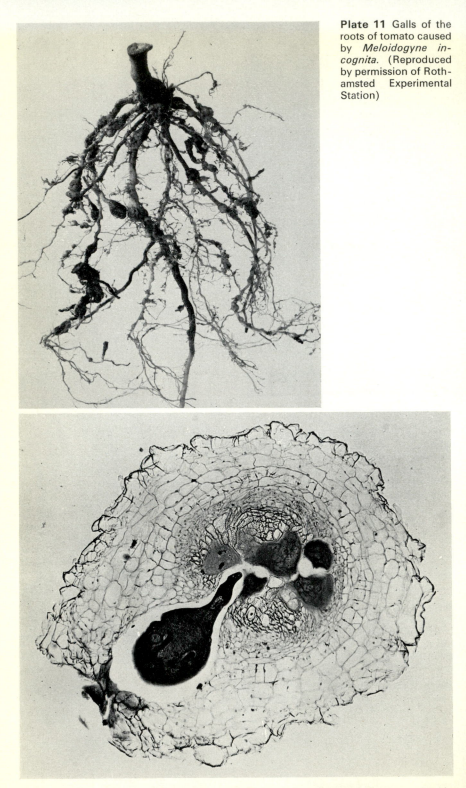

Plate 12 Transverse section of tomato root showing female *Meloidogyne sp.* Darkly stained giant cells are grouped near the head of the nematode. (Reproduced by permission of Rothamsted Experimental Station)

whether the data conform to the Poisson distribution, if they do the parasites are randomly distributed. One of the features of the Poisson series is that the mean equals the variance. If the variance is less than the mean, then the distribution is more uniform than random, and if the variance is greater than the mean, the distribution is more patchy than random.

The distribution of the patchy population can often be expressed as a negative binomial. This distribution is described by two parameters, the mean and the exponent k which is a measure of the degree of patchiness. Generally values of k are in the region of 2; as they become larger the distribution approaches and is eventually identical with that of the Poisson, whilst fractional values of k lead into the logarithmic series (Southwood, 1968).

Let us now look at some of the things the animal parasitologists and the plant pathologists have to say about kinds of distribution and their causes.

Some aspects of distribution

In animal hosts, specificity is determined by innate or natural resistance and the immune response, and it seems likely that the same factors decide where the parasite will exist within the host. Variations in the environmental components of the animal intestine such as pH, CO_2 and concentration and nature of food substrate may also influence distribution within the host. Read (1971), for example, describes the small intestine as an environment where organic compounds are regularly secreted into the intestinal lumen and subsequently reabsorbed, where there are linear gradients of pH, oxidation-reduction potential and certain chemical components, where the chemical nature of the region near the mucosa differs from the central lumen and where there is a high degree of regulation. There is also evidence that there is a circulation of nitrogen compounds from the body into the intestine with a subsequent reabsorption, and that there are concentration gradients of amino acids and bile salts. Clearly, the vertebrate digestive tract is a complex environment and not merely 'a tube running through the body', as Read puts it. Consequently, it is not surprising to find that several species of parasitic nematodes, each with specific requirements, can coexist in the same intestine but in different parts of it. The distribution of species of the nematode *Tachygonetria* differs radially and longitudinally in the colon of the tortoise, *Testudo graeca* and, even where their distribution overlaps, their different feeding habits ensure coexistence (Schad, 1963). Similarly, the nematodes *Strongyloides ratti* and *S. venezuelensis* occupy different parts of the same rat intestine (Wertheim, 1970). A cestode and an acanthocephalan living in the same intestine of a stickleback fish have different preferences for feeding sites. From studies of the separate distribution of the two parasites it is apparent that their distributions overlap whereas, in concurrent infections, their distributions are more restricted indicating a possible interference between the two species (Chappell, 1969). Comparable data from plant pathology is sparse. There is little information on the micro-environment within the plant that influences the endo-parasite. We know little of how much changes in soil conditions are reflected by changes within the plant close to the parasite. There is little information on the relationships between biochemical and physical gradients within roots and the distribution of endoparasites. We do know that plants are frequently infected by more than one parasite and that they often interact so that one parasite is suppressed. In fact, Rishbeth (1963) achieved successful control of the wood-rotting fungus *Fomes annosus* in pine stumps by inoculating the stumps with the oidia of *Peniophora gigantea*, another fungus. Here, *F. annosus* was suppressed because *P. gigantea* was a successful competitor in that it consumed nutrients (cellulose and lignin) that are also required by *F. annosus*. There are also numerous references in the literature to antagonism, antibiosis and fungistasis, but little mention of how such processes might influence the distribution of parasites within the host plant. In the soil at least, the contrary opinion has been expressed that competition is unlikely to occur between many species of micro-organisms. Thus, Clark (1965) suggests that food specialization makes possible the existence of a large number of ecological niches within the soil. Clark goes on to say that even in such a restricted and specialized habitat as the rhizoplane of an individual plant, it is probable that most of the microbial species that are present therein are not competitive.

In spite of Clark's opinion it seems advisable that, when we consider the distribution of nematodes in plants, we should be aware of the possibility of interactions between different species. Even individuals of the same species may influence each other if, during feeding, fluids from the host's tissues are released that attract other individuals to the same place. Conversely, overcrowding may repel others from the feeding site. Such factors probably contribute to the non-random patchy distribution of parasites in the host and within particular organs of the host. To understand such distribution it is necessary to understand not only the parasite's requirements but the variable nature of the environment within the host.

There may even be a patchy distribution of parasites in tissues which appear to be fairly uniform. Thus, the nematode *Nippostrongylus brasiliensis* occurs in clumps within the small intestine of the rat because of thigmo-kinetic responses and sexual attraction (Alphey, 1970).

The picture of the distribution of a parasite within the host at any one time is one frame, so to speak, in a long film showing a continuous series of arrivals and departures, of localized movement and of accumulation and disintegration of localized populations. The rate of such activity is influenced by the innate ability of the parasite to move, its speed of locomotion and its responses to various stimuli. Dispersal is thus an important feature of distribution. Dispersal may be passive when parasites are carried in the gut contents or the blood stream to a particular site where features of the environment elicit the response of attachment and feeding. Other parasites, using their power of locomotion, may have a long and devious route through various organs and tissues of the host before they finally establish themselves. The systemic spread of viruses through the host plant, the passive movement of fungal spores in the plant's translocation stream and the growth of fungal mycelium through leaf and root tissues are similar, if less dramatic, processes. In both parasitology and plant pathology however, little is known of the factors or stimuli that determine the direction a parasite will move in the host or where it will eventually settle. In other words, the distribution of motile parasites in an animal or plant may be known but the preceding events are largely unknown.

The environment of the pasture, the river, the forest or the crop may seem a far cry from intestines, livers, xylem and phloem but basically the problem of distribution follows the same ecological principles. In attempting to explain the distribution of a parasite, say a nematode in a pasture, we need to know whether the distribution of individuals is random or uniform or clumped. We need to know whether the distribution of components in the nematode's environment account for the nematode's distribution. Are levels of soil moisture, density of plants, soil temperature, concentration of host faeces and the numbers of other organisms significantly correlated with the numbers of nematodes? We also need to know what the nematodes' requirements are for food and how the environmental factors influence their locomotion, reproduction, survival and invasion of the host. Their behavioural responses to temperature and moisture gradients may also be important.

Most likely, the frequency distribution of such nematodes will be patchy, as Donald (1967) found for strongyloid larvae. The variance of the population was substantially greater than the mean indicating a non-random patchy distribution. Environment being what it is, we might expect most parasites, fungi, bacteria or nematodes, whatever their hosts, to be distributed in the soil or above ground in a patchy fashion.

The distribution of diseased plants or animals in a host population is worth mentioning too, because it raises the question—why are some animals or plants infected, whereas others seem to escape? With plants, the distribution of disease may be correlated with the distribution of the pathogen, or there may be some other factor in the environment that favours invasion or predisposes the host to disease. The helminth parasites in long-tailed field mice from Wales tend to have a clumped distribution (Lewis, 1968). The frequency distribution of the cestode *Caryophyllaeus laticeps* in a population of the fish *Leuciscus leuciscus* (dace) was independent of the size of the fish, but greater numbers occurred in the females because of variations in feeding habits between the sexes. The negative binomial appeared to give a satisfactory model of the parasites' patchy distribution (Kennedy, 1968). The study of aerial photographs such as those of Brenchley (1968) emphasize the non-random and non-uniform nature of the patterns of diseased plants in space.

So far we have used the word distribution in a somewhat indiscriminate way to describe the relative occurrence of parasites in space whether it be a continuum like soil or a discontinuous environment like fish. However, we could study the distribution of parasites in relation to soil type or, in the case of the dace, in relation to feeding behaviour. In such studies, we might find a closer correlation between clay content of the soil and numbers of nematodes, and a close association between feeding behaviour and numbers of cestodes. In other words, we have accounted for most of the observed variation in spatial distribution in terms of some environmental factor or behavioural characteristic. This procedure, as we will see later when we discuss etiology, plays an important part in the search for causes of disease. It helps, as Brenchley (1968) says, to determine the nature and sources of disease and, by revealing correlations with environmental factors, to indicate possible methods of avoiding or controlling it.

The quantitative relationships between parasites and their hosts that produce non-random distributions, such as the negative binomial, have been discussed by Crofton (1971) who indicates the sorts of events that might give such distributions. These are worth repeating here because they may suggest what we might look for in plants and their nematode parasites. These events are:

(1) As a result of a series of exposures to infection in which each exposure is random but the chances of infection differ at each exposure or wave of infection.
(2) As a result of infective stages not being randomly distributed.
(3) As a result of infection increasing or decreasing the chance of further infection occurring.
(4) As a result of the variation in host individuals which makes the chances of infection unequal.
(5) As a result of the chance of infection of individual hosts changing with time.

These situations are obviously relevant to plant nematodes and their hosts.

Little need be said about geographical distribution of parasites or their diseased hosts because basically it is similar in the ecological sense to distribution within the individual host, in the host population and in a local land area such as a field, orchard or county. The only difference lies in the environmental components that determine distribution and dispersal. That we are once again faced with patchy distribution is evident in many of the maps produced in the supplements of the *Plant Disease Reporter* that show the distribution of many important plant parasites in the U.S.A. There are also many suggestions on the factors that might influence such distributions. Holdeman (1970), for example, found that two bacterial diseases of Persian walnut, bark canker and phloem canker were widespread in California's hot central valley. He suggested that the absence of susceptible varieties and cool summer temperatures were the major factors limiting their geographical distribution to the central valley. Thus, in geographical distribution we may relate the incidence of a parasite to the distribution of its host, temperature, rainfall, altitude, direction of prevailing winds, day-length, vectors, the human population and human activities, whereas in an orchard we are more concerned with the distribution of trees, soil type, soil moisture, drainage, salinity, soil fertility and so on. In other words the scale of the area in which distribution is being measured is matched by the scale of variation in the environmental components that determine distribution, e.g. rainfall is unlikely to determine the distribution of diseased plants within a one-acre (0.4047 hectare) field but rainfall may be a very important factor influencing distribution in a country the size of Australia with its rain forests and deserts. The same can be said of temperature and other climatic factors, plant distribution and the distribution of human populations. Within such large geographic areas there are smaller areas in which distribution of pathogens and diseased hosts is also patchy because of variations in the environmental factors just mentioned. We can in fact continue to study distribution and environmental variability in even smaller areas until we reach a clod of soil or the individual plant. Thus, there are patches within patches within patches, and to account for the distribution of an organism within any area we need to look for environmental factors that have a similar degree of variability within the area.

As well as distribution in space we can also speak of the distribution of parasites with respect to time. Just as the distribution of parasites and diseased plants may be non-random or patchy in space, so can they be non-randomly distributed in time. Numbers of organisms fluctuate as the seasons change. To take just a few examples: cercariae of digenetic trematodes have peaks of infection in snails in June and August in South Wales, and Pike (1968) attributes the cause of the fluctuations to seasonal variations in rainfall, temperature and the numbers of the intermediate host. Seasonal changes in the infection of dace by the cestode *Proteocephalus torulosus* were attributed to seasonal variations in the river temperature (Kennedy and Hine, 1969). In plant pathology, annual cycles in the density of parasites are common; their numbers go up regularly in the summer and down in the winter or vice versa. The variation in density from year to year often varies considerably however, and one of the chief problems in epidemiology is to account for this variability in terms of the variation in environmental components. Weather often plays a large part. With some parasites their numbers are so largely determined by weather that forecasts of 'good' and 'bad' years can be made. For example, weather is a predominant factor in controlling the incidence of potato blight and the downy mildews and prediction systems now operate for these parasites (Bourke, 1970). The question is—does the rise and fall of populations occur in a manner which is more regular or less regular than would be expected by random chance? In some vertebrates, the oscillations in numbers with time are *less* regular than would occur in a random series, thus, like patchy distribution in space, distribution of these animals in time is excessively irregular, there being a lack of periodicity in the phase of the oscillations. And, like patchy distribution, we have to look for environmental factors that account for such irregular oscillations. At the other extreme there are variations in numbers with time that are non-random because they are highly regular or periodic. The maxima and minima occur at similar intervals and if the intervals are very close we can call the oscillations a cyclical series, especially if the heights of the peaks and troughs are also similar. Bliss (1958) provides a very useful paper on periodic regression in biology and climatology. Andrewartha and Birch (1954) also discuss this aspect of distribution in detail and with clarity; they suggest that it is best to attempt to explain all the variability in the recorded numbers of animals and to take into account all the environmental components that seem relevant. Studies of the long series of records for animals may be alluring, but in the future, progress may depend on getting more precise information about the animals themselves and their environments.

Such advice is certainly applicable to plant nematology where it is necessary to unravel the ecological factors that determine the numbers of nematodes if we are to ascertain the role nematodes play as causes of disease in plants.

In looking for those factors that influence the fluctuation of numbers of parasites and diseased plants with time we have to consider the direct influence of seasonal changes in environment on the parasites' various activities—hatching, spore-germination, migration, wind dispersal, survival and so on. Included in the parasite's environment is the plant itself which is also subject to its own environment, plus those inherent temporal changes such as maturation and senescence and, if we are studying animal nematodes, pregnancy in animals that have a profound influence on their parasites. Furthermore the parasite itself may have adaptations such as diapause or response to host exudates that integrate its growth and development with that of the host. In looking at the distribution of parasites with respect to time, it is likely therefore, that there will be many examples of a regular periodicity because the parasite is so closely dependent on another organism, the host, which in the case of annual plants at least, may have an essentially cyclical existence. In other words we might expect the populations of a nematode to have regular oscillations if it lives in association with a wheat crop that is grown continuously on the same land. On the other hand, variations in weather may impose differences, directly or indirectly, through the plants on the heights of the peaks and troughs of nematode numbers between different years.

When it comes to dispersal over larger distances such as between fields or orchards plant parasites, unlike insects, are not particularly adept at migrating under their own locomotory powers. Yet disperse they must if they are not to become overcrowded nor succumb to one of those extremes in environment such as drought that occurs in every locality now and again. Ability to disperse is thus an important factor in the survival of any organism, parasites included, and it has an important influence on their distribution.

Although parasites, like nematodes that infect animals, are not particularly mobile at least their hosts are, so they are transported from place to place and dispersed in the hosts' faeces. Plant parasites, on the other hand, have immobile hosts, so the problem of dispersal is even more acute. Consequently, there is a greater dependence on passive dispersal by wind, water or other animals including man himself. Even with actively moving animals like insects that sometimes migrate in particular directions and can detect their food plants at considerable distances, the process of locating their food is a chancy business. With parasites that disperse passively it is even more chancy, hence the production of large numbers of infective propagules which, it is argued, increase the chance of infection occurring. The much discussed topic of inoculum potential is based on this idea. Thus, according to Dimond and Horsfall (1965), the sizable numbers required to start an infection reflect the distribution of inoculum over many sites that are not susceptible, and competition for susceptible sites by more than one unit of inoculum. Rather than setting a threshold for the number of fungal spores required to produce a lesion, it is better to say that infection is chancy. Most nematodes, unlike the spores referred to by

Horsfall and Dimond, live underground all their life so the chances of dispersal, even passive dispersal, are further reduced. On the other hand, plant nematodes like fungal zoospores and some bacteria are motile and can orientate towards host roots, hence, because of the adaptations, infection is less chancy, but we will consider the question of adaptation in the next chapter. Now let us look at the distribution and abundance of plant nematodes bearing in mind the various ideas and approaches of parasitologists and plant pathologists.

The distribution and abundance of plant nematodes

The distribution and abundance of an organism are only two aspects of the same problem, as Andrewartha (1970) has pointed out. Thus, the environmental components that determine the limits of distribution of a species are the same as those that determine the numbers of individuals within the area of their distribution. This is an important point because, whenever we read about the influence of environment on the population density of a particular nematode, we are at the same time being presented with information about the distribution of the nematode. Distribution of nematodes in space is thus a consequence of environmental influence; in a later chapter we will discuss the influence of environment from another point of view, the incidence and intensity of disease in the host.

WITHIN THE HOST

The picture of a parasite invading an animal host and then proceeding along a route through the body until it eventually reaches a place where it settles down, is not applicable to most plant nematodes, even those that migrate within the host tissues. Thus, distribution within the plant is often closely related to the invasion site. Kirkpatrick and his colleagues (1964) have explained that many plant nematodes show a preference for feeding or penetration at particular zones on the root and at specific stages in the root's ontogeny. Some species prefer the meristem, some the zone of elongation and others the region of maturation. Preferences are also shown for tissues and cells within a particular region of the root, e.g. the apical meristem, the epidermis, the cortex or the stele. The distribution of larvae of *Heterodera schachtii* in the roots of rape (*Brassica rapus*) and sugar beet (*Beta vulgaris*) was determined by Kampfe (1960) who examined the root tips, the points of origin of lateral roots and intervening regions separately. Although similar numbers occurred in these three regions, the larvae were clumped in groups at the points of origin of lateral roots thus giving a patchy distribution within the whole root system. Presumably sites of lateral root formation are particularly attractive to migrating larvae of *H. schachtii*. Kinloch and Allen (1972) provide us with another example of differential attraction and invasion; *Meloidogyne hapla* is not attracted to and does not invade galled tissue of tomato roots to the same extent as *M. javanica*. Consequently, there is a more rapid invasion of the host by *M. javanica* and, in a population containing both species, *M. javanica* is likely to predominate and its distribution in the host is likely to be more widespread.

Although distribution of nematodes within the plant is probably influenced to a large extent by preferences for particular types of tissue, it would be wrong to assume that other factors are of little importance. Thus, *Heterodera trifolii* is usually found in the roots of its host but Ross (1960) found cysts of this species on both surfaces of white clover leaves. Giant cells were formed, so presumably development proceeded in a similar way to that in the root. *Meloidogyne incognita* can cause galls on the leaves of *Siderasis (Tradescantia) fuscata*. The galls contained adult females, viable eggs and larvae; giant cells were formed; what is more, the roots were not infected (Miller and Di Edwardo, 1962). Similarly, Wong and Willetts (1969) describe the formation of galls in the aerial parts of tomato, French bean and *Capsicum* seedlings inoculated with *Meloidogyne javanica*. In these species at least, distribution within the host is not restricted by tissue specificity; more likely, it is influenced by the inability of the nematodes to migrate to and invade the leaves, except on those few occasions when the leaves touch the soil. Wallace and Doncaster (1964) have suggested that nematodes can be divided arbitrarily into three groups; those that are active enough to swim in deep water; those like *Ditylenchus* and *Aphelenchoides* that can swim in thick water films, escape from the soil and ascend plants above ground level; finally, those that are too inactive to swim, the crawlers, which are largely confined to the soil. Furthermore, the nematodes that have the propulsive power to escape from the soil are able to survive desiccation for long periods. They can therefore tolerate exposure to dry conditions when they are exposed to the air on the plant surface. Thus, locomotory activity and adaptations for survival can be added to the list of factors that influence the distribution of nematodes within the host plant.

The presence of other organisms within the same host plant may also influence the distribution of a nematode species. This is an obvious statement, however it is less obvious how frequently it happens. Judging by the large number of papers on coexistence, antagonism, synergism and association between nematodes and other pathogens in diseased plants, it seems likely that such situations are common. Slack (1963), for example, goes as far as to say that in soil especially, the single organism—plant relationship does not exist. The same may be true within the host.

The invasion of and development within virus-infected plants may be different from that in uninfected plants. Bird (1969), for example, has shown that more larvae of *Meloidogyne javanica* invade beans infected with tomato ring-spot virus than virus-free controls, although subsequent growth of the nematodes was the same in both sets of plants. In tomatoes infected with tobacco mosaic virus on the other hand, rate of invasion of *M. javanica* was similar to that in virus-free plants but the nematodes grew more rapidly. It seems likely that some change in the physiology of the host has a marked influence on the nematode as a consequence of a virus—host interaction.

Plants infected with fungi have similar influences on nematodes. In some associations the numbers of the nematode are reduced. Thus, in a study of the association between the causal fungus of brown root rot of tomatoes and *Heterodera rostochiensis*, James (1968) demonstrated that the nematode did not increase the susceptibility of the roots to invasion by the fungus, however, the fungus decreased the rate of hatch and invasion by the nematode and the number of new cysts that were subsequently produced. James suggested that the fungus possibly produced a factor that inhibited the nematode. Ketudat (1969) studied the same nematode and plant and showed that *Rhizoctonia solani*, *Verticillium albo-atrum* and a 'grey sterile fungus' caused an increase in the ratio of males to females. Such a response usually indicates that the nematode is unable to get sufficient quantities of some resource, i.e. it is under stress, and Ketudat suggests that the resource in short supply is space within the root for development (Fig. 14). Similarly *Fusarium oxysporum* in sugar beet seedlings appears to inhibit invasion and development of *Heterodera schachtii* (Jorgenson, 1970).

There is plenty of evidence that the numbers of nematodes in a plant increase when another parasite is present. Higher populations of *Heterodera glycines* developed in soybeans grown in soil infested with *Fusarium* than in *Fusarium*-free soil (Ross, 1965). Significantly higher numbers of *Pratylenchus penetrans* occurred in egg-plant roots infected with *Verticillium albo-atrum* than occurred in plants without the fungus (McKeen and Mountain, 1960). Similarly *Verticillium dahliae* in egg-plant and tomato was associated with an increased rate of reproduction of *P. penetrans* (Mountain and McKeen, 1962). The authors suggest that the nematodes are influenced by changes in the physiology of the host plant induced by the parasitic activities of the fungus. What sort of parasitic activities is not known but Tu and Cheng (1971) put forward the hypothesis that a small amount of an IAA-like substance is produced by the fungus *Macrophomina phaseoli* in its host *Hibiscus cannabinus*, thereby stimulating root growth and making the roots more favourable for penetration by the nematode *Meloidogyne javanica*. According to Tu and Cheng this may account for the increased numbers of the nematode in the fungus-infected roots.

Such views are reminiscent of the picture I drew in the previous chapter on resistance, where a disturbance in the plant's metabolic machinery produces change. In the present discussion change is produced by two organisms entering the system and in some situations the nematode

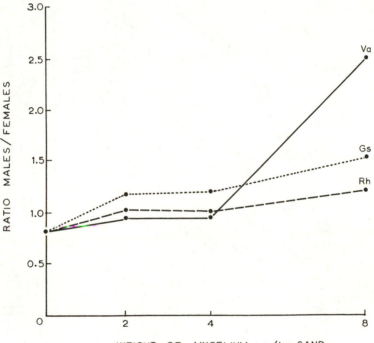

Fig. 14 The influence of soil-borne fungi on the sex-ratio of *Heterodera rostochiensis*. Va = *Verticillium albo-atrum*, Rh = *Rhizoctonia solani* and Gs = grey sterile fungus. (After Ketudat, 1969)

is inhibited, in others it is stimulated. Put another way we can say that the incursion of the fungus into the plant system may produce a plant which is more resistant or more susceptible to the nematode. We know little of the nature of such changes which is unfortunate because there may be a clue here to the nature of resistance.

That we are involved in a situation where both nematode and fungus contribute to physiological changes in the same plant, is indicated by Faulkner and his coworkers. The rate of reproduction of *Pratylenchus minyus* is greater in plants infected with *Verticillium dahliae* than in plants infected with *P. minyus* alone and the release of growth promoting substances is suggested to account for this (Faulkner and Skotland, 1965; Faulkner and Bolander, 1969). Later work (Faulkner *et al.*, 1970) showed the same trends. Detached peppermint stems were rooted at two places to provide the plant with two root systems. The root systems were placed in

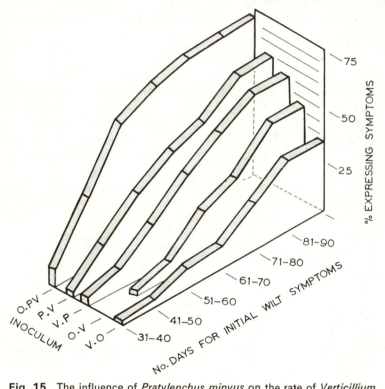

Fig. 15 The influence of *Pratylenchus minyus* on the rate of *Verticillium* wilt development on double rooted peppermint plants. In the inocula, *P* = *P. minyus*, *V* = *V. dahliae f. menthae*, *O* = no inoculum. The respective locations of each inoculation (terminal or basal) are shown on either side of the dots. Plants in treatments *PV · PV* and *V · V* received standard inoculum dosages on each root system and these results are not directly comparable with the other treatments. (After Faulkner *et al.*, 1970)

soil in separate pots and inoculated with various combinations of *Verticillium dahliae* and *Pratylenchus minyus*. The nematode numbers were greater in the plant containing the fungus, even though each parasite was contained in separate root systems (Fig. 15). This experiment shows very nicely that the influence of another parasite, that coexists with a nematode in a plant, is not just a question of competition for some resource in short supply but that physiological processes are at work. The analogy between the nematodes sharing the space within the intestine of some animal and the nematode and fungus coexisting in the same host plant is not a useful one. Parasites and their hosts meet at the biochemical level and interaction between parasites in the same hosts is likely to be through the host's biochemical machinery rather than at the ecological level where two organisms might compete for food or space.

In coincident infection with two or more nematode species most observations suggest that at least one species is suppressed. Freckman and Chapman (1972) however studied invasion by *Heterodera trifolii* and *Pratylenchus penetrans* in the same red clover plant and found no influence of either nematode on the other. Prior infection by *H. trifolii* did not affect invasion by *P. penetrans* and the distribution of *P. penetrans* was unaffected by the presence of *H. trifolii*. In this example there is no indication of competition. When equal numbers of *Pratylenchus penetrans* and *Tylenchorhynchus martini* were introduced into red clover and lucerne plants, *P. penetrans* increased as well in the presence of *T. martini* as it did when alone, but *T. martini* in the presence of *P. penetrans* increased only 10 to 25% as much as it did when alone (Chapman, 1959). There are similar kinds of observations with other nematodes: the reproduction of *Meloidogyne incognita* decreased in the presence of *Pratylenchus brachyurus* (Johnson and Nusbaum, 1970), *Heterodera tabacum* was suppressed by *Pratylenchus penetrans* when it occurred in 90% of a population of the two; however, *H. tabacum* at moderate to high levels, suppressed and eventually replaced a smaller number of *P. penetrans* in the same population (Miller, 1970). Experiments with three species of nematodes on the same host plant have been tried. Thus Johnson (1970) infected six Bermuda grasses with the ectoparasitic nematodes *Criconemoides ornatus*, *Tylenchorhynchus martini*, and *Belonolaimus longicaudatus*. The reproductive rate of all three was suppressed, *B. longicaudatus* least of all. Although the factors influencing the interactions between nematode species are unknown, it seems possible that if numbers and distribution are ever determined at the ecological level, it will be most apparent with ectoparasitic nematodes which are likely to occur close together on the root feeding on the same cells, without that intimate physiological relationship between host and parasite as in the *Heteroderidae* for example.

OUTSIDE THE HOST

Information about the distribution and numbers of nematodes in the host helps us to understand the nature of disease by identifying the location of the initial disturbance in the individual plant. Outside the host, the distribution and abundance of nematodes is important in studies on the etiology of disease in plant populations. We need to know whether the nematodes are distributed uniformly, randomly, or occur in patches and the use of the Poisson distribution provides us with a way of answering this question. Barker and Nusbaum (1971) provide excellent data to illustrate this aspect. They marked off test fields to give 576 small grids each measuring 5 by 5 m. The numbers of *Tylenchorhynchus claytoni* in each grid are given. By determining the variance of the 576 counts $(\Sigma(x-\bar{x})^2/n-1$, where x = count in any one grid, $\bar{x}$ = mean and n = the number of counts) it is possible to see whether the variance is less than, equal to or greater than the mean, i.e. whether the distribution is uniform, random or clumped. In this case analysis of the data showed that the variance was greatly in excess of the mean, indicating a clumped distribution, and a calculation of $X^2(\Sigma(x-\bar{x})^2/\bar{x})$ indicated that this difference was highly significant. A similar test with data provided by Barker and Nusbaum for *Meloidogyne javanica* showed that the distribution of this species was even more patchy within the field. It is likely that other field data will give similar results so we now ask the questions—why are nematodes more abundant in some areas than in others and is this non-uniform distribution associated with the distribution of diseased plants? If it is, we might suspect that the nematode was at least partly contributing to the observed incidence of disease in the plants.

To explain why the numbers of a nematode are higher in one place than another is a familiar but difficult ecological problem. There are so many environmental components that could influence the nematode, and in any situation it is likely that several do in fact have some influence on the distribution and abundance of a particular nematode. Satisfactory explanations of distribution must therefore take into account as many as possible of these components and, furthermore, assess their relative contribution to the observed distribution. To make the problem more difficult the existing distribution of a nematode might have been decided many years ago by some factor that no longer exists and which cannot be measured at the time the nematode samples are taken. However from previous records it may be possible to deduce possible reasons for distribution patterns. Thus, Brown (1958) showed that there was a correlation between the present distribution of *Heterodera goettingiana* in East Suffolk in England and those districts which grew the most beans during the latter half of the nineteenth and during the early twentieth century. The populations of this nematode, so Brown suggests, were built up many years ago and have been maintained since that time by the occasional crop of field beans. Similarly in a survey in Bedfordshire, populations of *Heterodera cruciferae* were greater and more fields were infested on farms of less than 20.234 hectare (fifty acres) than on larger farms (Winfield and Coppock 1970). *Brassica* crops were probably grown more frequently on the smaller farms. Such explanations of distribution are plausible but impossible to test experimentally because of lack of data on other factors that might have been important at that earlier time. If distribution is the result of previous introductions on planting stock, then the main factor determining distribution might be missed altogether. Hannon (1962), for example, suggests that *Tylenchulus semipenetrans* is distributed in citrus groves by infested nursery stock rather than because of its endemic existence. This, Hannon argues, might account for the observation that infested groves often adjoin uninfested groves. Such an explanation would be valid if there was evidence of the level of nematode infestations in the nursery stock when they were planted out. Without such data there are too many other possible explanations to allow us to accept the hypothesis of infested nursery material too readily.

These examples serve to make the point that in some situations the problem of accounting for distribution may be insoluble. We might measure and correlate all the environmental factors we can think of and find significant correlations and still miss the most important component because it no longer exists to be measured. Hopefully there are not too many situations like this and of course we can never know without historical data which are and which are not.

Let us now look at some of the environmental components that influence the distribution and abundance of nematodes outside the host.

In making surveys of nematode distribution and in any field problem, the most obvious factor that asks to be measured is soil type. There are in fact a large number of references to correlations between the distribution and abundance of various plant nematodes and the sort of soil from which they were recovered. Rebois and Cairns (1968), for example, took soil samples from soybean fields in 28 major soybean producing counties in Alabama, Northern Florida and in Georgia. The number of genera and the total number of plant nematodes that were recovered per pint of soil were higher in the lighter-textured soils than in the clay soils. Similarly, there is a close relationship between the distribution of five species of *Xiphinema* and soil type in Israel, and Cohn (1969) attributes this to the fact that the smaller species occur in the heavier soils whereas in the lighter soils, nematodes of greater body volume are more abundant (Fig. 16). Cohn suggests that oxygen content and water holding capacity might determine the ability of a species of *Xiphinema* to survive. Thus, larger nematodes might require well aerated soils and be unable to survive as well in the heavier clay soils. Although Cohn does not say in so many words why large nematodes require a well aerated soil, he is presumably thinking of relative decrease in surface area to volume of the body as nematodes increase in size, and the consequent relative reduction in available area through which gases can diffuse through the cuticle. Thus, it is not soil type that determines distribution and abundance but some other factor associated with soil type. In Cohn's studies, distribution of the *Xiphinema* species was associated with body size and soil aeration. This is a plausible suggestion, although there is no evidence to test the hypothesis; we might have suggested that the larger size of pores in the ligher soil might better accommodate the larger *Xiphinema* spp. by enabling them to move about in the soil from root to root more quickly. The distribution of *Heterodera avenae* in Victoria, Australia, has been shown by Meagher (1968) to be closely correlated with soil type. The nematodes are more frequent in

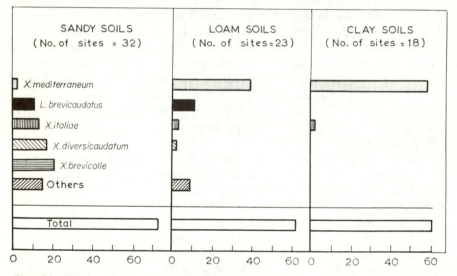

Fig. 16 The mean population size of nematode species in three soils of different texture. (After Cohn, 1969)

areas with sandy solonized brown soils or friable grey soils and Meagher suggests that soil structure may be the main factor determining distribution. In similar studies, where nematode distribution is related to soil type, Fidler and Bevan (1963) have stressed the importance of water holding capacity and phosphorus; Ferris and Bernard (1971b) mention soil moisture and Kimpinski and Welch (1971) soil moisture, nitrogen and plant growth.

From these few examples emerges a picture of a complex web of inter-acting soil factors, all of which are associated with soil type and could influence the nematode. However, as correlations do not indicate causality, we are left with the problem of deciding which, of all the numerous components, are the ones which determine the distribution and abundance of the nematodes in any particular situation. Furthermore, it is possible to imagine that some soil factors that are not closely correlated with soil type may have a large influence on nematode distribution in some areas; consequently, there may be no correlation with soil type. Brzeski (1969), for example, found that the distribution of nematodes in cabbage fields in Poland was most closely related to pH and independent of soil type. Similarly Whitehead (1969) found that the relative frequencies of *Meloidogyne javanica* and *M. incognita* in East Africa were not correlated with soil texture but with altitude, rainfall and temperature. *M. incognita* seemed to be more successful in hotter soils and *M. javanica* in the cooler wetter soils. In such studies, Whitehead states, it is necessary to survey a fixed range of crops in different climatic regions. In other words it is necessary to make some early decisions about what is worth measuring and what can be handled in the time available and with the facilities at our disposal.

In general, the following factors might be measured, soil texture, soil structure, air and soil temperature, rainfall, soil moisture, evaporation, soil conductivity, pH, plant material and topography. Some of these factors might not be worth measuring in some areas, whereas others not mentioned here like crop rotation (Ferris and Bernard, 1971a) and salinity might be important in some situations. Initial surveys, discussions with local farmers and extension workers and the examination of published data help in this initial decision.

It is also important to take samples of sufficient number and volume so that any correlations stand a chance of being statistically significant. It is therefore necessary to take some initial samples so that variability in numbers of nematodes between samples can be assessed and the sampling procedure adjusted accordingly. The vertical distribution of nematodes must also be taken into account because some species appear to prefer certain depths. Richter (1969) found that *Trichodorus* spp. occurred in greater numbers in the deeper soil layers compared with species of *Tylenchorhynchus* and *Pratylenchus*. Furthermore, the males of two *Trichodorus* spp. had different vertical distributions, *T. viruliferus* was most prevalent at depths of 10–40 cm whereas *T. pachydermus* was most prevalent at 30–60 cm. Flegg (1968a) found that *Xiphinema diversicaudatum* and *X. vuittenezi* decreased in numbers with increasing depth whereas *Longidorus macrosoma* increased with depth to 70 cm. Koen (1966) found that seasonal variations from summer to winter and the consequent change of soil temperature and soil moisture influenced the pattern of vertical distribution of *Meloidogyne javanica* in the soil. During winter, the highest population density was found at a depth of 30 to 45 cm compared with 15 to 30 cm during summer. Sometimes such distribution patterns can be attributed to some environmental change; Griffin and Darling (1964) suggest, for example, that the degree of fluctuation in soil moisture and temperature may be important, and numerous authors have stated that vertical distribution is probably correlated with the distribution of the host's roots. Whatever the controlling factor, however, it is clear that, in our initial survey for nematode distribution, we must decide on the best sampling depth by determining the depth of soil within which the population occurs, otherwise apparent differences in horizontal distribution may only reflect differences in vertical distribution of similar numbers.

Already it will be apparent that research projects on distribution and abundance are likely to be complex and time consuming and, if we attempt to assess the numbers of all species in the samples, there is a distinct possibility that the task will prove to be beyond our practical capabilities. However, the initial survey of species in the soil should indicate which species predominate and which are most likely to be important. Thus, as well as collecting vital information in the initial survey, we simultaneously produce an hypothesis that relates the variables we intend to measure. In fact, we construct a story of how we think the ecological system works in determining the distribution of nematodes. The nematodes occupy the centre of our attention and we postulate which factors we think are most likely to influence their numbers. We then collect data so that the necessary statistical correlations can be made between nematode numbers and environmental components.

The collection of data on nematode distribution in space is much more useful if there are factors that we can correlate with such numbers because they suggest where we might look for causal factors. Analysis of the data by simple correlation, multiple and stepwise regressions is the next phase. In the chapter on etiology of disease we will discuss these processes in more detail when we consider the problem of assessing the causes and determinants of disease in plants. Here we are concerned with the causes and determinants of the distribution of nematodes.

I will give three examples that indicate how data might be analysed to produce conclusions about distribution and abundance. Ferris *et al.* (1971), used two mathematical methods, a resemblance equation and community ordination, to study the community structure of plant nematode populations in soybean soils in Indiana and Illinois. The methods enabled the relative densities of different species to be measured at fourteen sites which were characterized by latitude, soil type, average frost free period, average annual temperature, average annual precipitation and average soybean yield with good management. According to the authors the reasons for taxonomic resemblance or lack of it are probably determined by soil factors. Although the quantifiable characteristics of the environment were not correlated with the location of the sites, some generalizations were made that provided possible explanations why certain sites had similar communities of nematodes. In particular, community structure tended to be similar on the dark-coloured, highly productive soils; on the lighter soils, the communities were different from those in the darker soils and from each other, possibly reflecting the more diverse nature of the lighter soils. Here then is a method whereby populations in different areas can be measured and the possible influence of environmental factors assessed through correlation. We might ask, however, whether the study of communities and the proportions of its members is more worthwhile than the study of populations of different species. If the relative number of species within a population has any biological significance then we might look for interactions between species in their effects on each other and on the plant. We have already mentioned interactions between different species in the host, and in the soil there are some indications of possible antagonism; for example Griffin and Darling (1964), suggest that *Xiphinema americanum* has a suppressing effect on *Criconemoides xenoplax* in ornamental spruce nurseries. However, it seems to me that the task of elucidating the causes of nematode distribution is complex enough without introducing, at this stage, community structure, a concept which some believe has contributed little to the understanding of the abundance and distribution of animals (Andrewartha, 1970). The alternative approach is to consider one species at a time, to try to explain its distribution and to treat other species as further environmental components of the single species under study.

The second example is provided by Norton *et al.* (1971). Here, soil factors were correlated with numbers of selected species of nematodes from 40 soybean fields over two years in Iowa. The soil factors measured were pH, percent sand, silt and clay, percent organic matter, cation exchange capacity, saturation percentage and percent saturation. The nematodes that were counted in the samples were total nematodes, non-stylet nematodes, *Dorylaimoidea* (excluding *Xiphinema americanum*), *X. americanum*, *Helicotylenchus pseudorobustus*, *Tylenchus* spp., *Aphelenchus avenae* and other groupings of nematodes. The objective of the work was to assess the influence of the various soil factors on the numbers of nematodes. The data were analysed by stepwise regression using logarithmic transformations of actual nematode numbers. Such a procedure is now used frequently in ecological studies of this kind because it allows conclusions to be made of the extent to which combinations of independent variables (in this case, the soil factors) account for variability in the observed numbers of the dependent variable (nematodes). The results of the analyses of the data indicated that organic matter, pH and cation exchange capacity were most consistently and highly correlated with the nematodes and there were also indications that the highest numbers of nematodes were usually found in the lighter soils except in the loamy sand where moisture was probably limiting. Norton and his colleagues discuss how cation exchange capacity *might* influence nematodes but they are careful to point out that there is no evidence that the correlations indicate causality as cation exchange capacity is closely linked to soil texture, pH and organic matter.

In the third example (Nyhan, *et al.*, 1972), the influence of specific soil and plant properties on nematode populations associated with soybean was studied. Two sites in north–central Iowa with known cropping history were selected with three adjacent rows of soybeans that extended as transects parallel to the topographical soil formation from the shoulder to the slope of the gradient. Core samples were taken along the transects and the numbers of nematodes were counted. Soil analyses and plant analyses were made to provide numerous variables including soil texture, soil structure, pH, soluble salts, top weight of plants and mineral content of plants. The statistical analysis involved the principle component method of factor analysis, a procedure frequently employed by plant ecologists. The 23 variables measured were grouped, and the analysis indicated that 67 to 73% of the total sampling variance could be accounted for by soil structure, root activity, soil fertility, dry matter production and nematode factors. However, nematode populations were more closely correlated with plant variables than with soil variables at each sampling site.

The papers of Ferris, Norton, Nyhan and their colleagues have different objectives but they all indicate ways in which ecological studies on nematode distribution can be tackled. That is not the end of the story however, there are two essential phases of such studies that usually receive less emphasis. The first we have alluded to already; the need for a careful appraisal of the ecological system to decide which environmental components should be measured. The other phase involves experimentation to test the hypotheses that arise from the analysis of data. Correlations enable plausible stories to be built around ecological systems but whether they are realistic, useful and true can only be established by further experiments designed to prove that the hypothesis is false. Laboratory experiments are therefore necessary to test hypotheses developed from field measurements and they may also indicate what environmental components are worth measuring. The laboratory experiments of Daulton and Nusbaum (1961, 1962), on the responses of different populations of the same nematode species to soil moisture and temperature, are good examples of the type of work that might follow a study of the geographical distribution of nematodes such as that of Whitehead (1969).

The distribution and abundance of nematodes in time

The distribution and abundance of nematodes are never static and, just as numbers inside the host change as the host matures and senesces, so do numbers of nematodes in the soil change as the seasons progress. In studies on the spatial distribution of nematodes, it is therefore necessary to sample several times during the growing season of the host and in several consecutive seasons. Account must also be taken of changes in distribution with time both horizontally and vertically.

There are numerous references in the literature to seasonal fluctuations in nematode numbers with suggestions for the factors causing them. Griffin and Darling (1964) have shown that *Xiphinema americanum* has two population peaks per season in ornamental spruce nurseries. One cycle extended from April to August, the other from September to January. The peaks became less obvious in the larvae and non-gravid females as sampling depth increased, whereas the gravid adults showed two distinct cycles at all sampling depths. *Meloidogyne naasi* may also have two population peaks in the soil because there are few nematodes in winter, a marked increase in spring, a decrease when host roots are invaded in the summer and a moderate increase in late summer (Franklin *et al.*, 1971). Flegg (1968*b*) found that eggs of *Longidorus* and *Xiphinema* spp. were produced only during a brief period in early summer but proportions of each larval and adult stage in the population showed no comparable annual cycle. In studies on the populations of *Pratylenchus penetrans* in soil and roots in rye–tobacco rotations in Canada, Olthof (1971) showed that populations were low in the summer and high in the autumn, although seasonal changes were not consistent from year to year. There is a distinct annual periodicity of high populations of *Radopholus similis* in *Citrus limon* rootlets with a peak in October to December and a trough in February to June. The particular month when peak populations occurred varied from grove to grove and from year to year (Ducharme, 1967). The seasonal emergence of *Heterodera avenae* larvae was studied over three years in wheat in Victoria, Australia (Meagher, 1970). Larval numbers were highest during late autumn and winter. Meagher attributes the increase to changes in soil moisture and temperature that favour hatch. Banyer and Fisher (1971), on the other hand, attribute the increase in such numbers to the onset of low soil temperatures in late autumn and they give experimental evidence that indicates that this change in temperature breaks dormancy in the eggs. They found no evidence of an inherent seasonal cycle of hatching.

There are many other records in this vein and most authors suggest what factors might be responsible for the observed fluctuations. It is usual for example to include rainfall and temperature data with graphs showing the changes of nematode numbers with time. However there has been no attempt in nematology, as far as I know, to account for population changes with time in a statistical way such as that done by Ferris (1971) and Norton (1971) and their coworkers for spatial distribution. Such analyses of data would indicate the relative contribution of the nematodes' various environmental components to the observed fluctuations—not only those periodic fluctuations associated with changes in the host but other less pronounced but important changes superimposed on the more uniform cycles. The statistical technique of periodic regression as described by Bliss (1958) would be a useful tool in such ecological studies.

Although the task of elucidating the ecology of distribution of nematodes is a formidable one, it is not impossible if the work is done by a team of workers. However, there is one facet of the work that should be considered very seriously—the methods used to extract the nematodes from the soil. The paper of Barker, *et al* (1969) indicates that the method of extraction greatly influences the numbers recovered during certain periods of the year. In addition to extraction method, rainfall, season, crop and cultural practices that influence apparent shifts in population densities of nematodes the interaction of extraction method and time of sampling may often be important; in other words, different extraction procedures might give different pictures of seasonal fluctuations. The only answer to this difficulty is to use extraction techniques that give high recoveries without depending on the nematodes' own movements as in the Baermann method.

Dispersal

Unlike insects, nematodes do not move very far or very quickly by their own locomotory power, they haven't evolved any characteristics that enable them to disperse quickly. In fact they appear to be more efficient at aggregating. Being obligate parasites, plant nematodes do not feed while in the soil in the absence of plants, hence, they have a limited time to actively move before their resources of chemical energy run out. Many adaptations, as we will see in the next chapter, appear to be related to reducing the time the nematode spends away from the host. Neither have they evolved any characteristics that enable them to escape from the soil nor for projecting themselves into the air like fungi. Some nematodes like

Ditylenchus, *Anguina* and *Aphelenchoides* can escape from the soil and, with their highly developed ability to resist desiccation, their chances of dispersal are correspondingly greater, but for the endoparasitic and ecto-parasitic nematodes that attack roots such opportunities rarely occur. The conclusion can be drawn therefore, that the survival of nematodes in the evolutionary sense has been successful for reasons other than those related to rapid dispersal. As has been stated before, the usual arguments for the selective advantages of dispersal are that animals live in a changing environment and that if a population did not disperse it would stand a chance of becoming extinct when the weather in any particular year was unusually severe or when ecological succession of plants in an area no longer provided sufficient amounts of the right food. We might therefore ask whether nematodes have any particular adaptations that enable them to overcome these hazards.

Most plant nematodes live in the soil where fluctuations in temperature and moisture decrease rapidly with depth, hence spectacular climatic changes above ground are likely to be less hazardous in the soil. Moreover, nematodes have the ability to migrate vertically in response to physical gradients and so escape the hazards, hence the seasonal changes in vertical distribution of nematodes that we have just discussed. When it comes to the hazard of diminishing food reserves the inability to disperse is a disadvantage and in a natural ecosystem it is likely that isolated populations of a species do in fact become extinct as succession of plant species occurs. However many nematodes have a wide host range and can therefore occupy a particular area even though the plant population is changing. The efficiency of crop rotation as a nematode control measure is an indication of how changing plant populations can influence populations of nematodes, but it is also true that a significant proportion of the nematode population always survives to build up again when suitable hosts are eventually planted. So inability to disperse is offset to some extent by escape in the soil from detrimental climatic conditions and by the ability to persist, perhaps in low numbers, on alternative hosts during times when preferred hosts are few. Some dispersal does occur however, even over long distances but it is passive and by chance. Wind-borne dispersal has been reported by Orr and Newton (1971) who found *Meloidogyne* larvae among 28 genera recovered from dust traps placed 2 m above the ground in Western Texas. Numerous plant nematodes were found and the authors suggest that the deposition of nematode-laden dust might explain the extensive occurrence of root knot nematodes in the area. Dispersal by surface run-off of water and by irrigation is also possible (Faulkner and Bolander, 1966; Meagher, 1967; Sauer, 1968). The primary source of plant nematodes in irrigation waterways, in the Columbia basin of East Washington, appears to be irrigation run-off returned into the irrigation system (Fig. 17). It is possible that dispersal by this means has contributed to the rapid spread of nematodes in this region over the past eight years (Faulkner and Bolander, 1970). In fact the most efficient ways for nematode dispersal appear to be a consequence of man's own activities, especially in his agricultural activities. Erosion of the land by wind with its dust storms, the movement of water in irrigation channels, the transport of infected plant material between different countries and the spread of nematodes on farm implements and vehicles all contribute to dispersal. Thus man, by creating artificial systems of plant culture, contributes to nematode dispersal and produces disease problems at the same time. The influence of dispersal on distribution of nematodes may be of little importance in areas of natural plant communities

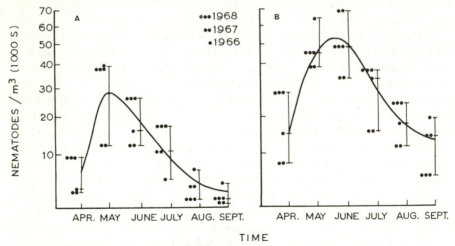

Fig. 17 Variation in nematode populations per m³ of drainage water at two locations during three growing seasons. (After Faulkner and Bolander, 1970)

but man's influence on the environment is now so extensive that, in agriculture at least, we cannot overlook the effects of our own activities on nematode distribution. Unfortunately, such activities are hard to measure and there is usually little quantitative evidence that enables us to assess this aspect of distribution.

References

ALPHEY, T.J.W. (1970). Studies on the distribution and site location of *Nippostrongylus brasiliensis* within the small intestine of laboratory rats. *Parasitology*, **61**, 449.

ANDREWARTHA, H.G. (1970). *Introduction to the study of animal populations.* Methuen, xiv + 275 pp.

ANDREWARTHA, H.G. and BIRCH, L.C. (1954). *The distribution and abundance of animals.* Univ. of Chicago Press, xv + 782 pp.

BANYER, R.J. and FISHER, J.M. (1971) Seasonal variation in hatching of eggs of *Heterodera avenae. Nematologica,* **17,** 225.

BARKER, K.R. and NUSBAUM, C.J. (1971). Diagnostic and advisory programmes. In *Plant Parasitic Nematodes* Edited by B.M. Zuckerman, W.F. Mai and R.A. Rohde. Vol. 1. Academic Press, xiv + 345 pp.

BARKER, K.R., NUSBAUM, C.J. and NELSON, L.A. (1969). Seasonal population dynamics of selected plant-parasitic nematodes as measured by three extraction procedures. *J. Nematology,* **1,** 232.

BIRD, A.F. (1969). The influence of tobacco ring spot virus and tobacco mosaic virus on the growth of *Meloidogyne javanica. Nematologica,* **15,** 201.

BLISS, C.I. (1958). Periodic regression in biology and climatology. *Connecticut Agric. Exp. Stn., Bull.* **615.**

BOURKE, P.M.A. (1970). Use of weather information in the prediction of plant disease epiphytotics. *Ann. Rev. Phytopath.,* **8,** 345.

BRENCHLEY, G.H. (1968). Aerial photography for the study of plant diseases. *Ann. Rev. Phytopath.,* **6,** 1.

BROWN, E.B. (1958). Pea root eelworm in the eastern counties of England. *Nematologica,* **3,** 257.

BRZESKI, M.W. (1969). Nematodes associated with cabbage in Poland. 2. The effect of soil factors on the frequency of nematode occurrence. *Ekologia Polska—Ser. A.* **17,** 205.

CHAPMAN, R.A. (1959). Development of *Pratylenchus penetrans* and *Tylenchorhynchus martini* on red clover and alfalfa. *Phytopathology,* **49,** 357.

CHAPPELL, L.H. (1969). Competitive exclusion between two intestinal parasites of the three-spined stickleback, *Gasterosteus aculeatus* L. *J. Parasit.,* **55,** 775.

CLARK, F.E. (1965). The concept of competition in microbial ecology. In *Ecology of soil-borne plant pathogens.* Edited by K.F. Baker and W.C. Snyder. Unif. California Press, 571 pp.

COHN, E. (1969). The occurrence and distribution of species of *Xiphinema* and *Longidorus* in Israel. *Nematologica,* **15,** 179.

CROFTON, H.D. (1971). A quantitative approach to parasitism. *Parasitology,* **62,** 179.

DAULTON, R.A.C. and NUSBAUM, C.J. (1961). The effect of soil temperature on the survival of the root-knot nematodes *Meloidogyne javanica* and *M. hapla. Nematologica,* **6,** 280.

DAULTON, R.A.C. and NUSBAUM, C.J. (1962). The effect of soil moisture and relative humidity on the root-knot nematode *Meloidogyne javanica*. *Nematologica*, **8**, 157.

DIMOND, A.E. and HORSFALL, J.G. (1965). Theory of inoculum. In *Ecology of soil-borne plant pathogens*. Edited by K.F. Baker and W.C. Snyder. Univ. California Press, 571 pp.

DONALD, A.D. (1967). Population studies on the infective stage of some nematode parasites of sheep. 1. The frequency distribution of strongyloid infective larvae in random samples of pasture. *Parasitology*, **57**, 263.

DUCHARME, E.P. (1967). Annual population periodicity of *Radopholus similis* in Florida citrus groves. *Pl. Dis. Reptr.*, **51**, 1031.

FAULKNER, L.R. and BOLANDER, W.J. (1966). Occurrence of large nematode populations in irrigation canals of South Central Washington. *Nematologica*, **12**, 591.

FAULKNER, L.R. and BOLANDER, W.J. (1969). Interaction of *Verticillium dahliae* and *Pratylenchus minyus* in *Verticillium* wilt of peppermint: Effect of soil temperature. *Phytopathology*, **59**, 868.

FAULKNER, L.R. and BOLANDER, W.J. (1970). Acquisition and distribution of nematodes in irrigation waterways of the Columbia Basin in Eastern Washington. *J. Nematology*, **2**, 362.

FAULKNER, L.R., BOLANDER, W.J. and SKOTLAND, C.B. (1970). Interaction of *Verticillium dahliae* and *Pratylenchus minyus* in *Verticillium* wilt of peppermint: Influence of the nematode as determined by a double root technique. *Phytopathology*, **60**, 100.

FAULKNER, L.R. and SKOTLAND, C.B. (1965) Interactions of *Verticillium dahliae* and *Pratylenchus minyus* in *Verticillium* wilt of peppermint. *Phytopathology*, **55**, 583.

FERRIS, V.R. and BERNARD, R.L. (1971*a*). Crop rotation effects on population densities of ectoparasitic nematodes. *J. Nematology*, **3**, 119.

FERRIS, V.R. and BERNARD, R.L. (1971*b*). Effect of soil type on population densities of nematodes in soybean rotation fields. *J. Nematology*, **3**, 123.

FERRIS, V.R., FERRIS, J.M., BERNARD, R.L. and PROBST, A.H. (1971). Community structure of plant–parasitic nematodes related to soil types in Illinois and Indiana soybean fields. *J. Nematology*, **3**, 339.

FIDLER, J.H. and BEVAN, W.J. (1963). Some soil factors influencing the density of cereal root eelworm (*Heterodera avenae* Woll.) populations and their damage to the oat crop. *Nematologica*, **9**, 412.

FLEGG, J.J.M. (1968*a*). The occurrence and depth distribution of *Xiphinema* and *Longidorus* species in South eastern England. *Nematologica*, **14**, 189.

FLEGG, J.J.M. (1968b). Life cycle studies of some *Xiphinema* and *Longidorus* species in South eastern England. *Nematologica*, **14**, 197.

FRANKLIN, M.T., CLARK, S.A. and COURSE, J.A. (1971). Population studies of *Meloidogyne naasi* in the field. *Nematologica*, **17**, 575.

FRECKMAN, D.W. and CHAPMAN, R.A. (1972). Infection of red clover seedlings by *Heterodera trifolii* Goffart and *Pratylenchus penetrans* (Cobb). *J. Nematology*, **4**, 23.

GRIFFIN, G.D. and DARLING, H.M. (1964). An ecological study of *Xiphinema americanum* Cobb in an ornamental spruce nursery. *Nematologica*, **10**, 471.

HANNON, C.I. (1962). The occurrence and distribution of the citrus-root nematode, *Tylenchulus semipenetrans* Cobb., in Florida. *Pl. Dis. Reptr.*, **46**, 451.

HOLDEMAN, Q.L. (1970). Varietal and geographic distribution of walnut phloem canker and bark canker in California. *Pl. Dis. Reptr.*, **54**, 373.

JAMES, G.L. (1968). The interrelationships of the causal fungus of brown root rot of tomatoes and potato root eelworm, *Heterodera rostochiensis* Woll. *Ann. appl. Biol.*, **61**, 503.

JOHNSON, A.W. (1970). Pathogenicity and interaction of three nematode species on six Bermudagrasses. *J. Nematology*, **2**, 36.

JOHNSON, A.W. and NUSBAUM, C.J. (1970). Interactions between *Meloidogyne incognita*, *M. hapla* and *Pratylenchus brachyurus* in tobacco. *J. Nematology*, **2**, 334.

JORGENSON, E.C. (1970). Antagonistic interaction of *Heterodera schachtii* Schmidt and *Fusarium oxysporum* (Woll.) on sugarbeets. *J. Nematology*, **2**, 393.

KÄMPFE, L. (1960). Die räumliche verteilung des Primärbefalls von *Heterodera schachtii* Schmidt in den Wirtswurzeln. *Nematologica*, **5**, 18.

KENNEDY, C.R. (1968). Population biology of the cestode *Caryophyllaeus laticeps* (Pallas, 1781) in dace, *Leuciscus leuciscus* L. of the river Avon. *J. Parasit.*, **54**, 538.

KENNEDY, C.R. and HINE, P.M. (1969). Population biology of the cestode *Proteocephalus torulosus* (Batsch) in dace *Leuciscus leuciscus* (L.) of the river Avon. *J. Fish. Biol.*, **1**, 209.

KETUDAT, U. (1969). The effects of some soil-borne fungi on the sex ratio of *Heterodera rostochiensis* on tomato. *Nematologica*, **15**, 229.

KIMPINSKI, J. and WELCH, H.E. (1971). The ecology of nematodes in Manitoba soils. *Nematologica*, **17**, 308.

KINLOCH, R.A. and ALLEN, M.W. (1972). Interaction of *Meloidogyne hapla* and *M. javanica* infecting tomato. *J. Nematology*, **4**, 7.

KIRKPATRICK, J.D., VAN GUNDY, S.D. and MAI, W.F. (1964). Interrelationships of plant nutrition, growth and parasitic nematodes. *Plant Analysis and Fertilizer Problems*, **4**, 189.

KOEN, H. (1966). The influence of seasonal variations on the vertical distribution of *Meloidogyne javanica* in sandy soils. *Nematologica*, **12**, 297.

LEWIS, J.W. (1968). Studies on the helminth parasites of the long-tailed field mouse, *Apodemus sylvaticus sylvaticus* from Wales. *J. Zool. Lond.*, **154**, 287.

MCKEEN, C.D. and MOUNTAIN, W.B. (1960). Synergism between *Pratylenchus penetrans* (Cobb) and *Verticillium albo-atrum* R and B in eggplant wilt. *Canad. J. Bot.*, **38**, 789.

MEAGHER, J.W. (1967). Observations on the transport of nematodes in subsoil drainage and irrigation water. *Aust. J. Exp. Agric. Anim. Husbandry*, **7**, 577.

MEAGHER, J.W. (1968). The Distribution of the cereal cyst nematode (*Heterodera avenae*) in Victoria and its relation to soil type. *Aust. J. Exp. Agric. Anim. Husb.*, **8**, 637.

MEAGHER, J.W. (1970). Seasonal fluctuations in numbers of larvae of the cereal cyst nematode (*Heterodera avenae*) and of *Pratylenchus minyus* and *Tylenchorhynchus brevidens* in soil. *Nematologica*, **16**, 333.

MILLER, P.M. (1970). Rate of increase of a low population of *Heterodera tabacum* reduced by *Pratylenchus penetrans* in the soil. *Pl. Dis. Reptr.*, **54**, 25.

MILLER, H.N. and DI EDWARDO, A.A. (1962). Leaf galls on *Siderasis fuscata* caused by the root-knot nematode, *Meloidogyne incognita incognita*. *Phytopathology*, **52**, 1070.

MOUNTAIN, W.B. and MCKEEN, C.D. (1962). Effect of *Verticillium dahliae* on the population of *Pratylenchus penetrans*. *Nematologica*, **7**, 261.

NORTON, D.C., FREDERICK, L.R., PONCHILLIA, P.E. and NYHAN, J.W. (1971). Correlations of nematodes and soil properties in soybean fields. *J. Nematology*, **3**, 154.

NYHAN, J.W., FREDERICK, L.R. and NORTON, D.C. (1972). Ecology of nematodes in Clarion-Webster toposequences associated with *Glycine max* (L) Merrill. *Soil Sci. Soc. Amer. Proc.*, **36**, 74.

OLTHOF, T.H.A. (1971). Seasonal fluctuations in population densities of *Pratylenchus penetrans* under a rye-tobacco rotation in Ontario. *Nematologica*, **17**, 453.

ORR, C.C. and NEWTON, O.H. (1971). Distribution of nematodes by wind. *Pl. Dis. Reptr.*, **55**, 61.

PIKE, A.W. (1968). The distribution and incidence of larval trematodes in the freshwater fauna of the Wentlong level, South Wales. *J. Zool. Lond.*, **155**, 293.

READ, C.P. (1971). 'The microcosm of intestinal helminths'. In *Ecology and physiology of parasites*. Edited by A.M. Fallis. University of Toronto Press, x + 258 pp.

REBOIS, R.V. and CAIRNS, E.J. (1968). Nematodes associated with soybeans in Alabama, Florida and Georgia. *Pl. Dis. Rptr.*, **52**, 40.

RICHTER, E. (1969). Zur vertikalen Verteilung von Nematoden in einem Sandboden. *Nematologica*, **15**, 44.

RISHBETH, J. (1963). Stump protection against *Fomes annosus*. 3. Inoculation with *Peniophora gigantea*. *Ann. appl. Biol.*, **52**, 63.

ROSS, J.P. (1960). *Heterodera trifolii* a foliage pathogen of white clover, *Phytopathology*, **50**, 866.

ROSS, J.P. (1965). Predisposition of soybeans to *Fusarium* wilt by *Heterodera glycines* and *Meloidogyne incognita*. *Phytopathology*, **55**, 361.

SAUER, M.R. (1968). Nematodes in an irrigated vineyard. *Nematologica*, **14**, 457.

SCHAD, G.A. (1963). Niche diversification in a parasitic species flock *Nature, Lond.*, **198**, 404.

SLACK, D.A. (1963). Introduction. Symposium on interrelationships between nematodes and other agents causing plant diseases. *Phytopathology*, **53**, 27.

SOUTHWOOD, T.R.E. (1968). *Ecological methods*, Methuen xiv + 391 pp.

TU, C.C. and CHENG, Y.H. (1971). Interaction of *Meloidogyne javanica* and *Macrophomina phaseoli* in Kenaf root root. *J. Nematology*, **3**, 39.

WALLACE, H.R. and DONCASTER, C.C. (1964). A comparative study of the movement of some microphagous, plant-parasitic and animal-parasitic nematodes. *Parasitology*, **54**, 313.

WERTHEIM, G. (1970). Experimental concurrent infections with *Strongyloides ratti* and *S. venezuelensis* in laboratory rats. *Parasitology*, **61**, 389.

WHITEHEAD, A.G. (1969). The distribution of root-knot nematodes (*Meloidogyne* spp.) in tropical Africa. *Nematologica*, **15**, 315.

WINFIELD, A.L. and COPPOCK, L.J. (1970). A survey of brassica cyst eelworm in Bedfordshire. *Pl. Path.*, **19**, 91.

WONG, C.L. and WILLETTS, H.J. (1969). Gall formation in aerial parts of plants inoculated with *Meloidogyne javanica*. *Nematologica*, **15**, 425.

7 Adaptation in nematodes

The numerous references in previous chapters to adaptations clearly indicate their importance in many aspects of the relationships between nematodes and plants. Thus, in discussing the response of the plant to infection we were in fact considering the adaptations of plants, now it is time to consider nematodes from this point of view.

Adaptation is a term frequently used by biologists to explain some characteristic of an organism that appears to have some beneficial value. Darwin and Lamarck, for example, regarded adaptation as any change in the structure of a living organism that better fitted it to its environment; and in the same sense R.A. Fisher considered that evolution was progressive adaptation and nothing else. Adaptation is thus concerned with change in the form and function of an organism, with increased chance of survival, and above all with environment. When we consider nematodes it is therefore apparent that what they do and how they are constructed are products of evolution, they are all adaptations, but in this chapter we are mainly concerned with characteristics that appear to have some *obviously* important function in the survival of nematodes as plant parasites.

Adaptation has three general meanings. The first type of adaptation, and one which we will not pursue further in this book, is used in the physiological sense to mean the ability of a physiological mechanism to respond to a change in some stimulus. When a receptor cell in an animal receives a stimulus, such as light for example, it initiates a train of electrical impulses which travel along a nerve away from the cell. If the light reaching the cell does not change in quality or quantity the cell eventually ceases to respond and is said to be adapted to the incoming light energy.

The second type of adaptation is called acclimatization. The limits of tolerance to a particular environmental factor such as temperature may be influenced by the temperature at which the plant or animal has been living previously. In general, plants and animals can better tolerate low temperatures if they have spent some time in low rather than high temperatures. The horticultural practice of 'hardening-off' glasshouse plants in a cold frame before exposing them to the rigours of cold conditions is an example of acclimatization. It enables the plant to adapt to the changing environmental conditions and thereby to have a greater chance of survival.

The third type of adaptation is evolutionary in nature and is achieved by genetic change, such as mutation or recombination of genes, independently of external influences. Acclimatization, on the other hand, involves a response with physiological mechanisms already in existence.

Evolutionary adaptation is essentially pre-adaptive; the variation in structure, behaviour or physiology occurs by chance, natural selection decides who survives. Thus, not all characteristics of an organism confer advantage, they may be in the process of selection or rejection. Populations of individuals adapt to new environmental circumstances through a systematic change in various gene frequencies within the population. In bacterial populations where an environmental stress can be met by single gene changes, and where the descendants of a given individual are genetically identical to the parent, adaptation of the population may occur in a single generation; those with the gene survive, the others die. In diploid cross-fertilizing individuals however, the correlation between phenotypes of parents and offspring is much less than that in bacteria and many environmental stresses are not met by single gene mutations. In these cases adaptation involves a gradual change in the gene pool of the population so that an ever-increasing proportion of adaptive gene combinations (individual genotypes) is formed in each generation.

Adaptation is a teleological concept because a sense of purpose is implied and the purpose or goal is an increased chance of survival through natural selection. Consequently it might be argued that adaptations, although interesting in themselves, are nevertheless historical events and unlikely to be of much use in solving research problems with pathogens and disease. This may be true if adaptation is used in discussion in a purely descriptive and uncritical way, which it often is. But we can look at adaptation in another way, as a form of problem-solving procedure. The organism is faced with some new environmental feature, to survive it too must change, so what possible solutions are there? Looked at in this way it is apparent that quite different organisms are faced with similar problems such as desiccation, high temperatures, low aeration, predators, scarcity of food and so on. The solutions to the problems moreover are probably limited hence it is not surprising that different organisms have evolved similar adaptations. Thus in research on a particular organism it is sometimes useful to find out how other organisms 'solved the problem'.

Frequently, an adaptation such as a new structure, enzyme or behaviour pattern is discovered and further research reveals the probable purpose of the adaptation, i.e. how it increases the chance of survival and the nature of the environmental factor that probably elicited the adaptation. Sometimes, however, it is useful to work backwards, so to speak, and ask the question, 'What possible adaptations *might* this organism have that would enable it to achive a particular goal, such as host-finding or survival in particularly rigorous climatic conditions ?'. In other words we recognize the goal first and then look for the adaptations that might help to achieve that goal.

Sometimes adaptations strike us as being somewhat complex as if evolution had come up with a solution to the problem of survival but had gone about it in an unnecessarily devious way. Some of the behavioural patterns of insects and birds for example seem very complex if not downright bizarre. Such a view may only be an expression of ignorance yet the adaptations are there and, what is more, they are sometimes vulnerable to interference by man. Some animals and plants may have become extinct because of disturbance of the environment that rendered the adaptation ineffective. Here then is a further reason for studying adaptations. By changing the environment in some way we might be able to interfere with some adaptation of a parasite and so control it to the benefit of the plant.

Therefore, let us look at some of these adaptations, viewing them as solutions to problems of survival that have risen in the host-parasite relationship.

Examples from parasitology and plant pathology

To survive, any parasite must proceed through a pre-determined chain of events involving hatching or germination, invasion of the host, growth, development, maturation, reproduction and dispersal. We will, take each of these activities in turn, therefore, identifying some of the problems associated with them and discuss the adaptations the parasites have evolved to overcome the problems.

The chance of survival would increase if eggs hatched or spores germinated, not at random, but in environments where the newly hatched helminth larva or the fungal hypha would be able to grow, develop and infect. Thus, eggs of some nematode parasites of the alimentary canal are stimulated by specific environmental components to produce a hatching fluid that enables them to escape from the egg shell. The stimulus for *Ascaris lumbricoides* is undissociated carbonic acid plus dissolved carbon dioxide at a particular concentration and pH (Rogers, 1960). Consequently, eggs hatch in the intestine of the host and not in the external environment. In the nematode *Trichostrongylus retortaeformis* on the other hand, eggs hatch outside the host and Wilson (1958) has shown that hatch is inhibited by high concen-

Plate 13 (top) Chrysanthemum variety Pennine Snow severely attacked by *Aphelenchoides ritzemabosi.* Other adjacent varieties show no apparent symptoms.

Plate 14 (bottom) The edge of a grove of 30-year-old orange trees in Florida showing margin of area with spreading decline caused by *Radopholus similis* (Reproduced by permission of R. F. Suit, photographed by Harriet Long)

Plate 15 (top) A field of barley at Cooke Plains in South Australia. Patches in the crop are probably associated with the presence of *Pratylenchus* spp., root-rot fungi, high salinity and low fertility. (Reproduced by permission of J. R. Harris, C.S.I.R.O. Division of Soils)

Plate 16 (bottom) A field of lucerne at Hilltown in South Australia. The factors associated with the stream patterns of unthrifty growth are not well understood but suppression of symbiotic nitrogen fixation in the highly saline subsoil is thought to be an important determinant of plant growth. The relative importance of plant nematodes and fungi is unknown. (Reproduced by permission of J. R. Harris, C.S.I.R.O. Division of Soils)

trations of electrolytes in the surrounding fluid. When faeces containing eggs are deposited, desiccation which increases the electrolyte concentration, inhibits hatch until the concentration decreases following rainfall at which time conditions are suitable for survival of the larvae and for their migration. This observation is of particular interest because many plant nematodes also occur in the soil as eggs, and face the same problem of larval survival in a fluctuating environment.

Germination in the fungi has similar adaptations. In some a specific external stimulus is required to break dormancy, e.g. *Neurospora* spores require a heat shock, whereas other stimuli are less specific in that removal of spores from the vicinity of the mycelium or colony, or from one another, allows copious germination (Robertson, 1968). In other cases microorganisms in the soil may provide the required stimulus; the chlamydospore-inducing substance for *Fusarium solani* may be produced by specific bacteria (Ford *et al.*, 1970); sporangia production by the fungus *Phytophthora cinnamomi* is dependent upon inducing substances produced by soil bacteria (Marx and Bryan, 1969). Apparently such substances are absent in axenically cultured roots of the hosts. The occurrence of these specific bacteria may be related to the presence of the host, thus ensuring that spore germination or sporangial production is more likely to occur when the host is present. The stimulus may come from the host itself. Thus the growth of the sclerotia of *Sclerotium cepivorum* does not occur in unsterile soil but they do germinate when removed from the soil or in unsterile soil in the presence of roots or extracts of the host, *Allium* (Coley-Smith and Holt, 1966).

In looking at adaptations in plant nematodes it will be worth considering therefore, the influence that the host and soil microorganisms might have as stimuli and as inhibitors of egg hatch. Furthermore, just as animal nematodes require a precise set of environmental conditions for hatching, so fungi have a well defined set of environmental conditions for germination and growth although the different phases of the life cycle may have different requirements (Burrage, 1970). We must consider also the possibility that the environmental conditions in which plant nematode eggs hatch may be related to their chances of survival in the next stage of their life cycle.

The newly hatched larva, or germinated propagule, now enters the next phase of its life with its attendant hazards. The host has to be located and invaded or, in the case of ectoparasites, penetrated. With mobile hosts like animals, adaptations may involve directional movements to localities where the parasites stand a better chance of being passively ingested by the host. The migration of such animal parasitic nematodes as *Trichostrongylus* spp. on to herbage is an example (Crofton, 1954). Rabbit fleas move slowly upwind to a host by their attraction to urine, hence they tend to accumulate in places where the rabbits live (Vaughan and Mead-Briggs, 1970). Where the hosts are immobile or nearly so the problem of reaching the host can be solved by chemokinetic responses. Trematode miracidia orientate to snail hosts under the influence of a water soluble substance released by the snails (Chernin, 1970). Fungal zoospores are attracted to their hosts too, although the magnitude of zoospore accumulation cannot usually be correlated with host or non-host, with resistance or susceptibility. Exudate appears to be the main factor inducing the zoospores to accumulate around roots. The degree of accumulation increases as the amount of exudate produced increases, especially behind the root tip and at the sites of wounds (Hickman and Ho, 1966). There is in fact a great deal of evidence that exudates from plants have a chemotactic influence on parasitic fungi (Wood, 1967) so we might expect that nematodes will respond in a similar way to exudates from plants.

For those parasites that have an active stage outside the host, survival of environmental extremes is a major problem. Most species have a so-called resistant stage in which morphological features such as the lipid membranes in the egg or the thick walls of the spore provide resistance to desiccation. At such times the organism often becomes quiescent and subsequently requires a stimulus to start growth and development again. Quiescence frequently occurs at times when the levels of some environmental components are outside the range which enable organisms to grow, develop and reproduce. High temperatures or dry conditions may induce a change in physiology that enables the organism to survive until conditions return to a state where physiological activities can be resumed. Quiescence or dormancy may end with a simple change in some environmental component; the organisms' activities fluctuate as the environment fluctuates. In some cases however dormancy ends only when some specific stimulus operates and when the organism has completed certain physiological processes or reached a particular stage of morphogenesis. The term for this type of dormancy in nematodes is diapause. The terminology for these various processes has been described by Van Gundy (1965) under the general heading of hypobiosis. They are all adaptations that increase the organisms' chances of survival in times of environmental stress.

One of the stresses to which parasites are exposed is absence of a host and the problem for the parasite may be summed up as follows: to ensure continuity in the train of events that constitute the life cycle, it is essential for the parasite to move from the environment outside the host to the environment within or on the host. During the time that this movement is being made, energy is consumed and, as there is a limited amount of energy available to each organism, it has a limited time to find a host. In some species of fungi with air-borne spores, where the process of reaching the host is passive, the organism may remain dormant until it reaches the host where stimuli from the host may end dormancy. Here, survival of the species is increased if there are a large number of organisms involved, i.e. the chance of survival is increased by sheer numbers. Where the potential pathogen is active outside the host and moves either by growth as with fungal hyphae or by locomotion as with nematodes and zoospores, survival is enhanced if the parasite can obtain nutrients from the external environment. Some animal parasitic nematodes and facultative parasitic fungi feed outside the host hence they are usually considered to be free-living saprophytes until a host appears when they can become parasitic. Where organisms are obligate parasites there is greater reliance on adaptations that ensure that the minimum amount of time is spent in finding a host. Hence, dormancy and chemotaxis increase the chance that the parasite will only expend its energy when it is close to a host. Furthermore the time spent by the parasite in reaching the host is reduced by moving towards the host along a path which is shorter than it would be if the parasite moved at random. Conservation of energy is in fact one of the main functions of adaptations in parasites when they are outside the host.

Except for those parasites that enter the host through natural openings such as the mouth of animals or stomata of plants, invasion involves a penetration of the host's outer skin or cuticle. Animal-parasitic nematodes such as hookworms have adaptations that provide secretions, destructive mouthparts, and body movements that enable them to achieve this objective. Fungi do the same kind of thing with their infection peg and secreted enzymes. The problem here is how to breach the host's outer barriers quickly, and in looking for solutions we have to think in terms of mechanics, how the forces available to the parasite can be applied most effectively and how the morphology and shape of the penetrating organ influence penetration.

Having invaded the host, the parasite enters a completely different environment from that outside. In animals it is a more stable environment influenced by homeostatic mechanisms that regulate temperature, concentration of body fluids, erythrocyte concentration and so on. In plants it is likely that the internal environment reflects more closely the environment outside. In both types of host however the main problem before the parasite is to obtain food. In animal nematodes at least, there is evidence that parasites have adaptations that help them to locate the required tissues. *Nippostrongylus brasiliensis* for example aggregates in the anterior part of the small intestine of rats under the influence of some directional stimulus. Experiments have shown that the worms recognize when they are in an unsuitable part of the intestine and that they can orientate, migrate and settle in more suitable sites (Alphey, 1970).

This cursory glance at adaptation indicates its problem-solving nature and suggests how we might consider adaptation in plant nematodes. It is a deliberately teleological way and somewhat anthropomorphic into the bargain. My reason for using this device is that I believe it is a useful way to consider adaptations in that it suggests what new experiments might be done to elucidate the relationships between nematodes, plants and disease. To support my argument therefore, I will describe some of what I imagine to be the problems that face nematodes, and the adaptations that have been evolved to solve them. There are three phases of the exercise: (1) identification of the problem, e.g. nematodes may have no host plants during the winter so how do they survive? (2) an indication that the problem has been solved, e.g. nematodes overwinter in the soil to infect the next season's crops (3) a description of the means whereby the problem is solved, e.g. the eggs become dormant, the nematodes feed on weed hosts. Sometimes we may not be able to see at once the solution to a problem which we imagine exists, e.g. how do nematodes overcome the problem of overcrowding when their ability to migrate in soil is so restricted? Finally we may come across some particular aspect of the nematode's behaviour or physiology that leaves us wondering what its function is, thus we have found the solution to some problem that is as yet unknown. What function does movement of larvae in the egg have? Perhaps it has no function, but this possibility should not stop us from looking to see what happens if we immobilize the larva in the egg. Such questions demand hypotheses that can be tested by experiment.

Obviously consideration of adaptations is no different from general scientific enquiry. Thus Medawar (1968) points out that in real life the imaginative and critical acts that unite to form the hypothetico-deductive method alternate so rapidly, at least in the earlier stages of constructing a theory, that they are not spelled out in thought. The adjustment and reformulation of hypotheses through an examination of their deductive consequences is simply another setting for the ubiquitous phenomenon of negative feedback. We may collect and classify facts, we may marvel at curiosities and idly wonder what accounts for them, but the activity that is characteristically scientific begins with an exploratory conjecture which at once becomes the subject of energetic critical analysis. These words of Medawar are clearly relevant to discussion on the nature of adaptation and they set the scene for what follows—adaptations in plant nematodes.

Adaptations in plant nematodes

LIFE IN THE EGG

The processes of embryonic and postembryonic development occur within the eggshell and other membranes that provide protection against desiccation. Apart from this obvious adaptation however, we might imagine that the chance of nematode survival would be increased if it reached a stage of development which, immediately following hatching, enabled it to migrate through the soil to a host plant root. What adaptations has the nematode got that might achieve this goal? There are at least three requirements: (1) the nematode's physiological machinery must be operating efficiently, (2) it must be highly mobile, (3) it must possess the anatomical requirements for subsequent locomotion and penetration. There is a useful parallel to be drawn here between embryogenesis in nematodes and in the vertebrate amphibians. According to Hamburger (1963) the S-flexure in the Salamander (*Ambystoma*) embryo is the antecedent of integrated swimming; a sequence of several S-flexures results in locomotion for a short distance while more vigorous S-movements result in sustaining swimming. Such behaviour, Hamburger suggests, is geared to an early readiness of the hatched *Ambystoma* larva to cope with life in the external milieu; the swimming performance, that is required after hatching, emerges from earlier motility in the most direct and rapid way. In the chick embryo on the other hand, development within the shelter of the amniotic cavity precludes exposure to selective pressure of the same sort as the salamander. Studies on the locomotion of *Meloidogyne javanica* within the egg (Wallace, 1968) indicate that there is a high degree of integrated movement whereby the unhatched nematode larva moves by undulatory propulsion in basically the same way that the newly hatched larva moves through the soil. For locomotion inside the eggshell, the muscles on the side of the body touching the eggshell must progressively contract to release potential energy for locomotion. If the eggs had a constant curvature this requirement would be denied, hence the asymmetrical kidney-shape of the nematode egg might be considered as an adaptation whereby locomotion is possible; the poles of such an egg have a change in curvature and so permit the muscles to shorten. Movement in the egg can thus be considered as an adaptation that enables the nematode to reach a pitch of physiological efficiency at the time it hatches. The obvious way to test this hypothesis is to inhibit movement in the egg without preventing the completion of embryogenesis. So far such experiments have not been attempted and may prove impossible if embryonic development is dependent on such movement.

Wallace (1970) has also suggested that the annulated form of the nematode cuticle is an adaptation that provides greater flexibility. The nematode is able to bend its body into curves of very small radius. It seems possible that the annuli are formed by the mechanical process of buckling of the cuticle during its early formation. So movement is also a prerequisite for morphological development of the cuticle. Once again, inhibition of such movement would test the hypothesis that annulation is the result of a mechanical buckling of the outer cortical layers of the cuticle.

The moult of the first stage larva within the egg also ensures that the hatching second stage larva is fully equipped to penetrate a host; the stylet, absent in the first stage larva, appears in the second stage larva.

So, like the salamander larva, the nematode larva on hatching is ready to cope with the external environment. In the case of the nematode this

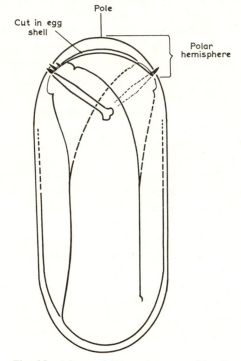

Fig. 18 A larva of *Heterodera rostochiensis* cutting a slit in the eggshell prior to hatching. (After Doncaster and Shepherd, 1967)

means migration and invasion of the host. However, we have overlooked one problem, how to escape from the confines of the eggshell. In posing this problem, and considering ways in which it can be solved, it is apparent that most of the adaptations that enable the larva to achieve physiological efficiency could equally be considered as adaptations that overcome the problem of hatching. Thus Wallace (1968) suggests that the propulsive forces achieved by the larva of *M. javanica* within the egg enable pressure to be exerted on the poles, which together with the penetration of the shell by the stylet, create an opening through which the larva escapes by un-dulatory propulsion. In *Heterodera rostochiensis* the larva makes a line of overlapping punctures with its stylet at the pole of the egg thus forming a slit through which the larva escapes (Doncaster and Shepherd, 1967, Fig. 18). A further adaptation that would assist hatching would be the release of enzymes that broke down the egg membranes. Bird (1968) has in fact shown that the lipid layer in eggs of *M. javanica* is absent in eggs in which the larva is moving actively just before hatching. Bird suggests that enzymes associated with the hydrolysis of lipids may play an im-portant part in hatching.

We may anticipate a further problem at this stage: the chance of survival would be greater if the larva on hatching entered an environment in which it could move efficiently without being exposed to hazards of desiccation, lack of oxygen or absence of a host. In *M. javanica* at least, the environ-mental conditions for maximum hatch, movement and invasion are similar, hence when an egg does hatch the larva is in an environment conducive to rapid migration to the root and to quick invasion (Wallace, 1966a). This is one solution to the problem, but there are too many observations in the literature where environmental requirements for different phases of the life cycle are different to speculate further. Thus, wide differences in the requirements for hatching and migration may indicate other types of adaptation or strategies for survival. In *Heterodera avenae* for example the optimum temperature in South Australia for larval development within the egg is about 10 °C (Fig. 19) whereas it is 20 °C for eclosion (Fig. 20). This difference in temperature requirement leads to an accumulation of unhatched larvae which, with the onset of rain, hatch within a short time (Banyer and Fisher, 1971a). The prerequisite of exposure to a temperature of 10 °C before eggs hatch in *H. avenae* is doubted by Meagher (1970) who found that although emergence did appear to follow a depression of temperature in autumn in Australia there was no evidence for a very low temperature requirement prior to hatching as described by Banyer and Fisher (1972). In spite of these conflicting views, however, it is clear that the rapid emergence of larvae of *H. avenae* from cysts in the Australian autumn, at a time when cereals are germinating, is probably an adaptation that increases the probability that when hatch does occur host plants are available for invasion. It is worth adding also that encysted eggs of *H. avenae* can survive the harsh conditions of the South Australian summer and that dormancy during this period is not interrupted by summer rainfall that might cause hatch at a time when no host plants are present (Banyer and Fisher, 1971b).

Baxter and Blake (1969a) demonstrated that the eggs of *Meloidogyne javanica* are well adapted to hatch over the same range of soil moisture

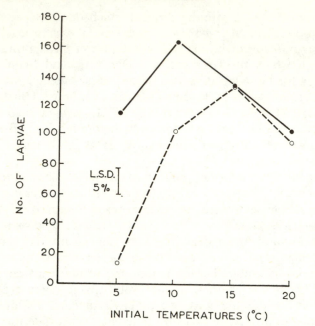

Fig. 19 The hatch of eggs of *Heterodera avenae* after 4 weeks at 5, 10, 15 and 20 °C followed by 4 weeks at 15 °C (continuous line) and the hatch after 8 weeks at constant temperatures of 5, 10, 15 and 20 °C (broken line). (After Banyer and Fisher, 1971*a*)

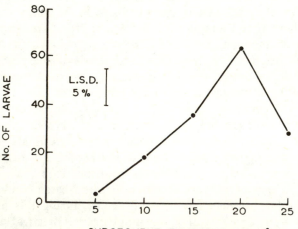

Fig. 20 The hatch of *Heterodera avenae* after 7 weeks at 5 °C followed by different subsequent temperatures for 1 week. (After Banyer and Fisher, 1971*a*)

regimes as those at which germination and growth of the host proceed. They showed that neither the development of larvae nor the hatch of single eggs were affected between pF o and 2.8. Wallace (1966*a*, 1966*b*), on the other hand, found that in the same species emergence from egg sacs was inhibited at pFs of 1.8 and 2.0, when migration was also inhibited; the adaptation suggested here is the one mentioned previously, that it is advantageous for nematodes to hatch into a soil in which they can readily migrate. Such contradictory results and interpretations are to be expected and welcomed, they provide the 'fun' part of research and above all they encourage progress. The experimental results of both lots of workers and the conclusions drawn from them, seem valid and plausible, so who is right? This is probably the wrong question however, it would be better to ask, what were the differences in the experimental procedures that produced the different results? In this case the chief difference is that Baxter and Blake used single eggs whereas I used egg sacs. So there is possibly something about egg sacs that makes them behave differently from single eggs, perhaps there is an adaptational reason why eggs of *Meloidogyne* are clumped together in a mass.

Watson and Lownsbery (1970) found that *Meloidogyne naasi* did not hatch over a range of constant temperatures but was stimulated by (1) a cold-warm treatment consisting of incubation at 6 to 9 °C for seven weeks followed by 21 to 24 °C, (2) treatment with 0.4% sodium hypochlorite. The authors speculate that stimulation by sodium hypochlorite may indicate the presence of an inhibitory substance in the egg matrix or eggshell. The temperature requirements on the other hand occur naturally in the field and it appears that hatch probably occurs with the onset of rising temperatures in spring when the host crop is germinating. *Meloidogyne javanica* requires oxygen concentrations above 10% for embryonic development, hatch and migration; thus a favourable environment for this nematode will be provided where moist soils drain rapidly and allow oxygen concentrations to increase above 10% (Baxter and Blake, 1969*b*). Such soils are probably ideal for seed germination too.

From these few examples it is evident that the integration in time of nematode hatching and host germination is an adaptation that helps to ensure that infective larvae are active at a time when the environmental conditions are suitable for migration and invasion and when the host is most likely to be there. Such an adaptation depends on the coincidental requirements of host and parasite, but it does not prevent the eggs hatching if the host is not there. Closer integration between host and parasite requires some response by the nematode to some stimulus from the plant.

The influence of root exudates on the hatch of *Heterodera* spp. is well known and has been reviewed recently by Shepherd and Clarke (1971).

Chemicals, released by the host root, stimulate hatch and where the stimulus is specific as it is for *H. rostochiensis* for example, the newly hatched larvae find themselves in the vicinity of the host plant. Furthermore, as the range of diffusion of root exudates is probably only a few mm, they are likely to hatch from the egg and emerge from the cyst within easy reach of a root. In *Meloidogyne javanica*, hatch in soil also proceeds at a greater rate when host roots are present, and in the absence of roots hatch is inhibited, possibly by microorganisms (Wallace, 1966a, Fig. 21). It seems clear that response to root exudates is a highly effective adaptation that is likely to be more widespread among plant nematodes than the literature would lead us to believe at present.

PATTERNS FOR SURVIVAL OUTSIDE THE HOST

Although the topic of survival has received much attention (Van Gundy, 1965; Cooper and Van Gundy, 1971) it will be worthwhile to consider briefly the kinds of adaptations that nematodes have evolved to solve the problem of living in a hazardous environment. The problems—desiccation, extremes of temperature, lack of oxygen, etc. are obvious, but the solutions are not always easy to identify.

There are three main ways in which a nematode can increase its chances of survival: (1) it can slow down or stop its activities and change its physiology or structure accordingly while the hazardous conditions prevail, (2) it can continue its activities but modify its physiology and behaviour in order to continue living under the changed conditions, (3) it may escape from the hazardous environment by migrating elsewhere.

The phenomenon of reduced activity and metabolism in times of environmental stress is called hypobiosis. At one extreme there are those species like *Tylenchus polyhypnus*, *Anguina tritici*, *Ditylenchus dipsaci* and others that can survive for long periods at very low temperatures and under very dry conditions. At the other extreme most species reduce their rate of development and metabolism when environmental factors temporarily move outside their particular range that permits activity. However, hypobiosis is more than a means of surviving hazardous conditions, it is also a means whereby activity of the nematode is made to coincide with that of the host thus increasing the chance of infection. The ending of hypobiosis is often associated with conditions that favour seed germination or plant growth, thus the renewed activity of nematodes in the spring following inactivity in the winter is an important survival process. As we have seen already, integration between the activities of nematode and plant may be more closely linked when hypobiosis in the egg is ended by stimulation from plant root exudates. Integration between host and parasite also

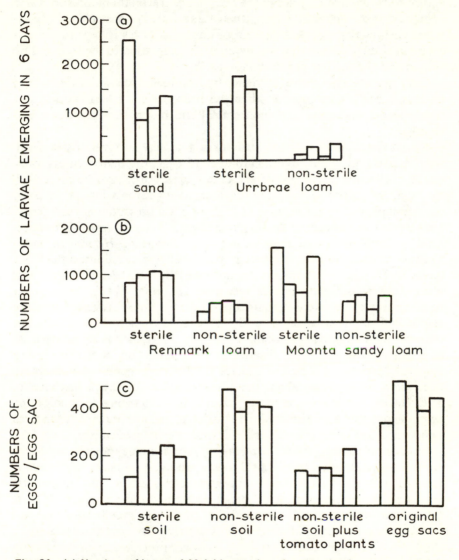

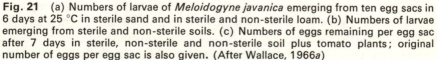

Fig. 21 (a) Numbers of larvae of *Meloidogyne javanica* emerging from ten egg sacs in 6 days at 25 °C in sterile sand and in sterile and non-sterile loam. (b) Numbers of larvae emerging from sterile and non-sterile soils. (c) Numbers of eggs remaining per egg sac after 7 days in sterile, non-sterile and non-sterile soil plus tomato plants; original number of eggs per egg sac is also given. (After Wallace, 1966*a*)

permits the conservation of the parasite's energy. Plant nematodes do not appear to feed while they are in the soil; hence it would not aid survival if nematodes were active at a time when there were no host plants. Hypobiosis ensures that the consumption of energy reserves is kept to a minimum until such time as they are required for migration to the host and its subsequent invasion or penetration.

How nematodes survive extreme environmental conditions for long periods is not understood but when the processes have been worked out it is possible that quite new biochemical and biophysical principles will emerge.

Nematodes appear to have structures that aid survival, particularly from desiccation. Thus lipid membranes in eggs, the matrix in egg sacs, or the cuticles of larvae and adults, could conceivably provide protection by forming a barrier around the organism that prevents loss of water in dry atmospheres or in solutions of high osmotic pressure or free energy. However, it is difficult to devise experiments that test such hypotheses. Ellenby (1968a) showed that second stage larvae of *Heterodera rostochiensis* survived desiccation better at all relative humidities than did larvae of *H. schachtii*. Experiments indicated that *H. schachtii* larvae lost water at a significantly higher rate than *H. rostochiensis*. Subsequent research using interference microscopy (Ellenby, 1968b) revealed that the eggshell of *H. rostochiensis* is freely permeable to water when wet, but becomes increasingly impermeable as it dries. Here then is an explanation of a mechanism whereby resistance to desiccation can be achieved, and comparison between different species of the same genus may enable a conclusion to be drawn about the adaptive value of such a mechanism. Such an approach may be more practicable than trying to modify the eggshell or cuticle of nematodes in order to change their resistance to desiccation and thereby assess the efficiency of the mechanism.

Studies on the egg sac of *Meloidogyne javanica* also indicate how eggs resist desiccation (Wallace, 1966b). Data from experiments on development, mobility in the egg, hatch, and volume changes at different osmotic potentials indicate that at some point between the development of first and second stage larvae the permeability of the egg membranes changes, probably because the lipid membrane is dissolved by enzymes secreted by the larva. The embryo and first stage larva are protected from desiccation by the lipid membrane but the unhatched second stage larva is also resistant to desiccation so it relies on its own mechanisms, whatever they are, for conserving water. The egg sac is a further barrier to loss of water from eggs. When soil pores around the egg sac drain, the moisture content of the gelatinous matrix around the eggs decreases only slightly. Reduction of the soil's hydraulic conductivity inhibits movement of water out of the egg sac thus maintaining a high level of moisture inside. At high suctions in the soil the egg sac shrinks and the enclosed eggs are subjected to pressure that inhibits increase in volume of the eggs that is a prerequisite for hatching (Wallace, 1968). Thus coupled with an adaptation that resists desiccation is one that inhibits hatching when the soil is too dry for movement. The hypothesis just described lends itself to experimental test and is one way in which an apparent adaptation can be studied to assess how it contributes to the nematode's survival. The main reason for describing these adaptations is to stress the inadequacy of statements that refer to structures as adaptations unless supporting experimental evidence is given. To say that a structure is an 'adaptation to parasitism' is either a truism or it may be false if the structure is a relic from some other environment which has changed and left a superfluous structure behind.

Physiological adaptation is another way in which nematodes increase their chance of survival. As the environment changes so the nematodes' physiological mechanisms change. *Ditylenchus dipsaci* can tolerate considerable desiccation and can withstand high osmotic pressures in its tissues. Thus as Viglierchio *et al.* (1969), say, it is adapted to tolerate whereas *Rhabditis* spp. appear to have a mechanism for ionic uptake and osmotic regulation, i.e. they have a physiological adaptation. Physiological responses to changes in the gaseous composition of the surrounding medium enable nematodes to survive in soil where fluctuations in soil water impose fluctuations of oxygen and CO_2. The fact that most nematodes have the capacity for both oxidative and fermentive metabolism enhances their chances of survival (Van Gundy, 1965). A further kind of adaptation is called acclimatization. Croll (1967) showed that when batches of *Ditylenchus dipsaci* were stored for 30 days at constant temperatures of 10 °, 20 ° and 30 °C respectively, a statistically significant proportion accumulated in a thermal gradient at the temperature in which they had been stored, Fig. 22. Here is a distinct response or adaptation whose function is obscure but it is possible that if by natural selection a strain arises that functions best at a particular temperature, survival will be enhanced if the individuals in the race subsequently tend to aggregate at that temperature. There is obviously room here for further experiments.

Experiments with larvae of *Meloidogyne javanica* (Wallace, 1969) suggest that the pattern and rate of muscular activity respond to change in soil environment thereby conserving energy reserves for infection and at the same time maintaining an efficient means of locomotion. Measurements of waves formed by the body indicated that the nematode increased its muscular effort to overcome increased resistance to locomotion, but its speed was reduced. Thus, there was little change in power output as the environment became more difficult to move in and consequently energy output was conserved. This is a speculative hypothesis that arose out of the idea that it would increase the chances of survival of this nematode if there was some means of regulating its energy consumption; otherwise the nematode would use up its energy reserves in striving to overcome the high resistance imposed by the water films in a drying soil. In other words the problem was recognized first and experiments were done to see if an adaptation had evolved to deal with the situation. In Croll's (1967) acclimatization experiments, on the other hand, the adaptation was recognized first but the problem that elicited the adaptation has not yet been found.

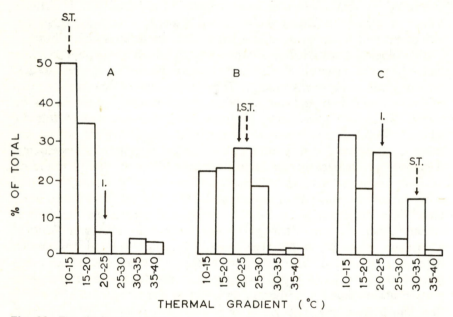

Fig. 22 The distribution of *Ditylenchus dipsaci* in a thermal gradient. Storage temperatures A = 10 °C, B = 20 °C and C = 30 °C. I = inoculation point, S.T. = storage temperature. (After Croll, 1967)

It is now becoming clear that nematodes have a wide range of possibilities whereby they can survive hazardous conditions. But there is one further solution, to avoid such stresses by escaping to less hazardous surroundings. This they can do by migrating. Thus Wyss (1970) found that the tolerance of migratory root nematodes towards increasing desiccation of the soil and high osmotic pressure varied between species. The Tylenchida were less susceptible to both factors than the Dorylaimida and the highest tolerance was shown by *Tylenchorhynchus dubius*. Moreover the more resistant species occurred nearer the soil surface. It is possible that the vertical distribution of nematodes in soil as described by Wyss and by other workers is merely the result of differential survival; that individual species have particular requirements for temperature, moisture and aeration which occur at particular soil horizons, and that if they move out or are carried out of this zone they perish. Alternatively, nematodes may actively migrate by orientation in physical and chemical gradients, to particular regions where their requirements are met. There is ample evidence to indicate that they are capable of such behaviour (Croll, 1970) but do they actually behave this way in nature? Only further research can answer this question.

FINDING A HOST

Having hatched, the nematode moves through the soil pores at speeds determined by moisture, temperature, aeration and other factors (Wallace, 1968). During this time, energy reserves are consumed and not replenished as all plant nematodes appear to be obligate parasites that do not feed during the freeliving stages (Van Gundy et al., 1967). Consequently we can recognize a problem in survival here that requires a solution in the form of an adaptation. The chance of a nematode surviving decreases as the distance it has to travel to reach a root increases. To decrease the distance travelled from egg to root requires a directional response and the orientation of nematodes to roots fulfils this requirement. There have been numerous reports on the movement of plant nematodes to their host roots (Klingler, 1965; Croll, 1970; Green, 1971) and in general root exudates have been proposed as the most likely stimulus. However negative electrical potentials (Caveness and Panzer, 1960; Jones, 1960) and temperature (El-Sherif and Mai, 1969; Klingler, 1972) have also been suggested. Furthermore, it is well known that CO_2 is an attractant (Klinger, 1963) so it looks as though orientation will not be specific in the way that hatch in species like *Heterodera rostochiensis* is only stimulated in root exudates from a narrow range of host plants. Thus, although the problem of finding a plant root has been solved by adaptation, there is no evidence that the problem of finding the right plant root, i.e. the host, has been solved. Of course they may not need to if some adaptation earlier in the life cycle ensures that hatch tends to be greater in the presence of the host. Hence, it is worth asking once more whether hatch in response to specific plant exudates is not more prevalent than the literature indicates at present.

INVASION OF THE HOST

Let us imagine that the nematode has successfully survived the hazardous journey from the egg to surface of the host plant root and that it has conserved enough energy for the final task of invading the host's tissues. The first problem is to locate that part of the root which presents the least obstacle to invasion or penetration and which at the same time is near to those internal tissues on which the nematode feeds. Species like *Hemicycliophora arenaria* and *Xiphinema diversicaudatum* prefer the meristem, *Meloidogyne* spp. and *Heterodera* spp. the zone of root elongation, while *Pratylenchus penetrans* and *Xiphinema americanum* appear to prefer the zone of maturation (Kirkpatrick *et al.*, 1964). Such adaptations have selective value but whether the chosen sites are in fact related to ease of penetration or choice of food is unknown, however it is an hypothesis amenable to experimental test. It may be possible, for example, to correlate the invasion sites for a particular nematode in different hosts with the thickness of the plant's cuticle or some other structural feature, or with the location of particular tissues like phloem and endodermis. As a nematode's preference for particular zones of the root varies between different host species, such a study may be worthwhile.

The penetration and invasion of host tissues is a problem in mechanics and the stylet is an obvious adaptation that provides the solution. However, the problem does not end there, quick penetration requires the application of the maximum amount of force. The pointed tip of the stylet enables the force to be applied over a very small area, hence pressure on the plant cell wall is increased. The stylet tends to be applied at right angles to the surface of the root thus providing maximum penetrative force (Fisher and Evans, 1967; Wallace, 1968). Further force may be achieved by a spiralling or corkscrew action of the body (Wallace, 1968) that provide shearing forces. The stylet combines sensory functions with mechanical ones; the labial papillae may be tactile, and by sensing the resistance to penetration of surfaces, regulate the strength of stylet thrusts (Doncaster, 1971). The reaction between stylet and the root surface must be opposed by equal and opposite reactions if penetration is to occur. Wallace (1959) has suggested that the thin water films in soil may provide the necessary reaction; Dickinson (1959) suggests that the nematode's lips act like a suction cup and attach the nematode to the root; Kisiel *et al.* (1971), found that *Hemicycliophora similis* attaches itself to cranberry roots by means of an adhesive plug circling the stylet. In *Meloidogyne javanica*, invasion of the root is achieved initially by propulsive forces developed by the body outside the root but when one fifth of the body has entered, the posterior end stops moving and the anterior end does most of the work; thus the nematode pulls itself into the root (Wallace, 1968). Finally it is possible that enzymes may be secreted that soften the root tissues and so facilitate penetration, but there is little evidence for this.

Aphelenchoides ritzemabosi is a leaf parasite that invades the host via stomata. Klingler (1970) posed the question, how do such nematodes find and enter the stomata under fluctuating environmental conditions? His experiments suggested the kinds of stimuli that might lead to successful invasion: random movement over the leaf surface, mechanical stimulation caused by the interruption in the water film at the leaf surface, cessation of movement and probing movements of the head at the stoma, tactile stimulation of the head at the stoma and eventual additional chemical stimulation by CO_2, activation of locomotion and passage through the stoma. Having described possible adaptations Klingler then posed another question that could initiate further experiments: when do the conditions for successful invasion occur under natural conditions, i.e. at what time of day, and under what weather conditions do thin water films, open stomata and CO_2 concentrations in the leaf's intercellular spaces fulfil the requirements for invasion? The problem is a plant physiological one, but to those interested in adaptations it is a common experience that answers to problems have often to be sought outside the field of nematology and even biology.

FINDING FOOD

As soon as we begin to consider adaptations of nematodes within or on the host plant, it is clear how little we know of the behaviour and physiology of nematodes as parasites and pathogens. The problem of finding the right cells on which to feed is an example. Are there directional responses that enable the nematode to reach particular sites? Is the choice of cells from which a nematode extracts nutrient a purely random business? Random feeding is likely to be destructive to the plant and disadvantageous to the nematode, so selection of feeding sites is desirable particularly in species like *Heterodera* and *Meloidogyne* where the development of syncytia may depend on the selection of particular cells. Is there, in fact, a particular number of feeding sites per unit length of root for such nematodes? Feeding may not be too destructive to the plant as a whole as long as vital tissues remain untouched; the migratory habits of *Pratylenchus* spp. may be considered an adaptation whereby those cells that are destroyed during feeding do not seriously impair the physiological efficiency of the plant unless numbers of nematodes are excessively high. The questions then arise: what factors prevent the nematode from destroying cells that are important in the plant's physiology? Has the nematode characteristics to counteract the plant's defensive mechanisms? Has the nematode adaptations that ensure that it does not destroy its host while destroying the cells on which it feeds? At this stage of enquiry we are almost overwhelmed with so-called problems without much indication that adaptations exist to solve them.

Ectoparasitic nematodes and the migratory endoparasitic nematodes move by undulatory propulsion; the body forms waves often with a small radius of curvature. Locomotion of this kind requires flexibility of the cuticle and Wallace (1970) has suggested that the annular structure of the nematode cuticle is an adaptation that provides such flexibility. As the nematode grows and develops, however, the cuticle is stretched and flexibility and motility would decrease unless the size of the annulations was increased. Moulting would appear to be one way to solve this problem because a new and larger cuticle would replace the older one. Shepherd and Clarke (1971) suggest that moulting may be an adaptation that permits growth in nematodes whose cuticle is only partially extensible but they point out that the animal parasitic nematode *Ascaris* increases in length by about 400 times, and after the final moult by 29 times. In *Ascaris* the cuticle is increased in size between and during moults, hence moulting cannot be considered as an adaptation solely for the purpose of accommodating increase in size. Crofton (1966) in fact believes that moulting is to allow more complex structural changes to occur and new organs (such as the mouth stylet) to be formed or modified.

In looking for 'problems' that have given rise to adaptations it must therefore be realized that different species may have similar adaptations for different purposes and that an adaptation might solve more than one problem.

It may be as well to reiterate at this stage that the consideration of adaptations as problem solving events is an artificial way (but useful) of viewing the host-parasite relationship. There is little danger in this approach as long as it is realized that variations occur first by chance and that the apparent problem solving nature of the adaptation is a consequence of natural selection.

In endoparasitic sedentary nematodes like *Meloidogyne* and *Heterodera*, the cuticle of the larva becomes almost structureless once the nematode adopts the parasitic life. Bird (1971) suggests that such a cuticle is capable of greater increases in surface area. Moreover, the muscles atrophy and hence provide a more useful source of energy for the developing nematode. Moulting does occur in these nematodes but it is rapid and the cuticles are not discarded. Is this an adaptation whose function we do not understand or is it a relic of a previous time when such behaviour had survival value? Questions like this may appear rather sterile because it is difficult to see how we could test the hypothesis by experiment. On the other hand future research may provide us with methods for controlling moulting and then the question could become pertinent. The fact that moulting in *Paratylenchus* spp. can be stimulated by root exudates indicates that progress in this field may occur in the near future.

REPRODUCTION

Where the number of nematodes in a population is low, sexual reproduction may be limited by the number of successful contacts between males and females. Klomp and colleagues (1964) have expressed the problem in the form of a mathematical model although they remark that the model is inappropriate for some species presumably because of lack of attraction between the sexes. In a pot experiment to study the multiplication of *Rotylenchus uniformis* on peas, Seinhorst (1968) found that at high initial densities the rate of multiplication was considerably higher than at lower initial densities. Seinhorst attributed these results to the decreased chance of a female meeting a male at low initial densities. Finding a mate is a real problem and there are at least two solutions: sexual reproduction may be abandoned for parthenogenesis or the sexes may attract each other and so reduce the hazards of meeting by chance.

The subject of sexual attraction in nematodes has been reviewed by Green (1971) hence I do not intend to describe it in detail. Instead, I will discuss some of the conclusions drawn by various researchers because they indicate how thinking of adaptations in terms of problem-solving can often be useful and stimulating.

Green (1966) demonstrated that females of *Heterodera rostochiensis* emit a chemical that is attractive to males. Perception of the chemical appears to be gustatory as it has a low vapour pressure and diffuses in the soil water. The chemical stimulus elicits a klinokinetic aggregation behaviour, i.e. the males react to decreases in chemical concentration by turning but they show no reaction to increases in concentration. The males also orientate by klinotaxis, i.e. regular lateral movements of the body enable the male to compare concentrations at successive time intervals, and so move towards the source of the chemical, the female. Green observed that males find even isolated females in soil so the problem of finding a mate is partly overcome by this adaptation. However, the further point is made that if newly emerged males were unresponsive to females, the chance of inbreeding, which is often harmful, would be decreased. Thus sexual attraction, while increasing the chance of survival in one direction, may decrease it in another. Perhaps the hazard of inbreeding is less than that of not finding a mate.

Although the chemical sex attractant in *Heterodera* spp. appears to have a low volatility, Greet *et al.* (1968), suggest that the volatile component may play an indirect role in soil by arousing the usually inactive males or stimulating them to emerge from the ensheathing cuticles of third and fourth stage larvae so that they move at random until they come to the aqueous gradient that leads them to the female. The volatile fractions of the sex attractant would be well fitted for this role because of their ability to diffuse through the air spaces in the soil to greater distances than their non-volatile counterparts in the soil water. In effect these authors are proposing the kind of problem that an observed adaptation might solve.

Evans (1970) too suggests that the sexual attractant might activate as well as attract males. As females may stop producing attractant once they are mated it is possible, Evans argues, that a stimulus is required to make males move as well as to attract them. Thus the system is doubly efficient, males do not exhaust themselves by moving unless females that can be fertilized are present.

The ability of males to mate with several females successfully are advantageous in species such as *H. rostochiensis* and *H. schachtii* in which the sex ratio ranges greatly and males may be outnumbered by 9 to 1 in sparse populations. Furthermore multiple mating causes a greater diversity of genes in the offspring of one female (Green *et al.*, 1970).

PATTERNS FOR SURVIVAL IN THE HOST

Once a nematode has entered the host plant its main requirement is food. Several factors may restrict this resource however. There may be insufficient food for the number that are present in the root; drought, lack of nutrients, or high temperature may inhibit plant growth and so reduce the quantity and quality of food for the nematodes. We have already seen in Chapter 3 that change in the sex ratio in some species results in fewer females and more males under conditions of crowding or when the plant is under stress. As males consume less food than females, the chance of some females reaching maturity and laying eggs is enhanced, thereby ensuring the survival of at least some individuals in the population.

Bird (1970) showed that the rate of growth of *Meloidogyne javanica* is related to the degree of stress to which the plant and nematode are subjected. Slight stress leads to an acceleration in the growth rate of the nematode, further stress leads to the production of males and a slowing down of the growth rate. Kirkpatrick *et al.* (1964), also point out that certain nutritional and other physiological conditions that result in reduced plant vigour can increase the rate of nematode development and reproduction.

Hence nematode populations that produce significant reductions in plant vigour apparently stimulate their own rate of growth. Bird (1971) suggests that accelerated growth of the nematode when the plant is declining permits the nematodes to survive when a more slowly developing species would perish. This is a plausible explanation that might be tested by experiment if species of nematodes can be found that infect the same plant but which have different growth responses when the plant is under stress. Alternatively, a particular species may not have the ability to react to stress by increasing its rate of growth on all hosts. Studies on population growth under these different conditions might indicate whether 'the race against time' hypothesis was realistic.

A further adaptation that increases the chance of survival when food is limiting is described by Evans and Fisher (1970). *Aphelenchus avenae* was cultured on two growth media with different nutrient content. Although egg production was the same on both media, the nematodes were smaller on the medium with least nutrient. Thus the demands for egg production take precedence over those for body tissues when nutrients are limiting. Although *A. avenae* is not an endoparasite, these experiments indicate a further way in which the problem of lack of food might be met.

When there is insufficient food to support a population of animals, migration to other areas often occurs. Nematodes may act in an analogous way by vacating a root if they are unable to find a feeding site or adequate food. If tomato plants inoculated with *M. javanica* are sampled at intervals to determine numbers of nematodes in the roots, the numbers increase for about a week and then decline sharply. There is no evidence of dead larvae in the roots hence it seems likely that in this species at least movement out of the root is as much a pattern of behaviour as invasion.

Information on the responses of nematodes to environmental factors, other than food, within the plant is markedly lacking. The characteristics of the internal environment of the host plant: moisture, aeration, pH, osmotic pressure are unknown. There are some data on the values of these components in the intact healthy plant but it seems likely that the picture will change markedly when cells are destroyed and cavities are formed or when hypertrophy and hyperplasia occur along with the inevitable changes in biochemical components. Unlike animal parasitologists, the plant pathologists know little of the influence of the fluctuations in the plant's internal micro-environment and what adaptations the parasite has evolved to achieve survival. It may be incorrect, for example, to imagine that on invading the root, the nematode enters a safe haven in which it is protected from the rigours outside. It may simply enter a different kind of environment with characteristics of its own that continue to exert selective pressures on the nematode.

Conclusions

Adaptations are events that arose in the past when some change in the organism afforded increased chance of survival in a changing environment. Taxonomists describe differences in structure between species and morphologists explore the structural intricacies of different organs and tissues and, occasionally, relate form and function. The student of adaptations however starts with such facts and speculates on how they may be beneficial, useful or efficient in terms of natural selection. In nematology, perhaps no one has stimulated as much thought on adaptations and form and function in nematodes as Harris and Crofton. The ideas that the elongated cylindrical form of nematodes is determined by mechanical considerations, and that the structure of their cuticle and their internal pressure are determined by the undulatory type of locomotion in these animals, appear in what must be regarded as a classical paper (Harris and Crofton, 1957). As Crofton (1971) says 'the most impressive feature to the fundamental morphologist is the ecological diversity achieved with economy of structure. Probably in no other group is the relationship between form and function so clearly seen'. Just as Harris and Crofton followed the lead of D'Arcy Thompson in relating structure to function, so have other authors subsequently produced research papers in a similar vein. For example, Roggen (1970) has asked the question: is there an upper limit to the diameter of the pharynx in nematodes? Roggen states certain assumptions, develops his argument and examines the facts to test his hypothesis. Predictions are then made which suggest useful experiments— this is where the real value of considering adaptations lies. In a similar vein, Wallace (1971) asked the question: are there mechanical or functional reasons why most plant nematodes have a similar length to width ratio of about 30? A hypothesis was then developed that explained this observation, but the real reward from the exercise came when ideas appeared for further experiments that might disprove the hypothesis.

What puts such questions into the head of the research worker in the first place is beyond the scope of this book but the habit of looking for functions in aspects of behaviour, structure and form is probably partly responsible. Furthermore it is not just questions about the function of structures like hemizonids or cephalids that invoke the most discussion but curiosity about aspects of nematodes that are more obvious, so obvious in fact that we take them for granted. Harris and Crofton's paper contained little that was not known already but the synthesis of the facts into a simple but vital hypothesis was the major accomplishment.

The study of adaptations has practical value as well. There is always the possibility that some aspect of nematode behaviour can be modified to the benefit of the plant; thus the study of sex attractants (pheromones) in nematodes may indicate a method of control as is used for insects. Furthermore, as the subject of models and systems simulation develops in plant nematology there will be a requirement for information about feedback and other relationships that influence the ecological or physiological system. Do nematodes regulate their own numbers in the plant and if so, how do they do it? Questions like this involve a study of adaptations.

References

ALPHEY, T.J.W. (1970). Studies on the distribution and site location of *Nippostrongylus brasiliensis* within the small intestine of laboratory rats. *Parasitology*, **61**, 449.

BANYER, R.J. and FISHER, J.M. (1971*a*). Effect of temperature on hatching of eggs of *Heterodera avenae. Nematologica*, **17**, 519.

BANYER, R.J. and FISHER, J.M. (1971*b*). Seasonal variation in hatching of eggs of *Heterodera avenae. Nematologica*, **17**, 225.

BANYER, R.J. and FISHER, J.M. (1972). Motility in relation to hatching of eggs of *Heterodera avenae. Nematologica*, **18**, 18.

BAXTER, R.I. and BLAKE, C.D. (1969*a*). Some effects of suction on the hatching eggs of *Meloidogyne javanica. Ann. appl. Biol.*, **63**, 183.

BAXTER, R.I. and BLAKE, C.D. (1969*b*). Oxygen and the hatch of eggs and migration of larvae of *Meloidogyne javanica. Ann. appl. Biol.*, **63**, 191.

BIRD, A.F. (1968). Changes associated with parasitism in nematodes. 3. Ultrastructure of the egg shell, larval cuticle, and contents of the subventral esophageal glands in *Meloidogyne javanica,* with some observations on hatching. *J. Parasit.*, **54**, 475.

BIRD, A.F. (1970). The effect of nitrogen deficiency on the growth of *Meloidogyne javanica* at different population levels. *Nematologica*, **16**, 13.

BIRD, A.F. (1971). Specialized adaptations of nematodes to parasitism. In *Plant parasitic nematodes* Vol. 2. Edited by B.M. Zuckerman, W.F. Mai and R.A. Rohde. Academic Press, xvi + 347 pp.

BURRAGE, S.W. (1970). Environmental factors influencing the infection of wheat by *Puccinia graminis. Ann. appl. Biol.*, **66**, 429.

CAVENESS, F.E. and PANZER, J.D. (1960). Nemic galvanotaxis. *Proc. helminth. Soc. Wash.*, **27**, 73.

CHERNIN, E. (1970). Behavioral responses of miracidia of *Schistosoma mansoni* and other trematodes to substances emitted by snails. *J. Parasit.*, **56**, 287.

COLEY-SMITH, J.R. and HOLT, R.W. (1966). The effect of species of *Allium* on germination in soil of sclerotia of *Sclerotium cepivorum* Berk. *Ann. appl. Biol.*, **58**, 273.

COOPER, A.F. and VAN GUNDY, S.D. (1971). Senescence, quiescence and cryptobiosis. In *Plant parasitic nematodes* Vol. 2. Edited by B.M. Zuckerman, W.F. Mai and R.A. Rohde. Academic Press, xvi + 347 pp.

CROFTON, H.D. (1954). The ecology of the immature phases of trichostrongyle parasites. V. The estimation of pasture infestation. *Parasitology*, **44**, 313.

CROFTON, H.D. (1966). *Nematodes.* Hutchinson Univ. Library, Lond., 160 pp.

CROFTON, H.D. (1971). Form, function and behaviour. In *Plant parasitic nematodes* Vol. 1. Edited by B.M. Zuckerman, W.F. Mai and R.A. Rohde, Academic Press.

CROLL, N.A. (1967). Acclimatization in the eccritic thermal response of *Ditylenchus dipsaci. Nematologica*, **13**, 385.

CROLL, N.A. (1970). *The behaviour of nematodes.* Edward Arnold. ix + 117 pp.

DICKINSON, S. (1959). The behaviour of larvae of *Heterodera schachtii* on nitrocellulose membranes. *Nematologica*, **4**, 60.

DONCASTER, C.C. (1971). Feeding in plant parasitic nematodes: mechanisms and behaviour. In *Plant Parasitic nematodes* Vol. 2. Edited by B.M. Zuckerman, W.F. Mai and R.A. Rohde. Academic Press, xvi + 347 pp.

DONCASTER, C.C. and SHEPHERD, A.M. (1967). The behaviour of second-stage *Heterodera rostochiensis* larvae leading to their emergence from the egg. *Nematologica*, **13**, 476.

EL-SHERIF, M. and MAI, W.F. (1969). Thermotactic response of some plant parasitic nematodes. *J. Nematology*, **1**, 43.

ELLENBY, C. (1968*a*). The survival of desiccated larvae of *Heterodera rostochiensis* and *H. schachtii. Nematologica*, **14**, 544.

ELLENBY, C. (1968*b*). Desiccation survival in the plant parasitic nematodes *Heterodera rostochiensis* Wollenweber and *Ditylenchus dipsaci* (Kuhn) Filipjev. *Proc. Roy Soc. B. Lond.*, **169**, 203.

EVANS, K. (1970). Longevity of males and fertilization of females of *Heterodera rostochiensis. Nematologica*, **16**, 369.

EVANS, A.A.F. and FISHER, J.M. (1970). Some factors affecting the number and size of nematodes in populations of *Aphelenchus avenae. Nematologica*, **16**, 295.

FISHER, J.M. and EVANS, A.A.F. (1967). Penetration and feeding by *Aphelenchus avenae. Nematologica*, **13**, 425.

FORD, E.J., GOLD, A.H. and SNYDER, W.C. (1970). Soil substances inducing chlamydospore formation by *Fusarium. Phytopathology*, **60**, 124.

GREEN, C.D. (1966). Orientation of male *Heterodera rostochiensis* Woll. and *H. schachtii* Schm. to their females. *Ann. appl. Biol.*, **58**, 327.

GREEN, C.D. (1971). Mating and host finding behaviour of plant nematodes. In *Plant parasitic nematodes*. Vol. 2. Edited by B.M. Zuckerman, W.F. Mai, and R.A. Rohde. Academic Press, xvi + 347 pp.

GREEN, C.D., GREET, D.N. and JONES, F.G.W. (1970). The influence of multiple mating on the reproduction and genetics of *Heterodera rostochiensis* and *H. schachtii*. *Nematologica*, **16**, 309.

GREET, D.N., GREEN, C.D. and POULTON, M.E. (1968). Extraction, standardization and assessment of the volatility of the sex attractants of *Heterodera rostochiensis* Woll. and *H. schachtii* Schm. *Ann. appl. Biol.*, **61**, 511.

HAMBURGER, V. (1963). Some aspects of the embryology of behaviour. *Q. Rev. Biol.*, **38**, 342.

HARRIS, J.E. and CROFTON, H.D. (1957). Structure and function in the nematodes: internal pressure and cuticular structure in *Ascaris*. *J. exp. Biol.*, **34**, 116.

HICKMAN, C.J. and HO, H.H. (1966). Behaviour of zoospores in plant-pathogenic phycomycetes. *Ann. Rev. Phytopath.*, **4**, 195.

JONES, F.G.W. (1960). Some observations and reflections on host finding by plant nematodes. *Meded. Landbhoogesch. Gent*, **25**, 1009.

KIRKPATRICK, J.D., VAN GUNDY, S.D. and MAI, W.F. (1964). Interrelationships of plant nutrition, growth and parasitic nematodes. *Plant analysis and fertilizer problems*, **4**, 189.

KISIEL, M., CASTILLO, J. and ZUCKERMAN, B.M. (1971). An adhesive plug associated with the feeding of *Hemicycliophora similis* on cranberry. *J. Nematology*, **3**, 296.

KLINGLER, J. (1963). Die orientierung von *Ditylenchus dipsaci* in gemessenen künstlichen und biologischen CO_2-gradienten. *Nematologica*, **9**, 185.

KLINGLER, J. (1965). On the orientation of plant nematodes and of some other soil animals. *Nematology*, **11**, 4.

KLINGLER, J. (1970). The reaction of *Aphelenchoides fragariae* to slit-like micro-openings and to stomatal diffusion gases. *Nematologica*, **16**, 417.

KLINGLER, J. (1972). The effect of single and combined heat and CO_2 stimuli at different ambient temperatures on the behaviour of two plant-parasitic nematodes. *J. Nematology*, **4**, 95.

KLOMP, H., VAN MONTFORT, M.A.J. and TAMMES, P.M.L. (1964). Sexual reproduction and underpopulation. *Archs. néerl. Zool.*, **16**, 105.

MARX, D.H. and BRYAN, W.C. (1969). Effect of soil bacteria on the mode of infection of pine roots by *Phytophthora cinnamomi*. *Phytopathology*, **59**, 614.

MEAGHER, J.W. (1970). Seasonal fluctuations in numbers of larvae of the cereal cyst nematode (*Heterodera avenae*) and of *Pratylenchus minyus* and *Tylenchorhynchus brevidens* in soil. *Nematologica*, **16**, 333.

MEDAWAR, P.B. (1968). *The art of the soluble*. Methuen, 160 pp.

ROBERTSON, N.F. (1968). The growth process in fungi. *Ann. Rev. Phytopath.*, **6**, 115.

ROGERS, W.P. (1960). The physiology of infective processes of nematode parasites; the stimulus from the animal host. *Proc. Roy. Soc. B. Lond.*, **152**, 367.

ROGGEN, D.R. (1970). Is there an upper limit to the diameter of the pharynx in nematodes ? *Nematologica*, **16**, 605.

SEINHORST J.W. (1968). Under-population in plant parasitic nematodes. *Nematologica*, **14**, 549.

SHEPHERD, A.M. and CLARKE, A.J. (1971). Molting and hatching stimuli. In *Plant Parasitic Nematodes* Vol. 2. Edited by B.M. Zuckerman, W.F. Mai and R.A. Rohde. Academic Press, xvi + 347 pp.

VAN GUNDY, S.D. (1965). Factors in survival of nematodes. *Ann. Rev. Phytopathology*, **3**, 43.

VAN GUNDY, S.D., BIRD, A.F. and WALLACE, H.R. (1967). Aging and starvation in larvae of *Meloidogyne javanica* and *Tylenchulus semipenetrans*. *Phytopathology*, **57**, 559.

VAUGHAN, J.A. and MEAD-BRIGGS, A.R. (1970). Host-finding behaviour of the rabbit-flea *Spilopsyllus cuniculi* with special reference to the significance of urine as an attractant. *Parasitology*, **61**, 397.

VIGLIERCHIO, D.R., CROLL, N.A. and GORTZ, J.H. (1969). The physiological response of nematodes to osmotic stress and an osmotic treatment for separating nematodes. *Nematologica*, **15**, 15.

WALLACE, H.R. (1959). The movement of eelworms in water films. *Ann. appl. Biol.*, **47**, 366.

WALLACE, H.R. (1966a). Factors influencing the infectivity of plant parasitic nematodes. *Proc. Roy. Soc. B. Lond.*, **164**, 592.

WALLACE, H.R. (1966b). The influence of moisture stress on the development, hatch and survival of eggs of *Meloidogyne javanica*. *Nematologica*, **12**, 57.

WALLACE, H.R. (1968). Undulatory locomotion of the plant parasitic nematode *Meloidogyne javanica*. *Parasitology*, **58**, 377.

WALLACE, H.R. (1969). Wave formation by infective larvae of the plant parasitic nematode *Meloidogyne javanica*. *Nematologica*, **15**, 65.

WALLACE, H.R. (1970). The flexibility of larvae of *Meloidogyne javanica* within the egg. *Nematologica*, **16**, 249.

WALLACE, H.R. (1971). The movement of nematodes in the external environment. In *Ecology and physiology of parasites*. Edited by A.H. Fallis. Univ. of Toronto Press, x + 258 pp.

WATSON, T.R. and LOWNSBERY, B.F. (1970). Factors influencing the hatching of *Meloidogyne naasi*, and a comparison with *M. hapla*. *Phytopathology*, **60**, 457.

WILSON, P.A.G. (1958). The effect of weak electrolyte solutions on the hatching rate of the eggs of *Trichostrongylus retortaeformis* (Zeder) and its interpretation in terms of a proposed hatching mechanism of strongyloid eggs. *J. exp. Biol.*, **35**, 584.

WOOD, R.K.S. (1967). *Physiological plant pathology*. Blackwells Sci. Publ., xi + 570 pp.

WYSS, U. (1970). Parasitierungsvorgang und Pathogenität wandernder Wurzelnematoden an *Fragaria vesca* var. *semperflorens*. *Nematologica*, **16**, 55.

8 Nematodes as a cause of disease in plants

A thorough knowledge of the ecology of a crop should include those factors that are chiefly responsible for the growth and yield of the plants; it should explain the distribution of unthrifty, dying or stunted individuals within the crop and identify the environmental components responsible for variations in plant density. To accomplish such a difficult task, a knowledge of plant physiology, plant ecology, soil science, plant pathology and statistics is required. Consequently, the individual who has the job of diagnosing the causes of poor crop growth, has to face a complex ecological problem in which the answers are seldom obvious.

First a word about causes, for it is important to explain what is meant by cause in the present context of plants, nematodes and disease. It is usual to think of causality in terms of the relationships between two factors, i.e. nematodes and plants, but it has already been emphasized that nematodes never act alone when they parasitize plants, and plants respond in many ways to damage. Thus although the idea of single causes and specific effects is attractive because of its simplicity, it is unrealistic, it does not happen in real life. Furthermore, it is tempting to think in causal chains; thus we might imagine a plausible story that goes: a warm wet spring caused a widespread hatch of *Heterodera avenae* that caused a massive invasion of young wheat roots that caused severe losses in yields over a wide area that caused the farmer to sell his farm and so on. But once again causal chains are unrealistic because there are numerous factors acting at any one point in the chain, hence a web of interacting events is closer to reality. Thus instead of using the expression 'cause of disease', we might substitute 'contributor to disease' thereby avoiding the notion of one cause, one effect and at the same time emphasizing the idea of a web of components that influence disease.

Let us imagine that we have been asked to find out what is wrong with a crop of wheat on a particular farm. According to the farmer there are several areas of poorly growing plants and even some patches with no plants at all. To clarify the objectives, we must first of all define the problem in more precise terms: we want to know what components of the cereal plants' environment are chiefly responsible for the observed variation in numbers and distribution of plants within the field.

The solution to the problem is not likely to be easy or obvious. Awareness of the complexities of the ecological web immediately deter any 'snap' diagnoses based on symptoms. We assume from the outset that several factors are responsible for the farmer's poorly growing wheat although we hope that only a few, perhaps one or two, will be of real importance.

Having made the mental resolution to be non-committal about causes, we then have a look at the wheat field. Our purpose at this stage is to obtain information from the farmer and through our own observations on what might be worth measuring when we come to sample the field. The farmer tells us that he has had *Rhizoctonia* and *Ophiobolus* in previous wheat crops and that the poorly growing areas often appear on the tops of the hills. On pulling up a few plants it is also obvious that *Heterodera avenae* is present and no doubt *Pratylenchus* will be about. Further enquiry reveals that during heavy rainfall ponding often occurs in some parts of the field, especially in areas where the soil is heavier. A picture is already building up of possible combinations of causal factors, of interactions and even the outside possibility of a single major factor. We have now decided what should be measured and how the area should be sampled so that we can obtain sufficient data of the right sort which can then be statistically analyzed and enable us to reach a conclusion that explains why the field of wheat is in such a sorry state. The results of our work may indicate that the main causes of poor wheat growth are a combination of winter ponding, damage from *Rhizoctonia* and low soil nitrogen, with nematodes (in spite of their numbers) having only a minor influence on the plant. Or it may turn out that of all the factors we measured, *Heterodera avenae* is by far the most important factor correlated with the incidence of poor wheat growth; it is in fact a nematode problem. The important point however is that it is impossible to decide whether we have a nematode, fungus, fertilizer or any other problem, until some quantitative measurements have been made. Sometimes a crop may be so severely infected with a parasite that it would be absurd to deny that the parasite was likely to be a major cause of disease but such occasions are rare, and we are still left wondering whether there is not some other environmental component that predisposed the crop to such a severe infection.

It seems to me therefore, that it is very important to establish the causal factors in a diseased crop before we give it a label and are committed to a particular line of research or even control. The importance of the extension worker as an ecologist equipped to diagnose causes of disease after adequate sampling and analysis has been largely overlooked in this respect. He is in fact the key man with one of the most complex biological problems in front of him. His conclusions should decide what control measures are required in a particular disease situation and further, he might also indicate where research should be directed within the system. The plant nematologists in particular require etiological information to help them decide whether they have a 'nematode problem', what aspects of the problem they should concentrate on and who they should collaborate with, to solve problems where other factors, in addition to nematodes, are involved.

In Chapter 6 the factors influencing the distribution and numbers of nematodes were discussed. In this chapter we consider the same problem except that the plant is now the target organism instead of the nematode; the nematode becomes part of the plant's environment. Thus the plant and the nematode are caught up in the same ecological web, each being part of the environment of the other and each sharing some of the other's environmental components. There are various definitions of environment in the literature but, in the present context, I define it as all those factors that influence an organism's chance to survive or reproduce. Of all the factors in the environment, some act more directly than others on the target organism, however this distinction does not imply that direct factors are more important; to explain why plants are more diseased in one locality than in another, the solution might lie in a single indirect factor such as soil moisture that influences the invasion of plant roots by nematodes.

In the context of such a holistic approach we will therefore be interested in multifactorial problems, with interactions between environmental components and with ways in which we can analyse data to arrive at simple and realistic conclusions which can be tested by further experiment. Recent work on the ecology of nematodes using principal component and factor analyses indicates that there is now an awareness of the contribution quantitative ecology can make to nematology. The same procedures can be used equally well in studies on the ecology of the plant where nematodes are part of the plant's environment. In fact, in such research as that reported by Nyhan et al. (1972) where the factors influencing nematode distribution were studied, it should be possible to use the same data to answer the question 'which factors are most closely correlated with plant weight or yield of soy-beans?'

Before we go any further however, let us look briefly at some aspects of medical science that deal with diagnosis and etiology.

Attitudes from medical science

In medicine diagnosis is concerned with the recognition of disease from signs, symptoms or laboratory data although in a broader sense it is concerned with the diversity of disease and its relationship to structural, physiological, biochemical, psychological and ecological aspects (Engle, 1964). In general there are three steps in medical diagnosis; taking of a history, physical examination and a scheme of investigation, part of which may be a trial of a treatment. Thus in making a diagnosis, the physician is faced with a large amount of information from which he has to make decisions about diagnosis and treatment in which a high level of uncertainty is involved. In making such decisions, reliance is placed on pattern recognition and at some point subjective probabilities, developed from past experience, are brought in and related to the weighting of the different components that make up the pattern (Lusted and Stahl, 1964). Thus diagnosis by the recognition of syndromes and patterns presents two major problems: ignorance of the number of diseases which produce the same signs and symptoms; difficulty in recalling all the diagnostic information from the various diseases (Lusted, 1968).

To help the physician cope with all the mass of information and with the factor of uncertainty, computer-based aids have been devised to help analyse medical data after the signs and symptoms have been weighted. Clustering methods that group related signs and symptoms and matching procedures and numerical taxonomy have been employed that enable diagnoses to be given in terms of probabilities. By this means, as Lusted (1968) says, probability quantifies uncertainty.

Thus medical diagnosis is mainly the collection, processing and analysis of data whereby conclusions about the causes of disease are deduced. Naturally, busy practising physicians tend to seek simple explanations when it comes to a decision about what causes a disease (Paul, 1966) but diagnosis should mean much more than the mere setting of a name to a disease; ideally the summing up should include the etiology of the disease state (Black, 1968). However, etiology (the science of causes of disease) necessarily involves a wider approach to the study of disease and its diagnosis. The numerous interacting factors that influence a disease become important, requiring observation and research outside the hospital and laboratory. The clinical epidemiologist now enters the picture because it is his job to measure the circumstances under which disease occurs, where diseases tend to flourish and where they do not (Paul, 1966). He is in fact an ecologist.

The diagnostic and epidemiological fields clearly overlap. Whereas the diagnostician is more concerned with data from the individual patient and thinks in terms of primary causes, the epidemiologist regards all factors as having some influence on the disease whether they be called causes or influences. In the field of plant pathology there is a similar distinction between the extension scientist and the field research worker; the extension man by necessity has to examine many problems in a limited time and give opinions and advice on the causes of disease. The research man on the other hand, because he has more time at his disposal, can measure the numerous factors in the ecological web of disease and, by analytical procedures, state in terms of probability which factors are the most important. As Paul (1966) states, it is the epidemiologist's '. . . responsibility to differentiate direct precipitating causes from supplementary causes and assign them priorities. These other causes are to be found in the characteristics of individual members of the population attacked, as well as in the environments in which both host and parasite find themselves. It is the sum or interaction of these influences that gives rise to disease'. It seems to me however, that the most cogent arguments on this aspect of disease have been made by Dubos (1970) who states that '. . . multifactorial etiology is the rule rather than the exception and apparently conflicting theories of disease causation can be reconciled'. In cancer, for example, Dubos speculates that '. . . the present piecemeal succession of apparently conflicting statements on the cause of neoplastic diseases will eventually be replaced by a larger view that several factors, acting simultaneously, are usually instrumental in their causation'. The similarity between these views and the conclusions reached in this book on the nature of disease emphasizes the similarity between etiological and epidemiological problems in the medical and plant pathological sciences. In effect, it is all ecology and the fact that one is concerned with humans and the other with plants is of less importance.

By elucidating the causes of a disease and the circumstances that are concerned with the appearance of the disease, the medical epidemiologist is contributing useful information from which the physician can make more reliable diagnoses. He also uses his skills to solve disease problems by finding out, for example, why a disease occurs in certain regions and not in others. The problem is far more than finding the pathogen which causes the disease; the control and prevention of disease are equally important. He may find that the main factor which determines where a disease occurs is correlated with the distribution of a vector (e.g. mosquito or tsetse fly) and that controlling the vector is a better way of controlling the disease than treating the patient for the disease. Changing or even eradicating some component in the ecological web of disease is always an exciting possibility for the epidemiologist.

Studies on the diagnostic process in medicine indicate the value of the orderly collection of data including epidemiological data. The practitioner can frequently refer to laboratories with specialized techniques in clinical pathology, radiology, human biochemistry, histology, haematology, etc.,

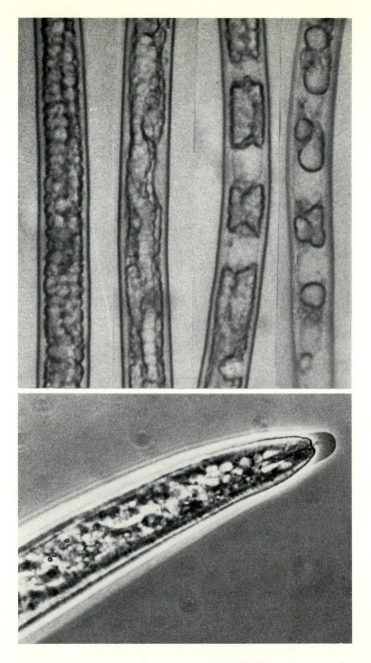

Plate 17 (top) Second stage larvae of *Meloidogyne javanica* showing, left to right, depletion of body contents from a newly hatched larva to a freeliving 10 days old larva. Body width about 18 μm.

Plate 18 (bottom) Second stage larva of *Meloidogyne javanica* within the first stage cuticle. The nematode was removed from the egg.

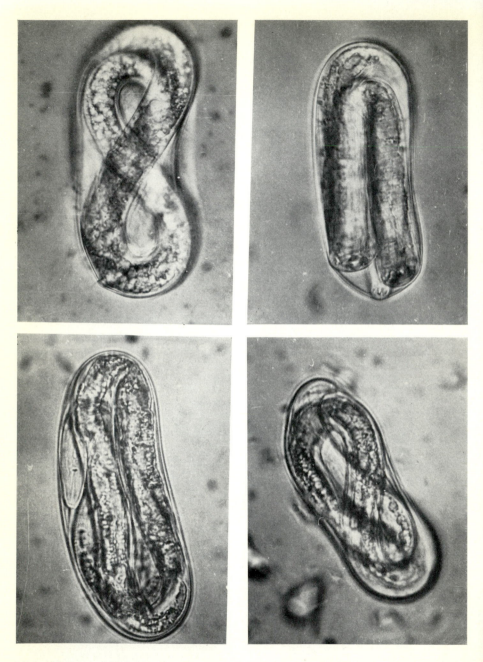

Plate 19 Eggs of *Meloidogyne javanica* showing body flexures of the unhatched second stage larva and asymmetrical shape of the egg. Eggs measure about 100 μm long.

from whom he can obtain additional information. However, diagnosis involves statistical procedures in the analysis of multiple variables if an opinion is to be given in terms of probability and, desirable as such procedures are, it is doubtful whether they are used anywhere other than in large diagnostic centres such as hospitals.

If the diagnostic processes in medicine and plant pathology are basically similar, so are the restraints on effective diagnosis. Like the medical practitioner, the extension scientist has too many problems to be able to apply even a few of the processes involved in the determination of the major components in a disease system. One solution may be to copy the medical scientists and establish regional centres where plant and soil analyses, parasite identification, data processing and statistical analyses might be made. In fact a few laboratories of this kind do exist already. Another solution is to determine what minimal amount of sampling and data processing is required to give conclusions that are more reliable than subjective on-the-spot conclusions. Perhaps the extension worker could then handle most disease problems without relying on the services of a central laboratory. However, whatever the solution, considerable research has to be done on the ecology of disease in the field to answer questions like: How do we decide what to measure? How do we sample the area? How do we measure the various components in the environment? What sort of data do we require for subsequent statistical analysis? What statistical analyses are available that enable us to form conclusions and make decisions about the causes of disease? When these questions have been answered we can then begin to devise ways of providing quick and reliable diagnoses for the diseases on farms.

Ideas from plant pathology and parasitology

Let us look at some disease problems to see how ecological data can be analysed to determine the relative importance of different components. Dirks and Romig (1970) set out to account for the variation in numbers of cereal rust urediospores in the Mississippi River Basin over several years. They discuss in general terms the influence of temperature, precipitation and initial inoculum on cereal rust epidemics in North America and their intention to develop models from the numbers of urediospores trapped on slides and from climatological data of temperature and precipitation. The object of the work was to ascertain whether prediction was possible and, if so, to select the most appropriate variables for the development of working models.

Linear multiple regression analyses were used to develop the models.

The dependent variables, i.e. the target organisms, were expressed as the log cumulative numbers of urediospores trapped per cm² on microscope slides. Eleven biological and climatological variables were developed from the urediospore data for the two species under consideration and from meteorological records of maximum and minimum temperatures and precipitation.

The eleven variables described by Dirks and Romig were thought to be correlated in some way with numbers of urediospores; the choice of the variables is extremely important of course, and an intimate knowledge of the biology and ecology of the target organism is essential in such a choice. From our point of view, however, the details of the variables need not concern us; we are more interested in the methods of treating the data. Dirks and Romig used the conventional linear multiple regression analysis to calculate (1) the total variance of the dependent variable (numbers of urediospores) attributable to regression, (2) the individual partition coefficients and (3) the tests of significance. Such a procedure indicates the contribution made by each of the independent variables to the observed variance of urediospore numbers. Thus if we plot a graph of the values of the dependent variable against those of an independent variable the dispersion of points about the regression line indicates the degree of variance that is accounted for by the independent variable. The correlation coefficient r gives a measure of the dispersion of points about the regression line whereas r^2 gives a measure of how much variance is due to the dependent variable in question. Thus a correlation coefficient of 0.7 accounts for 49% of the variance ($0.7^2 \times 100$). The multiple regression analysis enables such quantitative assessments to be made of several variables and a further procedure called stepwise regression enables the contribution of groups of factors to be assessed. Thus we can determine which combination of variables is most closely correlated with the observed variation in the numbers of the target organism. These are very valuable tools at the disposal of the ecologist and as long as it is realized that a relation does not indicate causality, that variables are often not independent and that the success of the exercise depends to a great extent on the variables that we choose to measure, then useful conclusions can be drawn from field data.

To return to Dirks' and Romig's experiment, their analyses indicated that a significant portion of the variation in final cumulative number of urediospores in the spring wheat areas could be accounted for as early as two weeks before the wheat formed a head. However in the winter wheat area, estimates made two weeks before heading were significant only for the 7- and 14-day predictions. For *Puccinia recondita*, the model using only biological variables accounted for a highly significant portion of the variation in the final cumulative number of urediospores two weeks before heading. The model based on six climatological variables was unsatisfactory for both species of cereal rust. Once again we are not particularly concerned with the plant pathological importance of these conclusions although it is clear that Dirks and Romig made a useful contribution to the problem of predicting outbreaks of cereal rust. The conclusions do indicate, however, what the multiple regression method can do for the ecologist.

The work of Kincaid and his colleagues (1970) should also be mentioned because it provides a useful example of how stepwise regression analyses can be used to study the influence of several independent variables on several parasites (dependent variables) at the same time. Regression equations were determined in a stepwise manner. The variable explaining the largest amount of variation in the total sum of squares was fitted first. Before selection of the next factor to be included in the model, the data were adjusted to remove the effect of the first variable. The procedure was continued until no further significant reductions were found. In this way equations were calculated for each of the three parasites thus indicating the factors that most influenced each of them.

In both of the examples just described the target organisms were parasites whereas our immediate concern is with the host plant as a target organism. Unfortunately for some reason there are few examples in plant pathology where estimates of the relative influence of the plant's environmental components, including parasites of various kinds, have been made. However, the following examples provide useful ideas.

Multiple linear regression analyses have helped to indicate the relative importance of different environmental components on disease in plants. A study of the influence of nine climatic or biological factors on lesion production in rice by *Pyricularia oryzae* (rice blast) gave a model expressed by the equation $Y = a + b_1X_1\ xb_2X_2 \ldots b_pX_p$ where there are p independent variables. Values of r^2 were of the order of 0.56 for all inoculum rates and, as before, r^2 represents the proportion of the variation in average number of lesions that is explained by the linear model given in the above equation. The environmental factors of most importance were: amount of dew; length of dew period; leaf area at time of inoculation (Asai, *et al.*, 1967). Studies on the incidence of wilt in hops caused by *Verticillium albo-atrum* indicated after multiple regression analyses, that low soil temperature rather than high rainfall was probably the cause of the commonly observed association of high wilt incidence with wet weather (Talboys and Wilson, 1970). A stepwise multiple regression computer programme was used by Eversmeyer and Burleigh (1970) to predict percent disease severity of wheat leaf rust (*Puccinia graminis* f.sp. *tritici*). Equations were generated for winter and spring wheats by analysis of biological and meteorological data from 24 winter wheat and 16 spring wheat locations.

When data from all sites were combined coefficients of determination (r^2) indicated that variation in disease severity, minimum temperature and either hours of free moisture or days of precipitation explained over 70% of the variation in epidemic development. James and his colleagues (1972) used multiple regression analyses to develop an empirical equation relating losses in yield of potatoes (dependent variable) with increase in disease caused by *Phytophthora infestans* during nine weekly periods (independent variables). Data were obtained from 96 disease progress curves in eastern Canada during 1953 to 1970, and the equations enabled estimates to be made of the loss in tuber yield caused by the late blight. The difference between estimated loss computed from the equation and actual loss, derived by weighing, was less than 5% in nine cases out of ten.

Statistical procedures of this kind help us to arrive at conclusions about the relative importance of particular factors on the host but they do little to explain the interactions between components or whether a factor acts directly or indirectly. To include these sorts of relationships demands the experimental testing of hypotheses built on a framework of biological experience and information. Here are a few examples that illustrate the nature of interactions and factors that act indirectly.

It is common experience that a well-fed animal or a well-watered plant stands a better chance of survival in a disease epidemic than its weaker neighbours. Similarly, it is likely that a vigorous animal or plant living in an amicable environment is better able to summon up defensive mechanisms to parasites than one living in a hostile environment. Consequently those environmental factors that influence the host's health in any way are likely further to influence its tolerance and resistance to parasites. Thus sheep fed on a high protein diet maintained the same rate of growth whether they were infected by nematodes or not, whereas on a low protein diet, infected animals had a lower rate of growth than uninfected animals. The sheep on the low protein diet may not have been able to repair damaged tissues or to constrain the parasite because of inefficient resistance mechanisms (Bawden, 1969). The size of cankers and the degree of mortality in cottonwood trees infected by fungi depend on the site in which the trees are growing and on environmental conditions during the attack (Filer, 1967). When cotton plants growing in soil at temperatures of 20 to 40 °C were subjected to soil water stress and inoculated with *Macrophomina phaseoli*, the severity of the subsequent root rot was much greater in those plants under stress (Ghaffer and Erwin, 1969). Similarly Bier (1959) has shown that reduced turgidity in willow bark is correlated with the increased development of canker diseases caused by *Cryptodiaporthe salicina*. Thus canker development was prevented during winter, when bark turgidity is usually low, by placing dormant twigs in water.

Environmental factors may therefore predispose the host to disease when infected by pathogens, although it is usually difficult to decide whether tolerance or resistance or both have been reduced or whether the pathogen has been directly affected. The host and the parasite may share the same environmental components; moreover the levels of the components for maximum infection by the parasite and for maximum growth of the host may be similar. Jordan (1968) for example, showed that the establishment of infections and sporulation by American gooseberry mildew, *Sphaerotheca mors-uvae* on blackcurrants were increased by relatively low soil moisture content, temperatures about 15 °C, 60% relative humidity, good illumination and high phosphorus and potassium nutrition, all factors that promote vigorous plant growth. Thus Jordan concluded that susceptibility of the host was positively correlated with its vigour. There are plenty of examples where the susceptibility of a plant decreases as its vigour increases and it is usually argued that the resistance mechanisms are less efficient when the host is under stress. The trouble with such hypotheses is that there are too many other explanations involving indirect environmental influences or interactions. Thus, Rotem *et al.* (1971) state that the effect of any one factor on fungal infection depends on other factors. Findings such as the minimum, maximum or optimum level for a factor, or the inhibitory effect due to too much of a good factor are likely to be valid only within a limited range of combinations of other factors and are therefore only meaningful if the other conditions of the experiment are explicitly stated. The problem of interactions between environmental factors is also stressed by Foster (1967) who showed that the susceptibility of *Chenopodium amaranticolor* was influenced by interactions between various nutritional elements. Schnathorst (1965) sums up the situation when he discusses the distribution and severity of powdery mildews. He emphasizes the dynamic state of environmental factors and suggests that there is a balance of favourable and unfavourable factors that directly affect germination, infection, growth, sporulation and dissemination as well as factors that indirectly affect the development of the parasite through their influence on host physiology.

In an attempt therefore to understand the major components in a disease situation and how they are interrelated in their influence on the crop we rely on two kinds of information: (1) Data derived from a sampling programme in the field. Having defined our objectives we decide (usually with the help of a statistician) what particular method of analysis would be most helpful. This may be multiregression, principal component or factor analysis, all of which are different aspects of multivariate analysis. (A clear description of the aims of factor analysis is provided by Brown *et al.* (1965).) The sampling requirements are then decided according to our choice of method and eventually, after the data have been analysed, conclusions can be made about the possible components and groups of components that most affect plant growth. (2) Data derived from individual field, glasshouse or laboratory experiments that help to explain particular relationships within the system, e.g. how different levels of nitrogen in the soil and different nematode populations interact to influence plant growth. A hypothesis or story can now be put together that explains in biological terms what we think is happening in the field to give rise to the observed distribution and intensity of disease in the crop.

We might even take the process a stage further and compose a model, often in the form of a flow diagram that depicts how we think the components in a system are interrelated. Such systems simulation, as it is called, involves relating the components in the model in mathematical terms. Thus the data from our field measurements and from our experiments are put to use. The model is then tried out with the aid of a computer to see whether with certain initial states and given inputs the subsequent outputs resemble what happens in nature. Adjustments are then made to improve the similarity between model and nature and finally the statement is made that the model is a reasonable imitation of what really happens. The model can then be used in an explanatory way to indicate how the ecological system works and experiments can be devised to test the validity of the model. The model can also be used for practical purposes to indicate what might happen in nature if a particular environmental component is altered, or to predict epidemics. Waggoner and Horsfall (1969) have produced such a model for a plant disease which they state provided a guide to the importance or influence of the characteristics of the fungus, the weather or the host; it also provided a predictor for the outcome of modified weather.

In the field of parasitology, Ractliffe *et al.* (1969) have described a model that provides a concise summary of present ideas about disease in sheep caused by a nematode, *Haemonchus contortus*. The host-parasite interaction was successfully simulated and it yielded useful hypotheses for testing. In both of the papers by Waggoner and Horsfall and by Ractliffe and coworkers, the narrative and the philosophy of systems simulation is expressed in a most lucid and interesting way as if the authors had felt the responsibility of presenting for the first time in their respective fields, a subject that was novel and complex.

Plant Nematology—environment and disease

Suppose we have a good indication from an initial ecological survey or from information passed on to us by previous investigators, that nematodes are an important component in the environment of a crop. Let us further suppose that we have been given the task of finding out whether the crop is yielding as well as it might and what factors are mainly responsible for reducing yield. Such information, we are told, is required so that the correct steps can be taken to increase the yield of subsequent crops. As plant nematologists, we are particularly anxious to know whether nematodes are having such a marked influence—if they are, we may be able to advocate measures that reduce the chances of serious losses from nematode damage. If, on the other hand, nematodes are not one of the major factors then we can suggest what other procedures should be considered.

We have just discussed what is involved in diagnosing the causes of disease and we have had some ideas from medical science, plant pathology and parasitiology. There now remains the question of what to measure, so let us look at those environmental components that are likely to influence the plant and at the same time examine their influence on nematodes.

PLANTS OTHER THAN THE HOST

The influence of plants such as weeds on the growth of a crop is to increase plant density and thereby reduce growth and yield. Reductions of 10% in yield are common in fields where weeds are not considered to be particularly dense. Weeds may also serve as alternative hosts for parasites providing a habitat in which they can reproduce during times when the host crop is absent or dormant. The wide host range of some plant nematodes for example, *Meloidogyne*, provides for a constant reservoir of nematodes in an area where rotational cropping occurs. Thus in a survey by Davidson and Townshend (1967), 34 species of weeds in 32 genera and 19 families were found to be hosts of *M. incognita*. The prevalence of such weeds in an agricultural crop where *M. incognita* occurred might have a marked effect on the association between nematode numbers in the soil and the growth of the crop plants; the weeds might act as a source of infective nematodes or possibly as a sink if they are more attractive to the nematodes. In any event the inclusion of weeds in the list of factors to be sampled in a crop may be necessary in some situations.

PLANT PARASITES

It is probable that at any one time, plants in a crop contain numbers of different parasites in the tissues or in the rhizosphere. Such disease complexes, as they are called (Powell *et al.*, 1971), are probably the rule rather than the exception, hence it will be useful to include measurements of the density of those parasites that experience tells us may be important. At its simplest the fungi, bacteria and viruses will, along with the nematodes, each account for part of the observed decrease in plant growth. Important interactions may, however occur between nematodes and other parasites. A survey of cotton fields containing stunted plants showed that various plant nematodes and soil-borne fungi were often associated with the stunted plants although no single organism was consistently associated with the disease (Bird *et al.*, 1971). The severity of cotton seedling diseases is seen by Cauquil and Shepherd (1970) as a synergistic effect between root knot nematodes and various pathogenic fungi. In disease complexes in tobacco involving *Meloidogyne incognita* and fungi, none of the fungi

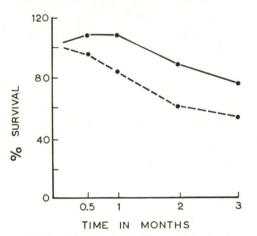

Fig. 23 Survival of viruliferous (continuous line) and virus-free (discontinuous line) adults of *Xiphinema index* maintained in fallow soil. (Das and Raski, 1969)

induced disease unless the nematode was present (Powell *et al.*, 1971). Thus in this example the nematode was the dominant predisposing agent. Our samples might show an equally close correlation between the nematode and plant damage and between the fungi and plant damage but only experiments will indicate the biological importance of the different pathogens in the disease.

Different species of nematodes may attack the same plant, and there may be unexpected and unpredictable interactions between them that influence their relative numbers in the host (Johnson and Nusbaum, 1970; Kinloch and Allen, 1972; Silora *et al.*, 1972; Estores and Tseh an Chen, 1972). It seems likely that the response of the plant to such mixed infections will also be unpredictable, consequently the numbers of each species in a sample should be counted.

Parasites may influence each other directly. Thus studies on the interaction between the grapevine fanleaf virus and its nematode vector, *Xiphinema index*, indicated that although the virus had no influence on the nematode's rate of reproduction it did influence its survival, possibly by increasing the RNA content of the nematode and thereby affecting its protein metabolism (Das and Raski, 1969, Fig. 23). Or, parasites may influence each other indirectly; propagules of *Fusarium oxysporum* f.sp. *lycopersici* were more numerous in the rhizosphere of tomatoes infected with *Meloidogyne javanica* than in the rhizosphere of non-infected plants. At the same time, numbers of actinomycetes were lower in the rhizosphere of galled roots but, on addition of chitin to the soil, the actinomycetes increased and there was a marked reduction in the secondary invasion of root galls by other micro-organisms (Bergeson *et al.*, 1970). The measurement of parasites in the plant's environment is obviously essential but, as these few examples indicate, the job of sorting out their role as causes of disease is likely to be difficult.

OTHER ORGANISMS

Although references to interactions between nematodes and other plant parasites are common, no mention has been made as far as I know, to interactions between nematodes and insects. A crop plant is likely to be attacked simultaneously by insects and nematodes and it seems likely that each will have some influence on the other through the plant. A severe infection of the plant's root system by nematodes may change the chemical composition of the leaves on which an insect like a caterpillar or locust may feed. Consequently the development of the insect may be changed, or the leaves may become more palatable, hence the damage done to the plant may be influenced by the nematode's activities. It is also likely that nematodes are influenced by the defoliating activity of insects. Such a hypothesis sounds more credible when the work of White (1969) is considered. White showed that unusually wet winters followed by unusually dry summers in Australia resulted in prolonged stress in eucalyptus trees (Fig. 24). Outbreaks of psyllids which feed on the leaves, were associated with years of high stress. The reason, White suggests, is because stress leads to an increase in the amount of nitrogenous food available to these insects. Thus unhealthy or stressed trees are more susceptible to insect attack than healthy trees. This is an example of how environment might influence susceptibility by influencing the nature of the host as a source of food. Perhaps nematodes, by causing stress in plants, produce changes in the amount of nitrogenous food available for insects. Apart from such interactions however, it is necessary to watch for insect damage that might necessitate including these organisms in the environmental components to be measured. I am sure that if an entomologist were writing this he would assume that insects are universal components of the plant's environment whereas nematodes are less important; however, such disciplinary loyalties are not particularly helpful to ecologists.

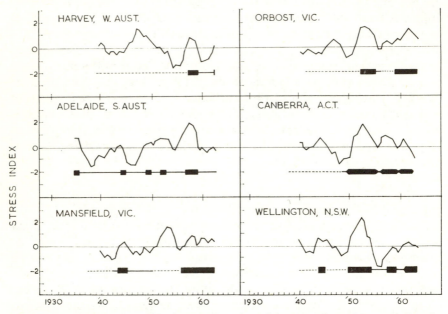

Fig. 24 Outbreaks of psyllids (Insecta, Hemiptera) in Australia and stress indices for various representative localities. In the horizontal graph a dotted line indicates no known records, a heavy black line indicates records but no outbreaks, and a black blocking indicates a recorded period of outbreak of one or more species of psyllids. Stress indices were calculated from meteorological data. (After White, 1969)

WATER

None would deny the importance of water in the environment; it is a major influence on plants, parasites and pests and on other physical and chemical properties of the soil, like aeration. The amount of water in the soil is the result of many events of which *precipitation* is the most obvious. Precipitation often varies widely from year to year and throughout the year, and in some places like South Australia the change from the dry hot summer to the cool wet winter is sufficiently marked to indicate when the wheat crop should be sown. In such situations, records of precipitation may be a useful pointer to soil conditions, and correlations between precipitation and plant growth and the numbers of parasites might be expected. Counteracting precipitation in its influence on soil water are *evaporation, drainage* and *run-off*. Loss of water from soil by direct evaporation and indirectly by transpiration from plants is determined primarily by wind and solar radiation which raises the temperature and reduces the relative humidity of the air. Run-off occurs when the rate of precipitation exceeds the *rate of infiltration* of the rainwater down through the soil. *Surface sealing*, through the mechanical action of raindrops or of certain fungi in so-called 'non-wettable soils', increases run-off. The *topography* of the land also influences run-off, the greater the slope the greater the chance that the water in the soil will fail to be augmented; furthermore soil solutes and the top soil itself may be washed to lower levels.

Within the soil, the amount of water that is retained and which is available for use by the plant is determined by several forces. The forces that attract water to the solid particles are called *adhesion* whereas the forces occurring at the interfaces between water and air are due to *surface tension* or *capillarity*. The forces of adhesion and capillarity are together referred to as matric forces or *matric potential, suction* or *pF*. There are also forces retaining water in the soil which are determined by *osmotic potential*. Thus the availability of water to plants is determined by the combined effects of the matric and osmotic potentials which together constitute the *moisture potential* of a soil. Because we are interested in water as a component of the plant's environment, moisture potential is a useful factor to measure out of all the others already mentioned. It will now be obvious that the water available to a plant in soil is at the centre of its own web of interacting factors and that we could measure many factors associated with soil water that might be correlated with plant growth. Rainfall for example is frequently recorded along with data on the seasonal growth of crops or the seasonal fluctuations in numbers of some parasite. But rainfall is likely to be a remote environmental factor in the plant's ecological web and, apart from the ease with which such data can be obtained, it has no advantages over the more direct component, available soil moisture. Furthermore this same expression of soil water is just as realistic when the environments of parasites are concerned. So the important question arises, how can we measure available soil moisture in such a way that it gives us a continuous record of the major changes in soil water over the time that we take our samples in the field? Soil tensiometers inserted in the soil at various depths and connected to a continuous recorder is one way but usually the number of sampling sites precludes this approach. What we want is a method that will enable us to determine the available soil moisture in soil samples extracted from the field. The same samples could also be used to assess numbers of nematodes and other parasites and various other soil characteristics such as salinity, pH, conductivity and texture. Baier and Robertson (1966, 1968) have described such a method which they call the versatile soil moisture budget. With the daily recordings of precipitation and estimates of potential evapo-transpiration and with some knowledge of the moisture characteristics of the soils, daily estimates of soil moisture can readily be obtained. The efficacy of the method was demonstrated by Baier and Robertson (1968) in their field experiments; higher correlation coefficients and lower coefficients of variation were obtained, in fact multiple correlation analysis indicated that soil moisture, as estimated by the soil moisture budget, was the best estimator of crop yields whereas rainfall was quite unsuitable.

When water is lacking the plant is subjected to moisture stress, the amount of water available from the soil being insufficient to meet the plant's demands. The plant's demands are in turn influenced by the rate of transpiration, which is influenced by atmospheric conditions and to some extent by the degree of stomatal closure. The depth to which roots penetrate the soil also influences water uptake and is important where pathogens are responsible for root destruction or proliferation of surface roots at the expense of the deeper ones. At the other end of the scale, water-saturated soil may inhibit plant growth through reduced aeration. Nematodes, too, apparently require intermediate soil moistures for maximum population increase. Thus Kable and Mai (1968) found that the rate of population increase of *Pratylenchus penetrans* was greatest at pF 2 to 3 and least at very low or high moisture tensions. Variations in soil moisture between soil types, because of differences in drainage possibly explain why *Radopholus similis* is more destructive to citrus seedlings in fine-sandy than in loamy-sand soils (O'Bannon and Tomerlin, 1971). Surveys in the field also emphasize the importance of water as a determinant of nematode numbers and distribution. Fidler and Bevan (1963) suggest that water holding capacity is the most important factor influencing the growth of oat crops infested with *Heterodera avenae*. Similarly, a comparison of plant nematode populations using a multivariate analysis technique indicated that total available moisture was probably an important influence (Ferris *et al.*, 1971). In general, plants and nematodes frequently have similar requirements for water but other organisms may have quite different needs; Griffin (1963) for example has shown that the majority of fungi can probably grow in soils that are considerably drier than the permanent wilting points of plants.

SOIL TEXTURE AND STRUCTURE

Soil texture or soil type is measured by the percentages of sand, silt and clay, and is frequently quoted as a factor associated with the occurrence of plant diseases. However, like rainfall, texture is not usually a direct cause but an important determinant of other environmental components. For example, texture influences structure, that property of the soil concerned with the geometry of pore spaces. Thus a fine textured clay soil may impede root growth and penetration because of the narrow pore spaces; it may also inhibit such parasites as nematodes which require a minimum pore diameter of about 20 μm if they are to move through the soil. The structure of the soil influences the infiltration and rate of movement of water, factors which are important in water uptake by the plant. The water-holding capacity of the soil is also influenced by soil structure; thus in fine textured soils there is a greater surface area over the aggregates and more points of contact than in coarser soils, consequently during a dry season the clay soils retain water longer and plants growing in them are less likely to wilt than in sandy soils. Parasites in the soil are less likely to succumb to desiccation where the water holding capacity is high. Temperature and aeration are also influenced by texture and structure hence it is not surprising that high correlations are often obtained between soil type and the growth of plants, incidence of disease and populations of pathogens; like rainfall, soil structure lies at the extremity of the ecological web exercising an all-pervading influence on almost every other environmental component of the plant.

In general, diseases in plants which are associated with the presence of nematodes are more prevalent and intense on sandy than clay soils, but whether this is caused by poor plant growth, lack of water, increased nematode reproduction or interactions between these various factors is largely unknown. Thus Townshend (1972) states that penetration of corn roots by *Pratylenchus penetrans* and *P. minyus* was greatest in soils with a low bulk density because in such soils the size of pores afford the best conditions for penetration. In studies on the structure of nematode communities in forest, Johnson *et al* (1972) suggest that soil type and drainage are possible determinants. Ferris and Bernard (1971) showed associations between soil type and the population densities of nematodes in soybean fields but noted that moisture was also probably involved. And there are many other examples of this kind indicating associations or statistical correlations between soil type and the numbers of nematodes, but usually other factors are mentioned as more probable causes. Kimpinski and Welch (1971) for example showed that nematodes were more abundant in clay than in sandy soil but they also pointed out that the sandy soils had a lower moisture content which increased the chance of desiccation, reduced nematode mobility and inhibited plant growth. The sandy soils were also deficient in nutrients thus restricting growth of the plants on which the nematodes fed. Studies on the movement and survival of *Pratylenchus penetrans* in three soil types differing in particle size distribution, moisture retention, aeration and pore-size indicated that survival increased with increasing soil dryness, whereas poor survival in the wetter soils was attributed to lack of aeration (Townshend and Webber, 1971, Fig. 25).

It can be concluded therefore, that measuring soil texture as a component in ecological field problems has little explanatory value; nevertheless, where correlations are high, the information may be of practical value; we may conclude for example, that it is economically impracticable

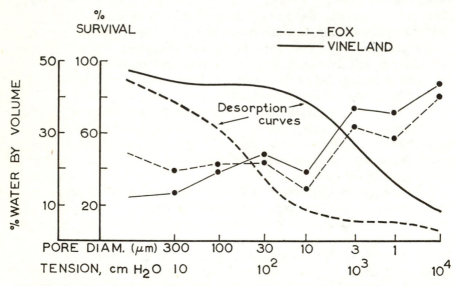

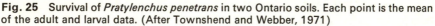

Fig. 25 Survival of *Pratylenchus penetrans* in two Ontario soils. Each point is the mean of the adult and larval data. (After Townshend and Webber, 1971)

to grow a particular crop on a particular soil type. The inclusion of soil structure in the list of factors to be measured is worthwhile because it may have a direct influence on the plant and pathogens as well as being a strong determinant of other soil factors.

THE SOIL PROFILE

Soils are differentiated vertically into three horizons, the A horizon at the surface in which most of the plant roots and organisms occur; the B horizon which contains plant material, some organisms and substances that have been leached from the layer above; the C horizon consisting of parent material of partially decomposed rock. How far the root system penetrates into the soil is determined to some extent by the structure and other physical properties of the various horizons together with distribution of water, height of water table, and fertility. In any event the pattern of root distribution varies considerably between sites and consequently the distribution of organisms, including parasites, will also vary. Furthermore, the vertical distribution of plant material and organisms changes with season. Thus Koen (1966) found that populations of *Meloidogyne javanica* were higher in the surface layers in summer than in winter and similarly the larvae of *Meloidogyne graminis* are most abundant in the top 5 cm of soil at times when the growth of Tifgreen Bermuda grass was most active

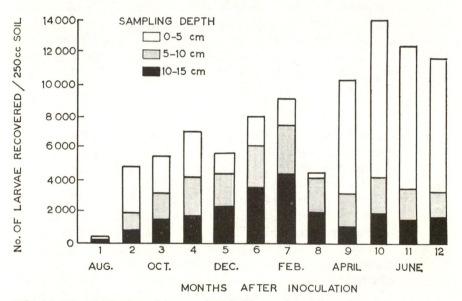

Fig. 26 The distribution of larvae of *Meloidogyne graminis* recovered from around 'Tifgreen' bermuda-grass roots growing in a sandy loam soil. Monthly samples were taken at three depths from August 1967 to July 1968. (After Laughlin and Williams, 1971)

and least abundant when the host was dormant (Laughlin and Williams, 1971, Fig. 26).

In taking soil samples in an ecological study, it is therefore necessary to remove soil to a depth which contains most of the root and organism population regardless of season and site. Usually samples of 20 cm depth meet this requirement but ideally, initial surveys that indicate depth distribution are required to suggest the most reliable procedure. Deep cores may yield other useful information too. An impermeable or a saline layer in the B horizon may help to explain variable growth in a crop and assumes importance as one of the plant's environmental components.

TOPOGRAPHY

Measurements of the slope of the land in the area under investigation may contribute to the understanding of an ecological situation in several ways. Run-off on sloping land affects the moisture content of the soil and tends to erode the surface. Water collecting at the foot of slopes may contain bases from the higher ground and so soils on the level ground will tend to be less acid. The slope of the land in relation to the direction of the sun's rays may markedly influence temperature in the soil and evapo-transpiration of water. Variations in the growth of plants and the density of parasites are often associated with topography; it is quite common for example, to see poorly growing plants on the tops of hillocks, and in such cases a soil physical factor is probably responsible. As far as nematodes are concerned, run-off on sloping land may contribute to their dispersal especially where stem and leaf nematodes are involved.

SOIL CHEMICALS

Malnutrition may be responsible for weak plant growth and low yields in a crop, hence measurements of nutrient elements in the soil are required. Major elements, nitrogen, phosphorus, potassium, sulphur, magnesium and calcium and trace elements like manganese, boron, zinc, copper and molybdenum are all essential. Fortunately symptoms of mineral deficiencies are often distinctive enough to provide a guide to what should be measured, although interactions between nutrients in their influence on the plants have to be considered. Thus symptoms of potassium deficiency are usually more severe where iron is lacking in the soil. Nutrient elements in excess may be toxic and in these days of increasing pollution of waterways and rivers it is not surprising that losses from this cause are more frequent.

Soil chemicals influence parasites through the plant but they may also influence them through other organisms. Nitrogenous compounds added to soil decreased populations of *Pratylenchus penetrans* by their influence on micro-organisms or their degradation products (Walker, 1969). Chemicals may also influence nematodes directly; addition of 70 and 700 p.p.m. of nitrogen to soil decreased populations of *P. penetrans* and Walker (1971) suggests that ammonification of the added compounds to produce ammonia is possibly responsible because of its nematicidal effects. Similarly Barker *et al.* (1971) showed that applications of $NaNO_3$ and NH_4NO_3 to soil reduced hatch, penetration and cyst development of *Heterodera glycines* on soybean; as nitrogen concentrations were below those necessary to give an inhibitory osmotic effect, the authors concluded that nitrogen had a direct inhibitory effect on the nematode. However, little is known about the influence of chemicals on nematodes in the soil (Wallace, 1971), but there are enough data to suggest that correlations exist between the levels of plant nutrient elements and the numbers of plant nematodes, therefore inclusion of chemical data in the sampling programme is justified.

DECOMPOSING PLANT MATERIAL

Organic matter may be worth measuring because it influences the growth of micro-organisms which may produce toxic by-products. In a recent review of biotic influences on nematodes in soil, Sayre (1971) discusses the control of nematodes by soil amendments. Reductions in nematode populations are recorded and attributed to the production of nematicidal compounds during breakdown of the organic material, to the multiplication of natural enemies that attack the nematodes and to the enhancement of resistance mechanisms in the host plant. On the other hand, plant material in the form of senescent roots may provide protection for such nematodes as *Pratylenchus penetrans* by increasing their rate of survival during winter (Kable and Mai, 1968).

OSMOTIC PRESSURE OF THE SOIL SOLUTION

The osmotic component of the moisture potential inhibits plant growth when there are excess salts in the soil solution. Excessive application of fertilizers or leaching of solutes may produce such a situation, thereby inhibiting the uptake of water by plant roots. High osmotic pressures (above 10 atm [$1013 \, kN/m^2$]) may in turn inhibit nematodes (Wallace, 1971). High osmotic pressures due to high salinity occur naturally in some countries particularly in arid regions with poor agricultural production. High salinity may give rise to concentrations of toxic ions, to high pH and to impermeability of soil to water; in such situations plant growth is inhibited. Nematodes may interact with salinity in their effect on the plant. Thus Heald and Heilman (1971) found that *Rotylenchus uniformis* occurred in similar numbers in relatively non-saline and in highly saline soils in Texas cotton fields. Nevertheless, glasshouse experiments indicated that nematode injury increased as the soil salinity increased.

HYDROGEN ION CONCENTRATION

There is good evidence of a correlation between pH and nematode numbers. Morgan and MacLean (1968), for example, state that *Pratylen-*

chus penetrans maintains itself over the pH spectrum of most agricultural soils (pH 5.1 to 6.5) but thrives best at pH 5.5 to 5.8; above pH 6.6 there is a rapid decline in numbers. Burns (1971) grew soybeans for two months in non-sterilized silt loam amended to pHs of 4.0, 6.0 and 8.0. The greatest numbers of *Pratylenchus alleni* occurred in soybean plants at pH 6.0. The low numbers at pH 4.0 were associated with high levels of potassium, manganese and phenols in the soybean plants and in addition a thick suberized outer layer developed on the roots. Such observations

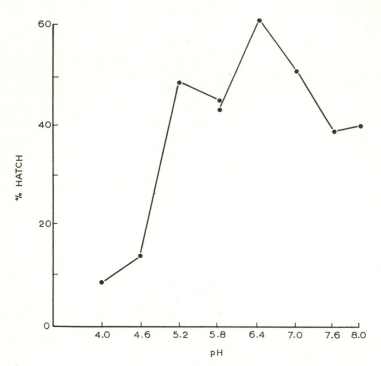

Fig. 27 The mean percent hatch of *Meloidogyne javanica* at different pH. (After Wallace, 1966*a*)

indicate that numbers of nematodes may be correlated with pH but there is no evidence that hydrogen ion concentration as such had a direct influence on nematodes. Where such experiments have been attempted (Wallace, 1966), there is evidence that pH may be inhibitory below 5.0 and above 8.0 (Fig. 27). Bacteria have similar requirements whereas actinomycetes are more sensitive to acid conditions. Fungi are usually acid tolerant, some species being able to tolerate pH 2.0.

Although soil pH and plant growth are correlated, there are good indications that the relationship is indirect. Thus the harmful effects of soil pH are shortage of available calcium and phosphate or excess of soluble aluminium, manganese and other metallic ions. In measuring pH in our sampling programme we must therefore accept that we are probably concerned with a factor that is an indicator of other variables in the environment and not a direct component of the plant's environment. However as pH, like rainfall and soil type, is readily assessed it should be included because it indicates what further factors (like calcium and phosphate) might usefully be measured.

AERATION

There is ample indication that aeration of the soil is an important factor controlling plant growth, but there are few quantitative data from the field relating oxygen and carbon dioxide concentrations in the soil solution to plant growth. The same can be said of plant nematodes although there is good evidence from laboratory and glasshouse experiments that poor aeration decreases survival and population density (Wallace, 1971). Lack of field data is probably due to the difficulties of measuring aeration *in situ*. The use of platinum electrodes to measure the rate of oxygen diffusion in soils has made a big contribution to our knowledge of the influence of oxygen and CO_2 on nematodes but such methods do not afford a practical way of dealing with a large number of sampling sites over the growing time of a crop.

Statements about the influence of aeration on nematodes are usually deductive and stress the importance of soil water. Cooper *et al.* (1970) state that soil-inhabiting nematodes appear well adapted to the variations of aeration encountered in soil, so it is not generally a critical environmental component. However, they go on to say that aeration may be important for nematode survival in irrigated agricultural soils because oxygen supply drops to low levels during periods of flood irrigation. As irrigation frequency increases, the period of adequate soil aeration for nematodes is decreased, and those in soil at depths from 30 to 61 cm and below may be exposed to continuous low levels of oxygen. Townshend and Webber (1971) also suggest that lack of aeration probably accounts for poor survival of nematodes where soils are saturated. As the rates of diffusion of CO_2 and oxygen are directly related to the moisture content of soil, moisture is a good indicator of aeration but other factors are involved too. The nearer plant roots or nematodes are to the surface the better their chances of receiving adequate aeration; size of soil crumbs and porosity also influence the rate of gaseous diffusion in soil, so it is conceivable that two different soil types might have similar moisture contents but quite different degrees of aeration.

What is needed, perhaps, is a method of estimating aeration using the soil moisture budget plus other parameters that influence gaseous diffusion. The statement by Cooper *et al.* (1970) that aeration is probably not a critical environmental component of the nematode is open to argument. In terms of survival alone this statement may be correct but in our concern with the rates at which nematode populations increase and their influence on plants, any modifying influence may be important; in other words survival is rather a harsh criterion by which to assess the importance of an environmental factor.

TEMPERATURE

Here is a factor which can be measured easily and which has a great influence on plant and nematode alike. Records of air temperature and soil temperature at various depths are often obtainable from meteorological or field stations close to the area under investigation. Temperature is likely to be an important factor in the seasonal fluctuations of plant growth and nematode numbers. Like other factors it may influence nematodes directly or indirectly. Thus temperature influenced the rate of development and sex ratio of *Meloidogyne graminis* in Tifgreen Bermuda grass; at higher temperatures more males were formed presumably because of the influence of temperature on the plant. However there may be a direct effect on the nematodes through changes in hormone balance (Laughlin *et al.*, 1969). The plants and their pathogens may have different temperature requirements; Ferris (1970) for example found that at 7 to 13 °C, fewer than 100 *Pratylenchus penetrans* per g of root caused significant reductions in the weight of onion roots by the fifth week. At 16 to 25 °C on the other hand 400 nematodes were required to produce comparable injury. Ferris suggests that low soil temperature slows the growth of the onion plants without markedly restricting the feeding and migration of the nematodes. Clearly, knowledge of the temperature requirements of the various organisms in the ecological system is required if useful explanations are to be given of the various correlations derived from the field studies. The work of Banyer and Fisher (1971*a*, *b*) on the temperature requirements for hatching in *Heterodera avenae* illustrates the inadequacy of field data and the need to understand the biology of the organism. In this species a cold period followed by a warm period is required, hence the seasonal changes in temperature play an important role in determining when populations of infective larvae reach their peak in the soil.

Measurements of temperature down the soil profile may be useful in the search for factors that influence the vertical distribution of nematodes but, once again, other factors like soil moisture that control the thermal conductivity and thermal capacity of soil may have to be taken into account. Air temperature may sometimes be a good indicator of soil temperature because usually the temperature at any depth varies with the same frequency as that at the ground surface although the amplitude of temperature oscillation decreases with depth and the phase of temperature change lags increasingly behind that at the surface with increasing depth. Moisture, because it increases the conductivity of soil to heat, may consequently alter these relationships.

Although data on temperature fluctuations in the form of continuous recordings on charts are easy to acquire, it is less easy to decide how to reduce them to some statistic that is biologically realistic. Average monthly maxima, average monthly minima, monthly averages, temperature summations, average frost free periods are the kinds of statistics that have been used. Occasionally temperatures are weighted; thus if we are concerned with survival at high temperatures the numbers of days that temperatures exceeded say 35 °C may be given more weight than those between 30 and 35 °C, and so on. In making such decisions a knowledge of the organisms' responses to temperature are required so that field measurements can be reduced to some realistic value that can be included in a statistical analysis.

POLLUTANTS

In agricultural areas close to cities and busy roadways, there is a real possibility of air and water pollutants playing an important part in influencing plant growth. Ozone, nitrogen oxide and peroxyacetyl nitrate are the most important phytotoxic components of the oxidant complex (Heck, 1968) and various other environmental factors like water stress, low soil fertility, light intensity, pathogens, temperature and humidity, influence the plants' sensitivity to the oxidants.

The use of waste water for irrigating crops can also raise serious problems by introducing parasites, altering the characteristics of the soil and producing phytotoxic effluents. Pollutants of this kind lead to increases in the prevalence of root decay and foliar diseases, predispose plants to pathogenic damage through increases in levels of nutrient elements and impair mycorrhizal synthesis (Cole *et al.*, 1969).

FARM PRACTICES

Information on what has been previously done to a soil has two benefits: it enables us to assess the importance of these factors on the observed variability in crop growth in the area under study and it also suggests possible ways in which the soil and crop might be treated to reduce the chance of poor crop yields. Data on previous cropping history, frequency of cultivation, applications of herbicides, pesticides, fungicides and nematicides, the seeding rate, the depth at which the seed was sown, the sowing time, fertilizer applications and so on may give useful correlations in the subsequent multivariate analysis. They may indicate for example, that over a large number of farms a particular seeding rate, depth and sowing time were correlated with low numbers of parasites, high soil moisture content and high crop yields. The implications are clear and a plausible story could be constructed to suggest why high crop yields were associated with these conditions. Further experiments would then be required to test the hypothesis. Factors concerned with farm practice (control factors) are therefore of practical as well as ecological significance.

THE HOST PLANT

We have now covered the more important factors that might need to be measured when we study the ecology of a crop and try to determine the major factors influencing growth and yield. However the chief object of our interest is the plant which has to be sampled too. The characteristics that we measure obviously depend on the type of plant; with trees it may be height, girth, yield of fruit, numbers of branches, time of flowering, time of bud burst, and so on. With annual crops which can be removed from the soil, we might measure the dry and fresh weight of roots, yield, numbers of tillers, numbers of leaves, numbers of nodes, height, root length, etc. Usually it is worthwhile to measure as many characteristics of the crop plant as possible because the influence of environment is usually unpredictable. Thus variability in a crop may not become apparent until a particular time of year or stage of development. In wheat in South Australia, for example, root proliferation and stunted tops are often characteristic of patches of poor growth in the crop. *Heterodera avanae*, *Pratylenchus minyus*, various pathogenic fungi, as well as low nigrogen and low soil moisture are all associated with the condition. Occasionally, however, patchiness in the crop is revealed in the amount of grain produced per ear, although in general height and appearance the high and low yielding plants were similar before grain production. It may also be useful to measure some physiological aspects of the growing crop by analysing the leaves for nitrogen, phosphorus and potassium or for photosynthetic rate or respiration. In this way early influences of environment on the plants may be detected. Aerial photography using infra-red film may serve the same purpose by indicating areas of incipient disease that are not apparent at ground level.

Summary

The various steps we might take to complete the task of determining the chief factors controlling the yield of a crop may be summarized as follows:

(1) Clarify the problem so that the objectives are explicit.
(2) Survey the area, collect information from farmers and extension workers and gather relevant published data.
(3) Decide on a sampling procedure and a probable method of statistical analysis.
(4) From the initial survey decide on the factors that need to be measured and how they can be measured. Sample the crop.
(5) On the basis of the statistical analysis of the data from the samples form a hypothesis on the relative importance of the factors on crop yield.
(6) Simulate the system by a model if the situation demands it (e.g. a recurring series of disease epidemics, or persistent crop failure of economic importance).
(7) Test hypotheses, diagnoses and models by laboratory, glasshouse and field experiments.

Adoption of such a scheme is no guarantee of success of course; important factors may be excluded from the sampling procedure through ignorance of their existence or lack of appreciation of their importance. Incorrect interpretation of analyses of the field data may lead to wrong hypotheses and wrong conclusions. Our attempts to understand the nature of the system may be thwarted by numerous interactions between parasites and other environmental components. Furthermore, even if our efforts meet with success as judged by future events, the time and resources spent in reaching a solution to the problem may indicate that the procedures I have described are impractical. We may have to be content with a less thorough approach, even if this means that a higher percentage of the answers to field problems are wrong.

It also becomes clear that when we are involved in looking for causes of poor yields in crops, we are not just plant nematologists, or even plant pathologists, but crop ecologists. Even when a particular disease situation is designated a 'nematode problem' the search for solutions inevitably involves these other scientific disciplines.

Mention should be made of Koch's postulates as their importance in disease problems was stressed (wrongly I now think) in an earlier publication (Wallace, 1963). Koch's postulates may provide good evidence that an organism is closely associated with some disease, but it is too remote from the field situation to explain causes in a system where multiple causation is the rule rather than the exception. Thus Koch's postulates may substantiate the pathogenicity of an organism which in the ecological field situation contributes little to the disease. Furthermore, failure to establish pathogenicity by Koch's postulates does not mean that in the field the parasite is not an important cause or determinant of the disease. The application of Koch's postulates may still be useful, however, in those experiments that follow the analysis of the field data; they may provide useful information about a vital part of the ecological web.

Finally, the application of fumigants, nematicides and sterilants to soil in field experiments may indicate a way in which yields can be improved. It might be argued that information about the causes of disease in a crop are rather superfluous as long as the disease is being controlled, at least from a practical and economic viewpoint. And there is some logic in the argument; however the application of chemicals to soil might have unpredictable long-term consequences that are unacceptable and which outweigh the initial benefits. For example, it has been shown by Kempton and Maw (1972) that soil fumigation with methyl bromide may result in an appreciable accumulation of bromide in lettuce. Such residues may present a hazard to health and necessitate regulations on tolerance limits. Furthermore there is enough information from the entomological field, for example, to suggest that such a pessimistic prognosis is not out of the question. Soil fumigation and sterilization are very useful expedients in some situations, especially those that require immediate and urgent attention, what is needed now are studies on the long-term ecological effects of such treatments. Such a statement might almost be a platitude if it were not for the fact that nematicides are sometimes used in field experiments to indicate the importance of nematodes as causes of disease. Once again, the effect of such a drastic disturbance in the ecological web precludes unequivocal statements about causes; for one thing the experiments are based on the assumption that one factor, nematodes, is responsible for the disease, and for another it is assumed that only nematodes will be affected by the chemicals. These objections alone, it seems to me, are sufficient to throw serious doubt on the validity of diagnostic work that is based on nematicide treatment.

References

ASAI, G.N., JONES, M.W. and RORIE, F.G. (1967). Influence of certain environmental factors in the field on infection of rice by *Piricularia oryzae*. *Phytopathology*, **57**, 237.

BAIER, W. and ROBERTSON, G.W. (1966). A new versatile soil moisture budget. *Canad. J. Plant. Sci.*, **47**, 299.

BAIER, W. and ROBERTSON, G.W. (1968). The performance of soil moisture estimates as compared with the direct use of climatological data for estimating crop fields. *Agric. Meteorol.*, **5**, 17.

BANYER, R.J. and FISHER, J.M. (1971*a*). Seasonal variation in hatching of eggs of *Heterodera avenae. Nematologica*, **17**, 225.

BANYER, R.J. and FISHER, J.M. (1971*b*). Effect of temperature on hatching of eggs of *Heterodera avenae. Nematologica*, **17**, 519.

BARKER, K.R., LEHMAN, P.S. and HUISINGH, D. (1971). Influence of nitrogen and *Rhizobium japonicum* on the activity of *Heterodera glycines. Nematologica*, **17**, 377.

BAWDEN, R.J. (1969). Relationships between *Oesophagostomum columbianum* infection and the nutritional status of sheep. 1. Effects on growth and feed utilization. *Aust. J. agric. Res.*, **20**, 589.

BERGESON, G.B., VAN GUNDY, S.D. and THOMASON, I.J. (1970). Effect of *Meloidogyne javanica* on rhizosphere microflora and *Fusarium* wilt of tomato. *Phytopathology*, **60**, 1245.

BIER, J.E. (1959). The relation of bark moisture to the development of canker diseases caused by native, facultative parasites. I. *Cryptodiaporthe* canker on willow. *Canad. J. Bot.*, **37**, 229.

BIRD, G.W., MCCARTER, S.M. and RONCADORI, R.W. (1971). Role of nematodes and soil-borne fungi in cotton stunt. *J. Nematology*, **3**, 17.

BLACK, D.A.K. (1968). *The logic of medicine.* Oliver and Boyd. Contemp. Sci. Paperbacks, vi + 88 pp.

BROWN, T., BARRETT, M.J. and DARROCH, J.N. (1965). Factor analysis in cephalometric research. *Growth*, **29**, 97.

BURNS, N.C. (1971). Soil pH effects on nematode populations associated with soybeans. *J. Nematology*, **3**, 238.

CAUQUIL, J. and SHEPHERD, R.L. (1970). Effect of root-knot nematode-fungi combinations on cotton seedling disease. *Phytopathology*, **60**, 448.

COLE, H., MERRILL, W., LUKEZIC, F.L. and BLOOM, J.R. (1969). Effects on vegetation of irrigation with waste treatment effluents and possible plant pathogen—irrigation interactions. *Phytopathology*, **59**, 1181.

COOPER, A.F., VAN GUNDY, S.D. and STOLZY, L.N. (1970). Nematode reproduction in environments of fluctuating aeration. *J. Nematology*, **2**, 182.

DAS, S. and RASKI, D.J. (1969). Effect of grapevine fanleaf virus on the reproduction and survival of its nematode vector *Xiphinema index* Thorne and Allen. *J. Nematology*, **1**, 107.

DAVIDSON, T.R. and TOWNSHEND, J.L. (1967). Some weed hosts of the southern root-knot nematode *Meloidogyne incognita. Nematologica*, **13**, 452.

DIRKS, V.A. and ROMIG, R.W. (1970). Linear models applied to variation in numbers of cereal rust urediospores. *Phytopathology*, **60**, 246.

DUBOS, R. (1970). *Man, medicine and environment*. Penguin Books Ltd., 173 pp.

ENGLE, R.L. (1964) Medical diagnosis. In *The diagnostic process*. Edited by J.A. Jacquez. Proc. Conference University of Michigan, 1963, vi + 391 pp.

ESTORES, R.A. and TSEH AN CHEN (1972). Interactions of *Pratylenchus penetrans* and *Meloidogyne incognita* as coinhabitants in tomato. *J. Nematology*, **4**, 170.

EVERSMEYER, M.G. and BURLEIGH, J.R. (1970). A method of predicting epidemic development of wheat leaf rust. *Phytopathology*, **60**, 805.

FERRIS, J.M. (1970). Soil temperature effects on onion seedling injury by *Pratylenchus penetrans*. *J. Nematology*, **2**, 248.

FERRIS, V.R. and BERNARD, R.L. (1971). Effect of soil type on population densities of nematodes in soybean rotation fields. *J. Nematology*, **3**, 123.

FERRIS, V.R., FERRIS, J.M., BERNARD, R.L. and PROBST, A.H. (1971). Community structure of plant-parasitic nematodes related to soil types in Illinois and Indiana soybean fields. *J. Nematology*, **3**, 399.

FIDLER, J.H. and BEVAN, W.J. (1963). Some soil factors influencing the density of cereal root eelworm (*Heterodera avenae* Woll.) populations and their damage to the oat crop. *Nematologica*, **9**, 412.

FILER, T.H. (1967). Pathogenicity of *Cytospora*, *Phomopsis*, and *Hypomyces* on *Populus deltoides*. *Phytopathology*, **57**, 978.

FOSTER, R.E. (1967). *Chenopodium amaranticolor* nutrition affects cucumber mosaic virus infection. *Phytopathology*, **57**, 838.

GHAFFER, A. and ERWIN, D.C. (1969). Effect of soil water stress on root rot of cotton caused by *Macrophomina phaseoli*. *Phytopathology*, **59**, 795.

GRIFFIN, D.M. (1963). Soil moisture and the ecology of soil fungi. *Biol. Rev.*, **38**, 141.

HEALD, C.M. and HEILMAN, M.D. (1971). Interaction of *Rotylenchulus reniformis* soil salinity, and cotton. *J. Nematology*, **3**, 179.

HECK, W.W. (1968). Factors influencing expression of oxidant damage to plants. *Ann. Rev. Phytopath.*, **6**, 165.

JAMES, W.C., SHIH, C.S., HODGSON, W.A. and CALLBECK, L.C. (1972). The quantitative relationship between late blight of potato and loss in tuber yield. *Phytopathology*, **62**, 92.

JOHNSON, S.R., FERRIS, V.R. and FERRIS, J.M. (1972). Nematode community structure of forest woodlots. 1. Relationships based on similarity coefficients of nematode species. *J. Nematology*, **4**, 175.

JOHNSON, A.W. and NUSBAUM, C.J. (1970). Interactions between *Meloidogyne incognita, M. hapla,* and *Pratylenchus brachyurus* in tobacco. *J. Nematology,* **2,** 334.

JORDAN, V.W.L. (1968). The life-history and epidemiology of American gooseberry mildew on black currants. *Ann. appl. Biol.,* **61,** 399.

KABLE, P.F. and MAI, W.F. (1968). Overwintering of *Pratylenchus penetrans* in a sandy loam and a clay loam soil at Ithaca, New York. *Nematologica,* **14,** 150.

KEMPTON, R.J. and MAW, G.A. (1972). Soil fumigation with methyl bromide: bromide accumulation by lettuce plants. *Ann. appl. Biol.,* **72,** 71.

KIMPINSKI, J. and WELCH, H.E. (1971). The ecology of nematodes in Manitoba soils. *Nematologica,* **17,** 308.

KINCAID, R.R., MARTIN, F.G., GAMMON, N., BRELAND, H.L. and PRITCHETT, W.L. (1970). Multiple regression of tobacco black shank, root knot and coarse root indexes on soil pH, potassium, calcium and magnesium. *Phytopathology,* **60,** 1513.

KINLOCH, R.A. and ALLEN, M.W. (1972). Interaction of *Meloidogyne hapla* and *M. javanica* infecting tomato. *J. Nematology,* **4,** 7.

KOEN, H. (1966). The influence of seasonal variations on the vertical distribution of *Meloidogyne javanica* in sandy soils. *Nematologica,* **12,** 297.

LAUGHLIN, C.W. and WILLIAMS, A.S. (1971). Population behaviour of *Meloidogyne graminis* in field-grown 'Tifgreen' Bermudagrass. *J. Nematology,* **3,** 386.

LAUGHLIN, C.W., WILLIAMS, A.S. and FOX, J.A. (1969). The influence of temperature on development and sex differentiation of *Meloidogyne graminis. J. Nematology,* **1,** 212.

LUSTED, L.B. (1968). *Introduction to medical decision making.* Charles C. Thomas Publishers, Springfield, Illinois, xxi + 271 pp.

LUSTED, L.B. and STAHL, W.R. (1964). Conceptual models of diagnosis. In *The diagnostic process.* Edited by J.A. Jacquez. Proc. Conference University of Michigan, 1963, vi + 391 pp.

MORGAN, G.T. and MACLEAN, A.A. (1968). Influence of soil pH on an introduced population of *Pratylenchus penetrans. Nematologica,* **14,** 311.

NYHAN, J.W., FREDERICK, L.R. and NORTON, D.C. (1972). Ecology of nematodes in Clarion–Webster toposequences associated with *Glycine max* (L.). Merrill. *Soil Sci. Amer. Proc.,* **36,** 74.

O'BANNON, J.H. and TOMERLIN, A.T. (1971). Response of citrus seedlings to *Radopholus similis* in two soils. *J. Nematology,* **3,** 255.

PAUL, J.R. (1966). *Clinical epidemiology.* Univ. Chicago Press, xix + 305 pp.

POWELL, N.T., MELENDEZ, P.L. and BATTEN, C.K. (1971). Disease complexes in tobacco involving *Meloidogyne incognita* and certain soil-borne fungi. *Phytopathology,* **61,** 1332.

RACTLIFFE, L.H., TAYLOR, H.M., WHITLOCK, J.H. and LYNN, W.R. (1969). Systems analysis of a host-parasite interaction. *Parasitology*, **59**, 649.

ROTEM, J., COHEN, Y. and PUTTER, J. (1971). Relativity of limiting and optimum inoculum loads, wetting durations, and temperatures for infection by *Phytophthora infestans*. *Phytopathology*, **61**, 275.

SAYRE, R.M. (1971). Biotic influences in soil environment. In *Plant parasitic nematodes*. Vol. 1. Edited by B.M. Zuckerman, W.F. Mai and R.A. Rohde. Academic Press, xiv + 345 pp.

SCHNATHORST, W.C. (1965). Environmental relationships in the powdery mildews. *Ann. Rev. Phytopath.*, **3**, 343.

SIKORA, R.A., TAYLOR, D.P., MALEK, R.B. and EDWARDS, D.I. (1972). Interaction of *Meloidogyne naasi*, *Pratylenchus penetrans*, and *Tylenchorhynchus agri* on creeping bentgrass. *J. Nematology*, **4**, 162.

TALBOYS, P.W. and WILSON, J.F. (1970). Effects of temperature and rainfall on the incidence of wilt (*Verticillium albo-atrum*) in hops. *Ann. appl. Biol.*, **66**, 51.

TOWNSHEND, J.L. (1972). Influence of edaphic factors on penetration of corn roots by *Pratylenchus penetrans* and *P. minyus* in three Ontario soils. *Nematologica* **18**, 201.

TOWNSHEND, J.L. and WEBBER, L.R. (1971). Movement of *Pratylenchus penetrans* and the moisture characteristics of three Ontario soils. *Nematologica*, **17**, 47.

WAGGONER, P.E. and HORSFALL, J.G. (1969). Epidem. A simulator of plant disease written for a computer. *Bull. Connecticut Agric. Exp. Stn.*, **698.**

WALKER, J.T. (1969). *Pratylenchus penetrans* (Cobb) populations as influenced by microorganisms and soil amendments. *J. Nematology*, **1**, 260.

WALKER, J.T. (1971). Populations of *Pratylenchus penetrans* relative to decomposing nitrogenous soil amendments. *J. Nematology*, **3**, 43.

WALLACE, H.R. (1963). *The biology of plant parasitic nematodes*. Edward Arnold, viii + 280 pp.

WALLACE, H.R. (1966). Factors influencing the infectivity of plant parasitic nematodes. *Proc. Roy. Soc. B. Lond.*, **164**, 592.

WALLACE, H.R. (1971). Abiotic influences in the soil environment. In *Plant Parasitic nematodes* Vol. 1. Edited by B.M. Zuckerman, W.F. Mai and R.A. Rohde. Academic Press, xiv + 345 pp.

WHITE, T.C.R. (1969). An index to measure weather-induced stress of trees sociated with outbreaks of psyllids in Australia. *Ecology*, **50**, 905.

9 The nature of disease

It is opportune at this stage to gather together the arguments and concepts presented in previous chapters to see if we can get a better understanding of what disease is. This seems essential if we are to do anything about curbing the undesirable effects of disease in crops where nematodes are involved.

Disease starts by disturbance of the plant's physiology during penetration, feeding or migration of the nematode through the host's tissues. Thus, through secretions, excretions or mechanical damage the plant's integrity is violated and the amount of subsequent disturbance is aggravated by their frequency and intensity. The numbers of nematodes that parasitize a plant influence the severity of disease and, in general, the more nematodes there are the more intense the malfunction they produce. However, the plant is not a passive recipient of disturbance by the nematode; through its abilities to compensate for, repair and generally absorb damage and to divert metabolites to infection sites it can tolerate a certain amount of damage without exhibiting marked physiological malfunction. The plant therefore, appears to have mechanisms that help to sustain its health. It is only when there are too many nematodes that it fails to cope and disease occurs. In addition, the plant opposes nematodes that produce disturbance by directly inhibiting them. This is resistance and, like tolerance, it appears to be a means of maintaining the plant's stability. Furthermore it is possible that in order to bring the factors of tolerance and resistance into play, the plant works harder thus revealing characteristics of an integrated self-regulating system that maintains homeostasis in the face of disturbance initiated by the nematode. Such characteristics may be imperfect or inadequate when, for example, environmental factors exert stress on the plant and prevent the homeostatic factors from working to their full efficiency. In particular, large numbers of nematodes may overwhelm the plant's defences, hence the distribution and abundance of nematodes in relation to disease within a crop is important. Such ecological features of nematodes are also influenced by environmental components, thus the variations in crop and soil factors play a large part in determining nematode distribution. The nematode, like the plant, has adaptations that increase its chances of survival; for example, stress due to lack of food at high population densities of nematodes is offset by changes in sex ratio.

In considering nematodes as causes of disease in plants, it is apparent that they are only one of several environmental components that influence the plant and contribute to physiological malfunction. Thus, in considering disease in plants associated with nematodes, we are always concerned with a multifactorial system and one of the major problems that confronts us is to determine which factors are most important in causing disease. The main cause of disease in plants infected with nematodes may not be nematodes but some other pathogen or some soil factor like lack of water or nutrients.

Disease, then, is involved with disturbance of a physiological system which is more or less stable, with activities that tend to restore and maintain stability, with the inability of the system to maintain stability in the face of overwhelming disturbance, with the influence of environment on these processes, with the interaction between host and numerous environmental components including parasites. If there is one feature which categorizes all these aspects it is homeostasis, hence it will be worth considering this concept in a little more detail. Finally, we can consider disease from two points of view, the individual plant which is a physiological topic, and the plant population or crop which is ecological in nature. Before we attempt to be more precise about the nature of disease however, let us cast our net a little wider and see what the medical scientists, the plant pathologists and the ecologists have to say on these characteristics of disease.

Some medical views

Disease means different things to different people and this is particularly true among medical scientists. Ryle (1948) for example says that disease is not merely a symptom or a group of symptoms, it is not a local injury nor the general poisoning which gives rise to symptoms, nor yet the bacterial invasion that produces the injury which causes the symptoms. Ryle then goes on to suggest that disease might be defined as the whole consequence of a conflict between man and the various agencies in his environment. Pneumonia or any other disease in an individual may be influenced in its course, not only by the type of invading microbe but also by the age and type of the patient, by his hereditary endowments, by his environment and by his psychology. Ryle thus recognizes the holistic nature of disease and the consequence of numerous factors acting on the human.

A somewhat similar view is expressed by Norton (1969) in a different way. He argues that in medicine the etiology of most of the diseases that have single predominating causes such as infections, deficiencies and genetic metabolic disorders is probably understood by now. A few may remain to be discovered and the search for these must continue as it must continue for secondary causes of such conditions as tuberculosis, accidents and lung cancer. However, Norton emphasizes that the concept of multiple causes, of combined and contributory causation, seems to fit the facts best. Thus in psychiatry it has long been accepted that a diagnosis cannot be expressed in a few words; it more often needs a sentence or two if it is to serve the primary purpose of diagnosis and prescribe a likely course, a probable outcome and useful therapy. Perhaps, Norton continues, the same stage has been reached in diabetes, in rheumatoid arthritis, arterial degeneration and chronic bronchitis. In these and many other illnesses it seems futile to hunt for a single cause as the preponderant cause in all cases. It is more constructive, Norton suggests, to assess the individual's illness in terms of a number of causes that may be concurrent, consecutive or interlocking.

Such views obviously agree with the concepts of the ecological web, multifactorial causation, their interacting nature and the playing down of the idea of single primary causes. They also emphasize the limited value of a diagnosis which consists merely of putting a name to a disease.

Dubos (1970) goes further; he suggests that multifactorial etiology is the rule rather than the exception and he makes the important point that the body is capable of only a limited range of reactions. Its responses to assaults of very different origin and nature is consequently rather stereotyped. Thus, Dubos states, intestinal lesions mimicking those of typhoid fever can be produced by introducing into the mesenteric nodes of animals almost any irritating substance, even a rose thorn. Symptoms, then are likely to be of only limited value in diagnosis and not always indicative of causes.

What can be said about disease in terms of the host? As Black (1968) points out, it is insufficient to define disease as a departure from health because we merely become conscious of our inability to define health. Disease, according to Black, is an abstraction that may have causes which are indefinable, multiple or unknown and therefore constitute part of the challenge of medicine and, we might add, plant pathology. White and Jordan (1963) define health as the state which results from the successful adjustment of body form and function to forces tending to disturb them, i.e. the multiplicity of disease-producing agents which arise within the host or exist in the environment outside it. There is a hint of homeostasis here especially when White and Jordan go on to say that failure to adjust successfully results in disease and that health and disease are the results of active processes in which the body tissues engage in a continuous struggle with diverse factors. Burnet (1962) sees disease in the same light when he describes it as a conflict between man and his parasites which in a constant environment would tend to result in virtual equilibrium in which both species survive indefinitely. However, as Burnet points out, man lives in an environment which is constantly being changed by his own activities and few of his diseases have attained such an equilibrium.

These few examples of views from medical science indicate the similarity between the nature of disease in humans and plants. The major differences lie in their physiology and in the fact that medical practitioners, unlike plant pathologists, are more concerned with individuals than with populations, but even here the differences are qualitative. The physiology of plants and animals may be different but they are both self-regulating systems and to understand disease in a population we must understand disease in individuals. However, let us now work closer to home and examine some ideas from the field of plant pathology.

Ideas from plant pathology

Gäumann (1950) considered that every disease originates primarily in a functional disturbance of the host which has the capacity to adjust and to retain and continue its normal development and metabolism. If disturbance occurs the host 'endeavours to return to its norm and to reinstate its threatened equilibrium'. Accordingly it was Gäumann's opinion that disease is an indication that the host has reacted to disturbing influences and deviated from its normal functional course. Gäumann's notion of disease as 'mutual conflict' between host and pathogen more or less reflects the ideas expressed in previous chapters; it conjures up the picture of disease as a lack of stability and the plant's inability to restore stability.

Other views of disease are less explicit. Stakman and Harrar (1957) describe it as any deviation from normal growth or structure of plants that is sufficiently pronounced and permanent to produce visible symptoms or to impair quality and economic value. However, words like 'normal' and 'sufficiently pronounced and permanent' are rather vague.

Walker (1969) thinks of diseased plants as those which have become altered in their physiological and morphological development to such a degree that signs of such effects are obvious as symptoms. Walker points out however that the degree of alteration from the norm that constitutes disease is largely a matter of definition and that there is no clearly defined distinction between normal or healthy plants and abnormal or diseased plants. In other words, we can infer that we should not think of plants as being either healthy or diseased but as being at different levels of health (or disease). This is a useful point to which we will refer later.

Horsfall and Dimond (1959), after refuting the idea that disease is a condition or a pathogen, conclude that it is a malfunctioning process caused by continuous irritation, thus distinguishing it from injury which is caused by transient irritation. This definition of disease is clear and precise but it seems incomplete and lacking in some of the ideas expressed by Gäumann (1950).

Agrios (1970) defines disease in plants as any disturbance brought about by a living entity or an environmental factor which interferes with the plant's physiology in such a way that the affected plant changes in appearance and/or yields less than a normal healthy plant of the same variety. We are once again faced with the problem of deciding what we mean by a normal healthy plant. If, as Agrios suggests, such a plant is recognized by its ability to carry out its physiological function to the best of its genetic potential then in nature the great majority of plants must be somewhat less than healthy.

It is not my purpose to compose a critique of definitions of plant disease that have been put forward by various authors but to see if useful ideas about disease can be found. In general, the view of disease as expressed by plant pathologists is one of deviation from a norm, of deviation that is sufficient to produce measurable affects, of deviation that is expressed as continuing malfunction, and of an attempt by the plant to return to the norm. What the norm is and how much deviation is required to qualify as disease is a matter of definition within the context of particular situations, e.g. we might specify the norm of a particular potato crop as x tonnes per hectare and the deviation as y tonnes per hectare but this does not prevent us from changing the values of x and y for another locality, for a different season or in different economic circumstances.

What is lacking in plant pathological discussions of the nature of disease is emphasis on multifactorial causation. In describing the evolution of ideas concerning the causes of disease for example, Allen (1966) traces progress from the time that particular weather conditions were thought to cause disease, to the recognition that the causes of disease were the result of specific agents, that disease was caused by toxic products released by the microorganisms and finally that it is largely the result of altered host metabolism that is the real cause of disease. We may suggest now that the idea of causality has evolved to the multifactorial stage where there are numerous direct and indirect causes that form a web of interacting components with the plant at the centre. It should be stressed that recognition of multiple causation in plant diseases is a matter of emphasis, not omission, as examples of etiological problems in the previous chapter indicate.

The concept of homeostasis as an important feature of disease has also received little emphasis although several authors are clearly thinking along these lines. Beckman (1964), for example, in discussing the respiration of infected plants, remarks that increases in tissue respiration follow infection of both resistant and susceptible plant cultivars. In resistant plants there is a localized, rapid and sizable increase in respiration followed by a rapid return to normal levels. In a susceptible type of reaction there is a slower rise in respiration that gradually spreads throughout the plant. This suggests that in the resistant reaction the respiratory mechanism is adequate to overcome infection whereas in the susceptible reaction the respiratory mechanism is not quite adequate to do the job. Beckman goes on to say that as the pathogen progresses through the susceptible plant the respiratory mechanism that is linked to defence is called into play in more and more host tissues, but it is always too little and too late to subdue or confine the invading organism. Beckman's narrative appears to support Gäumann's idea of disease as the inability of the plant to restore its equilibrium. Furthermore, the inability of a diseased plant to function as a self-regulating system is implicit in the description by Uritani (1971) of disease. In some combinations of plants and parasites, infection extends to adjacent non-infected tissues gradually and at this stage, Uritani suggests, plants are incapable of regulating their metabolism which is altered in an abnormal way.

It will be worthwhile therefore to consider the topic of homeostasis further, especially those aspects that deal with regulation, stability, deviations about a norm and restoration to a norm.

Homeostasis

Animals and plants have physiological characteristics that enable them to maintain a constant internal environment at a norm in the face of external disturbing influences. The norm is an inherited characteristic of the organism. This is what homeostasis is about but a more precise definition was given at the eighteenth symposium of the Society for Experimental Biology (Hughes, 1964). It states that 'homeostasis in its widest context includes the coordinated physiological processes which maintain most of the steady states in organisms. Similar general principles may apply to the establishment, regulation and control of steady states for other levels of organization. It must be emphasized that homeostasis does not necessarily imply a lack of change because the 'steady states' to which the regulatory mechanisms are directed may shift with time. But throughout the change they remain under more or less close control'. The definition then affirms that 'the concept can be applied to organizations at cellular, organ system, individual and social levels. It may be considered in relation to time intervals ranging from milliseconds to millions of years. Its essential feature is the interplay of factors which tend to maintain a given state at a given time.'

We might expect therefore, that the attributes of a plant such as size, shape, growth, photosynthesis, respiration and so on are regulated and that if an outside disturbance (such as parasites) upsets the equilibrium then responses will be initiated that restore equilibrium. Moreover the degree of response is likely to be determined by the degree of the disturbance. In warm-blooded animals, for example, a constant temperature is maintained in environments where temperatures fluctuate widely. In hot weather, the blood capillaries at the surface of the skin dilate and sweat is produced that evaporates, both of which processes help to cool the body. In cold weather, shivering increases heat production which warms the body. These and other responses keep the temperature within narrow limits. When the body temperature begins to change under the influence of some external factor the control mechanisms begin to operate and their performance is governed by the extent of the change in temperature. Thus, like a machine which is automatically regulated, the operation of the body is determined by its performance immediately before. This type of operation is called feedback, and if the regulatory action opposes the change thereby correcting excess or deficiency it is called negative feedback. Conversely, a reaction that increases change is called positive feedback. Equilibrium or a steady state may also be achieved by a feed forward or open loop process in which a reaction compensates for change without opposing the change. We have previously noted that resistance to disease in plants is an example of negative feedback whereas the ability to replace damaged tissues (tolerance) is of the feed forward variety.

Each system, whether it is temperature regulation or control of numbers of parasites by antibodies, has what is called an input or stimulus and an output or response. The response may be proportional to the magnitude of the stimulus, e.g. more parasites, more antibodies; the response may depend on the rate of change of the stimulus and there may be a delay in response, the lag time. A further feature of homeostatic control by feedback is the oscillation of some physiological characteristic about a mean or a norm which is a genetic characteristic of the organism. Thus regulatory mechanisms are never so efficient or so prompt in their response that fluctuations never occur.

In the context of disease it seems likely that the host plant has numerous mechanisms of compensation, repair and resistance that by feedback and feed-forward processes tend to resist change in physiological function and so maintain equilibrium at a norm. Such stability might be called health. Disease occurs when parasites, as a disturbing factor, occur, in such numbers or intensity that the host's homeostatic responses are insufficient to maintain stability. Or, some environmental components may adversely influence the organism's ability to respond effectively to other environmental components. Lack of nitrogen may, for example, reduce the mechanisms of compensation and resistance to parasites attacking a plant. Thus, we might conclude that any factor that upsets homeostasis is a cause of disease, consequently, the distinction between the transient nature of insect damage and the prolonged irritation of a pathogen seems untenable. The scarab beetles that destroy roots and the nematodes that penetrate roots causing necrotic cavities may have similar influences on the ability of the plant to maintain its top growth.

Such notions, presented here in the context of homeostasis, have already been mentioned in terms of multifactorial causes of disease, of horizontal resistance and of interactions between environmental components in the ecological web. That is why the concept of homeostasis in disease is so appealing; it readily accepts all the concepts of disease that have been discussed so far without being so all-embracing as to lose effectiveness as a useful hypothesis.

If the pathogen has caused instability in the host's physiology, i.e. caused disease, and continues to maintain the upper hand so to speak, death may follow. If, on the other hand, the host is tardy in responding to the disturbance of infection then disease may eventually subside as the host's homeostatic mechanisms resume control. Lack of homeostasis in one particular physiological function may lead to a series of biochemical and physiological reactions that culminate in visible signs of instability; we call these symptoms.

Such a view of disease is useful because it is testable by experiment. The previous discussion on tolerance and resistance that suggested that plants infected with low numbers of nematodes may show physiological responses related to the size of the inoculum, is really a test of the homeostasis hypothesis.

It would be a mistake, however, to become too idealistic about homeostasis. Although Dubos (1970) approves of the concept of homeostasis, he asserts for example, that organisms do not always return to the exact former state following a disturbance; the response may be inadequate and may be inappropriate for the welfare of the organism. Disease, Dubos states, is commonly the consequence of inappropriate responses.

It is probably true to say that homeostasis has received more consideration from the animal physiologists than their botanical counterparts, hence plant pathologists are at a disadvantage, for to understand abnormal physiology (disease) of plants, it is necessary to understand the plant's normal physiology (health). The concept of what is normal is difficult to resolve and define and yet the idea of a norm is necessary if we are to consider stability and fluctuations about a norm. It will therefore be useful to consider briefly the nature of stability and disease, especially as the norm and stability are ultimate objectives in the control of disease.

From what has already been said about homeostasis, stability might be said to be the ability of an organism to return to its norm following disturbance. An infected plant which maintains its rate of growth and yield in spite of environmental factors that cause disturbance, is stable; there may be marked changes in the rates of physiological processes but these are corrective processes that 'absorb' disturbance and allow other processes to proceed thereby ensuring the survival of the plant. On the other hand, an infected plant that fails to reach maturity and eventually dies is unstable. Between these two extremes there is a range of instability or disease. We might go further and define the norm and the deviation from the norm that we would still designate as 'healthy', by stating values for a particular plant grown under particular conditions. However, such values are arbitrary and, although useful in experiments where plants have to be categorized as healthy or diseased, they have little physiological meaning. In fact we might conclude that the question 'is this plant diseased or healthy?' is a bad one, it should be 'how healthy is this plant?'. The word disease is excluded because it is too emotive. It should also be added that the question is not asking whether the plant is infected or has diagnostic symptoms.

A ready solution to the question of 'diseased' or 'healthy' would be available if plants had a distinct tolerance level as described by Seinhorst (Chapter 3) but there is some doubt about the frequency with which this characteristic occurs in plants. Hence, this solution, although attractive, may not be applicable in many disease situations.

The concept of homeostasis is easy to grasp whereas stability and norm are not, but perhaps this need not concern us too much if our chief aim is to understand the causes of disease, the characteristics of disease and eventually how we might control it. Perhaps our attention should be primarily directed to those mechanisms in the plant that oppose change and so maintain the plant's integrity and we should attempt to find out why some individuals succumb to disease quicker than others and what some plants have in their physiological makeup that enables them to grow and yield well when others succumb. In this context norm and stability assume less practical importance.

Homeostasis and disease in populations

Homeostasis in the infected plant is largely a question of physiology but homeostasis, as the definition by the Society for Experimental Biology states, can be applied to other levels of organization. We might therefore consider the plant population or crop as a system and enquire whether it too has properties that confer stability. Browning and Frey (1969) favour the idea of the plant population because they claim that plant pathologists have been preoccupied with individual plants, whereas it is populations of plants that feed increasing populations of people. They also favour the concept of population resistance to describe the situation where the fungus population cannot increase and damage the well-buffered host population which may possess vertical resistance, horizontal resistance or combinations of them. What we are looking for then, are characteristics of populations of plants as distinct from those of individual plants, that compensate for damage and resist the cause of damage to the crop. One such characteristic has been referred to already, the capacity of a crop to maintain yield when a considerable number (40%) of individual plants has been removed or destroyed. This is achieved by increased root growth of the remaining plants that colonize soil previously occupied by the dead plants.

Factors such as insects, rodents, birds, parasites, soil nutrients, water, soil structure, in fact all the plant's environmental components, may at particular levels or numbers cause disturbance to the crop. Evidence of such disturbance may be apparent as patches of stunted, discoloured or dead plants. We have already mentioned the significance of such patches in discussing the distribution of pathogens and diseased plants and in searching for ways to determine the causes of such variable growth. But does the crop as such have regulatory mechanisms, like the individual plant that tend to maintain steady growth and yield?

There has been much controversy in animal ecology about this problem as a review on attitudes to populations and environment indicates (Clark et al., 1968). However, there seems to be general agreement that the numbers of animals in a population may be influenced by negative feed-back processes. Thus, resources in short supply or parasites and predators have an increasingly restrictive influence on the numbers of animals as the density of animals increases. The extent to which such regulatory mechanisms occur in natural populations is unknown, although Andrewartha (1970) thinks that when the ecology of more species is more fully known, density-dependent reactions will be found to be important in relatively few of them. Others, perhaps most, hold opposite views but until the information asked for by Andrewartha is available, it seems rather untimely to adopt either view. The arguments resemble in many ways those on health, disease, norms and stability and, as in those aspects, I suggest it will be more useful to search for possible mechanisms whereby populations of plants are regulated rather than to be too preoccupied with concepts like equilibrium density.

Furthermore, in our consideration of disease in plants we are mainly interested in the agricultural crop which, unlike the insect population for example, is a highly artificial system. Thus, we might not expect crops to have much in the way of homeostasis other than that conferred by the collective contribution of individuals. For one thing, populations of agricultural plants have not had time to evolve such characteristics as those exhibited in wild populations; thus it is commonly recognized that there is greater stability in populations of plants containing many species and that mono-cultures are more prone to devastation by disease epidemics. There is a great deal of information on how environmental factors influence individual plants and how agronomic practices influence yield in crops but, as Donald (1963) says, there is surprisingly little information on the basic relationships among plants within a crop.

How relevant then is the concept of homeostasis in the crop? In my opinion it is both relevant and useful to think in these terms. The farmer's goal is to achieve the biggest yields he can but of course his expectations are never met, he has good years and bad years according to the vagaries of the environment; and weather and disease are often responsible for his disappointments. Over the long term a farmer learns how much on average he can expect from his crops; years of drought and epidemics are offset by years of good rains and little disease. The long term average might be increased by improving the fertility and structure of his soil but he is still exposed to the unpredictable restraints of climate and disease. He can overcome the influence of drought by irrigation and mulching may lower soil temperatures, but such measures are often impracticable, especially where a crop occupies a large area as in a forest or a wheat belt. Insect damage may be reduced by insecticides, and diseases too may be counteracted by the use of chemicals. What the farmer is doing then, is to impose his own environmental influence on the crop to restrain those factors that reduce plant growth. If a crop is left alone entirely it will certainly give a yield, but usually it is too low to be economically acceptable; the crop has to be weeded, thinned out, pruned, fertilized, treated with pesticides and so on to remove the subtractive influence of environment. In other words, the farmer aims to produce a good crop every year and to reduce marked fluctuations in yield from year to year. He is aware of the best way to prepare seedbeds, when crops should be sown, when thinning should occur, and so on. He watches the crop for weed development and the appearance of the first symptoms of disease or insect damage and takes the necessary measures to try and overcome them. In fact he acts like a sense organ in an organism, responding to events by taking action to counteract undesirable changes. We might therefore, consider the farmer and his crop as a self-regulating system with homeostasis; and the farmer is the key regulator. This is a useful way of looking at the situation because it is immediately obvious that if homeostasis is to be achieved on the farm, the farmer must know which factors he should try to alter out of all those that influence his crops. Here the etiologist and extension worker can supply useful advice. Acting on this advice the farmer must also be informed of methods whereby he can influence those factors that depress yields and upset homeostasis. In one sense then, the agronomists, soil scientists, entomologists and plant pathologists are attempting to provide the farmer with better homeostatic tools. The greater the efficiency of these tools the better the chance the farmer has of reaching his expected yields. Of course, the higher the target that is set the more difficult it will be to reach and, if the target is 'as high a yield as possible', then naturally the chances of success will be less; the desired yield is in fact an asymptote, something that is never attained but for which we strive. These however are abstractions; for practical purposes crop management aims to increase the average yield and to reduce the fluctuations in yields from one harvest to the next. Control of disease is clearly one area that contributes to this objective. Unlike the entomologists and plant pathologists however, the farmer is attempting to increase populations and yields of plants by removing restraints whereas the control of insects and pathogens aims to decrease populations by applying restraints. The two processes are complementary but they may also be incompatible. A chemical which kills nematodes is of little use if it inhibits plant growth. Account has therefore to be taken of the influence of any control method or agronomic practice on the whole system, and to do this we may have to resort to the strategies of systems analysis and simulation mentioned earlier. Such approaches to crop production are now being made (Dent and Anderson, 1971) but it is evident that plant parasites have got little recognition so far in the scheme of things. Perhaps this is not surprising in a subject still in its early infancy.

Conclusions

We might describe disease as a lack of homeostasis in physiological function, or departure from a norm which is measured in terms of some component of the plant. If any component is plotted against time to give a development curve which we accept as our standard or norm because of its subsequent acceptable yield or rate of growth or quality of some attribute, then curves for other plants which do not lie within a particular range of the norm are considered to be diseased. Inclusion of the time factor in disease recognizes the fact that disease develops like the plant. Thus, we can include in our description of disease those examples where a plant may be growing weakly early in its life and be designated as diseased and yet make up lost ground later in the season to assume the characteristics of health. Such recovery from disease is a common feature in wheat in dry climates like South Australia, for example, where early drought sometimes markedly retards growth in plants on sandy soils but where subsequent rains enable the plants to increase their growth rate and eventually yield as well as those plants which had not had an initial setback.

In some situations physiological malfunction, although slight and insufficient to justify calling the plant diseased, may nevertheless be indicative of serious malfunction to follow at a later date. Experience may tell us for example, that tomatoes grown in well irrigated sandy soil containing high numbers of root knot nematodes will probably yield very poorly if early in their life they have even a few galls on their roots. However, it is probably unwise to categorize the young tomato plants as diseased even if their subsequent failure seems inevitable, there is always the chance that some unexpected change in the environment may enable the plant to maintain its homeostasis. Such a change may even be produced by man in the form of nematicides or chemical fertilizers.

It seems clear that physiological disturbance varies in intensity from zero to the ultimate stages in the process of dying. However, at the lower intensities certain features of the plant, like growth and yield, may be largely unaffected although there may be profound changes in the physiological processes that reflect the plant's attempts to maintain stability. What is meant by 'largely unaffected' is an arbitrary expression of the reduction in growth or yield that for theoretical or practical reasons we give a number to; this is the departure from the norm just mentioned. This value which demarcates health and disease is not fixed; nor can it be fixed because there are no measurable criteria which indicate any sort of interface except in those few cases where a distinct tolerance level occurs. Moreover, the multifactorial nature of disease causation, environmental variability and differing standards for the reduction in yield that can be accepted, probably preclude any formula that might distinguish health and disease. This, in part, is why these states are difficult to define. Nevertheless it follows from these conclusions that we might describe health as that level of physiological change which does not produce reductions in some plant component (e.g. yield) beyond a predetermined amount, in other words the converse of disease.

Plant nematodes are one of many factors that, acting concurrently, can cause disease. There is probably nothing about the *nature* of such diseases that is unique although what nematodes do to cause disease may be different from other parasites, and the plant responses and subsequent symptoms may sometimes be indicative of these differences. As these aspects are very important in the etiology of a disease and sometimes offer opportunities for controlling disease, there will always be a requirement for specialized knowledge from nematologsts, virologists, bacteriologists and mycologists. However, I suggest that where we are concerned with crop protection and with increasing yields a good case can be made for greater emphasis on the interdisciplinary, etiological approach to define problems so that maximum use can be made of the few specialists we have.

In discussing the nature of disease and in attempting to define it we have set the stage for the important problem of how to cope with the unpleasant consequences of crop diseases to man. This is the subject of the next chapter.

References

AGRIOS, G.N. (1970). *Plant pathology*. Academic Press. xiv + 629 pp.

ALLEN, P.J. (1966). The role of the host in the development of disease symptoms—a review. *Phytopathology*, **56**, 255.

ANDREWARTHA, H.G. (1970). *Introduction to the study of animal populations*. Methuen, x + 283 pp.

BECKMAN, C.H. (1964). Host responses to vascular infection. *Ann. Rev. Phytopath.*, **2**, 231.

BLACK, D.A.K. (1968). *The logic of medicine*. Oliver and Boyd, vi + 88 pp.

BROWNING, J.A. and FREY, K.J. (1969). Multiline cultivars as a means of disease control. *Ann. Rev. Phytopath.*, **7**, 355.

BURNET, F.M. (1962). *Natural history of infectious disease*. Cambridge Univ. Press, 377 pp.

CLARK, L.R., GEIER, P.W., HUGHES, R.D. and MORRIS, R.F. (1968). *The ecology of insect populations in theory and practice*. Methuen, xiii + 232 op.

DENT, J.B. and ANDERSON, J.R. (1971). *Systems analysis in agricultural management*. John Wiley, xv + 394 pp.

DONALD, C.M. (1963). Competition among crop and pasture plants. *Adv. Agron.*, **15**, 1.

DUBOS, R. (1970). *Man, medicine and environment*. Penguin Books, 173 pp.

GÄUMANN, E. (1950). *Principles of plant infection*. Crosby Lockwood & Son Ltd., xvi + 543 pp.

HORSFALL, J.G. and DIMOND, A.E. (1959). *Plant Pathology*. Vol. 1. Academic Press, xiv + 674 pp.

HUGHES, G.M. (1964). Preface to *Homeostasis and feedback mechanisms Symp. Soc. Exp. Biol.*, **18**.

NORTON, A. (1969). *The new dimensions of medicine*. Hodder and Stoughton, 288 pp.

RYLE, J.A. (1948). *The natural history of disease*. Oxford Univ. Press, xiv + 484 pp.

STAKMAN, E.C. and HARRAR, J.C. (1957). *Principles of plant pathology*. Ronald Press Co., xi + 581 pp.

URITANI, I. (1971). Protein changes in diseased plants. *Ann. Rev. Phytopath.*, **9**, 211.

WALKER, J.C. (1969). *Plant Pathology*. McGraw Hill, xi + 819 pp.

WHITE, E.G. and JORDAN, F.T.W. (1963). *Veterinary preventive medicine*. Baillière, Tindall and Cox, ix + 334 pp.

10   Living with disease

Control of disease is a branch of applied ecology and as ecology is concerned with systems in which there are numerous interrelated factors, it follows that there are likely to be many ways in which change in such factors might either be deleterious or beneficial to plant growth. In chapter 9, disease was described as lack of homeostasis in physiological function caused by a complex of factors. The plant was imagined to occur at the centre of a web of such factors, some of which acted directly on the plant whereas others, at the edges of the web, acted indirectly. Factors influencing plant growth constitute the plant's environment and include soil properties as well as climate and pathogens. Some of the environmental components restrain plant growth whereas others stimulate it. Moreover, the same component may act as a restraint at one level of intensity and a stimulant at another; interactions with other factors may also influence the way in which a particular factor affects a plant.

In considering the control of disease we have to think of ways in which the web might be changed to the plant's benefit; in other words the plant's environment has to be modified to lessen the effects of restraining factors and, where possible, to increase the effects of beneficial factors. Thus, nematodes, when they cause serious damage, restrain plant growth, and to control disease it may be necessary to kill them with nematicides. Alternatively, we might control the same disease indirectly by adding soil amendments that encourage the increase of antagonists that kill nematodes. Or, the plant itself might receive attention to make it more resistant or tolerant to nematode attack, by breeding new varieties.

In another situation we might find that a parasitic fungus and lack of soil fertility are equally responsible for disease in a crop; the options for disease control are now greater and whether we choose to apply fungicides, fertilizers or both may be determined by economics.

Control of disease then, involves the reduction of restraints on the plant to acceptable levels, or changing the genetic constitution of the plant itself. It is more than just control of parasites, although this is usually the most satisfactory way where a parasite has been shown to be the chief cause of disease and where there are techniques to control the parasite both efficiently and economically.

Reduction of disease in a crop is difficult for many reasons, not the least of which is the unpredictable nature of weather which produces profound changes in the plants' environment. Consequently, how well disease is controlled is likely to fluctuate from year to year. Even when satisfactory control of a disease is achieved, other undesirable consequences may arise that pose further problems; applying fungicides to plants, for example, may make them more susceptible to nematodes (Brzeski and Macias, 1967) and there is always the spectre of pollution. Furthermore, whether control is feasible often depends on socio-economic conditions, for the business of containing disease is usually expensive. For these reasons I have called this chapter 'living with disease' rather than 'the control of disease', as it implies that there are wider issues in control than just increasing crop production. It is even possible that there are disease situations where doing nothing is more advantageous than attempting control, especially where information about the components in the system is lacking.

Knowledge of the crop and its environment, including parasites and soil factors, is essential if satisfactory control is to be achieved without undesirable consequences. This statement, like those that advocate more research on the ecology of nematodes, sounds rather trite but it is certainly relevant to ask how much of this sort of information is required before a programme of control can be recommended to the farmer. How satisfactory, for example, is it to recommend soil fumigation on evidence from a few plants that happen to be heavily infected with nematodes or some other parasite? How much information is required before a reliable decision can be made? Do we need to identify the major causes of disease in every situation?

The random collection of data on the behaviour, physiology and ecology of nematodes in the hope that a method of control will somehow emerge, is unrealistic if control is our major objective. So the question: how much and what sort of information is required before control can be attempted? —is important. However, our conclusions are likely to be so tentative in this problem that perhaps there should always be a few people who are making 'shots in the dark' and looking for the unexpected so that novel ways of control can be devised. It is the old question of achieving a balance between effort and returns; there is no simple answer. Before we do that, however, let us look at some views on living with disease and its control.

Some other views

In clinical medicine the attention of the physician is largely fixed on the individual patient. Following diagnosis, usually of a so-called primary cause, a treatment is prescribed that aims to control the disease, i.e. to reduce physiological dysfunction to a level which can be designated as healthy. In epidemiology on the other hand, the population or group is the unit and the objective here is to identify the associations that may lead to the development of disease. Paul (1966) suggests that in medicine, epidemiology is concerned with measurements of the circumstances under which diseases occur, where diseases tend to flourish and where they do not. Epidemiology is also concerned with the spread of diseases, how they are inhibited and what factors are responsible for them. Such information, Paul states, lies in the area of preventive medicine and the care of public health. According to Roger (1963), the main use of epidemiology is to discover populations with high and low rates of disease in the hope that causes for disease, and for freedom from disease, can be postulated. Control therefore depends on an understanding of the natural history of the disease, of the multiple causative factors involving the agent, host and environment during periods of pre-pathogenesis and pathogenesis in man. Paul's and Roger's views are similar to those expressed in the previous chapter on the nature of disease in plants, but we are still left with the question of how much understanding we require before a method of control is adopted that will have a reasonable chance of success. The idea expressed by Roger of studying disease severity in different populations emphasizes the importance of understanding why some populations remain healthy. The answer does not always lie in the absence of some parasite, nor in high levels of resistance or tolerance within the hosts; there may be some factor in the environment which inhibits the parasite at some stage in its life cycle. Apparently there are thousands of people in New York who are carrying parasites such as the blood fluke, *Schistosoma*, and the hookworm, *Ancylostoma*, but populations of these helminths have not increased in New York since the means of transmission are lacking (Cockburn, 1963). Control in the epidemiological sense therefore entails the maintenance of restraints on parasites, thereby preventing disease. Study of the healthy population may indicate ways in which disease may be prevented from spreading in the population, just as study of the healthy but infected individual may suggest ways in which health might be maintained and disease controlled.

Dubos (1970) also affirms that disease cannot be successfully controlled without considering man in his total environment, although such an ideal is rarely attainable because most medical situations are so complex that their determinants can never be understood in all their details. Hence, Dubos argues, precise scientific knowledge of the body machine must be supplemented with a more empirical attitude in the practice of medicine.

Dubos is saying in effect that the medical practitioner, like the plant pathologist, has to compromize between what is theoretically desirable and what is practically possible. If, Dubos goes on to say, all important responses have multiple determinants, new scientific methods will have to be developed to investigate complex systems in which various factors act simultaneously. Perhaps the new methods of factor analysis in statistics will now enable such problems to be tackled. But this hardly helps the man who has to prescribe treatments or methods of control for several patients or plant diseases every day. It is possible of course that intensive studies of disease situations will permit generalizations to be made so that identification of the key factors and determinants causing disease can be made in a relatively short time. Thus, having examined in detail the ecology and etiology of a disease situation, it may be possible to advise methods of control if the data can be readily stored, retrieved and then applied when further problems arise in the future. Perhaps computers may one day be the stock in trade of the diagnostic centres for plant diseases as they are for many medical centres today. Lusted (1968), for example, suggests that because of the increased volume of medical information, the physician must make decisions about diagnosis and treatment under conditions of uncertainty; and the supply of more and more information does not in itself decrease this uncertainty. Thus to help the physician, Lusted advocates the use of computer-based aids to help in the processes of making diagnoses and treatments and furthermore, research should be done on the physician himself as a decision maker.

Plant pathologists face the same problems. There is now a large amount of information on the ways in which particular diseases in particular crops in particular areas have been successfully controlled, but how can all these data be put to the best use? In other words we have the tactical means of tackling disease; what we want now is strategy. If an orange grower asks for advice about a slow decline in yield, how do we decide which of all the published data are relevant to the conditions that exist in his particular orange grove, and how much extra etiological work should be done to ascertain what is relevant? It is easy to prescribe a method of disease control with fumigants and fertilizers of course, but how do we know it is the best method? If we could in some way draw on all the previous experience and data relating to slow decline we might go some way to reaching our objectives. In discussing this problem in medicine Black (1968) indicates that there is no hard-and-fast line between medical and general biological research and that analogue and digital computers have found many applications in these fields. It is likely that before long a detailed medical history of anyone who has come under medical observation may be obtainable from a national record store. When this happens,

Black points out, a living clinical epidemiology will be possible, based on verifiable statistics about disease. Perhaps, a farm or group of farms might be considered analogous to the human patient, in the sense that the extension worker will be able to retrieve previous data, ascertain the successes and failures of control procedures in the past and add his own contribution to the store of information that future extension workers can use.

In discussing control of disease, most plant pathology text books categorize the methods into quarantine, eradication programmes, cultural practices, chemical control, use of resistant varieties, biological control, soil treatment and so on. It is generally agreed that the aims of such measures are to reduce the amount of disease within the crop, rather than in the individual plant. Moreover, of necessity, control of disease in plant pathology is concerned more with prevention than with cure, thus agreeing with the views of the medical epidemiologists.

The difference between prevention and cure is only a question of time within the development of a disease. Prevention aims at changing the plant's environment or the plant itself so that interacting factors in the crop system, or the incursion of new factors, have less chance of causing disturbance. Curative methods, on the other hand, only come into effect when disease has occurred. Prevention thus aims to maintain existing homeostasis in the crop, whereas cure aims to restore homeostasis. Of the two, prevention seems preferable. The maintenance of homeostasis in the crop clearly demands a thorough knowledge of the crop's ecology so that the various control measures can be used simultaneously to the best advantage. Baker (1968), in discussing biological control, emphasizes the lack of information on such situations. Baker asserts that except for one or two instances long term effects of crop sequence on inoclum density, capacity and disease proneness are not known for any example of biological control. Thus he argues, we should visualize a systems analysis for applying biological control to diseases in which the interaction and behaviour pattern of inoculum and host in different soils can be studied to uncover possible regimes for control.

The reasons for studying the ecology and etiology of disease and for comparing healthy and diseased populations therefore are clear. We wish to understand the nature of the restraints in the crop that maintain health and the circumstances which cause them to fail. Menzies (1970), in discussing the factors affecting populations of plant parasites in soil, suggests that to use biological controls in the field we need to find the key factors involved and then to devise means of applying them at a much greater intensity than nature provides. In many diseases living pathogens may be the key factors, but to control the disease it may be more effective to alter some other component of the plant's environment. Schmitthenner (1970), for example, suggests that *Phytophthora* and *Pythium* might be controlled more easily by manipulating soil moisture than by attempting to eradicate the parasites, because high soil moisture by lowering soil aeration makes the plants more conductive to disease. Drain-pipes, not fungicides, might be a better proposition. Similarly adding fertilizers to soil might occasionally be a useful method of control; Huber *et al.* (1968) showed that the percentage of winter plants infected by *Ophiobolus graminis* was reduced with increasing rates of nitrogen fertilizer. Moreover, fungicides and pesticides may have undesirable side effects. Thus Dubey (1970) suggests that repeated applications of pesticides probably change the microbial population in the soil so much that mineralization of soil nitrogen is inhibited resulting in nitrogen starvation of sugar cane crops. Increasing nitrogen applications may not always be beneficial, however, for Sewell and Wilson (1967) found that such a treatment increased the infection of hops by *Verticillium* and the severity of wilting; the recommendation was therefore to reduce the traditionally high nitrogen applications as this reduced wilt without any detectable influence on yield.

I have mentioned these few examples from plant pathology to illustrate that the *tactics* of control vary between disease situations and to emphasize that the *strategy* of control through the use of systems analysis supported by adequate retrieval of data is at least worth considering. At present there is little in plant pathology to support these somewhat abstract suggestions; the entomologists and ecologists on the other hand seem to have progressed much further, hence I have selected a paper by Geier and Hillman (1971) to make my point.

Geier and Hillman attempted to produce a quantitative model of the life system of the codling moth in south-eastern Australia. The life system of a pest, as explained by Clark *et al.* (1968), is composed of the population of the target organism and its effective environment including all the external factors influencing the population. The system was simulated 'by expressing the processes of the life system as simple algebraic functions capable of digesting the assessed features of a situation in early spring (input), into predictions regarding the demography and injuriousness of a population throughout the following season (output)'. The numbers of codling moth in seven study orchards were changed experimentally by applying an insecticide, the plant extract ryania. Consequently, the model was used to determine schedules of ryania sprays required to achieve stated levels of crop protection under given field conditions. The model is thus concerned with the life system of a particular pest which was known, following many years of research, to cause serious losses in pome-fruit orchards. There is no reason why similar procedures could not be adopted with a particular nematode, fungus, bacterium or virus known to be an important cause of disease in a crop. Alternatively the host crop might be specified as the target organism with parasites and other environmental factors forming the life system.

Geier and Hillman in critical tests, obtained predictions from the model which were close enough to subsequently observed values to confirm the model as a substantial reproduction of the natural system. The model was then used to analyse some practical problems in the control of codling moth, such as the assessment of current control methods and devising new strategies. Geier and Hillman claim that the successful quantification of the model validates the concept of life-systems. They also suggest that the exercise was worthwhile because it shows that using relatively simple methods enough knowledge can be gained about a key species to predict quite accurately how it may be expected to perform from season to season through a vast region and how it would respond to a particular strategy of control. The model was thus an aid to the management of insect pests, and indicated a means of ecological investigation. Thus selection of the best control strategy for a given set of conditions could be made. Ecological studies of this sort, as Geier and Hillman point out, are costly in manpower, material resources and time; they are only justifiable if they help with the difficult task of choosing what to do in a particular situation, and if they contribute to the solution of practical problems.

There is little doubt that the success of the Geier-Hillman model can be attributed at least in part to the amount of detailed work that preceded the final phase. This does not contradict my previous contention, however, that large quantities of accumulated ecological data are not necessarily the most effective for a subsequent model. A certain amount is required to form a conceptual hypothesis on which a model can be based, but it is usually evident very soon in the exercise that the sort of data the model requires have not always been obtained, nor was it possible to foresee that such data would be needed. We are now faced with the same kind of problem posed earlier which was—how much ecological information is required before a programme of control can be recommended to the farmer? Enough apparently to form a hypothesis which can be readily tested by running the model to see whether its predictions correspond to values subsequently observed in nature. Similarly, in devising control procedures without systems simulation we need enough data to form an hypothesis that can be tested by field experiments. In either case the hypothesis will need revision followed by further experiments. Whether we proceed from an initial accumulation of data to a model such as that achieved by Geier and Hillman and finally to a control strategy, or whether we omit the model, depends on the resources available and the seriousness of the disease problem.

There are still too few reported studies on the systems simulation approach in pest-control to decide whether it is a useful answer to many of these problems and the same can be said of the related topics of management in agriculture and natural resources. Nevertheless, current views (Watt, 1968; Dent and Anderson, 1971), strongly suggest that systems analysis and simulation may enable decisions to be made about complex systems which hitherto were impossible. Watt (1968), in discussing the problems of managing resources such as fisheries, forests, agricultural crops and wildlife, concludes that many can be reduced to the basic problem of deciding between alternative solutions and combinations of solutions. In each of these problems, Watt says, there is a dependent variable that is a function of a considerable number of variables, only some of which are subject to manipulation by man. There are also constraints on the solution to the problem because of economic feasibility, equipment characteristics, side effects of the process or some other factor. Furthermore, every time some factor in the system is manipulated all the other variables are altered too, hence subsequent procedures are likely to be different and depend on the frequency with which they are applied. To handle such complexities, some type of systems simulation is required to assess the consequences of a range of conditions on yields.

Such views are applicable to plant disease problems, whether we are concerned with the management of a resource, the agricultural crop, and the manipulation of restraints like pathogens, or whether we are concerned with the control of a pathogen or pest that we know to have an important influence on the crop. In fact pest and disease control are part of the wider subject of crop management, as pests and disease form only part of the group of factors that restrict plant growth.

Dent and Anderson (1971) identify the various stages in system research: (1) recognizing a problem, (2) defining the boundaries of the system, (3) analysing the system and synthetizing a model, (4) coding for the computer, (5) validation, (6) experimentation, (7) interpretation. In the context of plant diseases these steps resemble those of (1) initial survey to assess the chief factors likely to influence the crop, (2) analysing the system, (3) defining the key factors influencing the crop, (4) simulating the system with a model, (5) field experimentation to test the model, (6) practical application following interpretation of the model.

Four conclusions emerge from this survey of views. First, the practical aspects of plant pathology and nematology form a part of the study of the management of agricultural resources. Second, the *strategy* of disease control is important; so far there has been little attempt in plant pathology or nematology to tackle disease problems in a rational way using existing *tactical* methods of control. Third, recognition of the relative importance of key factors in a system should precede any attempted control of a disease. Fourth, restraints from lack of resources and time will determine the choice of control procedure. In discussing systems simulation in relation to the management of crops and control of disease, little consideration has been given to such restraints because it is worth looking first for procedures that might give the most efficient control before assessing the influence of abbreviating such procedures.

Plant nematodes

To those of us who are concerned with immediate problems of disease in crops the idea of systems simulation might seem too remote from reality, 'ballooning in the absolute' as the late Tom Goodey used to say. This is a valid criticism which deserves consideration. First of all a distinction will be made between two types of disease problems: (1) those that are recurring, of great economic importance, occur over wide areas and for economic reasons demand urgent solutions, (2) those that are of local importance, restricted in their range, appear sporadically or infrequently and have little national economic importance (although they may be important to a few individuals). In the first category *Heterodera avenae* in cereals, *H. rostochiensis* in potatoes, *Radopholus similis* in citrus and *Meloidogyne javanica* in tobacco may be examples. In the second category, *Aphelenchoides ritzemabosi* in chrysanthemums and *Helicotylenchus* in sports-turf will serve as examples. Between these extremes are diseases of varying economic importance. It is impossible to be more precise than this, and the only reason for making this distinction at all is to indicate that some problems may deserve more attention than others, some may even need the systems simulation approach. What diseases qualify for such intensive treatment depends on a variety of scientific, political and socio-economic factors that will not be discussed here. What will be discussed however is a series of possible strategies from the simplest to the most complex with the idea that, even if we cannot do what we would like to do with a problem, at least we should try to find out what ought to be done. In discussing the control of disease in which nematodes are involved, we shall therefore emphasize strategies; less will be said of tactics or methods of control as these are well documented in other texts.

STRATEGY

Major problems or side-effects caused by procedures to control plant nematodes have not so far been reported, possibly because they haven't been sought. However the numerous examples of such events in the pest control field indicate what might happen if attempts to control nematodes involve radical disturbances of the environment. For these reasons Osstenbrink (1964) has advocated harmonious or integrated control in which different methods of control are applied simultaneously and at levels that (1) avoid the excessive stresses that cause nematode populations to develop resistance, (2) remove natural enemies and other stabilizing factors of the nematode populations and (3) also deplete soil productivity factors and the quality of the harvest. The hazards of chemical treatment of the soil are probably the main justification for considering harmonious control. Oostenbrink further suggests that all present control measures can be used in a way that causes less disturbance of the environment. Thus soil fumigants could be used at lower dosage rates, selective nematicides should be sought that do not kill other micro-organisms and plants should be bred for tolerance rather than high resistance. The idea of harmonious or integrated control is not new and has been used by the entomologists in an empirical way to avoid further problems of the kind just mentioned. There is little indication, however, in this concept of how harmonious control might be achieved. The concept appears sound but lacks theory.

How to apply existing methods of control to the best advantage, i.e. adequate disease control with the minimum of environmental disturbance, is therefore important. That we may have enough information to formulate useful control programmes is mentioned by Ducharme (1969) who stresses the urgency of obtaining more food now, especially in hungry nations. He suggests that present information should enable us to keep land free from nematodes and to restore the productivity of infested soils. Ducharme may be right, in fact there are frequent references today from a variety of disciplines that what we need now is not more technology but greater use of existing technology for man's benefit. The same can be said in plant nematology; how can we best apply what we know now?

A further reason for the simultaneous application of several control methods lies in the interactions between different parasites in the same crop. Powell (1971) concludes that nematodes are of great importance as components of diseases complexes along with other disease-causing agents; in fact, such interactions may be the major economic hazard posed by these pathogens. Powell clearly believes that disease complexes will turn out to be more common than is apparent at present; I would go further and suggest that all disease problems are complexes in which factors in the plant's environment interact to produce disease—and nematodes may be one of these factors. To achieve this goal however, the diseased crop has to be sampled to ascertain the key factors in the system that depress plant growth or productivity and thereby cause disease. The nature of the disease problem can then be defined. We have already discussed these aspects in earlier chapters but to indicate their importance in the search for a control procedure I shall describe some features of a disease, 'Docking disorder', that has received much attention for many years. Whitehead and his colleagues (1970) have reviewed the problem.

Docking disorder appears in seedlings of sugar beet which show poor growth, signs of nutritional deficiencies especially in magnesium and nitrogen and discoloured, misshapen rootlets. The condition recurs in the same fields and the same areas in fields, but its severity differs greatly from year to year. Other crops often grow poorly where sugar beet was previously affected.

The authors state that as any kind of damage to roots can slow plant growth and lead to nutritional deficiencies, it is not surprising that early work on Docking disorder done in different places led to seemingly contradictory conclusions, or that the role of ectoparasitic nematodes as a prime cause took long to establish, even though the beneficial effects of treating soils with DD fumigant were already known. Experiments with fungi like *Fusarium oxysporum* and *Pythium* spp., the application of fungicides, and organic manure in the form of wool-waste, or farmyard manure were examined to assess their influence on the diseased plants. *Trichodorus* was suspected to be involved but their numbers were not correlated with the disorder, possibly, the authors suggest, because of inadequate extraction from the soil. Fungi and nematodes isolated from roots were similar in affected and unaffected roots. Diseased beet taken from the field, recovered in compost but grew poorly in pots containing the field soil, even after it was autoclaved thus suggesting unusual chemical or physical conditions in the soil. Viruses were not considered to be responsible for poor growth but the fact that *Trichodorus* damaged sugar beet in the Netherlands led to a reassessment of the relationships between nematodes and 'Docking disorder'.

This account by Whitehead and his colleagues clearly indicates the large amount of survey and experimental work that was done on this disease of sugar beet. We can imagine the sequence of successes and failures that followed each attempt by workers from different disciplines, each no doubt hoping that he would be the one to reveal the cause of the disease. The account reads like a detective story where various experts are called in to try and reveal the criminal. But is the situation really like this? Is it not more likely that several factors in the sugar beet seedling's environment influence its growth and contribute to the various symptoms? The account of the various experiments suggests so, and the fact that Whitehead and his colleagues separate Docking disorder into six types according to the shape of the patches, presence of *Longidorus* or *Trichodorus*, cultivation effects and areas of excessive drainage merely affirms that the sugar beet's environment is extremely variable and that the chief causes of diseased patches are likely to vary between fields and farms. The authors chose to restrict the name Docking disorder to the situation where *Longidorus* and/or *Trichodorus* occur on the seedling roots, although it is pointed out that the amount of stunting in the plants might be influenced by variations in soil moisture that influence nematode activity; poor soil structure, lack of nutrients or herbicide damage might also reduce the plant's tolerance to nematode damage. Finally, the authors give a list of factors that affect yield of the sugar beet.

The considerable amount of work on Docking disorder undoubtedly indicates what would be worth measuring if an attempt were made to assess the relative importance of factors as causes of disease. There is no indication that an attempt was made by multiple regression, factor analysis or any other methods to reach such a conclusion, hence the notion that *Trichodorus* and/or *Longidorus* are the primary causes of Docking disorder is still questionable. This does not mean to say that the systematic analysis of the sugar beet crop as described in earlier chapters would automatically have given an unequivocal answer. If, as the authors say, extraction of the nematodes from soil is difficult, and if yield losses are more closely correlated with the time the seedlings are attacked and with their vigour rather than with nematode numbers, then an incorrect assessment of the disease situation might easily have been reached. Nevertheless with what is known now, it might be useful to analyse the system, identify the key factors and define the problem more fully than has been done so far, especially as the conclusions will influence subsequent control procedures.

Support for these views comes from the paper of Cooke and Draycott (1971) who point out that although Docking disorder has been controlled by soil fumigation, the improvement in the crop might not be due only to killing of nematodes. The authors state that fumigation also retards nitrification of ammonium ions to the more readily leached nitrate ions thus causing more mineral nitrogen to be retained in the soil surface. Thus the use of fumigants to assess the importance of a parasite in a disease situation may not be reliable

Having decided that *Trichodorus* and *Longidorus* were the prime causes of stunting (Docking disorder) in plants on which these nematodes occurred, a programme of possible control procedures was given. Killing the nematodes in the soil is the only reliable way of controlling Docking disorder, Whitehead and co-workers suggest, and there is good evidence that treatment of soil with nematicides gave marked increases in yield. Damage may also be ameliorated by: avoiding practices that weaken plant growth (sowing seed too deeply or too late, using too much herbicide, harming soil structure), adopting all practices that encourage plant growth (control damage from other pests, apply organic matter, apply extra nitrogen), minimizing the amount of nematode feeding by providing additional feeding areas (inter-row cropping, denser sowing, etc.).

The problem of Docking disorder has been solved in the sense that control procedures are now known which give substantially greater yields of sugar beet, although there is still a possibility that factors other than nematodes may contribute to the disease. But need this concern us as long as the main objective, to control the disease, has been achieved? I think it should, because the essential features of control are its economic practicability, its efficiency and its ability to disturb the stability of the plant's environment. It is likely that the control procedures described by Whitehead and his colleagues will greatly improve yields of sugar beet in areas where Docking disorder occurs, but it is also likely that it would improve yields in most other crops whatever their soil conditions and parasites. So the real problem is to decide which of all the tactical methods available is the best combination, that is, to say the most efficient, the cheapest and the least environmentally-disruptive.

There are at least two procedures in which this problem can be solved: First, the process of analysis and problem definition, in which the key factors are identified, is followed by field experimentation. Many treatments are incorporated in a multifactorial design that indicates treatment effects and more importantly their interactions. We might imagine, for example, an experiment with treatments like: times of sowing seed, depths of seed, plant spacings, fertilizer levels, nematicide dosage rates, varieties of plant and tillage. Such experiments are often impracticable however, because of the sheer volume of work involved. Nevertheless if there are a few important key factors influencing disease in a crop it would probably be useful to attempt a multifactorial experiment along these lines. I know of no example in the literature that illustrates such a procedure, but the experiments of Tarjan and Simmons (1966) come close. These authors were concerned with the problem of 'spreading decline' of citrus caused by *Radopholus similis*. The disease had been controlled by removing infected trees, burning them and chemically fumigating the soil. Attempts were also made to eliminate sources of infected plant material and to prevent their introduction into non-infested groves. Barriers in the form of buffer zones were also used around groves to restrict the migration of nematodes. In spite of these measures the disease persisted, hence Tarjan and Simmons considered the possibility of coexistence between the nematode and the citrus trees, and they started a research programme to study the effect of various cultural materials and practices on the performance of mature orange trees infected by the burrowing nematode. This research thus changed the emphasis from control of a single parasite, the nematode, to control of the disease by influencing the plant's environment, thereby increasing the tolerance and possibly the resistance of the orange trees to pathogens including the burrowing nematode. A multifactorial experiment was started with five treatments: one application of four tonnes of high calcium lime, a single root pruning to a depth of 45 cm, an annual application of two tonnes of manure compost, applications three times yearly of a 40% synthetic organic nitrogen fertilizer or a 40% natural organic nitrogen fertilizer, and spraying three times yearly with a soluble fertilizer. Various responses of the tree and its fruit were measured annually. Each of the responses was subsequently shown to be influenced by specific combinations of treatment but no one combination was found to be the best. The experiments continue with the objective, Tarjan and Simmons say, of enabling the grower to manipulate certain cultural practices within nematode—infested groves to give adequate yields. Such procedures, integrated with current efforts to control the burrowing nematode, could, the authors claim, result in logical management. Several questions arise from this undoubtedly useful experiment. (1) Would an analysis of the system have indicated which factors should be manipulated; why was root pruning included in the treatments, for example? (2) Tarjan and Simmons examined the literature to ascertain the various cultural practices that benefit nematode-infected plants, but how is the relative importance of each factor in such a list decided? (3) If a systems analysis were done what would be the relative importance of burrowing nematodes to, say, plant nutrients or water? (4) If nematodes are the key factor in 'spreading decline' in orange groves, how do we manipulate the various cultural treatments and nematode control practices to optimize yields? The answer to the first three questions lies in the analysis of the orange grove system prior to experimentation. The fourth question cannot readily be answered by multifactorial experiments; it is the province of the modellers and systems simulators.

If a disease problem is economically very important it may be worthwhile to resort to models to arrive at hypotheses about complex systems in which optimization procedures are required. This is the second control procedure which, in the order of events, lies between systems analysis and field experimentation. It is a means of making statements about the various treatments that can be applied simultaneously, and at what levels and how frequently they should be applied to give the best chance of obtaining maximum yields from a crop. Jones et al. (1967) used such a method to decide the frequency with which resistant varieties of potato should be grown within crop rotations to control populations of *Heterodera rosto-chiensis*. Resistant varieties derived from *Solanum tuberosum* ssp. *andigena* grown in soil infested with *H. rostochiensis* provided the controlling factor. A computer programme was written to include three mathematical relationships: (1) a law relating multiplication to pre-cropping density, (2) two mathematical models of inheritance of ability to overcome resistance, (3) a law relating the proportion of larvae able to become females to pre-cropping population density. The programme also included four parameters, (1) maximum possible reproduction rate, (2) fraction of the population (eggs) not participating in reproduction and carried over to the following year unchanged when potatoes are grown, (3) fraction carried over annually when other crops are grown, (4) frequency of larvae able to become females in the initial population. The computations led Jones and his coworkers to suggest that the best policy for potato growers who have fields suitable for resistant varieties is to alternate resistant with susceptible varieties in a crop rotation containing potatoes every three or four years. Here then is a hypothesis on which decisions can be based. Imperfect and incomplete as the data and the model are, it is probably the best advice that can be given with what information we have now. Furthermore, it is now clearer what other experiments need to be done to improve the model. The model must be tested of course to validate its conclusions, i.e. field experiments must be done to confirm that the recommendations of Jones and his colleagues are better than other possible procedures. Resistant and susceptible varieties would presumably have to be grown at various frequencies in different rotations and the effects on populations of *H. rostochiensis* assessed. Thus modelling and systems simulation does not replace field experimentation, its purpose is to indicate the direction field experiments might take, and to produce hypotheses on which decisions about control can be made. The model is not the end of the road to control but a useful step towards that goal, especially where the disease problem has numerous interacting factors that have an important influence on a disease which is economically very important.

Sayre (1971), in discussing the evaluation of antagonists in biological control of nematodes, suggests that modelling and computer programming of nematode-parasite or nematode-predator relationships may be useful. He concludes however, that such methods can only be used when we have a lot more information on every step in the life cycles of the parasite and host. Sayre is probably correct but it may be unwise to delay modelling until we feel we know 'all about' the system. As soon as modelling starts the experimenter becomes aware that the model is demanding information he does not have and that much information he does have is not required in the model. Hence Jones and his coworkers, in my opinion, were fully justified in attempting a model even though some necessary information was not available and some guesses had to be made.

CURRENT STRATEGIES

The more we know of a crop system, the factors restraining plant growth and the interactions between such factors, the more able we are to suggest how existing control methods might be used to the greatest advantage in improving yields. The most complex, time-consuming and expensive method involves the stages of (1) Survey, (2) Field or systems analysis, (3) Problem definition, (4) Modelling, (5) Field experimentation, (6) Practical control. The simplest, quickest and cheapest method involves an initial survey on the spot when the problem is defined and a control recommendation is made. Between these two extremes there are procedures of increasing complexity. Thus survey, field experimentation and control is a common procedure. So far there have been few attempts at field analysis to define the key factors. In my opinion greater use should be made of this stage because it is not necessarily time-consuming or expensive. Modelling is somewhat of a luxury and should probably be confined to economically important or intractable problems.

The most complex procedure that leads to a control programme is not necessarily the best, because the expenditure of effort and resources should match the demands of the problem. Thus it would be unrealistic for the extension worker to think in terms of models or detailed field analysis when he has many problems to contend with every year. On the other hand some extension workers may be given the job of dealing with important intractable problems in which situation they will require all the weapons that can be mustered to solve the problems. As long as it is realized that the control recommendations are only as good as the work that has been put into them, then what is best or what is likely to be most efficient is a question of available resources in time and manpower. However, it is possible that within these constraints more effective use can be made of resources and it is my opinion that more consideration should be given to field analysis and problem definition.

TACTICS

Chemical control

In the opinion of Good and Feldmesser (1967) there is a need for non-specific chemicals or combinations of selective pesticides that control nematodes, insects, weeds and parasitic soil fungi. There is also a need for nematode-selective systemics, repellents and sterilants as plant chemotherapeutants, because on low value and perennial crops nematode control has not been particularly successful. In such situations nematicides have been insufficiently effective, too expensive, phytoxic or they leave undesirable residues in plants when applied to the growing crop.

Such specific chemicals would be useful for they could be applied to control a particular factor that was an important restraint on crop production without disturbing other factors in the system that might give rise to other unpredictable and undesirable consequences. The kind of events that might ensue following fumigation are described by Sutherland and Adams (1966). They comment that it is common practice to use soil fumigants such as methyl bromide to sterilize seedbed soil in forest nurseries. Soil so treated is rapidly colonized by fungus- and bacterium-feeding nematodes. Forms like *Aphelenchus* may be beneficial by feeding on plant pathogenic fungi such as *Rhizoctonia* while avoiding beneficial fungi such as *Trichoderma*. However, fungus-feeding forms could reduce the development of mycorrhizal fungi; bacterium-feeding nematodes like *Cephalobus* might be involved in damping-off by feeding on certain bacteria that antagonize damping-off fungi, and so on. In other words Sutherland and Adams suggest that general fumigants might have major influences on the soil system and subsequently create disease. So far there is little indication of the influence nematicides might have on the ecology of soil micro-organisms and their plant interactions. Williams' (1969) experiments with formalin on cereal growth indicated that although grain yield was increased two-fold, this desirable result was not caused by controlling *Heterodera avenae* as populations of this nematode increased eight times. On the other hand yield increases, following the application of extra nitrogen, were not associated with such big increases in nematode numbers as in the formalin treated plots. Thus, Williams concludes, formalin probably influenced *H. avenae* through factors other than increased plant size or vigour. Chemical treatment of soil certainly appears to cause marked changes in the soil system. If we accept the principle that control procedures which cause marked changes are undesirable because they are likely to initiate further unwanted changes including disease, then perhaps we should try using nematicides at much lower dosage rates, as suggested by Oostenbrink (1964). According to Brudenell (1969) the idea of eradication of nematodes became widely accepted even though eradication was only temporary. Consequently, the idea of growing economically worthwhile crops in the presence of nematodes lost favour but it is now clear, says Brudenell, that nematodes can and must be lived with. And to achieve this end, lower doses of nematicides that give economic returns should be considered. Brudenell's view corresponds to that of Tarjan and Simmons (1966), mentioned previously; they too consider that living with disease is a desirable aim. Some may consider it a sign of defeat but this is unrealistic if it is accepted that although it may be possible to control nematodes by drastic measures the results in the long term may not be beneficial. That is why 'living with disease' is a more realistic outlook in my view than outright control of one factor and why we should be looking for more refined chemical control practices.

Biological control

Success in the control of insect pests by so-called biological control has probably prompted many nematologists to ask whether the same can be done to control nematodes. Furthermore, although the evidence that nematicides may have undesirable side effects is largely anecdotal, there are valid reasons why greater stress should be placed on the search for biological control methods. Whether control can be achieved by the use of sterile males or natural chemicals like pheromones, repellents or attractants does not, at first sight, seem likely. Nematodes, unlike insects, are not very mobile; they live in an environment, the soil, that is not conducive to rapid or widespread diffusion of chemicals. In fact the pace of life in the soil proceeds at a much slower rate than above ground; nematode populations increase and disperse much more slowly than insects. For these reasons, biological control of plant nematodes may be feasible only if the controlling factors occur in or on the plant roots. Jones (1969) is more optimistic because he suggests that lack of nematode mobility and their inaccessibility might be partly countered by spraying the soil with a water suspension containing sterile male nematodes; sexual sterilization may be possible, but the main problem is that of producing large numbers of nematodes at a reasonable cost. The use of pheronomes and plant attractants are also feasible according to Jones, although these are long term projects.

One aspect is clear, more will have to be known about the soil system if biological control is to be achieved. The initial attempts at controlling nematodes by the application of nematode-destroying fungi has been replaced by a more cautious approach. Thus Cooke (1968) emphasizes that there is no simple labile equilibrium between the amount of soil amendment, the number of freeliving nematodes and the predacious activity of fungi. Thus the arbitrary addition of fungi or organic amendments to soil is likely to prove no more fruitful in the future than it has in the past. Cooke concludes that although the soil environment might possibly be altered to favour nematode-killing fungi, the means of doing so are not known at present. Huber and Watson (1970) have indicated the sort of events we might look for in research of this nature. They suggest that organic amendments and crop rotation probably influence the severity of soil-borne diseases by (1) increasing the biological buffering capacity of the soil, (2) reducing parasite numbers during anaerobic decomposition of organic matter, (3) affecting nitrification, which influences the form of nitrogen predominating in the soil, (4) denying parasites a host during the interim of unsuitable crops. Like all research, however, there is always the chance that someone will stumble on some novel event that may open up new possibilities in control.

Conclusions

The control of plant nematodes has been reviewed in Publication 1696 of the National Acadeny of Science (Anon, 1968). This book is a valuable source of practical information, although some of the recommendations need consideration. For example, there are two factors that are seen as primary obstacles to effective nematode control: first, lack of recognition that plant nematodes are seriously limiting the potential yield of crops. The book suggests that the main reason for this is the shortage of agriculturists at all levels who recognize and understand nematode diseases. The second obstacle is lack of capital to invest in equipment and nematicides. The situation in my opinion can be better expressed as a lack of information on how seriously nematodes limit yields, because of a shortage of extension workers with the training to achieve this end. To the present, our assessment of the importance of nematodes in agriculture relies mostly on faith, or on those situations where the crop is decimated; perhaps the less dramatic losses that miss our notice, and which cover much larger areas, are in the long run the most important. If quantitative assessments of the role of nematodes as causes of disease in crops are made along the lines we have already discussed, we might even find that they are a bigger menace than we imagined. It is not surprising that many disbelieve statements by plant nematologists that nematodes seriously limit crop yields; there is little real evidence to suggest that they do. It might be argued that nematicide trials have shown what yields crops can achieve when nematodes are removed from the system, but there is always a nagging doubt that perhaps other parasites have been removed too.

The National Academy of Science booklet also suggests, quite rightly, that well trained nematologists are absolutely essential to fruitful research programmes; but trained in what? I suggest that we need more people who are trained in quantitative ecology with specialization in plant pathology, particularly nematodes. They would have a multi-disciplinary approach to field problems and be trained not to categorize a disease as a 'nematode problem' or 'wet feet' or 'die-back' or 'virus disease' but to wait until the requisite samples had been taken and analysed statistically so that a statement on causes could be made in terms of probabilities and the requisite control procedures given to the grower. Such extension workers might need to work as mobile teams of specialists as Radewald (1969) suggests, but in any event they would require the same resources as any other research worker because their tasks are among the most difficult in biology.

One important advantage of this approach would be to indicate what further research is required in particular nematode–plant associations. Research on physiological and biochemical aspects of plant nematodes might then make a more direct and useful contribution to the control of nematodes than it does at present.

References

ANON. (1968). Control of plant–parasitic nematodes, in vol. 4 of series *Principles of plant and animal pest control*. Publ. 1696. Nat. Acad. Sci. Wash., 172 pp.

BAKER, R. (1968). Mechanisms of biological control of soil-borne pathogens. *Ann. Rev. Phytopath.*, **6**, 263.

BLACK, D.A.K. (1968). *The logic of medicine*. Oliver and Boyd, vi + 88 pp.

BRUDENELL, P.B. (1969). A reappraisal of established soil fumigants—a temperate challenge to the tropics. In *Nematodes of tropical crops*. Edited by J.E. Peachey. Commonwealth Agricultural Bureaux. Tech. Comm., No. 40.

BRZESKI, M.W. and MACIAS, W. (1967). The increased attack of *Ditylenchus dipsaci* on onion caused by some fungicides. *Nematologica*, **13**, 322.

CLARK, L.R., GEIER, P.W., HUGHES, R.D. and MORRIS, R.F. (1968). *The ecology of insect populations in theory and practice*. Methuen, xiii + 232 pp.

COCKBURN, A. (1963). *The evolution and eradication of infectious diseases*. Johns Hopkins Press, Baltimore, ix + 255 pp.

COOKE, D.A. and DRAYCOTT, A.P. (1971). The effects of soil fumigation and nitrogen fertilizers on nematodes and sugar beet in sandy soils. *Ann. appl. Biol.*, **69**, 253.

COOKE, R. (1968). Relationships between nematode-destroying fungi and soil-borne phytonematodes. *Phytopathology*, **58**, 909.

DENT, J.B. and ANDERSON, J.R. (1971). *Systems analysis in agricultural management*. Wiley, xviii + 394 pp.

DUBEY, H.D. (1970). A nitrogen deficiency disease of sugarcane probably caused by repeated pesticide applications. *Phytopathology*, **60**, 485.

DUBOS, R. (1970). *Man, medicine and environment*. Penguin books, 173 pp.

DUCHARME, E.P. (1969). Nematode problems of citrus. In *Nematodes of tropical crops*. Edited by J.E. Peachey. Commonwealth Agricultural Bureaux. Tech. Comm., No. 40.

GEIER, P.W. and HILLMAN, T.J. (1971). An analysis of the life system of the codling moth in apple orchards of south-eastern Australia. *Proc. ecol. Soc. Australia*, **6**, 203.

GOOD, J.M. and FELDMESSER, J. (1967). Plant nematocides and soil fumigants. In *Developments in industrial microbiology*, **13**, 117.

HUBER, D.M., PAINTER, C.G., MCKAY, H.C. and PETERSON, D.L. (1968). Effect of nitrogen fertilization on take-all of winter wheat. *Phytopathology*, **58**, 1470.

HUBER, D.M. and WATSON, R.D. (1960). Effect of organic amendment on soil-borne plant pathogens. *Phytopathology*, **60**, 22.

JONES, F.G.W. (1969). Some reflections on quarantine, distribution and control of plant nematodes. In *Nematodes of tropical crops*. Edited by J.E. Peachey. Commonwealth Agricultural Bureaux Tech. Comm., No. 40.

JONES, F.G.W., PARROTT, D.M. and ROSS, G.J.S. (1967). The population genetics of the potato cyst-nematode, *Heterodera rostochiensis*; mathematical models to simulate the effects of growing eelworm-resistant potatoes bred from *Solanum tuberosum* spp. *andigena. Ann. appl. Biol.*, **60**, 151.

LUSTED, L.B. (1968). *Introduction to medical decision making*. Charles C. Thomas Publishers, Springfield, Illinois, xxi + 271 pp.

MENZIES, J.D. (1970). Factors affecting plant pathogen population in soil. In *Root diseases and soil-borne pathogens*. Edited by T.A. Tousson, R.V. Bega and P.E. Nelson. Univ. California Press, 252 pp.

OOSTENBRINK, M. (1964). Harmonious control of nematode infestation. *Nematologica*, **10**, 49.

PAUL, J.R. (1966). *Clinical epidemiology*. Univ. Chicago Press, xix + 305 pp.

POWELL, N.T. (1971). Interaction of plant parasitic nematodes with other disease-causing agents. In *Plant parastic nematodes* vol. 2. Edited by B.M. Zuckerman, W.F. Mai and R.A. Rohde. Academic Press, xii + 347 pp.

RADEWALD, J.D. (1969). The role of agricultural extension in nematology—past, present and future. In *Nematodes of tropical crops*. Edited by J.E. Peachey. Commonwealth Agricultural Bureaux Tech. Comm., No. 40.

ROGER, F.B. (1963). *Epidemiology and communicable disease control*. Grune and Stratton, viii + 104 pp.

SAYRE, R.M. (1971). Biotic influences in soil environment. In *Plant parasitic nematodes.* Vol 1. Edited by B.M. Zuckerman, W.F. Mai and R.A. Rohde. Academic Press, xiv + 345 pp.

SCHMITTHENNER, A.F. (1970). Significance of populations of *Pythium* and *Phytophthora* in soil. In *Root diseases and soil-borne pathogens.* Edited by T.A. Tousson, R.V. Bega and P.E. Nelson. Univ. California Press, 252 pp.

SEWELL, G.W.F. and WILSON, J.F. (1967). *Verticillium* wilt of the hop: field studies on wilt in a resistant cultivar in relation to nitrogen fertilizer applications. *Ann. appl. Biol.,* **59**, 265.

SUTHERLAND, J.R. and ADAMS, R.E. (1966). Population fluctuations of nematodes associated with red pine seedlings following chemical treatment of the soil. *Nematologica,* **12**, 122.

TARJAN, A.C. and SIMMONS, P.N. (1966). The effect of interacting cultural practices on citrus trees with spreading decline. *Soil and Crop Sci. Soc. Florida,* **26**, 22.

WATT, K.E.F. (1968). *Ecology and resource management.* McGraw-Hill Book Co., xii + 450 pp.

WHITEHEAD, A.G., DUNNING, R.A. and COOKE, D.A. (1970). Docking disorder and root ectoparastic nematodes of sugar beet. *Rep. Rothamsted exp. Stn.,* **219**.

WILLIAMS, T.D. (1969). The effects of formalin, nabam, irrigation and nitrogen on *Heterodera avenae* Woll., *Ophiobolus graminis* Sacc. and the growth of spring wheat. *Ann. appl. Biol.,* **64**, 325.

Index

Index